A COMPANION TO
OLD AND MIDDLE ENGLISH STUDIES

THE LANGUAGE LIBRARY

EDITED BY DAVID CRYSTAL

A. C. Partridge

A COMPANION TO OLD AND MIDDLE ENGLISH STUDIES

BARNES & NOBLE BOOKS
TOTOWA, NEW JERSEY

First published 1982 by
André Deutsch Limited
105 Great Russell Street London WC1

Typesetting by King's English Typesetters Limited, Cambridge.
Printed in Great Britain by
The Thetford Press Limited, Thetford, Norfolk

Partridge, A. C.
A companion to Old and Middle English.
1. English language – History
I. Title
427'.02   PE1075.5

ISBN 0-233-97411-3

First published in the USA 1982 by
  Barnes & Noble Books
  81 Adams Drive
  Totowa, New Jersey, 07512
  ISBN 0-389-20287-8

Library of Congress Cataloging in Publication Data
Partridge, A. C. (Astley Cooper)
  A companion to Old and Middle English studies.

  Bibliography: p. 439
  Includes index.
  1. Anglo-Saxon philology. 2. English language – Middle English, 1100–
1500 – History.   3. English literature – Middle English, 1100–1500 – History
and criticism. 4. Anglo-Saxons. 5. England – Civilization – To 1066.
6. England – Civilization – Medieval period, 1066–1485.
I. Title.
PE123.P37   942'.01   82-1682
ISBN 0-389-20287-8   AACR2

Trackway and Camp and City lost,
  Salt Marsh where now is corn;
Old Wars, old Peace, old Arts that cease,
  And so was England born!

Rudyard Kipling

Tell me the Acts, O historian, and leave me to reason
upon them as I please.

William Blake

For times so remote as those before the Conquest, it is
difficult to get the background. We must use every scrap
of information we can find, which may teach us what
manner of men the pre-Conquest Englishmen were.

R. W. Chambers, *The Continuity of English Prose*

I wish to save history; we cannot approach literature
innocent and naked. We must know what a poem meant
before we can fully know what it means.

Morton W. Bloomfield, *Essays and Explorations*

Contents

𝕾𝕾𝕾𝕾𝕾𝕾

Preface

A PERIOD AS REMOTE as the one here considered calls for an holistic approach. The primary purpose of this study is to provide a background to Old and Middle English, when cultural life was largely dominated by the Church at Rome. The nine hundred years that followed the arrival of St Augustine at Canterbury are far from adequately reflected in the limited number of texts an undergraduate is able to read in the original language. The more thoroughly his language work is done, the less feasible is the study of documents that confirm or deny the legends that surround historical figures.

Though the 'Dark Ages' lie partly outside the Christian era in England, knowledge of these formative centuries is necessary to the student of English. Even if he has no intention of becoming a medieval specialist, it is essential that he bridge the gap between the cultural dimension and the linguistic one.

The plan has been to attempt a synthesis of cultural, political and language elements, in the belief that formative ideas are as influential as climate and environment in a nation's evolution. In recent studies there has been a resurgence of interest in the literary products of the Late Old English period (the tenth and eleventh centuries). Writers then aimed at a high standard of speech for expository prose, and displayed a propriety of style that implied a training centre of some importance among users of the West-Saxon tongue. This is one of several movements that call for historical explanation. To anyone who knows this period well, it should be obvious that West-Saxon partiality makes it essential to supplement, from other sources, the knowledge one gleans from *The Anglo-Saxon Chronicle* (see p 38).

The admonition contained in the first essay of F. W. Maitland's *Domesday Book and Beyond* (CUP, 1897) is a landmark in the concept of medieval history:

ix

The doctrine that our remote forefathers, being simple folk, had simple law, dies hard. Too often we allow ourselves to suppose that, could we but get back to the beginning, we should find that all was intelligible, and should then be able to watch the process whereby simple ideas were smothered under subtleties and technicalities. But it is not so. Simplicity is the outcome of technical subtlety; it is the goal, not the starting point. As we go backwards the familiar outlines become blurred; the ideas become fluid, and instead of the simple we find the indefinite.

To sharpen the outlines, and disentangle the truth from the indefinite, is another principal aim of this essay. *Puck of Pook's Hill* and *Rewards and Fairies* were Kipling's inimitable way of instructing the young, and making the wisdom of the past illuminate the blindness of the present. In *Rewards and Fairies* there is, for example, 'The Conversion of St Wilfred', the Anglian missionary who converted the pagans of Sussex. Here, and in Shaw's *Androcles and the Lion*, animal fables are used to illustrate the legends associated with Saints and Desert Fathers. Kipling's narrative carries the message, not only of religious forbearance, but of loyalty to principles, which the gods of *whatever* faith are supposed to reward. The miracle that Kipling records may well represent one of the ploys used to facilitate the work of proselytizers like St Wilfrid. The real instrument of conversion was, however, the missionary's tactful handling of Saxon kings or tribal chieftains. Kipling's moral 'Law', by which social groups are thought to be governed, was taken to be a man-to-man relationship, like that of freemasonry; but this could hardly have found much kinship with Angles, Saxons and Jutes.

The linguistic results of racial admixture in England arose from incursions described in this study. Most significant, for change, were the Anglo-Saxon and Norman invasions, the first differing from the second in occupying a much longer period. Families and kinsmen came as settlers of occupied territory, and the acquisition of land was in both invasions a cogent factor. Native inhabitants disappeared from public office, and were reduced to a lower social status, one important effect being replacement of the upper and middle classes.

When the Britons were displaced by Anglo-Saxons, the language of the conquered was looked upon as servile, and had little influence on that of their overlords; for the Britons were either expelled from their lands or absorbed.

The Normans, coming in smaller numbers, were instantly rewarded by the grant of land. Most of their aristocrats owned estates both in England and Normandy, and when the latter was absorbed by France, there was divided loyalty. The Anglo-Norman barons, as rulers, found it impractical and undiplomatic to impose their language on the defeated majority, whose culture, in literature at least, was superior to their own. Though the Normans passed on to the English terms connected with the army and government, their language was eventually lost in England.

The Norman conquest, in some respects, resembled that of the Roman imperial armies. The Britons found it commercially and culturally profitable to know Latin, but used a British variation; educated Britons thus became bilingual. Both the Roman and Norman invasions were responsible for sound-substitution in the language of the occupied country, but this phonetic facility does not fundamentally influence the differentiation of languages.

Under the Holy Roman Empire religious aspirations and ethnic groupings replaced the old imperial aims. National consciousness spelt linguistic isolation, of which the different Romance languages provide the best examples. The extent to which sound-substitution alters lexical borrowings from other languages is seen in loan words, which are usually introduced by literate persons with a command of alien pronunciations; but poorly educated imitators falter and favour approximate sounds familiar to them.

I have tried to limit my account of the phonological changes caused by these invasions to the barest minimum, in the belief that too much philology can prove a barren field to the student. Equally, I have sought to avoid contentious religious issues like the murder of Thomas Becket. Chaucer's use of *blissful* in the phrase 'the holy blissful martyr' can only mean 'blessed', not 'happy'. For Becket was a man of towering ambition, who probably sought to be honoured by posterity through martyrdom.

My deepest obligation is to Professor David Crystal for his patient encouragement in bringing this study to completion. For the typing, indexing and proof-reading of the book, I am indebted to my wife, who made frequent suggestions for improving the balance and usefulness of the final version. Principal instruments for the use of material sources have been the British Library, the Municipal Library, Johannesburg, and the Library of the University of the Witwatersrand, to whose willing hands educators like myself are perennially grateful.

A.C.P.

January 1981   *Johannesburg*

Part One
TO THE CONQUEST

CHAPTER I

The Romano-Celtic Prelude

𒐫𒐫𒐫𒐫𒐫𒐫

THE ANNALS OF ENGLAND, from the first Roman expedition in 55 BC to the death of Richard III (AD 1485), occupy a period of over fifteen hundred years, about three quarters of the country's known history. It is important that this time-scale should be seen in perspective, against the background of the earlier Celtic settlement, which lasted some eight hundred years. Although there is no literature in an indigenous language to represent the period of Roman occupation, Latin contributions in administrative planning, law and communication are so unmistakable, that an account of the internal situation is the most appropriate introduction to subsequent linguistic changes.

Some account of the situation immediately before the Roman conquest is essential to the understanding of Rome's imperialistic aims. The roving Celts were partly invaders, partly refugee settlers. Compared with Rome's well-organized colonies, Celtic society during the Iron Age was primitive, as it was dependent entirely on what the enviroment could provide. The Ordnance Survey map of Roman Britain shows that the Midlands and the South were heavily wooded, and seldom more than eight hundred feet above sea-level. Here was a territory teeming with wild beasts that had to be hunted. Lines of communication consisted almost wholly of ridgeways and rivers.

Celtic settlements in Britain resulted from successive cultural waves during the fifth, third and first centuries BC, emanating from northern France, between Brittany and the Rhine. One group settled in Cornwall, Devon and Somerset, and began building numerous hill-forts in Wessex, at a time of considerable tribal unrest. The most progressive Celts, the Belgae, were the last to arrive, about 75 BC, settling in Kent, Essex and Hertfordshire; Caesar styled them the Catuvellauni, and their principal centre was *Camulodunum* (Colchester). Caesar's envoy, Commius, a chieftain

1

of the Atrebates, made the crossing a generation later, and settled his Belgic people, from Northern Gaul, in the Thames Valley, Hampshire and the western part of Sussex, where they mixed with the earlier Celtic inhabitants.

The principal builders and users of the British camps or hill-forts (called *oppida* by the Romans) were the peasant farmers, a particular *sept* (sub-division of a tribe) in the Celtic social scale. The peasants kept in contact with their Belgic forebears in Gaul, to whom they were indebted for the first use of a coinage system. There was trade across the Channel in precious metals, cattle, corn, slaves and hunting dogs. In the early first century AD, King Cunobelin ruled over most of southern England and the Midlands, as far north as Huntingdonshire and Northamptonshire. The Iceni were masters of East Anglia and Lincolnshire.

To the Romans, Britain was an outpost of Empire, a province to be subdued and governed by military power, and inevitably exploited. Julius Caesar realized the necessity of extending the Atlantic frontier of Rome's dominions to Britain; for its Gaulish inhabitants were in constant league with rebellious forces on the Continent. Caesar's plan was not, however, put into effect by Augustus, one reason being that the expansion of the Roman Empire was at that time predominantly eastward; it was considered that the future of the Empire's prosperity lay in Asia.

The more purposeful of the two invasions was that of Claudius's four legions, which took place in AD 43, under the command of the senator, Aulus Plautius. Claudius hankered after military triumph at the expense of tribal dissidents in Britain, and coveted the mineral resources of the country; he was encouraged by the anti-Roman stance of Cunobelin's son, Caratacus, who had ousted the Roman ally, Bericus. The Roman landing was at first unopposed, but a delayed engagement took place at the crossing of the Medway, in which the future Emperor, Vespasian, played a notable part. The Roman forces were eventually drawn up on the south bank of the Thames, until the pre-arranged arrival of Claudius from Rome, via Ostia, Marseilles and Gaul. The Thames was then crossed in three ways, by swimming, by a bridge and by a ford at Westminster. The awaiting Britons were easily defeated by Claudius, Camulodunum was entered, and peace negotiated. Claudius returned to Rome for his triumph and received the cognomen 'Britannicus'; the rest of the campaign was left in the hands of Plautius, Governor of the new province. Invariably, a Roman advance was secured by the building of a substantial road. One of the first was Ermine Street, which ran due north from London. It was five years after the first landing before the ninth legion established itself in Lincoln, which lies on Ermine Street.

The conquest of the south and south-west of England was entrusted to Vespasian and the second legion. He subdued the Isle of Wight, using the harbour at Fishbourne, near Chichester, as a supply base; he overcame the Durotriges in what was to become Wessex, successfully stormed twenty of their fortified *oppida*, including Maiden Castle and Hod Hill, and advanced westward as far as present Devonshire. The historian Suetonius described Vespasian as the hero of thirty battles. The other two legions were deployed along Watling Street in the direction of Wroxeter. According to the *Annals* of Tacitus (Book XII), the western boundary of the province was by AD 47 established along the Trent-Severn line, later to be called the Fosse Way, a dependable route connecting Exeter with Lincoln.

With the best farming land in the possession of the Romans, including the rich corn-producing area of East Anglia, succeeding Governors pursued a policy of consolidation, negotiating with client chiefs on the British border, such as Queen Cartimandua of the Brigantes and King Cogidubnus, who was based at Chichester. Auxiliary troops used on the frontier were drawn from all parts of the Empire, but principally Gaul, Germany, Spain, Syria and North Africa; in engagements these cohorts were placed in the front line, with the seasoned Roman veterans immediately behind them. It took auxiliaries twenty-five years of exemplary service to acquire Roman citizenship, and their origin is often recorded on the ubiquitous stone inscriptions.

Gradually the frontier was pushed forward by the establishment of legionary fortresses at Gloucester (AD 49), Wroxeter (before AD 60) and York (AD 71). The new military centres were intended as bases for the conquest of Wales in the west and Brigantia in the north. During the fourteen years AD 71–84 (the age of the Flavian Emperors, Vespasian, Titus and Domitian), three Governors were responsible for carrying out the expansionist programme dictated from Rome; these were Petillius Cerialis, Julius Frontinus and Julius Agricola. The object of these campaigns was to secure all the lowland areas, suitable for farming and food production, by occupying the adjacent uplands and subjecting them to control from fortified positions.

The Brigantes, who were in possession of practically all northern England, were not a homogeneous people, but a confederation of Celtic tribes, warlike and numerous, ruled by a dynastic chieftain. The area was coveted because it was well adapted to the grazing of cattle and sheep. Cerialis advanced from York in AD 71 and defeated the usurping ruler of the Brigantes, Venutius, at Stanwick, just north of present-day Scotch Corner; this enabled him to continue his advance in a north-westerly direction towards Carlisle. The subjugation of the north of England in three years was a considerable military achievement.

In AD 74 Frontinus, author of a treatise on strategy, moved into Monmouthshire against the Silures of South Wales; this he did by landing troops on the coast and occupying the mouths of the rivers Wye and Usk. He then advanced up the valleys and secured his position by establishing the second (Augusta) legion at *Isca* (Caerleon-upon-Usk). The word *Caerleon* is Welsh for *castra legionis*.

It was left to Agricola in AD 78 to overcome the Ordovices of north Wales, with the second (Adiutrix) legion, a body of European soldiers, which had been stationed and tested at Lincoln, but was now installed in a new fortress at Chester. Agricola was himself a native of Gaul, from Fréjus on the Mediterranean coast; he was born in AD 40, had served in Britain with distinction, and recently been Governor in the Gaulish province of Aquitania (south-western France). In north Wales he established forts at Flint, Denbigh and Caernarvon, controlled from the new military centre he created at Chester.

Although Eric Birley in *Roman Britain and the Roman Army* (1961) has taken a moderate view of Agricola's generalship, the latter's energetic persistence during seven successive summers marked the peak of Roman aggression. In AD 79 Agricola gained most success by adroit pressuring of opposition forces, and by the genius he invariably displayed for sound reconnaissance. He moved his troops by sea along the west coast of England to southern Scotland, sending the ninth legion, under Caristanius Fronto, on the east side of the Pennines, to establish fortifications at Corbridge on the Tyne, and Newstead on the River Tweed, near the Eildon Hills. The latter became one of the principal centres of Roman power in Scotland. In the Lowlands, from east to west, the Votadini, Selgovae and Novantae were pacified.

In the summer of AD 80 Agricola advanced from the Clyde-Forth line to the Tay (*Tanaus*), again without a struggle. He was a tactful general and a Governor of temperate personality, anxious to romanize the Celts by bestowing upon them the benefits of education and the amenities of civilized life. With an eye to strategic significance, he erected a legionary fortress at Inchtuthil, and spent his fourth and fifth summers building roads, strengthening the isthmus that made the north of Scotland virtually an island, and exploring the west coast. This was achieved with only minor skirmishes, leading Agricola to believe that the Ireland he could see from the coast might be taken with the strength of a single legion.

It was not until AD 83 and 84 that Agricola met with desperate opposition from the Caledonians, first in a night attack, and then at Mons Graupius, where the Romans, about twenty thousand in number, were confronted by. an army of thirty thousand. The Roman legions were below strength, for detachments had been withdrawn to aid Domitian's campaign on the Rhine. But he had secured his retreat by building a fort to block each of the entrances to the highland valleys. The battle of Mons Graupius, near the Moray Firth, took place immediately in front of Agricola's camp and resulted in considerable slaughter of the enemy. Ten thousand were killed, against the invaders' loss of only 360, few of whom were of Roman blood.

Shortly after this victory, Agricola was recalled to Rome, where he died in retirement ten years later. The speech which Tacitus put into the mouth of Calgacus, a Caledonian chieftain, before the battle of Mons Graupius is fictitious, but a notable indictment of imperial military government. Under this system Celts from the Continent and Britain were conscripted and trained for what was little more than organized plunder of their own kindred. But Highland resistance, in the course of time, prevailed. As A. R. Burn wrote, in *Agricola and Roman Britain* (1953), 'Calgacus and his friends and the men who fell at Mons Craupius [note the approved spelling] might have lost a battle, but they had won the war' (p 157).

There is no record of what happened in Roman Britain after the withdrawal of Agricola, until the building of Hadrian's Wall (AD 122–33). One reason seems to be that the scene of large-scale military operations now moved to the Danube. But inscriptions show that at the beginning of the second century AD, the war of resistance was renewed in Britain, in the reign of Trajan. One of the unsolved mysteries of this period is the disappearance after AD 108 of the ninth legion, Hispana, from the Roman roll of geographical units. This was supposed by some writers to imply a disaster that occurred during the second British rising between AD 119 and 125; but the probable explanation is to be found in transference of Hispana to the Jewish uprising in AD 132, and the legion's subsequent dispersal, because of the depletion of its numbers.

The Lowlands of Scotland continued to be occupied until about AD 100; but the rebellious north was so troublesome that Hadrian personally surveyed the situation four years after he became Emperor. He decided to strengthen the strategic Stanegate road, constructed by Agricola from Corbridge to Carlisle, by building a fortified line, seventy-six miles long, on the north side of it. Hadrian's wall extends from Wallsend to Bowness-on-Solway, what remains being about fifteen feet high, with a ten-foot-deep ditch in front of it, on the north side, and a Vallum (demarcation line) and 'military way' on the southern side. Several British tribes seem to have had a hand in its construction.

Built mainly by the second, sixth and twentieth legions, the Wall is the most elaborate Roman frontier work anywhere in Europe, comprising dozens of forts, mile-castles and turrets, spaced at regular intervals. Indeed, the Stanegate and most other forts, and the Vallum, were probably built first, and the connecting wall added later by Platorius Nepos, Governor of Britain from AD 122–26 (see R. G. Collingwood, *A Guide to the Roman Wall*, 3rd edn 1933, p 10, and E. Birley, *Research on Hadrian's Wall*, 1961, p 120ff). But the Wall was not merely defensive in a military sense; its object was to prevent cattle-rustling and petty raids, and at the same time to act as a customs barrier.

One of the reasons for the impending dismemberment of the Roman Empire was the strain on its expanding frontiers; they had become too extensive for control by a largely non-Roman army, opposing half-conquered or disaffected tribesmen. In the time of the Emperor Antoninus Pius (AD 138–61) a determined attempt was made at north-British consolidation. The Governor, Lollius Urbicus, recovered the Lowlands of Scotland about AD 140; but the Antonine Wall, which was constructed in 143, had not the strategic advantage of its predecessor; it was too far from the legionary bases in northern England. This was shown in the year 155, when Roman armies met with disaster after disaster, and had to be reinforced from the Continent. In AD 181 the Scottish Wall was severely damaged by the Picts; but neither bastion was finally abandoned until fifteen years later.

The capture of Hadrian's Wall in AD 196, the first of three reverses that punctuate the decline of Roman power in Britain, was due to dissension arising from military autocracy and personal ambition within the body politic. Gibbon, in *The Decline and Fall of the Roman Empire*, traces the beginnings of disruption to Augustus's creation of the Praetorian guards, and the established principle that the Emperor should be elected by the authority of the Senate *and the consent of the soldiers*. His reasoning dates the onset of the decline from the assassination of Commodus in AD 192, when rival claimants used the military strength they possessed to get themselves elected. One of these claimants in the year 196 was Clodius Albinus, Governor of Britain, who crossed to France with a large army of Roman legions and Britons, to press his candidature; another was Septimus Severus, Governor of Moesia, who defeated his rival at Lyons in the next year.

The withdrawal of legions from the north by Albinus enabled the Maeatae and Brigantes to breach Hadrian's Wall in many places and overrun part of the Roman province, as far south as York. The situation was not fully restored until the arrival in Britain of the Emperor Severus in AD 208; he remained until his death in York in 211. His campaign against the Caledonians was continued for a while by Severus's sons, Caracalla and Geta. The strategy was similar to that of Agricola, in establishing supply bases on the Tyne, the Forth and the Tay, and transporting the bulk of the troops by sea. A Roman coin depicts Caracalla crossing a river by a bridge of boats, and it is supposed that the Firth of Forth is here represented, at a point near where the bridge now stands. Though peace was restored in the northern province and Scotland, Severus and Caracalla had demonstrated how vulnerable the east coast of Britain was to attack by armed ships.

The disturbed period of Severus's activities followed a century called by Gibbon the 'Age of the Antonines' (AD 98–180), which he described as Rome's most peaceful and progressive era of enlightened despotism. Gibbon's study of Severus shows him to have been acquisitive and inflexible, but just, especially to the oppressed. He was a tireless builder and restorer of towns, roads and public amenities.

The passing of Severus saw the beginning of many civil settlements in the north of England, especially in the neighbourhood of Hadrian's Wall. There was a steadier mingling of interests, and better recruitment to the Roman garrisons from the British inhabitants. A contributory reason for this was an edict of Severus that legionaries should be allowed to marry while on active service, and even to lease land, provided their sons enlisted in the army. Severus was in this way responsible for the creation of garrison towns like Carlisle, and the promotion on the northern border of peasant farmers disposed to a more peaceful way of life.

There is little documentary history of Britain for the next eighty years, often regarded as the most prosperous era of the Roman occupation; but during the first half of the third century the principal fortresses of Caerleon, Chester and York were either strengthened or rebuilt, and towns with little military significance began to be enclosed with stone walls. These were necessary precautions, because Germanic invaders made their first inroads in the earlier half of this century. They were mainly Saxon and Frisian pirates from the country between the Rhine delta and the mouth of the River Elbe. The whole of the east coast of Britain lay open to them; but the first marauders came to the south-east. Depredations were encouraged by the inability of the military defences in western Europe to contain the migrating land-hungry tribesmen. In 286 the Roman authorities appointed a Belgian, named Carausius, as admiral of the British Fleet, because of his knowledge of the North Sea coast; and he for a time successfully defended the exposed eastern and southern shores.

Like many naturalized citizens in responsible office, Carausius was corruptible, and Rome indicted him for collusion with the pirates whereby he was able to share in their spoils. He then took the bold step of declaring himself Emperor of Britain and parts of Northern Gaul. During the years AD 287–93 he was acknowledged as such until killed by Allectus, a member of his own staff. Three years later Allectus himself was removed from power by Constantius Chlorus, Caesar of the western half of the Roman Empire. He defeated Allectus in the south of England, and then moved north to retake Chester and restore Hadrian's Wall, which had fallen to the native tribes on the withdrawal of its garrisons to sustain the civil war. Constantius died during another campaign in Britain at York in AD 306, and his son, Constantine, was immediately proclaimed Roman Emperor. Constantine later defeated his rival Maxentius at the battle of the Milvian Bridge outside Rome in AD 313, and it was before this battle that Constantine claimed he saw the vision that converted him to Christianity.

In the second half of the third century, the plight of the disintegrating Roman Empire, already suffering economically from inflation, was desperate. The Goths had invaded the Balkan provinces; the Alamanni and Franks had crossed the Danube and Rhine and entered Gaul, penetrating as far as north-east Spain. From AD 259 to 274 a separate Gallic Empire came into being, which included Britain and Spain, until its independence was terminated by Emperor Aurelian. The later secession of Britain under Carausius was not therefore without precedent; there had also been previous attempts at rebellion against Probus (276–82). Whenever there was civil war of this kind, the Picts and their allies took the opportunity of raiding Britain, and the Saxons were quick to increase their pressure on the coastal towns from the North Sea.

Under the brief British Emperorship of Constantius Chlorus (AD 296–306) the so-called Saxon Shore was placed on the alert; it extended from the Wash in the east to the Isle of Wight in the south. Forts were already in existence at Richborough and Reculver, and new ones were erected at Dover and Lympne; a little later also at Porchester, Pevensey, Bradwell, at Walton and Burgh Castles, and at Brancaster. Others were soon provided at strategic points on the west coast, to ward off attacks by the Irish.

The situation again became serious in AD 367, when there was a co-ordinated assault upon Britain by Picts, Irish, Scots, Saxons and Franks. Hadrian's Wall was completely overwhelmed by the Picts; the Scots from Ireland attacked England's north-west coast, while Saxons and Franks landed on the shores of Kent. The Count of the Saxon Shore was killed, and the Duke of Britain (head of the home forces stationed at York) was encircled and taken prisoner. The Emperor Valentinian was compelled to send a Spanish military expert, Count Theodosius, with a strong army, to restore order in Britain, where the bewildered auxiliaries threatened desertion.

Theodosius found that London was already beseiged; it took him three years to reconquer the five provinces into which Britain was now divided for administrative purposes, and to rebuild Hadrian's

Wall. But the role of this great bulwark was coming to an end. The solution to the border problem was found in the creation of buffer-states, which took the form of nominally independent British kingdoms on the northern frontier. On the English side of the Wall thirty-four peasant villages (partly romanized) sprang up during the fourth century, including Chester, Lanchester, Housesteads, Penrith, Bowness, Ravenglass and Ambleside. Knowledge of the progress of this period depends largely on the testimony of the historian Ammianus Marcellinus in *Rerum Gestarum Libri*, substantiated by inscriptions unearthed by the archaeologists.

Theodosius restored confidence by pardoning the auxiliary troops that had defected; he constructed signal-stations, about a hundred feet high, along the Yorkshire coast, to keep a constant watch on sea-raiders, one of the better preserved being found near Goldsborough. But in AD 383 the rule of law was once more disrupted. Magnus Maximus, a high-ranking officer of Spanish origin, who had been enrolling recruits for the army among the Atecotti of the client-kingdom of Galloway, seized power as the Emperor of Britain. Whatever his motives, Maximus claimed the right to control the western sector of the imperial government; he crossed to France with an army, and defeated the Emperor Gratian near Paris. Relying on troops he had drawn from Britain, he overran Gaul and Spain in the next four years. In AD 388 he invaded Italy, only to lose the decisive battle of Aquileia against Theodosius I, ruler of the Eastern Empire in Constantinople. When Theodosius the Great (son of Count Theodosius) died in AD 395, the effective power of Rome in Britain had virtually ended. A considerable Saxon raid on England had taken place in AD 390. At this time of crisis, the new Emperor Honorius being a mere boy, pretenders and usurpers made unavailing bids for power. One of them, the usurper Constantine III (407–410), was British, but he was captured and killed at Arles.

For Britain, already drained of its defending legions, the final blow came with the withdrawal of Rome's military officials in AD 410, the year in which Rome itself was sacked by the Gothic leader, Alaric. Romanized towns in England were told by Honorius to organize their own defences, and some hired Anglian and Saxon mercenaries. A sporadic return of Roman military support was made in AD 429 under St Germanus; but at this stage the political figure who mattered was the Romano-Celt, Vortigern.

The document which throws most light on the internal changes is the *Notitia Dignitatum* (date undetermined, but possibly AD 395). It shows that the Duke of Britain (*Dux Britanniarum*) was, in fact, the head of the *foederati* (frontier or auxiliary army), whose soldiers were known as *limitanei* (Latin *limes*, 'a boundary'). The *Comes litoris Saxonici* (Count of the Saxon Shore), the office that arose out of the invasion of 367, was in origin a naturalized Roman, tested as a responsible leader. The effect of Honorius's message, recommending self-reliance, was to repeal the law that unknown Celtic tribesmen were not allowed to bear arms. For practical purposes, the termination of Roman rule in Britan dates from about AD 415, and its direct cultural influence from 450.

The principal source of information about Vortigern is Gildas's *De Excidio Britanniae*, though this jeremiad may be prejudiced in blaming him for the Anglo-Saxon invasions. The Latin form of the name (according to Bede) is *Vertigernus*, and the Saxon *Wyrtgeorn*, meaning 'overlord'. When the Romans left the province, Vortigern became the undoubted ruler of the greater part of romanized Britain, and the presence of Saxons in the territory at that stage was due to their employment as mercenary soldiers. Archaeological evidence suggests that, as early as the beginning of the fourth century, Saxons used in this way were actually granted rights as settlers, but remained in regular contact with their people across the North Sea.

Vortigern had married Sevira, daughter of Magnus Maximus, who was revered as a British champion. In legend Magnus was known as Maxen Wledig, ancestor of Welsh kings, the only Celtic rebel who had killed a Roman Emperor (Gratian). Vortigern assumed the role of arch anti-Romanist, and was probably a defender of the British Pelagian heresy which rejected the doctrine of Original Sin. Hence the dual mission to Britain of St Germanus, as military leader and protector of the orthodox Christian faith, and the Augustinian belief in divine grace (see G. P. Fisher, *History of the Christian Church*, 1908, pp 135–7).

It remains to assess the impact of the Roman occupation on British society, its religion, military organization, language and culture.

At the time of Cicero and Caesar, the Graeco-Roman religion of the Republic was polytheistic, a synthesis of different cults and creeds; and the western sector of the Empire, which controlled a body of largely Celtic peoples, became the melting-pot of many different forms of worship.

The religious awe of the Roman people, embodying its fears and superstitions, was not profoundly metaphysical. There were two aspects of observance, the personal and the public. The earliest belief was in *numina* or spiritual forces, which were peculiar to places (woods, groves, rivers and mountains) and indispensable to domestic felicity. The household gods, such as the *Vesta* (guardians of the hearth) and the *Penates* (who provided food and other necessities), were especially revered; but there were also gods of mystic force, such as *Ianus* ('the spirit of the door', from which January is derived), who initiated human activity. In honour of *Lar*, the spirit of the fields, the rural community celebrated their seasonal festivals, and adorned a figurine with flowers. Respect for the household shrine was more important to the Roman people than public worship. Prayers were said twice daily, and the perpetual fire on the hearth was only extinguished and relit by the *paterfamilias* once a year, on March the first, which was the beginning of the Roman New Year.

This simple, but picturesque, ministration of rites which was the source of *virtus*, remained a patrician, and not a plebeian privilege, and for this reason it could not survive the advent of civil strife, when *Fortuna* (Fate or Chance) became one of the presiding deities. It was about this time that religion tended to be linked to the State, rather than the family, and the number of public holidays was irrationally increased. There were about a hundred a year in Cicero's day, with the result that many were not observed. By this time anthropomorphic gods, based on those of Olympus, enjoyed more favour in the popular fancy than the *numina* of high moral purpose. It is believed that the worship of mythological gods in terracotta and the practice of augury began with the Etruscans (700–400 BC), and splendid examples of Apollo, Herakles and Hermes were found at Portonaccio in 1916. The Romans, as great cultural borrowers, were particularly partial to Jupiter, Juno, Apollo, Venus, Mars, Diana, Neptune, Ceres, Minerva, Vulcan and Mercury; and they later appropriated from sculpture abstract representations, such as Justice, Hope and Victory, which were not unlike *Fortuna* in supernatural potentialities.

After the Punic Wars and the expansion of the Empire under

militarists such as Julius Caesar, further alien gods made their appearance in Rome, now a cosmopolitan city resembling Alexandria. In the second century BC came Cybele from Phrygia, whom the Romans called *Magna Mater*; then there was Serapis, of Egyptian origin; and the Persian god, Mithras, who became important objects of veneration. From Asia, too, the pomp and luxury of religious ceremony was first introduced, along with public games and spectacles. Materialistic culture was encroaching on the religious life of the community, and high offices, such as that of *Pontifex Maximus*, became available for public election. Cicero in his books *Of the Nature of the Gods* and *The Laws* rebuked the nation for its unrestrained absurdities of superstition and corruption. From the rule of Augustus to that of Tiberius, it was the custom to deify mighty Emperors during their life-time, and to expect demonstrations of loyalty through offerings of incense upon the altar.

In the provinces it was not an easy matter to reconcile Roman practices with the local pagan forms of worship; but as polytheism was common to the religions encountered, a compromise was effected, whereby new gods were incorporated in the Roman hierarchies, e.g. *Mars Leucetius* (the god of lightning). The keynote was flexibility in the modification of beliefs and ritual. A number of Latin inscriptions testify to the diversity of Romano-Celtic religious practices in Britain during the occupation, the deities principally honoured being Mars and Mercury. *Minerva Sulis* was the presiding goddess of Bath and its healing waters. The centre of orthodox Roman worship was undoubtedly Colchester, where a huge stone temple was dedicated in AD 50 to the worship of the ruling Emperor; but the British Celts, unlike their forebears in Gaul, were not attracted to the cult of Emperor worship. This may have been a contributory reason for the rising of the Iceni under Queen Boudicca; for the British had to bear the cost of the imported stone. The practice among the Britons was not to elevate any god above another; their deities being tribal, no hierarchy was feasible. The Celtic gods rather resembled the domestic *Penates* of primitive Roman worship.

The Germanic soldiers enrolled in the auxiliary units were located mainly in the north among the Brigantes, and their presence is recorded by inscriptions to such deities as Viradecthis. Soldiers from the Eastern Empire were remembered in military areas principally by their worship of Mithras and Isis when the cult of the former was widespread in Italy and Provence. In England, Mithra-ism, which was a religion for men only, appears to have been practised in London and amongst the Batavi stationed at Carraw-burgh (*Brocolitia*) on Hadrian's Wall; both of their small temples were probably desecrated by Christians. At the eastern end of the Wall, on the River Tyne, altars to Asiatic and Egyptian gods were fairly common. Archaeological evidence indeed suggests that the Romans were tolerant of nature-worship, and other alien forms of religion, unless Rome opposed such manifestations on political grounds; as it did, at first, in the case of Judaism and Christianity, whose devotees refused reverence to the Emperor. Druidism was probably suppressed for humanitarian reasons.

Constantine's recognition of Christianity, when he became sole Emperor (AD 324), did not mean that the ruler was officially a Christian; he accepted baptism on his deathbed, but in the daily conduct of affairs was content to enjoy the best of both worlds. The first note of Christianity as a religion in England is the report that three bishops, from London, York and Lincoln, attended the Church Council at Arles in AD 314. Christianity was slow to gain a footing, both in Gaul and Britain; but once established its followers adhered more strictly to the spiritual disciplines than did churches and monasteries of the eastern Mediterranean and Italy. Christian monasticism, based on that of the Essenes of Judaea, did not reach Rome until AD 340 (St Athanasius); and Gaul, through St Martin of Tours, about twenty-five years later.

There was a temporary pagan reaction during the reign of Julian the Apostate (AD 361–3), who revived the cult of Apollo. In Britain the return of heathenism was accelerated by the combined invasion of AD 367, and a large temple to the Celtic god Nodens was erected at Lydney, overlooking the Severn estuary. The British were sympathetic to the old-fashioned Roman reverence for the spirits of place, which accounts for the survival of Celtic names of rivers, mountains, springs and places of natural interest. But the fourth-century pagan setback was far from universal, for churches and private chapels in villas survived until the early fifth century, when the Pelagian heresy excited the interest of anti-Roman British followers.

In the fifteenth chapter of *The Decline and Fall of the Roman Empire*, Gibbon appraises the zeal of early Christians, and cites their 'pure and austere morals' as one reason for their 'victory over the established religions of the earth'. Another reason was their 'just confidence in immortality', important, because it was widely prophesied that the end of the world was approaching, through fire and earthquake. The prediction was partially fulfilled by the destruction of Pompeii and Herculaneum in AD 79. The untiring missionary activity of Christians within the Empire was facilitated by the efficient communications system of the legionary roads, along which the apostles travelled from urban centres such as Jerusalem, Antioch, Alexandria, Corinth, Rome and Marseilles; they spread the gospel from the Euphrates to the shores of Britain. By the middle of the third century, there were more than fifty thousand adherents of the faith in Rome; and it was calculated by Chrysostom, that in the Roman domains of Theodosius, pagans and Jews combined were outnumbered by Christians. Ecclesiastical government was highly organized, and the Church became wealthy in landed property, precious vessels, ornaments and coin.

The disabilities of Christian communities from Nero to Diocletian, and the scant attention accorded to them in the writings of Seneca, Tacitus, Pliny and Plutarch, make their rise to influence improbable, but for the protection of Constantine. The Edict of Tolerance in Milan in AD 313 was only less revolutionary than the Emperor's division of citizens into clergy and laity, allowing the former autonomous juridical power over the spiritual welfare of the people. The status of women was irrevocably enhanced, their role in the Church being a decisive factor in the spread of Christianity. Constantine restored to the Christian laity all property of which they had been deprived by Diocletian. He also endowed the clergy with exceptional privileges (such as the censorship of morals) and immunities (such as the right of asylum), which helped to swell ecclesiastical ranks at the expense of the army. The power of the Emperor was reciprocally increased through the moral support of bishops and presbyters from the pulpit.

It was Constantine who caused the first basilicas to be built over the relics of St Peter and St Paul in Rome. So conservative was the capital, and so rooted in paganism were the Senate and leading citizens, that Constantine took the far-reaching step of founding a holy city for his dynasty on the site of ancient Byzantium. Though he had endowed many temples of Apollo, his victorious armies began to be feared because they marched under the banner of the Cross, known as the *Labarum*.

The effect of Constantine's more than three hundred enactments was felt throughout the Empire; and though the immediate repercussions in Britain were less momentous, they were often permanent. Partly by rendering the Senate innocuous as a political influence, Constantine set the pattern of absolute monarchy that dominated the Dark and Middle Ages; at the same time his enactments accorded the Roman Catholic Church a temporal power that was unforeseen. The Empire was being maintained at considerable expense to the establishment, and the burden of taxation, which supported the Church and the new city of Constantinople, was heavy. Diocletian and Constantine were apparently the first fiscal progressives to levy taxes on the profits of trade.

Rome's policy had never been to enslave conquered peoples, but rather to enlist them as allies and draw upon their resources in commodities and manpower. The auxiliaries raised among Celtic and other alien tribes were not mercenaries, but prospective Roman citizens, enrolled for twenty years and finally rewarded with a pension and a grant of land. The professional soldiery in Gaul and Britain was fired by a disciplined loyalty to commanders; for the *peregrini* (auxiliaries) regarded themselves as sharers in a political enterprise, to expand Roman citizenship in the provinces, of which the army soon became fully representative. Originally, a large army meant continuous employment for semi-literate plebeians of *Italian* towns, who had little share in patrician government; in the end the replacement of these Italians by provincials became a potential risk to the state. Both discipline and resourcefulness suffered from a lack of romanizing motivation. By the time of Constantine, army officers had become conscious of their power to make and unmake Emperors, who like Constantine and Diocletian were sometimes not of Italian origin.

Before the onset of political anarchy initiated by war-lords, the demands made upon the provinces for feeding and transporting the Roman legions were not excessive. Transport was occasionally necessary for the rapid movement of troops, predominantly infantrymen, carrying equipment weighing some sixty pounds. The use of cavalry was limited to 120 *equites* per legion, until the age of Constantine.

When Augustus died (AD 14), the strength of the entire Roman army was twenty-five legions, or approximately 150,000 men. By Trajan's reign (AD 98–117) the legions had been increased to thirty, and Roman citizens were already outnumbered by the tally of auxiliary cohorts. Hadrian drafted a force of about 33,000 auxiliaries to the Wall area alone, but only a small proportion is likely to have been British, since in this period it was not the army's policy to use indigenous recruits in the home country. A rough calculation will show that there was then a cohort (about 500 men) for each mile of Wall to be patrolled. Besides campaigning, every auxiliary cohort in defence of a frontier had to help in the construction of fortifications. The Antonine Wall, completed in AD 144, was built by special detachments of *peregrini*, known as vexillations; and the manning of this line imposed a much heavier strain on the depleted strength of the army in Britain.

Caerleon, headquarters of the Second Augustan Legion, is a typical example of a permanent military fortification in Britain. It was built in AD 75 during the governorship of Sextus Julius Frontinus, when Wales was being pacified, and was used as a military reserve for technicians, as well as a garrison town, containing an amphitheatre for games and ceremonies. Outside the walls there grew up a settlement of traders, workmen and other camp-followers, known as a *vicus*; beyond there were wheatfields stretching to the Severn, to supply the essential granaries of the legion. This body of men was under the command of a *legatus legionis* of senatorial rank, who received regular despatches by the hand of a mounted messenger. No less than sixteen routes were served by this postal service in the third century. There was constant communication with neighbouring forts, such as *Glevum* (Gloucester), *Corinium* (Cirencester) and *Viroconium* (Wroxeter) near the Wrekin. Caerleon, being in a uniquely strategic position, could receive all its heavier supplies by boat from the mouth of the Severn.

Severus, at the beginning of the third century, first separated the British territory into two provinces, Britannia Superior and Britannia Inferior, for the purpose of more efficient military control. Although the boundaries are unknown, these corresponded roughly to the highland and lowland areas. In the reign of Diocletian, at the end of this century, when the Empire became a tetrarchy, Britain (by now divided into four provinces) fell under the civil jurisdiction of a *vicarius* in London, responsible to the Praetorian Prefect at Trier. This official's authority extended to transalpine Gaul and Spain, the three countries thus forming a western administrative bloc. A fifth province, called Valentia, beyond Hadrian's Wall, was added to the Romano-British system of control at the conclusion of the Pictish War (AD 367–70); and thereafter a fleet based on Boulogne, known as *Classis Sambrica* (from the Roman name for the River Somme), patrolled the whole of the north Gaulish seaboard.

The importance of the British provinces to Rome, in agriculture, trade and industry, can be gauged by the large body of armed forces retained in some eighty forts at the height of the Empire's power. For more than a century after the death of Severus (AD 211) the lowland areas enjoyed a measure of security and prosperity, and a considerable number of towns and villages came into being, commencing with the *coloniae* of retired veterans at Colchester and Lincoln.

A reliable picture of Romano-Celtic culture is to be obtained from studying the archaeological remains of *coloniae* and towns in the east, south and midland parts of the lowlands. The generals who commanded the legions did not disturb the Celtic way of life, but used tribal aristocrats to divert public energies into profitable channels. This was achieved by allowing them to retain the reins of local government; but also through education, the development of agricultural estates, and respect for religious institutions. The amenities of life were splendidly preserved in such towns as *Camulodunum* (Colchester), *Naviomagus* (Chichester), *Calleva Atrebatum* (Silchester), *Verulamium* (St Albans) and *Aquae Sulis* (Bath). Of these Silchester, ten miles south of Reading, disappeared as a town in the fifth century.

As recently as 1960 a workman digging a trench for a water-main near Fishbourne, a few miles from Chichester, uncovered the remains of a Roman palace occupying several acres. Its size, the elaborate baths, audience chamber, mosaic pavements, interior decorations and colonnaded garden, show that the owner was a man of considerable wealth and importance, probably a client-king, who enjoyed cordial relations with the Roman authorities. The most likely person was King Cogidubnus of the Regnenses, whose seat was on the Sussex coast. No harbour better meets the requirements than Fishbourne, which was used by Vespasian as a base for his conquest of south-western England. The first stage of development here has been dated, by the discovery of Claudian coins, as between AD 43 and 75. An inscribed stone now preserved in the Chichester Museum, bearing the words *Tiberius Claudius Cogidumnus, rex et legatus Augusti in Britannia*, indicates that this man had been granted Roman citizenship of senatorial status, and was therefore a trusted ally of the imperial government.

The Fishbourne river mouth has now receded; but in Vespasian's time the harbour was first a military depot, then a civil settlement for trade with Brittany, the Channel Islands and Cornwall. The palace on the river, judging by its earliest Neronian style, was probably begun about AD 65; but Carrara marble from Italy and breccia from France were later imported for dressing by skilled masons. The magnificent mosaic floors, with which most of the rooms were paved, could only have been the work of craftsmen from the Mediterranean, first, of the Flavian period (about AD 75), later, of the second and third centuries AD. The palace appears, from archaeological evidence, to have been demolished about AD 270.

When Julius Caesar defeated Cassivellaunus in 54 BC, there was a Belgic settlement at Prae Wood, near the present city of St Albans. Here King Cunobelin operated a mint, from which some moulds have been found. The first Roman construction at Verulamium was a fort, with a wooden tower on Watling Street, overlooking the River Ver. The town was laid out in square blocks in the first century and established by the middle of the second century. Among the archaeological finds made by S. S. Frere when excavating the town's defences in 1956 were timber shops and a coin of the Emperor Septimus Severus (AD 193–211) in perfect condition. The shops were destroyed by fire about AD 155, but a bronze figurine of Venus, discovered by Frere in 1961, survived the conflagration (see I. Anthony, *The Roman City of Verulamium*, 1970, pp 9–11).

The next stage was to provide Verulamium with houses built of flint (AD 50–100); to this period belongs a small private chapel dedicated to some undetermined pagan cult. In the next century the homes became more elaborate, with decorated walls, mosaic floors and hypocausts (under-floor heating). Verulamium was provided with public baths; and during the rule of Agricola a basilica had been erected for meetings of the *Municipium*. After the fire of AD 155 the amenities were improved by the addition of an amphitheatre, which accommodated over five thousand spectators.

This was used in association with an adjacent temple, which had become a place of Christian worship by the time St Germanus visited St Albans (AD 429) for discussions on the Pelagian heresy.

London, in spite of an earlier Celtic trading settlement there, is essentially a Roman town, strategically located as the radiating centre of a road system that has always been of commercial importance. *Londinium*, a place-name recorded in AD 60, was ideally situated as a port of entry for a military power emanating from the Continent; its first bridge was therefore placed near the tidal limits of the River Thames. In AD 43 the Roman army must have crossed the river just below London Bridge, near the City area (see p 2); Watling Street was constructed along the line of the present-day Edgware Road, further to the west, because it was a route to Verulamium through surrounding forest, already in use by the Celts. The bridge referred to by the Greek historian Cassius Dio, writing one hundred and fifty years after the event, was probably a temporary one supported by boats, not an existing structure. Only the western wing of the army, under Vespasian, is likely to have made the crossing by the gravel ford at Westminster. The whole operation was uncontested by the Britons; for Claudius, who was accompanied by a corps of elephants, spent only sixteen days on the island, and could not have been involved in any hard-fought engagement.

Archaeologists have suggested that the military base of the legions was established in the Walbrook area, though few finds are dated before the beginning of the second century. Forty years previously Londinium was one of three youthful Roman towns sacked by British rebels under Queen Boudicca, the others being Camulodunum and Verulamium. At some stage an east-west road parallel to the Thames was constructed under present Lombard Street. London soon became the financial centre of the province of Britain, and consequently the place of residence of the procurators; one, Julius Classicianus, was buried there after the rebellion, according to the inscription on his tombstone. It is probable that the City was the administrative capital of Hadrian's province early in the second century AD, when a basilica five hundred feet long was erected to serve as a town hall, law court and civic centre. London was by this time the largest city in Roman Britain, its nearest rival in population being Cirencester; but it was again destroyed by fire about AD 130. When the city was rebuilt, Walbrook became a fashionable residential area.

Some seventy years later (probably in the time of Severus and Caracalla) London's most enduring monument, the Wall, was built to defend the city against internal, rather than external, aggression. It has been suggested that this enterprise coincided with the granting of Roman citizenship to all free inhabitants of the Empire, under the *Constitutio Antoniniana* of Caracalla (AD 212); but this date is probably too late. The Wall reached a height of fifteen to twenty feet, and was seven to eight feet wide, stretching for a length of slightly over two miles. On the northern side of the river there was no stone defence, only an embankment.

As a trade centre, London was from the beginning cosmopolitan, and this prevented it from becoming a *colonia*. When Theodosius raised the siege of London in AD 367, he made the city his base, and its status was raised by the addition of the imperial epithet *Augusta*.

In cities the traces of Roman occupation are generally obliterated by the superimposition of modern buildings and in Britain the vestiges of Roman life are better preserved in the villas or farms. They were of two main kinds, productive farms and retreats for veteran soldiers retired from the army. Farms employing a large labour force were owned mainly by Britons, who had been instructed in the principles of farm economics. The Romans were responsible for introducing the scythe and the spade with a metal blade. Many farms were located on the chalk downs of southern England, where livestock, fruit and grain were the principal sources of revenue. By the third and fourth centuries romanized agriculture was a profitable business, for the Romans introduced many varieties of trees, fruit, flowers and vegetables, whose names indicate Continental sources. Apples, cherries and plums are known to have been grown. Grain was carefully dried and stored, and wine was actually produced. A farm at Ditchley in Oxfordshire covered as much as a thousand acres.

The architectural style of the country dwellings was simple and functional, resembling that of houses in northern Gaul, which were either on the corridor or courtyard plan. In Lullingstone villa, Kent, the owners were not Celts, but immigrants, possibly from the eastern Mediterranean, who took over a first-century farm about AD 280. They introduced mosaic floors and mural decorations, one being illuminated by a text from Vergil. One room was later transformed into a Christian chapel. Some of the Romano-Celtic

21

villas have hunting scenes, which indicate that the sporting tradition
has not changed; nearly every farm had its horses and dogs, and
comfortable houses were invariably provided with baths and
hypocausts.

There is evidence on large estates of a peasant-tenant and owner
relationship, but what it was has not been recorded. In Dorset and
highland areas several early Celtic villages have been unearthed, and
they all show houses with round, wooden frames and mud walls.
On the estates the peasant homes were either *tuguria* or *casae*,
depending on whether they were turf-covered hovels or cottages.
The latter seem to have disappeared in the lowlands during the
second century, when master and servant probably came to live
under the same roof, rooms being provided with separate entrances.
The day of the medieval country village had not yet arrived in the
Romano-Celtic agricultural system, because the villa was sufficient
to house a small community itself. Over six hundred of the latter
have been identified or excavated, though there are few in the Weald
of Kent, in eastern Sussex and the territory west of Dorset, and also
north of the Wroxeter, Leicester and Norwich line.

The Roman organization of the East Anglian grain farms has not
yet been fully investigated, though several valuable coin-hoards
have been unearthed. The Fens became important for the supply of
corn to the troops on the Rhine. This rich fen-land was drained by
means of canals, of which the Roman engineers were the first
builders. Car Dyke extends from Cambridgeshire to Lincolnshire, a
distance of seventy miles. Foss Dyke was then constructed from
Witham to the river Trent, making it possible to travel by inland
waterway from Cambridge to York. Britain was valued by the
imperial government both as a granary, and as a land plentifully
endowed with minerals.

With the exception of coal, which was mined but not exported,
the mineral resources were severely drained, first by the Celts, then
by Roman exploiters, principally the imperial government. All
minerals were regarded as the property of the State, and the mines
were apparently worked by slave or convict labour, organized by
companies. The most profitable of the commodities exported were
silver, lead, copper and tin. Lead was the most plentiful because it
was easiest to obtain by the open-cast system, and has always been a
by-product of the mining of silver, the metal most required for the
minting of coins. What the Romans transhipped were ingots of

oblong shape, made by pouring the extracted metal into moulds; these are known in the trade as 'pigs'. The principal sources of silver and lead were the Mendip Hills, Flintshire, Derbyshire, the Nidderdale area of Yorkshire, and Northumberland. Fairly large deposits of copper were available in Shropshire, Anglesey and Caernarvonshire, which accounts for the importance of north Wales to the Romans. The tin, for which Celtic Britain was famous, came from Cornwall, but during the earlier part of the Roman occupation a rival source was exploited in north-west Spain. Iron was mined principally in the Forest of Dean and the Weald of Kent and Sussex, though it was not regarded as so valuable a commodity as the other metals.

Since the provincial authorities left much of the local administration in the hands of trusted Britons, it is worth examining the kind of organization they set up. The earliest responsible bodies are to be found in the four *coloniae* of Colchester, Lincoln, York and Gloucester, where there were sizable communities of Roman citizens. In Verulamium the founders were a Celtic body of long standing, and the privileged group were granted a charter or *municipium*, which conferred the rights of Roman citizenship. Lesser towns of mainly Celtic inhabitants, such as Wroxeter and Silchester, were allowed the status of *civitates*, which afforded no rights of citizenship, the control being effectively in the hands of British aristocrats. All three shades of local government were based on a central urban authority of some size, controlling a surrounding territory, which might be as extensive as an English county. The tribal canton was apparently the basis of this system.

The *ordo*, or local council in charge of such an area, usually consisted of a hundred *decuriones*, who collected taxes in money or goods; they were mostly ex-magistrates, who had held office for a period of one year. Magistrates were elected officials, two for the administration of law and order, and two for finance and public amenities. As regards legal functions, serious cases of crime or civil action were sent to the higher court of the governor's legal deputy, known as *legatus iuridicus*.

The co-ordinating authority for all local bodies was the *concilium provinciae*, which met once a year to ensure that the state religion was observed. Through this council, complaints from the local bodies could be brought to the notice of the Emperor, without passing through the hands of his provincial governor – a system which provided a useful check on the latter's power. This scheme of autonomous local control prevailed throughout the Roman occupation, and was not affected by the reforms of Severus and Diocletian.

All taxation in the shape of money formed part of the imperial revenue, the amount of the land tax and the poll tax being assessed by Roman officers, called *censitores*. Each cantonal community was made responsible for the upkeep of trunk and subsidiary roads in its area, under the supervision of the army's engineers. Changing-stations for horses and rest-houses had to be maintained by the *civitates* at intervals of twelve miles on the principal roads. The impositions were by no means light, but were submitted to in the interests of progress and the preservation of justice. The postal service was in no way *public*, but designed exclusively for imperial use and for military communication.

It is noteworthy that *Lindum* (Lincoln), a model of early planning, is the only town that provides evidence of a sewerage scheme compatible with the Romans' reputation for civic amenities. It also possessed a municipal water supply, pumped from several springs. Aqueducts were not built in Britain, most towns being supplied with water, either by gravitation, using wooden underground pipe-lines, or by open conduits.

The system of local government was flexible enough to permit considerable variation, without destroying the basic Roman pattern. This needed to be the most stable of institutions because the governorship of the Roman province was, in its inception, a short-tenure appointment, and tied to military command. From the civilian point of view, the officer, whose independent status is significant, was the *procurator Augusti* (Receiver of Revenue), to whom the local finance magistrates and *decuriones* were responsible. A large proportion of the population, however, consisted of slaves, who were the backbone of the labour force; with no incentive to improve their techniques, the economy made little progress. The inducements to material prosperity were similarly curtailed for the Celtic aristocracy, the followers of loyal chieftains who had no longer retained any significant authority.

What advantages were the Romans able to promote in the arts and education? It is certain that they did much to extinguish the native arts of decorative design wherein Celts excelled, particularly in metal work. Roman efficiency did not encourage the attitude of mind or the domestic leisure in which the arts flourish; it favoured mass-produced articles, such as Samian pottery from Gaul, which was introduced as tableware. British makers, on the whole, yielded to this influence, though a few isolated groups of ceramic workers did evolve a distinctive Romano-Celtic style, using Greek mythological motifs and scenes from the chase. In general, however, pottery and jewellery designs tended to be conventional and repetitive.

The curative waters of *Aquae Sulis* (Bath) were responsible for the preservation of exceptions to this monotony. This spa was one of the most splendid in western Europe; in order to attract visitors, who came from as far afield as Gaul, it was dignified with Roman architecture and sculpture of a nobler tradition. As the amenities were constantly altered and improved, many novelties were introduced, including an altar of Minerva on which coals from Somerset were burnt. The pediment of the goddess's temple is sculpted in an unusual Celtic style, quite unlike anything preserved in Gaul.

Not much is known about education in Britain during the Roman occupation; but it is unlikely that the state made much provision for it, as it did in Gaul. Yet Agricola, hailed by Anthony Birley as the founder of British education, valued the intelligence of the islanders above that of the Gauls. According to Tacitus (*Agricola*, 21) he introduced a system of education for the sons of British chiefs, who aspired to mastery of the Latin language. He is said to have brought a Greek tutor, Demetrius of Tarsus, with him to care for the upbringing of his own children. Schools there undoubtedly were in Britain, since Martial boasted that his works were read in this remote province. Schoolmaster-slaves from Gaul or Italy first taught Britons to read and write, when the *litteratores* had introduced the Roman alphabet. Cursive writing was found on tiles made by such lowly citizens as brickmakers at Silchester. St Patrick, whose birthplace is uncertain, but who seems to have come from the neighbourhood of Hadrian's Wall, was modest about his latinity; but he was reasonably educated, though not as good a linguist as the heretic Pelagius.

The Latin language was acquired by townsmen principally through lessons in grammar and rhetoric, initiated by the disciples of Agricola. There is no doubt, however, that the Celtic dialects survived among romanized tribesmen, yet not a single Celtic inscription survives from the Roman period in Britain. This, and the existence of numerous graffiti, suggest that the public and official language was Latin, predominantly in the towns. In the country, Latin was probably employed only by the upper stratum of society. In Kenneth Jackson's *Language and History in Early Britain* (p 76) it is estimated that about eight hundred words were borrowed by Brittonic speakers from the Latin tongue, of which six hundred occur in Welsh. As the Romans were in occupation of the province for nearly four hundred years, during most of which Latin was the official language, this represents a small proportion. After AD 425, Latin was preserved in Britain by the Church and its historians; consequently Christianity supplied a large number of the loan words borrowed from the standard Latin of the schools.

Jackson points out that the Latin used in Britain by some 140,000 speakers may have been markedly different from that heard on the Continent; for instance, classical Latin *v* was preserved in stone inscriptions, whereas it had been changed to *b* (e.g. in *Danubius*) in the Latin of the European provinces, from about the first century AD. As most troops were recruited from Gaul, Spain and the Danubian provinces, the bulk of their forty thousand must have been speakers of vulgar Latin, whose influence would have been quite significant. The sons of the British aristocracy learnt classical Latin at school; but the parents of St Patrick apparently used Celtic with their younger children. Jackson concludes that the sound-system of British Latin must have appeared archaic by Continental standards.

Vulgar Latin, which played so significant a part in the evolution of western European languages in the Middle Ages, was not a degraded form of the classical (and, in a sense, 'artificial') language used by poets, orators and prose-writers; it was the speech of the man in the street, and of the surrounding rural areas. One source of innovation was the language of Greek settlers in southern Italy; and it should be remembered that Greek teachers were commonly employed to instruct Roman pupils, who wished to become bilingual.

Mixed populations invariably produce hybridization of speech. Moreover, rapid speakers of Latin often attempted to be racy, vigorous or picturesque by using the slang or table-talk of comic characters in plays. Such a speaker was Trimalchio in the second part of the *Satyricon* of Petronius. The vocabulary of vulgar Latin preserves many novelties of meaning, spelling and grammar that do not suggest regional peculiarity. In the fourth and fifth centuries a fruitful source of oddities was the technical jargon of writers who treated such subjects as agriculture and natural history.

In *The Latin Language* (1954, ch. VI) L. R. Palmer shows that the first sign of laxity in usage was the failure to recognize the quantity of long vowels. Then came the levelling of genders, the loss of some declensions of nouns, the disappearance of the final nasal consonant *n*, and the development of certain periphrastic constructions, using prepositions. The evolution of a two-case system coincided with the loss of inflexions. Verbs showed a tendency to employ the subjunctive for any kind of subordination. Such changes were conveyed abroad by Roman soldiers, settlers and tradesmen, the provinces being responsible for only minor modifications, except in additions to the Latin vocabulary. The words *brun, carpa, flasca, harpa, helm* and *hosa* were among many borrowed from Germanic sources.

The written *koiné* of vulgar Latin, in administrative use throughout the Roman world, continued to spread after the decline of the Empire. The anxious struggle between pagan and Christian faiths had already resolved itself in favour of the latter by the enactments of Constantine the Great. The Church became chiefly responsible for the form that the Latin language thereafter took. Palmer describes the early Christians as a kind of 'secret Society, evolving a species of Latin which was largely incomprehensible to outsiders' (ibid., p 183). One reason was the familiar style of the Greek New Testament, especially the Gospels, for which the Latin translators required new words, including abstract ones, not associated with pagan religions. The Christian Church found that it had to invent a large number of semi-technical terms for its ceremonies and organization. The Greek of the New Testament was itself the *koiné* of the post-Alexandrian world, and Biblical Latin tended to develop as a specialized form of vulgar Latin in order to reach the common man. In *The City of God*, Augustine of Hippo named it *ecclesiastica loquendi consuetudo.*

Important writers of the Christian Church, such as Cyprian and Lactantius, began in the mid-third century to compose their works in Latin, whereas their predecessors, such as Clement of Alexandria, the Christian Platonist, wrote in Greek. In the intervening period, Tertullian was a bilingual author, whose Greek writings did not survive. It so happened that many Latin-speaking Church Fathers were either natives of north Africa, or made their spiritual home in places like Carthage. Most were skilled in rhetoric, and their contribution to ecumenical idiom of the Church was important for the evolving Romance tongues in Spain and Gaul.

The greatest masters of ecclesiatical Latin were undoubtedly Jerome (345–419) and Augustine (354–430). To gain the attention of a large body of converts, less educated than their pagan neighbours, it became essential to break with the literary tradition of Cicero and the Augustan age. Models of Church Latin are to be found in the sermons of St Augustine, but they are couched in a more intimate language than the same author's doctrinal works and *The City of God*.

Jackson's survey of the linguistic situation in Britain at the end of the Roman period shows that by AD 410 the towns had become depopulated for economic reasons, as well as the threat of invasion. This meant a decline in the public use of Latin as a means of communication. A return to Celtic, under the influence of the anti-Romanist Vortigern, representing the Welsh-highland tradition, is a feasible supposition. The promotion of Latin was in the hands of its eloquent defenders, the Christian Church, which assumed the civilizing role of *coloniae* and *civitates*; but one should not overlook the support of enlightened civilian leaders, who considered themselves the guardians of Roman culture. They had the advantage of carrying this banner into the intellectually starved highland zone. In this way Latin borrowings were multiplied, and the educated were able to counter the recrudescence of paganism in regions where Christianity had been regarded with mistrust.

Palaeographers affirm that the Latin alphabet and the system of writing, used to transmit the vulgar language in the period 410–600, was a modification of the practice of the Dorian Greeks. The 'villa' civilization of England that survived the Roman departure was maintained by private collections of manuscript books, and by teachers from the romanized schools of Gaul, the most important of which were at Marseilles, Arles, Vienne, Autun, Toulouse, Bordeaux and Lyon. The book, as we know it, was a development of the vellum codex, which replaced papyrus rolls in the third century AD, because it was more durable and easier to handle.

The schools of Languedoc, Aquitaine and other southern cantons of Gaul, were at first pagan, but most had been christianized by the fifth century. The change followed logically from the introduction of monasticism, the most notable reformer being St Martin of Tours. Elementary teaching of writing consisted of the making of letters with a stilus on wax tablets. The industry must have been prodigious, since secretaries and transcribers of books were in great demand throughout romanized Europe. Founders of the church schools in Britain were nearly all Romano-Celts, the principal names being those of St Ninian, St Patrick, St Illtud and Paulinus. The first known writing in Latin actually penned in Britain is said to have been Fastidius's *On the Christian Life* (c 420–30).

The Roman alphabet used in British scriptoria was based on the lettering found on Latin stone inscriptions dating from the monuments in Trajan's time; it is thought to have been in vogue by the end of the Roman Republic. Scribes in Britain, as elsewhere, copied literary documents in a form of calligraphy styled bookhand, which initially employed capital letters (majuscule). A system of rounded letters (uncial) was soon evolved as more suitable for a lengthy work. The Latin word *uncia* signified both 'inch' and 'ounce', and indicates a duodecimal system of calculation, which persisted in some basic English measurements.

The uncial letters of Greek and Roman script were not joined together, but for correspondence or business, cursive styles of penmanship, in running hand, were employed by the scribes of both nations. The cursive style, which obviously enables one to write more quickly, was the source of minuscule bookhand. With the symmetry of an attractive calligraphy, this proved ideal for vellum or parchment, and was consequently favoured by the European monks of the seventh century.

Cursive forms were introduced according to scribal taste, often leaving only about half the letters in pure uncial. Mixed hands like this were already in use by the sixth century AD, and have been conveniently named Roman half-uncial. Substantially, this became the national bookhand of the Irish scribes for literary purposes, and was transported to Scotland (Iona) and northern England (Lindisfarne) by Celtic missionaries.

The Celts in Britain never acquiesced in romanization as fully as

those in Gaul; it would be a mistake to imagine that they understood the benefits of humanism for which Cicero, Vergil and
Horace strove. As in all empires, colonialism acquired a bad name,
because it exploited the subject people. The Romans in Italy
thought colonialism necessary to material progress; it far more than
compensated for the costs of a province's development. Improve-
ments, such as the network of roads and canals, were not the
product of voluntary enterprise which was adequately rewarded,
but of enforced labour by tributary workers, using the materials
that came to hand. Although, by the fifth century, many Roman
provincials had risen to the rank of emperor (Hadrian, Constantine
and Diocletian among them), the mass of the suppressed peoples
was conscious of loss in their cultural identity.

Empires cater for cosmopolitan life, racial tolerance and individual mobility, with many opportunities for their citizens, but
these are available only if there are waves of prosperity. Rome's
territorial gains and economic development were badly handled
at the political level. Inflation gave rise to dangerous disparity in
the standard of living, which bred dissatisfaction among subject
peoples. In Britain, dissidence was sometimes fomented by political
exiles, who had been trouble-makers in their own country. Not
only auxiliaries, but the legions themselves, were known to rebel,
especially when civil war offered an opportunity of opposing the
central government.

As early as the end of the first century there were twelve
thousand Britons serving in the Roman continental armies, chiefly
in Germany. When trained, these were highly esteemed as a fighting
force, and thoroughly loyal to their immediate commanders. The
Romans, though not themselves conspicuous as a sea-faring nation,
first taught the British the use of sea-power. The *Classis Sambrica*,
based on Boulogne, was a Roman institution, with a partly British
fleet, patrolling the French coast from the mouth of the Somme to
St Malo. This protected the valuable sea-routes that passed through
the English Channel – an important instance of co-operation that
reveals how closely the British were connected, by ties of blood as
well as economic interests, with the Celts on the western seaboard
of Europe.

Among the enduring bequests of the Romans to the Britons were:
(1) the concept of unity, and consequent need for husbanding
internal resources; (2) an improved food supply, affording the

people a diet both varied and nourishing; (3) respect for silviculture, which introduced the laurel, box and plane trees to supplement the useful indigenous ones; (4) the social benefits of Christian culture, which combined Hebrew piety with Greek philosophy and Roman church organization. It would be tempting to add education to this credit list, if one knew more about the Romans' provision for it in Britain. Tacitus thought that Agricola was one governor who was sad to relinquish his post in Britain; concern for the country's welfare is witnessed by his furtherance of learning for the people he governed. The Celts were assiduous learners of Latin, perhaps realizing that the Italic languages were the nearest in kin to their own.

Agricola was recalled from Britain because the pusillanimous Domitian (afterwards deposed) was allegedly jealous of his prowess, and would suffer no other power near the throne. An Empire torn by such power-politics could not have endured. The prestigious *Pax Romana*, the justice of its laws and the consolations of its new faith, were unable to survive the bitter struggles of the fifth century. At the end of chapter 35 of the *Decline and Fall* Gibbon rightly observed that the over-burdened taxpayer and the greedy landlord spell inevitable dissolution for the imperial idea. His summary of the situation in chapter 38 is strikingly perceptive:

> The Empire of Rome was firmly established by the singular and perfect coalition of its members. . . . But this union was purchased by the loss of national freedom and military spirit; and the servile provinces, destitute of life and motion, expected their safety from the mercenary troops and governors who were directed by the orders of a distant court. The happiness of an hundred millions depended on the personal merit of one or two men, perhaps children, whose minds were corrupted by education, luxury, and despotic power. The deepest wounds were inflicted on the empire during the minorities of the sons and grandsons of Theodosius . . . The splendid days of Augustus and Trajan were eclipsed by a cloud of ignorance.

Gibbon goes on to add the abuse and factions of Christianity, monastic refuge, and the passivity of Churchmen, as contributory causes of the imperial collapse.

Gibbon's 'servile provinces, destitute of life and motion' does less than justice to the northern and highland Celts of Britain, whose resistance to Roman rule, however sporadic, was perennial.

31

Apart from the punitive campaign of Suetonius Paulinus, in Anglesey, just before the revolt of Boudicca in AD 61, the reduction of the Celtic population in Britain was not considerable; for the Britons and Picts, who used small-scale guerilla tactics, were elusive opponents. Agricola even commented on the general mildness of the Celtic temperament. But the indigenous population was rapidly being diluted by Roman importations of foreign troops and the admission of ubiquitous European traders. The population of Britain had never been so cosmopolitan, and racial inter-marriages must have been numerous. Before the arrival of the influential Belgae, there was already a strong admixture of German with their Celtic blood.

CHAPTER II

The Anglo-Saxons and their Distribution (450–850)

൬൬൬൬൬൬

To ASSESS THE EFFECTS of the Anglo-Saxon invasions, it is imperative to realize the situation that had developed in Britain in the first half of the fifth century AD. Kipling in *Puck of Pook's Hill* imaginatively depicted one aspect of decline in the demoralization of the Roman legions during the aggrandizement of Magnus Maximus, which followed upon the territorial restorations of Theodosius. Many, but not all Roman towns were forsaken by the insecure inhabitants; the country's economic activity consequently moved to areas where the self-supporting owners of villas were able to survive the pillaging of invaders and of robber bands, which were the product of a period of depression. Samian pottery from Gaul disappeared from the market, and was replaced by the ephemeral wooden platter and leather bottle. Building restoration was of the crudest efficiency. Money of inferior design and minting had to be brought into circulation.

Though information about the sub-Roman period AD 410–50 is difficult to obtain, even from archaeologists, there are a few biographical sources to eke out the distressing account of Gildas in *De Excidio et Conquestu Britanniae* (*c* AD 547), written more than a century after the Roman departure. This writer's record of events before 450 is sometimes discredited, because of its known lapses of fact and its rhetorical animus. But various sources agree that Britain's haphazard attempts to administer its own affairs were not edifying. The principal reason was that co-ordinated local government had broken down. The political leaders of a disturbed society were opportunists, with instincts characteristic of Celtic individualism; there was a general tendency to react against the levelling influence of Rome. Fatalistic Romano-Celts were not averse to relapsing into the paganism that threatened them on every side; but most remained Christians, because exemplary missionaries had demonstrated the consolations of this religion in times of distress.

At first the Church had small organizational hold on the illiterate majority, especially in highland areas. But a fairly reliable picture of the period is to be reconstructed from the lives of St Germanus and Pelagius, and the *Confessio* of St Patrick, all of whom were actively engaged in the controversies of the time. They were able to derive from the perennial devastation of their land by Picts, Irish and Saxons, certain moral lessons which their congregations would accept as signs of hope. In the end they were able to achieve more than such dynasty-founders as Welsh Cunedda, and consular reformers like Stilicho, who was a high-ranking Roman citizen of Vandal origin. Not all of Roman England was ravaged and laid waste. There remained aristocratic pockets of Romano-Celtic afflu- ence and luxury in the domains of five British kings, whom Gildas rebuked for their debauchery and *carpe diem* attitude.

Pelagius was a British theologian of unaggressive temperament, born about AD 360, who probably received his training from an Irish monastic order, before going to Rome at the beginning of the fifth century. He was distressed by the low standard of Church morality on the Continent, especially in Italy. He therefore opposed, in his writings of AD 405 and 409, St Augustine's doctrine of Original Sin, as tending to condone human frailty. Having experienced no problem of discipline in his own life, Pelagius proposed individual responsibility for wrong-doing as a corner- stone of Christian ethics. The Church took notice of this doctrine when Pelagius's lawyer-disciple Coelestius, a more fanatical thinker, went to North Africa and confronted Augustine himself. Rome had recently fallen to the Goths (AD 410), and the blame for this had some religious implications. By this time Pelagius had gone to live in Palestine, where he was in contact with St Jerome, and he never returned to Britain. The Bishop of Carthage summoned a synod, which recommended the excommunication of Coelestius; but in Palestine Pelagius was so respected that he was not con- demned, after protesting that his views differed from those of his disciple. The issue resolved itself into a lengthy clash on the respective merits of grace and free will, St Augustine waging persistent theological campaigns for acceptance of the former.

St Germanus, Bishop of Auxerre in southern Champagne, was sent by the Pope in AD 429 to controvert Pelagianism in southern

Britain, the doctrine having spread rapidly during the rule of Vortigern. The *Life of Germanus* by Constantius of Lyons (written about 480) appears in Surius's *De Probatis Sanctorum Historiis*, vol. IV. Here one learns that the reverence Germanus enjoyed in the Church of Gaul was due to his hospitality, coupled with austerity in his personal habits, including abstinence from wine, vegetables, wheat bread, salt and oil. He and his colleague, Bishop Lupus of Troyes, preached by the roadside, and eventually confronted the Pelagians in debate at Verulamium, gaining the argument. In AD 430 the two bishops baptized the non-Christians in the home army, and without a blow defeated the Picts and Saxons near the Chiltern escarpment, by instructing their troops to use the Alleluia war-cry, which struck terror into the hearts of their foes. This legendary victory was remembered when Germanus revisited Britain eighteen years later; on this occasion he was successful in getting Pelagians banished from the island. He greatly extended the influence of the Church of Rome, and is credited with founding schools and colleges.

The life of St Patrick is dependent largely on tradition, and on his own account in the *Confessio* of his capture by pirates, with thousands of others, in north-west England. He tells of enslavement in Ireland, and escape to Britain, where he wandered for four weeks through territory devastated by invaders. These harsh experiences converted him to a life of prayer and a firm belief in guidance through visions and the admonitory voice of God. Though the escapade of many years is briefly related, it presents a lively picture of the state of England in a period of rapine and insecurity. It also confirms that Christian institutions and education, as well as civilization by Roman standards, were yet available to those with the means and the will to seek these advantages abroad.

The Welsh chronicles of Gildas, Nennius and Geoffrey of Monmouth tell the historian much about contemporary events on the west coast of Britain, but little is available about the happenings on the eastern seaboard. The advent of the Anglo-Saxon tribes, described by Gildas, Bede and Nennius, was no unexpected incursion; settlers had been arriving for over a century, and German legionaries had become a factor in the composition of the Roman army. The date and place of the first large-scale settlement, and the identity of the newcomers cannot be determined with certainty. Bede, in *The Ecclesiastical History of the English Nation,* always a more sober witness than the exasperated monk Gildas, does not exactly repeat the latter's account, though he relies on it, as does the compiler of *The Anglo-Saxon Chronicle.* Bede, in chapter XV, supplies a possible, but not reliable date (AD 449) and names of the protagonists, Hengest and Horsa, allegedly invited by the British ruler Vortigern to help quell the Picts. Unfortunately, Bede's chronological framework is not now thought dependable. If there were Caledonians in Kent, it is most likely that they came south by sea, and not overland. Hengest and Horsa were apparently *foederati* (allies of foreign tribal origin), and the mercenaries who landed at Ebbsfleet in the Isle of Thanet (according to the *Chronicle*) were trained and equipped forces, decribed by Bede as Jutes. They may well have arrived a decade earlier than Bede states, but no written document makes it clear whether they were exiles as well as allies. The Welsh historian Nennius had no additional facts to offer in *Historia Brittonum,* but garnished the tale with a romantic account of love and treachery, in which three hundred British noblemen were sacrificed to Vortigern's misguided diplomacy.

Bede does not clearly distinguish Jutes from Saxons, because he uses the latter as a generic term for the people of 'Old Saxony', which comprised the territory between Friesland and the mouth of the Elbe. Nowhere is it stated that the Saxons were a tribe; they were simply a regional group who used the *seax* or short sword. The Jutish invaders, dissatisfied with the rewards of their services and their provisions, according to Bede (Book I, ch.15):

> began to turn their weapons against their confederates. . . . They plundered all the neighbouring cities and country, spread the conflagration from the eastern to the western sea, without any opposition, and covered almost every part of the devoted island. Public as well as private structures were overturned; the priests were everywhere slain before the altars; the prelates and the people, without any respect of persons, were destroyed with fire and sword; nor was there any to bury those who had been thus cruelly slaughtered. Some of the miserable remainder, being taken in the mountains, were butchered in heaps. Others, spent with hunger, came forth and submitted themselves to the enemy for food, being destined to undergo perpetual servitude, if they were not killed even upon the spot. Some, with sorrowful hearts, fled beyond the seas. Others, continuing in their own country, led a miserable life among the woods, rocks, and mountains, with scarcely enough food to support life, and expecting every moment to be their last.

This account describes a holocaust of greater magnitude than the occupation of Kent and Hampshire, opposite the Isle of Wight, by the Jutes. More light is needed than the written documents can supply, and the evidence of archaeology has been invoked to determine the ethnological sources of the invasion.

Cremation was the general practice of the tribes of north-west Germany by the middle of the fifth century; but this means of disposing of the dead has left only a few traces south of the Thames. The Jutish invaders apparently preferred inhumation, as practised by the Franks and by other tribes of the middle Rhine. Moreover, the burial trappings, jewellery and glassware found in Kentish graves resemble those discovered in the Frankish cemeteries, and not the work of craftsmen in the Anglo-Saxon homelands. All this suggests that the Jutish invaders had long since left their original home (where they gave their name to Jutland) and that they must have been settled for a considerable time on the Rhine, as well as to the north on the Frisian coast. Different burial practices discovered in Kent reveal a very mixed population during the fifth and sixth centuries.

The Frankish and Frisian impact on the Jutes of Kent is reflected also in their laws, social stratifications and language. Place-names ending in -ing or -ling are characteristic of the Kentish dialect, being especially clustered around the River Medway, which is likely to have been the strategic base from which the leaders operated. Hengest was the principal strategist; but the Jutes' occupation of the Isle of Wight and the Southampton coast was undoubtedly of later date, and may have been initiated from Kent early in the sixth century. It is noteworthy that the Jutes did not give their name to the kingdom established in southern England. It is extremely unlikely that a Roman-style monument to Horsa (mentioned by Bede) was still in existence in the eighth century; for the Anglo-Saxons left no inscribed stones to commemorate the dead elsewhere.

The first Jutes invited to Britain arrived in Kent in three long ships; they were the only foreign help available to Vortigern at the time, for the Roman consul in Gaul, Aëtius, was fully occupied restoring order on the Continent. One of many appeals for assistance had been made to Rome in AD 446, during the rule of the Emperor Valentinian III.

For the sequence of events in the Jutish and Anglo-Saxon

conquests the historian is dependent on the dates recorded in two works: (1) *The Ecclesiastical History of the English Nation* by the Venerable Bede (AD 673–735), written in Latin and completed in AD 731; and (2) *The Anglo-Saxon Chronicle*, an anonymous collection of vernacular annals, begun in the ninth century AD, possibly at the instigation of Alfred the Great. An Old English translation of Bede's *History* was made in the last quarter of the same century. Bede's work is significant, *inter alia*, because he was the first historian in Britain to date events from the Incarnation of Christ.

The *Chronicle* briefly describes the take-over of Kent by the Jutes during the years 449–88. The revolt against Vortigern of Hengest's augmented forces is dated AD 455. Two engagements were then fought against the Britons, the first at Aylesford, where Horsa was killed, and the second at Crayford (457), which left four thousand British dead on the battlefield; the remains of the home force are said to have taken refuge in London. Æsc, Hengest's son, stepped into Horsa's shoes as a military leader, and became the founder of the Kentish dynasty of kings in AD 488. The campaign was extended westwards, for eight years later Hengest and Æsc overcame the 'Welsh' on the river *Wippedesfleot* (location unknown), and 'slew twelve Welsh nobles', as well as the thegn Wipped himself. This onslaught was repeated in another battle (AD 473), but the *Chronicle*'s use of *Wālas* 'Welsh' (original meaning 'foreigners') implies no more than British (Celt), since the territory seized was the Sussex Weald, not Wales. In each Jutish victory no mercy was shown to the defenders. Æsc is said to have remained King of the Jutes until 512, and it was largely in his time that the Romano-Kentish tradition of culture, in advance of the rest of England, was created.

The next invasion recorded in the *Chronicle* is that of the Saxons, a more extensive group than the Jutes, though they were likewise part of the Great Migration of Baltic peoples westwards that took place in the fifth century. All who participated were populous tribesmen in search of *lebensraum*, land more fertile and habitable than their own. Contact with the Romans had made them emulous of power over less favoured peoples, and they were ready to seize their opportunities in Gaul and Britain, when they realized that the Roman Empire was crumbling. In their land-hunger and adventurous enterprise, the Saxons were closely associated with the Angles from Schleswig, on the north side of the River Eider. Ptolemy in his *Geography* described this territory as 'the neck of the Cimbric peninsula'. The minstrel of the famous duel on the River Eider, and the Mercian King Offa, who figure in the Old English poem *Widsith*, are supposed to have been of Anglian descent.

The original home of the Saxons was the western half of Holstein, between the Rivers Eider and Elbe. They waxed powerful, crossed the Elbe, took over the territory of the Lombards around Hamburg, and eventually overcame the Chauci (eulogized by Tacitus) occupying both sides of the River Weser. Much of the new Saxon coast consisted either of fenland, like that around the English Wash, or of salt-impregnated soil. The archaeology of the territory supports the links of these inhabitants with the Saxons who settled in England (see R. H. Hodgkin, *A History of the Anglo-Saxons*, vol. I, pp 9–12).

Eventually the migrant Saxon pirates extended their domain to several parts of the Frisian coast, to the land neighbouring Boulogne in Gaul, and to the hinterland of the Normandy beaches where the allies of the Second World War were later to land on D-Day 1945. Port-en-Bessin, Arromanches, Caen and Bayeux had once been Celtic settlements, and it is worth observing that the earliest known school established at Caen was of Saxon origin. These settlements in Gaul were undoubtedly the dwelling-places of Saxons with whom Carausius had been in league, before he became Emperor of Britain (see p 8).

Like the Jutes, the Saxons in the late fifth century had probably lived opposite the south-east coast of Britain for generations, and were induced to leave the Continent because of the advancing Franks under Clovis. From the mouths of the rivers Rhine, Meuse and Scheldt they could have made short-distance incursions upon Britain. The Nydam long boat, seventy-seven feet long and just under eleven feet wide, excavated near Flensburg Fiord in Schleswig, and now in Kiel Museum, suggests the kind of craft the Saxons used for such a sea-journey of perhaps 130 miles. It was constructed of oak and clinker-built, with fourteen oars on either side. Typically Saxon swords were unearthed in the peat bog, and there were spears, long-bows and arrows, and a wooden shield, without its usual covering of tough hide.

By the end of the fifth century, when the Saxons invaded the south of England, they were the most feared enemies in western

Europe, and the word 'saxon' had become a term of reproach in Britain for any freebooter who disturbed the peace, whatever his origin. The *Chronicle* records that the South Saxons arrived in AD 477; and it is clear that Britain's commerce with the Continent was effectually severed by the turn of the century. The landing was made by Ælle, and his three sons Cymen, Wlencing and Cissa, in three ships, south of Selsey Bill. Fourteen years later *Anderida* (Pevensey), one of the Saxon-shore ports, was captured, and the most arable part of the Sussex coastal plain occupied by Saxons; the villages of Lancing and Cissbury testify to the presence of the second and third of Ælle's sons. Bede records in Book IV, ch. 13, that by AD 681 seven thousand pagan families were settled in this area, which had once been dotted with Roman villas.

The West Saxon invaders, under Cerdic and his son (or grandson) Cynric, landed on the coast of Hampshire from five ships in AD 495; but the details in the *Anglo-Saxon Chronicle*, from this date until 560, are meagre and vague. There were innumerable skirmishes and one or two battles with British defenders, resulting in the establishment of the Saxon kingdom of Wessex in AD 519; from 530 this kingdom included the Isle of Wight. Four years after the latter date King Cerdic died, but Cynric reigned for another twenty-six years. The Laud manuscript of the *Chronicle* informs us that he was the first Saxon king to be baptized into the Christian faith in AD 552. From this date Wessex began to extend its territory westwards. The date would roughly correspond to the recovery of Saxon prestige, after the setback of the defeat of Mount Badon, when the victory of Ambrosius Aurelianus, according to Gildas, ushered in forty years of comparative peace in southern Britain.

The Saxon move into Wessex began in Wiltshire, where Cynric and his son Ceawlin (the next king from AD 560) gained victories at Old Sarum, outside present Salisbury, in 552, and at Fort Barbury, on Marlborough Down south of Swindon, in 556. Twenty-one years later Ceawlin, the creator of Wessex, fought the decisive battle of Dyrham, near the mouth of the Severn, which led to the capture of three Roman towns, Bath, Cirencester and Gloucester. This conquest of three British kings took the Saxons to the western coast of Britain for the first time, and to the forest of Selwood, which divided Wiltshire from Somerset. The Wessex kingdom now incorporated present-day Hampshire, Berkshire, Wiltshire and Gloucestershire, but the seat of the royal house, ancestors of Alfred the Great, remained in Winchester. The attention devoted in the *Anglo-Saxon Chronicle* to the Wessex line was stimulated by the verse genealogies of minstrels, who borrowed from Latin annals recorded in the seventh century. The evidence of Latin originals is the peculiarity of some of the grammatical constructions. From the year 547 several genealogies were embodied in these annals, which have all the characteristics of contemporary writing. The acquisition of present-day Dorset, Somerset and Devon by Wessex belongs to the seventh century.

The Saxons' achievement in the south of England should·not, however, overshadow their success in the valley of the Thames as far west as Oxford; and their progress north of the Thames, between the river Lea and the Chiltern Hills, enabled them to inhabit the greater part of Essex, Hertfordshire, Middlesex and Buckinghamshire. Though the *Chronicle* is silent on the sixth-century history of these areas, archaeology is more helpful (except in Essex) than in the Saxon south. The remains are richest near the Roman road known as the Icknield Way, north of the middle Thames. This road connected the river ways of the Wash with Berkshire. The culture of the many settlements is linked with that of Berkshire; and some archaeologists have needlessly assumed that the Saxons of the Thames valley reached their destination by traversing East Anglia, via the rivers Cam and Ouse. There was a Saxon river settlement at Dorchester before AD 500, but most of the newcomers arrived during the sixth century, and probably sailed up the Thames. Because of the proximity of London, there was from the earliest times an affinity between the people of Surrey and Middlesex, and Middlesex and Essex.

The utility of the *Chronicle*'s Saxon genealogies, and the feasibility of intermarriage between Saxons and Jutes, are illustrated by Asser's account of the parentage of Alfred the Great, in his biography of the King. Alfred's maternal grandfather Oslac, and his mother Osbury, were Jutes, descended from Stuf and Wihtgar, rulers of the Isle of Wight. These latter are inexplicably introduced into the *Chronicle* (AD 534) as nephews of the Saxon King Cerdic, whose patronymic suggests that he may have been of British blood. His name is associated with Charford, near the Hampshire Avon, between Old Sarum and Southampton Water. Early in the sixth century Cerdic, the lineal founder of the present English monarchy, acquired suzerainty over existing Saxon settlements north of the middle Thames; but how extensive they were is not clear. If the Battle of Mount Badon was a logical exercise to stem the principal Saxon advance up the Thames valley, it may fairly be concluded that much of this area was repossessed by the Romano-Britons after their victory. There was certainly a considerable repatriation of Saxons to Germany. No explanation but recapture is feasible for the entry in the *Chronicle* under the year 571, which reads: 'Cuthwulf fought against the Britons at Bedcanford and captured four villages, Limbury, Aylesbury, Benson and Eynsham.' Cuthwulf has not been identified in any royal genealogy, but Bedford, from its military proximity to the four places mentioned, may well be identified with Bedcanford.

The Chilterns and territory westwards to the Severn valley were never firmly in Saxon hands; during the seventh and eighth centuries this part of Wessex fell to the rising power of the Mercians. The turning point in the *Chronicle* seems to be the period AD 584 to 592, beginning with the Battle of Adam's Grave (Alton Priors) and ending with the Battle of Woodborough in the vale of Pewsey, after which Ceawlin was expelled from the Wessex kingdom. It seems that the second phase of West-Saxon expansion, begun in the middle of the sixth century, ended with a southern limitation of their influence. Quite early the Saxons had acquired the dynastic name of *Gewissae*, (see Bede's *Ecclesiastical History*, Book III, ch. 7), derived from their legendary king, Gewis (*Chronicle* AD 597), meaning 'confederate'. This appellation was, however, confined to the Saxons of Hampshire; their less distinguished countrymen who lived in acquired territory became known as West Saxons.

Essex calls for separate consideration, largely because its archaeology reveals very few Saxon and Roman remains. The kingdom contained not only the area east of the Lea as far as the treacherous North Sea coast, but Middlesex and the greater part of Hertfordshire. A principle reason for the rise of Essex as a monarchy in the second quarter of the sixth century, a period about which the *Chronicle* is strangely silent, was the importance of London as a seaport and commercial centre. The hinterland towards Colchester was still heavily wooded, and the river estuaries of the Crouch and Blackwater were flanked by swamps. Roman villas had been conspicuous by their absence in this largely clay area.

Essex was probably one of the British cantons surrendered to the

Jutes by Vortigern in return for the hand of Hengest's daughter, and it must have been only sparsely occupied by Saxons before about 550. The duplication of place-names ending in -*ing*, such as *Barling* and *Terling*, indicates a mingling of social interests north and south of the eastern Thames. There are few remains, except unidentifiable bones, in Essex, as well as parts of Wessex, because the furnishing of graves with weapons and jewellery went out of fashion several generations before the Saxons became Christians. In this respect they were clearly influenced by prevailing Romano-Celtic practices.

It is most unlikely that London was totally destroyed early in the fifth century, as some archaeologists have argued. There is reason to believe that the Saxons who used the Thames as a waterway in the sixth century either bypassed London, as a down-at-heel Romano-British enclave like Verulamium, or favoured its south (i.e. Surrey) bank to initiate new settlements. In an important way small Saxon settlements were differently sited from Celtic ones – they were not on hill-crests, but, wherever possible, in valleys near rivers. The characteristic villages of medieval England undoubtedly had their origins in Saxon times, and are well represented in the southern counties.

In *Germania* (AD 98) Tacitus described the population distributed along the North Sea coast as *Ingaevones*, and seems to have implied that the north-western German tribes were speakers of Anglo-Frisian dialects. Three hundred years later, the people whom Tacitus called *Anglii* were living north of the River Eider in the Danish province of Schleswig. They must have been pushed farther north by the gradual expansion into upper Germany of the Celtic Gauls, during the intervening centuries. The Angles, who invaded the east coast of England and Scotland, were in the fourth century grouped round the river-inlet known as the Schlei in east Schleswig, and are said in *Widsith* to have coalesced with the Swaefe on the west coast. In this way they retained their outlet on the North Sea coast, and a close relationship with Saxons and Frisians.

The earliest Anglian invaders entered England by the rivers that flow into the Wash, the Witham, Welland, Nene and Ouse; almost certainly they shortened their journey by using the *terpen* (reclaimed land) of Friesland as their base. Fifth-century remains of these invaders have been found in graves near the Ouse, in the part of East Anglia of which Cambridge is the centre, and at Sleaford in the case of Angles who proceeded north-west, via the Witham, towards *Lindum* (Lincoln). Named after this Roman town was the kingdom of Lindsey, between Lincoln and the Humber, whose king, Cædbæd, bore a British name. This confirms that there was some mingling of Angles with Romano-Celts.

The Mercians were a branch of the Angles who favoured a landfall in the River Humber, and then rowed down its tributary, the Trent, the upper reaches of which became the heart of their kingdom. The name is derived from *Merce* (Marchmen), which signifies that the Mercians were 'borderers'. Many settled in what is now Nottinghamshire, Leicestershire and east Staffordshire; others penetrated to the foothills of the Derbyshire Peak district. Points of contact between the Mercians and West Saxons led to boundary contentions in the south-west, late in the sixth century. The *Chronicle* records (AD 597) that the Angles and West Saxons were constantly at war. Between the kingdoms of Mercia and East Anglia the river Cam was the principal boundary.

Other Anglian settlers travelled from the Humber, up the northern Ouse, to York, where they took over the fertile areas of the British kingdom of Deira, including its name. Pockets of Britons on less arable land were left untouched, and some inter-marriage undoubtedly took place. In the centre of northern England, between the rivers Aire and Wharfe, the small British kingdom of Elmet was left independent, until absorbed by King Edwin of Deira before the middle of the seventh century. The Romans called this canton *Loidis regio*, from which the modern name Leeds is derived.

The River Humber was not the natural dividing-line between north and south that it is today; it was the centre of a fan-like Anglian expansion that developed in both directions. In the north there was persistent conflict between Deira and Bernicia, caused by the claims of rival dynasties of the mid-sixth century. There seems to have been a family connection between the kings of Wessex and Northumberland, while the latter was part of Bernicia. The first mention of Northumbria in the *Anglo-Saxon Chronicle* occurs in the years 560 and 593; but Angles had settled on the east coast between the rivers Tees and Forth before the earlier date. According to Bede's *Ecclesiastical History* (Book V, ch. 24) the kingdom of

Bernicia dates from the accession of Ida, who ruled for twelve years and founded Bamburgh. The arrival of the Angles in Scotland could not have been much earlier than Ida's kingship.

Because the Celtic influence was strong north of the Tees, and the Britons were still resisting attacks by the Picts and Scots, Northumbria was not occupied overland. The Anglians found it preferable to make raids from the sea, the focal points being the Tyne estuary, and the coast between Lindisfarne and the Tweed. When King Æthelfrith, who died in AD 616, had established footholds in Bernicia soon after the close of the sixth century, Anglians from further south (including Deirans from the Humber) settled along the shores of the kingdom; Bernicia was therefore not colonized directly from the Continent. Though the tributary Celts were under military rule, they were too numerous to suppress, and this accounts for the survival of the British tradition in the north-eastern Anglian region.

Perhaps the most orderly Anglian domain was the Cambridge district of East Anglia, where the density of population, even in the fifth century, bespoke a stable community. Burial urns, both holed and windowed, tally with discoveries between the rivers Elbe and Weser, suggesting that Saxons and Angles were mingled in this part. The indications are that an infiltration of Saxon settlers from Germany took place early in the sixth century; about a hundred years later the group came to be known as 'Middle Angles'. According to R. H. Hodgkin in *A History of the Anglo-Saxons* (vol. I, p 117), these Saxons gradually extended their influence westward, in the neighbourhood of the Icknield Way, until they linked up with the West Saxons on the upper Thames. The Roman road crossed the river between Wallingford and Goring, where there was a large West-Saxon settlement. Dorchester-on-Thames was shortly to become the seat of the first Saxon bishop.

In the Middle Ages the fenland that surrounded the Wash was so vast that it had to be reclaimed by systematic drainage, in emulation of the Roman practice. Such extensive fens did not exist when the Angles arrived, as modern air photography has disclosed; there were not only habitable sites, but ancient villages and Celtic cultivated fields. Undoubtedly the Roman system of dykes contributed to this prosperity; and when they were neglected by the Angles, they deteriorated, helped by a possible submergence of the eastern coastline. The evidence shows that the terrain began to change towards the end of the fifth century; the desolate condition of the fens is graphically described in Felix's *Life of St Guthlac* (663–714), the latter being a royal ascetic who lived for fifteen years on a slip of rising ground known as the Isle of Crowland.

The East Anglian area of settlement, east of the Ouse and south of the Fens, incorporated Norfolk, Suffolk and Cambridgeshire. It is extremely rich in burial and other remains, if not in documentary history. Over two dozen investigated cemeteries have shown Anglo-Saxon habitation before the end of the fifth century. As a result of the Roman road system, the distribution of population was similar to that under imperial rule; but there is evidence of decline in industry (especially pottery), as well as in the clearing of forests for agriculture. The patronymic of the East Anglian royal family was Wuffa, whose kingship began in the second quarter of the sixth century; but Rædwald seems to have been the most progressive of the East Anglian rulers.

The identity of ceramic work found in Frisia and Deira leaves no doubt of the Continental origins of the Humber group of invaders. But here, as in Lindsey, a cross-fertilization of Roman culture remained during the earliest period of Anglian occupation, owing to traditional ties with York and Lincoln, where the Christian church gained ground in the seventh century. By this time the Anglo-Saxon kingdoms, through consolidation, had become seven in number: Kent, Sussex, Wessex, Essex, East Anglia, Mercia and Bernicia (Northumberland).

The new kingdom of Northumbria was the result of Æthelfrith's incorporation of Deira with Bernicia in the first decade of the seventh century. He was a ruthless warrior-champion of the Bernician cause, and gained a notorius victory over the Welsh near Chester in AD 613. The epithet 'notorious' is deserved because he countenanced the slaughter of 1250 unarmed spectator monks, who had come from Bangor to offer prayers for a Welsh victory. Bede's account rebukes the holy men for their unwillingness to participate in the conversion of the Anglo-Saxon heathens. Æthelfrith's aggression was eventually his undoing; for Edwin, the exiled ruler of Deira, had sought refuge with Rædwald, King of East Anglia, who killed Æthelfrith in battle at the River Idle, on the Mercian border, in 616.

During the sixteen years of Edwin's reign, the king and his court were baptized into the Christian faith (*Chronicle*, AD 627), and Northumbria became the leading Anglo-Saxon power of the seventh century. Anglesey and the Isle of Man were conquered, and the Welsh expansion eastward was halted. But Cadwallon, King of Gwynedd, joined forces with the Mercians of King Penda, and marched to Hatfield Chase (632), where Edwin was defeated; the line of Deiran kings ended with his death. This reverse brought into power the Bernician monarch, Oswald (633–41), a Christian who sponsored Columban Christianity in Northumbria; he began his reign by overthrowing Cadwallon at the battle of Hexham, near the Roman Wall.

Gradually the Angles were able to absorb Lowland Scotland in the Clyde area, where the Welsh had been dominant; and they actually invaded Meath in Ireland in AD 684. By that date present-day Westmorland, Cumberland and Lancashire were in their hands. The attempt of Ecgfrith to expand Anglian influence north of the Firth of Forth was, however, foiled by the Picts at Dunnichen Moss in 685, where the Northumbrian king was killed.

In the south the Northumbrians had been under considerable pressure for more than twenty years from King Penda of the Mercians, one of whose expeditions penetrated as far north as Bamburgh. King Oswald died in doing battle against Penda, at Oswestry, in 641. Oswiu, his successor, bided his time; then with a large army, he overwhelmed the combined Mercian, East Anglian and Welsh forces near Leeds, in AD 654. Penda and Æthelhere, King of East Anglia, were both killed in a fluctuating battle that involved many thousands of men. By 670, when Oswiu (Bede's *Oswy*) died, Northumbria had exhausted its military might in both aggressive and defensive wars. The growing strength of Mercia enabled it to regain prestige in an onslaught near the River Trent, where Ecgfrith was decisively beaten in AD 678. He was the last of the ambitious Bernician and Deiran rulers, who could command political stability; their interest in religion and education had done much to encourage scholars like Bede to create and preserve literature and art.

Bede's *Ecclesiastical History* states that the Mercian king and his nobles accepted Christianity in AD 653; but the beginning of Mercian hegemony dates from the accession of King Æthelbald in AD 716. Between them, Æthelbald and Offa ruled for eighty years, and reduced the surrounding kingdoms to a state of vassalage. Although Æthelbald was a Christian, his rule was extortionate, and he was murdered in 757. East Anglia, Essex and Lindsey had already been absorbed into Mercia, and three kingdoms south of the Thames (Kent, Sussex and Wessex) acknowledged the suzerainty of the new King Offa (757–96). The influence of bishops, abbots, the monastic system, and widespread Christianity undoubtedly helped to bring about this federation, and with it greater social and political order.

Offa is now regarded as the most renowned Anglo-Saxon ruler before Alfred the Great. He was invited to be father-in-law of one of the Emperor Charlemagne's sons. A firm boundary between Mercia and Wales was defined by the construction of the frontier wall known as Offa's Dyke. Offa chose the central town of Lichfield as an episcopal see, and by introducing the first silver penny furnished the realm with a respectable coinage that remained in currency until the time of William the Conqueror. But there were ominous signs of change when the Vikings first raided the east coast of England, and sacked Lindisfarne in AD 793.

Wessex was the next power to bid for control of the confederate kingdom, but was unable to do so until the ninth century, because of a clash of interests with Mercia. In spite of expansion westward into Somerset and Devon during the seventh and eighth centuries, Wessex had entered a period of comparative obscurity, in which two kings, Cynegils and his son Cenwalh, reigned for sixty-one years. The former became a Christian in AD 635, and to mark his conversion, established the first bishopric in Wessex at Dorchester-on-Thames. Seven years earlier he had boldly engaged in battle at Cirencester with the Mercian king Penda, but was compelled to forfeit the territory gained by Wessex at the victory of Dyrham in 577. Wansdyke, the great earthwork extending from Wiltshire to Gloucestershire, is said to have marked a new boundary-line between the two kingdoms.

Cenwalh, who was a pagan, married into Penda's family in order to preserve peaceful relations; but the match was unsuccessful, and this Wessex king was driven into exile in East Anglia for a period of three years. Here he was baptized, and when he returned to power established a second bishopric at Winchester. By the time of Cenwalh's death in 672, Mercia had won all of the Wessex territory north of the Thames, including the Dorchester bishopric. Cenwalh's loss was compensated by an advance into Devon as far as Exeter, where the king founded a monastery. The pressure on Wessex from the Midlands was continued when Penda's son, Wulfhere, occupied the Isle of Wight and awarded it to the satellite kingdom of Sussex. The island was, however, recaptured by Cædwalla, a king of mixed British blood, in AD 685. In the three years before his abdication, this warrior-king, who died a Christian in Rome in 689, overcame Sussex and Kent, and created the ideal of a unified kingdom in England, south of the Thames.

The eighth century opened auspiciously for the improvement of Saxon England, in religion, education and agriculture. It was generally accepted in the lowlands that the German invaders had come to stay, and that they were sufficiently powerful to hold the land on which they settled. The next Wessex ruler, Ine (688–726), wisely consolidated his kingdom and, though not the first to do so, framed a code of laws, indicating a felt need for civilization. The ecclesiastical aspect of Ine's reforms was left in the hands of a distinguished scholar, Aldhelm, whom the king made Bishop of the new see of Sherborne. Aldhelm, who afterwards moved to the famous Irish foundation at Malmesbury, was in constant touch with learned ecclesiastics in the north. Cædwalla and Ine set the example in England (already practised in Ireland) for kings to retire by abdication, and end their days peacefully in a religious community; a third king, Ceolwulf of Northumbria, became a monk at Lindisfarne in 737.

In AD 792 the West Saxon prince, Ecgberht, returned from exile among the Franks of Charlemagne's kingdom, into which he had been sent three years earlier by the will of Offa. A decade later he succeeded to the kingdom of Wessex and ruled for the next thirty-seven years, the first twenty of which were uneventful. Ecgberht was building up resources for a final clash with Mercia, which came in 825, when he defeated Beornwulf, with heavy losses, at Ellendun near Swindon. The Mercian king fled to East Anglia, and was there murdered. This victory led to the annexation of Surrey, the reassertion of West-Saxon power over Kent and Sussex, and a declaration of protection for East Anglia. Consolidating his position in the south, Ecgberht four years later subdued Mercia and Northumbria, and invaded north Wales.

Ecgberht's real authority over these kingdoms was, however, short-lived; for in 836 the Wessex king unwillingly assumed the mantle of English defender against the Vikings. An isolated inroad began in Dorset on the south-west coast about AD 789, when three shiploads arrived and killed the reeve of Dorchester, who had questioned their intentions. The northern and western islands of Scotland suffered heavily, and religious communities were attacked at Lindisfarne, Jarrow and Iona. As will appear later, these raiders were Norwegians, not Danes. But Danes seem to have landed in Cornwall in large numbers in AD 838 and joined forces with the local British inhabitants, until put to flight by Ecgberht at the battle of Hingston Down. When Ecgberht died in the following year he was succeeded by two of his sons, Æthelwulf becoming King of Wessex, and Æthelstan becoming King of Essex, Kent, Surrey and Sussex.

When Ecgberht conquered Mercia in AD 829, the *Chronicle* observes that he was the eighth king to become *Bretwalda*, i.e. 'Overlord of Britain'; the names of the other seven, taken from Bede's *Ecclesiastical History* (Book II, ch. V), are: Ælle, King of Sussex; Ceawlin, King of Wessex; Æthelberht, King of Kent; Rædwald, King of East Anglia; and Edwin, Oswald and Oswy, Kings of Northumbria. West-Saxon bias against Mercia was palpably the reason for the omission of such distinguished rulers as Æthelbald and Offa. Both records contain a list of 'overlords', and not merely of personages of large territorial authority; but control over the important kingdoms south of the Humber was undoubtedly implied. Kings regarded themselves as rulers over people, and not of parcels of land; they achieved popular acclaim through their courtesy, generosity and probity in dealing with their thegns, as well as through their commanding presence in warfare. When a victorious ruler exacted the submission of a conquered people, it was conceded as a loyalty due to his personal might, and not to his unproven successors. A Bretwalda had the right to grant safe-conducts through affiliated kingdoms, and to prevent the alienation of land without his permission, for instance by the gift of property to the Church.

In the period 450–850, which was one of ruthless warfare, disputed succession, and frequent deposing of kings, it should be remembered that the Anglo-Saxon invaders were not organized tribes owing fealty to their rulers, but adventurers, operating in small bands of a few hundred, undisciplined except by a desire for their common advantage. Power was the criterion of success for an aspirant ruler, who was expected to possess all the qualities of leadership. The German newcomers were more aggressive oppor- tunists than the Celts, with few religious compunctions until their acceptance of Christianity. Their kings, when they acquired terri- tory by armed force, could claim no rights of primogeniture in the succession, but invariably nominated a kinsman or noble in whom they had confidence. In setting up their independent domains, the Anglo-Saxons continued the pattern of political instability estab- lished by Vortigern and northern British kings after the termination of Roman rule.

Pre-Christian English society reveals a degree of impermanence, which the archaeology of the fifth and sixth centuries confirms. The pagan invaders left no material remains to compare with those of the Romans, who built in stone and brick; and their graves can be identified only when there are relics of jewellery (such as cruciform brooches) and weapons, which disappear after the heroic age that is depicted in the poetry of the seventh century. This age had virtually come to an end before the German invaders arrived in England. The themes of their sagas are all Germanic in origin, but the minstrels who recited them enjoyed a traditional popularity throughout the Anglo-Saxon period (see chapter VIII).

The British opposition to the Saxon invasion (AD 465–500) occasioned heroic legends of a different kind – those of Ambrosius Aurelianus and Arthur of Britain. They belong to a period too poorly documented for any historical certainty. Ambrosius, who was of the resistance movement, and was known to the Welsh as Emrys, must have been the son of the Roman-British emperor who opposed Vortigern a generation earlier. King Arthur could have been no lesser person than a Romano-Celt of noble blood, and probably an experienced commander of cavalry. While it is known that sixth-century Gauls and Britons employed mounted units in military operations, there is no archaeological evidence of horse soldiers, or even of the use of stirrups, a century earlier. Welsh heroic poetry of the sixth century, however, confirms the tradition of the mounted warrior; horses were bred and trained in some southern regions of England, in the Cotswolds and Gloucester- shire, during the time of Ambrosius the younger. It would appear, therefore, that the Cymry to which Arthur belonged, and the

51

south-western owners of Roman villas, equipped their own cavalry-men to defend the country against Saxons, who had no knowledge of horses in warfare. The mobility of such a force of individualists, under a skilful leader, and operating from strong defensive positions such as the hill-fortress of Cadbury, would secure distinct advantages over small bodies of infantry, especially in the sparsely populated terrain of the west and north of England.

Speculation about the historicity of Arthur includes the belief that he succeeded Ambrosius as commander-in-chief of the British resistance movement sometime in the 470s. He is credited with twelve famous British victories. A Welsh verse legend, written about a hundred years after the event, recounts an unsuccessful battle fought by King Arthur at Portchester about AD 480, in opposing a Saxon landing; in this lament, the 'Elegy for Geraint', the death is recorded of Gerontius, the Prince of Dumnonia, who hailed from Devon. The celebrated siege of Badon, which Gildas describes, took place near Bath; the English probably invested an encampment of British cavalry on the isolated Solsbury Hill. The Arthurian warriors must have numbered not many more than a thousand, and the besieging Saxon army was bound to have been many times larger. The siege is said to have lasted three days, after which Arthur's cavalry made a determined charge downhill, and routed the Saxon infantrymen, killing 960. Not many Saxons on foot are likely to have escaped the aftermath of this defeat, which was decisive enough to ensure twenty-one years of stable government, modelled on that of Roman Britain.

If the Arthurian legends of the twelfth century, written by Geoffrey of Monmouth, are to be credited, some of the King's most notable exploits were connected, not only with the north of England and Scotland, but with much of western Europe as well. The code of chivalry of the Round Table and the tournaments of jousting should be recognized as Plantagenet anachronisms, designed to boost the imperial dreams of Norman kings. Some events, however, enshrine late British history, for example the death of Peredur of York in AD 580, and the tragic Cornish history of Tristan and Iseult (the scene is King Mark's castle at Fowey), which belongs to the close of the sixth century. It was Thomas Malory, a knight of Warwickshire, who dressed Arthur's knights in the fifteenth-century trappings of the Wars of the Roses (see chapter XIV). Despite this obvious romantic fiction, its worth is not to be minimized; the tradition of Arthur as a just British ruler in an age of corruption cannot be altogether discredited.

Whatever Arthur's origin, he would have ruled over some portion of lowland England east of Wales, and been disliked as a tyrant principally in remoter areas, such as north of the Clyde, where he had appeared in the guise of a conqueror. It is very likely that northern campaigns induced him to remain in the Carlisle-Penrith area for a considerable time. Nennius mentions that he fought battles in the Cheviot hills and Lowlands north of Hadrian's Wall, the main object of this campaign being to reunite the Welsh kingdom of the Clyde with Britain. It is said that Irish settlers in western Scotland, northern and southern Wales and Devon were enlisted as Arthur's allies in attempting the reunion of Celtic peoples in Britain. One of Arthur's generals in Wales, Cornwall and Brittany was a Goth called Theodoric, presumably from Gaul. The name was common, especially in the age of Theodoric of Ravenna, King of the Ostrogoths (c 454–526, see p 248). *Leon*, in north-west Brittany, to this day recalls Arthurian Lyonesse. The English name corresponding to French *Avallon* would be 'Appleton'.

The Arthurian legend, revived in France, was commonly known as 'the Matter of Britain', to be set beside indigenous tales, 'the Matter of France', and classical literature, 'the Matter of Rome'. Two French writers of the twelfth century, Chrétien de Troyes and Marie de France, adapted some Arthurian romances in their verse tales (see p 367). Chrétien de Troyes' principal contributions were *Lancelot, Ywain* and *Perceval*, composed between 1169 and 1175. All these extol the code of chivalry, and the last-mentioned introduced the legend of the Holy Grail, a vessel supposed to have been brought to the West by Joseph of Arimathea, after the Last Supper. Marie de France was a woman of noble rank, probably born in Anjou, but resident in Britain. Her songs are less indebted to the Arthurian legends than her contemporary's, her main title to fame resting on fourteen delicate narratives, known as the *Lais of the Bretons*. They were dedicated to an English king, thought to be Henry II.

The attempt of the established Church to show Arthur in a disreputable light is explicable. Though Arthur was a Christian, the Celtic church was not in sympathy with ecclesiastics of Rome, who recorded anecdotes about him in the monastic age after his death. Disparagement occurs in the Lives of Saints, mostly of Welsh provenance, written by monks of plebeian origin, who were inveterate haters of dynastic military authority. They shared the sentiments of St Brigit, who said: 'All subjects serve the Lord . . . the children of kings are serpents, save a few whom God hath chosen.'

After the battle of Mount Badon, the English settlers held the territory south of the Humber and east of the Trent, the whole of East Anglia, Kent and Surrey, and part of Sussex, Hampshire and Berkshire. Except for a few Anglian groups on the north-eastern seaboard, the rest of England, including Suffolk and most of Essex, remained under British control.

Towns and cities were sadly depopulated and people tended to live in small communities, in which distinctions of class were not great. This was fortunate, for a devastating bubonic plague spread through Europe about AD 550. The Roman system of *civitates* was partially revived; but the Arthurian court had no appointed seat, the policy of its tenure being that of a mobile military force, operating vigilantly in the lowlands. The aim was to prevent a recurrence of civil war. That such a government was short-lived was not surprising; its end is thought to have come at the unlocated battle of Camlann (meaning 'crooked glen'), twenty-one years after Mount Badon. This was the time of the great migration of Cornish Celts to Brittany, formerly Armorica, the Romano-Gallic word *Armorici* meaning 'dwellers by the sea'.

Gildas (c 516–73), who initiated the Arthurian legends, is supposed to have been born in Dumbarton, the son of Pictish King Clau. Tutored by St Illtud, he is said to have visited Ireland, and founded a monastery at Ruys in Brittany, of which he ultimately became Abbot. Here his principal work was probably written, and judging from the Cymric flavour of his Latin, he might equally have been born in Wales. He was esteemed as a man of wisdom and learning in a sermon of Wulfstan, and the *De Excidio et Conquestu Britanniae* was consulted by Bede for his *Ecclesiastical History*. The book, which he likened to an epistle, abounds in quotations from the Bible, and shows that Gildas was acquainted with the Arian heresy, and that he had also read the *Ecclesiastical History* of Eusebius, Jerome's *Letters* and Orosius's *Universal History*, works unlikely to be available in English libraries.

All that is known of Gildas's successor, Nennius, is that he was a Welshman of the Mercian border, active during the latter half of the eighth century; he says that he was a disciple of Elvod, Bishop of Bangor. Three important copies of his *Historia Brittonum* are to be found in the Cambridge, Harleian and Vatican manuscripts; but it is doubtful whether Nennius wrote more than the Prologue and Apology (sections 1 and 2). A marked difference of style is perceived, when the History itself begins. Nennius would appear to be only the compiler of some earlier records that contain no events after the middle of the seventh century; the problem of the given date (858) is at present insoluble. The compiler excuses himself by saying that he was instructed to undertake the work in spite of his limitations. He claims to have consulted the works of Jerome, Eusebius, Isidore of Seville (*c* 570–636, poet historian and encyclopaedist), Prosper of Aquitaine (*c* 390–463, poet and defender of St Augustine), as well as annals of the Scots and the Saxons. Observations in the History that provoked most discussion are: the locations of the thirty-three towns of Britain (§ 7); the curious relationship of Vortigern with Hengest and Horsa (§§ 36–49); King Arthur's battles (§ 50 – the first eight are said to have been fought on the Scots border); and the genealogy of the leading Anglo-Saxon kings (§§ 57–65).

No history of the time seems to have the potential to illuminate the complex situation by which the Germanic culture was assimilated into the Romano-Celtic life that preceded it. Bede, as a monastic historiographer, had little of the humanist's tolerance. He called the pagans among his own people 'a barbarous, fierce and unbelieving nation' (*E. H.* Book I, ch. 23). He could not be expected to have sympathy for the causes of social disharmony, such as differences of blood, of worship and of mythology. His account of the miracle of Cædmon's hymn (Book IV, ch. 24) shows that he was artist enough to understand inspiration in a scop or minstrel. He may also have been aware of the Church's plan to transform an early version of *Beowulf*. The *Ecclesiastical History* is silent on Anglo-Saxon poetry in its Continental origins, though some of these poems make reference to a Christian God.

In *Widsith*, *Deor* and *Waldhere* the dominant mood is heroic, but also elegiac. The earliest poems show that the Celtic Church of Northumberland, in whose scriptoria they were probably recorded, had come to terms with a powerful mythological culture, Scandinavian in origin, and oral in tradition, which embodied a belief in magic. The transposing of *Beowulf* into something consonant with the New Testament is explicable on the best of all grounds – the fusion of religious ideas among ecclesiastics with vision.

The Germanic mythology was earthy and close to nature, but fundamentally pessimistic, one reason being the nostalgia of a people living in exile from the *penates* of the domestic hearth. Heorot, the mead-hall in *Beowulf*, was a symbol of tribal togetherness, a place for the evening occasion when gifts were distributed to loyal followers and distinguished guests, the scop being an honoured entertainer of the clan. In *The Lord of the Rings* J. R. R. Tolkien recaptures the mood of this Nordic twilight, its belief in courage and loyalty, its mystic vagueness and terror of the unknown. His British Academy lecture 'Beowulf, the Monsters and the Critics' (1936) was the germinal work of a creative mind, fascinated with the lost values of pagan antiquity.

The thirteenth and fourteenth chapters of Tacitus's *Germania* (AD 98) describe the institution of *comitatus*, which is most characteristic of the heroic age.

> 13. There is rivalry also among the chiefs as to who shall have the largest band of followers and the most valourous. This is honour, this is strength, always to be surrounded by a great band of chosen youths. This confers distinction in peace and help in war. . . .
> 14. When they go into battle, it is shameful for the chief to be surpassed in feats of valour and for the followers not to strive to equal the courage of their chief. Moreover, it is a lifelong infamy and shame if any of the followers survives his chief and comes uninjured from the battle. Their sacred oath of loyalty requires them to defend and protect him and to attribute their bravest deeds to his fame. . . . The table of the chief with its plain but plentiful dishes is regarded as salary. The source of rich gifts is war and plunder. They could hardly be persuaded to work the soil and earn the yearly harvest; they are more easily moved to challenge an enemy and earn glorious wounds. They consider it dull and senseless to gain by their labour what they might obtain by their blood.

The *Germania* of Tacitus expanded its influence throughout the Rhineland, Friesland, Flanders and northern Gaul, and this area became the melting-pot of several cultures, most already under the spell of Latin and in contact with Britain. The Goths and the Franks had rulers who promoted the festive arts of poetry and song. The spirit of the age reflects an Anglo-Saxon community in England not yet severed from its native past. Once the invaders had become literate under Christian tuition, they found the Old Testament congenial to their indigenous culture; for instance, the genealogies that trace rulers back to some patriarch or god. In Old English no secular literature survived that was not transcribed by some monk with a religious motive.

The mingling of cultures resulted in a conflation of mythologies, which was negligent of time and history; hence the abundance of anachronisms in literature, which lasted even beyond the Middle Ages.

The earliest of the Germanic poems is probably *Widsith* (143 lines), found in the Exeter Book; it seems to be a product of Mercia in the seventh century, but its West-Saxon manuscript seemingly belongs to the tenth. The theme concerns a travelled harpist of Continental Anglia, sufficiently skilled in his art to give the poem its title. But the narration presents little more than a catalogue of notables, among them three heroic kings, Attila of the Huns, Eormanric of the Goths, and Theodoric of Ravenna, who dominated Europe in the fourth to sixth centuries. This is a fictitious array of the minstrel's supposed acquaintances.

The language of *Widsith* is simple, but at the same time a technically competent display of stylistic conventions. In line 1 (second hemistich) *word-hord onleac* 'unlocked his word-hoard' expands the sense of *maðolade* 'spoke' in the first hemistich. Anglo-Saxon *kennings* of this sort have been called parallelisms, and sometimes contain metaphors of remarkable vividness. *Kenning* is an Old Norse term for what is really a periphrastic expression, most frequently in apposition to a significant noun. The device is not simply an ornament, but a way of connecting a verse line semantically with the preceding one.

Deor, or 'the minstrel's lament', is a poem of forty-two lines and uncertain date, also appearing in the Exeter Book. The minstrel laments that he has been superseded by a rival, and has therefore lost his patron and his prestige; in bemoaning his fate, he displays heroic acceptance of life's vicissitudes. Mutability, he shows by historical examples, is the common lot of man; every instance cited ends with the refrain: 'That passed away, so can this.' Kemp Malone properly observes: 'It is hardly justifiable . . . to look upon the refrain as a metrical device, serving to divide the poem into stanzas or strophes, because the sectional division is determined by the matter, not the form.' (*Deor*, Methuen ed., 1933, p 17.)

The originality of *Deor* consists, not in its strophic structure, but in the brevity, blend of heroic and lyric elements, and optimistic tone, intended to lighten the poem's didactic purpose. In lines 28–34, a message of hope reminds the despondent one that his misfortune is not singular or endless; the wise Lord, who is responsible for change, designs honour for some, sorrow for others.

A peculiarity of the poem, which some attribute to archaism, is the absence of definite articles. Though this author, too, reveals acquaintance with classical examples of Old English poetry, a later date is suggested for *Deor* than for *Widsith*. Legendary figures that appear in the poem are Weland the Smith, whose craftsmanship was associated with magic, and Theodoric, King of the Ostrogoths, who overcame Odovacer in Italy; both appear to have had dealings with the Geats and a share in the tragedy of Hygelac, mentioned in *Beowulf*.

Another heroic poem recalling Weland and Theodoric is the fragmentary *Waldhere* (Walter of Aquitaine). The manuscript consists of two vellum folds in the Royal Library of Copenhagen, discovered in 1860. It represents a transcript into West Saxon of what was probably a mid-eighth century Anglian poem. F. Norman, who edited the Methuen edition in 1933, believes the spelling may be that of a Northumbrian scribe, who copied *Waldhere* as late as the eleventh century.

There are Latin and Bavarian versions of this Walter legend, the latter in Old High German; Walter and Balder are the names of one and the same person. The strained relations between Huns and Burgundians in the fifth century provide the background. The famous swords of legend all bore names; Waldhere's was Mimming, Weland's masterpiece, and it was presented by Theodoric to Widia, Old English for the Visigothic warrior, named Vidigoia. In the *Heldenbuch*, and South-German epos of the *Nibelungen* and Weland legends (13th century), Theodoric of Verona becomes Dietrich of Berne, Attila is named Etzel, and Ravenna is Raben.

The language contains much dramatic exhortation, the putative writing of a monk who introduced into a pagan work this confession of faith: he who trusts to God for help, finds it at hand, if only he takes thought how to deserve it.

The runic alphabet adopted by Germanic peoples is a phenomenon that occurs sporadically in Anglo-Saxon remains. The word *rune* is found early in Ulfilas's Gothic Gospel of St Mark; then in *The Wanderer* (line 111), where it has the sense of 'secret meditation'; and in *Beowulf* (line 172), with a similar meaning, suggesting a connection between runes and pagan magic.

Runic inscriptions are reported to be more numerous in Norway, Sweden and Denmark than in Britain, where most occur in the formerly Norse-ruled islands of Orkney and the Isle of Man. The Norse inscriptions are older than any other extant examples of Germanic languages. Some Scandinavian runes have furthermore proved to be of much *later* date than any from Germany, Friesland and England; for runes continued in use long after the Norse people had been Christianized. The conversion of these pagans was comparatively late. In 994 the Norwegian Olaf Tryggvason (see p 213), was among the first Christians of his people in England. Latin script was not introduced into the Scandinavian countries until the eleventh century.

Runes on the Ruthwell Cross, an ecclesiastical monument of the first half of the eighth century, and on the Franks Casket in the British Museum, are famous. The casket, made of walrus bone, was bought in France by the donor (Monsieur Franks) in the middle of the nineteenth century. The scenes carved on its sides are from Roman, Germanic and Christian history or legend, each provided with a short runic description. The so-called Old English *Runic Poem* consists of short stanzas, illustrating, through the initial letters of words, the various characters of the runic alphabet; verses of this kind are still in use in elementary education.

Runes were angular in shape, convenient for carving inscriptions on wood, stone or bone. Research has shown that the earliest runes in northern Italy were a modification of the Greek alphabet, and were brought from the Black Sea area by Gothic mercenaries in the third century AD; a little later runic characters appeared among the northern peoples. The *futhark* or runic alphabet of twenty-four letters was known to the Anglo-Saxon invaders of the sixth and early seventh centuries; indeed the settlers added nine more to the British system; the name of the alphabet is derived from the first six runes, *f, u, th, a* (primitive OE *æ*), *r* and *k*.

Runic characters in England were replaced by the Irish system of writing, when the latter was taught by the Celtic missionaries of Northumbria. As has been said, the Roman alphabet proved more convenient for everyday purposes, but there were modifications in the case of *d, f, g, i, r, s* and *t*. The modern English letters *j, v* and *w* were not, however, employed.

St Augustine's missionaries in the south had introduced a sixth-century Italian hand, which remained in use at Canterbury, in the writing of Latin texts, for nearly two hundred years. This style then gave way to the narrow, pointed Irish hand that prevailed for Old English script until the Norman conquest. About the year 900 the Roman digraph *th* was superseded by the runic character þ *(thorn)*, but failed to maintain its intended voiceless function, becoming interchangeable with its voiced counterpart ð (eth). The latter symbol was lost in the Middle Ages, but þ persisted until the close of the fourteenth century.

Roman type for printing Old English texts did not become acceptable until about 1850; but the OE characters þ, ð, æ and sometimes ʒ have been retained. Earlier printers, beginning with John Day in 1567, had special characters cut for the printing of Old English literature.

CHAPTER III

The Conversion of the
Anglo-Saxon Peoples

𝕊𝕊𝕊𝕊𝕊𝕊

A FEW PARAGRAPHS from the fourth chapter of W. E. H. Lecky's
History of European Morals will serve as an introduction to the
present survey:

> What Europe would have been without the barbarian invasions, we may
> partly divine from the history of the Lower Empire, which represented,
> in fact, the old Roman civilisation prolonged and Christianised. The
> barbarian conquests, breaking up the old organisation, provided the
> Church with a virgin soil, and made it, for a long period, the supreme
> and indeed sole centre of civilisation. . . .
> Rude tribes, accustomed in their own lands to pay absolute obedience
> to their priests, found themselves in a foreign country, confronted by a
> priesthood far more civilised and imposing than that which they had
> left, by gorgeous ceremonies, well fitted to entice, and by threats of
> coming judgment, well fitted to scare their imaginations. Disconnected
> from all their old associations, they bowed before the majesty of
> civilisation; and the Latin religion, like the Latin language, though with
> many adulterations, reigned over the new society. . . .
> The priests, in addition to their noble devotion, carried into their
> missionary efforts the most masterly judgment. The barbarian tribes
> usually followed without enquiry the religion of their sovereign; and it
> was to the conversion of the king, and still more to the conversion of the
> queen, that the Christians devoted all their energies. Clotilda, the wife
> of Clovis, Bertha, the wife of Ethelbert, and Theodolinda, the wife of
> Lothaire, were the chief instruments in converting their husbands and
> their nations. Nothing that could affect the imagination was neg-
> lected. . . .
> Hope, fear, gratitude, and remorse drew multitudes into the Church.
> The transition was softened by the substitution of Christian ceremonies
> and saints for the festivals and the divinities of the Pagans. . . .
> (Longmans, Green, 1886, vol. II, pp 178–81.)

Orthodox Catholicism was not, at first, the mode of worship
which the Germanic kingdoms of Europe readily accepted. Among

the Goths who inhabited the Baltic coast between the rivers Vistula and Elbe, and later migrated southwards into the Balkans, Italy, southern France and Spain, Arianism became the recognized religion. The gist of the Arian heresy ('The Son is not co-eternal with the Father') was held to discredit the doctrine of the Trinity, upon which the Catholic mouthpiece, St Augustine of Hippo, grounded his faith. The heresy was confirmed by the Council of Nicea in AD 325, but it continued to hold conviction for influential churchmen, among them Ulfilas (311–83), who converted the Goths in about 348.

Theodoric (c 454–526), the Ostrogoth King whose capital was first at Ravenna, later at Verona, was an Arian, and so were his allies the Visigoths and Burgundians. Arian Christianity was therefore widespread in Western Europe, and might have remained so, had not Clovis, King of the Salian Franks, who emerged from the low country at the mouth of the Rhine, decided to become the first militant monarch to associate his people with orthodoxy and the Pope. The religious influence of Theodoric's kingdom began to wane, an event which has been regarded as unfortunate by some historians, since the tolerant Ostrogoth ruler had proclaimed: 'Religion is not a subject for edict, for nobody can be forced to believe against his will.'

Theodoric had spent ten years in exile at the Byzantine court in Constantinople and became thoroughly latinized; Boethius and Cassiodorus were the ablest classical authors of his time. He was subsidized by the Emperor to maintain an army in defence of the Eastern Empire's frontiers. The Germanic tribes, who successfully invaded Italy and the old imperial provinces, thoroughly assimilated the superior Roman culture, including its system of administration and law. In their new habitations they sacrificed the use of their own language. No literary language emerged in German-occupied territory on the Continent until the Old High German examples of the eighth to the twelfth centuries. Antoine Meillet in *General Characteristics of the German Languages* (p 5) says, in particular, that: 'German speakers remained for a long time faithful to the Indo-Europoean custom of not writing things having to do with religion.'

The pagan myths of the Germanic peoples are seldom reliable pointers to actual religious beliefs. The immortality of their gods was patently inconsonant with their anthropomorphic actions. But supernatural beings there had to be to account for disharmony, or actual conflict, in the forces of nature. There was no evidence of personalized philosophical ideas in the form of moral principle.

Unlike the Celtic culture, that of Germanic society was patriarchal; the gods were subject to a father-figure, like Zeus of the Olympian hierarchy, or the *paterfamilias* of the old Roman household. The *Gesta Danorum* of Saxo-Grammaticus ('the learned one'), written in the thirteenth century, gives a sceptical account of the deities, and their subordinate creatures, the giants and elves; the latter were capable of all manner of distortion.

Before their adoption of Christianity, the Romans invariably respected the religious observances of the people they conquered. When the Angles and Saxons came to Britain, the hero-cult was displacing the old faith in Woden and his son Thor, the oak-god. Woden was, in origin, a war-god, but animistic according to E. B. Tylor's *Primitive Culture* (Murray, 1920), in the sense of 'breathing' the spirit or soul into all forms of life. The ash and the alder were trees of his special care, from which sprang the humans, man and woman.

The pessimism of Germanic mythology may have been due to the perennial conflict between light and darkness, day and night which had special significance for people living through northern winters. Supernatural creatures included dwarves, the children of Ivalde, who were skilled in the magic of metal-work. Of their kindred must have been Volund (Weland), the maker of swords and armour.

Beowulf, whose hero was probably an historical figure, could only have been conceived, or reconstructed, from mythical memories, after the Angles had come to England. Though the intrepid liberator anticipates Dietrich of Berne, he is totally absent from the German cycle of sagas. The many Christian references in *Beowulf* are not interpolations, but necessary to the transformed concept of a gifted traditional poet. *Beowulf* contrives to incorporate many legends, by supposing them to be the songs of minstrels at the festive board.

The Anglo-Saxon peoples who overcame British resistance in the third decade of the sixth century, seem to have had little contact with the life of the Roman Empire; their arrival in Britain was marked by a pagan recession lasting for at least three generations. Genealogies reveal that most of the Anglo-Saxon leaders attempted to trace their descent directly from Woden, who gave his name to the middle day of the English week. The gods worshipped in timber sanctuaries were of Scandinavian origin. Though the priests sacrificed animals, there is no evidence that the German invaders, after settling in England, still practised the fertility cult of Nerthus, the goddess whose rites were described in Tacitus's *Germania* (ch. 40). The 'month of sacrifice' was November, because in the autumn the surplus cattle were culled. Like the Celts, the Anglo-Saxons were overawed by the mystery of forests, and evinced a superstitious dread of marshes and meres, which they peopled with dragons and other evil powers.

Tuesday and Thursday are etymologically derived from the Germanic gods Tiw and Thunor ('the thunderer'), while Friday owes its name to the goddess Frig. Another goddess, worshipped at the vernal equinox or spring festival, was *Eostre* ('of the dawn') whose name survived in 'Easter', after the heathens had been converted to Christianity. The Anglo-Saxon New Year began a week earlier than at present, on 25 December, and the following evening was known as 'the night of the mothers'. Yuletide comprised the last month of the Old Year and the first month of the New. Whether this religion inculcated ethical principles, or led to belief in a life hereafter, is uncertain. The practice of burying men with their weapons, and women with their jewellery, suggests the latter probability, while ethical values are implied in dying men's regard for favourable reputations.

A priest in Northumbria was not permitted to bear arms, or to ride any horse but a mare. There may have been a professional priesthood, but the religion of the Anglo-Saxons in Britain was not apparently organized; it is impossible from the slender records to assume ecclesiastical unity. All the evidence suggests that Sussex and London strongly opposed the introduction of Christianity. Some kings wavered in their allegiance, through lack of understanding; for example, Rædwald of East Anglia allowed both Christian and pagan altars in the same church. Fanatical converts, such as the high-priest Coifi of Northumbria, occasionally became desecrators of ancient gods, as Bede indicates in the *Ecclesiastical History*, Book II, ch. 13:

> I have long since been sensible that there was nothing in that which we worshipped; because the more diligently I sought after truth in that worship, the less I found it. But now I freely confess, that such truth evidently appears in this preaching as can confer on us the gifts of life, of

salvation, and of eternal happiness. For which reason I advise, O king, that we instantly abjure and set fire to those temples and altars which we have consecrated without reaping any benefit from them . . .

Then immediately, in contempt of his former superstitions, he desired the king to furnish him with arms and a stallion; and mounting the same, he set out to destroy the idols . . . The multitude, beholding it, concluded he was distracted; but he lost no time, for as soon as he drew near the temple he profaned the same, casting into it the spear which he held; and rejoicing in the knowledge of the worship of the true God.

R. H. Hodgkin in *A History of the Anglo-Saxons* (vol. I, p 245) describes the conversion of these Germanic people to Christianity as 'the most decisive event in the history of the English before the Norman Conquest'. Thanks to Bede and the biographers of saints, it is also the best documented. Once Christianity was firmly rooted in Roman Britain at the beginning of the fourth century, it was never expunged; the monastic orders of the fifth and sixth century spread their influence in a westward movement, inspired by the Roman church in Gaul, of which the monasteries at Auxerre and Tours were outstanding examples.

Archaeology has shown that there were a number of private churches in the southern villas of England during the Roman occupation. One had the earliest representation of Christ (now in the British Museum) which was found as the centrepiece of a mosaic floor at Hinton St Mary in Dorset. Behind the head of this figure is the Chi-rho monogram, which represents the two initial Greek letters in *Christos*. Long before the Romans left Britain, they had given titles to most of the church officers, such as bishop and rector; while organization of the Christian church in the south and north-west regions of England, as well as in Wales, continued unbroken during Anglo-Saxon domination of the lowlands. Private chapels, monastic communities and organizing bishops thus brought about important changes in institutional Christianity during the sixth century.

The newly established monasteries were places removed from the political conflict. The philosophy of the austere life, dedicated to religion, had its origins in the persecution of Christians in the Roman provinces of Egypt and the Near East; the believers withdrew in considerable numbers from cities to desert places.

The most important early monastic development was, however, that of St Benedict of Nursia (480–549), who founded monasteries at Monte Cassino and Subiaco. They were thoroughly democratic institutions, welcoming all classes, from the rich to emancipated slaves. A visionary Benedict may have been, but the *Regula* he introduced was practical as well as timely. A fundamental principle of the Rule, written in popular Latin, was that a portion of the day must be spent in manual labour, so that a monastery should be self-supporting, as well as capable of helping the needy in its environment. The monks' tillage of the soil and poor relief became unsurpassed, without sacrifice to devotional exercises.

Such monasteries helped to save Italy at the height of the barbarian invasions, and at critical times they had the same effect in Britain. The cardinal disciplines instilled were humility, obedience and silence in seclusion. The practice was initiated by Benedict of having one of the monks read to the others at meal times; a magnificent library was thus assembled. The English name Seymour is derived from St Maur, one of Benedict's disciples, who left Italy to found a monastery on the banks of the River Loire in France.

Many of the small islands in the Mediterranean became retreats for ascetics, one of the best-known being that of St Honoratus on Lérins, off the south coast of Cisalpine Gaul. Here the celebrated missionaries, St Patrick and St Illtud, founders of early British and Irish monasteries, are believed to have studied. The name of Illtud is surrounded by legend, which makes him a one-time soldier of King Arthur; but his claim to remembrance was the exemplary education he gave to St David (520–88), who became the patron saint of Wales. The discipline that David enforced upon his community at Menevia (probably on Caldy Island) was the severest possible; but he believed it insignificant when compared with the cruelties and hardships suffered at the hands of the Saxons in the disturbed period AD 450–550, which Gildas described.

Like owners of Roman villas, rich Britons endowed the *llans* or *minsters* of the monasteries they founded, their ·motive being a desire for peace and salvation. Monastic Christianity offered the only facilities for education, and appealed particularly to the suffering Celtic peoples. Bede records that there were over two thousand monks at the monastery of Bangor. But withdrawal from the world was condemned as escapism by missionaries of the Church in Northumbria, who tackled the more difficult task of spreading the gospel among militant Anglo-Saxons. There is no doubt, however, that the earliest monasteries in Britain were Celtic, and founded on the west coast of England and Wales. Their abbots were men of high estate and sound education. Among the earliest foundations may have been the monasteries of Tintagel on the north coast of Cornwall (about AD 470) and Glastonbury. Archaeologists have shown that Samian pottery used by these communities came from the eastern Mediterranean, from Athens, Antioch, Tarsus and Constantinople, and not from the west.

Early in the sixth century Gallic monasticism, implanted by St Germanus and St Illtud, passed from south Wales to Ireland, where the principal missionary zealots were St Patrick and St Columba. From Iona in AD 634 Aidan was sent to Northumbria, at the invitation of King Oswald (see p 47), who had received his Christian education while exiled among the Scots of Dalriada. The monastery founded on Holy Isle, Lindisfarne, emulated the religious life practised by Columba's community, and the site was chosen because it was near Bamburgh, the seat of Northumbrian kings. Lindisfarne soon became the English home of the missionary movement, which established monasteries in the western lowlands of Scotland and the north of England. The monks were both English and Irish; and Diuma, Cedd, Chad, Wilfrid and Cuthbert carried Christianity into Mercia, East Anglia and Wessex, as well as Frisia, the Netherlands and Germany. Wilfrid was of noble birth, and most of the emissaries later became bishops. The bishop's *see* is derived from the Latin word *sedes*. His chair became the symbol of his office, which was to ordain priests and to teach the faith, and when the bishop travelled, his chair was usually taken with him. In the British Church, the bishop did not ordain priests under the age of thirty years.

It should not be forgotten that St Augustine's foundation at Canterbury in AD 597 preceded that of Aidan at Lindisfarne by a generation. The moving spirit behind Augustine's mission was the Benedictine Pope Gregory I (540–604), whose aim was to curb isolationism among the Christian Celts and to restore the ideals of the Graeco-Roman church of Constantine, whose fountain of inspiration was in Rome. Gregory was an able administrator and a devout Christian, but reactionary in certain opinions, as expressed in *Moralia*, on literature and the arts of language. On the grounds of their appraisal of paganism, he wanted to suppress the writings of Cicero and Pliny, and was openly contemptuous of grammarians like Donatus, who had trained brilliant pupils, such as Jerome.

Gregory was the first of a line of revivalist popes, and a

philanthropist who had divested himself of riches to found the monastery of St Andrew in the city of St Peter. One of his first steps was to halt the trade in Christian slaves, among whom he encountered in the market place some fair-haired Anglian youths from Deira. This is the account given by F. Contard in *The Popes* (Barrie and Rockcliff, 1964, p 164); it has some elements of unlikelihood, but the gist of the story is supported by Bede's *Ecclesiastical History.*

> One day, before he became pope, Gregory saw at the market-place in Rome some slaves with fair skins, blue eyes and flowing hair. He asked them of what tribe they were. 'Angles,' they replied. '*Non Angli sed angeli*', cried Gregory. 'They shall be companions of the angels.' He asked them the name of their province. 'Deira,' they said. '*De ira*,' exclaimed Gregory, 'from the anger of God they shall be released.' And the name of their king? The Anglo-Saxon slaves told him it was Ælla. '*Alleluia* shall they sing one day,' said Gregory, and he bought the slaves.

Before he became the chief pontiff, Gregory had intended to go himself to Britain; but his desire being frustrated through indifferent health, he persuaded the Pope to divert Church funds from Gaul for buying young Anglian slaves, educating them in Rome, and returning them to work among their own people.

Augustine's mission left Rome in April AD 596, but lost courage at Lérins before reaching its destination. Reassured by Gregory, the party of forty, bearing a large silver cross, reached the Isle of Thanet at Easter 597, and were cordially received by Æthelberht, King of Kent. He permitted Augustine to use the Roman church of St Martin at Canterbury and to preach to his subjects. Augustine's fears had been prompted by a lack of English, and his difficulty now was to convert through a Frankish interpreter. Nevertheless, by the end of the same year, the King and ten thousand of his people had been baptized into the Christian faith. Part of this success was due to the fact that Queen Bertha was a Frank and a Christian; there were extremely good relations between her homeland and the kingdom of Kent. As a result of his achievement, Augustine was created 'Archbishop of the English Nation', by the pontiff at Arles, and Canterbury became the seat of the new Church province.

For a circumstantial account of the conversion of the Anglo-Saxon peoples during the next century, history is indebted to the *Ecclesiastical History* and *Life of St Cuthbert* of Bede (673–735). He completed the *Ecclesiastical History* in Latin in AD 731, and an Old English translation was made available by King Alfred a little more than a century later.

Pope Gregory was discerning in sending a civilized evangelist like Augustine to convert the barbarian Teutonic people, for men of understanding, as well as saintliness, were needed to harmonize Christian teaching with the heroic tradition, whose code of ethics was loyalty to a leader. Augustine's priests succeeded in transferring the core of this loyalty to the figure of Christ, but were able to do so only when the admired leader became a Christian. Cædmon, Aldhelm and Bede succeeded in infusing much of the heroic tradition of vernacular poetry into religious themes. Yet the success of Augustine's experiment hung in the balance for a generation, the reason being that warlike kings identified honour with tribal feuds and personal aggrandizement; they were a permanent threat to religious peace, and the pliant populace, especially in defeat, tended to relapse into heathenism. It was nearly a half-century before any king could order the destruction of images of the pagan gods.

Gregory entrusted his missionary with entire responsibility for the conduct of Church government. His tolerance and breadth of vision are revealed in the replies sent to Augustine's nine queries, some of which arose from want of experience in human relations outside of monastic rule. Gregory quotes from the apostolic maxims of St Paul, but offers much homely wisdom of his own, for example in resolving Augustine's bafflement about different customs in several Christian churches. The advice given to Augustine took nearly four years to arrive, but is so practical and germane to Christian ethics in the Church of England, that some examples are worth citing:

(1) 'Things are not to be loved for the sake of places, but places for the sake of good things. Choose therefore from every church those things that are pious, religious and upright.
(2) 'At this time the Holy Church chastises some things through zeal, and tolerates some through meekness, and connives at some things through discretion, that so she may often, by this forbearance and connivance, suppress the evil which she disapproves . . . In spiritual affairs, we may take example by the temporal, that they may be wisely and discreetly conducted.'
(3) 'As for all the bishops of Britain, we commit them to your care, that the unlearned may be taught, the weak strengthened by persuasion, and the perverse corrected by authority.'

(4) 'All sin is fulfilled in three ways, viz., by suggestion, by delight, and by consent. Suggestion is occasioned by the Devil, delight is from the flesh, and consent from the mind . . . Man is, as I may say, a captive and yet free. Free on account of justice, which he loves, a captive by the delight which he unwillingly bears within him.' (See Bede's *Ecclesiastical History*, Dent, 1939, Book I, ch. 27, pp 39–49.)

Christian humanism of this kind was part of Rome's contribution to English civilization. In the Dark Ages figures such as Gregory the Great were towers of salvation. Indeed, the turmoil and violent change of the seventh and eighth centuries would have extinguished the tradition of learning, but for Charlemagne's Frankish power, Alcuin's and Bede's teaching, and the courage of Christian missionaries.

In AD 601 Gregory turned from the diverse problems of preserving the faith in Italy to the organization of the Church in England. As the author of *Cura Pastoralis*, he was peculiarly fitted for this task, and he was anxious to create in Canterbury a school for the training of ministers of religion. He therefore sent to Augustine, Mellitus, Justus, Paulinus and Rufinianus, who brought books, sacred relics of martyrs, vessels and vestments for church services, and instructions for the expansion of the Church's work. Gregory no doubt felt that the conversion, thus far, had been principally a mission to the court in Kent; it was necessary to spread the idea of national unity, through Christianity, wherever the Germanic pagans were settled. He desired Augustine to ordain twelve bishops under his personal jurisdiction, among whom those of London and York were to enjoy eminence, as metropolitans. A directive was given that heathen temples should not be destroyed, but sanctified to the new faith. The Pope expressed opposition to impressing converts through miracles, because he thought the exploitation of a special gift was not the main purpose of Christian teaching.

To the east of Canterbury Augustine built the monastery of St Peter and St Paul, and furnished its church as a mausoleum for the burial of Kentish kings and bishops of Canterbury, Augustine himself being the first to be buried there in AD 604. In that year a second Kentish see was established at Rochester, Justus becoming its first bishop; the church, with its foundations under the present cathedral, was provided by King Æthelberht, after conversion. All Augustinian churches were small and of Italian design, with eastern characteristics. There were side-chambers opening from the nave or chancel, and behind the altar was a semi-circular apse. Surviving Roman brick-work suggests that the churches were constructed by builders from Italy.

One of Pope Gregory's less fortunate decisions was to assume that the British churches could be assimilated by the Roman dispensation. The approaches made by Augustine, through Æthelberht, in AD 603 met with a rebuff that was largely due to misguided diplomacy. He convened a meeting with bishops and learned ecclesiastics on the borders of Wessex, and rebuked the Celtic Church for observing Easter at the wrong time (from the fourteenth to the twentieth day of the lunar month of four weeks), for irregularities in the ceremony of baptism, and because the Celtic monastic system placed individual power in the hands of abbots, thereby inhibiting effective church organization. Although Augustine prevailed in a demonstration of righteousness when he restored the sight of a blind man where the Britons had failed, he was told that traditions could not be abandoned without the consent of the people.

At a second meeting, Augustine haughtily remained seated upon the arrival of the British delegation, which was mainly from the monastery of Bangor; the Britons regarded this as an affront to their dignity, and a minimizing of their religious status. Further reasoning became impossible, and Augustine, with less than his usual tact, predicted the destruction of the British cause by their Anglo-Saxon enemies. A principal reason for the breakdown of negotiations was undoubtedly the unwillingness of British monks to co-operate in the conversion of their hated German foes.

Just before Augustine's death Æthelberht laid the foundation of St Paul's in London, where Bishop Mellitus had been proselytizing among the East Saxons with some success; their ruler was a nephew and vassal of the Kentish king. Upon the death of Æthelberht in the fifty-sixth year of his reign (AD 616), both kingdoms reverted to paganism, compelling Justus and Mellitus to depart for France. Both were shortly recalled by the pious Laurentius, new Archbishop of Canterbury, who unfortunately died in 619, and was succeeded by Mellitus. Mellitus was, in turn, followed by Justus (AD 624); there had been no less than four Archbishops of Canterbury in twenty-seven years.

Æthelberht had been overlord of all the kingdoms of England south of the Humber, and when he died religious as well as political influence moved to Northumbria. Here Bishop Paulinus was most active as missionary among the Angles of Deira, when in AD 625 pagan King Edwin married the Christian princess Ethelberga of Kent, daughter of King Æthelberht. The marriage was given royal assent, provided the new queen retained her faith, and Paulinus's party accompanied her to ensure that this condition was fulfilled. The following Easter, when his wife presented him with a daughter, Edwin had a narrow escape from assassination. He revenged this attempt by defeating the West Saxons, when he was urged by the Pope, by Paulinus and his chief-priest Coifi to accept the Christian faith (see p 64). In a wooden church specially built for the occasion, he and his nobles were baptized at York in 627; this building was afterwards replaced by a stone edifice.

Paulinus's mission was so acceptable in the north that he was occupied for thirty-six days baptizing Bernicians in a river glen near Yeavering. These people are thought to have been of British descent, not Anglians. Nevertheless, the desire for Christian conversion spread in the next two years to the people of Essex and Lindsey. There was no constraint on the part of missionaries, most of whom had a single collaborator; the example of the king and queen was of paramount importance to the people. The circumstances favouring conversion were similar in Kent and Deira; both kings were overlords of the greater part of England, and had married Christian wives. Their reigns, as converts, were productive of peace, security and prosperity, but regrettably short; in Edwin's instance only six years. His overthrow at Heathfield in AD 633, by Penda of Mercia and Cadwallon of north Wales, was a disaster to national unity; and Paulinus's return to Kent was a setback to Roman Christianity in Northumbria. A disadvantage of Augustine's mission to Kent had been imperfect mastery of the English tongue.

In AD 634 the conversion of the Anglo-Saxon peoples entered its second phase, at Lindisfarne in Bernicia, and Dorchester in Wessex. The first was initiated by the Celtic Church of Scotland, the second from Rome by Birinus, a missionary who seems to have been of German stock. Birinus baptized King Cynegils in the presence of King Oswald of Northumbria in 635, but made little headway except in the royal house of Wessex; his status as a bishop in

Dorchester was independent of the see of Canterbury.

The Celtic mission to Northumbria and Mercia, during the century 635 to 735 AD, was made possible by individual self-sacrifice and monastic co-operation, in conditions of political unrest that were both dangerous and discouraging. For twenty years Northumbria was at the mercy of the pagan King Penda of Mercia, and the overthrow of his thirty legions in 654 alone enabled the Bernician dynasty to reap the harvest of Christian humanism. Most of the leading figures in the Northumbrian revival, including King Oswald himself, became saints, and were personalities of remarkable diversity.

Bishop Aidan is described by Bede (Book III, ch. 3) as 'a man of singular meekness, piety and moderation'; he introduced the practice of fasting on Wednesdays and Fridays, and when he preached in the Scots dialect before Oswald, the king interpreted his words 'to his commanders and ministers'. Upon the exposed tidal island of Lindisfarne, chosen for security, the life of the Christian community in its timber and thatch dwellings, was austere, and unlike that of the monastery at Canterbury, where the disciplines of penance were less exacting. In the best sense, Aidan and his monks were Christian socialists; indeed, many disciples were slaves whom Aidan had ransomed. All wordly goods were distributed to the poor, and travelling was invariably on foot. Once Oswald's successor, King Oswin of Deira, gave Aidan a horse, with splendid trappings, but learnt that he had presented it to the first beggar he met by the wayside. Aidan preached the gospel throughout Bernicia and Deira, using the king's *vills* (centres of local administration), and he enrolled numerous volunteers in his religious community. He died at Lindisfarne in AD 651, only twelve days after the gentle King Oswin, whose death he foretold.

Wherever a bishop could establish harmonious relationships with a ruling monarch, Christianity made considerable progress among the people. The monastery of Lindisfarne was Aidan's most valuable asset, because after his death it became a training ground for preachers and teachers, who had learnt to speak the English tongue. Aidan selected a dozen disciples to continue his mission, and to spread the Celtic influence throughout Anglo-Saxon England. The first mentioned by Bede was Cedd, a man of English birth, who in 653 and 654 resuscitated Christianity among the East Saxons, where it had been extinguished for thirty-six years. Cedd caused churches (such as Bradwell-on-Sea) and monasteries to be built in Essex; when he became bishop, he moved from one to another, having no appointed see. He died of the plague at the monastery of Lastingham, on the Yorkshire moors, in AD 664.

Among the Middle Angles a royal marriage between Peada, son of Penda, and Alhflæd the daughter of Oswy, was conditional on the former's conversion, and Diuma, a Scots disciple of Aidan, accompanied the bride to safeguard her Christian integrity. This led to the baptizing by Bishop Finan of Lindisfarne of many influential Mercians, and the founding of the important monastery of Peterborough. The need for conversion was increased by Oswy's defeat of Penda at the Battle of Winwæd in 654. In thanksgiving for his victory, Oswy set aside twelve parcels of land for the building of monasteries, six in Deira and six in Bernicia. Bede does not say what happened to the 120 families dispossessed (Book III, ch. 24), but the assumption is that they became converts. By this time Christianity had been accepted in every Anglo-Saxon kingdom except Sussex and the Isle of Wight, chiefly through missionaries of the Celtic Church. Contact with the Roman Church seems to have been made only by King Sigeberht of the East Saxons, to whom Bishop Felix of Burgundy had been sent by Archbishop Honorius of Canterbury, twenty years before the arrival of Cedd.

Bede's *Ecclesiastical History* reveals that there were frequent discussions and disagreements about matters such as the dating of Easter, the ceremony of baptism, the convention of the tonsure, and the rights of bishops in the organization of church government. These were among the problems that gave rise to the Synod of Whitby in AD 664. The controversy is described by Bede in Book III, chs. 25 and 26, of the *Ecclesiastical History*; it apparently flared up when Colman succeeded Finan as Bishop of Lindisfarne. A practical difficulty arose when King Oswy's court found it necessary to observe two Easters that overlapped. This created a contretemps about the time of fasting, the king being of the Scots persuasion, and Queen Eanfleda, of Kentish origin, being of the Catholic. The initiative in summoning the Synod to meet at the monastery of the king's kinswoman, Abbess Hilda, was taken by Oswy and his son Alcfrith (sub-king of Deira and pupil of Wilfrid), who happened to hold opposite views on the dating of Easter. The Old English name of the place was *Streoneshalh*, 'The Bay of the Lighthouse', identified with the later Viking settlement of Whitby.

The issues do not appear to modern readers of primary significance; but they were to recent converts, both Anglo-Saxon and
Celtic, who believed, because they were told, that devotions and
good works were nullified by error; in short, that they should not
hope to enter the kingdom of heaven. Although the Celtic party
(headed by Bishop Colman of Lindisfarne) was the stronger, the
new enlightenment had begun to have doubts of the veracity of its
judgement, and the wisdom of isolation from the rest of the
Catholic world. The leader of the latter group was Wilfrid, a man of
high social standing and an accomplished debater, who had studied
in Rome and France. Colman's faction was undoubtedly handicapped by indifferent knowledge of English, in which the proceedings were conducted.

King Oswy presided, and the principal delegates, except Hilda,
were bishops: Cedd (who acted as interpreter), Cuthbert,
James (the disciple of Paulinus) and Agilbert of Wessex (a Frank),
who was accompanied by two. priests Agatho and Romanus. The
clash between Colman and Wilfrid, as recorded by Bede, is valuable
because the Easter debate illustrates the disparate appeals to
authoritarian tradition and reason. When Colman cited the authority of Father Columba and others for his practice, Wilfrid replied:

> I do not deny those to have been God's servants, and beloved by Him,
> who with rustic simplicity, but pious intentions, have themselves loved
> Him. Nor do I think that such keeping of Easter was very prejudicial to
> them, as long as none came to show them a more perfect rule; and yet I
> do believe that they, if any catholic adviser had come among them,
> would have as readily followed his admonitions, as they are known to
> have kept those commandments of God . . .

The sagacious king ruled in favour of the Catholic convention, and
England fell into line with the rest of Christendom. The Easter
controversy was not, however, amenable to a rational solution, as
Wilfrid thought; the adaptation of the Jewish Paschal festival to
Christian needs was, in reality, arbitrary.

The Jewish Christians of St Paul's time regarded Christ's death in
the light of the redemptive sacrifice of the paschal lamb, but
departed from the Old Testament tradition in the matter of dating.
Christian churches of the Mediterranean world soon found themselves divided on this issue, those in the east following the Jewish
custom, those in the west the practice of the Judaeo-Christians. In

AD 325 the Council of Nicea decided in favour of the latter. The important days for Christians had become Easter Sunday (day of the Resurrection) and the preceding Good Friday (day of the Crucifixion); the proper occasion for observance was thought to be the day of the month in the first case, and the day of the week in the second.

Because Alexandria was the home of astronomy, its bishop was invited to calculate the date of Easter Sunday each year, and to communicate it to the Roman see, which would then circulate the decision to the Christian world. The first Sunday after the spring equinox thus became the festival of Resurrection. But as this day varies in different longitudes, the calculators invoked different cycles of years (8, 84 and 532), when the changes of sun and moon appeared to repeat themselves. The Jewish cycle of 84 years, observed in Rome until AD 457, was recognized by the British and Celtic churches. Without justification, they were accused of stubbornly observing an Asiatic practice, when they consistently obeyed the Nicene decree of Constantine the Great. By the seventh century Rome had, however, adopted the more accurate cycle of 532 years. No satisfactory solution was found until the adoption of the Gregorian calendar in 1752.

The decision of the Synod of Whitby, with the king as arbiter, left the government of the Church largely in the hands of the Roman group, with the result that York replaced Lindisfarne as the northern diocesan centre; Chad, the brother of Cedd, became its first bishop. The die-hards of Colman's party, including thirty English monks, withdrew to Scotland, and later founded a new monastery at Mayo in Ireland. Eata of Melrose became Abbot of Lindisfarne, and later its bishop. Henceforward the Celtic Church remained a spiritual force through examples of frugality and asceticism. The schism was not healed by the Synod of Whitby; its effect was valid only for the domain of King Oswy. Picts, Scots, Strathclyde Welsh and Northern Irish did not change church or monastic practices until the ninth century.

The different parts played in their various offices by important English figures such as Cuthbert (625–87) and Wilfrid (634–709), are worth considering, for they illustrate antithetical qualities. Cuthbert, born on the banks of the Tweed, was of humble origin and little education. Brought up as a Christian by his foster-mother, Kenswith, he was first a shepherd on Lammermoor Hills and then a soldier. He had been taught by his mother to venerate the monks of the new monastery at Melrose, a religious house founded by St Aidan in AD 635, and he voluntarily emulated their fasts and prayers. This small house was situated at Old Melrose, three miles east of the present abbey, and its prior was the holy Boisil, after whom the village of St Boswells was named. It was Boisil who supervised Cuthbert's religious training, when he entered the monastery in 651.

The great plague of AD 664 decimated not only the lay population of Britain, but its religious houses. Boisil was taken, but Cuthbert recovered, largely through his faith, athletic strength and determination, and became the new prior. Bede records in his *Life* (ch. 8) that Cuthbert and Boisil spent their last week together studying quarto sheets of John the Evangelist: 'they sought therein only that simple faith which operates by love, and did not trouble themselves with minute and subtle questions.' The figure of St Cuthbert which appears above the east window of Melrose Abbey, shows him holding the head of St Oswald in his left hand. King Oswald was killed when Cuthbert was a youth, and was the first Saxon ruler to be canonized; his severed head was for long venerated, and finally placed in Cuthbert's wooden coffin, still preserved in Durham Cathedral. The legend was confirmed in 1899, when the contents of the coffin were examined.

For thirteen years prior to the plague Cuthbert, with his small portable altar, evangelized the Lowlands of Scotland, from east to west coast; the town of Kirkcudbright (meaning the church of Cuthbert) was named after him. No parish churches existed when Cuthbert walked or rode from village to village; sacraments had to be celebrated in open spaces or private homes, depending on the weather. The face of the pious St Cuthbert inspired confidence, and the warmth of his personality was communicated in conversation; the gentleness of his nature, like that of St Francis, was apparent even to animals.

Shortly before the Synod of Whitby, Cuthbert had been invited by Eata to become prior of Lindisfarne and to supervise the training of missionaries; for twelve years he laboured, with exemplary patience, to restore peace between the Augustinian and Columban churches. He accepted the new Easter as immaterial to his conception of Christianity, preserving the Celtic austerity of his upbringing by undyed garments and personal hardships. In AD 676 he resigned his office, and was granted permission to use a hermitage on the uninhabited Island of Farne, several miles out to sea, as Aidan had done before him. A round habitation was built out of the unhewn stone and turf, and here he was visited by so many brethren, that he considerately provided a landing-place and a building to accommodate them.

In AD 684 the Synod of Twyford allocated four bishoprics to Northumbria, and Theodore, Archbishop of Canterbury (since 669), visited all the regions of England to organize dioceses, so that bishops might function under the authority of the primate, and not by the goodwill of kings. Cuthbert was elected to the See of Hexham, but declined, as he did not wish to leave his cell on the island. King, bishop, nobles and brethren from Lindisfarne then landed on the island, and pleaded with the recluse to change his mind. He reluctantly yielded, and was consecrated by Theodore at York in March 685. For two years he served with characteristic zeal and endless visitations, but he had exchanged sees with Eata, Bishop of Lindisfarne, his lifelong friend, in order to retain the island hermitage, where he subsisted on a diet of barley and onions.

Nearly all of the forty-six chapters of Bede's *Life of St Cuthbert* contain authenticated accounts of his miracles, prophecies and cures. We learn that St Cuthbert was left-handed; that he was gifted with second-sight and remarkable healing powers, which continued to operate at his shrine after his death in AD 687. No testimony omits to mention Cuthbert's forbearance, sympathy, love and holiness. Haggard and careless of his appearance, he was the most typical and venerated example of a Celtic anchorite. It was to honour St Cuthbert that the Lindisfarne Gospels were produced by Bishop Eadfrith from 698 to 721.

The cult of St Cuthbert endured long after his burial in a stone sarcophagus, on the right of the altar of St Peter's, Lindisfarne. There were no less than five inspections of the saint's tomb, in 698, 1104, 1539, 1827 and 1899, the first in order to bring the remains above ground level. On the opening of the coffin, eleven years after his death, the body was found to be uncorrupted, and the limbs still flexible. The next two inspections produced similar testimony; undoubtedly, these discoveries helped to confirm Cuthbert's pre-eminence among the English saints. When in AD 875 the ravages of the Danes compelled the evacuation of Lindisfarne, the bones of St Aidan and the head of St Oswald were placed in Cuthbert's coffin; and during the next eight years the monks devotedly bore the relics from place to place. For a time they reposed at Old Melrose, and for 112 years at Chester-le-Street, the new episcopal see. Finally, they were laid to rest in Durham church (995), before the building of the present cathedral. The coffin was despoiled of its treasures during the Reformation (1539); when finally opened in 1899, only the bones of the saint and the skull of the king remained.

Wilfrid was a prelate who in many ways anticipated Cardinal Wolsey. He was the son of a Northumbrian land-owner, with an aristocratic ambition and restlessness that led him to the service of Queen Eanfled. Not appreciating the virtue of austerity in his training at Lindisfarne, Wilfrid spent the years 653–8 journeying to St Peters in Rome, and improving his understanding of the faith in France. He became a dedicated Romanist, and on his return was made abbot of the monastery at Ripon and Bishop of Northumbria. As he had received the tonsure in Rome, he objected to installation by bishops of British training, and in AD 665 proceeded to Compiègne in France to be consecrated by twelve bishops of Gaul. He was accompanied by 120 armed men and a choir, and conformed to the Gallic practice by being borne on a golden throne, shouldered by nine bishops. During Wilfrid's prolonged stay in France, Chad, the brother of Cedd, was appointed Bishop of York (see p 76). This bishopric was unsuccessfully claimed to be under Wilfrid's jurisdiction; but the latter was not reinstated by the Archbishop of Canterbury until AD 669.

Wilfrid soon became a builder and restorer of churches. He built in stone, introduced glass windows to keep out birds, and invited an expert from Rome to teach the singing of sacred music. The church at Hexham (only the crypt remains) was his lasting memorial, magnificently endowed with ornaments; the stone for its building was taken from the Roman Wall. There were constant complaints to Canterbury of Wilfrid's sumptuous way of living, when it became clear that he was an extremely wealthy man. In AD 678 his power was curtailed by the appointment of three other bishops, at York, Lindsey and Hexham. After doing missionary work in Frisia and Sussex, Wilfrid appealed to Rome for the restoration of his domain, obtaining a papal decree, which the King of Northumbria rejected, on the grounds that it had been bought. Wilfrid was imprisoned for nine months in 681 and went into voluntary exile. For five years he lived in Sussex, and helped to convert the South Saxons and Jutes of the Isle of Wight (see preface, p x), who were the last of the Anglo-Saxon peoples to accept Christianity. On the death of King Ecgfrith in 685, Wilfrid was, however, restored to the monasteries of York, Ripon and Hexham; but still dissatisfied with his minor role, he settled in Mercia as an evangelist.

The primate who bore the brunt of Wilfrid's wrangles was Theodore of Tarsus, who arrived in England as the nominee of Pope Vitalian in AD 669. The English candidate, Wighard, had died of the plague in Rome, and the Pope selected an African abbot, Hadrian, as his replacement. The latter withdrew in favour of his colleague Theodore, a scholar of great reputation, aged sixty-six years; but Hadrian offered to serve as his understudy, being better acquainted with the need of the western church. On the way, they were joined by Benedict Biscop, a Northumbrian monk who had been studying monastic discipline at Lérins. No better team could have been chosen to revivify the Church in the aftermath of the great plague of 664, which depleted the churches and monasteries, and caused a large number of converts to lose faith in Christianity.

After a five-year break in the continuity of the Archbishop's office, Theodore took time to become acquainted with the ecclesiastical state of his province. He found only three bishops in the recognized dioceses, Wine (London), Wilfrid (Ripon) and Chad (York); he quickly established a new see at Winchester. On 26 September, 672, he called a national synod of the English clergy at Hertford, which, though not representative, adopted ten canons of ecclesiastical rule that proved to be of lasting value. They concerned the universal acceptance of Roman Easter, the guaranteed integrity of a bishop's territory, the independence of consecrated monasteries, the abolition of peripatetic monks, bishops and clerics, regular assemblies of the clergy, equality of bishops subject to their seniority, the desired proportion of bishops to the Christian laity, and the proprieties of lawful matrimony..

These canons, based on the decrees of the church fathers and long experience, were a means of removing church separatism and providing an example of national unity to political leaders. Seven bishoprics were now recognized; Canterbury, Rochester, London, Winchester, Dunwich (East Anglia), York and Lichfield; Lindsey and Hexham were added in 677, and Worcester in 680. Aware of the power of Northumbrian kings and the recalcitrance of Wilfrid, Theodore moved warily when creating bishoprics in areas that were not preponderantly Christian. Wilfrid had done more than any other cleric to win the north from the Celtic to the Roman cause; his missionary and educational work was widely recognized, and his influence over the monasteries that favoured Benedictine rule was immense.

It is thought that Wilfrid aroused the ire of King Ecgfrith when he advised Queen Æthelthryth to found the monastery of Colding-ham, and encouraged her to withdraw from the world to become its abbess. The accepted view is that the king's second wife was Wilfrid's most bitter opponent; that she stimulated royal suspicion of the bishop's growing riches and armed following; and that Wilfrid was expelled from Northumbria as a power menacing the throne. It would have been undiplomatic for the primate to become involved in such squabbles, and Theodore wisely remained in the background. He was uncompromising, however, in supporting the need for four bishoprics in Northumbria; at the same time, he regarded with disfavour the king's rejection of the papal decree calling for Wilfrid to be reinstated.

Theodore was a humanist, and with Hadrian as his ally, immeasurably raised the status of the monastery outside Canter-bury as a seat of learning. After returning from Lérins, Benedict Biscop spent two years studying at St Peters, before establishing his institutions at Wearmouth and Jarrow, where Bede received a scholarly education. Before Theodore died in AD 690, he and Wilfrid were reconciled; but the Northumbrian bishop was still not agreeable to the division of his province. He was again expelled, this time by King Aldfrith, in 691; a second appeal was then made to Pope Agatho, who referred the quarrel to Aldfrith's Council at Austerfield (702), without much redress.

At the age of nearly seventy Wilfrid went on foot to Rome, and for four months pleaded before the papacy (704). The issue dragged on until AD 705, when a serious illness induced Wilfred to accept the compromise of his restoration to the churches of Ripon and Hexham. He died at a monastery in Oundle four years later. Like Becket and Wolsey, he was dour in relationships with the secular powers; but though his opposition to Christian monarchs was partly personal, there was more at stake for ecclesiastical efficiency. Wilfrid was a capable administrator and his material service to the

Church was the importation of craftsmen to embellish the architecture and sculpture of new churches. Though an individualist, he did not aim at independence for the Northumbrian church; a separate archbishopric was not, in fact, achieved until twenty-six years after his death, when the great educator, Egbert of York, received the pallium from Pope Gregory III. This symbol was a woollen band, embroidered with crosses, first conferred by the Pope as a sign of his favour, later as a symbol of the archbishop's authority.

Bede reported this episode with the characteristic impartiality of a sound historian. But two facts emerge from this episode in church history:

(1) The opportunity for Christianity to reach the people depended on the interest or tolerance of the reigning king.
(2) The state of the faith in any diocese was the result of the energies exerted by the bishop.

The Christian invariably sought admission to a community and a sacramental way of life, in which self-denial, as practised by the Celtic saints, was a powerful stimulus. The bishop's function was to baptize and to confirm converts.

In spite of the labours of St Cuthbert, the time of the parish church, with the priest as principal activist, had not yet arrived. In the eighth century, the encouragement and generosity of kings and nobles made the existence of the minster and field-church possible. The latter arose out of the expansion of agriculture in new areas, and might be regarded as a satellite of the minster or monastic church of a community. As a result of the Danish invasions, many monasteries disappeared soon after their founding; but the minster was fortunate enough to survive.

Not all Christian communities were monasteries in the sense that their worshippers were monks. Common interest and security urged many clergy of lesser churches to band together in Christian religious groups. The churches were usually endowed by noblemen, who regarded themselves as owners. The patron appointed the priest, who was expected to render part of his income in return for arable land allotted to the church. If no graveyard was provided, however, the patron was held responsible for the priest's stipend. It was not until the Council of Clofeshoh in AD 746 that the parish priest was granted economic independence, and placed under the jurisdiction of his bishop.

Many Christian communities remained without a church until the ninth century; the attendant priest then served mass 'in the field', before a cross of wood or stone erected for that purpose. Surviving stone crosses, without inscriptions, were probably the work of Italian craftsmen, who had been imported by St Wilfrid or Benedict Biscop; some are memorials to the dead, others recall the site of an earlier church, rebuilt in a more convenient area. But most mark the locations of altars for field services. The Northumbrian church at Escomb on the river Wear is one of few surviving seventh-century minsters.

A parish church was commonly a foundation supported by the voluntary contributions of farmers, including the priest himself; the hide allotted to him was known as the *glebe* (Latin *gleba*, 'a clod'), his dwelling being described as the 'glebe-house'. When a man of property died he might bequeath a portion of his goods to the priest by way of *sawol-sceat* 'soul-scot', which was probably a substitute for the pagan practice of burying valued possessions with the dead. Archbishop Theodore, however, ruled that a bequest of this kind was to be reserved for the poor, for the church, or for pilgrimages. The payment of a *tithe*, or tenth part of a Christian's goods, to the church was originally a matter of conscience, the payer alone determining the purpose to which the tithe should be devoted. By the tenth century, however, the tithe had become an obligation, enforceable by law.

These provisions, incorporated in the bishop's parish rules, were important to domestic economy and civil liberty, as well as to church revenue. But just as significant for society was the increasing number of monasteries, and the responsibility they assumed for education. The church did not envisage such communities as essential to the furtherance of religion; they arose from the exigencies of the times, which were harsh and brutal, because of the ambitions of the ruling class. The citizen, whether farmer, craftsman or merchant, must have regarded a life of endless warfare as futile and repressive of man's nobler instincts; if he was stirred by heroic exploits, he preferred to enjoy them in his imagination. Christianity offered opportunities for the fulfilment of worthwhile human relations, and a life of contemplation rich in spiritual experience.

When a monastery was established, it formulated its own discipline of co-existence, sometimes based on the ideals of its founder.

A whole family might devote itself to the religious life, as did the community of Little Gidding in the seventeenth century. In England, Benedictine rule proved most acceptable to Christian humanists; in such a community the anchorite was not encouraged to become an eccentric. Even Celtic foundations, such as Lindisfarne, came to regard the rule of Benedict as congenial for its multifarious tasks, chiefly missionary. Queens and ladies of noble households were frequent founders of monastic orders, of which they became cultured and disciplined abbesses, such as St Hilda. Women invariably headed dual monasteries, in which there were separate houses for the sexes, with a unified purpose. The ruler of a monastery was the abbot or abbess, the bishop being responsible mainly for the elevation of monks to the priesthood. He would enquire also into canonical practice and the use of sacraments; he would consecrate church buildings, and protect the property rights of religious institutions.

The golden age of the Anglo-Saxon church was the period AD 535 to 755. In Europe it expanded the work of the Irish Celtic church of Columbanus and of Egbert, the exile; it motivated the Carolingian foundations, and maintained Anglo-Irish church ascendancy on both sides of the Rhine and Danube, until the Reformation. The importance of the monastic movement on the Continent was its international and predominantly Benedictine character. The missionary work took deepest root among peoples from whom the original migrants to Britain had come, and there is no doubt that language and cultural affinities contributed to the success of this evangelical movement. The monks in their cells provided individualists and scholars, seeking direct access to God; bishops and priests mingled with the world, and through contacts with rulers shaped the developing relationships between Church and State.

The Latin language and the spread of Graeco-Roman culture were among the greatest benefactions to the semi-barbarous people of Europe, largely of Germanic stock. Linguistically, the Germanic group of dialects was probably the least unified; their very origin is a matter of surmise. Germanic invaders, who became settlers, were not numerous, and were ill-fitted to impose their household speech on the subjected. In such an interchange of culture, the language problem is usually one of articulation; some modification of pronunciation, and later of spelling, invariably takes place. Speakers of Germanic dialects were little influenced by the grammatical and inflexional systems of other Indo-European languages, finding them too subtle and complex to be acquired by anyone not educated in Greek or Latin.

Boethius was the last classical writer of Latin, whose scholarship testified to a sound knowledge of Greek; his *Consolations of Philosophy* (*c* 524) was one of the first works to be translated into the new vernacular languages of Western Europe. He is thus an important link between Graeco-Roman and medieval culture, when the latter was born during the second half of the eighth century. After Boethius, the Latin of the Church became the literary vehicle of the whole of Charlemagne's empire, as well as England; and with it some of the individualism of authors was lost. In the monasteries, a scarcity of parchment led to the obliteration of pagan writings by scraping, to make way for Christian writings. Laborious compilers and hagiographers were, in the ninth century, responsible for the bulk of the new literature.

It is possible that outmoded ecclesiastical and monastic teaching was responsible for the encroachment of authority in the form of the feudal system. The Church had to compromise with ruling monarchs, and countenance the cruelties of war, as compatible with the maintenance of Christianity. As the popularity of Old Testament legends in Old English literature testifies, the Church was active in teaching that spiritual progress depended on absolute obedience to the Supreme Power. The governance of a principality was regarded as a microcosm of this autocratic order. Hence the struggle for power between Church and State in the Middle Ages, and militant Rome's organization of Crusades that endowed the participants with special privileges of absolution, despite their previous crimes.

The works of Anglo-Latin authors before 850 are not to be assessed solely by their literary value. Aldhelm (640–709) is an instance (see pp 49, 69, 111, 195). He first studied under Maeldubh, an Irish scholar, at Malmesbury Abbey, before becoming the pupil of Theodore and Hadrian at Canterbury. He travelled to Rome in 692, built the still-existent Saxon church at Bradford-on-Avon, and is said to have spoken and written Greek fluently. A long dialogue on

the technicalities of Latin verse reveals the scope of his interest in
the Latin classical poets. A number of diverting, but culturally
instructive, riddles are contained in a letter to King Aldfrith of
Northumbria. His title to fame, however, rests on *De Laudibus
Virginitatis*, a treatise on chastity addressed to the Abbess and nuns
of Barking, which is preserved in a verse text as well as prose. This
extols biblical and historical exemplars, as well as saints, men as well
as women, but is now of no more than ecclesiastical interest.

A display of conventional rhetorical devices infects both the verse
and the prose. Long periods and 'thundering words' exhaust the
patience of the reader not equipped to commend the correctness of
the Latin. Aldhelm is what critical analysts now call a mannered
writer, undoubtedly under the spell of his earlier Celtic education; a
weaver of long words and periphrases that do not often obscure
meaning, because the structure of sentences is simple. A pleasing
inevitability is lacking in the precious phrases, for which
Aldhelm was as much a borrower from Ovid and Vergil, as master
of his own invention. A florid vocabulary, metaphorical adjectives,
and amplified or varied rhythms, display technical expertise that is
nearly always obtrusive. Alliterative pairs of words, to which
English prose has ever since been prone, may be traced to Celtic
sources, beginning in Britain with Gildas and the anonymous
Hisperica Famina, a curiosity of the sixth century. Hisperic latinity
is notable for its artificial vocabulary, and borrowings from Greek,
Hebrew and other languages. A large number of Aldhelm's out-
landish words were included in Old English glossaries of the tenth
century. Being a man of noble birth, he was able to absorb the
benefits of Greek, Latin and Irish cultures of the seventh century,
but not always with felicitous results.

Christian scholarship provided a finer flowering in the *Ecclesiastical History* of Bede (673–735), a book that, as we have seen, is
indispensable to an understanding of the time. Bede was born near
Durham, but spent most of his life in the Benedictine monastery of
Jarrow, established in 682. His love of books was instilled by his
tutors, Benedict Biscop, a Northumbrian nobleman, and his successor Ceolfrid.

Bede wrote treatises on poetry, mathematics, chronology and the
natural sciences, and was the most widely educated man of his time
– master of a lucid style with the pedagogical aims of an encyclopaedist. He was the first English Church historian with an

international reputation, being mentioned by Dante in the *Paradiso* (X.131) six centuries after his death.

Bede makes known his sources and often evaluates their documentary worth. He quotes frequently from papal and epis-copal letters. The miracles of St Cuthbert and others he regarded as a test of faith. His style is at opposite poles to that of Aldhelm, excelling at plain narrative, whose fervour of simplicity has a genuine ring of truth. A balanced judgement in Bede compensates for a general want of originality in his ideas. He appears as the English counterpart of St Augustine of Hippo, and the biblical commentaries (his life-work) are in the patristic tradition. Yet his English environment was very different from theirs, lacking their indigenous Latin background, while his knowledge of Greek seems to have been limited.

In *De Naturis Rerum* Bede revealed his dependence on Pliny's *Natural History*, chiefly as an aid to interpretation of passages in the Bible. His other classical Latin stimulus was Vergil, whose poetry he admired for its tolerance. Bede's *De Temporum Ratione*, a handbook on geography and chronology, introduces a topical discussion on the dating of Easter. Much slighter are the writings on *Metrics, Orthography* and *The Tropes of the Scriptures*. The first discusses the types of poetry and classical metres, both rather conventionally treated. *Orthography* is a teaching manual, almost exclusively devoted to the Roman alphabet. The study of tropes is partly an exhortation to revere the Bible. Rhetorical definitions are occasionally useful, but disproportionate space is accorded to allegory, so much biblical interpretation being of that nature.

Celtic Christianity in Northumbria was a selfless endeavour to sublimate warlike emotions among the Anglian people and divert their thoughts to civilized channels. The crusade of Bede and his colleagues was only partly successful; but the picture he gives of the Church's dutiful stand for ethical values has a graciousness that reflects an early trend in the English character.

Monasteries supplied most of the recruits to the missionary movement, and were responsible for the Christian conversion of Frisia by Willibrord, the Northumbrian, and of western Germany and Austria by Wynifrith of Exeter, afterwards known as St Boniface; he became Archbishop of Mainz in AD 747. Boniface founded the monastery of Fulda, famous for its learning, and helped to reform the Frankish church, being on terms of amity with

Charles Martel and his son, Pepin, ancestors of Charlemagne. This king defended St Gregory's papal state, the Duchy of Rome, from aggression by the German King of the Lombards. Boniface's letters, in the florid style of Aldhelm, show that the cultural influence of Wessex was beginning to be felt by the middle of the eighth century.

After Boniface, the most memorable impact at the Frankish court was made by Alcuin, whose Latin name was Albinus (735–804). Known in England as Alwhine, he was educated at the Cathedral School of York, founded by Bede's pupil, Archbishop Egbert, brother of Ceolwulf, King of Northumbria. At this school Alcuin enjoyed the benefit of working in the best equipped library in his own country. Although his work and thinking tended to be derivative, he earned the reputation of being a learned cleric, an excellent teacher, and able administrator in the sphere of education; he therefore succeeded Egbert as head of the Cathedral School.

On a visit to Italy, Alcuin met Charlemagne at Parma in 781, and was induced a year later to become head of the king's Palace School for the education of young noblemen, afterwards emulated by Alfred the Great. At this time Charles was King of the Franks and the recently-conquered Lombards, a north Germanic people who had occuped the Po valley in northern Italy. The king loved to have thinking men about him to talk with and to consult; and he thought to improve the educational standard of persons he could use as administrators. He himself took lessons in Greek, Latin, music, versification, biblical criticism, astromony, and was interested in natural history and the elementary science that was available in his time. He aspired to be a 'universal' man centuries before the advent of Dante. In short, Charlemagne was responsible for a minor Renaissance in Frankland, which he expanded, through his complex operations, into the Holy Roman Empire.

It was Alcuin who introduced the seven liberal arts into Frankland, the name Charlemagne had chosen for his kingdom. Through the monasteries, he also conceived the idea of free education in Latin to German-speaking sons, most of whom used the *lingua teudisca* of the *Nibelungenlied*. There were other of the king's subjects, who spoke the *lingua Romana rustica*, from which French was derived. Alcuin had little tolerance for Vulgar Latin or indigenous dialects; he taught the accepted range of grammar, rhetoric, dialectic, arithmetic, geometry, astronomy and music, using the late classical Latin of Boethius, which he had acquired through the Anglo-Saxon Church. He compiled manuals of instruction, usually in the form of a colloquy or dialogue; one between the 'Noble Youth Pepin' and Albinus, the schoolmaster, survives, in which the former asks questions, and the latter provides model answers. This rather naive teaching bridged the gap between the speech of the people and the written language required of clerks and scholars.

After fifteen years as director of the Palace School and general adviser on education, Alcuin retired, ending his days as Abbot of the wealthy and important monastery of St Martin at Tours. In Church government he had never risen above the status of a deacon. Charlemagne's magnanimous plan for uprooting barbarism through Christianity and education was but partially successful, the principal beneficiaries being the peoples of France, Italy and Spain, who were congenial to romanization.

Alcuin's main contributions to scholarship were ecclesiastical and liturgical. He had a hand in revising the Vulgate Bible and the Gregorian Sacraments, which form the basis of the Catholic Mass at the present time. Surviving letters (see p 195) and his life of St Willibrord, in verse and prose, are the surest indications of his quality as an author. A long poem in Latin on 'The Saints of the Church of York' has no great literary merit. Nevertheless, the influence Alcuin indirectly exerted over Alfred the Great has never been fully appreciated; for the personality and charm of the churchman and teacher outlived the worth of his written endeavours.

Social and cultural change are sometimes reflected in the lexicography of a language, or related group of languages, such as the Germanic. The Franks who invaded northern France were probably so named from their use of the javeline (OE *franca*), as the Saxons were from their weapon the sword (OE *seax*). But the adjective *frank*, meaning 'free, open', of the same ethnic origin, did not appear in English until the beginning of the fourteenth century. This sense was derived from med. Latin *francus* 'free', since political freedom was granted only to persons of Frankish tribal origin (see *OED*, vol. IV, p 511).

Though the conversion of the Germanic tribes was, at first, sporadic, phonological transmutation of borrowings can be observed in the names of places, public offices, festivals, domestic utilities, acts of worship and the like. Changes in religion were not always radical, as is shown by the giving of a new dress to some traditional customs.

The Anglo-Saxon settlers of the fifth century came into contact first with the Celts, whose language was the closest in the Indo-European family to the Italic group, represented by Latin. Anglo-Saxon borrowings from the Celts were chiefly names of geographical features, such as rivers and mountains, OE *Temes*, Old British *Tamesa* 'The Thames', and OE *penn*, O.Brit. *penno* 'hill', being instances. *Ancora* 'anchorite' is from O. Irish *anchara*. Priority of British or Latin origin is often difficult to determine.

The instinct of Old English and other Germanic languages was to avoid foreign borrowings. Though loan words were increased by the advent of Christianity, adaptations from indigenous sources were as common, e.g. *ālȳsend* 'Redeemer', *dǣdbōt* 'penance', *sundorhalga* 'Pharisee'.

Anglo-Saxon invaders were not unacquainted with the impact of Christianity before they came to England, as pagans. The OE word *hǣðen* (Bede's *Ecclesiastical History* in OE, Book I, ch. 7) occurs also as a compound in the Anglian Lindisfarne Gospels (Luke 10, 33): 'Samaritanus, þæt is *heaðinmonn*.' In different orthographies, this word is found in all Germanic languages, to which it apparently spread after the Gothic-Arian conversion by Ulfilas, who used the form *haithno* 'one who lives on the heath' (Gothic Bible, Mark 7, 26). In chapter 21 of *The Decline and Fall of the Roman Empire* Gibbon explained that Christianity soon became a religion of the towns, while most countrymen continued to worship pagan deities. A parallel semantic development took place with the Latin word *paganus* 'villager', from Doric *paga* 'fountain'. The word *paganus* appeared early in the ecclesiastical writings of Tertullian and Augustine; then the Roman army contemptuously extended it to rustics who were not enrolled in its ranks. It was next borrowed in a similar sense by Christians who, thinking of themselves as 'soldiers of Christ', dubbed all non-believers *pagani*.

OE *Crīst*, from Greek *Kristos* 'The Anointed', was the source of the adjective *crīsten*, which occurs in Alfred's *Orosius* 6, 12: 'him sealde Justinus āne *crīstene* bōc.' No noun was employed in Old English corresponding to the sixteenth-century borrowing of *Christian*. According to Acts 11, 26 this name arose in Antioch from the movement's heathen opponents. There are only a few early words borrowed from Greek in the Germanic languages, and they are usually regarded as the outcome of the Gothic conversion. In Old English these are: *cirice* 'church', *Crēcas* 'Greeks', *dēofol* 'devil', *engel* 'angel', from *kuriakon* 'the Lord's house', *Graicoi*, *diabolos*, and *angelos*. But all the latter were adopted also in Latin, and borrowing from that source is feasible, as A. Campbell has pointed out in his *Old English Grammar* (p 199). *Reogol* 'rule', and *scrifan* 'write', are borrowings from Latin *regula* and *scribere*.

There was a lively assimilation of loan words from early Germanic contacts with Gaul. The *lingua Romana rustica* was responsible for the introduction into Anglo-Saxon of *biscop, munuc, mynster* and *prēost*, though what the intermediate forms were can only be conjectured. The words were undoubtedly descended, through ecclesiastical Latin, from post-Alexandrian Greek.

After the arrival of the Anglo-Saxon peoples in England, there were fewer borrowings until the seventh century; the absence of written documents makes it difficult to estimate how many. During the next five centuries, the adoption of loan words from Latin was uninhibited by the Danish invasions; to this period belong *clīroc* 'clergyman', *dēacon, apostol* and *Ādam*. From Gallo-Roman, Old English apparently took *ælmesse* 'alms', *lǣwed* 'lay' and *nunne* 'nun'.

New words, composed of native elements, again outnumber loan words from foreign sources. Among the most appropriate are *boda* 'prophet', *leornere* 'disciple', *cynna* 'Gentiles', *gāstlic* 'spiritual', *godspell* 'good tidings', *hirde* 'pastor', *sawol-sceat* 'burial fee' and *tungol-witga* 'astrologer'. For Peter's Pence (the levy due to the Church in Rome) there were such alternative terms as *Rōm-feoh* or *heorð-penig*.

A special feature of Latin loan words still needs to be noticed – the substitution of native suffixes for the original Roman ones, e.g. *-ere* for *-arius* (and other endings) in *cāsere* 'emperor', *fullere* 'fuller', *scolere* 'scholar'. There are several OE suffixes so combined with Latin roots; for instance: *mentel* 'cloak', *eosol* 'ass', *fæcele* 'torch', *Arabisc* 'Arabic' and *papig* 'poppy'. Native prefixes are not so common.

Curiously, the *sermo plebeius* which Tertullian introduced into ecclesiastical Latin for his vigorous rhetorical prose, was not transmuted into English forms until the Middle English period, e.g.

confessor and *creatura* (1300), *glorificare, humiliatio, protector, sanctificare* and *transgressor* (C 14). The assimilation of many Latin polysyllables into the English vocabulary reflects a sophisticated, non-Germanic trend, which followed from the Norman conquest and the Italian Renaissance.

Aldhelm, Bede and Alcuin were examples of a distinctive Anglo-Saxon culture, enlightening a dark age – Aldhelm, a latinist of humour and poetic insight; Bede, a scholar who lived by faith; Alcuin, an educator whose mission was the promotion of human dignity. All were lovers of books and good sense, but not of fine writing for its own sake. The civilization they endeavoured to sustain was essentially a selective service to the community through religion. What they achieved was not in conflict with the ethnic patterns of behaviour disclosed in *Beowulf* and *The Seafarer* but a sublimation of its violent elements. Their gentleness is that of Christian sensitivity, yet marked by different qualities in the language. Aldhelm's is extrovert and arresting; Bede's plain, fervent and reclusive; Alcuin's dialectical and social. Linguistically, all were of Low German descent, spreading their humble yet compelling culture to correct thoughts and refine uncouth expressions, on both sides of the North Sea.

W. P. Ker, in the opening chapter of *The Dark Ages* (1904), perceived the essence of this mission. The 'Gothic night' was not, indeed as long or hopeless as our forefathers thought. The writer suggests that the year 1100 was the turning point, marking as it does the end of aggressive Germanic migrations, and the harmonizing of Christendom with Teutonic self-will. 'One chief agent in this change [he writes] is not religious doctrine nor politics, but the new languages. . . . The Teutonic nations brought new languages and new subject-matters into the system of European literature; they also brought originality . . . The Latin literature of the Dark Ages has not a definite character of its own, in the same way as the old Teutonic poetry . . . The Dark Ages are *really*, not merely conventionally, separate from what came after' (pp 6–17).

CHAPTER IV

Alfred the Great and the Viking-Saxon Condominium (850–900)

𒀭𒀭𒀭𒀭𒀭𒀭

THE TERM *viking* is of doubtful etymology, but likelier to be from Anglo-Frisian *wic* (a 'settlement') than Old Norse *vik* (a 'bay'). The compound *sǣ-wicingas,* in the OE poem *Exodus,* is the earliest eighth-century evidence; Icelandic *vikingr* does not appear before the tenth century. With or without the final -*r, viking* is not found in English literature until the second quarter of the nineteenth century, the citations in the *OED* being from Chalmers's *Caledonia* (1827) and Longfellow's *Skeleton in Armour* (1840).

The Vikings of the eighth century were linguistically a cohesive group that inhabited territories at the entrance to the Baltic sea, i.e. parts of modern Norway, Sweden and Denmark. The Geat dynasty that had apparently ruled their independent nation in Southern Sweden did so no longer. The main Swedes had conquered them, and migratory movements had spread their people east and south, where they founded the Russian state, and advanced through Poland and the Balkans as far as Constantinople. Norwegians and Danes, on the other hand, harried the coasts of Germany, Britain and France before Charlemagne conquered Frisia and Old Saxony, to make himself master of all western Europe, except Spain.

From the sixth to the mid-eighth century Frisians controlled the northern waters, their power extending from the Rhine delta to the mouth of the Elbe. When the Frisians were incorporated in the Frankish kingdom, their influence declined, and the larger ships of the Vikings took over.

King Ecgberht of Wessex, ruler of all England, had the protection of Charlemagne during his three years' exile among the Franks (see p 49), but neither monarch took the precaution to equip himself with a defensive fleet. The Vikings were unopposed when they sailed up the rivers of England and north-western France, landing sizeable forces for ruthless plunder. The economic cause of what became a vast Norse migration was probably overpopulation of a limited arable homeland; but domestic restlessness was aggravated by political issues, chief of which was the rivalry of warlike tribal leaders.

Each spring the Norsemen descended upon the eastern, western and southern shores of the British Isles, and the monasteries that had sought security on islands were the first to be sacked and robbed. The Vikings were pagans, but there was no religious motive behind their pillaging; the destruction of the Northumbrian culture at the end of the eighth century was the principal reason for Alcuin's departure for the court of Charlemagne. The earliest attacks were made by Norwegians on Lindisfarne and Jarrow in AD 793–4. In the next year Norse raiders landed on Lambay Island off the north coast of Ireland and invaded Skye, beginning their long hold on the northern and western islands of Scotland, which was eventually extended to Sutherland, Caithness, Ross and Cromarty. The Isle of Man was raided in 798, and Iona was twice plundered, in 802 and 806.

Danes began their attacks on the east coast of England in AD 835, four years before the death of King Ecgberht, and a year after their initial assaults on Frankland. The first Danish invasion was led by the sons of Ragnar Lothbrok, who devastated the island of *Sceapig* (Sheppey), east of the Medway estuary. No less than twelve recorded landings took place during the next generation, especially in Kent, where the Danes spent the winter on the isles of Thanet (850) and Sheppey (854). During the reign of Æthelwulf (839–58) some raids were repulsed with considerable loss, for example at Wigborough and Sandwich, and at *Acleá* (Ockley, Surrey) in 851; but according to Asser's *Life of Alfred*, Canterbury and London were sacked. There was no organized defence by those held responsible, the ealdormen of the shires, and consequently the Danes landed with impunity in East Anglia, Lindsey and Southampton.

King Æthelwulf, the father of Alfred the Great, was followed by four of his sons, and it was during the reign of the third, (Æthelred) in AD 865, that the Danes determined to settle permanently in England. Under Lothbrok's sons, Ivar and Halfdan, the great army landed in East Anglia. Including kings and nobles, they remained for a year and equipped themselves with local horses, before proceeding to York. They occupied York for four months, until engaged by combined Northumbrian forces under King Osberht and his rival Ælla, in March 867. Both the Anglo-Saxon leaders were killed in the attack. Always on the move, the Danes chose to spend the next winter in Nottingham. In the following year they defeated and humiliated the East Anglian king, Edmund, at Hoxne in Suffolk; his appalling martyrdom is generally ascribed to defiance of the invaders on the ground of religion. A festival is still accorded to this saint in the Anglican calendar, and Bury St Edmunds is named after him.

At this point Alfred became a prominent figure in the defence of Wessex. He was born at Wantage in AD 849. Both Asser and the *Parker Chronicle* record that his father sent him to Rome at the age of four, where Pope Leo 'adopted him as his spiritual son'. He again accompanied Æthelwulf on a pilgrimage to Rome in 855, where the king remained for twelve months, expressing in his actions a preference for the religious life, which his son inherited. Alfred's mother, Osburga, who was of Jutish descent, died when Alfred was only seven years old, and his father died two years later. The prince's education at court was so neglected that he was a poor reader until his adult years. There were, he complained, no good teachers available to satisfy his insatiable desire for learning. At the age of twenty he married Ealhswith, daughter of the Mercian nobleman Mucil, who lived near Gainsborough.

Alfred first entered the war in 871 at the Battle of Ashdown, which he prematurely initiated from unfavourable ground, while his brother, King Æthelred, was still at mass. The Danes were quelled and driven from central Berkshire; but they retaliated a fortnight later by winning a skirmish at Basing. In Easter of the same year Alfred became King of Wessex, on his brother's death after a reign of five years. The new king was in his twenty-fourth year, and within a month lost his first engagement at Wilton. He realized that nine battles in a year had thoroughly exhausted his troops; so in 872 he and the Mercians entered upon the first of many treaties with the enemy. The Danes agreed to withdraw and to winter, first in London, where the first Danish coins were struck, and in the following year in Lindsey. It seems that from this year the Danish leader, Halfdan, began to exact tribute.

During the respite, Alfred built ships and trained an army in anticipation of renewed hostilities, which began with the occupation of Mercia and Northumbria by the Danes in AD 875. Always ubiquitous, they spent the next winter as far south as Cambridge. By this time the 'great army' had made such progress that it was able to divide itself into two forces, one for Northumbria and the Scottish Lowlands, the other for the Midlands and south of England. From AD 874 these operated as separate units. Alfred, to buy time with the southern force, once more resorted to diplomacy, but in spite of hostages offered, the Danes broke the treaty, and Halfdan then occupied Exeter, in order to winter his army in Devon. From this base the Norwegian, Rollo, attacked Normandy in AD 876.

The Danes received annual reinforcements from the homelands, and were masters of unexpected attacks on vantage points, which they then fortified and used as bases for further aggrandizement. Wherever they took foothold, they set up Quislings as puppet-rulers to collect dues and maintain order. Alfred came to the conclusion that he would have to forestall landings by attacking the invaders at sea. He planned a combined sea and land attack on Exeter during the winter of 877, when a hundred and twenty Danish ships were lost in a storm near Swanage. Alfred's army laid siege to the town, in the hope of starving out the enemy. The Danes agreed to abandon Exeter, exchanging hostages for tribute. After occupying Gloucester, the Danish army proceeded to Mercia, where they partitioned the realm into northern and southern regions, settling soldiers of all ranks on the coast of Yorkshire and Lincolnshire.

At the beginning of 878 Alfred's fortunes were at a very low ebb; the Danes, under King Guthrum, made a surprise mid-winter march from Gloucester to Chippenham on the Wiltshire Avon, their aim being to dismember fertile Wessex, as they had done to Mercia. Alfred was compelled to retreat to the difficult terrain west of Selwood, which contained the swampy region of Athelney, near Taunton. For seven weeks he and his faithful thegns lived in great distress, attempting no more than guerrilla raids on the enemy. He then rallied volunteers from Hampshire, Wiltshire and Somerset and won a decisive victory at Eddington, south of the Danish base at Chippenham, to which the enemy retreated with great loss. A fortnight later Guthrum surrendered; the following passage from

Bishop Asser's Latin *Life* illustrates Alfred's magnanimity:

> . . . The pagans, driven by famine, cold, fear, and last of all by despair, asked for peace, on the condition that they should give the king as many hostages as he pleased, but should receive none of him in return, in which form they had never before made a treaty with any one. The king, hearing that, took pity upon them, and received such hostages as he chose; after which the pagans swore, moreover, that they would immediately leave the kingdom; and their king, Guthrum, promised to embrace Christianity, and receive baptism at king Alfred's hands. All of which articles he and his men fulfilled as they had promised. For after seven weeks Guthrum king of the pagans, with thirty men chosen from the army, came to Alfred at a place called Aller, near Athelney, and there king Alfred, receiving him as his son by adoption, raised him up from the holy laver of baptism on the eighth day, at a royal villa named Wedmore, where the holy chrism was poured upon him. After his baptism he remained twelve nights with the king, who, with all his nobles, gave him many presents.

It is worth noting that Asser, as this passage shows, closely followed the *Anglo-Saxon Chronicle* up to the year 887.

Guthrum and his still considerable army remained in the royal vill of Chippenham during the summer of AD 878, and then moved to Cirencester in Mercia, which they occupied for a year, before settling in and partitioning East Anglia. Of the four kingdoms existing at the beginning of the century, only Wessex remained independent and intact; the rest of England, which came to be known as the Danelaw, was shared by Angles and Danes, the latter already being recognized as permanent colonists. The condominium lasted for nearly two hundred years, and was gradually moulded to the West-Saxon type of rule, with Scandinavian modifications.

Alfred's fifteen years of warfare (871–86) was shortly renewed by the arrival of a large Danish force in the Thames, late in 878. It was quartered at Fulham until the following spring; but, after a conference with Guthrum, this army was diverted to the Continent, and spent the next year at Ghent. For five years the Danish drive was now directed at northern France and the Low Countries; then a detachment was landed in Kent (884) to capture the fortified position of Rochester, at the mouth of the Medway. The siege was soon raised by Alfred, who immediately put to sea to punish the East Anglian Danes for supporting this new invasion. Two engagements were fought near the mouth of the Stour, but only in the first was Alfred's fleet victorious.

As the Thames estuary made the south-east vulnerable to Danish invasion, Alfred's next step was to occupy the Mercian city of London, causing much destruction; the city had harboured a contingent of Danes for more than a decade. Alfred's court in Winchester was deemed too distant from the scene of likely hostilities; but, as a centre of international trade, London was not then incorporated in the kingdom of Wessex. The city was virtually rebuilt after its sacking, and the king ensured that the walls were strengthened. In 886 the government of the city was entrusted to Æthelred, ealdorman of the English part of Mercia, who married Alfred's eldest daughter, Æthelflæd, in 889.

The second treaty negotiated with Guthrum was more enduring than the first, as it safeguarded the rights of English subjects living in Guthrum's kingdom of East Anglia, Essex and Danish Mercia, by an undertaking that they would not be taxed at a higher rate than the Danish settlers. The southern boundary agreed upon with Wessex ran along the Thames, as far as London, then up the line of the river Lea to its source; thence westward to Bedford, and along the River Ouse, as far as Watling Street. Beyond the latter line, in the north-west Midlands, lay English Mercia. Both Northamptonshire and Leicestershire were included in the Danelaw. Unauthorized migration of citizens from one kingdom to the other, except for the purpose of trade, was strictly forbidden.

Alfred enjoyed a short respite from campaigning during the period AD 886 to 892. For a man of such energy and accomplishment, these were not years of rest, but of arduous endeavour for the reform and consolidation of his kingdom. Yet Asser devotes much space to the poor state of Alfred's health. His unknown malady was contracted in childhood, but afflicted him after marriage, in an alleviated form, until his fortieth year; the biographer describes it as 'an unusual kind of fever', of whose onset he had fearful premonitions. The son of pious parents, Alfred was deeply religious, and during this period resolved to spend half of his day in prayer and the usual canonical devotions.

Five children survived Alfred, three of them daughters, one of whom, Æthelgifu, entered monastic life. The younger of the sons, Æthelweard, profited in learning from his father's guidance. Asser records that the Saxon tongue was studied as well as Latin; and it is probable that many of the translations Alfred commissioned were the work of members of his Palace School. Attention was directed principally to writing skills and the liberal arts (in Latin) of grammar, logic and rhetoric. Alfred encouraged the reading of the Psalms and Anglo-Saxon poetry, as suitable for a young nobleman's training; but he insisted on physical education, especially the craft of hunting, to which he was devoted. In this way he laid the foundations of what was to become a typical English education.

Asser mentions especially Alfred's talent for 'mechanical inventions', which included ship design and improved building techniques. The seaport towns of London, Rochester, Southampton and Exeter required to be reconstructed, and among the new institutions founded was a commemorative monastery at Athelney.

Like Charlemagne, Alfred ruled by consultation with men of understanding, whom he gathered about him and made his friends. The bulk of these were learned Mercians or theologians from France, such as Grimbald and John. Seven are named by Asser, including himself; he eventually spent half of the year at Alfred's court, and spoke with admiration of the king's generosity. Alfred would 'read with' his intellectual superiors, and learn by disputation; possibly he introduced the tutorial system.

Asser writes deprecatingly of the indolence and neglect of their duty of the West-Saxon upper-class; they were dilatory in fortifying their areas at Alfred's behest. A notable decay of monastic life had set in towards the end of the ninth century, as a result of prosperity under the king's rule. The extent of the royal revenues is reflected in Alfred's thoughtful disposition of them. One third of the secular share went to the payment of the army, the king's administrators and the nobles whose services he retained at Court. The last category comprised three groups, which were called upon in rotation, each being on duty for a period of one month. The second third of secular revenue went to the skilled workers, largely introduced from abroad, who put into effect Alfred's ambitious scheme of reconstruction. Asser is vague about the final third of the king's secular expenditure, but the fact that it went to foreigners, shows that he imported many specialist advisers, and was lavish in hospitality to visitors at Court.

The other half of the king's income was divided into four parts, all devoted to charitable or religious ends. The first was to relieve poverty; the second to support two monasteries which were royal foundations; the third to maintain in the Christian tradition the school for noblemen's sons; the last to foster monasteries in regions of English influence other than Wessex, including Gaul and Brittany.

According to Asser the most unusual of Alfred's attributes was his concern for the execution of justice. His biographer writes:

> The king was a most acute investigator in passing sentence, as he was in all other things. He inquired into almost all the judgments which were given in his own absence, throughout all his dominion, whether they were just or unjust. If he perceived there was iniquity in those judgments, he summoned the judges, either through his own agency, or through others of his faithful servants, and asked them mildly, why they had judged so unjustly; whether through ignorance or malevolence; i.e., whether for the love or fear of any one, or hatred of others; or also for the desire of money. At length, if the judges acknowledged they ha given judgment because they knew no better, he discreetly and moderately reproved their inexperience and folly.

Alfred's second war with the Danes lasted four years, their attack being the aftermath of an invasion of France and the Low Countries, which in AD 885 culminated in the siege of Paris. The division of Charlemagne's empire into French and German kingdoms, and the consequent dynastic rivalries, provided an incentive to attack defenceless territory between the Scheldt and the Seine. The Danes penetrated as far as Burgundy and Aquitaine, and were not turned back until defeated by King Arnulf of Germany at the Battle of the Dyle near Louvain, in November 891. After forty years of relentless piracy in France, the Danes reassembled forces in Boulogne, and crossed the Channel to Lympne the following year. The size of this force can be estimated by its transportation in 250 ships. Later in the year another party, under the command of the warrior Hæsten, sailed up the Thames in eighty ships and settled at Milton Royal. The two camps were separated by the forest of Andred in the Weald of Kent; Alfred's army therefore encamped half-way between them.

Alfred followed his custom of demanding hostages from East Anglia, to ensure non-co-operation with the newcomers; but this precaution was invariably unavailing. To be nearer his source of supply, Hæsten crossed the Thames into Essex, and encamped at Benfleet, where he was joined by the Danish force from Lympne; he placated Alfred and Æthelred by offering his two sons for

Christian baptism. Had it not been for the collaboration of Danish settlers, the ensuing war would have been earlier terminated by famine. The invaders were apparently determined to find English territory on which they could settle, but Wessex and English Mercia alone remained in Anglo-Saxon hands. Their first search was in Berkshire, Hampshire and Surrey, but this was foiled by Alfred's son Edward, aided by Æthelred of Mercia.

Throughout the military campaigns, the Wessex forces had been troubled by problems of recruitment; the bulk of the soldiery being farmers, they were unwilling to serve beyond their district, or left the army prematurely to attend to their crops. Alfred's solution was the conscription of only half the men liable for service, leaving the remainder on the land to safeguard the economy. Agriculture suffered from ravages largely because there were insufficient fortified camps to which the farmers could retreat in times of danger.

While Alfred was in the south-west relieving a blockade of Exeter by diversionary naval assaults from Northumbrian and East Anglian fleets, Edward and Æthelred captured the Danish camp at Benfleet, with large supplies of equipment. The wife and sons of Hæsten were then despatched to the king; but as he had sponsored the baptism of the boys, and presented gifts to the family, Alfred would not keep them as hostages, and had them immediately returned to the Danish leader. Hæsten ungraciously mobilized all remaining forces in Essex and marched them to the upper Severn, where they built a fortification near the Shropshire border. Here they were besieged by an army under Æthelred, until food became scarce, when the Danes escaped by strategem or sortie, and returned to their new base at Shoebury in Essex.

By 893 the invaders were intent on finding a foothold in English Mercia, and in the autumn of that year moved quickly by day and night marches to Chester, where they ensconced themselves behind the old Roman fortifications. This time Æthelred tried a scorched-earth policy, and forced the besieged to take refuge in north Wales, until the summer of 894, when they made their way, by devious routes, back to Essex and encamped on Mersea Island. In the autumn they sailed up the Thames and the Lea to a position about twenty miles north of London, and there wintered until the summer of 895. By diverting the river, Alfred left their ships high and dry, and cut them off from return by that route. The Danes, in a desperate situation, made their way to the west and halted on the

101

River Severn at Bridgnorth, in Shropshire. They finally abandoned the struggle in 896, realizing that there was no land to be had outside the Danelaw, where most of the disbanded eventually settled; the rest returned to France for renewed depredations in the valley of the Seine.

In his second campaign Alfred's losses from the enemy were slight; but a recurrence of the plague carried off many of his ablest citizens. Perceiving that the power of the Danes rested on control of the sea, Alfred next designed warships which were double theirs in length, mustering sixty oars. They were in action by the end of the war, but nine went aground, through lack of experience in handling.

This mishap took place in the first recorded naval engagement of English annals. The *Anglo-Saxon Chronicle*, under the year 896, notes that a Danish squadron of six ships was attacked on the English south coast, by nine of King Alfred's new warships, some apparently manned by Frisians. The situation of the battle is not mentioned, but it took place at the mouth of a river, reputedly near the Isle of Wight. A. J. Wyatt, however, suggested Poole Harbour, twenty-five miles to the west (*Anglo-Saxon Reader*, 1919, p 206). The men of three Danish ships beached their craft at high tide to ravage the countryside; and English ships were then sent in to prevent the marauders from rejoining their vessels. Entering the inlet at an ebbing tide, Alfred's large ships found themselves stranded on different shoals, six of them on the opposite shore. A fight took place on the spit of land at the entrance to the harbour, 120 Danes and 62 English and Frisians being killed; but the Danish ships managed to escape on the incoming tide. With depleted crews, two of them were unable to round the Sussex coast; when they landed the Danes were arrested and summarily hanged (see F. P. Magoun's article in *Modern Language Review*, xxxvii, 1942, pp 409–14).

Three years later, on 26 October, 899, the most respected and resourceful of the Saxon kings died. His reign proved a turning-point in English cultural history, and the state of the realm at the end of the ninth century should therefore be reviewed.

There is no record of the ordering of life of the Anglo-Saxon peoples before the seventh century, when Kings Æthelberht of

Kent and Ine of Wessex proclaimed their laws. In the OE *dōm-bōc* (Doombook) of Anglo-Saxon laws, the first element seems to have meant 'that which is set up', or 'statute'. This compilation, written in English, not Latin, is often attributed to King Alfred, being mentioned in the Preamble to the *Laws of Edward* (*c* 925). It contains enactments of the sixth to the ninth century, based on the Teutonic customs outlined by Tacitus in *Germania*. *Dōm* is a word common also to Old Frisian, Old Saxon and Old High German, and appears in the West-Saxon translation of Bede's *Ecclesiastical History* (Book IV, ch. 5), in the derived sense of 'judgement'.

Æthelberht's laws, codified on the advice of the Christian bishops sent to Kent by Pope Gregory I, contained some important measures to protect the peaceful right of assembly, as well as the security of Church property and priests. The deterrent was a system of fines by way of compensation, though in some cases the money went into the royal coffers. The effect of this code was to safeguard the rights of the king's free subjects, through appointed officers. Murder, physical violence and theft were the principal offences; and the penalty for selling men or women into slavery was a necessary step to prevent that kind of victimization. A freeman was held responsible for the misdemeanours of servants, among whom brawling was a fairly common occurrence.

The next lawgiver of note, King Ine of Wessex, at the close of the seventh century, had the assistance of Erconwald, Bishop of London. Hence the law's insistence on the baptism of children, the observance of Sunday as the Lord's day of rest, and respect for the Church as a place of sanctuary for persons fleeing from the condemnation of death. The straying of cattle owing to improper fencing was a more mundane offence. Much more significant was the protection newly given to Britons, even those who owned no land; for many persons of Celtic origin were employed as the king's retainers.

Marauding was at this time so general, especially on the well-wooded border between Kent and Wessex, that the death penalty had to be imposed for serious cases of theft; the king, however, could exercise the option of selling the offender as a slave in some other country. Under the laws of Alfred, the king and his officers were held solely responsible for the peace and order of the kingdom, including the administration of justice.

The king's authority, as a ruler, was sacrosanct, especially when, in the eighth century, there was adopted the Continental practice of a church coronation; this, from the tenth century, included anointment and the swearing of a royal oath (see p 126). Until Alfred's death, the kings were elected from members of the royal family, and it was not until the reign of Edward that the eldest son was accepted as the hereditary heir to the throne. In matters of state the later kings deferred to their *Witan* (Council), which began as an ecclesiastical synod, and later developed into a body of 'wise men', consisting in Christian times of archbishops, bishops, abbots of important monasteries, ealdormen, thegns of high rank, and royal chaplains, who accompanied the king on his travels. The king's court did not meet in one place, and Wessex coronations were at times held in such convenient centres as Bath and Kingston. A dignified ceremonial was observed to impress subjects, ambassadors and visitors from Europe. Presenting gifts to cement good relations was an ancient practice, punctiliously honoured by important monarchs, such as Alfred. The most effective rule resulted from the monarch's diplomatic recognition that affairs of Church and State were interdependent.

The earliest evidence of a hierarchy in Anglo-Saxon society is found in the laws of Æthelberht, which were formulated specifically for Kent; each rank had a price, representing its value to the community for the purpose of compensation, should such a person be killed. The *wergeld* of a Kentish nobleman (*eorl*), expressed in cash or kind, was three hundred shillings; a freeman (*ceorl*) was valued at only a third of that sum. The companions of a king, who served diligently in war or peace (first known as *gesithas*, later as *thegns*) were regarded as a privileged class, lesser in the wergeld scale than an *eorl* or *ealdorman*. When the Danes conquered Northumbria, they brought their wergeld valuation into line with that of Wessex. By King Alfred's reign, the moneys of account had varying values in different kingdoms, a shilling's equivalent being twenty pence in Kent, five in Wessex, and four in Mercia. The scale of fines payable for offences was based on the wergeld scale.

The free peasant or *ceorl* was the backbone of the country, perhaps the ancestor of the medieval English *yeoman*. He was liable for military service in the *fierd* (home army) and contributed to the king's revenue by payment of a *feorm* or 'food-tax'. The *hide* that supported a farmer's household consisted in Wessex of about forty acres; but its size depended on the fertility of the land and the standard of living of the owner, who was responsible only to the king. It would appear that the regional term *hundred* signified that number of English hides, implying an area capable of accommodating a hundred families. Except in the north of England, an open-field system entitled the peasant farmer to grazing rights in meadows, while forestland was available for the pasturage of swine, an important source of food supply.

Country villages, as centres of social life, began to appear in the river valleys in the eighth century, and they explain the existence of small township-moots, which became necessary, *inter alia*, for the assessment of the king's feorm, and for good relations with the reeve, or steward of the royal property in each region. The feorm was regarded as an amount sufficient to support the king and his retinue for twenty-four hours, and became payable in kind once a year. It consisted of oxen, sheep, poultry, corn, cheese, butter, ale, honey and fodder, and sometimes included luxuries such as salmon and eels. Originally, kings required entertainment without charge, whenever they passed through a district. When resident vills were introduced, this privilege was relaxed, but it was still enjoyed by royal officers, and even high-ranking ealdormen, who travelled on the king's business. In addition, every community was expected to contribute labour for the erection of buildings, bridges and fortifications in their neighbourhood, and equally important, to provide cartage for the king's goods. A system of shires for local administration was in existence in Wessex by the end of the eighth century; the -*y* at the end of many shire- and place-names, such as Surrey and Ely, is a reduced form of OE *ge* (German *Gau*), meaning 'district'.

There is no account of the organization of an Anglo-Saxon army, but its mainstay was the warrior class (eorls and thegns), the rank and file being made up of peasants, like St Cuthbert, who preferred militia service in their district to enslavement by the enemy. A ceorl would have been unable to leave his land during military service, but for the employment of slave labour. He had to provide his own equipment, such as horse, shield and spear. By the ninth century, when Danish invaders were active, the Anglo-Saxon *burh*, a defendable centre for persons not on active service, became significant in military operations, as well as agricultural life. Burhs were initiated by King Alfred, and proved not only indispensable refuges for the families of ceorls, but training grounds for garrisons that could be moved, at need, to hard-pressed areas of siege.

By King Alfred's time, land tenure in England had become complicated by grants of property to the king's thegns, or to monastic founders, such as Benedict Biscop, whose religious purpose included services to education (see pp 80, 111). In the course of events this produced the manorial system. Hereditary eorls of noble blood, with armed retainers, were peculiar to Kent; elsewhere gesithas owed their status to kingly favour, with the grant of an estate. As a result of Guthrum's treaties with Alfred, all land-owning freemen, whether Danes or Saxons, were raised to the condition of thegns.

The granting of an estate was legalized by a royal charter, hence the term *bocland* (literally 'bookland') or land held by title-deed; in effect, a generous monarch was bestowing a private lordship, and he would often transfer, in perpetuity, the feorm, cartage services, fines and royal perquisites, for which the peasant dwellers were liable. Usually, however, the king retained the subject's obligation for military service, and labour in the construction of bridges and fortifications. In this way many landed proprietors acquired the control of villages and their communities. Any owner who dedicated land to a monastic foundation, or other religious purpose, usually sought a special charter exempting the property from taxation and all services, except public works.

The Anglo-Saxon legal system was designed to maintain the pattern of kinship peculiar to most primitive societies. A family was responsible for the conduct of its members, and for fines or ransoms imposed upon them; it was expected to honour the blood-feud incident to any quarrel that caused the death of a relative, even in civil war. Alfred the Great sought to restrain vendettas by requiring contestants to apply to the court within thirty days for compensation, while the Church insisted on penance for acts of violence. But family feuds were not easily abolished.

In the tenth century loyalty to one's lord and protector was second only to family ties. The efficacy of the law depended largely on the power of the lords spiritual and temporal, representing the Church and the upper classes, who sat on the Witan; they were the sole defenders of serfs and labourers. Baptized members of the latter class shared in the Church's sacramental life, and were entitled to its protection. In every shire of Wessex, Alfred ensured that an ealdorman was in charge of the administration of justice, working in collaboration with the responsible bishop.

The Alfredian legal code, which came into operation soon after AD 890, claimed to be founded upon the ten commandments of Moses, interpreted by Christ and his Apostles. It affirmed the ideals of Æthelberht of Kent, Offa of Mercia and Ine of Wessex, all Christian monarchs, and based its validity on the sanctity of a man's oath, in testimony as well as contractual agreements. In trials for murder, Alfred urged a wergeld penalty instead of capital punishment. Yet he sanctioned the killing of witches and magicians, following the biblical injunction in the book of Exodus.

Alfred prefaced his laws with the following admonition:

> What you would not other men should do to you, do not to other men. From this one precept a man may learn to judge righteously; he needs no other law-book. Let him simply remember that he attribute to no one what he would not that another should attribute to him, if he were in quest of a legal decision upon himself.

Public holidays proclaimed in King Alfred's laws celebrated Church festivals, such as Yuletide (Christmas Day to 6 January), the Feast of St Gregory (12 March), Holy Week, Easter, the Feast of Saints Peter and Paul (29 June), the Feast of St Mary the Virgin (a week in autumn), and All Saints Day (1 November).

The tenant-farmer of Wessex was in existence by King Ine's time, his relationship to the landlord being of historical importance. Under the stress of Danish invasions, and consequent disruption of trade, unfree peasants increased, a principal reason being that in many parts of Wessex and Mercia the independent farmer felt insecure enough to sell his land. Ceorls owning five or more hides of land were unlikely to belong to this depressed group; they were actually privileged during military service to be placed in the thegn class.

The serf, in spite of his usefulness to the economy, figures very rarely in Old English writings. As he was a chattel, valued at about eight oxen, he did not appear in the wergeld scale. Slaves changed hands, before witnesses, at a rate of approximately one pound, sales tax being imposed on each transaction, as with all merchandise. An owner who ill-treated, injured or killed a slave was subject to no secular law, but only ecclesiastical penalties. Serfs did not enjoy relaxation on religious holidays, their leisure being confined to four Wednesdays of the Ember Weeks, or fasting time, following Lent, Whitsun, Holy Cross Day (14 September) and St Lucia's Day (13

December). Archbishop Wulfstan was incensed at this inhumanity, and told his countrymen that the Viking invasions were God's punishment for their callousness. Slaves sometimes escaped during these attacks and joined the Danish forces; the majority of Anglo-Saxon slaves must have become serfs after capture as British prisoners of war. But often family poverty compelled the selling of children as slaves. Although it was legal for the Church to own serfs, Archbishops were earnest pleaders for their *manumission*, with the result that Christian owners often released bondmen in their wills. Several extant manumissions were recorded on the fly-leaves of church service-books.

Women had considerable rights of independence in Anglo-Saxon society. They could own and dispose of property, including slaves, in their own right, and appear in court, without permission of husbands. No maiden could be compelled to marry any man she disliked though, once married, she was obliged to obey her husband. When a marriage was contracted, two stages were universally accepted, first betrothal, then the actual giving of the bride. The term *wedding* applied to the first stage, namely, the pledge of acceptance of the dowry or 'bride-price'; the subsequent gift of the bride by her father or his deputy came later, and involved a ceremony and a feast. Responsibility for the latter ceremony was taken over by the Christian Church, but its blessing was not essential to the contract. It was Pope Gregory who determined the degrees of consanguinity permissible in a Christian marriage, and the crown's rules of divorce and remarriage were based upon his recommendations. But Anglo-Saxon and Danish customs of pagan origin in some respects conflicted with the laws of Æthelberht and Alfred; for instance, Germanic practice permitted a man to marry his stepmother. Saxons and Danes regarded divorce as comparatively easy to obtain by unilateral choice, the division of property and the custody of children being decided by the court, as at the present time. A woman might claim half the family's property, if children were left in her care, but only the same share as a child, should the husband desire custody.

The economy of Anglo-Saxon England is difficult to trace, except in broad outline, until the appearance of the Domesday Book. Farmers avoided clay soils, because they were too heavy to work and usually covered with dense vegetation; neither did they care to cultivate heathland, with its dry, sandy terrain. They preferred sandstone, loam or chalk areas, easily drained, yet accessible to a regular water supply from river or stream. Ploughing was done by a team of eight oxen, drawing the wheel-plough of northern Europe; but on lighter soils the Mediterranean wheelless plough was still in use. The water-mill for grinding corn seems to have been introduced in the eighth century. Wheat and rye for bread, oats for porridge and horses, and barley for ale were the principal crops, though flax for linen was also cultivated. There was apparently no grassland cultivation for hay. Beans are the only vegetables mentioned in Ælfric's *Colloquy* of the tenth century.

Some information about the economy is to be gleaned from the *Colloquy* just mentioned. The ploughman reports that he is a serf, and is expected to plough an acre or more a day. The hunter is an employee of the king, and snares animals principally in nets, into which they are driven by trained dogs. The fisherman, because of the size of his boat, takes most of his catch in rivers, consisting of eels, pike, minnows, trout and lampreys. The merchant is an importer of dyed garments, silk, precious stones, gold, spice, wine, oil, ivory, brass, copper, tin, sulphur and glass from abroad. The shoemaker is in reality a utility leather-worker, who trades in gaiters, leather bottles, reins, spur-straps, halters, bags and purses, as well as shoes and slippers.

The staple diet of the Anglo-Saxon freeman consisted of meat, bread, butter, cheese and ale, pigs, sheep and geese being the principal animals of slaughter. The domesticated pig had longer legs and hair than its modern counterpart, and the flesh, very popular among the poorer classes, was leaner. As meat was forbidden on Fridays, there was a considerable demand for fish, lobsters, oysters and other sea food. The horse was not used for its flesh, nor as a draught animal, being bred for hunting, distance travel and warfare. Wine and mead were both produced in southern England, but as they were expensive, they were drunk mainly by the upper classes.

Nearly all the shires of England, and most kingdoms, were separated from each other by rivers, which provided routes of transportation by medium-sized boats. The major Roman roads, paved with stone, were employed for long journeys, but on the South Downs ridgeways provided suitable tracks for traders and travellers on horseback. Roman fortified towns such as London and York survived into Anglo-Saxon times, if they were convenient centres of trade, at the junction of important roads and rivers.

Nottingham came into prominence when the Danes established a stronghold there in AD 867.

Anglo-Saxon market towns usually began as fortified settlements or royal boroughs; even in Danish occupied territory burgesses were exempted from the payment of danegeld. A different scale of taxation applied to borough-traders, because for centuries they remained renters of crown tenements, who were held responsible for defending a stretch of the town walls. They were forbidden to exchange goods outside the market town, and transactions had to be before creditable witnesses. Cultivable lots within the walled borough were naturally limited, and tended to become expensive; hence the requirement in a Kentish charter of AD 868 that no building should be less than two feet from the owner's boundary, to allow for 'eavesdrip' (water from a thatched roof). An *eavesdropper* was one who lurked inside this limit to listen to secrets.

The largest towns in England before the Norman conquest were Winchester, London and York; they were chief among the 'twenty-eight noble cities' referred to in the first chapter of Bede's *Ecclesiastical History*; but even in London the population had not yet attained 25,000. Houses were built of wood, though stone was in use for ecclesiastical buildings as early as the seventh century. Gradually quarrying became as important an industry as the trade of blacksmith. It is known that the monasteries at Monkwearmouth and Jarrow provided training for craftsmen in glasswork and woodwork. Weavers, dyers and seamsters were originally homeworkers; but as trade developed, co-operatives sprung up in the market towns.

Unfortunately, Ælfric's *Colloquy* does not discuss the co-operative industries of mining, timber-felling, salt-making and ceramics, which flourished, as in Celtic times. The dialogue is in Latin, with interlinear glosses in Old English, and was written a century after Alfred's reign. One of the interlocutors, presumably a pupil, enacts the role of a monk, the idea being to improve command of colloquial Latin.

Education owed much to the Roman and Celtic Christian churches. Every bishop abroad was obliged to maintain a school in his diocese for the benefit of those who needed instruction, and the discipline observed was strict. Schools in Kent and Northumbria were generally supported by monasteries. A third class were royal foundations, one of the earliest being established by King Sigeberht

110

of East Anglia in AD 635, under the guidance of Bishop Felix. Children sometimes learnt their letters at the early age of three or four; the maturer pupils were taught Latin, scripture from the Vulgate, enough arithmetic to grasp the computation of seasonal cycles, and a variety of church music. In monasteries, such as St Peter's of Canterbury, students were taught the rudiments of Greek from Eusebius's *Ecclesiastical History*. At Malmesbury Bishop Aldhelm had encouraged the reading of Latin authors, secular and religious; he himself was the first Englishman to write Latin verse.

By the end of the seventh century scholars and teachers were drawn mainly from Ireland and France. During the eighth century many lives of saints became available for study, and Bede was able to read such hagiographies, as well as Orosius's *Universal History* and the writings of Gregory of Tours, chief of which was the *History of the Franks*. Among the books imported into England by scholars who visited Rome were Latin grammars; Benedict Biscop made at least five journeys to Italy, among other things to replenish his library. Most schools had library facilities for a limited number of students, so that Bede was able to spend his life as a scholar, teacher and writer, corresponding with colleagues in other kingdoms of England. The copying of manuscripts in scriptoria was endless, though few examples of penmanship and illumination survived the Danish holocaust in Northumbria.

The importance of Alfred's educational reforms was the shift in emphasis from Latin to English studies. To make this possible it was necessary to multiply the number of English texts by translation. Latin scholarship had seriously declined by the latter half of the ninth century, especially among ecclesiastics, and medical knowledge was tinged with superstition and magic. The King realized that intelligible reading-matter was indispensable, and that vernacular translation was preferable to illiteracy. A number of derivative Latin books continued to appear in the monasteries, and some were produced in English for the benefit of women, whose schooling tended to be neglected. (See Rudolf's *Life of St Leofgyth*, Leofgyth being an assistant to Boniface.)

Alfred's unrivalled asset was humility in personal relationships. A king who wished to educate his subjects must first acquire learning himself. He was, indeed, the earliest English advocate of adult education, and much of his leisure was spent improving his skill in Latin. Asser, his personal tutor, was not a classical scholar, but a

111

teacher of enthusiasm and immense pride in the achievement of his pupil; in the words of St Gregory he 'did not think the burden of teaching light', because he 'knew the power of its impact'. As a priest of St David's in Pembrokeshire, he was always a patriotic Celt; but his ruler, King Hyfaidd of Dyfed, had been compelled to seek Alfred's protection against Viking invaders, probably from Ireland. According to Asser, Alfred kept about his person a commonplace book, in which he accumulated passages of human and divine wisdom that appealed to him; the manuscript is said to have been in existence as late as the twelfth century. The Old English translations that Alfred is believed personally to have made, soon after 890, are: Gregory's *Pastoral Care*, Orosius's *Universal History against the Pagans*, Boethius's *On the Consolations of Philosophy* and parts of St Augustine's *Soliloquies*. Some detailed parts of the *Anglo-Saxon Chronicle* are also attributed to the king, but may owe no more to him than encouragement.

The model of Alfred's Palace School was the similar institution of Charlemagne. In the ninth century the abbeys of the Midlands had acquired a reputation for learning, and four Mercian luminaries, who participated in this scholastic venture, are mentioned in Asser's *Life*:

> Werefrith, bishop of the church of Worcester, a man well versed in divine scripture, who by the king's command, first turned the books of the Dialogues of Pope Gregory and Peter, his disciple, from Latin into Saxon, and sometimes putting sense for sense, interpreted them with clearness and elegance. After him was Plegmund, a Mercian by birth, Archbishop of the church of Canterbury, a venerable man, and endowed with wisdom; Æthelstan also, and Werewulf, his priests and chaplains, Mercians by birth, and erudite. These four had been invited out of Mercia by King Alfred, who exalted them with many honours and powers in the kingdom of the West-Saxons, besides the privileges which Archbishop Plegmund and Bishop Werefirth enjoyed in Mercia. By their teaching and wisdom the king's desires increased unceasingly, and were gratified. Night and day, whenever he had leisure, he commanded such men as these to read books to him; for he never suffered himself to be without one of them, wherefore he possessed a knowledge of every book, though of himself he could not yet understand anything.

The collaborators from Gaul, chosen for their Saxon connections and mastery of Alfred's language, were men of a different stamp. Grimbald, who arrived in 887, was selected by Archbishop Fulk of

Reims, with whom Alfred carried on a lively correspondence, often critical of Anglo-Saxon life. He came from the abbey of St Omer, in the district of Calais, and spent most of his English career as a priest in Winchester, where he was promised a 'new minster' that did not materialize in Alfred's lifetime. He was an admirable scholar, singer and interpreter of the Scriptures, and was honoured as a saint after his death in AD 901.

John was born in Old Saxony, and is thought to have been a priest in the monastery of Corvey, near Amiens, then part of the West German kingdom. He was rewarded for services to Alfred by becoming abbot of the monastery at Athelney, which had no more than half a dozen scholars. It was never popular, because inaccessible and damp; but Athelney did attract a number of foreign students, among them Danes, who sought its seclusion.

The study of Old English dialects, on a phonological basis, began in 1871, when Henry Sweet edited King Alfred's translation of St Gregory's *Cura Pastoralis* for the Early English Text Society. As far as is known, *Pastoral Care* was the first literary work undertaken by the king, and the Hatton manuscript in the Bodleian Library is indubitably the earliest (AD 891) on which one can rely for grammatical knowledge of the dominant West-Saxon dialect spoken in the late ninth century. Nearly all the surviving Old English writings are preserved in the latter dialect, and the majority belong to the tenth century, when there was a revival of the Benedictine monasteries. The works of Ælfric and Wulfstan show that by this time there was a classical or literary prose in West Saxon, using what C. L. Wrenn has described as the *koiné* (or standard language).

The Kentish and Anglian dialects seem to have been the earlier in writing, but the areas of use were ravaged by the Danes, and few documents survived. All that remains of Kentish before 900 are names in Latin charters, such as those selected by Sweet in *Oldest English Texts* (1885); after 900 the dialect is preserved in the *Kentish Psalm* (No. 50), the *Kentish Hymn* and glosses to *Proverbs* (Vespasian MS D6).

The Anglian dialects are commonly distinguished as Northumbrian and Mercian. Mercia seems to have given rise to different types, which are difficult to formulate from the evidence available. The commonest form of Mercian was unmistakably a west-midland dialect. Practically nothing is known of East Anglian speech until the Middle English period. Variations in spelling of the same words in the manuscripts of different dialects were not very significant for pronunciation and understanding in all parts of the country. The phonological differences of the four Anglo-Saxon dialects are indicated by A. Campbell in his *Old English Grammar* (1959).

Sweet's *Oldest English Texts* contains most of the pre-Alfredian remains, from which it is seen that the non-West-Saxon dialects occur in fragmentary charters and interlinear glosses of biblical texts. Internal evidence, e.g. northern dialect forms, suggests that most Old English poetry, such as *Cædmon's Hymn*, paraphrased by Bede in Book IV, ch. 24, of the *Ecclesiastical History*, would have been written in an Anglian dialect; but it is preserved in West-Saxon copies.

The Northumbrian texts include *Cædmon's Hymn*, *Bede's Death-Song*, the *Leiden Riddle* and the interlinear glosses of the Lindisfarne Gospels, the *Durham Ritual* and a few runic inscriptions. Mercian texts include glosses to the Rushworth manuscript of the Gospel of St Matthew and the Vespasian Psalter.

The copying of Old English manuscripts in insular script continued until about AD 1150, and their classification is important for the history of the language. First come the Northumbrian glosses; except for *Cædmon's Hymn*, of which seventeen manuscripts exist, they are without parallels in other dialects for the purpose of comparison. More significant is the second group – the Alfredian West-Saxon writings, which Sweet and Joseph Wright regarded as the criterion for the compilation of their Old English grammars. The late West-Saxon manuscripts of the tenth century (those of Ælfric and his contemporaries), however, contain the bulk of Anglo-Saxon literature; their literary language provided the basis, not only of George Hickes's eighteenth-century studies, but of Randolph Quirk and C. L. Wrenn's *Old English Grammar* (1955). This has the further advantage of greater uniformity in the spelling.

It should perhaps be added, that most extant MSS of Old English verse preserve it in a mixture of late West Saxon and forms from other dialects. This may imply either that Anglo-Saxon poetry was copied from other dialects, or that it was conventional for scribes to use some antique non-West-Saxon forms in poetry.

* * *

The principal authority for the history of the period AD 850–1050 is the *Anglo-Saxon Chronicle*, whose provenance has not yet been described. It was a collaborative work, probably designed as a history of the West-Saxon dynasty, in relation to happenings in the rest of the island. The Parker manuscript, written in a single hand up to the year 891, was presented by Archbishop Parker to Corpus Christi College, Cambridge, during the reign of Elizabeth I. The genealogical preface and the years 1 to 443 (from the birth of Christ to the arrival of Hengest and Horsa) were composed about the time of King Alfred's *Orosius*, from which it borrows freely. That this part was inspired, if not written, by Alfred is shown in the year AD 81, where the sentence 'he who said that he lost the day on which he did no good' was inserted after 'Titus succeeded to the kingdom'. The same interpolation was made in the *Orosius* translation.

From AD 449 to 601 the *Chronicle* is an independent authority, and the reliability of the Ceawlin story has been much debated. Some statements come from Bede, others from regnal tables. From 601 to 721 (the first Christian period) the main source is the chronological recapitulation in the last chapter of Bede's *Ecclesiastical History*. But interspersed with such events, especially after 648, are entries that describe contemporary incidents, from annals compiled in Canterbury, Winchester and Mercia. This sense of immediacy continues from AD 722 to 858, when King Æthelwulf passed away; but there are a few entries, such as the first coming of the Danes, which are retrospective. The age of Wessex dominance begins with Egbert's victory at Ellendun in 823; from this point the accounts are much more detailed. A peculiarity of the annals from 858 to 899 is that they favour events in Somerset and Dorset, rather than in Winchester and Hampshire.

In 892 Alfred had copies of the *Chronicle* circulated, along with his *Pastoral Care*, to the principal seats of learning, with the request that they should help to keep the records up to date. The Parker manuscript contains four historical poems between the years 937 and 973, including the patriotic one on the *Battle of Brunanburh*, where Æthelstan defeated the Vikings and Scots from Ireland. Although the record from 875 to 1001 is scanty, it has the merit of being independent of all other witnesses. The principal annalist seems to have continued to work in Winchester until the year 1001, when the longest of all the episodes was penned.

In the main, the seven extant copies of the *Anglo-Saxon Chronicle* seem to have come from monastic sources, and in no less than ten different hands. The most significant complement to the Parker document is the Laud manuscript, donated to the Bodleian Library, Oxford, by Archbishop Laud in the seventeenth century. This manuscript, in the hands of two different scribes, was copied at Peterborough, between 1121 and 1154, from a document lent by St Augustine's library at Canterbury, which is now lost. It contains the most lively of all the early historical accounts, the state of England in the reign of King Stephen (see p 234).

With the creation of the Palace School, and invitations to scholars from the Frankish empire, Alfred shifted the focus of cultural life from the North to Wessex. His motive in choosing Gregory's *Pastoral Care* as the first of a planned programme of translations is mentioned in the Preface.

> I began, among other various and manifold troubles of this kingdom, to translate into English the book which is called in Latin *Pastoralis*, and in English *Shepherd's Book (Hierdebōc)*, sometimes word by word, and sometimes according to the sense, as I had learned it from Plegmund my archbishop, and Asser my bishop, and Grimbald my masspriest, and John my masspriest. And when I had learned it as I could best understand it, and as I could most clearly interpret it, I translated it into English; and I will send a copy to every bishopric in my kingdom; and in each there is a book-mark (*æstel*) worth fifty mancuses. And I command in God's name that no man take the book-mark from the book, or the book from the monastery.

The Preface is a fatherly injunction to the bishops to join the king in re-educating the people through the mother-tongue.

The word *æstel* appears in Ælfric's *Glossary* opposite Latin *indicatorium*, both terms being nonce-forms. There is a reasonable suggestion that OE *æstel* was derived from Latin *hastula* 'a little spear'. OE *mancus* (from med. Latin *mancusus*) recalls an Arabic system of valuation which was recognized throughout Europe.

Alfred's translations were the first significant prose works in Old English, indeed in any Germanic language. The tone of this preface is moralistic, but masculine; the syntax is halting on account of the anacoluthia (primitive incongruity in the parts of a sentence). To bring translations up to date, Alfred was constrained to make additions to the received text, without sacrificing fidelity to the original.

The englishing of Paulus Orosius's *Universal History against the*

Pagans was a formidable undertaking, which Alfred approached with invariable practicality. Orosius was a Spanish churchman, a disciple of St Augustine, who wished him to write a book refuting the suggestion that Rome's calamities were retribution for discarding the traditional gods and acquiescing in Christianity.

Alfred condensed the history, omitted unreliable passages or those of negligible educational use, and added what he considered relevant to a better geography or history of the known world. A Norwegian, Ohthere, and a Danish traveller, Wulfstan, visited his court and gave him first-hand accounts of their respective voyages along the northern coast of Norway, as far as the White Sea, and along the southern shore of the Baltic to Danzig, then the country of the Estonians. Alfred's version is still of anthropological interest.

It is probable that one source of Alfred's geographical knowledge of Europe, Africa and Asia was Books 11–20 of the *Etymologies* of Isidore, Bishop of Seville, who wrote at the turn of the sixth century. One observation of Orosius, taken over by Alfred, is that the climate of Ireland was more temperate than that of Britain. Many historians seemed credulous enough to accept the legend that the crater of Mount Etna was the entrance to Hell. Often the etymology of place-names led Orosius to erroneous location of the places themselves. In making diplomatic changes, Alfred apparently had before him a map of the world upon which he thought he could depend; there has been much speculation as to the cartographer and the date. There are reasonable grounds for doubting whether Alfred translated Orosius at all.

The *De Consolatione Philosophiae* of Boethius (475–524) was a moral treatise, in dialogue form, that appealed to harassed monarchs for a millennium (see p 85). Five hundred years after Alfred's reign, Chaucer translated it, as did Queen Elizabeth towards the close of the sixteenth century. Boethius's book was much esteemed by Dante, Sir Thomas More and Spenser. There are two versions in Old English, Cotton Otho in the British Library (much the older) and the Bodleian manuscript in Oxford. The former preserves in alliterative verse the alternating metrical portions of the original, retaining the rest in prose; the Bodleian copy is entirely in prose. The author of the Latin work is characterized in Alfred's paraphrase as *heretoga* 'leader of men', which signifies that Boethius was of noble rank.

In the last quarter of the fifth century, Boethius was a Roman of many parts, poet, music-lover, and orator, as well as philosopher, who translated into Latin works of Plato and Aristotle. He was Roman Consul in 510, and King Theodoric put him in charge of his civil administration. But in 523 he was charged with undermining the government, by conspiring with the Eastern Emperor in Constantinople, who was the persecutor of Arians, to whose heretical faith Theodoric belonged. Boethius was imprisoned in Pavia, where he wrote the *Consolations*, and was shortly afterwards executed.

He was not a Christian, but a Senecan Platonist, who believed in Providence, and probably sympathized with Christian martyrs. In this stoical dialogue with the divine image of Philosophy, he reflects upon the attitude of mind that should be sought by men of adversity, who anticipate death. The spirit of the writing struck a sympathetic chord in the heart of Alfred. The seventeenth chapter of the translation is almost wholly his contribution, and illustrates the king's essentially Germanic outlook:

> Every kind of skill and power quickly grows old, and is passed over in silence, if it is devoid of wisdom; because no one can manifest any skill without wisdom, since whatever is done foolishly can never be accounted as skill. Now to speak most briefly, this it is that I have desired – to live worthily while I lived, and after my life to leave to the men who should follow me my memory in good deeds.

Alfred's plan of the work is somewhat different from the author's; it consists of forty-two short chapters (again sub-divided) instead of five books, and eight of the choric poems are sacrificed. The expansions seem to give Alfred's simple style its fullest scope. The primitive cult of the Golden Age (Book II, Metre 5) appears in chapter 15 of Alfred's version; the versified myth of Orpheus and Eurydice (Book III, Metre 12) is in chapter 35. The 'lying stories' (*lēasan*), he concludes in a characteristic neo-Christian approach to pagan literature, 'teach everyman who will to flee from the darkness of hell and seek the true light of God, lest he betake himself to his old sins'. Alfred undoubtedly anticipates the Christian thinking of Thomas à Kempis.

The translation of St Augustine's two books of *Soliloquies* resembles in style that of Boethius; it is found in the B.M. codex Cotton Vitellius A XV, and was copied by a scrivener sometime after the Norman conquest, probably in the reign of Henry I. The

Old English it preserves is therefore of the transitional kind, and the translator modestly claims to offer only a selection. Alfred, in the Preface, justifies this procedure on the analogy of a woodman who enters a forest, choosing the timber he desires to take home for a specific task. The most exacting exercise is Augustine's discussion on the nature of God and the immortality of the soul. Supplementary material, which Alfred assigns to a third book, is taken mainly from Augustine's *De Videndo Dei* and the *Dialogues* and *Morals* of Gregory the Great.

Alfred, by individual amplification, sought to establish basic truths about the nature of man and the freedom of his will. Thematic consistency is not the only merit of his unsubtle style, which is that of a man of affairs, not of letters; his achievement undoubtedly suffers from a restricted vocabulary. The English language did not yet possess a capacity to handle the philosophical and theological problems, to which Augustine dedicated his life. In word-formation, especially of abstract conceptions, King Alfred was the father of popular Anglo-Saxon adaptations, rather than foreign locutions. Thus it is unusual to find him borrowing from Greek, through Latin, the word (and even the spelling of) *philosophe* in *Orosius* III.7.2.

CHAPTER V

The Danish Ascendancy (900–1050)

𑀽𑀽𑀽𑀽𑀽𑀽𑀽

THE TIME IS OPPORTUNE to consider the Danes, and the condition of the occupied territory known as the Danelaw. The pillaging of monasteries in the north of England was by Norwegians; but all the Vikings were guilty of piracy, while not in open hostility to Christianity. The Danes had enjoyed some benefits of civilization from contact with the Frankish empire, and were beginning a lively and enduring trade with the rest of western Europe. In AD 826 the Danish king, Harald, became ruler of the part of Frisia known as Rüstringen, and Walcheren was occupied by him in 841. Wherever the Vikings made their assaults they were encouraged by the inefficiency and dilatoriness of the forces raised to oppose them. Paris, being on a well-fortified island in the Seine, withstood the long siege of 885–6; but in AD 911 the Norwegian Christian leader, Rollo, had to be placated by a grant of land now known as Upper Normandy. The pirates had by then decided to become settlers and farmers.

In England the organization of the Christian Church broke down in southern Northumbria, eastern Mercia and East Anglia; the bishoprics of Hexham, Whithorn and Lindsey disappeared, and York and Dorchester exercised only a shadow of their former control, because most of the churches were dispossessed of their estates. Yet Guthfrith of York, the first Danish king of Northumbria, who died in 895, is said to have been a Christian. In spite of conversion, Vikings often continued to practice polygamy, taking their further wives from among the local inhabitants. But it is not easy to ascertain the extent to which Danes were assimilated to the native population of England.

At the beginning of the tenth century the area between the Tees and the Thames was increasingly settled with Danes. Scandinavian place-names probably date from the ninth century, though the Norse influence on vocabulary and accidence was not strongly felt until the reign of King Cnut, at the beginning of the eleventh century. The truth is that, with the dissolution of northern and eastern monasteries, education there was in abeyance. The Danish aspect was so terrifying that little missionary work was attempted among them, for which English bishops were rebuked by Rome. At the instance of the Pope three new dioceses were created in the south-west, always open to Viking attack, when Edward the Elder, son of Alfred, came to the throne; these were at Sherborne, Wells and Crediton.

There was no political cohesion in the Danelaw, though a state of military preparedness among the farmer-warriors did exist. The principal strongholds were Nottingham, Leicester, Lincoln, Stamford (Lincolnshire) and Derby, which had been strategic places in the Roman defensive system. These centres, forming the core of the Danelaw, came to be known as the 'Five Boroughs'. Yet in AD 907 settlers in the Danelaw were attacked by Norwegians from across the Irish Sea. North of the Tees, as far as the Firth of Forth, the country was governed by English ealdormen, whose rule along the east coast area was not disturbed by invaders. In the tenth century, invaders continued to come from Ireland, and when allied with forces from Dumbarton on the Clyde, had no difficulty in annexing Cumberland, Westmorland and Lancashire. Hence the prevalence of Scandinavian place-names in these areas, especially Cumberland.

The origin of the Danelaw can be traced to the division of the great Danish army in AD 876, when Halfdan, according to the *Chronicle*: 'shared out the lands of Northumbria, and they were engaged in ploughing and in making a living for themselves'. The diversity of social, legal and administrative practice implied a lack of unity; yet the Danes prospered agriculturally, because they farmed areas previously undeveloped. Neither the open-field system, nor the occupation of land, was disturbed, except in East Anglia, where the arable ground was unfamiliar to them. Here they implemented units called 'ploughlands', each capable of cultivation by eight gangs of oxen; in the Domesday Book the technical name of these throughout the area of Danish influence is *bovata*.

Edward, first hereditary king of England (see p 233) reigned for a quarter of a century, beginning with a fruitless civil war against his cousin Æthelwold. No doubt questioning Edward's inheritance of the throne, Æthelwold seized the royal estate of Wimborne, and when besieged escaped to Northumbria, where he enlisted the sympathy of the Danes. In AD 901 he brought a fleet of ships from the Continent, and gained a foothold on the coast of Essex. At the head of an East Anglian army, he invaded English Mercia, which in 902 comprised the present-day shires of Oxford, Gloucester, Worcester, Hereford, Stafford, Shrewsbury and Chester. The territory was ruled by Æthelred, ally of Alfred, until his death in AD 911, when it was absorbed by Wessex. In retaliation, Edward overran Cambridgeshire, as far north as the Fens; but the Kentish part of his force was confronted by the Danish army. Whatever the outcome, Æthelwold was killed, and so was the Danish king Eohric. This was the first occasion when Danes participated in an English dynastic dispute.

Edward next prepared for the liberation of the Danelaw by inducing Englishmen to purchase tracts of land in occupied territory, to which the administration raised no objection. His first campaign against Northumbria (909) lasted only five weeks, but it compelled the Danes to agree to terms favourable to Wessex. The following year a Danish army again attacked English Mercia, as far south as the Bristol Avon. It was challenged by Edward at Tettenhall in Staffordshire, where the Danish force was destroyed with great loss, enabling the king to reoccupy the south-east Midlands and East Anglia, virtually unopposed.

When Æthelred of Mercia died in AD 911, he was succeeded by his capable wife Æthelflæd, who was King Edward's sister; she became known as 'The Lady of the Mercians'. In the ensuing years she established ten fortresses at important points in west Mercia, and personally conducted military expeditions. The occupation of London enabled Edward to consolidate his position in the north and east by fortifying the banks of the River Lea at Hertford, mobilizing ships in the Blackwater estuary and strengthening positions at Maldon and Colchester. In the summer of 914 he established an army at Buckingham in the Midlands, as a *force majeure* for bargaining with the Danes. In diplomacy Edward was both skilful and successful, for he managed to occupy Bedford in AD 915, and secured the evacuation of Thurketil and his army from England.

A well-documented campaign against the Danes was begun in AD 917. Edward himself was not in charge until the autumn, but assaults were made on Northampton and Leicester, from Towcester on Watling Street. The Danes tried to seize the initiative by counter-attacking prepared positions in Bedford and East Anglia; but their unco-ordinated efforts failed. In July, Æthelflæd struck at the northern Danes and captured Derby and the surrounding country, which she annexed to English Mercia. This proved to be the turning-point in the campaign, the Danes being simultaneously harried on several fronts. In August an East Anglian army was defeated with considerable loss at Tempsford. The last Danish stand was made near the coast, when an English force was unsuccessfully besieged, from land and sea, at Maldon. The war was virtually over when Edward in person took the field in the Midlands, and forced the surrender of the defenders in Northampton and Cambridge. South of the Humber, the only Danish forces undefeated were stationed in the boroughs of Stamford, Nottingham and Lincoln. Edward fortified a position opposite the first, on the River Welland, and had received the garrison's submission, when the news came of Æthelflæd's death (June 918). Not only English Mercia accepted him as king, but several rulers of Wales acknowledged Edward as overlord, because they feared Viking inroads from Ireland. It was York that bore the brunt of the Irish attack in AD 918. But for the first time the Midlands and the South of England were united, and Danes actually shared in the new garrisons.

Viking attacks were next concentrated on the north-west of England, where Norwegians from Ireland settled in alarming numbers; their stay is recalled by several sculptured stones on which Irish and Norse designs are happily blended. Within a generation settlers had appropriated the whole of the territory from the Wirral to the Solway Firth. The aggressive invader from Ireland was a warrior known as Rægnald, who between 913 and 915 successfully conducted campaigns against the Scots and Bernicians, gaining a victory over them at Corbridge. In 919 he captured York and made himself king. This encouraged further Irish inroads by the River Mersey, on which Edward proceeded to erect fortifications. By 920 he had consolidated his defensive system, and was able to advance to Bakewell in the Peak District, where he established a garrison. Such was the reputation he had now acquired that he was met by all Norse rulers south of the Clyde-Forth line, including Rægnald, and acknowledged as their overlord.

Four years later King Edward put down a rising in Chester, but he died at Farndon-on-Dee, and was buried in Winchester. The king had proved himself a great strategist, who patiently safeguarded positions, and enlisted disaffected elements in his progress. This cautiousness he had learnt from participation in his father's campaigns. His garrisons were encouraged by grants of land, and were regarded as the king's tenants. The shires of the Midlands derived their names from the fortified centres in which Danes had quartered their armies.

Rægnald died in 921, and his cousin-successor, Sihtric, six years after. The latter cemented an alliance with the new Wessex king, Æthelstan, by marriage to his sister. Æthelstan had been brought up in the household of the English Mercian ruler, and was therefore acquainted with Midland affairs; he had been thoroughly instructed in the duties of a king by his grandfather, Alfred the Great.

At Eamont, near Penrith, in 927 he was acknowledged by the northern rulers as overlord of all the territory protected by his father; and he bound them to an undertaking to stamp out paganism. This agreement, however, lasted for only six years. Æthelstan then occupied York and took possession of ancient Deira. He also compelled the Welsh princes to pay tribute in return for protection from the Vikings, and to accept the River Wye as the natural boundary, since Offa's day, between England and Wales.

Æthelstan's show of strength in Scotland, to impress dissident elements beyond the Firth of Forth, followed the Roman plan of combined invasion by land and sea. The army gathered at Winchester, with five Scandinavian earls and four Welsh princes, advanced as far as Kincardineshire, without engagement, while the fleet raided Viking seaports as remote as those of northern Caithness. Æthelstan became the only monarch in Europe successfully to repel the Danes, and this prestige led to Continental alliances in France and Germany, through offers of marriage with the king's sisters.

In consolidating his kingdom, Æthelstan made enemies in Ireland and Scotland. One was the exiled Olaf, son of Sihtric of York, who had established himself as King of Dublin; another was King Constantine of Scotland. Olaf had a large fleet, with which he planned to invade northern England and recover his father's inheritance, by means of an alliance with the Scottish king and the Strathclyde Welsh. The extent of his penetration in AD 937, and the location of Brunanburh, where the decisive battle took place, are uncertain, but Olaf seems to have landed in the Solway Firth.

Æthelstan and his brother Edmund (then only sixteen) commanded a composite force of West Saxons, Mercians and Danes. According to the well-known OE poem *The Battle of Brunanburh*, there were heavy losses on both sides, including two of Alfred's grandsons; but Olaf and his allies left dead on the field five kings, seven members of the Irish aristocracy and the son of King Constantine.

Æthelstan, like Alfred and Edward, kept court in many places, twenty-three being recorded in a reign of fifteen years; there were always Danish earls from the east present, as appears from eleven Scandinavian names that witness charters. He had every confidence in his new subjects, and he tried to make his assemblies representative of the whole nation. The Council for the transaction of state business consisted of bishops, abbots, ealdormen in charge of provinces, thegns of Wessex, and other persons considered of specific importance. The king's charters are notable for their florid, legalistic Latin language, for which a body of educated clerks was responsible. The intimate council of Alfred the Great was a thing of the past.

The laws of Æthelstan were concerned principally with felony and social problems arising from a complex population. The tenor of legislation was the preservation of peace; but there were several enactments concerning gilds in London, as instruments of responsible trade conduct. The constitutional importance of Æthelstan's reign exceeded its territorial gains, for the laws were designed to promote goodwill and unity.

When he died in 939, Æthelstan had proved himself to be a great king of Wessex, with strong family ties, and abounding energy and vision. The gifts from foreign rulers contained many Christian relics, of which he was a zealous collector; his benefactions included generous donations of books to religious institutions.

The new king, Edmund I, was only eighteen when he ascended the throne, and the death of Æthelstan was therefore the signal for a renewed attack by King Olaf Guthfrithson of Dublin. Within months he occupied York, unopposed. In 940 he invaded Northamptonshire; but when confronted by Edmund's army, the Archbishops of York and Canterbury negotiated a truce, whereby the shires surrounding Nottingham, Leicester, Lincoln and Derby were ceded to Olaf. This shameful arrangement was the work of an anglicized Danish earl, named Urm, and it enabled Olaf in the following year to invade the eastern Lowlands of Scotland; but he died before the expedition was concluded. Two successors to Olaf were baptized at Edmund's court, with the king as sponsor in AD 943. But it was only in the following year that York was recaptured, along with the shires of the four boroughs.

In England as well as Ireland, Danes and Norwegians were at loggerheads. As the Norse dissidents were in league with the Strathclyde Welsh, Edmund and the Welsh king of Dyfed successfully invaded the Strathclyde kingdom in AD 945, and placed it under the suzerainty of Malcolm, King of Scotland, as long as the latter remained England's ally. In the following year (946) Edmund was stabbed to death in Gloucestershire; according to tradition, he was defending his steward from attack by a returned exile. His children being young, he was succeeded by his brother Eadred, about whose short, but bloody reign, ending in 955, the *Chronicle* records little; but he 'reduced Northumbria to subjection', and had cause to imprison Archbishop Wulfstan for disloyalty at a time when Eric Bloodaxe of Norway ruled as usurper in York. The handsome but ineffectual King Eadwig (son of Edmund) then ruled for less than four years, and was succeeded by his brother Edgar in 959.

From 955 England enjoyed a quarter-century of peace; for there were no further Scandinavian attacks until AD 980. During this period there was a revival of interest in monastic life, stimulated by Dunstan, Abbot of Glastonbury; the return to private devotions is said to have been due to the example of King Edgar himself. Edgar wished to retain Dunstan at court as adviser, and made him first Bishop of Worcester and London, then Archbishop of Canterbury (963), in order to support his reformed ecclesiastical policy. The *Laud Chronicle* (see p 116) observes that Dunstan 'came to King Edgar and asked him to give him all the monasteries which the heathen had destroyed, because he wished to restore them'. A long list follows, beginning with Ely.

Dunstan designed the coronation ceremony, introducing the anointing of the king for the first time, to confer on him divine sanction similar to that bestowed upon priests at their consecration. Such power could not be conferred until the recipient had reached the age of thirty; and probably for this reason Edgar's coronation at Bath was delayed until AD 973, fourteen years after his accession. After the ceremony he went by sea to Chester to receive the homage of eight kings of Britain; according to tradition, they symbolized their acquiescence in his supremacy by rowing Edgar upon the River Dee, the English king being at the rudder; but the gesture was a promise of peaceful co-existence, rather than of submission.

The cession of the Lothians (territory between the Tweed and the Firth of Forth) to the King of Scotland, took place in Edgar's reign, and designedly introduced a strong Anglian element into the Celtic kingdom. But the granting of legal autonomy to the Danish provinces of England was probably the most far-reaching of Edgar's enactments; it explains the origin of the term *Danelaw* (OE *Dena laȝe, c* 1050).

Edgar died suddenly, two years after his coronation, and his passing was commemorated by a long poem in the *Chronicle*. He left only minor sons, Edward and Æthelred, who were the issue of successive wives, and both had partisans at court. Though Edward was crowned, he was murdered three years later (978) while on a visit to his stepmother and her son at Wareham. Much suspicion attended this deed; miracles were performed at the martyr's burial place and the 'stripling' Edward quickly became a saint.

Æthelred II, only thirteen, became king at a difficult period. He was irresolute and mistrusted, and as it proved, incapable of military prowess, at an unfortunate time when warlike passions were irrupting in Scandinavia. There the aggressiveness of Harold Bluetooth, King of Denmark and Norway, unwisely forced Christianity upon the people. Many dissenters fitted out small expeditions to England, from 980 to 982, chiefly along the south and west coast. The attacks, lasting ten years, were made from Norman ports, which produced friction with the Duke of Normandy in which the Pope had to intervene. The first army arrived in 991, and assumed such power that a tax of ten thousand pounds was imposed on their English co-inhabitants.

One of these raids is recalled in a short heroic poem, *The Battle of Maldon* (AD 991, see p 212). The Danes attacked Ipswich, sailed up the Blackwater estuary and landed east of this fortress. They had to cross a causeway, which was defended by Byrhtnoth, the ealdorman of Essex, who gallantly permitted the passage before high-tide, to enable the opposing forces to meet on open ground. The result of the conflict was virtually decided when Byrhtnoth was killed. Then for four months the Norsemen, under Olaf Tryggvason (a Norwegian) raided southern England, until a treaty could be arranged by the Archbishop of Canterbury, favourable to the invaders. They were to receive twenty-two thousand pounds in gold or silver, and the right to whatever merchant shipping they were able to take, provided that the present Danes helped the English to resist further seaborne attacks from their compatriots. Olaf did not observe the last of these provisions; for in 994 he returned at the head of a fleet of ninety-four ships, some to the coast of Northumberland, others to Lincolnshire; he was accompanied by Sweyn, son of Harold, King of Denmark. The combined strength was about two thousand men, and London was strong enough to resist it; but raids on undefended positions were destructive, and the invasion was only bought off by payment of a sum of sixteen thousand pounds. A disgruntled Sweyn returned to Denmark; but Olaf, after his baptism at Andover, undertook that he would not return in a warlike capacity; he was soon to become King of Norway.

Each summer, from 997 to 1001, a Viking army now ravaged the south coast of England, from Kent to Cornwall; fortified Exeter alone was able to withstand these assaults. Æthelred *Unræd* ('the ill-advised', not the 'unready') had not the fleet to oppose the large naval force stationed at the Isle of Wight. Once more he negotiated, and in 1002 secured an armistice at the cost of a further twenty-four thousand pounds. In the same year he married Emma, sister of Richard II, Duke of Normandy, in the hope that the alliance would be politically useful; but the situation was aggravated by the king's November decree that all Danes in England should be massacred (see Stenton, *Anglo-Saxon England*, pp 374–5). Æthelred's motive was an alleged threat to his life. The decree could be carried out only in part; but that killings did take place is attested both by the *Laud Chronicle* (AD 1002) and the Cartulary of St Frideswide, Oxford (ed. S. R. Wigram, Oxford Historical Soc. 1894, vol. I, p 2). Gunnhild, sister of King Sweyn of Denmark, was one of those killed, and the latter retaliated in AD 1003–4, by leading a punitive expedition, which overran Wessex and East Anglia, and destroyed Norwich by fire.

Sweyn's army returned to Denmark in AD 1005, but was back the following year, landing in Kent and ravaging southern England during the winter months, as far west as Wiltshire, and despoiling towns such as Reading and Wallingford. This raid cost the English people a further thirty thousand pounds in tribute. A large part of this sum was raised by the sale of estates, purchased by families of Danish settlers. The outcome of these extortionate demands was the decision in 1008 to build a new armed fleet, a warship being demanded from the proprietors of every 310 hides. This fleet was concentrated on Sandwich, where the last landing had been made. But twenty ships turned to piracy, and eighty were wrecked in a storm; the rest of the weakened fleet was in 1009 transferred to London, whereupon the Danes occupied the key port of Sandwich.

The largest of the Danish armies, under Thorkell and Hemming, attacked England in the same year. Kent offered them three thousand pounds to be left in peace, but Oxford was sacked before the invaders turned once more to East Anglia. This army remained in England until 1012, reducing the whole of the south-east Midlands, and then laying siege to Canterbury, where they exacted a fine of forty-eight thousand pounds before they would leave the country. They held Archbishop Ælfheah up to ransom, but he would not allow the demand to be met. It was, in fact, made by the troops without the authority of their leader. In a moving passage, the *Chronicle* recounts how the Archbishop was cruelly pelted to death at Greenwich 'with bones and the heads of cattle'. As a result, Thorkell, who offered everything but his ship to prevent this sacrifice, did not return to his homeland, but joined Æthelred with forty-eight ships.

The pusillanimity of the English commanders before the invaders, and the many acts of treachery and cowardice, were partly due to lack of confidence in the king. The entrenched position of the Viking aristocracy in Normandy made it impossible for later invaders to acquire land there, and the fertile tillage of southern and eastern England proved too attractive an alternative. The Danish conquest being inevitable, Sweyn took the initiative in 1013 of making himself king. He planned a two-pronged attack, first on Sandwich, then in the Humber estuary, where, sailing up the Trent he landed at Gainsborough, in the heart of Danish England. He was immediately accepted as ruler by the Five Boroughs. With a secure supply of food and horses, he captured Oxford and Winchester. Hostages were taken in every centre to assure allegiance, a precaution learnt from the Romans. London, strengthened by Thorkell's fleet, was able to halt Sweyn's advance, but the western thegns surrendered at Bath, and the campaign was virtually over. Æthelred and his wife, with the aid of Thorkell's ships, escaped to Normandy. Then Sweyn suddenly died on his return to Gainsborough early in 1014. He was succeeded by Cnut, the younger of his two sons; the elder, Harold, became King of Denmark.

The death of Sweyn emboldened the ealdormen of England to request the return of Æthelred, upon his promise of a juster and more efficient government. A pact was made between subjects and king, which in some ways anticipated Magna Carta. Æthelred came back from Normandy at the head of a loyalist force, which landed in Lindsey, at the very time the inexperienced Cnut had decided to abandon his supporters in Gainsborough and the Five Boroughs; many paid for this with their lives at the hands of Æthelred. Cnut, more savage, put his hostages ashore at Sandwich, after cutting off their hands, ears and noses. The king then bought off the army at Greenwich by paying twenty-one thousand pounds.

In 1015 Cnut returned with a Danish army to Poole, accompanied by the seasoned Norwegian warrior, Eric of Hlathir, and the very Thorkell who had left the Danes for Æthelred. The desertion of Eadric, ealdorman of Mercia, with all his forces, enabled Cnut to possess himself of Wessex in four months. Æthelred, though ill, himself entered the field with his resourceful son, Edmund, but he was too late to save the Danelaw and Northumberland. Cnut planned an assault on London and the south-east, but before he could arrive with his fleet in the Thames, King Æthelred's unhappy reign ended (April 1016). It is one of the best documented in Anglo-Saxon history, and proved that a mobile administration need never collapse.

Although Edmund was chosen to succeed the king in the beleagured city, the council at Southampton chose Cnut to rule them, satisfying itself that he would govern justly. Edmund Ironside, as he came to be known, decided that attack was better than defence, and abandoned London in order to recover Wessex, on which he relied for loyal troops. In this he was several times successful; the strategically important city of London was blockaded and its satellite port of Greenwich, captured. After an indecisive campaign in Wiltshire, where there were two costly engagements, Edmund reapproached London from the north through the woods of the Tottenham area, and surprised the Danes, who were compelled to evacuate their positions, and retreat to the south bank of the Thames. Here and at Otford in Kent, Ironside defeated the enemy heavily, though sadly depleting his own army; but the Danish hold on London was abandoned in favour of more profitable logistics in East Anglia. The ensuing Battle of Ashingdon in Essex might have been won by the English, had Edmund not been joined by the treacherous earl, Eadric, who again deserted with his west-midland army just before the clash began. Ironside lost the battle and became a hunted man. But his prowess in building four redoubtable armies was respected, and Cnut offered him an honourable peace, with a kingdom which comprised the Wessex-dominated portion of England, south of the Thames, though this agreement left London in the hands of the Danes. The wearied Edmund died the same year, after seven months of arduous but valiant resistance.

Cnut became King of All England in 1017, and Æthelred's widow, Emma, was brought to court to be his lawful wife, and so cement an alliance with Normandy. The tribute imposed was slightly less than eleven thousand pounds on London, and seventy-two thousand on the rest of the country. This meant that the country had been bled for more than a quarter of a million pounds in twenty-five years. Decentralized control was envisaged, by placing Wessex directly under the king, and East Anglia, Mercia and Northumbria under Thorkell, Eadric and Eric respectively. The country as a whole was made subject to the Wessex law of King Edgar, and Cnut found it politic to become a pillar of the Church. There was, however, a merciless streak in his nature, and he removed without trial several persons who might threaten his right to rule. Among these was the unpopular Eadric, killed in London in the first year. Thorkell was outlawed four years later, but reconciled to Cnut in Denmark in 1022. For the first ten years of his reign Cnut treated England as a conquered province, which could be left to look after itself, while he attended to dynastic interests in the Scandinavian homelands, resulting from the death of his brother Harold in 1019. He headed four military expeditions to Denmark and Norway, its tributary state, and in 1025 suffered a serious reverse in the Battle of Holy River. But he survived, and managed to make his son, Harthacnut, King of Denmark (1028).

Cnut maintained cordial relations with Conrad, the Holy Roman Emperor, whose coronation he attended in Rome in AD 1027. The Emperor's son, Henry, married his daughter Gunnhild in 1036, and Cnut had negotiated the cession of Schleswig to Denmark before his death in November of the previous year. His sister, Estrith, had married Robert, Duke of Normandy, much earlier, but this marriage proved a failure. During Cnut's reign there was a notable codification and improvement of the Anglo-Saxon laws, and stability of rule brought back prosperity to the Anglo-Danish state. The *danegeld* was renamed *heregeld* (an army and navy tax), collected annually until 1051, when it was abolished by Edward the Confessor. A further national levy was made to meet the salaries of the king's 'housecarls' (retainers and bodyguard), many of whom also received grants of land. At this time the word *eorl* replaced OE *ealdorman*, as witnessed charters show; but the majority of this local ruling-class were Danes. On the other hand, two of the king's chief advisers, Godwine and Leofric, were English.

When Cnut died, his elder son, Harthacnut, was preoccupied in the defence of Denmark against Magnus of Norway; it was not feasible for him to desert his kingdom. The English Council's choice fell on Harold, an illegitimate son of Cnut by Ælgifu of Northampton, before he married Emma of Normandy. The latter was to live at Winchester, and watch her son Harthacnut's interests, should he later lay claim to his inheritance; but she was soon forced to seek protection in Flanders. The Church was not happy at the election, but accepted it; in effect, the power behind the scene was Ælgifu, a forceful and influential personality. There was no need for Harthacnut to press his claims, when free to do so, because Harold died in 1040, after a reign of less than five years. The Danish king was then twenty-three, but he lived another two years only; his short tenure of the combined kingdoms was marred by a revolt in Worcester against oppressive taxation, needed to support his navy of sixty-two ships and the housecarls. He was magnanimous, however, in requesting his half-brother, Edward, son of Æthelred, to live in the king's household, which he did from 1041. When Harthacnut died in June of the following year, the line of Danish kings ended. Edward was unanimously elected to succeed him, and was crowned at Winchester nine months later.

The disruption of religion, through comparative impotence of church organization, was one of the worst effects of the Danish invasions. Danes were mostly pagans, and some remained indifferent to Christianity until the twelfth century. Converts, such as Guthrum, were often nominal Christians, from motives of policy, though King Cnut appears to have been sincere. A sympathetic Danish King of York, Guthred, allowed the Church of St Cuthbert to find a home at Chester-le-Street in 882; but this community's life was precarious, until in 990 Earl Uhtred made it possible for the Church to move to Durham, and to a highly defensible site on the River Wear. Hexham and Ripon went out of existence, and the impoverished diocese of York enjoyed minimal influence in its heathen environment. In Lindsey, East Anglia and the eastern half of Mercia, ecclesiastical property was seized, and the disintegration of the Christian church was inevitable. Only in Wessex, including Kent, were a few new bishoprics created, during the reign of Edward the Elder; but it was not until the late tenth and early eleventh century that the kingdom of Wessex made progress towards monastic revival.

The principal explanation for the lack of missionary zeal in educating the Danes was fear of their violence, and their habitual mobility. Settled Danes were more amenable to the civilizing influence of the Church, where it was available. By the time of King Alfred's reign so many monasteries had disappeared that a heavy burden was placed on parochial churches, with the result that the parish system began to flourish from the eleventh century. Bishops saw the wisdom of allocating areas of activity to priests from the regional *minster*. This word seldom implies 'church', but rather a centre of religious activity, and it survives as an appendage in place names, for instance, in Westminster, Axminster and Ilminster. The building of new churches was dependent on lay patronage and the generosity of landlords. In general, the parish churches belonged to noblemen or the crown, and the priest appointed was expected to collect the dues. This was not an ideal arrangement, but became an indispensable adjunct of the Church's pastoral responsibility.

The priest, as well as the bishop, needed to be English-speaking, because his duty was to expound the Gospels, the sacraments and the Lord's Prayer in the home-language. Bishops and priests invariably received their training in monasteries, with the result that, at the beginning of the eleventh century, more than half were monks, whose Celtic asceticism strongly influenced the future of the English Church. Among the provisos of St Benedict's rule, one required that priests should remain celibate. This proved to be a rule difficult to enforce during the Danish disturbances, although the conduct of priests was under the surveillance of the bishop, his archdeacon and deacons, who acted as administrative assistants in the diocese.

On the Continent, as well as in England, two concepts of religious life appeared to be in conflict, the monastic or devotional view, and the practical or secular one, which encouraged closer contacts with the outside world. When the strict monastic system declined at the close of the ninth century, other communities, calling themselves monasteries, came into being, consisting of secular priests or clerks, who anticipated the cathedral canons or prebendaries of the thirteenth century. The *prebend* was a share of church revenues for services in administrative or pastoral capacities. Secular priests acquired the title because they assumed the rights to possess property and to marry (often secretly), from which privileges monks were debarred. Quasi-monastic communities of this kind, though they admitted some laxity, were important to diocesan activities, and to the preservation of Christianity in England and the rest of Europe during the dark period of the tenth century; yet they were condemned in English writings of the eleventh century, nearly all emanating from the monasteries.

In the larger centres, such as Canterbury and Winchester, communities were usually mixed, though New Minster at Winchester had more secular priests than monks. Predominantly canonical communities existed in the tenth century at St Albans, Rochester, Abingdon, Bath and Exeter. Members of the community of St Cuthbert's, Durham, were nearly all married; they lived in their own homes, and passed on their estates to their descendants. Yet they were respected and responsible clerics of the Church and the collegiate school at Durham was among the best in England. North of the Humber the prebendary system was the invariable pattern, the regulations adopted being those of Archbishop Chrodegang of Metz (*c* 755), a modification of the Rule of St Benedict.

The movement for Benedictine reform began in Wessex in the tenth century, during the reigns of Æthelstan, Edmund and Eadred, reaching its peak in AD 975 under the complaisant Edgar. The guiding spirits were Dunstan, Æthelwold and Oswald, who died in 988, 984 and 992 respectively, and whose *Lives* were written about the year 1000. Though the monastic renaissance they fathered enjoyed royal favour, it was far from being a popular movement; only twenty-eight monasteries had accepted the sterner discipline by the time of Edgar's death. The inspiration for the reforms came from Ghent, where Dunstan had been exiled after a quarrel with King Eadwig; and from Fleury, where Oswald studied, and made the acquaintance of the learned monk, Abbo, whom he afterwards brought to Worcester. The three principal figures were influential because they were of royal or noble descent, and were able to secure large endowments of land for the monasteries they recreated. This led to the abuse of power by the monk class, injected in considerable numbers into the ecclesiastical system of England. Such a situation was not allowed to develop on the Continent.

Æthelwold proved to be the most intolerant and ruthless of the reformers; when he became Bishop of Winchester in 963, he dismissed the clerks and secular priests and replaced them with monks. Oswald, Bishop of Worcester, introduced changes more gradually. Dunstan's major innovations were made while Abbot of Glastonbury, when he transformed the foundation into an admirable seat of learning; later, as Archbishop of Canterbury, he was preoccupied with diocesan affairs of growing complexity. In the Midlands, principal centres of reform were Evesham and Ramsey. There was great monastic activity in the Fen areas of East Anglia, resulting in the revival of such foundations as Ely, Peterborough and Bury St Edmunds. An important outcome of the reform movement was the Synodal Council of Winchester (970), which framed a common rule to be observed by the monasteries; this was named *Regularis Concordia*, and was devised by Æthelwold on the basis of rules practised at Ghent and Fleury. It invited the king to become the protector of monastic orders, and included procedures for the election of bishops that would ensure strong monastic bias in the episcopy.

Much of this work of reform was neutralized by new Viking invasions in the last decade of the tenth century, when monasteries were again pillaged. But King Cnut, under the influence of Archbishop Wulfstan of York, proved sympathetic to the reform movement. In 1020 he consecrated a new church on the site of the Battle of Ashingdon, where Edmund Ironside had been defeated four years earlier. The levy of 'Peter's Pence', which he proclaimed in 1027, became England's annual contribution to the Church in Rome. But Cnut was diplomatic in giving equal recognition to both orders of clergy, the secular and the monastic.

The role of the Church in moulding customs, traditions and institutions, was important, because it was an organized body of educated men with a powerful hold upon the laity. Its ability to initiate or halt change by advice to kings, Saxon and Danish, grew with the accession of status through property. By the eleventh century, the Church possessed a sixth of the wealth of England. Teutonic sanctions, inherited in Anglo-Saxon England, were unwritten, but did not confer absolute power on the monarch. Christianity would appear to have limited despotic rule further, by anointing a priest-king, who became responsible both to God and his people; but this, like the divinity of the Roman emperors, was later to prove a dangerous innovation. There were two recorded depositions for unjust rule, Sigeberht's in 757, and Æthelred's in 1013. Momentous decisions of this kind were taken by the Witan, on which the highest ecclesiastics served.

Under normal conditions, decisions of policy were taken by the king without official consultation; his travel from one place of residence to another would have made him familiar with the needs of the realm. The method of government consisted of decrees through business-like *writs*, which were letters penned by the king's scribe, issued under his seal. The Witan was not in constant attendance on the king, as its composition varied from time to time, according to choice. He called it to session (*witenagemot*) two or three times a year, usually at festival seasons. An unfortunate decision was taken in AD 991, when Archbishop Sigeric of Canterbury advised King Æthelred to placate the invaders by means of danegeld, thereby creating a precedent for further demands, which had to be met instantly, to the embarrassment of the treasury and the suffering people.

Most of the young princes were educated by abbots in the liberal arts of Grammar, Rhetoric, Dialectic, Arithmetic, Geometry, Astronomy and Music. Many churchmen fought in the king's armies; and a few such as Archbishop Wulfstan of York, were, for justifiable reasons, go-betweens with Danish enemies, a situation that partly arose from the desire to secure Christian converts. There is very little evidence of a conflict between nobles and ecclesiastics on the king's council.

The impact of the Viking language upon Old English is worth considering, both being Germanic languages, with a largely common vocabulary, but different in grammar and pronunciation.

Educated Englishmen could understand Danes, as was shown when the Norse bard, Gunnlaug, recited a poem, with acclaim, at the court of Æthelred the Unready. Most Norse borrowings cannot be traced in English until after the Norman Conquest, for the reasons that (a) writings in Norse did not survive before the Middle English period; and (b) Old English manuscripts were preserved in the dominant dialect of Wessex, where the Danes made no political headway.

Because they had been Continental neighbours, Anglo-Saxons and Vikings were more adaptable to each other than were the English and Celtic Britons. There was a good deal of intermarriage. The Danes were, in fact, readily assimilated by the English they conquered, because the two peoples had a common cultural tradition, as traders, freebooters and farmers, and communication was always possible. The likeness of their languages makes it difficult to determine whether some words are actually of Scandinavian origin; in a glossary, especially modified by phonemic translation, they do not strike one as borrowings, as French, Latin and Greek words usually do.

The Danish invasion helped to re-model the English dialect system, especially the morphology of verbs. The origin of the plural inflexions -*en* and -*es* in Mercian and Northumbrian respectively, was probably associated with Scandinavian linguistic influence.

Danes predominated in Northumbria south of the Tees, and in the Five Boroughs of Mercia; in this region, and Norfolk, there is a concentration of Danish place-names, the commonest suffixes being -*by* 'village', -*thorp* 'hamlet' and -*dale* 'valley'. In Cumberland, Westmorland and Lancashire north of the Ribble, which were never areas of Anglo-Saxon settlement, the names of places and geographical features are Norse or Celtic, e.g. in the use of the suffixes -*beck* 'stream', -*fell* 'mountain', -*force* 'waterfall', -*garth* 'enclosure', -*gill* 'glen', -*keld* 'spring', -*scale* 'house', -*scar* 'rock', -*thwaite* 'paddock'.

Some of the commonest words in the English language (mostly nouns and verbs) were borrowed from the Viking invaders, for example:

Nouns: anger (O. Norse *angr*, C 13); *awe* (ON *agi*, cf. related OE *eʒe*, C 13); *billow* ON *bylgja*, Dan. *bölge*, C 16); *birth* (ON *byrðr*, C 13); *boon* (ON *bón*, C 12); *egg* (ON *egg*, OE *æʒ*,

C 11); *fellow* (ON *félage* 'one who shares monetary responsibility', cf. OE *feoh*, 'fee', C 11); *gait* (ON *gata*, C 15, earlier spelt *gate*, C 13); *husting* 'house meeting', (ON *húsþing*, C 11); *law* (ON *lag*, C 11); *loan* (ON *lán*, cf. obsolete OE *lǣn*, C 13); *root* (ON *rót*, C 12); *skill* (ON *skil* 'distinction', C 12); *skin* (ON *skinn*, C 13); *skirt* (ON *skyrta*, C 14); *sky* (ON *ský*, C 13); *swain* (ON *sveinn*, C 12); *window* (ON *vindauga*, C 13); *wing* (ON *vængir*, C 12).

Adjectives: awkward (ON *afug* 'turned the wrong way' + *ward*, C 14); *bleak* (ON *bleikja*, C 16); *cross* 'fierce' (ON *kross*, O.Irish *cros*, C 16); *ill* (ON *illr*, C 13); *odd* (ON *odda*, C 14); *rotten* (ON *rotinn*, C 13); *sly* (ON *slǽgr*, C 13); *ugly* (ON *uggligr* 'to be feared', C 13); *weak* (ON *veikr*, C 14).

Pronouns: both (ON *baðar*, C 13); *same* (ON *same*, C 13); *they* (ON *þeir*, C 13); *them* (ON *þeim* C 13); *their* (ON *þeira*, C 13).

Verbs: bait (ON *beita*, cf. related OE *bǣtan*, C 13); *bask* (ON *baðask* 'bathe oneself', C 14); *bathe* (ON *baða*, cf. OE *baðian*, C 13); *batten* 'grow fat' (ON *batna* 'get better', C 16); *call* (ON *kalla*, C 11); *cast* (ON *kasta*, C 13); *dawn* (ON *daga*, C 15); *droop* (ON *drúpa*, C 14); *egg* 'urge' (ON *eggja*, C 13); *gape* (ON *gapa*, C 13); *get* (ON *geta*, C 13); *hit* (ON *hitta*, C 11); *ransack* (ON *rannsaka* 'search a house', C 13); *scare* (ON *skirra*, C 13); *snare* (ON *snara*, C 14); *take* (ON *taka*, C 12); *want* (ON *vanta*, C 13).

Relation words: aloft (ON *á lopt*, C 13); *athwart* (a+ON *þvert*, C 14); *fro* (ON *frá*, C 13).

It can be seen from the above loan cross-section that only a limited number of the Old Norse borrowings recorded in documents such as the *Anglo-Saxon Chronicle* belong to the transition period (the eleventh century); the bulk appear in writing in Middle English (thirteenth to fifteenth century). The few that belong to the sixteenth century, e.g. *batten, billow, bleak* and *cross*, are assumed by the *OED* to have been in unrecorded dialect use during the intervening period.

The Danelaw was responsible for some technical words entering the language, one of the most interesting being *vapnatak* (OE of the tenth-century *wæpentac* 'wapentake') meaning 'the flourish of weapons'. In Leicester, Nottingham, Lincoln and Derby, a wapentake was a rural area, with an administrative village as the centre. There assemblies and courts met, and decisions were taken, which were announced by such a display. The laws of Cnut mention hundreds, shires and wapentakes as administrative divisions, depending on the custom of the majority in each area.

Scandinavian legal terms abounded, one which appeared frequently in documents of the eleventh century being *sokeman*. This class was a freeman-tenant of some lord, and a respected member of the peasant aristocracy. He paid a nominal rental for his land, contributed labour at the busiest seasons of the year, and was liable for the king's taxes; but he could dispose of his land and was virtually independent. By Cnut's time many Danes had settled south of the Thames, and the term 'sokeman' also appears in such areas as Kent and Surrey.

Æthelwold's School at Winchester has recently been credited with a wider influence on late West Saxon than was hitherto thought; Helmut Gneuss regards it as the sponsor of Standard Old English (see *Anglo-Saxon England* I, Cambridge, 1972, p 63 et seqq). So many Old English manuscripts (Gneuss says 169) belong to the late tenth century that he believes the industry of the Winchester scriptorium was responsible. Furthermore, Æthelwold must have been a more than competent instructor in Old English usage, judging by the quality of his translation in the *Benedictine Rule*, commissioned by King Edgar and his wife.

The homiletic skill of Winchester's leading scholars indicates that West Saxon was no longer one of the regional dialects; it had become the vehicle of cultural maturity, which the translations of Alfred obviously lacked. In the last quarter of the tenth century, the ecclesiastical school provided aspiring monks from three Winchester monasteries with a sensitivity to good writing. Virile prose is characterized by a feeling for sentence rhythm, for balanced syntax and varieties of subordination that lessen the monotony of the paratactic structures, which burdened Alfredian narrative. Pleasing modulations are secured by the inversion of word order. The secret

139

of Ælfric's skill lay in conscious use of the periodic structure of sentences; it stretches the retentive power of both minds – the writer's and the reader's. A remarkable regularity among late West Saxon prose writers is to be seen in the use of inflexions, spelling and vocabulary.

The Winchester school was talented in the use of rhetorical devices, learnt from Latin classics after Cicero, as well as Tertullian. The first evidence is to be seen in the unknown author of the *Blickling Homilies* (971), the manuscript of which belonged to the Marquis of Lothian at Blickling Hall, Norfolk, but has now gone to the United States. One of the sermons, 'The End of the World is Near', plays on the public fear that the Day of Judgement was at hand, and that it would probably fall in the year 1000. A typically rhetorical passage from this homily illustrates the point:

> Nor let any man here in this wordly kingdom be in thought too rash, nor in body too strong, nor in enmity too ready, nor in strife too bold, nor of deceits too full, nor of wickedness too fond, nor of wrongs too subtle, nor of artifice too skilled. . . . He will await doom when the Almighty God wishes to bring about the end of the world, and draws his flaming sword . . . and cleaves this universe; and the dead will stand up; then will the body be made clear as glass, and naught that is wrong will be hidden.

The scheme of amplification in the first sentence is *congeries*, what the classical rhetoricians preferred to call *synathroismus*; it is a single instance of the flowery devices that coloured the language of this preacher.

Alfred the Great's manuals and translations had been deliberately designed for an educational purpose. The prose writers who succeeded him at Winchester were monks or clerks, whose taste was less utilitarian, who tired of a narrative style so much given to co-ordinated clauses and sentences. As W. P. Ker rightly observed, 'prose literature taught and presented so much that it lost all spring and freshness' (Introduction to H. Craik's *English Prose Selections*, 1893, vol. I, p 12).

Ælfric (955–1020) was the literary spokesman in the vernacular of Benedictine reform. Educated under Æthelwold at Winchester, he later became an instructor at Cerne Abbas in Dorset. At the age of fifty he was invited to be the first abbot of a new Benedictine monastery at Eynsham in Oxfordshire, where he lived until his death. His voluminous *Catholic Homilies* were grounded on the precepts of Saints Augustine, Jerome and Gregory the Great. In the disastrous years of the Danish military occupation, scholars in Wessex found consolation in evangelical pleading and the production of fine books. Æthelred's was a great age for both these activities.

Ælfric's prolific output included theological and scientific treatises, like that on the seasons of the year, *De Temporibus* (a version of Bede), the pedagogical *Colloquy* mentioned in the last chapter, and the first Latin-English grammar, based upon Priscian. The works are couched in a style remarkable for clarity and variety. The admirable translations of the first seven books of the Old Testament show that Ælfric was adept at suiting the syntax of prose to its tone. His final, and probably most ambitious work, the vernacular adaptation of the *Lives of Saints*, was completed in AD 998. The English Preface to this hagiography ends with an exercise in free alliterative verse, which he also used in the homilies, perhaps to facilitate declamation. An ear for rhythm, and a penchant for matching synonyms, are characteristic of Ælfric's later style, but the persistent alliteration is a novelty not welcome to readers attracted by the earlier artlessness. A fault of most Anglo-Saxon theological writing is its lack of original thinking; there is a heavy dependence on the Church Fathers, and an apparent unawareness of the illogicality of some reasoning.

G. K. Anderson in *The Literature of the Anglo Saxons* (Princeton, 1949) and C. L. Wrenn in *A Study of Old English Literature* (Harrap, 1967) rightly suggest that Ælfric's *Grammar* (c 1000) is a unique document; but it is largely a paraphrase of Priscian, who borrowed the eight parts of speech from Donatus (see pp 67, 423, 432). The time was not yet ripe for getting to grips with the essential differences between Latin and the Germanic languages; indeed, Ælfric assumes that Latin and Old English are on all fours as regards the assigning of parts of speech. The most valuable contribution of Ælfric is the *Glossary*, which is appended to a few of the fifteen extant manuscripts; the lists comprise equivalent terms in Latin and Old English, classified under common headings, such as 'parts of the body' and 'names of animals'.

Donatus, who lived in the fourth century, was concerned in his *Ars Minor* and *Ars Grammatica* to define grammatical terms. In the next century a more precise concept of the parts of speech was

offered by Priscian in the *Institutiones Grammaticae*. Neither
grammarian pretended that the relation of grammar to logic was
important. Ælfric believes that grammar is of paramount importance in the understanding of languages; his procedure in the
categories is exemplified in the definition of a *verb*:

> *Verbum* is word, and word getacnað weorc oððe þrowunge oððe
> geþafunge. Weorc byð, þonne ðu cwest: *aro* ic erige . . . þrowunge
> byð, þonne ðu cwyst: *verberor* ic eom beswungen . . . geðafung
> byð, þonne ðu cwyst: *amor* ic eom gelufod.

> *Verbum* means verb, and the verb signifies action, or passivity or assent.
> Action is when you say *aro*, I plough . . . passivity is when you say
> *verberor*, I am beaten . . . assent is when you say, *amor*, I am loved.

Another Benedictine, this time from East Anglia, was Wulfstan
of Ely, who attained the highest offices in Church and State. He
became Bishop of London in 996 and Archbishop of York in 1003,
where he was most influential for the last twenty years of his life.
He was frequently consulted by both Æthelred and Cnut, and was
skilful in drafting their codes of laws. In twenty-one sermons,
Wulfstan adopted the role of a Hebrew prophet, in a style hortatory
rather than persuasive. He chose public occasions as suitable
opportunities to be heard. Sometimes he rewrote Ælfric's homilies
in the style of a pulpit orator.

Wulfstan would occasionally append the pseudonym *Lupus* to his
writings, as he did in the title *Sermo Lupi ad Anglos*, which he
circulated to bishoprics in 1014, describing the miseries of the
nation during the Danish spoliations of Æthelred's reign. For a
statesman, the language of this diatribe is unusually emotive and
vehement; but it was written to rally the nation at the time of
Æthelred's flight to France in 1013.

Of this much-quoted *Address to the English* there are no less than
five manuscripts of different length, in the Bodleian, Cambridge and
British Libraries; they are all in West Saxon, and the differences seem
to reflect Wulfstan's own revisions. In her edition of the *Sermo*
(Methuen, 1939), Dorothy Whitelock points to a number of Old
Norse adaptations such as *þræl* 'slave' and *nydmage* 'kinswoman',
which were probably due to Wulfstan's long residence at York.

Most of Wulfstan's homilies are eschatological – they deal with
death, the Last Judgement and the after-life; but this address does
not, though it does end on a homiletic note. Wulfstan does not

142

favour colloquial Old English, but a florid, legalistic rhetoric, derived from Latin court denunciations, both strenous and factual. He is patriot-scourge to his countrymen for their contumely, vices and deplorable absence of leadership; he does not hesitate to use the catch phrases of a demagogue.

A single prose work that stands apart from the Church school, but belongs to the late tenth century, is the romantic fragment, *Apollonius of Tyre*. It represents about half of what was translated by an anonymous author from a Latin tale, of Greek origin. About this time there were many Greek Christian houses in Rome. The medieval vogue for Greek romances was just beginning in the desperate time of the new Danish irruptions. The third-century romance of *Apollonius* is one of the sources of Shakespeare's *Pericles, Prince of Tyre*; the Old English version, ending with a humble epilogue, is transparently Christian in tone. The manuscript of fourteen folios in Corpus Christi Library, Cambridge, represents a copy dated about the middle of the eleventh century. The Appollonius legend was retold in the Middle Ages, in *Gesta Romanorum* and Gower's *Confessio Amantis*.

It is a pity that this romance of adventure, of shipwreck, piracy, portentous dreams and fidelity in love, is known to students only in brief extracts. It is not without humour, and is told in a gracefully simple style. The conception is that of many picaresque oriental tales, such as those in the *Arabian Nights*. Fiction was an innovation in Old English literature, and love between the sexes had not previously been an emotion of epic and elegiac poetry, much less a theme of prose.

Literature is only one evidence of the reputation Anglo-Saxon culture acquired in western Europe. Two examples of artistic remains that have survived from the ninth and seventh centuries must suffice. Alfred's Jewel, preserved in the Ashmolean Museum, Oxford, was discovered in the parish of North Newton, near Athelney, in 1693. This jewel, about six centimetres long, is made of gold, embellished with cloisonné enamel-work; and it bears the inscription *Ælfred mec heht gewyrcan* ('Alfred ordered me to be made'). On one of its sides there is a figure clad in green and red, with a sceptre or staff in each hand; this probably represents either a saint or Alfred himself. The gold surface on the reverse side bears a delicate branching design. The jewel is believed to be a pendant originally attached to one of the book-marks (*æstelas*), delivered to bishops with a copy of Alfred's *Pastoral Care*.

The second exemplar, the Sutton Hoo Ship Burial, is even more memorable, since its discovery coincided with the outbreak of the Second World War. The long ship, twenty-nine metres in length and just over four and a half metres wide, was built of oak planks as much as an inch thick, and tapered to a point at each end. No nobler example of Anglo-Saxon craftsmanship exists. That it was a clinker-built vessel was established by the rusted clench-nails, still held in position by sand, after the woodwork had decayed. The ship was concealed under a mound of earth, with an east-west axis, on a site near an inlet of the Deben River, east of Woodbridge in Suffolk; it had been dragged from the estuary about the year AD 650. At this time a residence belonging to the King of East Anglia existed at the nearby village of Rendlesham, and many of his subjects had already been converted to Christianity. Yet the ship-burial has all the indications of celebrating a pagan rite, as such ceremonies did in Scandinavian countries.

An exceptionally varied treasure-hoard was uncovered at the stern-end of the ship; it consisted of personal weapons (spears, shield and sword), a magnificent iron helmet and armour (with jewelled epaulettes and sword-belt), the remains of a harp, a very large silver dish and a ceremonial whetstone, with bearded heads carved at one end. Among the imported objects were a bronze bowl from Egypt, of Coptic design, ten Byzantine silver bowls, and two silver spoons, engraved with the names Paul and Saul in Greek letters. Some reconstructed drinking horns, with silver mounts, proved to have the record capacity of nearly seven litres; and a huge golden buckle weighed nearly half a kilogram. Thirty-eight gold coins in a purse were discovered to be of Frankish origin, minted by Merovingian craftsmen. It was partly on this evidence that the date 650 was arrived at.

Strangely, however, the buried ship contained no evidence of human remains, and is therefore classed as a cenotaph, or memorial to an eminent ruler who may have died at sea, or been killed and buried elsewhere. The engraved silver spoons suggest that the absent victim may, indeed, have been given Christian burial prior to observance of the hereditary pagan rites. King Æthelhere of East Anglia, who is known to have been killed at the Battle of Winwæd in Yorkshire in AD 655, was a pagan, but his father, Anna, was a Christian.

The considerable historical value of the Sutton Hoo find exceeds its intrinsic worth; for it is of earlier date than all other known English regalia. It was therefore a munificent act of the property's owner, Mrs Pretty, to donate this find to the nation. The significance of the treasure in confirming accounts in the contemporary poem, *Beowulf*, is worth noting; for lines 36–48 of the epic describe a similar honour conferred on the Spear-Danes' ruler, Scyld Scefing, who belongs to the fifth century AD:

> They laid then the beloved chieftain, giver of rings, on the ship's bosom, glorious by the mast. There were brought many treasures, ornaments from far-off lands. Never have I heard that a vessel was more fairly fitted-out with war-weapons and battle-raiment, swords and coats of mail. On his bosom lay a host of treasures, which were to travel far with him into the power of the flood.

Anglo-Saxon decorative art resembles that of Scandinavia in its liking for animal motifs, such as appear on the Sutton Hoo helmet. By the time the Danes settled in England, their native art tended to be abstract, rather than naturalistic. Designs of most periods are, however, to be found on coins, for the Vikings, as traders throughout tenth-century Europe, preferred not to barter. They minted coins to augment those collected from foreign shores, and some attractive specimens were coined in York. Domestic utensils, especially with ornamental metal-work, were of the finest craftsmanship, if tending to puritanical simplicity. Sword-blades were imported in large numbers from the Franks, until in 864 their king, Charles the Bald, forbad the trade, because these splendidly-forged weapons were being used against his own people.

Viking exports were principally of skins, furs, whale or walrus tusks, and dried fish. Haithabu (Hedeby) in Schleswig became the principal trading-centre of Denmark, and Kaupang of Norway; while Birka and Gotland were soon to appear as the principal exchanges of Sweden. These were the defensible, strategic points and clearing-centres that yielded to archaeologists the greatest finds in Viking material culture.

CHAPTER VI

The Norman Conquest (1050–1100)

𝕊𝕊𝕊𝕊𝕊𝕊

VIEWS ARE DIVIDED on the merits of the reign of Edward the Confessor (AD 1042–66). Some hold that unfortunate errors were responsible for William the Conqueror's coup; others that the Danes introduced changes in the economy that were responsible for the feudalism of Norman times. Anglo-Saxon legal codes tended to endorse Germanic custom, which was rooted in the right of a *ceorl* to possess and cultivate his land, provided he assented to a period of military service. These codes entrenched, as precedents, decisions on common law taken in the courts. Undoubtedly the disorganization to the economy of continuous warfare, and the large tracts of land granted to housecarls, minsters and monasteries, helped to upset this traditional order before Edward the Confessor came to the throne. As early as Cnut's time the freeman lost much of his independence.

Edward was a gentle, peace-keeping ruler, whose piety was in the Alfredian tradition; but unlike his great predecessor, he seemed uneasy in office. This is not surprising, for he had lived twenty-five years in Normandy, only one in England. His private joy was to watch from his new residence the building of Westminster Abbey, a monastery founded west of London, on a marshy corner of the Thames, called Thorney. When he married in 1045, he produced no heir, and he delegated much of his authority to three provincial earls, Godwine of Wessex, Leofric of Mercia (husband of Lady Godiva) and Siward of York, who had inherited their titles from the king's predecessors. Edward reposed no trust in Godwine, who had been responsible for the death of his brother, Alfred, during the reign of the Danish king, Harold I. Although he married Godwine's daughter, Edith, Edward succeeded in ousting the father from power in AD 1051, when Godwine and his family took refuge in the Flemish town of Bruges.

In the first five years of his reign the danger to Edward's

succession came from Magnus of Norway, whose claims were pressed by Edward's wealthy mother, Emma. Her only son by Cnut had died; but a supposed plot with Magnus deprived her of property in Winchester, where she died in 1050. The threat of invasion from Norway ended with the death of Magnus in 1047, and two years later the king decided to disband the larger part of the navy, by reducing it from fourteen to five ships. In this way he was able in 1051 to relieve the country of heregeld; but by disastrously weakening the defence of the realm, he encouraged the Norman invasion. At this time, however, Edward considered himself secure in the friendship of the Duke of Normandy; a solitary security measure was to endow the populations of Sandwich, Dover, Fordwich and Romney with money from local court fines, in return for reserves of ships and seamen.

The gravest error of Edward the Confessor's rule was the bestowing of influential church offices on ecclesiastical friends, partly of foreign birth. Cnut had favoured priests from Lorraine, and Edward offered bishoprics to Normans; for instance, London to Robert, Abbot of Jumièges, and Dorchester to the royal priest, Ulf; and it was not long afterwards that Robert was made Archbishop of Canterbury. The unpopularity of these two appointments produced the crucial revolt of 1052, which resulted in the expulsion of both from office. Unwisest of Edward's pronouncements was, however, the promise in 1051 that the Duke of Normandy would be his successor; it was assumed that the appointment of a Norman as Archbishop of Canterbury was the first step to this end.

As primate of England in succession to Robert, King Edward appointed Stigand of Winchester, a politician whose choice was instigated by Earl Godwine. The exiled Robert appealed to Pope Leo IX, who immediately excommunicated the new archbishop; and so did three of Leo's successors. The clergy were disillusioned by this contretemps, and from 1052 to the Norman conquest newly-appointed English bishops were reluctant to be consecrated by Stigand. In fact, Edward's successor, Harold II, was crowned by the Archbishop of York, and not by Stigand, as stated in the Bayeux tapestry.

Archbishops were expected to travel to Rome to receive the pallium from the Pope, those of Canterbury from AD 925, and those of York from the early eleventh century. During Edward's reign successive Popes, by judicial acts, began to exert Rome's authority over the Church in England. From 1049 representatives had to be sent to the papal councils; and Robert, Archbishop of Canterbury, was forbidden in 1051 to consecrate Abbot Spearehafoc of Abingdon as Bishop of London, although the new bishop was the king's nominee.

Under the Danish dispensation, kings assumed the right to appoint by writ bishops and abbots to vacant offices, overriding the provisions of *Regularis Concordia* (Synod of Winchester, 970), which assigned to the relevant monks the right to elect such successors, subject to the king's assent. Historians have therefore blamed the Church for not contesting the prerogative of patronage; but the assumption of divine right, through the coronation oath, and the evident piety of both Cnut and Edward the Confessor, enabled these rulers to declare themselves as the Church's protectors.

In local administration the situation was different. Involvement being complex, the same kings delegated authority to political supporters, whose appointment as earls was in the king's gift. Such was the wealth of land and strength of arms acquired before the Conquest, that these earls assumed the right to hereditary succession, from which arose the power-struggle between Edward and Earl Godwine. The substitution of Morcar for Tostig, Godwine's second child, as Earl of Northumbria, in 1065, to which Edward agreed, was virtually under political duress. Earls did not, however, enjoy the privilege of appointing the king's sheriffs to collect their taxes, and supervise the administration of justice; though the sheriff invariably acted for an absent earl when the latter's political activities were thought to be in the national interest. In Norman times these sheriffs became presidents of shire courts.

The fall of Godwine arose from an instance of pardonable insubordination, when the earl refused the king's order to punish the town of Dover, which was part of his domain. Count Eustace of Boulogne, returning home from a visit to Edward, sought quarters for the night in Dover in a truculent manner; a scuffle ensued, in which twenty men were killed, and many wounded. Eustace complained to the king, who, without investigation, told the earl to punish the inhospitable offenders, his compatriots, with violence. At the time the king was in court at Gloucester, and Godwine gathered a force in the Cotswolds to demand the surrender of

Eustace and his followers. A delicate situation was saved by the arrival of armed detachments of earls Leofric and Siward. A meeting of the Witan was called in London, but Godwine and his son Harold declined to answer for their conduct, unless their safety was guaranteed by the giving of hostages. The Council's answer was to allow the recalcitrant family five days to leave England. Harold did not go to Bruges, but sailed from Bristol for Ireland; while Queen Edith (Godwine's daughter) was sent to reside in Wherwell Abbey. The estates of the entire family were confiscated.

In the following year Duke William of Normandy, with a large retinue, paid a courtesy visit to the court of Edward. Although the *Chronicle* does not mention it, the visit was undoubtedly to confirm the right of Norman succession. Edward had been strengthening his hold on Wessex by introducing Norman officials to control affairs, with which they were unfamiliar. Their poverty of English speech made them unpopular; and there was an unwelcome resurgence of sympathy for Godwine, whom the popular imagination saw as the champion of the Englishman's heritage.

In midsummer 1052, provided with a small Flemish fleet, Godwine was able to land, first at Dungeness, later on the Isle of Wight and at Portland; in the west country he was joined by Harold and a force from Ireland. He then mustered a well-manned fleet from southern ports between Southampton and Sandwich; and the weakness of the royal resistance enabled him to enter the Thames and anchor at Southwark. Stigand, then Bishop of Winchester, intervened, by arranging for the exchange of hostages. The Witan was called, and Godwine given an opportunity to plead his defence. The result was that king and council agreed to his reinstatement as Earl of Wessex, and the return of his confiscated estates. Civil order was restored with a promise that Norman officials, except those in the king's personal household, would be outlawed, one of these being Robert, Archbishop of Canterbury. King Edward never recovered from the humiliation of this reverse; for his troops had actually declined to fight against Godwine and their countrymen. This display of Anglo-Saxon fervour placed the house of Godwine in a powerful bargaining position for the rest of Edward's reign.

When Godwine died in April 1053, he was succeeded in Wessex by Harold, previously Earl of Essex; but control over East Anglia passed to Ælfgar, son of Leofric of Mercia. The loyal Danish earl, Siward of Northumbria, died in 1055, soon after his defeat of

Macbeth in 1054; three years later Malcolm ascended the Scottish throne. England's help was acknowledged by Malcolm's visit to Edward's court in 1059.

Harold soon became an influential personality on the Witan; his first show of strength came, however, in 1055, when he triumphed over a Welsh invasion of Herefordshire by Gruffydd ap Llywelyn, king of Gwynedd and Powys, who had made himself master of all Wales. In this attack Gruffydd was disloyally aided by Ælfgar, the new Earl of East Anglia, who was outlawed for an unspecified offence against the crown. The Welsh sacked Hereford and killed a number of clerics, before Harold could expel them to the Black Mountains; here the campaign petered out, and an amicable treaty was arranged between Harold and Gruffydd. By a later agreement, the latter acknowledged Edward as overlord, in return for the cession of territory between the rivers Dee and Clwyd in North Wales. The pact further restored Ælfgar to power, as Earl of Mercia, on the death of his father Leofric in 1057. Herefordshire became part of the earldom of Wessex, East Anglia was given to Godwine's fourth son, Gyrth, and the northern Thames counties were granted to Leofwine, a younger son.

Tostig, Godwine's second child, was already Earl of Northumbria. This placed the administration of all of the north, part of the Midlands and Southern England in the hands of the Godwine family, imposing a threat of isolation on Mercia. When Ælfgar was expelled in 1058, he was speedily restored by a combined force of Norwegians from Ireland, and Welsh under Gruffydd. Much damage was done to the countryside in this offensive. Ælfgar married the Welsh king's daughter, but died four years after his restoration.

The death of Ælfgar removed one of Harold's principal rivals, and enabled him to wipe out the Welsh threat to England's safety in the west. In 1063 Harold attacked and burnt Rhuddlan, the seat of Gruffydd's power in the north, destroyed many of his ships, and harried the whole of the Welsh coast. In the latter part of the campaign he was aided by a force of Tostig's cavalry from Northumbria. The invasion occupied three months, and was ended when Gruffydd was killed by his own men.

In 1064 King Edward employed Harold on a diplomatic mission to William of Normandy, the purpose of the journey being unknown; but the Bayeux tapestry states unequivocally that it was 'to confirm to Duke William his succession to the throne of England'. This embroidery (not a tapestry) was worked in coloured worsted on linen in England during the latter half of the eleventh century, at the desire of William's half-brother, Odo, Bishop of Bayeux, later Earl of Kent. Intended for public exhibition, the tapestry is seventy metres long, and just under half a metre wide; it is said to have been the handwork of the court ladies of William's queen, Matilda. It recounts, in pictures and words, events from the time of Harold's mission, to the culminating battle of Hastings, covering a period of approximately two years. Since some of the embroiderers were contemporaries of these events, their testimony, though biased in favour of William, has been regarded as reasonable evidence, unsupported by the *Anglo-Saxon Chronicle.*

According to the Bayeux tapestry, Harold, sailing from Bosham, is carried by wind 'to the unfriendly shores of Count Guy of Ponthieu', who sends men to seize and imprison him at Beaurain, where he is held to ransom. A spy informs Duke William, and the Count is ordered to release Harold, on payment by the Duke himself of the required sum. Under escort, the prisoner is taken to William, and received as a guest, with promise of marriage to the Duke's daughter. Harold assists William in a campaign against Duke Conan of Brittany, involving an adventure in the quicksands of Mont-Saint-Michel, and successful sieges of Rennes and Dinan. For these services Harold is knighted by William. A scene in the Cathedral of Bayeux depicts Harold touching two shrines and swearing allegiance to William, whom he recognizes as the future English king. On his return to England, Harold presents an account of his mission to King Edward, of which no record survives.

The remaining months of the Confessor's reign reveal a man of pious pursuits abandoning affairs of state to counsellors, of whom the most resourceful was Harold. A dangerous situation arose from internal revolt in Northumbria, which alleged excessive taxation. Cospatric, a respected northern thegn, had been killed under suspicious circumstances, and a group of rebels was determined to avenge his death. Taking advantage of Tostig's absence in Salisbury, they broke into his home, and boldly declared him an outlaw, by choosing Morcar of Mercia, brother of Edwin the Earl, as their man. Under his banner, the malcontents raided Danish Mercia, and took Northampton. Harold was asked to negotiate, but lacking bargaining power, failed. The king had no alternative but to acknowledge

Morcar as *de facto* earl; but the rebel force did not return without despoiling Northamptonshire.

King Edward died at Westminster within three months, without being able to attend the consecration of the abbey he had founded. He was in his sixty-fourth year, and during his last illness the Witan had already decided to elect Harold, as a tried leader, capable of dealing with any invasion from Norway or Normandy. He was crowned the day after the king's death, this being the first coronation to be celebrated in Westminster Abbey. As events turned out, his reign was to last less than a year; yet no king, except Edmund Ironside, used his time more energetically.

The beleaguered and beggared state, and the rise of landed proprietors, had rendered the country ripe for change. Too much land had been alienated from the peasants and the royal estates to housecarls, bishops, abbots and thegns, rewarded for services to the king. Dues, for which independent ceorls were liable, had become so burdensome, that many of this class preferred the protection and responsibility of a landlord. The feudal trend did not appear first in England, but in Normandy, France and Germany. Throughout western Europe petty principalities, supported by armed local horsemen, became the recognized defence against attacks from Norsemen in the north and west, Magyars in the east and Saracens in the south.

The *Anglo-Saxon Chronicle* has a reasonably full account of events that followed Harold's coronation on January 6, 1066; it records, as a popular ill-omen, the appearance of Halley's comet on April 24. The severe winter months had prevented invasive action from Harold's rivals, Harold Hardrada of Norway and William of Normandy. English Harold was not of royal blood, but his title, because conferred by the Witan, had more legality than the claims of his rivals. On his deathbed Edward the Confessor had placed his queen and realm under Harold's guardianship. The king busied himself visiting the northern part of his realm, introducing reforms, and entering into good relations with the Church. He consolidated his hold on the Midlands by marrying Ealdgyth, daughter of Ælfgar, the late Earl of Mercia, and endeavoured by resolute measures to promote national unity and discountenance civil factions. Ships were manned, and coastal defences strengthened, against invasion.

Norman William cannot be accused of precipitate action; he is said to have pondered the situation carefully, before sending a protest to Harold, on the ground of alleged perjury. There was no reaction from England, but William obtained support for his claim from Pope Alexander II and Henry IV, Holy Roman Emperor. He had secured immunity from southern attack on his duchy, by establishing overlordship in Maine and Brittany; and he had inherited from his father a substantial navy, with command of the important French Atlantic seaports. The building of his force of invasion took six months.

Meantime Tostig had been active raising Flemish troops on the Continent, with which he attacked the Sussex and Kentish coast in May, 1066. He was joined by seventeen Norwegian ships from Orkney and a number from Sandwich, until sixty were at his disposal. Sailing up the rivers Burnham (Norfolk) and Humber, he ravaged the neighbouring territory, until defeated by Earl Edwin of Mercia. With the dozen ships left to him, he then went to Scotland, to plan another offensive. Harold was not active in repelling his brother, but in preparing for a Norman attack, and decided in September to move his fleet to London, nearer to his headquarters.

A tragic interruption of the king's organization was caused in the same month by the Norwegian invasion under King Harold Hardrada; it was encouraged by Scotland and the disaffected Tostig. Hardrada had a European reputation as a warrior, having fought and governed in Sicily, Asia Minor, Persia and Constantinople. Over three hundred ships landed forces at strategic points on the Northumbrian, Yorkshire and Lincolnshire coasts. The King of Norway himself disembarked at Riccall, ten miles from York, which he captured; he defeated Edwin of Mercia at Fulford, two miles to the south, and induced the local inhabitants to join him in an attack on southern England. This did not get far, because Harold, advancing by forced marches, met him at Stamfordbridge, on the river Derwent, north-east of York. Not only were the invaders completely routed, but the King of Norway and Tostig were killed; so decimated was their army, indeed, that twenty-four ships carried the remnants home.

Harold was in York when he heard the news of William's landing in England on 28 September, first at Pevensey Bay, then at Hastings, where the Duke hastily constructed a fortification. Harold's southward march began on 1 October, and the two hundred miles to London were covered in less than a week. The troops he mustered came principally from the Home Counties and East Anglia, and contained many Danes; the force could not have exceeded nine thousand. Unfortunately, the king did not wait for reinforcements from remoter parts to join him; and the army that marched to Sussex was weary by the time of its arrival. Though William's array was somewhat smaller, it had a large proportion of trained horsemen, experienced archers and heavily armed infantry. In up-to-date equipment, this force of Normans, Bretons and French mercenaries, was superior to Harold's English army, which consisted almost entirely of infantry, without the archers that had been useful at Stamfordbridge. The only dependable force was the king's housecarls and those of his brothers, Gyrth and Leofwine. A motley array of peasants was capable of hurling stones attached to sticks.

Contact between the armies was made on 14 October, ten miles from Hastings, at Sandlake in Sussex, which Orderic, a French historian of the twelfth century, called *Senlac*. The saddle on which the historic engagement occurred was uninhabited, and on the fringe of a forest; the town of Battle derived its name from the Domesday Book's mention of the 'Battle of Hastings'. The principal descriptions of the battle are to be found in *Gesta Willelmi Ducis* of William of Poitiers, and the Bayeux tapestry. The inadequate account of the *Anglo-Saxon Chronicle* merely states that the struggle took place by 'a grey apple-tree', and that 'William came upon him [Harold] unexpectedly, before his army was set in order' (*Laud Chronicle*, manuscript D). Tradition has it that Harold's standard was planted on rising ground where the high altar of Battle Abbey now stands.

A reliable early description of the Battle of Hastings, the most significant ever fought on English soil, is not available, as French sources are one-sided, and the West Saxon chronicles understandably reticent. Modern reconstructions vary in interpretation of the events, the most convincing being that based on full investigation of the terrain by a military expert, Lt. Colonel C. H. Lemmon, in *The Norman Conquest* (Eyre & Spottiswoode, 1966). The fighting area of few other English battles can be more precisely located.

One account says that Harold's brother, Gyrth, tried to persuade the king to adopt a defensive role, until the expected reinforcements from country districts could reach him. The plan involved harassing the enemy by denuding the surrounding land of provisions; but

Harold declined to harry his countrymen, already pillaged by William, and decided on an immediate clash – his first strategic error. If surprised by the appearance of William's army on Telham Ridge (now Blackhorse Hill), the choice of a position for his troops was well conceived. Near the village of Battle the road from London to Hastings, in those days, as now, ran along a saddleback, and crossed a hill over 275 feet high; here is a natural watershed, with a south-facing front of eight hundred yards, falling away at a gradient of one in fifteen. The position seemed ideal for defence against cavalry, because the slope on the two flanks and rear was even steeper. There can hardly have been time to build the controversial palisade, to which writers, such as Wace in *Roman de Rou*, refer; but Harold hastily contrived a staked ditch, supported by an *abatis* of felled brushwood, with the branches facing outwards.

Around the royal standard on the crest of the hill were grouped the housecarls or professional troops, numbering just over two thousand, who wore helmets and coats of mail, and were fully armed, with spears, swords and battle-axes. The *fyrd*, or supporting army under thegns, were protected only with leather jerkins, and indifferently equipped with javelins, slings and agricultural implements. Harold adopted the traditional phalanx formation of housecarls, which presented a wall of shields some ten ranks deep; this had to be broken in hand-to-hand fighting. The Bayeux tapestry shows that the men actually stood sideways, because of the narrowness of their shields. Having fought with William in Brittany, Harold was well acquainted with the Normans' tactics and use of cavalry, which dictated his plans and choice of ground. He had visited the area only the year before.

According to the tapestry, William's column advanced 'in battle order, headed by the Duke and Bishop Odo of Bayeux'. It was accompanied by munition wagons with fresh supplies of weapons. The professional knights wore hauberks, protecting them to the knees, and pointed helmets with metal guards for the nose; and they carried shields that were kite-shaped. Cavalry were armed with lances, swords and maces; infantry, with spears, axes, swords and daggers. Archers used a short bow with slender arrows, whose range was a little over a hundred yards. The invading army was deployed in three divisions, Bretons under Alan Fergant on the left, Normans under William himself in the centre, and Flemish under

Roger of Montgomerie on the right. The respective strengths have been estimated at about 2100, 4300 and 1600, a total of eight thousand men, of which at least a third were mounted. In each unit archers were in front, and horsemen in the rear. The battle commenced at 9 a.m. and lasted eight hours – an unusually long period for hand-to-hand fighting. It implies that there were breaks for regrouping and reconsidering of tactics, and in this aspect William proved himself a master of flexible manoeuvring.

The battle can conveniently be divided into four phases. The first attack was delivered by the Norman archers, whose range-limitations brought them to close quarters and compelled them to shoot uphill, with little effect. Phase two was therefore an assault by the infantry, and this was met by a hail of varied missiles, more violent than the attackers expected. In hand-to-hand fighting the Saxon battle-axe proved a deadly weapon, because coats of mail were of inadequate strength. The Bretons, first on the scene, were in terrified confusion; furthermore, their flight encumbered the advancing cavalry. Perceiving an initial panic, part of the fyrd rushed downhill – a pursuit now thought to have been unauthorized. A rumour went around that William had been killed; but appearing without his helmet, he soon dispelled doubts, and led the cavalry to demolish the disorganized English pursuers. On foot, the ill-armed stragglers were at a disadvantage against the horsemen, who cut them to pieces. If this was a planned Saxon counter-attack, it was a tactical error, and premature; it meant parity of losses on either side.

Probably there was a lull in activities at this stage, to restore order. The third phase consisted of a cavalry charge by the Normans' finest horsemen; and the Duke's valorous minstrel, Taillefer, was granted the boon of striking the first blow. He seized a lance, jumped on his horse, and single-handed attacked the Saxon ranks, killing two Englishmen, before he was mown down by the housecarls. Because it was uphill, the cavalry charge lacked momentum; it was repulsed by the steadfast defenders. Another undisciplined sortie by the fyrd followed, which historians have interpreted as Harold's move to end the battle. It failed for the same reason as the first; headlong infantry can invariably be picked off by mobile cavalry. Most accounts state that the Norman retreat in this phase was feigned, and that it was the same horsemen who turned and mauled their pursuers. According to Lemmon, planning and co-ordinating such a ruse, in such circumstances, was most unlikely; a charge by reserve cavalry, on orders from the resourceful Duke, more probably turned the day. Lemmon argues that a 'retreat according to plan' is the chronicler's euphemism for an unforeseen flight.

The planning of the final phase was William's trump; it proved to be a combined operation by archers, infantry and cavalry, against the contracted defence on the crest of Caldbec Hill, displaying a weakened western flank. This move became necessary because the Norman knights had lost many horses. Infantry and cavalry advanced under a barrage of arrows fired over their heads; and one of these falling shafts struck Harold in the eye. It did not kill him instantly, as the tapestry suggests; for he plucked the arrow out, and slumped over his shield. The moral effect was disastrous. The cavalry surged up the easier slope on the west flank at about 3 o'clock in the afternoon, while Eustace of Boulogne attacked on the east side. This three-pronged assault overpowered the depleted English housecarls, and both the king's brothers were slain. Eustace, Giffard, Montfort and Guy of Ponthieu brutally hacked the body of the dying Harold, until it was unidentifiable. To make amends, William later ordered the altar of the abbey to be erected on the spot. The housecarls stood their ground, but according to tradition, nearly the entire body died with Harold. The remainder, and the bulk of the fyrd, escaped to the woods by sunset. There was an attempted rally, by some newly arrived troops, at Malfosse ('evil ditch'), a furlong east of the road; but the situation was once again restored by the Duke's presence of mind. He returned to the battlefield and erected a cairn of stones, his Mountjoy, to commemorate the victory; and Caldbec Hill has been called by that name ever since.

William slept upon the field of slaughter that night, and the next day (Sunday) was spent in burying the dead of both sides. Permission to remove bodies was sought by relatives and friends, and among the latter were two monks from Waltham, whose abbey Harold had recently founded. So mangled was the king's corpse that no one could recognize it, until Edith Swan-neck, Harold's mistress, was called; she had had three sons by the king before his marriage, and identified the body by a mark that she alone knew. According to William of Poitiers, the monks' request was refused, because the Duke wished Harold, as a man foresworn, to be buried on the seashore. Whether the Conqueror relented, or whether the body was secretly removed, is unknown; but it was interred later at

Waltham Abbey, and remained there until the dissolution of the monasteries.

Harold was a great king and an able strategist, to whom his followers were devoted, although he was of Danish blood. He lost the battle of Hastings through tactical misjudgements, and the very impulsiveness that so often had carried him to victory. William was astute, resolute and cool under adverse circumstances. Two horses were killed under him in that battle, and in the final incident of Malfosse, he appeared at great personal risk, brandishing a broken lance. He out-generalled Harold, because he had wisely refused to move from the commanding base he enjoyed on the south-east coast; his enemy was wrong in seeking him out before adequate preparations had been made; for cavalry and superior equipment turned the scales in William's favour. On 16 October, he withdrew for five days to the security of his fortress at Hastings and rested his army, the remnants of which Lemmon calculated as 5400 men. In another fortnight cavalry reinforcements from Normandy disembarked at Fareham.

Cautiousness and statesmanship are revealed in the Duke's next moves, which were against the towns of Dover, Canterbury, Winchester and London, in that order. His army had to live off the land, and his route has been determined from the Domesday Book, since it records the areas of spoliation. A week was spent at Dover, repairing the defences, and there a garrison was left. By the end of October, Canterbury submitted, and William then sent a sufficient force to occupy the south bank of the Thames at Southwark and Battersea; this was to keep London under observation. Under the influence of Edith, Edward the Confessor's widow, who was also Harold's sister, Winchester surrendered early in November. The Duke then crossed the middle Thames and strengthened positions at Wallingford, Goring and Dorchester, in the event of attacks being attempted from the north-west by the earls of Mercia and Northumbria. He then turned eastward and established observation posts on the Roman route through Cambridge to the River Ouse.

When he had virtually sealed off London from the rest of England, William was able to control access with as small a force as 1500 men, which he posted in the neighbourhood of Westminster, some two miles from the eleventh-century city. At Berkhamsted in early December, he was met by a deputation, among whom were Ealdred, Archbishop of York, and the heir apparent, Edgar the

Ætheling, grandson of Edmund Ironside. They guaranteed the hostages William required, handed over the city, and invited the Duke to become king. As his position in the south was still insecure, he at first refused the crown; but he accepted it later, on advice, when Mercia and Northumbria acknowledged him. He was crowned by the Archbishop of York on Christmas Day, 1066. Thus two million English people had been militarily overcome by a couple of thousand well-armed Norman knights.

That part of the Tower of London, known as the White Tower, built to overawe the people of London, is one of William's most memorable monuments; and during its construction he resided at Barking. At the end of the winter (1067), he returned to Normandy, taking with him Archbishop Stigand, whom he distrusted, and the leading English earls, lest they should foment a rebellion in his absence. Before he left, he imposed heavy taxation on the people, and confiscated the land of those who had fought against him. Others who had been sympathetic to Harold's cause were required to find redemption money. The deputy appointed was William fitz Osbern, the new Earl of Hereford, and Odo of Bayeux was made Earl of Kent, to guard the Saxon shore against threatened Danish invasion.

When the king returned in December, 1067, he had a not unexpected revolt to suppress. At Exeter he was able to arrange a treaty in three weeks by his military presence, in which English as well as Norman soldiers participated. A second rebellion in York broke out in 1068, which was more serious, because Edgar the Ætheling had defected to Scotland. William retaliated with caution by building castles at Warwick and Nottingham to support his advance; his entry to York was not resisted, and this city was again fortified. By negotiation, the king came to an agreement with Malcolm of Scotland not to press Edgar's claims. Returning south through east Mercia, William built castle-mounds at Lincoln, Huntingdon and Cambridge; they were gestures of power rather than potentially effective.

Up to this point William had tried to rule England through its established earldoms; but the rugged independence of the north looked to Scotland rather than southern England. When a major insurrection occurred in 1069, the king's first step was to make Robert de Comines, Earl of Northumbria; but in spite of an armed escort, he was trapped in the Bishop of Durham's house and burnt to death by the insurgents, who also killed his men. William re-entered York and restored order, leaving fitz Osbern to deal severely with the rebels.

The next threat to the crown came from Scandinavia, when a combined Danish and Norwegian expedition asserted its right to place Sweyn Estrithson, heir of Cnut, on the throne. A fleet of 240 Norse ships established itself in the river Humber, York once more being at stake; but the fearful Norman garrison of the castle set fire to the city. English rebels joined the invaders, and killed most of the Norman defenders. Such was the prestige and sternness of the king, that he contained this revolt, and another in the Mercian counties of Staffordshire, Shropshire and Cheshire. He conducted punitive campaigns in person, and ordered the mercenaries he employed to use scorched-earth tactics to quell what he regarded as treason. Much of northern England, and most of Yorkshire, were so devastated that the economy did not recover in William's lifetime.

Early in 1070 Sweyn himself appeared in the Humber and joined the Danish fleet, with which the king had made a non-offensive pact. In order to harass William, the Danes broke their bond and moved into East Anglia, using the Isle of Ely as the hub of their activities. Their plan was to rally English resistance leaders, such as Hereward the Wake, a thegn who took refuge in Ely from Lincoln. Aided by the new invaders, Hereward captured Peterborough, and managed to hold out on Ely until 1071, well after Sweyn had agreed with William to abandon his mission. Hereward was joined by the fugitive earl, Morcar of Northumbria; but the leaders were encircled by a besieging force, and had to make their escape by stealth.

It became clear that William would have to subdue Scotland, its king being in league with the pretender, Edgar the Ætheling, whose sister, Margaret, Malcolm had married. By 1070 the border raids between the Scottish Lowlands and Northumbria had become menacing to William's conception of orderly government. In spring 1072 the king decided to invade Scotland by land and sea, in order to stabilize the situation; there was no attempt to resist his advance, which took him as far as the River Tay. Malcolm offered hostages and terms, one of which was to refrain from sheltering Edgar at his court. The young prince then went to live at the court of Count Robert of Flanders, whose relations with William were cooler than those of his predecessors. There was a further precautionary invasion of Scotland eight years later, by the king's eldest son,

Robert. To protect the east-coast approach to the north, the latter built a fortress on the Tyne estuary, from which Newcastle-on-Tyne is named.

Partly to placate the Scots ruler, the king appointed, as Earl of Northumbria, Siward's son, Waltheof, who married William's niece, Judith. Six years later, this man betrayed the king's confidence by plotting with earls Ralf of East Anglia and Roger of Hereford, son of fitz Osbern, to dethrone him. So far as is known, Waltheof was the only English nobleman to be executed for treason.

Between 1072 and 1084 William was forced to spend a large part of his time in Normandy, to oppose political threats to his power from neighbouring principalities. The Count of Anjou disputed his right to the province of Maine, annexed before the English conquest. The struggle of rival potentates lasted for eight years, during which William was loyally supported by English as well as Norman armies. Philip of France disputed the possession of part of eastern Normandy, and defeated William in 1076, establishing Edgar the Ætheling as a vassal ruler.

The bitterest pill was, however, the disaffection of William's eldest son, Robert, to whom the opportunist, Philip, became an exasperating ally. Robert had already acted as his father's deputy in Normandy, and was virtually in control of the province of Maine, by the Duke's own dispensation, though he did not enjoy its revenues. The son's discontent found an outlet in an unsuccessful attempt to capture the Tower of Rouen, which ended in flight to the Count of Flanders, an uncle on his mother's side. Philip's provocations culminated in 1078 in William's second defeat, and his being wounded while attempting to capture the castle of Gerberoy on the border. He had lost none of his cunning in negotiation, however, for he managed to persuade King Philip to change sides. Two years later he was reconciled to Robert, who joined him at the English court.

From 1077 to 1080 the king lived mainly in Normandy, and temporarily neglected his English business. He could not have done so without an able deputy in Archbishop Lanfranc of Canterbury, an Italian scholar born in Pavia, who had formerly been Bishop of Caen. He was called to be primate in 1070, and soon became William's confidential friend and adviser on secular as well as ecclesiastical affairs. The correspondence of Lanfranc is a useful additional source for the history of the time.

Wales offered two decades of resistance to the Norman occupation, but was subdued by the active fort-building and military pressure of fitz Osbern, Earl of Hereford, and Hugh of Avranche, Earl of Chester. In 1081 the king himself was in command of an expedition to St Davids, the last of his territorial expansions in Britain.

Not until twenty years after the Conquest did William require the survey of his realm's resources contained in the Domesday Book. His life of campaigning made it necessary to enrol large numbers of mercenaries, which in England were used for the defence of the coast against Norwegian invasion. Quarters had to be found for them in various parts, and at one time he ordered them to lay waste the neighbouring country. He had, moreover, to devise an effective system for assessing and collecting dues and taxes. To this end he appointed disinterested commissioners for each shire, whose returns, based on personal testimony, were checked by the king's auditors. The ulterior purpose was, however, to watch the dealings of land magnates, at a time when many estates were changing hands. On 1 August 1086, all landowners of account, and tenants of earls or barons, were summoned to assemble at Salisbury, and ordered to swear fealty to the king. Although the number that attended could not have exceeded some hundreds, the king succeeded in limiting the power of the feudal lords, to whom hitherto the loyalty of tenants had been due. It was a shrewd move to make every citizen of substance responsible to the king, as well as to his barons. But recent research has shown that the purpose of the Domesday Book was more complex than at first supposed.

Before the end of 1086 William returned to Normandy, and the struggle for power in northern France was renewed; it had repercussions in England for centuries. The new contention with Philip of France concerned the border province of Vexin, which the French king annexed. William stormed the town of Mantes and set it in flames; but his horse stumbled as he rode through the town. He was thrown against the pummel of his saddle, and sustained an internal injury, from which he died at the Abbey of Gervaise on 9 September, 1087. He was buried at Caen in the Abbey of St Stephen, then in his sixtieth year, having been Duke of Normandy for forty-one years. In his duchy he was succeeded by the eldest son Robert; while William, his second son, was designated King of England.

Though the Laud manuscript of the *Anglo-Saxon Chronicle* charges William with avarice, extortion, power-seeking and savage game and forest laws, his solid merits are also recognized. He was (the unctuous cleric records):

> a man of great wisdom and power, and surpassed in honour and in strength all those who had gone before him. Though stern beyond measure to those who opposed his will, he was kind to those good men who loved God. . . . Among other things we must not forget the good order he kept in the land, so that a man of any substance could travel unmolested throughout the country with his bosom full of gold. No man dared to slay another, no matter what evil the other might have done him.

Order and stability were indeed social benefits, but the claims just made were not entirely true. There was violence, and frequent crimes were before the courts, largely over the redistribution of land. The 'cold heart and bloody hand' of the oppressor, so feelingly recalled by the Norse poet, Thorkil Skallason, were amply demonstrated by the savage game and forest laws, which punished minor offences of hungry peasants with blinding or castration; such whimsical cruelty was not alleviated until the signing of Magna Carta. The regulations were not the design of a conservationist, but selfish indulgences of the king's passion for the chase; 'the peace of the king's venison' was a cant phrase invented in William's day. A large part of the wooded kingdom became a royal game preserve, the only shires unable to contribute being Kent, Suffolk and Norfolk. In Hampshire two thousand people were expelled from sparsely populated areas to enlarge the New Forest, and it can scarcely be coincidence that two of the king's sons, Richard and William Rufus, were accidentally killed there.

The population between York and Durham was so decimated in retribution that a large part of Yorkshire appeared in the Domesday Book as 'waste' land. It is difficult to reconcile William's zealous churchmanship with the inhumanity shown to honourable opponents, whom he himself described as 'a fine race of people'. According to *The Ecclesiastical History* of Ordericus Vitalis, William confessed on his deathbed:

> I have persecuted its native inhabitants beyond all reason. Whether gentle or simple, I have cruelly oppressed them; many I unjustly disinherited; innumerable multitudes, especially in the county of York, perished through me by famine or the sword.

The principal instruments of the Conqueror's oppression were the shire court and its sheriff, whose fiscal and judicial function was often obscured by his police activities. After 1071 sheriffs were invariably foreigners of the baron class, and the king's most feared and hated officials. They were allowed to pay for the privilege of farming the shire, and some were guilty of corruption. Bishops and earls had long ceased to preside at shire courts, whose function became exclusively secular, with the establishment of separate ecclesiastical courts.

By 1100 the prolonged migration of Germanic tribes had ended. The following centuries saw the consolidation of western feudal kingdoms, mostly of German origin, and the gradual evolution of national languages, English being one. Most peoples of Teutonic stock who moved south became romanized; and with their assimilation to Latin culture a clearer picture of the linguistic situation in north-western Europe begins to emerge. The Germanic languages that advanced into the Middle Ages were: Gothic (until about the sixteenth century), Old Norse, Old Saxon, Old English and Old Frisian (sometimes grouped as Anglo-Frisian), and Old High German, a west Germanic form of speech that developed in the southern mountainous regions of the Alamanni and Bavaria. Written records of the seventh and eighth century only partly reveal how the languages of Germanic dialects survived; tracing their descent from the parent tongue, conjectural Primitive Germanic, is extremely complex.

Some part of the Nordic peoples must have settled early in the Scandinavian peninsula; but finding the climate inhospitable, they moved first to the Baltic islands of Gotland and Bornholm, and then to the north coast of Germany. These were the East Germanic speakers, Goths and Burgundians, whose tongue was closer to North Germanic (Scandinavian) than to the Western branch, from which English is descended.

As Tacitus showed in the first century AD, the structure of Germanic society was tribal. However aggressive and mobile the different tribal warriors were, they were conscious of an underlying unity through their idiomatic form of speech. As efficiently as Rome, *Germania* demonstrated that language is a powerful cohesive social force. The differentiation of Germanic divisions of speech nevertheless began many generations before the written documents appeared in the seventh century; in all linguistic aspects, these indicate innovation as the prime characteristic of the Germanic family. Regional differences arose, sometimes quickly, as in England, through contact with alien peoples; but an important factor much more often was the dominance of Latin as the universal language of those who were able to read, write and teach. Politics was not, up to the eleventh century, an influential factor in guiding the future of a language. The stability of late West Saxon writings was due to the discipline of a small intellectual aristocracy that controlled the monastic scriptoria. Cultural ambition alone enabled Charles the Great and Alfred to influence (not to mould) their respective languages; their helpers in both cases were Latin scholars.

After the fifth century, the people who occupied the land on both shores of the North Sea, the *litus Saxonicus*, largely determined what the future of English was to be. By AD 400 Saxons had moved down the Continental coast as far as northern France; and from this shore the invasion of southern England took place. The Saxon substratum of English is succinctly described by the pioneer of modern English studies, R. C. Trench, in *English Past and Present* (1855, pp 21–2):

> Anglo-Saxon is not so much one element of the English language, as the foundation of it, the basis. All its joints, its whole *articulation*, its sinews and its ligaments, the great body of articles, pronouns, conjunctions, prepositions, numerals, auxiliary verbs, all smaller words which serve to knit together and bind the larger into sentences, these, not to speak of the grammatical structure of the language, are exclusively Saxon.

Throughout the period of late Old English, the Scandinavian linguistic influence described in the last chapter was oral, since no significant contribution came from literature until the Icelandic *Eddas* of the latter half of the thirteenth century. It is significant that not one instance of a Scandinavian charter has survived in England.

There are, however, two Icelandic works of the fourteenth century that throw light upon important events leading up to the Norman conquest, and tell of an interesting sequel overlooked by many historians. The *Jatvarðar Saga* and the *Væringja Saga*, though discrepant in some details, record that an Anglo-Saxon emigration to Byzantium, of considerable dimension, took place sometime after 1075. Both sagas were edited by Gudbrand Vigfusson for the Rolls Series (1887–94), but the gist of what is here described comes from carefully researched papers by Christine Fell in volumes 1, 3 and 6 of *Anglo-Saxon England* (CUP, 1972, pp 247–58; 1974, pp 179–96; and 1977, pp 223–36). Several collateral sources are drawn upon and evaluated by the writer, including William of Malmesbury's *Gesta Regum Anglorum*, the *Speculum Historiale* of Vincent of Beauvais, and the *Chronicon Laudunensis* of an English monk of Laon, preserved in two thirteenth-century manuscripts.

After the conquest William, Duke of Normandy and King of England, had to contend with resistance movements already noted, some undoubtedly underground. Siward, Earl of Gloucester, sent messengers to King Sweyn of Denmark, entreating him to send help, but none was at the time forthcoming, because William also sent envoys, with offers of tribute in return for non-interference. After years of fruitless negotiation, a large contingent of dissatisfied Englishmen, including a dozen of aristocratic class, assembled a fleet of about 230 ships, and sailed down the coast of France and Portugal, through the Straits of Gibraltar, to Majorca, Minorca and Sicily. Arrived at Septem, on the north coast of Africa, they learnt that the Christian Emperor of Byzantium, Alexius (from 1081) needed help in beating off his pagan enemies; it is not clear whether these were Turks or Normans, but it was well known at the time that Norsemen, like the earlier Harald Hardrada, were already in the military service of the Emperor. Thus, exiled Englishmen of standing, such as earls and barons, came to join the powerful body of the Varangian Guard, and to distinguish themselves in battle.

Others of the party asked for land to farm, and were advised to seek it in the Crimea, once under Byzantine rule, but then occupied by heathens. Hugging the coast, they made their way past the mouth of the Danube, journeying for six days. They occupied fertile land free of tribute, named it Nova Anglia and called such settlements as they had London and York. Finally they sought churchmen to minister to them from Hungary, because they did not favour the eastern orthodox religion. In the course of generations they lost their English way of speech.

How different was this adventure from the better-known rebellion of Hereward the Wake, and how typical of the English need for liberty of thought and religion! The eleventh-century emigrés who anticipated the Pilgrim Fathers were not all Anglo-Saxons; it is clear from the accounts mentioned that the emigrants were accompanied by a large number of dissident Danes.

In the Old English vocabulary some five hundred loan words were incorporated from Latin, and may be conveniently allocated to two periods – early (450–650) and late (650–1100). It is safer to determine the period of the early borrowings, because of certain phonological transformations in the words. Sound change, together with the semantic character of the word itself, is a better criterion of approximate date than the borrowing's first appearance in literature. To the earlier period belong *cæppe* 'cap' (Lat. *capistrum*, 'halter'); *ceaster* 'walled town' (Lat. *castra* 'camp'), the second element in many place-names; *Læden* 'Latin'; *mæssa* 'mass' (Lat. *missa*); *sacc* 'sack' (Lat. *saccus*); *strǣt* 'road' (Lat. *strata* 'paved way'); *tæfl* 'gaming board' (Lat. *tabula* 'table'); *weall* 'wall' (Lat. *vallum* 'rampart'); *wīc* 'village' (Lat. *vicus*). Over a hundred of such words seem to have been borrowed from Vulgar Latin.

The loan words from monastic Latin during the later period were more numerous, and are characterized by a fairly general retention of the Latin vowels. The borrowings include a number of verbs, such as *aspendan* 'spend' (Lat. *expendere*); *pinsian* 'weigh' (Lat. *pensare*). Among the commoner noun words were; *cealc* 'chalk' (Lat. *calx*); *fenix* (Lat., from Greek, *phoenix*); *leahtric* 'lettuce' (Lat. *lactuca*); *lilie* 'lily' (Lat. *lilium*); *postol* 'apostle' (Lat. *apostolus*); *tigle* 'tile' (Lat. *tegula*). The eleventh century also saw considerable borrowings of a learned kind, including medical, zoological and botanical terms; e.g. *cancer* 'crab and cancer' (Lat. *cancer*); *plaster* (Lat. *plastrum*); *scrofula* (Lat. *scrofulae*, from *scrofa* 'sow'); *camel* (Lat. *camelus*); *lamprede* 'limpet' (Lat. *lampreda*); *cellendre* (Lat. *coriandrum* 'coriander'); *petersilie* 'parsley' (Lat. *petroselinum*).

The adoption and transformation of Scandinavian loan words, which began in the eleventh century, must be left to a later chapter.

CHAPTER VII

Some Aspects of
Old English Grammar

🝿🝿🝿🝿🝿🝿

GERMANIC LANGUAGES, such as Old English, are distinguished as a branch of the Indo-European family by the following characteristics:

(1) A sound-shift affecting the plosive consonants, which took place over a long period up to 500 BC. It therefore had no influence on words borrowed from Latin. The modifications are thought to have arisen among dwellers of the Bronze Age on whom the proto-Germanic language was imposed.

(2) A series of vowel changes, observable in strong verbs and elsewhere, which are reflected in Gothic, Old English, Old Norse and Old High German.

(3) Confining of the accent to the first or root syllable of words. The accent had been movable in the historical period of Indo-European, e.g. in Greek.

(4) Simplified declensions and conjugations, the effect of which was to restrict the number of forms in use; for example, loss of the dual number (except in the first and second personal pronouns of Old English), and of the vocative, ablative and locative cases. The Germanic group of languages has two numbers and four cases. The verb forms have been reduced; there are only two tenses, past and present; while an optative mood and passive voice are not required, the function of the former being supplied by the subjunctive in Old English.

(5) In the evolution of weak verbs the preterite was formed by the addition of a dental suffix, probably developed from the verb *do*.

(6) A weak declension of adjectives is added.

Old English, belonging to the Ingvaeonic or Western group of the

Germanic languages, was closely related to Old Frisian and Old Saxon; but differentiation into the regional dialects suggested by Bede took place for the most part in England. The boundaries were not, however, clearly defined, as a study of the language of the poems in particular shows. Prosody reveals, through metrical stress, the relative values of parts of speech in sentences, primary stress being located on nouns, in preference to verbs and adjectives. Stress or its absence is of real importance in determining the quality of Old English vowels and diphthongs.

So far as is known, there were no silent letters in Old English, the language being approximately phonetic. All the vowels of modern English were in use, with the addition of *æ* (ash). The diphthongs of standard West Saxon were *ea*, *eo* and *ie*; the conventional stress is on the first element, the second being only slightly heard. The quantity of vowels and diphthongs is significant, especially in the scansion of verse. At the end of short syllables all consonants might be doubled, except *w*. Voiced *f*, when doubled, usually became *bb*, and g doubled was written *cg*.

It is essential to grasp the phonemic structure of Old English to understand the complexities of its grammar. Vowels and consonants had, in the main, their continental quality; but some letters served a double function, voiced and unvoiced e.g. ð (eth) is the voiced form of þ (thorn). *S* and *f* are always voiceless in final positions; but initially, before vowels, they may have been voiced in West Saxon and probably also in Kentish. Medially, between vowels or other voiced sounds, they were always voiced e.g. *hafað* and *ōsle* 'ousel'. In reading, however, the usual practice is to voice these symbols only when they occur between vowels. When doubled, *s* was unvoiced, as in *cyssan*. In *libban*, *bb* was a voiced labial consonant [β], approaching modern *v*.

H was originally a back voiceless spirant [χ], the sound in *loch*. Initially, before vowels, it became the aspirate of the present day [h]; but medially and finally, before and after back vowels, as in *feohtan*, it retained its original pronunciation. It had this pronunciation [χ] also before *w*, as in *hwæt*. Medially and finally, before and after front vowels, it was a voiceless front spirant, as in *gesiht* 'sight'.

The main inconsistencies in the OE vowels were these: (1) when lengthened *æ* was raised to [ɛ:]; (2) the vowel *a* underwent rounding before *n*, becoming [ɔ:]; (3) in LOE *y*, long or short, was unrounded, and fell together with *i*.

What appears to be the irrational Indo-European system of grammatical gender is preserved in Old English, and had nothing to do with personification. Certain classes of names were probably grouped, because of an abstract or general meaning. Such words ended in *-a*, and according to the German grammarian, Brugmann, in *Das Nominalgeschlecht in den indogermanischen Sprachen*, these became feminine because of association with some common words, e.g. *mama* and *gena* 'woman'. Masculine nouns were simply those that were not feminine, and neuter nouns were a later development. Under the system of grammatical gender, compound nouns took the gender of the last component.

Originally there were two declensions of nouns in Old English (a) for stems ending in vowels, and (b) for stems ending in consonants. The nouns whose stems ended in vowels all belonged to the *Strong Declension*. The nouns whose stems ended in consonants were of the *Weak Declension*, if the final letter of the stem was *-n*, and of the *Minor Declensions* if the stem ended in any other consonant. Owing to the loss of final short vowels and consonants in primitive Old English, many different stems fell together in the nominative and accusative singular, and the characteristic distinctions of declensions fell away, unless they were classified according to their Primitive Germanic origins, thus leaving Strong and Weak groups as the only valid division in the period of literary OE.

In the so-called *-ja* stems, e.g. *here* 'army', the original j- sound occurs in oblique cases as *-i*, *-g*, or *-ig* e.g. genitive sing. *heries*, *herges*, or *heriges*, though *heres* is also found. In the *-wa* stems, the *u* or *o* in the nom. case is the original *w*, which remains in oblique cases before a vowel e.g. *bearu* 'grove', gen. sing. *bearwes*; *þeo* (sometimes *þeow*) 'servant', gen. sing. *þeowes*.

Among neuter nouns, the nominative and accusative plural in Primitive Germanic ended in *ō*. This inflexion later became *u*, which was retained in Old English after short stem syllables (those ending in single consonant), and lost after long stem syllables (ending in two consonants) e.g. the plurals *hofu* 'dwelling' and *word* 'word'. The loss of inflexion in the latter case took place about 700 AD. In plurals of nouns with short stem syllables, inflexional *-u* was sometimes weakened to *-o* in EOE and to *-a* in LOE.

The phenomenon of *umlaut*, considered later in this chapter, affected the declension of several very common nouns; *bōc*, *fōt*, *brōþor*, *mōdor* and *dohtor*. The radical vowel was mutated to *e* in the dative singular, and the nominative and accusative plural, though occasionally the latter did appear as *broþru*, *modru* and *dohtru*.

Sound changes are held to be of two kinds, isolative and combinative. A sound modified without the influence of a neighbouring sound in the word or phrase, is isolative, e.g. the diphthongization of pure vowels in OE. A combinative change is brought about by the juxtaposition of some other sound, e.g. the rounding of *a* before *n* in *land*. The chief reasons for phonological change may be summarized under the following heads: economy of effort, physical differences in the organs of speech, greater ease in production, the need for distinctness, or the instability of certain sounds in themselves. An unusual sound or form often owes its currency to a borrowing from another dialect, for instance the ME spelling *bury*, with the pronunciation *bery* [berɪ].

An initial problem in translating Old English is the multiple use of the demonstrative pronoun *se, sēo, ðæt* (masculine, feminine, neuter). It represents also the definite article of modern English; it may be used instead of the third personal pronoun; and its neuter form is frequently employed as a relative pronoun. In addition, the neuter form *ðæt* may serve as a conjunction, meaning 'in order that'; and the adverb *ðā* ('then' or 'when') is identical in form with the nominative and accusative plural. The context invariably determines function.

The evolution of the English relative pronouns is a complex study, beginning with several OE makeshifts. A true relative pronoun did not, in fact, exist in primitive Germanic or its descendants. Some Anglo-Saxon writers made do with the indeclinable conjunctive particle *ðe*, which was applicable to all numbers, cases and genders. The *OED* describes relative *ðe* as 'an unstressed or worn-down case or derivative formation from the stem *þa-* of *That* demonstrative' (vol. XI, p 260). Other OE writers, if referring to the third person, used this particle in combination with the personal or demonstrative pronoun; e.g. 'se guma *ðe hine* he healp'; or 'se guma *þone ðe* he healp'. But as such periphrases were strictly redundant, there were scribes who favoured the demonstrative alone: 'se guma *þone* he healp'. If the relative concerned the first or second person, the construction was usually *ðe ic* 'I who' or *ðu ðe* 'you who'. The periphrastic forms above-mentioned did not survive beyond the year 1100.

OE *hwā* and *hwilc* were interrogative pronouns, not relative; the derived forms ('who', 'which'), now used as relatives, began their dual function in the twelfth century. About the same time Middle English 'that' (OE *ðæt*) was appropriated for use in all genders, rendering the forms *se, sēo* and *ðe* unnecessary. 'That' for persons and things is the oldest of the relative pronouns in modern use.

The division of Germanic verbs into strong and weak was first suggested by Jacob Grimm in 1822; he accounted for tense change by means of changes in the radical vowel of stems of strong verbs, and showed that in the parent tongue such verbs had simple, primary meanings. The thirty forms in which regular strong verbs appeared in Old English are derived from four tense-stems: present (17), past singular (2), past-plural (10), past-participle (1). Grammars also describe the strong category as *ablaut* verbs, and distinguish seven classes, the last with some reduplicating examples. Ablaut, better known as vowel gradation, was the phenomenon uncovered by Grimm, and its importance to the Germanic languages will be discussed later.

Contracted strong verbs may be readily placed in their proper classes (1, 2, 5, 6 and 7) once their full form is identified. Contraction took place because the stem-final was *h*, which, owing to a phonological law, disappeared before vowels. The radical vowel of the stem was then amalgamated with the inflexional vowel, producing either the diphthongs *ēo, ēa* or the vowel *ō*. In class 1 are *lēon* 'lend', from *līhan*, *tēon* 'censure', *ðēon* 'thrive', *wrēon* 'cover'. In class 2: *flēon* 'flee', from *flēohan* and *tēon* 'draw'. In class 5: *gefēon* 'rejoice', from *gefehan*, *plēon* 'venture' and *sēon* 'see'. In class 6: *flēan* 'flay', from *flahan*, *lēan* 'blame', *slēan* 'strike', *ðwean* 'wash'. In class 7: *fōn* 'seize', from *fanhan* > *fōhan* and *hōn* 'hang'.

Weak verbs, peculiar to Germanic languages, and much more numerous, were derivative, since their stems were supplied by other words, such as nouns or adjectives. They are assigned to three classes; but the subdivision should not be pressed, since knowledge about them is partly conjectural. In class I the stem vowel in the present indicative had invariably been mutated. Thus *dēman* 'judge', is derived from *dōm* 'judgement'; *scierpan* 'sharpen', from *scearp* 'sharp'. The umlaut change of the radical vowel was

SOME ASPECTS OF OLD ENGLISH GRAMMAR

occasioned by an *i* or *j* in the primitive OE ending, as illustrated in Gothic:

Endings	Infin.	Past	Past Participle
OE	-an	-ede, -de, -te	-ed, -d, -t
Gothic	-jan	-ida, -ta	-iþs, -ts

Another feature of the class was *gemination*, i.e. doubling of the consonantal root final, which began before the differentiation of the various Germanic languages. Any single consonant, except *r*, tended to be doubled, if the preceding vowel was short, and the succeeding vowel happened to be *j*. Vowels long by nature (marked with a macron) have in OE to be distinguished from those that are long by position (followed by two consonants). The effect of gemination must have been to prolong the sound of the stem syllable; this again is evident in the scansion of OE verse, on the accepted principles of Eduard Sievers.

There are a number of weak verbs with *-ian* infinitives in this class, such as *nerian* 'save', Gothic *nasjan*. Some passed over into the second class of weak verbs in West Saxon. In this second class the infinitive always ends in *-ian* or *-igan*, and none of the stem vowels is mutated, unless mutation had already taken place in the noun or adjective from which the verb was derived. Examples are *lufian* 'love', and *lōcian* 'look':

Endings	Infin.	Past	Past Participle
OE	-ian	-ode	-od
Gothic	-on	-ōda	-ōþs

The third class contains only the four common weak verbs *habban* 'have', *libban* 'live', *secgan* 'say' and *hycgan* 'think'.

There are twelve important defective verbs in Old English, grouped as a past-present class. They were originally strong, but like similar verbs in Greek and Latin, lost their present tense, and came to use the preterite in all its six forms with present meaning. These forms determine the strong class to which the verbs once belonged. Many lack the present or past participle, or both.

173

Infin.	Present	Past	P. Part.	Orig. class
wītan† (know)	wāt	wiste	gewiten	1
dugan (avail)	dēah	dohte	—	2
cunnan† (know)	can	cūðe	cunnen	3
durran† (dare)	dearr	dorste	—	3
ðurfan (need)	ðearf	ðorfte	∸	3
unnan (grant)	an	ūðe	unnen	3
munnan (intend)	man	munde	munen	4
sculan (had to)	sceal	sceolde	—	4
mugan (can)	mæg	meahte	—	5
nugan† (suffice)	neah (3rd p)	nohte	—	5
mōtan (may)	mōt	mōste	—	6
āgan (possess)	āh	āhte	āgen	prob. 7

† signifies hypothetical infinitive

The anomalous verbs of Old English are *bēon/wesan* 'be', *willan* 'will', *dōn* 'do' and *gān* 'go'. *Wesan*, which supplies the past tense *wæs* of the verb *be*, must originally have been a strong verb of class 5. The verb 'to be' is derived from three different Indo-European roots, *es* 'exist', *bheu* 'become' and *wes* 'remain'. The significances here offered are obviously approximate. There is a semantic distinction between the two forms of the OE present tense *eom* and *bēo*. In late West Saxon *bēo* signifies futurity 'I shall be', as well as actuality; *eom*, suggesting existence, implies the present moment only.

In the outline given here prominence is allowed to the verbs, because they best demonstrate the Germanic nature of the language. Progress in the understanding of early Old English is not feasible without some knowledge of its phonology. Two of the sound changes (Grimm's Law and Verner's Law) serve to distinguish the Germanic languages from other members of the Indo-European family.

Accent. By accent is meant the degree of stress or pitch placed on certain syllables of a word; there are three degrees: principal, secondary and weak (more correctly, absence of) accent. Except in compound words, a secondary accent is separated from the principal by one syllable. *Stress* is expiratory production, *pitch* musical height or depth. In their accentuation, all Germanic languages use partly pitch and partly stress; but in the parent tongue stress accent is thought to have predominated. By the time of early Greek and Sanskrit, however, pitch accent had come into vogue. In Germanic speech, sometime before the operation of Verner's Law, stress accent was again the dominant one.

The early history of the Indo-European languages shows that the principal accent did not always fall on the same syllable of an inflected word. Movable accent was still operative at the time when the phenomenon known as Verner's Law came into being. At a later stage, however, the principal accent was restricted to the stem syllable in the Germanic group, and this very early caused the weakening, and finally the loss, of vowels occurring in unaccented syllables. The tendency is alive in Germanic languages today. Certainly, by the time Old English came to be written, the principal accent was on the stem syllable (invariably the first) and was not shifted, even when suffixes or inflexions followed. There was, however, a single exception to this rule, which resulted from word compounding, especially when an adverb or preposition preceded the substantive word, as in the verb *apéncan*.

Fronting of ă. This low-back vowel *a* of West Germanic occurs also in Gothic, Old Icelandic and Old High German. In Old English, however, it was fronted to *æ*, probably before the crossing to England, unless the *a* sound was rounded before a nasal consonant. In the case of short *ă* the influence of other neighbouring sounds, however, at some stage discouraged this fronting; for instance, when a back vowel originally followed in the next syllable, this syllable beginning with *p*, *w* (labials), *g*, *k* (velars), *l* or *r* (liquids). Phonology accounts for the different stem vowels of past tenses of cognate strong verbs; thus *lāgon* and *sāwon*, but *ǣton* and *trǣdon*.

The next six sound laws are important, and are placed in their probable chronological order:

(1) *Influence of nasal consonants.* This change apparently took place before the crossing to England.

   (a) e > i before nasal + consonant; e.g. *bendan* > *bindan*.

   (b) ŭ > ŏ normally, if a, o, e, long or short, occurred in the next syllable; *but it did not change if a nasal or a nasal combination came in between.* This accounts for the different forms *holpen* and *bunden*, past participles of class 3 strong verbs.

(c) In groups consisting of one of the vowels a, i or u + nasal + h, the vowel was nasalized (often shown thus ~), then lengthened, and finally the nasal disappeared; e.g. -unh > ūh. Thus from the old verb *þyncean* came the hypothetical preterite *þunhta*, giving OE *þūhte* (seemed).

(d) A similar loss of nasal, with compensatory lengthening of the preceding vowel, took place in groups consisting of vowel+nasal +voiceless fricative f, s or þ. Compare OE *ōþer* with Gothic *anþar*, *fīf* with Gothic *fimf*, *ūs* with Gothic *uns*.

(e) Other changes took place in combinations of a vowel before a nasal, not followed by the voiceless fricatives mentioned:
(i) ǣ (from Germanic ā) was rounded before a nasal consonant and became ō. Thus in the past plural of class 4 strong verbs are found *bǣron*, but *nōmon*.
(ii) ǎ before a nasal was rounded to a sound closely resembling [ɔ]. Lack of clarity concerning the sound is reflected in different orthographies *land* and *lond*, *dranc* and *dronc*.
(iii) ě before m > i. This explains the difference of the infinitives of class 4 strong verbs *beran* and *niman*.
(iv) ǒ before a nasal > u; therefore the same class of strong verbs has past participle *boren*, but *numen*.

(2) *Fracture or breaking.* This occurred before primitive OE back consonants *h*, *r* and *l*. When one of them was preceded by a front vowel, there was apparent difficulty in pronouncing the combination. The result was a glide sound to ease the transition, which eventually combined with the vowel to produce a diphthong. This diphthongization or fracture of the vowel took place in early OE, after the crossing to England:

(a) ě > ěo before r + consonant (e.g. *weorþan*, strong 3); before lc and lh, but not before other l groups (e.g. *meolcan* 'milk', *sceolh* 'wry'); and before h or h + consonant (e.g. *seoh* 'see thou', *cneoht* 'boy').

(b) ǣ (Gothic ǎ) > ěa before r + consonant (e.g. *stearf*, 'starve', *bearn* 'child'); before l + consonant in W. Saxon (e.g. *healdan* 'hold'); before h or h + consonant (e.g. *seah* 'saw').

(c) ĭ>ĭo before r + consonant (e.g. *liornian* 'learn'); before h or h + consonant (e.g. *miox* 'manure', from the hypothetical form *mihst*).

The corresponding long vowels were fractured only before h (e.g. *flēoh* 'flee'; *nēah* 'near'; *tīoh* 'censure').

(3) *Influence of initial palatal consonants (diphthongization of front vowels after c, g, sc)*. Next to a front vowel the consonants mentioned became respectively [tʃ], [j] and [ʃ]. The sound law considered deals only with the transformation of front vowels that *follow* these palatalized consonants. To facilitate pronunciation, a glide was developed in primitive OE, which combined with the succeeding front vowel to form a *rising* diphthong, one in which the stress falls on the second element. Later, this became a falling diphthong, by a normalizing stress shift. Thus

ǽ>ĕa, e.g. *ceaster* (originally *cæster*); ǣ>ēa, e.g. *gēar* (orig. *gǣr*); ĕ> ie, e.g. *giefan* (orig. *gefan*).

(4) *I or j mutation (palatal umlaut)*. This change probably became effective in the sixth century, about a hundred years before any written records of Old English. The modification of the accented stem vowel was due to the influence of *i* or *j*, which originally followed in the next syllable. The speaker probably anticipated the second vowel sound, while making the first. There is abundant evidence that early Old English was spoken deliberately, and it should be remembered that *i* and *j* are the highest front vowels.

I-mutation may be readily observed in the second and third person singular, present indicative of strong verbs, where the old endings were *-ist* and *-iđ*. The *i* became assimilated and caused fronting of the stem vowel. Examples are as follows:

ŭ>ў, *cuman*, but *cymst* (orig. *cumist*)
ŏ>ĕ, *dohtor*, dative sing. *dehter* (orig. *dohtri*)
ă/ŏ>ĕ, *mann*, but plural *menn* (orig. *manniz*)
ǽ>ĕ, *steppan* (Gothic *stapjan*)
ū>ȳ, *brūcan*, but *brȳcst*
ō>ē, *dōm*, but *dēman* (orig. *domjan*)
ā > ǣ, *hāl* (whole), *hǣlan* (heal). Gothic *hailjan*.
ĕa >ĭe, *eald*, but *ieldra*; *gelēafa* (belief), but *geliefan*
ĕo>ĭe, *weorpan*, but *wierpđ*; *hrēowan*, but *hrīewđ*

(5) *U or o mutation (back umlaut).* The explanation of this phenomenon is similar to the last. The change affects the accented short vowels *a*, *e* or *i*, for the reason that *u* or *o/a* follows in the next syllable. The vocal organs, anticipating a back vowel, developed a back glide that combined with the preceding front vowel (*a* by this time had become *æ*) and produced diphthongs:

ă>ĕa, *caru (cæru)>cearu* 'care'
ĕ>ĕo, *weruld > weoruld* 'world'
ĭ>ĭo, *miluc>mioloc* 'milk'

This change took place about the end of the seventh century, usually before single consonants. It is exceptional rather than regular in West Saxon.

(6) *Influence of w.* This follows as a further development after u-mutation. A preceding *w* often changes *ĕo* to *o*, *u* or *y*, and *ĭo* to *u*; e.g. *weoruld* may be found written *woruld*. Early OE *widuwe* 'widow'>*wioduwe>wuduwe*.

The six sound laws just described trace the early descent of Old English from the Germanic group of languages. The next section will briefly consider the Indo-European family itself, taking the history of Old English back a step further. This is desirable to get to grips with the problem of *ablaut*, or vowel gradation.

Vowel Gradation. In his *Old English Grammar* (p 107) Wright says: 'every syllable of every word of whatever part of speech contains some form of ablaut.' This is plausible, though a difficult pronouncement to prove.

Owing to conservatism regarding the free accent of primitive Indo-European, Greek, Sanskrit and Balto-Slavonic are more closely related to the parent tongue than other members of the family. Those three branches in consequence faithfully adhered to grammatical inflexion. Languages such as the Germanic, Latin and Celtic groups, on the other hand, early fixing the accent on the root syllables of the word, underwent loss or simplification of inflexions. It is logical that this loss should result from the weakening of that part of the word which was habitually unaccented.

Greek seems to have preserved with great fidelity the vowel

system of primitive Indo-European, but the consonant system changed greatly. Of Sanskrit the opposite is true. In Germanic, vowel change was slight, but consonant change considerable. Complexity of grammar and inflexion is a characteristic of a language in an early stage of development.

Vowel gradation is found in all languages descended from primitive Indo-European; consequently it must have existed in the parent speech. It occurs in both stems and inflexions, and implies an order of variation in the *quantity* or *quality* of vowels in words etymologically related. Both kinds, quantitative and qualitative, are caused by free or shifting accent. The first studies the lengthening or shortening of vowels that took place in primitive Indo-European itself, and was due to the sensitiveness of vowel sounds to accent. According to the degree of strength with which any syllable was uttered, its vowel tended to preserve or increase its length. Vice versa, where the volume of stress was decreased; and the vowel tended to vanish where stress was lost completely.

Qualitative gradation is a variation of the vowel itself, probably due to sound changes in primitive Indo-European, of which the causes are unknown. There may have been a grammatical function, as in Semitic languages; but other factors, such as pitch or stress, were more likely the source. The full-grade vowel *e* may have occurred in a syllable with rising tone or stress, whereas the second-grade vowel *o* might appear in a syllable with falling tone or stress.

The first gradation is known as the e-o series, in which OE verbs like *beran*, and nouns such as *nest*, are located. For Germanic languages this is the most important series.

In the second or o-series, quantitative gradation is found only. Latin *ŏculus* and *atrōx* ('fierce', literally 'black-eyed') exemplify the incidence.

To the third, or a-o series, belongs the class 6 OE strong verb *faran*, and many etymologically related words.

The causes of the phenomena were widely separated in time, and specimens taken from different languages are like fossils in successive stratifications. The student of OE has the not always rewarding task of tracing the vowel-sound considered, first to its immediate forebear, Germanic, and then to its Indo-European original. Vocalic vowels are those that became so weakened by the shifting of stress to another syllable that they combined with the succeeding consonant *l*, *m*, *n*, *r*, by means of an intervening back glide. In primitive Indo-European the vocalic sounds belonged to the vanishing grade. A modern English example may help to illustrate the phenomenon. Partners A and B are engaged in a doubles game of tennis, and in the course of a rally the following interchange takes place (the heavily stressed words are italicized):

A. *Can* you?
B. No! C'n *you*?

The accent being shifted to *you*, *a* in *can* is no longer pronounced.

Classes 1 to 5 of the OE strong verbs belong to the e–o series of vowel gradation, subsequent variations being due to sound changes in the Germanic languages. The sixth and seventh classes employ a mixture of the ablaut series, not always easy to distinguish, owing to the falling together in primitive Germanic of Indo-European *a*, *o* and [ə].

An instructive word to trace to the original is 'tooth'; from OE *tōþ*, from Germanic *tanþ*. By influence of the Germanic nasal consonant, *ă* was nasalized and lengthened to *ō*, the *n* being dropped before *þ* (Change (1) above). Going further back, the phonologist will conclude that the hypothetical Indo-European stem was *dont* (cf. Greek stem *odont-*), because:

Ger. t<IE d (by Grimm's law, see next section)
Ger. ă<IE ŏ

Owing to the shifting of stress to the inflexion, the Indo-European stem *dont* was, at some time, weakened to *dnt*. The later history of the stem is traced, for instance, through Latin *dent* and Gothic *tunþ*; but Germanic *tanþ* is shown to be phonologically unrelated to either. All known forms of the word revert to the Indo-European syllabic stem *dnt*, and the vowel in OE *tōþ*, in spite of its length, is said to belong to the vanishing grade of the o-series.

Grimm's Law (First Germanic sound-shift). Jacob Grimm's interest in historical grammar was aroused in 1812, when he was called upon to review Rasmus Rask's *Introduction to Icelandic Grammar*, published in the previous year. The first volume of his own *Deutsche Grammatik* appeared in 1819, and was the beginning of a full-length investigation into the development of the Germanic languages. Grimm tabulated the results of observations on the behaviour of Germanic plosive consonants; but the findings only partially illuminate Grimm's law, as known to modern philologists. The research was nevertheless worthwhile because it vindicated Germanic as an off-shoot of the Indo-European family.

The first Indo-European consonants affected by the sound-shifting, sometime before 500 BC, were the voiceless plosives *p, t, k*. The various changes covered about six centuries, and came about in four stages:

(1) By the first shift the three voiceless plosives became aspirated – *ph, th, kh* [χ]. The voiced plosives *b, d, g* then followed suit.
(2) The aspirated voiceless plosives of (1) became the corresponding fricatives *f, þ,* and *h*.
(3) About the same time as (2) *voiced* aspirated plosives (*bh, dh* and *gh*) became the corresponding voiced fricatives (except at the beginning of a word) – the result was *β* [v], *ð* [originally dh], and *ʒ* [the g-sound in *rouge* is only an approximation].
(4) About the second century AD the voiced fricatives just mentioned became unvoiced – *p, t, k*.

In summary, the outcome was as follows:

Indo-European				*Germanic*		
p	t	k	>	f	þ	h
b	d	g	>	p	t	k
bh	dh	gh (of Sanskrit)	>	β	ð	ʒ

At first sight one does not readily perceive how OE *ēa* (river) is related to Latin *aqua* [akwa], in which the medial consonant was obviously aspirated [khw] by Grimm's law. The following suggests what probably happened:

First *aqua*>Gothic *ahwa* (changes (1) and (2)). The Germanic stem *ăh*>*æh* (fronting)>*eah* (fracture)>*ēa* (by loss of *h* between vowel and semi-vowel *w*; the latter was then vocalized to *u* at the end of a syllable, which combined with the preceding diphthong and lengthened it). All changes are accounted for by the preceding phonological laws.

There were certain exceptions to Grimm's law:

(a) In the case of *s* + voiceless plosive, the latter was not shifted: e.g. Latin *stare*, OE *standan*. Sometimes an unexplained intrusive *s* was added before the stem, giving rise to related forms in Old English:

e.g. OE haga 'hedge'   scaga 'wood'
       þeorf 'want'   steorfan 'starve'

(b) The consonant *t* was unshifted in the combination *tt*, but became *ss*, e.g. in the past-present verb wītan: preterite witte > wisse > wiste.

Philologists act upon the assumption that sound laws should admit of no exception; there should be an explanation of variations. If apparent exceptions to established rules do occur, they may be due to (1) forms taken from another dialect or language; (2) changes brought about by the influence of other sounds in the same word or sentence; or (3) analogy. By analogy is meant causal association, according to either grammatical use, meaning or similarity of sound. Nouns declined, verbs conjugated, and adverbs formed from adjectives according to a recognized system, are said by grammarians to invoke the principle of analogy.

In 1876 Karl Verner, a Danish philologist, in a paper entitled 'An Exception to the First Sound Shift', explained certain exceptions to the law of Grimm, which the latter himself did not understand.

Verner's Law depends on the fact that the accent had not yet been fixed on the stem syllable of a word in Primitive Germanic. The law would then have come into operation after the first two changes of Grimm's law, because it affects the voiceless fricatives brought about by these changes. The probable time was between the fourth century BC and the second century AD. The law is in two parts:

(1) A voiceless fricative tends to become voiced, if the vowel immediately preceding the fricative does not bear the principal accent of the word.
(2) In addition, a voiceless plosive standing next to the fricative usually becomes voiced also.

Examples of the latter tendency are frequently met with in modern English; e.g. exalt [gz], but exaltation [ks]; a*b*solve [bz], but a*b*solution [ps]. The exceptions to (2) of the above law are the combinations *fs*, *ft*, *hs*, *ht*, *sk*, *sp*, *ss*, *st*; they were not subject to this change.

The law operated regularly in Primitive Germanic; but in its descendants various changes occurred. In the following table, reflecting what took place in Old English, the final column shows variations according to the position of the accent:

Primitive Germanic		Primitive OE	Variations
(1) f > β[v]	>	f	f : f (because f and v fell together)
(2) þ > ð	>	d	þ : d
(3) s > z	>	r	s : r
(4) h > ȝ	>	g	h (or loss of h)* : g
(5) nþ > nȝ	>	nd	þ : nd [see nasalization (d)]
(6) nh > nȝ	>	ng	h (or loss of h) : ng [nasalization (c)]

*h fell away between vowels, and between r or l and a vowel, e.g. fanhan > fōhan > fōn.

The variations of the last column are found most commonly in strong verbs. For some reason the accent in the past tense plural, the past subjunctive, the past participle, and sometimes in the infinitive, did not originally fall on the stem syllable, but on the *last* syllable. In such cases the second variant is found; but in other parts of the verb, where the accent fell on the stem syllable, the original Germanic variant appears.

The examples follow the sixfold tabulation above:

(1) The f variation disappeared.

(2)	snīþan	snāþ	snidon	sniden	'cut'	class 1
(3)	cēosan	cēas	curon	coren	'choose'	class 2
(4)	flēon	flēah	flugon	flogen	'flee'	class 2
(5)	fīþan*	fand	fundon	funden	'find'	class 3
(6)	fōn (fehð)	fēng**	fēngon	fangen	'seize'	class 7

*fīþan is the hypothetical form which originally must have existed (cf. Gothic finþan, O.Saxon fīþan). The -nd- in *findan* and *fand* (infinitive and past singular) arose by analogy with the past plural and past participle.
**fēng in the past singular was formed by analogy with the past plural.

The results of Verner's law were often disturbed by analogy in Old English.

Many causative verbs which are weak of the first class, with mutated stem vowels, demonstrate the operation of Verner's law, because the accent was originally on the suffix. Examples of causative formations are:

> līþan (class 1, 'go'), pret. lāþ, whence old causative verb laþjan, which became lǣdan (by umlaut), meaning 'lead' (to cause to go).
>
> rīsan (class 1, 'rise'), pret. rās, whence causative verb rasjan, which became rǣran (umlaut), meaning 'raise' (to cause to rise).
>
> genesan (class 5, 'recover') pret. genæs, whence causative næsjan, which became nerian (umlaut), meaning 'save' (cause to recover).

In nouns, Verner's law explains many consonantal differences between Old English and other Indo-European languages:

> OE lagu 'sheet of water', Latin lacus 'lake'; cf. modern English lagoon and lake; g < h (Verner's law) < k (Grimm's law).

In OE magu 'son', Gaelic Mac- (e.g. Macdonald), the change came about in the same way.

SYNTAX

It is impossible to define syntax in a way that will satisfy all students of language; one begins modestly by suggesting that syntax is a way of combining words, in order to convey meaning to a listener or reader. In speech, a conventional order and intonational stress are the primary psychological factors; in writing, acceptable literary relationships of words, or word-groups, make for greater intelligibility. Orderly sequence, and a rhythm determined by motivated stress, have always made for clarity of understanding. But the interpreter decodes for sense, whether he reads or listens, and audience response depends largely on what Edward Sapir calls his 'inventory of experience' (Language, 1921, ch. V). Parts of speech, concords and clausal relationships are always ex post facto judgements, but none the less valuable.

The syntax of Old English has to be deduced from written documents. Ælfric's *Colloquy* is one of few dependable examples of everyday dialogue, but it is a gloss used in teaching Latin, an instance of *langue*, rather than *parole*. If de Saussure was right in holding that language and writing are two distinct systems of signs (*Course in General Linguistics*, 1960, ch. VI. 2), there is no alternative to a grammatically oriented and diachronic treatment of OE syntax.

The logical terms *subject* and *predicate* did not enter English grammar until the seventeenth century; and this is not surprising, since logical procedures are less than adequate to describe the early development of language, as phonology alone demonstrates. The symbolism of language may have the tacit approval of society; but no rational community is likely to have sanctioned an artificial system of communication so unconnected with the facts of nature, if the function of language was information only.

For the purpose of this section, it is assumed that syntax means the arrangement of words in sentences, including the functional relationships of smaller groups, with a view to conveying sense. Three main aspects will be considered: word order; flexional modifications in cases, tenses and moods; and the symbolic relationships of words. Phrasal idiom, which much extends the subtlety of thought, comes under the last head.

Word Order
Like Latin, Old English was an inflected language, and the same importance did not attach to the order of words as in modern English. The inflexion of the primary parts of speech – nouns, pronouns, adjectives and verbs – was not, however, deemed sufficient to determine every function in the sentence. In considering word order, the lesser parts of speech are customarily grouped together as particles (P).

S. O. Andrew in *Syntax and Style in Old English* (CUP, 1940) shows that there were some important principles of order, more especially in OE prose. The common word-collocation of modern English (subject-verb-object) was operative, though with lesser frequency, as early as the writings of King Alfred. But the order SVO was departed from under certain circumstances, both in principal and subordinate OE classes. Adverbs derived from the demonstrative pronoun, *ðā, ðonne, ðǣr*, if used at the beginning of a principal clause, were invariably followed by the finite verb, not the subject; the most frequent order then is PVOS. This applies, however, only if the adverb concerned is the first word; when *ond* or any other word precedes it, inversion of the subject does not take place. In temporal sentences, *ðonne* always has present or future implications; when used in the past tense the sense is frequentative. *Ða* is employed for a single event.

In subordinate clauses, including relative ones, the subject is usually retained after the conjunction, but the finite verb is placed at the end (PSOV). Often the same order obtains in the second principal clause of compound sentences. The notion of subordination, as different in function from the main clause, was not fully understood, especially when the latter was introduced by an adverb of time or place. *Beowulf* 1188–91 reads as follows (Klaeber's text):

> Hwearf þā bī bence, þǣr hyre byre wǣron,
> Hrēðrīc ond Hrōðmund, ond hæleþa beorn,
> giogoð ætgædere; þǣr se gōda sæt,
> Bēowulf Gēata be þǣm gebrōðrum twǣm.

Andrew observes (p 23) that editors punctuate before *þǣr se gōda sæt* (1190) as though this was a principal clause, whereas the best sense and better word order are secured by regarding this as a subordinate one:

> Then she turned to the bench, where her sons were, H and H, and the sons of the heroes, the younger men together, *where* the noble Beowulf of the Geats sat by the two brothers.

The narrative style of Ælfric, as the following extract on St Gregory shows, bears a close resemblance to that of modern English:

> Hē wæs swīþe wacol on Godes bebodum, þā þā hē sylf herigendlice leofode, and hē wacollice ymbe manegra þēoda þearfe hōgode, and him līfes weig geswutelode. Hē wæs from cildhāde on bōclicum lārum getȳd, and hē on þǣre lāre swā gesæliglice þēah, þæt on ealre Rōmana-byrig næs nān his gelica geþuht. (H. Sweet, *Selected Homilies*, p 56.)

> He was very circumspect in God's commandments, since he himself *lived* praiseworthily, and he watchfully *meditated* on the needs of many peoples, and *manifested* to them the *way of life*. He was from childhood *instructed* in book-learning, and *throve* so happily on that learning that in every Roman city no man *was thought* his equal.

The principal difference in these passages is in the positioning of the verbs, three of which (*hōgode, geswutelode* and *þēah*) are in the principal clauses of compounded sentences.

In Old English the chief other causes of inverted word order are imperatives followed by the second personal pronoun and interrogative sentences. To limit the frequency and awkwardness of many interrogative constructions, the function-word *do* gained ground in modern English, partly because it preserved the subject before the infinitive of the notional verb. Periphrastic exigencies in Old English will be discussed later.

The place of personal pronouns in relation to the verb in principal clauses is either immediately before or after. As subject, a personal pronoun would normally come first in affirmative sentences, except after the demonstrative adverbs already mentioned. When several pronouns appear in a clause (principal or subordinate) the order of precedence is (1) subject (2) direct object (accusative) and (3) indirect object (dative), unless a particular pronoun is given prominence through stress. Pronouns were usually unstressed words.

Negation is of special interest in Old English, because the particle *ne* served as a kind of prefix to the verb, and was sometimes combined with it. To make sure that this negative combination was recognized, it became the first word of a principal clause; e.g. Ælfric, *Catholic Homilies*, vol. II, p 36, line 6: 'Ne magon wē mid ānum mūðe bletsian and wyrian.'

Flexional Syntax
This is the most significant aspect of Old English syntax. Only the major potential is here noticed.

Nouns – Cases
(1) *Accusative.* In addition to employment as the object of a transitive verb, the accusative is found in several circumstances similar to Latin usage – (a) to express duration of time; (b) with impersonal verbs; (c) as an object cognate to the verb; and (d) as the subject of another verb, invariably in the infinitive, to complete the predicate, e.g. hē hierde þæt cīld sprecan. The prepositions which in some circumstances have the following noun in the accusative case in OE are *for* when it means 'in place of', *fore* 'before', *geond* 'throughout', *in/on* 'into' – motion towards, *ofer* various contextual meanings, *ongēan* 'towards', *oð* 'until', *ðurh* 'through', *wið*

'against', *ymb* 'about', *ymbutan* 'around', and *undenneoþan* 'below'. *Fore, ongean, oð and ymb* sometimes also take the dative. *Đurh* may occur with the accusative, but only when used in a temporal sense.

(2) *Genitive.* Many categories are somewhat arbitrary.

(a) *Partitive.* This resembles the usage of Latin. Idiomatic use of this genitive, with numerals is common in OE: e.g. Đā rād hē in wīce ðreora sum (Then he and two others rode into the village). 'Each one' appears in OE as *ānra* gehwilc. Grammarians sometimes regard as partitive genitives the use after verbs that express emotional states, e.g. *brūcan* 'enjoy', *gefēon* 'rejoice', *willan* 'desire'.

(b) It is difficult to classify semantically the many other verbs followed by the genitive case. Such are *beniman* 'deprive', *hrinan* 'touch', *onfōn* 'take', *wealdan* 'rule' etc; e.g. Cynewulf benam Sigebryht his *rīces* (kingdom).

(c) *Origin and relationship.* This is the commonest use of the genitive, e.g. hē wolde gesēcan *helle* godu 'he wanted to find the god of Hades'; *Pharāōnes* dohtor 'Pharaoh's daughter'.

(d) *Quality or state.* Usually after adjectives, e.g. *wīges* heard 'brave in war'.

(e) *Adverbial uses,* e.g. *ānstreces* 'continuously', *nihtes* 'by night'.

(f) *Prepositional uses.* It would be hard to name a preposition that governs only the genitive; but the case is found with *andlang/ andlanges* 'along/alongside', *tō* 'to', *tōweard* 'towards', *wana* 'lacking', *wið* 'towards'.

A number of OE verbs govern two objects, one of which is the genitive, the other either accusative or dative. *Biddan* 'ask' belongs to the gen.-acc. group, *onlēan* 'lend' and *þancian* 'thank' to the gen.-dat. one: (i) ðā suna *fultumes* biddan 'to ask the sons for help'; (ii) Apollonius hiere *þæs* þancode 'Apollonius thanked her for that'.

(3) *Dative.* Many uses of the instrumental were absorbed by the dative, owing to the paucity of distinct inflexional forms for the latter case. As the name of the case suggests, 'giving' of a kind is generally implied.

(a) *Indirect object.* This may be regarded as a dative of advantage e.g. hlāf *lēodum* dǣlan 'to distribute bread to the people'.

(b) *After certain verbs* (some intransitive). This is a disparate group, a few signifying deprivation. The verbs include speaking, thanking, promising, serving, benefiting, obeying, pitying, requiting, receiving, pleasing, suiting, seeming, opposing, betraying and deserting.

(c) *After adjectives.* Proximity and resemblance invariably warrant the use of the dative: e.g. *fugole* gelīcost 'very like a bird'.

(d) *After prepositions.* A majority of prepositions take the dative; but *innan* 'within' and *wið* 'against', 'opposite', 'near', etc govern all the oblique cases, according to sense. If the preposition implies 'motion towards', it governs the accusative; if 'rest in', it takes the dative. The commonest forms using the dative are *æfter* 'after', *ǣr* 'before', *betweonan* 'between', *bi* 'beside', *butan* 'outside', *for* 'before', *fram* 'from', *mid* 'with', *of* 'from' and *tō* 'for'.

(e) *Dative absolute.* This infrequent construction was influenced by the ablative absolute in Latin. A noun and a participle are put in the dative case, but are unconnected with the main sentence structure. The group acts as a substitute for an adverbial clause, usually of time.

(4) *Instrumental.* The function of this case was to indicate agency, manner or means. In OE times, the form, but not the function, tended to fall away. Substitute forms, with the preposition *mid*, sometimes took the place of the inflected case, especially in prose. Examples of the inflected case are seen in 'for *hwy*' 'wherefor' and 'ðȳ ilcan wege' 'by the same means'; relics remain in modern idiomatic expressions, such as '*the* sooner *the* better'.

Regularly the instrumental inflexion *-e* was used to form adverbs, as is shown in ðy seofoðan dæge 'on the seventh day'. The case was also used to indicate extent of difference, e.g. *micle* lengran, literally 'longer by much'.

VERBS

From a flexional viewpoint, the morphology of verbs is the Achilles heel of traditional grammar, since notion and function are more important than form.

(1) *Tense.* By the time of Ælfric the poverty of the tense system,

consisting only of present and past, was undoubtedly recognized. OE absolute tenses, those which indicate time from the point of view of a speaker's utterance, had no flexional form for the future, of which writers must have been aware in the classical languages, from education in Latin. In Old English the simple future was generally expressed by the present tense; but *sculan* and *willan*, with the infinitive, were being used as auxiliary verbs by the LOE period. There are examples of the *willan* usage in the last few lines of Alfred's Preface to Gregory's *Pastoral Care*; but the intended sense is volition. The past tense was originally a perfect tense, and retained that function in OE, along with the imperfect.

C. T. Onions, in *Advanced English Syntax* (§118.2, pp 107–8) explains the Old English tense-practice very clearly:

> So long as the language remained simply a means of expressing thought in speech for everyday purposes, these two tense-forms were adequate enough, as the various shades of time, present, past, or future, could be readily indicated by means of adverbs or adverb-equivalents. But when language began to be committed to writing, ambiguities would arise, which, with the increasing complexity of the thoughts to be expressed, made a more elaborate and accurate system of tenses necessary. Sentences which might be perfectly understood when spoken were not intelligible when written. Therefore we find in the more advanced OE authors a number of Compound Tenses coming into use, to express more accurately the meanings of Present Perfect, Pluperfect, and so forth, and towards the close of the OE period we have the Tense system developed almost to its present extent. In some writers, however, the two Simple tenses are almost the only ones actually employed.

(2) *Voice.* Composite forms are employed in OE to supply the want of a flexional passive voice; the auxiliaries are appropriate forms of either *wesan* or *weorðan* (become), added to the past participle. The alternative impersonal construction *hine man ofslōg* was just as common.

(3) *Number.*

(a) A double subject, standing for the same notion, often has the verb in the singular, e.g. Ælfric, *Colloquy* (Methuen 234–5): *sȳ sibb and geþwærnes* betweoh ūs, 'let there be friendship and peace among us'.

(b) Sometimes a neuter sing. introduces the verb *be* and compliment in the plural, e.g. *ðæt wæron* engla gāstes, 'they were the spirits of angels'.

(4) *Mood*.

(a) The *indicative* is factual, in that it expresses a reasonable judgement of reality. It is used not only in principal clauses, but in relative, noun and adverbial clauses also. *Mood* and *mode*, words of the same Latin origin, were used in English for logic and grammar, but not earlier than Sir Thomas More's refutation of Tyndale. The adaptation of the Latin modal system to English was not altogether happy, because modality expresses a psychological state, and distinctions so nice involve the thought processes of individual languages.

(b) *Subjunctive*. In Old English the subjunctive was used extensively, but examples have since shrunk to a handful of fossilized forms, overwhelmed by substitutions known as modal auxiliaries. The subjunctive was not confined to subordinate clauses, though these are the more frequent; they are of two main kinds, noun clauses and adverbial ones. As both subordinations may be introduced by ðæt, function has to be determined by context. Meaning 'so that' or 'in order that', this conjunction signals an adverbial clause; in other senses, it introduces a noun or relative clause.

The following circumstantial uses cover the majority of examples of the subjunctive that occur in Old English texts:

(i) The action or state indicated by the verb is hypothetical, e.g. Ða ondrēd þæt mægdan þæt hēo næfre eft Apollonium ne gesāwe, 'Then the girl feared that she might never again see Apollonius'.

(ii) A degree of uncertainty is implied, e.g. Wēn is þæt ðū *gemete* sumne þæt ðē *gemiltsie*, 'Perhaps you will meet someone who will pity you'. Here the second subjunctive *gemiltsie* is used by attraction with the first.

(iii) Expressing what is proper or ought to be, e.g. Tīma is þæt ðū mid þīnum brōðrum *wistfullige* on mīnum gebēorscipe, 'It is time that you should feast with your brothers at my banquet'.

(iv) After the conjunction ǣr, e.g. þone būr ūtan beēode, ǣr hine þā menn *onfunden* þe mid ðām cyninge wǣron, 'surrounded the bower before the men who were with the king discovered him'.

(v) Expressing a command or compulsive wish, e.g. *Hliste* se þe *wille*, 'Let him heed who may wish'.

(vi) In adverbial clauses that express time, place or manner, or whose function is conditional (*if*), concessive (*though*), final (in order that), or consecutive (so that), e.g. Ne biŏ swylc cwēnlīc þēaw/idese tō efnanne, þēah ŏe hīo ænlicu sȳ, 'That is no queenly custom for a woman to practise, peerless though she may be'.

(c) *Infinitive and Gerund.* The infinitive is treated as a neuter noun, but in origin it was a Germanic dative. As in modern English, the infinitive may be either the subject or the object of a verb.

(i) When the infinitive follows one of the defective verbs, *cunnan, durran, magan, sculan, þurfan*, and the anomalous verb *willan*, they act as a kind of auxiliary to it.

(ii) After verbs of causation and intention the Latin accusative and infinitive construction is common, and it is possible for the infinitive to be employed in a passive sense.

(iii) After verbs of motion the infinitive often has the significance of a present participle in modern English, e.g. ŏā cōm inn *gangan* ealdor þegna, 'then the prince of the thanes came walking in'.

(iv) In verse (e.g. the maxims of the Exeter Book) there is often idiomatic omission of the infinitive *be*, and less frequently of the verbs of motion also, e.g. Cyning sceal ᷄on healle/bēagas dǣlan, 'the king shall be in the hall to distribute rings'; fram ic ne wille ᷄ 'I will not away' – showing similar omission in modern English.

(v) The inflected infinitive, preceded by the preposition *tō*, serves as a gerund in Old English, the usual function being to amplify an adjective, or to signify purpose, e.g. wynsum *to sprecanne*, 'pleasant to talk'; wē winnaŏ rihtlīce wiŏ þysne cyning *tō āhreddenne* ūre lēode, 'we are fighting righteously against this king to save our people'.

(vi) Used with the verb *be*, the gerund denotes necessity or duty in a passive sense, e.g. monige scylda bēoþ *tō forberanne*, 'many sins have to be borne'.

PHRASAL SYNTAX

Being of a miscellaneous nature, this is no subject to be handled in a small compass. Many uses of nouns and adjectives are obviously phrasal, and countless examples of flexional verbs have a place here also. The categories overlap.

(1) *Apposition.* Usually words or phrases in apposition take the same case as the noun or pronoun to which they refer. Sometimes, however, words in apposition are left undeclined e.g. hē wearþ ofslægen fram Brytta cyninge, Ceadwealla gecīged, 'he was killed by the king of the Britons, called Cadwalla'.

(2) *Adjectives.* There is no vocative case in OE. When direct address is used in the nominative, any qualifying adjective there may be is usually preceded by the demonstrative pronoun, and is consequently in the weak form, e.g. *se mǣra* maga Healfdene, 'O famous sŏn of Healfdene'.

(3) *Adverbs* (negation). The double negative was regular to re-inforce the notion of negation. Under the influence of logical theory, the practice was discountenanced in the seventeenth century (see Subjunctive (i) above).

(4) *Pronouns.* Personal pronouns are often dispensed with in subordinate clauses.

(5) *Prepositions.* A preposition that comes after its object is said to be in post-position; when placed before or after the verb, it is likely to be mistaken for a prefix or an adverb. A subordinate clause introduced by relative particle *ðe*, takes the post-position regularly, e.g. Titus . . . sǣde þæt hē þone dæg forlure, þe hē nōht tō gōde *on* ne gedyde, 'Titus said that he wasted the day, on which he did no good'. A rather clumsy construction.

In post-position there were several prepositions combined with the demonstrative pronoun used adverbially, such as *þǣron,, hērinne*. Compound prepositions are frequently sep-arated in prose and verse into preposition and adverb, e.g. *ymb* hīe *ūtan*, instead of *ymbūtan* hīe.

(6) *Conjunctions* (correlative). To avoid any confusion, both cor-relatives were regarded as indispensable. *Swa . . . swa*, 'the . . . the' or 'as . . . as', is distinct from *swa-swa . . . swa* 'so . . . as'. In modern English the second of the pair is often omitted, e.g. *ðā . . . ðā* 'when . . . (then)', and *ðēah . . . ðēah* 'though . . . (yet)'.

Every living language is subject to change, which is sometimes so slow that it is not perceived from one generation to another, though it is much later by the linguistic historian. The changes here discussed affected forms, sounds and syntax, and there is no need to argue that morphological change is of importance to synthetic grammar, which concerns itself with the inflexion, function and notion of words. The most useful application of syntax is to the study of stylistic patterns. The morphemic approach is now more esteemed to express the relationship between ideas, syllables and sounds; but this study is difficult to utilize in ancient languages, where there is no spoken evidence.

In an epoch-making dissertation, *Progress in Language* (1909), Otto Jespersen argued: 'grammatical meaning was first expressed by certain more material instruments [inflexions], then by the same instruments with the words arranged in a fixed order, and finally by order independent of those original instruments.' (§85, p 111). In the record of written English, West Saxon represents the second stage of development towards an analytical language. By the end of the English Middle Age, the order of words in sentences had become relatively fixed, and demonstrably subtler in functional nuance than was the paratactic prose of King Alfred. One of the major gains was a better grasp of the concept of subordination.

CHAPTER VIII

Old English Poetry
and its Prosody

🌀🌀🌀🌀🌀🌀

OLD ENGLISH POETRY is the earliest extant literature of the West
Germanic peoples. The manuscripts that preserve its thirty
thousand lines belong mainly to the tenth and eleventh centuries,
though much of the poetry is undoubtedly of earlier origin than
Alfredian prose. By the end of the sixth century, heroic poems,
such as *Beowulf*, appear to have exhausted their creative possibilities. But this was not because of the so-called formulaic theory
of oral composition.

During the seventh century Aldhelm appears to have realized the
scop's possibilities as an entertainer. According to William of
Malmesbury, he made rapport with a bored congregation in an
unusual manner. The anecdote is said to have come from King
Alfred's Commonplace Book, now lost:

> The people, at that time semi-barbarous and too little interested in
> divine sermons, were accustomed to return to their homes immediately
> after the singing of Mass; therefore the holy man took up his stand
> before them on a bridge which connected the town and country like one
> professing the art of minstrelsy; and by doing this more than once he
> won the favour and presence of the people.
>
> (*Gesta Pontificium*, Rolls Series 52, 336)

In the eight century Alcuin (in a letter to the Bishop of
Lindisfarne) commented humourlessly on the 'frivolities' with
which monks were regaled in their leisure hours; the rebuke was
typical of the narrower Christian orthodoxy:

> When priests dine together let the words of God be read. It is fitting on
> such occasions to listen to a reader, not to a harpist; to the discourses of
> the fathers, not to the poems of the heathen. What has Ingeld to do with
> Christ?

Old English poetry has come down to us in four manuscripts, important because, in most cases, only one copy of the poem exists. The manuscript collections are all dated between the late tenth century and 1050 AD.

(1) The British Museum manuscript of *Beowulf* and *Judith*, found in the seventeenth-century Robert Cotton Collection, and known as MS Vitellius A 15. It contains a number of prose pieces, and bears the signature of Lawrence Nowell, dated 1563. Nowell was a well-known Old English scholar of the sixteenth century, but how he came by the manuscript is uncertain. An early record of its existence appeared in Wanley's *Catalogue of Anglo-Saxon Manuscripts* (1705).

(2) The Bodleian MS, Junius XI, so called because it was presented to Oxford University by François du Jon (1589–1677), son of a Huguenot professor at Heidelberg; he took the name Franz Junius, when he qualified as a theologian at Leyden university. He arrived in England in 1620, became Librarian to the book-collector, the Earl of Arundel, and edited the MS in 1655, when (he says) it was given to him by Archbishop Usher of Armagh. Sometime before 1651, the manuscript, which emanated from the Canterbury or Winchester school, seems to have been in the possession of Sir Symonds D'Ewes, a member of the Long Parliament and lover of Anglo-Saxon antiquities. It contains *Genesis*, *Exodus*, *Daniel* and three shorter poems, which were amalgamated as *Christ and Satan* by C. W. M. Grein (*Bibliothek der angelsächsischen Poesie*, 1857).

(3) The Codex Exoniensis or Exeter Book, preserved in Exeter Cathedral, to which it was presented by Bishop Leofric of Cornwall and Devon, who was Chancellor of Edward the Confessor. The donation seems to have been made shortly before the Norman Conquest; the Bishop's See was transferred from Crediton to Exeter in 1050. The manuscript, first printed in 1842, contains a number of unique, shorter poems: *Christ*, *Juliana*, *Phoenix*, *The Wanderer*, *The Seafarer*, *Widsith*, *Deor*, *The Ruin*, *Gnomic Verses*, *Riddles*, *The Wife's Complaint*, *The Husband's Message*, and *Address of the Soul to the Body* (part 1).

(4) The Codex Vercellencis or Vercelli Book (perhaps the oldest of

the four), lodged in the cathedral library of Vercelli, near Milan. Most likely this manuscript was brought there by Cardinal Guala, papal legate to King John and Henry III, between 1210 and 1218; for on his return to Italy, this cleric built the church at Vercelli, and dedicated it to St Andrew. The manuscript contains twenty-nine pieces, among them *The Dream of the Rood, Elene, The Fates of the Apostles, Address of the Soul to the Body*, and a prose *Life of St Guthlac*. There are also a number of Homilies, among which the poems are distributed, without any apparent plan.

Most aesthetic judgements of Old English poetry are founded on the accepted principle that the alliterative measure has a cultural identity more distinctive than the style of prose, being earlier, and therefore closer to the Germanic origins of the people. Heroic poems, of which *Beowulf* is the prototype (see p 55), are figurative in a special way, besides being dramatic and often spectacular. The professional minstrels who recited them were itinerant, and visited various courts, where they were generously treated as entertainers with a flair for narrative verse. Their wares were, at first, the legends of Germanic tribes and their chiefs, before the Anglo-Saxon peoples came to England. *Beowulf* vividly links the Anglo-Saxon world with that of the Scandinavian tradition in the north, and was perhaps a synthesis of Continental lays, Anglian Offa (the ancestor of King Offa of Mercia) being the only 'English' person mentioned in its three thousand lines (see line 1949b). The poem was much too long for a single session, and what we have is a much later transmission than the original. The work reveals considerable classical and Christian influence.

The Celtic aspect of Old English poetry is occasional, and evokes a different spirit; it is marked by a certain romantic tenderness in natural description, especially in the elegiac poetry of the Exeter Book. Among the *Riddles* there is one on 'The Swan', which in R. K. Gordon's modernized version reads as follows:

Silent is my garment when I tread the earth or inhabit the dwellings or stir the waters. Sometimes my trappings and this high air raise me above the abodes of men, and the power of clouds then bears me far and wide over the people. My adornments resound loudly and make melody; they sing clearly when I am not near the flood and the earth – a travelling spirit.

(*Anglo-Saxon Poetry*, Everyman, 1926, p 323)

The Seafarer abounds in strains of feeling that suggest the Celtic touch most strongly:

> He who sets out on the waters ever feels longing. The groves put forth blossom; cities grow beautiful; the fields are fair; the world revives; all these urge the heart of the eager-minded man to a journey . . . The cuckoo exhorts with sad voice; the harbinger of summer sings, bodes bitter sorrow to the heart . . . And yet my heart is now restless in my breast, my mind is with the sea-flood over the whale's domain.
>
> (ibid. p 85)

Much of the early poetry was composed in the north, where the influence of the Irish Church was strongest. Insemination of Celtic feeling is suggested in the melancholy thoughts of those who traversed the seas, and thought of life as a pilgrimage and a penance.

The dominant influences on Old English poetry were, however, the Christian religion and the classical tradition. Without the Church and the industry of its monks, little of the poetry of the pre-Alfredian times would have survived. The greatest of the heroic poems, *Beowulf*, was filtered through the Church creed, and structured with some long-standing technical expertise. The one poem of this class that may have eluded religious sanction was the *Finnesburh* fragment. So orthodox is the competence of the alliterative measure, with enjambed lines and natural speech rhythms, that one has to relinquish any idea that the poetry was 'primitive'. Knowledge that minstrels accompanied it with the harp raises speculation as to how poetry of such varied content was delivered. Nothing seems more unlikely than that verbal composition, as we observe it, was spontaneous, or inspired in the way that the Cædmon story suggests. J. R. R. Tolkien makes the point forcibly in *Beowulf, the Monsters and the Critics* (Appendix (b), p 44):

> Before *Beowulf* was written Christian poetry was already established, and was known to the author. The language of *Beowulf* is in fact partly 're-paganized' by the author with a special purpose, rather than christianized (by him or later) without consistent purpose. Throughout the poem the language becomes more intelligible, if we assume that the diction of poetry was already christianized and familiar with Old and New Testament themes and motives. There is a gap, important and effective poetically, whatever was its length in time, between Cædmon and the poet of *Beowulf*.

In copying manuscripts, the monks seem to have mastered the design of alliterative poetry and perfected it in biblical paraphrases of their own choice. As they adapted existing buildings to their own religious ceremonies, so they diplomatically preserved heathen elements in heroic poetry, tolerating some conflict of doctrine, for the sake of artistic tone and mass effects.

The classical influence in Anglo-Saxon writing needs more scrutiny. Since the disappearance of rhetorical studies in schools of the eighteenth century, the term *classic* has become too vague to describe an antiquated stylistic discipline such as that of Old English. The early rhetoricians distinguished two principal styles in Greek and Latin literature, the Attic and the Asiatic, the latter detected by its florid and romantic attributes; both occur in Old English poetry. Latin and Greek poetry, which learned churchmen like Archbishop Theodore knew, could hardly have exerted much influence before the close of the seventh century, and then only through individualists, like Aldhelm, who were competent to exploit both styles. Classical discipline could have been effective only through the scriptoria, whose impact was to diffuse appreciation of orderliness and formality, virtues that are associated with the well-structured Attic style in English poetry.

Two classifications of Old English literature are possible: (a) according to chronology, and (b) according to spirit. Early literature of the seventh and eighth centuries, including some of the finest poetry, is thought to have emanated from Northumbria; but unfortunately manuscripts of this period perished in the sackings of the Danes, or the later destruction of monastries during the Reformation. Kenneth Sisam has shown how precarious it is to assign the composition of the earlier poems to any particular dialect ('Dialect Origins of the Earlier Old English Verse', *Studies in the History of Old English Literature*, pp 119–39). One test is the survival of full forms of inflexion in the second and third person singular present indicative of verbs, in Anglian, and corresponding contracted forms in West Saxon, especially in the ninth century. Vocabulary tests have proved to be somewhat unreliable. Sisam suggests (p 138) that there was a pool of anonymous poems 'independent of local interest, which was the common stock for the entertainment or instruction of the English peoples'.

The other classification, into pagan and Christian poetry, is heavily loaded in favour of the latter. The heathen spirit, warlike and aristocratic, but also melancholy, left little scope for lyrical elements, except in isolated patches of the heroic poems, or in the form of shorter elegies. The gloomy undertone of *Beowulf* is part of the Germanic heritage, one aspect being the fatalistic nature of the pre-Christian religion. The multifarious use of *wyrd* ('fate' in a hostile sense) in early English poetry has been much discussed, and its relation to death explained by B. J. Timmer (see *Neophilologus* XXVI, 1940 and 1941, pp 213–28). *Wyrd*, after the Christian conversion of the Anglo-Saxon peoples, became an instrument of God, modified in meaning to imply something less menacing, for instance 'fortune' or 'lot'. This was desirable, since Christians were now without the protection in emergency of the old deities of Germanic mythology. The ingrained belief in inexorable fate had, indeed, made it easy to bring Christianity to them. Conversion had the secondary effect, however, of producing a tendency to seriousness, without the leavening of humour; and this led to the moralizing that has always been apparent in didactic literature.

In heroic poetry, posthumous fame was one of the principal ends of life. An *eorl*, or man of distinction, believed in the virtue of self-control and the suppression of emotions; but when the mead-cup circulated at the festive board, he was not averse to boasting. A change and expansion of theme occurs in the Christian poetry, which is noticeable in greater humility, cheerfulness and resignation. In most of the changes, impetus came from Latin literature. Romantic attachment to nature was toned down, and narrative strength supervened, especially when the rousing episodes of Old Testament history became the popular themes of poetry.

The known life of Old English poetry, about two hundred and fifty years, was long enough to witness the birth of allegory in English poetry. The coming of Christianity to settlers who were once nomads had something to do with the rise of this genre. St Augustine of Hippo had been dead a hundred and fifty years, when Augustine of Canterbury came to England, steeped in the principles of Gregory the Great, who was a dedicated student of the African theologian. As J. H. Wilson has shown in *Christian Theology and Old English Poetry* (pp 19–30), Father Hippo's use for literature other than the Bible was solely to interpret the language allegorically, and make it serve the end of the dogmas which he equated with truth. Vergil and Ovid, far from being rejected, were made to illustrate the Christian apologists; indeed, all recorded experience could be given religious significance, by applying a symbolic meaning to the words. The Church in England invoked the same maxims for the pagan poetry of the Anglo-Saxons; any original composition, including the lives of saints in verse, was to be didactic, or exemplary, in the patristic exegetical tradition. There were Latin models for *Andreas, Elene* and *The Dream of the Rood* in writers such as Prudentius, Lactantius, Juvencus, Fortunatus, Arator, Marius Victorinus, and Paulinus of Nola, the last of whom initiated the elegiac strain reflected in the Exeter Book. Alcuin must have been acquainted with these Latin writers, some of whose works were in the library at York (see Wilson, pp 37–47).

There were thus two classes of person involved in poetic productivity, the scop and the monk. Credibility presented few problems, since tales with a didactic purpose were regarded as true, whether or not they contained fiction. It would have been an indifferent story that involved no marvels, for marvels are by no means outside the Judaeo-Christian tradition. Nearly all Old English poetry was thus intended to improve conduct, or to control the forces of nature, and M. W. Bloomfield in *Essays and Explorations* (Harvard University Press, 1970) finds the bulk of the thinking much neglected as 'wisdom' literature. This category is not confined to gnomic verses, riddles, charms, proverbs and dialogues, and is indebted to the Wisdom books of the Old Testament, as well as to the *sententiae* of Seneca and Boethius; the last was sympathetically translated by Alfred the Great. Bloomfield regards *The Seafarer* and *The Wanderer* as poems of this class, rather than elegies.

Though alliterative measures are the only ones found in Anglo-Saxon poetry, the technique is varied for different kinds of theme. In heroic poetry the lines are 'run-on', with plentiful use of kennings, and the sense-pause is midway in the line. In elegiac poetry, however, the thought generally ends with the line. Alliteration was designed as an aid to memory, as well as a guide to the reciter as to where he should place the emphasis; it is undoubtedly responsible for a specific diction, not to be found in the prose. A peculiarity of this poetic diction was the formation of picturesque compounds, which are not simply synonyms or expletives, but parallelisms to secure variation, and simultaneously to enhance description. By the use of kennings (repetitions in a slightly different form), the subject or object was deemed to be improved, as well as fixed in the memory. If the kenning is not always a metaphor, it invariably expands some aspect of the conception.

Not all Old English poetry is vivid or vigorous; but when it is, the image tends to be enlarged by personification. By the animation of things such as weapons, vividness is given to action, and magic to the potency of nature in all its forms. This enrichment of the early compositions, such as *Beowulf*, sometimes fades in the later poetry; if the ornamentation is colourless, it may be because it is derived from classical exemplars. Ruggedness is the common disadvantage of alliterative poetry for the ear; there is little liquidity in the measures of such verse; not for the reason that alliteration is usually consonantal, but because the accented position is rhythmically awkward for the perception of sense. The robustiousness of the early poetry invokes sensations of the open air; but limitations of vocabulary in some poets lead to stock phrases and ritual epithets, which encourage the formulary theory.

It should be borne in mind that the speech-group represented by the hemistich or half-line in Old English poetry has a rhythm that is emotional, as well as syntactic and rhetorical. Alliterative poetry does not, however, cultivate a deliberate clash between sense rhythm and metrical pattern, as does the syllabic verse of post-Renascence poets. The beauty of sound for the scop seems to have depended more on the proper observance of quantity, than on the evocative effect of words in context.

What J. R. R. Tolkien says of *Beowulf* is true of many other Old English poems:

> The very nature of Old English metre is often misjudged. In it there is no single rhythmic pattern progressing from the beginning of a line to the end, and repeated with variation in other lines. The lines do not go according to a tune. They are founded on a balance; an opposition between two halves of roughly equivalent phonetic weight, and significant content, which are more often rhythmically contrasted than similar. They are more like masonry than music . . . *Beowulf* is indeed the most successful Old English poem because in it the elements, language, metre, theme, structure, are all most nearly in harmony. Judgement of the verse has often gone astray through listening for an accentual rhythm and pattern; and it seems to halt and stumble . . . We have none the less in *Beowulf* a method and structure that within the limits of the verse-kind approaches rather to sculpture or painting. It is a composition not a tune.
>
> (*Beowulf, the Monsters and the Critics*, pp 31–2)

A version of *Beowulf*, by an unknown compiler, probably existed by the early eighth century (the time of Bede) though the pseudo-historical events belong to a time not earlier than the fifth. The epic was not, therefore, composed in the dark period of European culture. Hrothgar's vast and stately hall of Heorot, which reminds the reader of archaeological finds at West Stow, Yeavering and Thetford, has obvious social significance; it typifies early life in Germanic society, warlike, yet gracious in the bestowing of gifts, and the reciprocal loyalties between warriors and their tribal leaders. What is unique in the Germanic hero-ethos is the mingling of physical courage with a civilized code of punctilious etiquette. Ceremony exists to show that courtesy, the product of reverence, is not incompatible with ordained violence. There are in *Beowulf* reflections on royal magnanimity and hospitality that surpass the cautious morality of James I's *Basilikon Doron*. Beowulf, who himself becomes a king, and rules his people for fifty years, is described at the end of his career as 'the mildest and gentlest of men, the kindest to his people and the most eager for fame' (3181–2).

The heroes celebrated were not strictly *national* leaders, since the period represented was that of the great migration of Germanic tribes, when there was no idea of a common nationality. The principal figures are authenticated in old Latin and Norse documents, such as Saxo-Grammaticus's *Gesta Danorum*, the *Historia Francorum* of Gregory of Tours, and *The Saga of Hrolf Kraki*; but the central figure and his exploits are fabulous. The monsters Grendel, his mother and the Dragon, suggest the grafting of folk-tale upon history; they are embodiments of evil, to which Beowulf, the strong and upright man, is the logical counter. The portrayal of his actions is not, however, without elements of the marvellous.

The poem was not called *Beowulf* until Kemble's edition of 1833, and Tolkien insists that it was the work of an Englishman (ibid. p 8). Fr. Klaeber in the Introduction to his edition (p cxxii et seqq) suggested that the poem was recited at the court of King Aldfrith of Northumbria, where the author is supposed to have lived, inspired by the 'warm-hearted, and tolerant spirit of Irish Christianity'. Dorothy Whitelock, in *The Audience of Beowulf*, prefers the court of the Mercian king, Offa II, which would partly explain the reference to his ancestor, Offa of Schleswig.

The Latin culture that tolerates pagan rites, such as Beowulf's funeral, is not connected with the Christian overlay of the poem, which some associate with the *Metra* of Boethius. A sensitive reading of *Beowulf* must place it in the first classical revival. The author of the tenth-century transcription stood by the fundamental Germanic conception, and there is no suggestion of clerical intrusion for the Christian element.

Beowulf does not conform to classical epic requirements; it is a poem *sui generis*. The poet possessed lofty sentiments and great dignity of style, as he brooded over the fate of man, the victim of hostile forces; his poem is, above all, a study in the ancient virtue of piety. Action may be halted by ceremony, and narrative interrupted by digression, but the picture of the times is skilfully amplified. It is a scene of strenuous endeavour, whose pagan moral is the nothingness of life.

No less than thirteen hundred lines of *Beowulf* are devoted to speeches, and in these the digressions sometimes appear obstructive to the progress of the theme. The long speech of Beowulf in lines 2000–2162, for instance, recapitulates what occurred in the first sixteen hundred lines of the poem, in which both Grendel and his mother are slain. It has been suggested that this recapitulation indicates a résumé at the beginning of another session, for the benefit of those who missed the scop's previous recital; but the real purpose of this episode was apparently to give the hero's psychological reactions to his own achievements. The speech incorporates a further digression, accounting for the blood-feud that arose from the betrothal of Freawaru to Ingeld, son of the late King Froda of the Heathobards.

Another restrospection in the narrative concerns the dialogue between Unferth and Beowulf about the swimming contest with Breca (506–58). This passage is a fine one, which serves to show how tactfully Beowulf could deal with the taunts of colleagues, by imperturbably presenting his own version.

The language, syntax and style of *Beowulf* all deserve close attention, because there is no other poem in Old English which presents a clearer picture of the poet's task. A remarkable aspect of the diction is the range of rhetorical devices that he calls upon to secure his effects. The Miltonic fecundity of expression in metaphor and simile is not present, but one has no right to expect it in a work that is heroic, without being truly epical. Nouns, adjectives, and the resources of compounding and apposition are exploited to the full, as Klaeber points out, to linger on situations that result from actions hinted at, but not fully described. This is effectually an un-Homeric procedure.

The considerable speech-making in the poem affords a pretext for gnomic utterance, as well as simplification of the syntax, by shortening the lengths of sentences, compared with those of the narrative portions. But examination will show that there is much narration in the speeches themselves. In *Postscript on Beowulf* (chapter VIII) S. O. Andrew demonstrates by quotation that the dominant rhetorical schemes of words are parallelism, litotes (understatement) and anaphora (repetition of words at the beginning of clauses), particularly in the forms of *se, sēo, ðæt*. The degree of understatement, implied in the use of negatives, depends on context; there are situations in which understatement intensifies, as in the modern English phrase 'not a little'; an example occurs in *Beowulf* 1575 'næs sēo ecg fracod/ hilderince' (the blade was *not without use* to the hero). This form of litotes is common in heroic poetry of Germanic inspiration, while it is relatively absent in Old English prose. There may even have been an intention in some situations to raise a wry kind of laughter (see F. Bracher 'Understatement in Old English Poetry', *PMLA*, LII (1937), pp 915–34).

This raises the question of irony in Old English poetry, but not of the kind to be designated 'exaggerated politeness'. The function of irony does not reside in verbal detail only, but, in a larger conspectus, from the Christian viewpoint of the inadequacy of pride in the pagan world. Life in the heroic ages seemed a succession of more or less tragic situations, in which men and women were doomed, at best to be noble failures. In the person of Beowulf, the poet contrasts the two worlds, and irony results from the perception of their opposition, not from any imitation of classical literature. The Danes, for instance, were powerful rulers, but ironically helpless when confronted with the natural, but evil, force of Grendel's inroads.

Judith is an heroic poem of a different order, a free rendering in 349 lines of the Vulgate *Judith*, chapters 12 to 15 of the Apocrypha; sections X to XII alone survive, from what may have been a minor epic of twelve books. The fragment is one of several religious narratives in West Saxon which show the power of Christianity to strengthen believers, especially brave women resisting oppression.

Lines are more often syntactically enjambed than in *Beowulf*; there are several instances of rhyme, and a more unusual resort to expanded lines than is common in other Old English poetry. The poem would appear to belong to the first half of the tenth century; Timmer's evidence for composition places it between 930 and 937.

Despite the heavily ornamented, conventional style, *Judith* has realism and great dramatic power. The central figure appears as a fanatical prophetess, rather than the cool and decisive leader of Christian legend. The savage nature of her mission is vividly revealed in the description of the slaying of Holofernes in his tent; in spirit, this episode is thoroughly Germanic. The verse reaches a climax in the exulting passage, where the Jews under Judith, overthrow the Assyrian army. Great skill is shown in the handling of crowds, and in the graphic account of all warlike exploits. The expanded line, for dignity, is at its best in Judith's prayer, ana-chronistically addressed to the Trinity.

In MS Junius XI, *Genesis* (a poem of 2935 lines), is of special interest, because it appears to be earlier than the tenth-century text of *Beowulf*. The poem has for long been associated with Cædmon, since Bede reported in chapter 24 of the fourth book of the *Ecclesiastical History* that this inspired poet versified many portions of the Bible; he specifically states that Cædmon 'sang of the creation of the world, and of the origin of the human race, and the whole narrative of Genesis'. All the other biblical paraphrases in allitera-tive verse, contained in the Bodleian MS, viz. *Exodus*, *Daniel* and *Christ and Satan*, were attributed to Cædmon by Junius himself; and the German authority on alliterative verse, E. Sievers, main-tained that 54 lines of *Genesis A* (the so-called *Elder Genesis*) were the composition of Cædmon. Detailed scholarship has since shown, however, that the four poems were written by different authors, who remain anonymous; the diction of each is not now held to resemble that of Cædmon's authenticated *Hymn*, nor does the method of construction.

A long passage in *Genesis* (lines 235–852) represents an interpola-tion by another hand, with many expanded lines, and so superior in style that another author is almost certain. This has been given the name *Genesis B* (or the *Later Genesis*), and a separate edition was prepared for Scrivener Press by B. J. Timmer in 1948. The theme of *Genesis B* is Satan's rebellion and fall, on similar lines to Milton's

Paradise Lost, which is clearly an independent version. *Genesis B* was the work of a translator from Old Saxon, as E. Sievers had maintained in 1875; he has been proved correct by the discovery of four ninth-century fragments in the Vatican Library, which were removed from the Heidelberg Bibliotheca Palatina in 1623. On reasonable grounds, Timmer suggests that the Old English translation in MS Junius XI was made during the reign of King Alfred, near to the date 900, a probable source of the original being John the Saxon, or a cleric who accompanied him (Introduction, pp 15–18). The composition of *Genesis A* is placed about a century earlier.

The homiletic influence in Old English poetry was largely due to the writings of Cynewulf, whose religious verse appears in both the Exeter and Vercelli codices. He is a shadowy figure of some early ninth-century monastery, who probably wrote in the Anglian dialect of Northumbria or Mercia, for traces remain in the West-Saxon texts. His thinly veiled identification, deciphered from the Old English names for runic letters and a few common terms, occurs in the epilogues of *Juliana* (731 lines) and *Elene* (1321), as well as in *The Fates of the Apostles* (122) and *Christ II* or *The Ascension of Christ* (426). These authentic poems run in all to just over 2600 lines. The poet was evidently steeped in Latin Christian models, for his extant remains have a deeply religious tone.

The school of ecclesiastical paraphrase that Cynewulf sponsored, perhaps in the reign of King Æthelstan, is temperate, civilized and didactic, in the balanced Anglo-Saxon way, quite different from the emotive Celtic. His themes have their origin in the Church calendar, but the narratives, other than *Elene*, are poor in structure, and tiresome as stories. The bookishness, evident in natural description, is made palatable solely by the orderliness of the verse, whose taste is that of a minor poet working conscientiously within the tradition.

Juliana, in the Exeter Book, is the life of a saint based on a legend recorded in the *Acta Sanctorum*, 16 February (ed. John Bolland, 1658). This Christian, the circumstances of whose death are told in Bede's *Martyrology*, was murdered during the emperorship of Diocletian; but few accounts were available in writing before the sixth century. She was the pagan daughter of Affricanus of Nicomedia, but turned Christian, and was then imprisoned, tortured and finally beheaded. Her remains were interred in a mausoleum at Pozzuoli, but removed to Cumae in 1207. The central event of the story is Juliana's temptation by the devil, disguised as an angel, the plan being to compel her to forego her virginity and marry the heathen Heliseus. Its prosaic monotony suggests that *Juliana* was an immature work, possibly Cynewulf's earliest; the style is signally devoid of figurative language, except for occasional resort to litotes.

Elene, in the Vercelli Book, is the longest and most craftsmanlike of Cynewulf's poems. There are elements of romance in the narrative which comes from the *Acta Cyriaci* (*Acta Sanctorum*, 4 March). It concerns the discovery of the Cross by St Helena, mother of Constantine the Great, when the site of the Holy Sepulchre was identified in AD 326. The account preserved in Greek patristic writings of the following century, involves Judas, brother of St Stephen, a man of Jewish origin, who attempted to frustrate the discovery, but was afterwards coerced to accept the truth.

Cynewulf's poem begins with the impending invasion of Rome by the barbarians, and the vision of Constantine before the battle of Milvian Bridge (lections I and II). The symbol of the Cross becomes so important to the Emperor that he sends Elene by sea to Jerusalem, with a considerable force, to find out where the true Cross had been buried, supposedly during the rule of Trajan, who died in AD 117. The *Elene* legend is notable for several chronological inaccuracies; e.g. Constantine, said to have been baptized by Silvester, did not receive baptism until his death-bed (see p 14); St Stephen was martyred centuries before the events in the legend took place.

Though the story lacks originality, and is marred by redundancies of phrase in the long speeches, the poem reflects a sensitive picture of the devotional state of mind. Most interest centres on the epilogue, which contains both assonance and leonine rhyme, while it affords an engaging self-revelation of the author in the following lines:

> I knew not fully the truth about the Cross, until, through illustrious power, God disclosed wisdom to the counsels of my heart, a deeper understanding . . . The radiant King of Might gave me knowledge, a perfect gift, as a comfort to my age, bestowed it upon me and set it in my mind, revealed it and from time to time amplified it. He unbound my body, unfettered my heart, unlocked the power of song, which I have gladly and joyously used in the world.

The Vercelli Book contains a kindred poem, *The Dream of the Rood* (156 lines), universally considered to be the finest religious composition in Old English. The title was given by B. Thorpe in 1836, when he produced the first edition of the Codex Vercelli. The word *rood* appeared in the *Vespasian Hymns* (c 825), and has the same etymology as the word *rod*, the original meaning of which was 'twig' or 'branch'. Excerpts from the poem appear in runic letters on the huge cross, housed in the Ruthwell church, Annandale, in Dumfriesshire. This cross had once been in the open, but was badly damaged by the Covenanters in 1642. Bruce Dickins and A. S. C. Ross in their edition of the poem (Methuen, 1934) say that the cross belongs to the golden age of Northumbria, and place its erection in the first half of the eighth century (Intro. p 8). The manuscript poem in the Vercelli Book almost certainly belongs to the latter half of the tenth century, and it contains a sprinkling of Anglian forms.

The latter half of *The Dream of the Rood* bears no relation to the citations on the cross, and points to the poem's expansion at a later date than the original composition. It was natural to associate this poem with Cynewulf, but the style indicates a more colourful imagination and a finer lyrical quality than he possessed. The Cross was a topical theme at the beginning of the eighth century, when Pope Sergius I claimed that he had unearthed a genuine fragment of it; another such was presented to King Alfred in the year 885.

The poem is a dream-vision, elegiac in character, and presented in monologue form, the major utterance coming from the tree in the forest, from which the instrument of Christ's crucifixion was made. There were models a-plenty in classical literature, secular examples being popular in the works of Ovid and Catullus. But the immediate progenitor of the Old English short monologue is the Riddle, for example Nos. 31, 56 and 73. In the first two of these, the actual solution is 'the Cross', in the last 'a spear'. Short monologues of this type were considered by clerical teachers to be useful exercises in rhetoric.

The power to transmute the secular into the Christian is splendidly illustrated in several poems of the Exeter Book, belonging to the *Physiologus* or *Bestiary* group, derived from a lost Greek animal mythology, written in Alexandria, and probably Egyptian in origin. *Phoenix*, a poem in two parts and 677 lines, is based on the fourth-century Latin poem of Lactantius, entitled *De Ave Phoenice*.

After a lengthy introduction on the Earthly Paradise, an attractive part of the composition, the poem develops into a Christian allegory, which is pleonastic to the point of tedium. Attribution of the poem to Cynewulf, on the ground of theme, is supported by no worthwhile stylistic evidence.

The phoenix, a symbol of resurrection, was earliest found in the sun-worship of the Egyptians, and associated by Herodotus with the temple in Heliopolis, on whose altar this unique creature was said to deposit its dead father every five hundred years. (There is no significance in the *Phoenix*'s extension of the period to a thousand years; many cognate legends had a different time-scheme.) European literature generally favours the version in Pliny's *Natural History*, which sends the Arabian bird of brilliant plumage and excellent voice to be consumed by fire in the desert of Syria; there it arises from the ashes, with renewed youth, through the instrumentality of a worm. Because of this power of resurrection, early Christian writers readily associated the Phoenix with Christ. The West-Saxon poet's picture of the Earthly Paradise, with abundance of water, vegetation and bird-song, represents an oasis, if at all relevant to the climate of Arabia. Here is Barbara Mackenzie's free verse translation of lines 50–65:

> There comes not age or hardship,
>   and unknown are griefs or woes,
> Or cruel death or evil,
>   or the heavy hand of foes.
> Nor with sin nor strife nor weeping,
>   nor the pinch of bitter need,
> Nor sickness nor weary sleeping,
>   nor the curse of an evil deed,
> Nor with wintry storms nor grieving
>   is the pleasant country marred
> Nor does frost with death-white fingers
>   on the earth below strike hard.
> And no dark clouds burst in showers
>   through the dim-oppresséd air,
> But the streams with stately flowing,
>   like clear wells upspringing there
> Still lave with their quiet waters
>   all the pleasant pastures green,
> Remote in the shady woodlands
>   in the depths of groves unseen . . .

(*An English Miscellany*, ed. B. S. Lee, OUP, 1977, pp 12–13)

Rhyme is not foreign to the *Phoenix*, as lines 15–16 show:

ne forstes fnæst,	ne fȳres blæst
ne hægles hryre,	ne hrīmes dryre

The original aspect of the poem is not the adaptation of myth to parable, but the Ovidian diction and romantic attitude revealed in the lush description of nature.

No account of Old English poetry is complete without consideration of the group of so-called elegies, of which *The Seafarer* and *The Wanderer* are the most representative; both are found in the Exeter Book, and seem to have been written in the first half of the ninth century. (The titles were again given by Thorpe in the 1836 edition of the Exeter Book.) There has been much speculation on the true nature and intention of these poems. In the modern sense, an elegy is a lyrical expression of the grief, either of an individual or of universal experience. The lyrical element is tenuous in Anglo-Saxon poetry, unless ruggedness may be accepted in exchange for melody of the line.

Both the poems are homiletic in character, and were probably the work of clerics, careful to supply a Christian message at the end of what began as a secular theme. *The Seafarer*'s 124 lines are curiously lacking in structural unity, though the meditations are couched in the first person singular. The notion of Kluge (1883) and Rieger (1894) that the first 64 lines represent a dialogue between an old sailor and a young one, because of the alternating moods of the poet, still has occasional supporters. But the thoughts of the speaker, according to Dorothy Whitelock's 'Interpretation of *The Seafarer*' (*Chadwick Memorial Studies*, eds Fox, C. and Dickens, B., pp 261–72) are those of a *peregrinus*, whose sentiments reflect the Christian view of life, a voyage on the road to Eternity, which is fraught with good and evil. A peregrinus, she adds, is more than a pilgrim visiting a shrine abroad, by way of penance. He is one for whom the roving life is a self-imposed duty, to renounce the luxuries of home, and embark on the sterner, Celtic religious life that entrusts all human safety to God. The trouble with the first half of the poem is that the allegory is never explicitly stated; and with the second that it lacks the dramatic imagery of the sea that made its predecessor so arresting.

The decisive change in *The Seafarer* is where moralizing supersedes realistic experience, and the speaker announces: 'Ic gelyfe no/þæt him eorðwelan ece stondað' (I have no faith that earthly riches will abide for ever, lines 66–7). Ezra Pound, who contracts the poem to 99 lines, translates in the archaic spirit of the original, 'I believe not/That any earth-weal eternal standeth' (*Selected Poems*, Faber, pp 52–3). The latter part of *The Seafarer* is full of gnomic utterance, as well as criticism of worldly values, such as: 'Fate is more strong,/God more mighty than any man's thought' (lines 115–16). Modern readers naturally prefer the impressionistic realism of the first 64 lines, believing that, under clerical influence, the form and spirit of Anglo-Saxon poetry are stylistically conditioned beyond the point of lay tolerance.

Perhaps to counter this attitude E. G. Stanley wrote an essay on 'Old English Poetic Diction' (*Anglia* LXXIII (1955), pp 413–66) which examines closely the nature of Old English figurative language, and the relation of symbol to the thing symbolized. In didactic poetry, he distinguishes between biblical paraphrase that is factual, and that which enshrouds doctrine. He finds that, for moods and abstract ideas, Anglo-Saxon poets freely employed metaphor that evokes natural phenomena; for example, the melancholy seafarer is said to be 'held prisoner by fetters of frost'. Invariably, the symbolic is so interwoven with the factual in descriptions of nature, that poets made no clear distinction between the real and the figurative.

Mutability, exile and loss are the themes of the elegiac poems *The Seafarer*, *The Wanderer*, *The Husband's Message*, *The Wife's Complaint* and *The Ruin*, the last of which is thought to have been inspired by the Roman remains at Bath. The elemental power and admirable control of emotions are Germano-Celtic in spirit; so is the occasional romanticism of the verse. But much that is admirable is weakened by the tendency to moralize. The homiletic rhetoric of this group suggests authorship by monks, who had well mastered the alliterative technique.

The fragmentary *Battle of Maldon* (325 lines) is the last of the poems in this survey, and one of the most important, because it deals with historical persons. As a late example of the heroic tradition, written near the end of the tenth century, and copied perhaps fifty years later, it did not appear in any of the four codices mentioned. It was preserved in MS Cotton Otho A XII, and had once been in the possession of John Leland and Archbishop Parker, but was destroyed in the Cotton Library fire of 1731. Fortunately, the text had been copied a year earlier by John Elphinston, and it then passed to Thomas Hearne, who printed an imperfect version in 1726.

The battle took place in the late summer of 991, between Norwegian invaders, nominally under Olaf Tryggvason, and Anglo-Saxon defenders, under Earl Byrhtnoth of Essex (see p 127). The scene was near the mouth of the River Blackwater, then known as the Panta. The poem has the stirring dramatic language and noble elegiac style of a characteristic Germanic epic; it is, in fact, a small scale counterpart of *Beowulf*, and not without its Christian message. In the figurative phrasing of the piece, kennings and conventional epithets are more sparing than in *Beowulf* and *Judith*. The language, full as it is of moral exhortation, is direct and forceful, and the patriotic motivation is extremely moving. The poet must have had eye-witness accounts of the battle, but did not himself take part in it (see line 117).

The ethics of the *comitatus* principle in *The Battle of Maldon* have come under fire, especially in two papers that call for close study: J. R. R. Tolkien, *The Homecoming of Beorhtnoth, Beorhthelm's Son*, Allen and Unwin, 1975; and J. E. Cross, 'Mainly on Philology and the Interpretative Criticism of *Maldon*', *Old English Studies in Honour of John C. Pope*, Toronto University Press, 1974. The *comitatus*, a term that owes its origin to Tacitus's account in *Germania*, was a bond of loyalty between an aristocratic leader and his men. The leader's honoured place in battle was before his house-carls, friends and retainers; any warrior was disgraced as a coward if he left the field before or after the commander's death. It was an instinctive duty of the retainers to publicly avow loyalty at one of the mead-drinking functions, in return for the earl's generosity towards them. This code is underlined in the speeches of Byrhtnoth's *heorðwerod* in *Maldon*, and the defection of the sons of Odda, described in lines 185–201, was a serious breach.

In lines 89 to 95 the poet criticizes Byrhtnoth's unwisdom in allowing the Vikings to cross the causeway and engage in battle, thereby negating the advantage of the situation he enjoyed. Tolkien writes of the earl's *ofermōd*: 'This element of pride, in the form of the desire for honour and glory, in life and after death, tends to

213

grow, to become a chief motive, driving a man beyond the bleak heroic necessity to excess – to chivalry . . . Magnificent perhaps, but certainly wrong. Too foolish to be heroic.' *Ofermōd* means 'pride' as well as 'overboldness', a fact borne out by Byrhtnoth's speech to the Viking messenger (lines 45–61). J. E. Cross maintains there is no ambiguity in the poet-critic's condemnation; he contrasts the situations of real men in a real battle, with noble heroes in a poetic battle (p 243). The glory in *Maldon* is the reward of the retainers, rather than their chief. If the poem was penned during the reign of Æthelred, Cross observes, it could well have been 'an indictment by implication of the policy of buying off the Danes, but also against Englishmen who lacked loyalty to their leaders in those times' (pp 247–48).

Taking Anglo-Saxon poetry as a whole, the reader will find it remarkably uniform in treatment, as well as limited in the variety of its themes. One cause of this was the West-Germanic tradition of alliterative verse, which resembles rhythmic prose. Then there was the Church's monopoly of literature, and the clerk's education using Latin literary models. Patristic specimens, from Tertullian to Augustine, were often rhetorical to excess, while the indigenous practice of verse tended to be stereotyped, if not in rhythm, in the choice of figurative language. The bulk of the poetry makes the same kind of appeal to the senses, and this creates an impression that the imagination had become ossified, not by technical convention alone, but by the evangelizing spirit of the Christian scholars who adapted or preserved poetry.

Louis Cazamian has been unforgivingly criticized by Anglo-Saxonists for his summing up of Old English biblical verse paraphrase:

> If, for a moment, these Anglo-Saxon poems are not read indulgently, if we cease to make allowances for them, almost as we do for the sketches of children and savage peoples, but, like some critics, overpraise them, the heavy pompousness of the paraphrases at once becomes evident, in contrast to the sober and sublime vigour of the Bible . . . Very often, the Anglo-Saxon has overlaid beauties not apparent to him with the weight of his words.
>
> (*History of English Literature*, Dent, 1933, p 38)

'Indulgently' and 'sketches of children and savage peoples' are unfortunate; but the gist of the indictment has the hall-mark of truth. The informality of the verse was largely determined by the phonetic structure of the spoken language; its characteristic feature being the prominence of consonants in stressed positions, tending to give them emphasis to the detriment of the vowels. The result was an almost complete inhibition of melody. The liberty poets took in devising figurative compounds, whether or not used as kennings, produced superfluous periphrases, which may be taken as a want of imagination. The riddling gift, designed to test the reader's capacity for observation, led to obscurity, artificiality and sometimes unwieldy syntax. Very few poets disciplined themselves to economy of phrase, or were able to exploit the most fecund use of metaphor, perception of the essential beauty of relationships.

Much has been written on the structure of Old English poetry, since Eduard Sievers produced his first paper 'On the Rhythm of Germanic Alliterative Verse' in 1885, followed by the monograph, *Altgermanische Metrik*, in 1893. The accuracy and usefulness of his examination have since been thoroughly vindicated. The exhaustive analysis of A. J. Bliss in *The Metre of Beowulf* does not show the quantity of stressed syllables, which is one reason for its super-subtlety. The relation of OE verse rhythm to that of prose is likely to remain a contentious issue.

All verse depends on a regularly recurring unit of rhythm, which is instinctive, and based on the language as colloquially spoken. The vitality and freedom of the rhythm, as well as the steps to modulate it, are linked partly with the mood of the poet (or reciter), and partly with the traditional scope of technical variation; a principal object of all art is to secure unity in variety. Modulation in Anglo-Saxon poetry is the result of variation, not only of the unit of rhythm, but of the combination of such units. Sievers found that five half-verse combinations, with suitable subdivisions, satisfy all needs.

Old English verse has a line to line development, like blank verse since the sixteenth century; it is never stanzaic. Sievers's types classify half-lines, and these have been accepted as the basic units of rhythm in Anglo-Saxon poetry. The two half-verses, usually label-led *a* and *b*, are separated by a pause or *caesura*; the term is not here used (as Bliss uses it) for the scanner's vertical stroke of foot-division, which is at the root of J. C. Pope's objection in *The Rhythm of Beowulf*, since rhythm is detected by the ear, not visually. A normal half-verse has none the less two metrical feet; where there happen to be more than two primary stresses, the half-line is held to be expanded. Any foot of the half-verse must have one primary stress, but may contain another syllable with secondary or medium stress. All other syllables are said to be unstressed. The binding together of two half-verses in a line is secured by the device of alliteration, the effective letters being referred to as *staves*.

According to Daniel Jones, 'Stresses are essentially subjective activities of the speaker' (*The Phoneme: Its Nature and Use*, Heffer, Cambridge, 1950, pp 134–5). On the other hand quantity is objective, and varies little from speaker to speaker. Bliss says that 'many of the conventional OE quantities are in fact prehistoric' (op cit., p 31, note 2). Old English verse is partly quantitative; but it does not, like Latin, depend *primarily* on the duration of time of a syllable. The main purpose in Old English poetry, as in all other, is to secure an equable distribution of stresses, without doing violence to the natural flow of speech. Within reason, the number of syllables in the half-verses is not important. Rhetorical stress is, of course, common in alliterative verse, as in any other; syllabic weight may, for instance, be modified in a particular sentence, because of a special relationship of the word on which it falls to other words. The actual degree of secondary stress can only be determined by the context.

Primary stress invariably falls on a long syllable; but as length is not always semantically available, *resolution* is permissible into two short syllables; the first of these bears the stress, the second being slurred, to produce what resembles syncopation. In an article 'Old Germanic Metrics and Old English Metrics' (*Grundriss der Germanischen Philologie*, II.2., 1905) Sievers says that resolution involves 'an acceleration of the tempo of the speech, which is itself shortened, since the two syllables are compressed approximately into the measure of a single long syllable'. It is essential to recognize what a *long syllable* in OE metrics implies; it is *either* one which has a naturally long vowel or diphthong, *or* a naturally short vowel or diphthong succeeded by two consonants; both are represented in scansion by a macron. A *short syllable* is one which has a naturally short vowel or diphthong, succeeded by a single consonant, and is represented by a breve.

A stressed syllable is simultaneously marked in scansion by an acute accent, if the stress is primary, and by a grave accent, if secondary. An unstressed syllable is marked by a cross. Primary stress customarily falls on the stem syllable of a word. Terminations and inflexions are invariably hurried syllables.

Henry Sweet, in the section on 'Metre' in the introduction to the seventh edition of his *Anglo-Saxon Reader* (1894, §§ 361–8), uses the appropriate terms *lifts* and *dips* to indicate the wave-like rhythm of OE verse. A normal foot contains one lift (stressed element) and one dip (unstressed element). A dip may be made up of any number of weak syllables. The sole necessity in the verse line is that it should contain at least two waves in each half-verse. The movement is not asymmetrical to those whose ear is attuned to it, but there are difficulties for some theorists in regard to Sievers's types D and E, where one of the feet contains a half as well as a full stress.

The second half-verse in Old English is more limited in structure than the first. It is generally the first half-verse that is expanded; for it permits of *anacrusis* (extra unstressed syllables at the beginning of the half-line); it also admits of more alliterative syllables than the second. Sweet calls one extra syllable at the beginning of a half-verse a *prelude*. Anacrusis is possible only where the half-verse begins with a primary stress, i.e. where the rhythm is falling; the same rule applies to a prelude. Bliss has shown that 'anacrusis is intimately linked to the question of double alliteration' (p 4), and that it 'is not to be expected' in type E of Sievers's classification (p 43).

The second half-verse has only one alliterative letter, called the *head-stave*; the first half-verse may have one or two, called the *under-staves*. The head-stave always commences the first lift, and should therefore be the most emphatic word in the second half-line. Only if there are two emphasized words in the first half-verse, will it contain double alliteration; nevertheless, this kind is the more common. Here are the rules for alliteration:

(1) Any vowel alliterates with any other vowel.
(2) Consonants must be the same, and *st, sc, sp* must be followed by identical combinations. *Sw*, however, may alliterate with *s* plus vowel, or *s* plus any consonant.
(3) *hw* is permitted to alliterate with *h*.
(4) *c* and *g*, when palatal i.e. fronted, are permitted to alliterate with back *c* and *g* (gutteral), respectively.
(5) Alliteration is always on the word that bears a primary stress.
(6) If a noun and a verb occur in the same half-verse, it is the noun

that alliterates.

(7) Similarity of initial letters in words that comprise the dip does not constitute alliteration.

The expanded or lengthened half-verse has three primary stresses, not two, and therefore differs from anacrusis. The additional foot may be either the falling or rising type, and alliteration is generally on the first and second stresses in the first half-line, not the third. In the second half-line, alliteration does not shift to the stress in the prefixed foot, but appears, normally, at the beginning of the second lift.

There are three poetic licences worth mentioning; the first two concern elision.

(1) Weak vowels are elided before a word beginning with another vowel.

(2) *h* in weak syllables is disregarded, probably to reduce the number of unstressed syllables in the dip.

(3) A vowel-like consonant after a consonant or parasite vowel (e.g. the *o* in *fugol*) may be disregarded for metrical purposes. Thus *setl* and *fæðm* are treated as monosyllables.

Sievers's classification of the five types of half-verse was based on prosodic analysis of the different combinations, as they occur in OE verse. Below are reproduced his final conclusions, taken from the 1905 article already quoted. The types are given in the order of their frequency of use:

(a) Types with equal feet, pattern 2+2.

(1) A ´ x | ´ x , double falling type

(2) B x ´ | x ´, double rising type

(3) C x ´ | ´ x , rising-falling type

(b) Types with unequal feet

(4) D ´ | ´ ` x } pattern 1+3
     ´ | ´ x ` }

(5) E ´ ` x | ´ } pattern 3+1
     ´ x ` | ´ }

The following variations on the above models, with examples from S. A. Cook's *First Book in Old English* (1906 edition) should be noted:

(1) *Falling rhythm* (A)

    (a) ᝽ x x | ∠ x (resolution of the first lift), cwicera cynna

    (b) x̆ x | ∠ x | ∠x (anacrusis), oððe sundoryrfes

(2) *Rising rhythm* (B)

    (a) x x ᝽ x | x x ᝽ x (resolution of both lifts), nū ic gumena
                                          gehwæne

    (b) x x x x ∠ | x ∠ (extra unstressed syllables), þæt hē in þæt
                                           būrgeteld

(3) *Rising-falling rhythm* (C)

    (a) x x ᝽ x | ∠ x (resolution of the first lift), on ðām
                                           sigewonge

    (b) x x x x ᝽ x | ∠ x (extra unstressed syllables, and resolu-
                     tion of the first lift), þe hīe ofercuman mihton

(4) *Type D*

    ᝽ x | ᝽ x ⊥ x (resolution of both lifts), hæleð higerōfe

(5) *Type E*

    ᝽ x ⊥ x | ᝽ x (resolution of both lifts), sigerōfe hæleð

Sievers considers that the West Germanic scops, in heroic verse, cultivated recitative to replace singing, and that only this kind of verse has survived in literature (ibid., 1905). For this reason every half-verse represents a grammatical unit of some kind. Sievers found that colloquial contractions need sometimes to be invoked to solve what appear as metrical corruptions in a text.

The following twenty lines, scanned, serve to show Sievers's system in operation:

          Raþe æfter þon (= þonne)
            ᝽ x | ∠ x ⊥   D

on fāgne flōr   fēond treddode
B x ∠ | x ∠ ‖ ∠ | ∠ ⊥ x D
ēode yrremōd;   him of ēagum stōd   (*e* of *ēode* elided)
D ∠ | ∠ x ⊥ ‖ x x ∠ | x   ∠ B
līgge gelīcost   lēoht unfæger.
A ∠ x x | ∠ x ‖ ∠ x | ∠ x A
        Geseah hē in recede   rinca manige
(prelude) A x | ᝽   x x | ᝽ x x ‖ ∠ x | ᝽ x x A
  swefan sibbegedriht   samōd ætgædcre
D ᝽ x | ∠ x x ⊥ ‖ ᝽ x x | ᝽ x x A
  magōrinca hēap.   Þa his mōd āhlōg
E ᝽ x ⊥ x | ∠ ‖ x x ∠ | x ∠ B

                (*Beowulf*, lines 724–730)

twēoda gifena
⌣ x | ⌣ x x A

in ðȳs ginnan grunde;
A x x | ⌣ x | ⌣ x‖

hēo ðār þā gearwe funde
x x x| ⌣x | ⌣ x A (anacrusis)

mundbyrd æt ðām mǣran þēodne,
A ⌣ x x x | ⌣x | ⌣ x ‖

þā hēo āhte mǣste þearfe
x x |⌣ x| ⌣ x| ⌣ x A (expanded line)

hyldo þæs hēhstan Dēman,
A ⌣ x x | ⌣ x | ⌣ x ‖

þæt hē hīe wið þæs hēhstan brōgan
x x| ⌣ ⌣ x x | ⌣ x | ⌣x A (expanded)

gefriðode, frymða Waldend;
A x| ⌣ x x | ⌣ x| ⌣ x ‖

hyre ðæs Fæder on roderum
⌣ x x | ⌣ x x | ⌣ x x A (expanded line)

torhtmōd tīðe gefrēmede,
A ⌣ x | ⌣ x x| ⌣ x x ‖

þe hēo āhte trumne gelēafan
x x |⌣ x| ⌣ x x|⌣ x A (expanded line)

ā to ðām Ælmightigan.
A⌣ x x |⌣ x x x ‖

Gefrægen ic ðā Olofernus   (elision)
x ⌣ x |x ⌣ x|⌣ x C (expanded half-verse)

(Judith, lines 1–7)

Swylce gēac monað   geomran reorde
A ⌣ x| ⌣ x x ‖ ⌣ x | ⌣ x A

singeð sumeres weard   sorge bēodeð
B x x ⌣ x|x ⌣ ‖ ⌣ x| ⌣ x A

(elision) bittre in breosthord. Þæt se beorn ne wāt
A ⌣ x | ⌣ x ‖ x x ⌣ | x ⌣ B

secg ēstēadig   hwæt þā sume drēogað
A ⌣ x| ⌣ x ‖ x x ⌣ x| ⌣ x C

þe þā wræclāstas   wīdost lecgað!
C x x ⌣| ⌣ x ‖ ⌣ x | ⌣ x A

For þon nū mīn hyge hweorfeð   ofer hreþerlocan
C x x x x x ⌣ x| ⌣ x ‖ x x ⌣ x|⌣ x C (defective foot)

(Seafarer, lines 53–8)

In the last four decades three scholars, C. S. Lewis, Marjorie Daunt and J. R. R. Tolkien, have published studies on Old English poetry of much relevance to the language of our time. In *Rehabili-*

tations and Other Essays, (OUP, 1939, pp 119–32) Lewis makes the
following useful observations:

(1) In the B type of half-verse 'the first dip may contain any
    reasonable number of unaccented syllables; but the second
    should normally consist of a *single* unaccented syllable . . . A
    predominantly "anapaestic" movement is to be avoided' (§ 8).
(2) In the D type, where there is only one dip, the theory of
    compensation is explained; 'the dip must be strengthened by a
    syllable nearly (but not quite) as strong as the lifts' (§ 10).
(3) 'No half-line of any type should end in a pure dactyl' (§ 16).
(4) 'The last half of a given line and the first half of the next are
    more intimately connected than the two halves of a single line'
    (§ 17.2).
(5) 'That two or more consonants make the *syllable* long is not a
    metrical rule, but a phonetic fact; that they make the preceding
    vowel long, as some say, is neither a rule nor a fact, but false'
    (Footnote 2).

These helps are counsels of perfection for anyone who wishes to
write alliterative verse in modern English, as Lewis does twice in the
essay. In § 18 he warns against attempts at accentual adaptation that
do not observe the rules of quantity; for these give the verse its
resonance.

Marjorie Daunt concedes that 'Old English verse is really conditioned prose' (*Transactions of the Philological Society*, 1946,
p 57); in her paper 'Old English Verse and English Speech Rhythm'
she discovers few signs of 'aesthetic' feeling at work. Poetry to the
scop was no more than colloquial speech, using alliteration as an aid
to remembrance. According to this writer, the five types of Sievers
are not essentially 'metrical', but simply the natural language
patterns one can identify in Cædmon's talk with the Angel, and
Alfred's conversations with Ohthere and Wulfstan. Hence the
predominance of noun-adjective groupings over finite verbs and
adverbs. The most inconspicuous parts of speech for metrical
emphasis are found by investigators to be the particles, and the
personal and other pronouns. Daunt believes that the scop chose for
recital 'groups of spoken language, arranged to run easily and not
monotonously'. The polysyllables that occur in extended lines
consist largely of compounds, which incorporate familiar nouns of

lesser dimension. Any example of ancient or modern colloquial speech in English may be segmented on the lines of Sievers's stress combinations, these being fundamental to the genius of the language. Daunt therefore suggests that the earliest verse was 'the spoken language rather tidied up', and untainted, as yet, by the latinate influx.

Tolkien, as a creative writer, late in his career assumed the role of a quaint, but sophisticated, gleeman. The thirty-four pages of the prefatory remarks he contributed to J. R. Clark Hall's modernization of *Beowulf* (1949) are more important than the notes on 'Metre' for understanding the epic, as experienced by the original audience. He noticed that, despite the comparative richness of *Beowulf*'s vocabulary, there is a paradoxical 'compactness' in the idiom of the poem, which few translators manage to capture without baldness. The unlikeness to modern English dawns upon the reader only when he wrestles with the composition in the original language; he will be troubled with finding semantic equivalents for the generative compounds, rather than the technical devices, though the right weight to be given to compound elements is never easy. Tolkien's 'philological knowingness', his ability to date words by their peculiar function, enabled him to appreciate the sensibility of the poet in assimilating what was already archaic by his time.

Like Lewis, Tolkien illustrates OE metre by reference to modern English examples; one reason is to show that the patterns identified by Sievers still exist. *Beowulf* is still a challenge to the literary stylist, and Tolkien met it by composing, in dialogue, a wry sequel to *The Battle of Maldon*, namely, *The Homecoming of Beorhtnoth, Beorhthelm's Son* (1975). The familiar style of most of it enabled him to disguise the 'artfulness' of the alliterative method. Here is his assessment of the lost hero of Maldon:

```
        His head was higher   than the helm of kings
    B   x   ⌣ | x  ⌣ x ‖  x   x ⌣ |x  ⌣   B
        with heathen crowns,  his heart keener
    B   x   ⌣| x   ⌣    ‖ x  ⌣  | ⌣ x C
        and his soul clearer   than swords of heroes
    C x    x ⌣ | ⌣ x ‖  x   ⌣  |x  ⌣ x B
        polished and proven;  than plated gold
    A  ⌣   x x |  ⌣ x ‖  x  ⌣|x  ⌣  B
        his worth was greater.  From the world has passed
    B  x  ⌣  | x  ⌣ x ‖  x   x ⌣ | x  ⌣   B
```

a prince peerless   in peace and war,
C x ∠ | ∠ x ‖ x ∠ | x ∠ B
just in judgement,   generous-handed
A ∠ x | ∠   x ‖ ∠̆ x x | ∠ x A
as the golden lords of long ago.
B x   x ∠ | x ∠ ‖ x ∠ | x ∠ B
He has gone to God   glory seeking
B x x x ∠ | x ∠ ‖ ∠ x | ∠ x A
Beorhtnoth beloved.
A ∠̆ ‿ x   x | ∠ x
or
E ∠   ∠̄ x | ∠̆ x

Note how skilfully the alliterated lines are run on. The difficulty however, is that modern spelling cannot be trusted for pronunciation; e.g. *generous* (line 7), alliterates phonetically with *just*. As regards quantity, *head* in line 1 is customarily a shorter syllable than *clear* in *clearer* (line 3); yet both have to be accorded the same theoretical weight, because metrical stress invariably lengthens the syllable on which it falls. There are eleven instances of type B, five of type A, three of type C, none of D and possibly one of E. This tends to confirm the dominance of iambic measures in modern English verse. The likelihood of a successful alliterative poem in the current idiom is as slender now as when Ezra Pound made his daring translation of *The Seafarer*.

Part Two

TO THE INTRODUCTION
OF PRINTING

CHAPTER IX

Transition

𝕚𝕚𝕚𝕚𝕚𝕚

THE NORMAN CONQUEST produced significant changes in the political superstructure, but the rank and file of English society continued to evolve as in the age of Æthelred, Cnut and Edward the Confessor. To the English ruling class the Norman revolution brought discipline as well as change, through the force of enlightened despotism. If the break with the past was a heavy burden, the consequences were the more enduring. The effects can best be seen in some institutions of English feudalism which date from the Anglo-Danish period.

The word *feudal*, though it did not appear in English until the seventeenth century, was derived from medieval Latin *feudum* 'fief' and was obviously related to OE *feoh* and Frankish *fehu*, meaning 'fee' or 'property'. No one had actually posited a 'feudal system' until Adam Smith published his *Wealth of Nations* in 1776. Though this system entailed no legislative confirmation of established custom until the thirteenth century, it was operative in the autocratic rule of European heads of state by the time of William the Conqueror. David Herlihy, in *The History of Feudalism* (1970) says that *feudal* 'identified an economy and a society marked by wide contrasts between rich and poor; a miserable and exploited peasantry; and an unresponsive, unproductive economy' (Introduction, p XVI). The origins of feudalism are still the subject of much historical debate.

William I's mind seems to have been Gallic and legalistic, and his dynamic rule was based upon money and power. Five years after the conquest he abandoned attempts at learning English and emulating the style of his predecessors. He spent less time in England, and before his death found a practical solution to political and dynastic squabbles in the division of his empire, three quarters of which was in Britain. No other king would have dared to claim one fifth of the kingdom as his personal property. He created a papal monarchy, in which the Church controlled a quarter of England's land; even the authoritarian Hildebrand, who became Pope Gregory VII, was compelled to respect William's autonomy. Half of the land that remained was distributed as 'honours' to his family and vassals, including Bretons and Flemish. By the time of his death only eight per cent of the country remained in English hands, and only two English landowners were left, one in Lincoln, the other in Warwickshire.

A principal barrier to social relations was the snobbish exclusiveness of the Norman and French privileged settlers, who were a trusted minority of about one hundred and seventy. Their fiefs were bounties for services at Hastings or elsewhere, and were intended to supply the backbone of William's military force. But earls and barons (the chief landed proprietors) were often abroad fulfilling military obligations in William's wars, and left the management of their estates to stewards, whose security lay in the Norman *motte* or mount-and-bailey castle, thirty-six of which were built in the Conqueror's reign. Not the Normans, but the English, built England's later stone castles, many of which still stand. Vassal barons farmed out their land to over five thousand professional knights, who in turn employed peasant labourers.

English aristocrats who did not emigrate to Ireland, Scotland, Denmark or other European states, were reduced to farmers, working for Norman lords. Their language and their Saxon names came to be regarded as barbarous and inferior; with the result that the ambitious learnt French, and many parents preferred to use the names of Normans for their children, e.g. Hugh, Richard, Robert and Roger. It should be observed that surnames did not come into favour until after the Norman conquest. By the fourteenth century they were commonly derived from trades, such as *Miller*, *Smith* and *Baker*; from place-names, such as *Holland* and *Lester*; or they represented patronymics, such as *Williamson*. Proper names derived from Norman functionaries at court or in noble households were: *Chancellor*, *Chamberlain*, *Butler*, *Marshall*, *Constable*, *Chaplin* and *Clark*.

The king's ingenuity in augmenting the royal privileges and revenues was sometimes regarded in a sinister light, especially when the danegeld, abolished by Edward the Confessor, was reintroduced. William claimed wardship over the minor children of deceased barons, and the right to determine whom they should marry. Most favours he granted had to be paid for in some form. It is not surprising that the Norman kings became wealthy; William's annual revenue from all sources (including fines, customs dues, sale of timber, etc.) was about £66,000. He was the first to appoint royal clerks, who later were to become secretaries of state, the chancellor becoming the Keeper of the Great Seal.

The common law applicable to public life remained that of Edward the Confessor, and during the first three years the royal writs were issued in English; but after 1070 official documents were prepared in Latin. Latin also took the place of the vernacular in church services. Many fine stone churches were pulled down and remodelled to Norman or Burgundian designs. The cathedral at Canterbury was under construction during William's reign. Though little remains of Edward the Confessor's nearly contemporary Westminster Abbey, it was reputed to be a magnificent edifice.

William's method of resisting papal interference in the affairs of his kingdom was to handle personally the policy-making of the church. He presided at councils and appointed trustworthy archbishops, bishops and abbots, on whom he relied to supply a quota of ecclesiastical knights for the army. Wulfstan of Worcester, an opponent of clerical marriages, was the only English bishop who remained in office at his accession. Archbishop Stigand of Canterbury, not having the papal blessing, was removed from office in 1070.

Three times a year, at Easter, Whitsuntide and Christmas, the king met the lords of the realm in session, called the *Commune Concilium*; this took the place of the West-Saxon *witena gemot*. These were ceremonial occasions, when the king was crowned, and a royal banquet held. The functions of this large *Concilium* were obviously limited, and consultations on public matters of immediate importance took place at the king's permanent court, the *Curia Regis*. The larger Council was, however, consulted at Christmas 1085, meeting in Gloucester, on the undertaking of the Domesday survey, an event of national significance, though it came too late to be of advantage to William himself.

The king's superior law-courts were usually presided over by Geoffrey, Bishop of Coutances, who had to deal with a large number of property lawsuits, and to assemble evidence pertaining to the rule of Edward the Confessor. The judge saw fit to co-opt

English assessors to help him arrive at a collective verdict, and these advisers are thought to have been the germ of the jury system. Such jurors, bound by oath, were employed in the Domesday investigations, of which the Ely Inquest provides a typical example. The following is taken from the title to this inquest:

> . . . the name of the manor, who held it in the time of King Edward, who holds it now; the number of hides; the number of plows on the demesne, the number of those of the men; the number of villeins; the number of cotters; the number of serfs; the number of freemen; the number of sokemen; the amount of forest; the amount of meadow; the number of pastures; the number of mills; the number of fishponds; how much it has been increased or diminished; how much it was all worth then; and how much now; how much each freeman and sokeman held and holds there. All this three times over, namely, in the time of King Edward, and when King William gave it, and as it now is, and if more can be had than is had.
>
> (Adams and Stephens, *Select Documents of English Constitutional History*, 1918, pp 2–3.)

The terms of this document are fundamental to an understanding of the Domesday Book, as well as the rise of English feudalism; the different ways in which persons could own, occupy or find employment on property were determined. The investigation showed how incomes from the land were derived, what assessment each tax-payer should bear, and whether the productive yield might be raised by improved management. Northumbria and urban areas such as London, Winchester and Shrewsbury were not included in the survey, which was little more than a bureaucracy's fiscal and tax register, directed at rural estates. The income derived from this geld is unlikely to have exceeded ten thousand pounds at the time of William's death.

The Domesday Book is of value because it grades the classes of rural England on a social scale. The types are freemen, sokemen, villeins, cottars and serfs. Maitland, in *Domesday Book and Beyond*, calls the eastern shires 'the home of liberty', because the first two classes were in greater numbers in that area than elsewhere. As the survey moved westward, the number of villeins, cottars and serfs increased, Gloucestershire and Cornwall having the highest proportion of the 25,000 serfs that existed in the whole country. Lincolnshire and Yorkshire recorded no serfs at all, though this is thought to be an oddity of nomenclature.

The *OED* holds that serfdom was a modified form of slavery. The serf, being attached to the soil, could not be removed from the lord's land, except by manumission; he had to be transferred when the land passed to another owner. *Serf* (Latin *servus*) and *slave* are both English words of OF derivation; the former is, however, the term used in the Domesday Book.

Historians often claim that serfdom had disappeared by the end of the twelfth century; but lines 9479–92 of *Cursor Mundi* and other documents suggest that this was not so:

> Now is man be-gylid alle / His owne synne made hym thralle / That first was fre as I told / Now hath hym satanas to hold / To whos service he hym yeld / His thralle he was to have in weld / While he his thralle in his service / he ne may be fre on no wyse / Thralle may be no law in lede / ffre Erytage asks of lord-hede / Synne he is us thralle by-comyn / his Erytage hym by-nomyn / In no court owy thralle be herd / Ne stond in dome to be answerd

Fuedalism radically transformed English social life for six hundred years, indeed until the reign of Charles I. It retained the manorial system and placed the peasant class (villeins and cottars) under manipulation of land-owning lords. This meant a progressive decline of individual rights and freedoms, though not always of the country's prosperity, which depended on the efficiency of individual rulers. One reason for the curtailment of liberty among the peasant classes was that they could no longer rise in the social scale, as was possible in Anglo-Saxon times. The papal church was not active in eliminating inequalities of the villein class until Pope Clement IV's proclamation on the Dignity of Human Nature in 1266. Women, too, were deprived under feudal law of many rights they had enjoyed during the rule of the Anglo-Saxon kings; for they were regarded as mere chattels of their husbands.

Separation of employments was very significant for the future structure of society. As in Saxon times, land remained the principal factor in the recognition of rank. A villein enjoyed the inalienable right to remain on the fuedal lord's estate, but had to pay the owner a non-increasable rent called an assize rent, to serve a stipulated number of days on the lord's demesne under the eye of the bailiff, and to provide his own team for the plough. In return he was given a parcel of land of his own to till on days when his lord did not require his service, and was allowed to share in any profits from the village meadows and adjoining woodland. So much forest land was, however, appropriated by William the Conqueror and his successors, that game virtually ceased to be a staple article of the peasant's diet.

The power struggle within the Roman papacy that involved Hildebrand, left the Church impotent to reform itself in the latter half of the eleventh century. William took advantage of the situation to entrench the power of the state-church in England. The siting of several cathedrals in rural areas was considered inappropriate, and Lanfranc transferred the bishops' dioceses of Selsey, Sherborne, Dorchester and Lichfield, to Chichester, Salisbury (Old Sarum), Lincoln and Coventry, respectively. The cathedral organization of Canterbury, Winchester and Worcester was largely controlled by Benedictine monks, with stricter rules, expecially in regard to celibacy, a condition which Lanfranc favoured. Rochester and Durham soon joined the monastic cathedrals, and others were added after King William's death (Bath, Ely, Norwich and Carlisle). The problems of this movement – limitation of the bishop's offices in secular affairs, and relaxed standards of discipline among monks – were to lead to endless dissension in the Church.

There were thirty-five self-governing monasteries and nine nunneries in England at this time, at which resided over twelve hundred monks and nuns, the institutions bringing in about £13,000 annually. Most English abbots, because they had supported Harold's cause, were replaced by Normans; three were left, one being Brand of Peterborough (died 1069), the uncle of Hereward the Wake. Æthelwig of Evesham (died 1077) and Wulfstan of Worcester, who survived William, were English ecclesiastics of considerable status, in Mercia and the Severn valley respectively. They were pillars of the Anglo-Saxon tradition, and owed royal favour to their integrity and charitable works. Wulfstan was canonized in 1203, and his *Life* by Colman was the last biography of a saint to be written in Old English.

When Norman abbots first assumed their charges, most were unpopular, because of their foreign characteristics, disrespect for the Anglo-Saxon saints and inability to communicate in English. Opposition to the less tactful abbots sometimes resulted in disobedience and even violence, as at St Augustine's in Canterbury, where the community had to be dispersed. Because the Pope required penance from the Normans for every Englishman killed at

Hastings, William founded Battle Abbey at his own expense, and colonized it with monks from Marmoutier on the River Loire. Furthermore, in about 1080, he established Cluniac orders of St Hugh at Lewes Priory (whose abbot was William de Warenne) and at Bermondsey, London. Between 1070 and 1083 monastic disciplines were reintroduced to the north of England, when Norman Reinfrid brought monks to Jarrow, Wearmouth and Whitby, rebuilding the churches that had suffered at the hands of the Danes. Lanfranc, realizing that the standard of education among the clergy had deteriorated, was instrumental in improving the facilities of monastic libraries. An Anglo-Norman librarian, William of Malmesbury, wrote his *Gesta Regum* during the reign of Henry I.

Several problems of the English succession and the theory of the divine right of kings had their birth in the reigns of the eleventh-century Anglo-Saxon kings. Germanic custom, inherited by the English, was both flexible and conventional on the subject of who should rule; there was no written law concerning the succession of kings. In theory, they were chosen by the Witan; in practice, however, the election depended on effective power that a member of the royal line could command. Though the claim of inheritance was a primary requisite, a nomination by a king with authority had overriding force; the king was bound, however, to designate a man of putative ability. Before Alfred the Great, brothers had been chosen to succeed, when the king's children were too young to rule.

In the short history of Normandy since Duke Rollo, there was no tradition of primogeniture. For that reason William I, claiming the support of both Edward the Confessor and Harold, had no compunction in ignoring the better title of Edgar the Ætheling, who in 1066 was a minor. Later William nominated his second son, William Rufus, as King of England, though his eldest child Robert was the obvious heir. William I's power in England was indeed *de facto* and despotic; he was an illegitimate son, and related to Edward the Confessor in the female line only. On the grounds of bastardy, he was lucky to have succeeded, at the age of seven, to the Duchy of Normandy.

When Edward the Confessor, on his deathbed, was pressured into changing his mind, and designated Harold as his successor, the Norman invasion was inevitable. In turn, this led to further

233

problems of succession, such as the disastrous one at the death of the Conqueror's third son, Henry I, in 1135. Henry had lost two sons, William and Richard, by drowning (on the White Ship) on 25 November, 1119. When he died in France, the king had over twenty illegitimate children, as well as a daughter, Matilda, by a nun of Romsey Abbey; the nun's marriage to the king was diplomatically legitimized by the pious Anselm, Archbishop of Canterbury, and by the Pope. In 1135, Matilda was the widow of the German Emperor, Henry V, remarried to Geoffrey, Count of Anjou; she was Henry I's only legitimate heir, but was apparently rejected on three grounds: (1) Normandy (conquered by the king at Tinchebrai in 1106) was at war with Anjou; (2) Matilda was a woman, whose husband, it was feared, would assume the real power; and (3) the Countess Matilda was a proud, difficult and quarrelsome woman, and deemed to be unsuitable as an English ruler. The upshot was that Henry's nephew, Stephen of Boulogne, grandson of the Conqueror by his daughter Adela (who married Stephen, Count of Blois), hurried to Canterbury and urged Archbishop William Curbeil to crown him, as legitimate successor to the throne. This hurried coronation is one of the inexplicable events of English history; for Stephen was not himself the eldest son. The nineteen-year reign of Stephen, as described in the *Peterborough Chronicle* under the year 1137 (see pp 245, 348), ended Norman rule with anarchy and every degree of cruelty, though Stephen was personally an amiable man.

In retrospect, William the Conqeror's dismemberment of his imperium for the benefit of separate rulers was an arbitrary act. It gave rise two centuries later to dynastic struggles between England and France, culminating in the tragic Hundred Years War (1337 to 1453) and the economic ruin of the latter country. This war, together with the Black Death of 1349, reduced the population of France and England by one-third, though England's total numbers are said to have remained static over the same period. In the quest for wealth and power, Norman rule proved alien to those who enjoyed the more settled life of the English under Edward the Confessor. During this king's reign, orderly local government and justice offered potentialities for peaceful development, unknown in the rest of Europe. Norman activity, on the other hand, was strenuous, restless and mercenary; under what A. F. Pollard described as an 'even-handed tyranny', kings at home were constantly taxing or restoring order (see *The History of England*, p 24); abroad, they fought with armies that increasingly demanded English co-operation and loss of blood.

In 1895, J. H. Round ascribed the origin of feudalism to the introduction of knight service into England (*Feudal England*, Sonnenschein, 1895, pp 225–314). Since then the subject has been warmly debated by historians. Obligatory military duty, resulting from the right of land tenure, had existed under Anglo-Saxon kings; but there were no fiefs. The Conqueror's arbitrary redistribution of land as fiefs to vassals, aggravated the agrarian problem, and created a political class of aristocratic landlords employing a wholly dependent peasantry to cultivate their estates. The country's economy was radically altered by the introduction of the manorial system, and the reduction of the ceorl to a condition of serfdom. The land policy of William differed widely from that of the Roman province of Britain, which the Anglo-Saxon peoples had largely inherited. For the Anglo-Norman *villanus* (or villager) enjoyed no civil rights, while his employer established himself as a member of the mounted affluent caste, which formed the backbone of the king's army. The Frankish rulers of the Continent were the undoubted creators of the feudal system.

Henry II aimed to resume control, after the anarchy of Stephen, by repudiating the absolute jurisdiction of the Church and barons. The murder of Becket, and the abasement and flagellation of the king at Avranche, in order to restore harmony with the Pope, were the price the monarchy had to pay for the important Constitutions of Clarendon in 1164. This document consisted of sixteen clauses, confirming the relationship between Church and State that existed in the reign of Henry I. One clause specifically forbade appeals to Rome without the king's permission; and this, Becket rightly maintained, conflicted with the Church's canon law. Henry II insisted on this agreement to ensure stable government and centralized justice, through clearer relations between secular and ecclesiastical powers; but these Becket's obstinacy denied.

This contretemps in English history needs no recapitulation; a realistic account is to be found in chapter IX of Arthur Bryant's *Makers of the Realm*. Clashes between Church and State constantly arose from the constitutional difficulties of Norman and Plantagenet kings, and were mainly responsible for the rise of a national consciousness.

Henry II, first of the Plantagenets, did not plan to remove all jurisdiction from the Church, as his subsequent actions showed; he was bent on ensuring that the ecclesiastical courts did not differ from those of the realm in punishing offenders. But beyond this, his object was to restrain the jurisdiction of feudal courts and place the administration of justice in the hands of the *Curia Regis*, thereby ensuring that the fines imposed would enrich the coffers of the royal exchequer. He needed this revenue to pay for the mercenaries that made him independent of military support from the baronage. The abuse of such royal power, for personal ends, ultimately brought about the downfall of his son, King John.

It has to be remembered that the first of the Plantagenet kings ruled England from France, where he held court most of the time, owing to the delicate state of royal possessions on the Continent. Henry I had an excellent Justiciar to represent him in the person of Roger of Salisbury, a Norman priest whom he subsequently elevated to the rank of Bishop; the positioning of such an official in Westminster may justly be regarded as the foundation of the English civil service. Henry II relied on Salisbury's nephew, Nigel of Ely, who proved to be the originator of English case-law; his son, Richard FitzNeal, Bishop of London, wrote the invaluable *Dialogue Concerning the Exchequer*, 'in the twenty-third year of the reign of King Henry II' (i.e. *c* 1177). The word *exchequer* (ME *escheker*, OF *eschequier*, from Med. Latin *scaccarium* 'a chess-board') first appeared in that sense in an English context in *Floris and Blauncheflur* (*c* 1300). The table used by the king's treasurer had a checkerboard surface, the squares of which were found useful for his accounting system. In the reign of Richard I the Justiciar, Hubert Walter (afterwards Archbishop of Canterbury), introduced officials known as *coroners*, specially appointed to conduct criminal inquests.

King John, though well educated, was a ruler less scrupulous and able than his father; his brush with the statesmanlike Pope, Innocent III, in 1207 was a disastrous blunder, which ended six years later in the monarch's complete humiliation. It concerned the appointment of Hubert Walter's successor as Archbishop of Canterbury, the King's nominee being John de Grey, Bishop of Norwich. The Pope proposed Cardinal Stephen Langton of Lincolnshire, who was a theological scholar of good reputation, and at the time Canon of York; but the King forcibly restrained him from taking office. Innocent III retaliated by placing the whole of England under an interdict, which meant a cessation of religious services. The vindictive reaction of John led to his excommunication, and a growing deterioration of his position in Western Europe. The Pope declared the throne of England vacant, and induced King Philip of France to mount an invasion, with the connivance of traitorous English barons. John was compelled to surrender his crown to the papal legate, and only after penance was it handed back to him in a feudatory capacity.

The rule of Common Law, based on custom rather than on statutes, dates from the signing of Magna Carta in 1215. This Great Charter, framed in French, initiated the use of French in official documents instead of Latin. It was not a charter of liberties, but an instrument to define by rule relations between the king and different classes of people, and to protect the rights of each in *public* courts. The *private* courts of the barons and Church were abolished; the privileges proper to each class were safeguarded; but Magna Carta did not aim at the welfare of all sections through equal rights. A court was deemed to be constituted when a man could be tried by his peers, under supervision of the king's officials, and not by a superior class of foreigners with vested interests.

Shakespeare's *King John*, which follows closely the earlier play, *The Troublesome Raigne*, does not mention Magna Carta, nor does it exploit the religious issue, as Protestants of the Reformation were to do. The central theme is Arthur, Duke of Brettany's claim to the throne, and its hero the patriot, Philip Faulconbridge, the natural son of Richard Coeur-de-Lion. King John is regarded merely as a usurper. What the play does show is that England, with the loss of all its French possessions north of the Loire, had become a unified national entity, which the king in future would have to rule with a more discreet feudalism than was usual on the Continent, in order to secure the goodwill of the nation.

Henry III, a vacillating king whom Matthew Paris of St Albans, in his *Chronica Majora* (c 1235) described as a man with 'a heart of wax', was nine when he came to the throne, at a time when King Louis IX of France was embarked on a fruitless invasion of England. Despite a feckless career, Henry reigned for fifty-six years (1216–72), in an age of humanistic revival, to which England contributed a fanatical adherent in Simon de Montfort, Earl of Leicester. This man, a friend of Robert Grosseteste, Bishop of Lincoln, was regarded by many as the 'foreigner' and self-seeker from Normandy. Though married to Eleanor, the King's sister, de Montfort had quarrels with Henry, and thought it wise to join the current crusade. Upon his return, he was sent to Gascony, a trouble-centre, where he successfully subdued a rebellion.

The Provisions of Oxford (1258), a landmark in constitutional history nearly as important as the Magna Carta of 1215, arose from the king's extravagance and incessant demands for money to impress his French favourites. De Montfort sat on the King's Council, whose terms were reactionary, being designed to transfer power to the barons, already on the point of open rebellion. A copy of Magna Carta, translated into English, was sent to each shire and read to the people.

In the Provisions of Oxford the word *parliament* made its first official appearance, though Matthew Paris had used the word in Latin writings. *Parliament* is distinguished in the Provisions from the *King's Council*, a consultative body of Anglo-Saxon origin; the evolution of the new body from the old is traced in the final chapter of Sir Maurice Powicke's *Medieval England*. Here are a few of the Oxford enactments:

> It is provided that from each county there shall be chosen four discreet and lawful knights, who on each day when the county court is held, shall meet to hear all complaints made by the sheriffs or bailiffs or any one else against all persons whatsoever . . . No knight of the aforesaid counties, shall be excused by writ of the lord king that he be not placed upon juries and assizes, nor be quit with respect to this provision thus made for the common advantage of the whole realm. . . .

> It is to be remembered that the twenty-four have ordained that there be three parliaments a year. . . . To these three parliaments the elected councillors of the king shall come, even if they are not sent for, to see the state of the realm, and to treat of the common wants of the kingdom, and of the king in like manner. And other times in like manner when occasion shall be, by the king's command.

These provisions sought to induce responsible barons to be less involved in their personal interests, and more in the affairs of the country; but few barons were as pragmatic as de Montfort. The twenty-four guardians of the agreement became a council of administration, which was neither an advisory nor a legislative body. The extent to which tenants-in-chief, like de Montfort, had become anglicized is shown by the zeal of the parliamentary representatives to rid the country of foreigners. The Pope, however, absolved Henry from his oath of acceptance, and the king repudiated the Provisions of Oxford in 1262.

In the Barons' War (1258–65) de Montfort defeated the king at Lewes, and became a virtual dictator. He packed the Parliament of 1265 with commoners representing the towns, thereby creating a precedent from which it was dangerous for subsequent kings to withdraw. But inevitable disagreement among the barons led in the same year to Simon de Montfort's defeat and death, at the hands of Edward, son of the king, who then became responsible for the government until the senile Henry III passed away seven years later.

A. F. Pollard in the *History of England* describes the Barons' War as 'a revolt of the half-breeds, not a revolt of the English' (p 40). Simon de Montfort was the champion of English cities and towns-folk, and the English undoubtedly profited by dissension among the foreigners; for their leader's policy was unequivocally 'England for the English', and his popularity was attested by the thirteenth-century political ballad, *The Song of Lewes*.

When Edward I's accession was announced, while he was on his way back from the last of the crusades, he showed his *bona fides* by determining that English should be the language of the Court. Within a quarter of a century, English had entered every sphere of public life, leaving French as the accomplishment of aristocrats and scholars.

Edward was popular with his people, never wearing the crown after his coronation. He became known as the Justinian of English kings, because he codified the country's laws. His further contribution was the Model Parliament of 1295, in which the people's representation was extended. Representation in Parliament was little valued up to this time; kings had had to issue writs enforcing attendance. The one sent out for the 'Model' parliament of 1295 was prefaced by a resounding rebuff to Philip IV's threatened invasion, and the French king's alleged intention to exterminate the English language.

Edward I's home policy was marked by expulsion of the Jews in 1287, on the ground of their infringement of the law indicting usury; the king showed that the usurers charged as much as thirty per cent on borrowed money. He was the first English monarch to tax church property, and this led to a drawn-out quarrel with Pope Boniface VIII. The despotic power of the papacy was thus undermined. In Edward II's reign the baronage was merged with the peerage.

The class system of the feudal world was seriously threatened, though a century was to elapse before the full impact of the change was appreciated in the political sphere. The writing was on the wall, in the reign of Edward II, when the single chamber invoked by his predecessor for the 'Model' parliament was divided into the House of Commons and the House of Lords, the objects being (1) to reduce the number of petitions against grievances, and (2) to obtain consent for taxation from counsellors in the shires, boroughs and cities. The Commons became a community of interests with which the knights or lesser barons associated themselves.

Members of the Commons in the fourteenth century were not chosen by an electorate, as in modern times; they were summoned by royal writ for each session, and were a 'talking' or advisory body, not a legislative one. The king summoned those only who might be of service to him, and this practice applied also to the House of Lords, to which Edward III and Richard II sometimes called judges and landed gentry. It was not until the parliament of 1387 that barons earned the right to be summoned to parliament. The House of Lords, which included the clergy (archbishops and bishops), was far from being a body of 'peers' or equals; but until the Wars of the Roses, some of the higher echelons (dukes, earls and marquises) considered themselves peers of the king.

The English language came into its own with the revival of characteristic English institutions. The basis of these was realignment of the class system, and recognition that each stratum constituted an order contributing to the prosperity of society as a whole. Politically, such institutions did not aim at democracy, in the liberal conception, but at feudalism more equitably applied, in which king, nobles, church, merchants and workers in town and country, accepted the principle of service as a co-operative enterprise for the benefit of all. This hierarchical concept was made articulate three hundred years later in the history plays of Shakespeare, especially in the speech on 'order' of Ulysses in *Troilus and Cressida*.

In the feudal hierarchies, land tenure, with service in produce or kind, was the foundation of their existence. In the English system, as elsewhere, the Lords spiritual, the Lords temporal and the Commons constituted an authoritarian pact to guarantee order and stability. In such a situation the impotent labouring class, which was large, had the least to lose: Gower said providentially, in Book V of *Vox Clamantis*: 'If justice does not discipline them through fear of punishment, the Lords will succumb within a short time.' But Common Law implied custom by tacit agreement, not a code committed to writing; and this was the law that manorial courts at first administered. By the late Middle Ages, charters gave the underdog a more equitable measure of political security. But they did not alter the basic assumption that all land belonged to the ruler, and that a citizen's safety depended upon a chain of obligations, not excluding military ones, which involved all three Estates.

Most of the titles of rank associated with the feudal system found their way into the English language from Continental sources. The prestige of noblemen was reflected in their order or precedence. Here are some notes on nomenclature, in order of rank:

(1) *Prince*. This title first appeared in English in the thirteenth century (*c* 1225), though a Latin borrowing, *princeps*, had appeared in LOE. *Prince* (not *Emperor*), was actually the civil title of the Roman head of state, Augustus, and became the general name for all feudal rulers, even if they were specifically styled kings (OE *cyning*). The eldest son of the English king became *Prince of Wales* from the late fourteenth century (reign of Edward III). James I extended the honour to all sons of the sovereign, and in 1885 Queen Victoria gave the title to grandchildren of both sexes. The title *princess* had been in common use since the beginning of the fifteenth century.

(2) *Duke*. The word appeared in the sense of 'leader', 'head of the army', in Layamon's *Brut* (*c* 1205). Later it became the official title of the royal sheriff among Carolingian kings, and was employed on both sides of the Rhine, replacing OE *heretoga* in fourteenth-century England. Except in France itself, the title was made hereditary when the Frankish principalities became independent duchies, e.g. Normandy, Burgundy, Saxony and Bavaria. But in Middle English, from the Conquest to the reign of Edward III, the invariable title was Earl, *Duke* being reserved for foreign noblemen; thus Robert of Gloucester refers to 'duc William' in 1297. The

Black Prince, when granted the Duchy of Cornwall in 1336, was the first English Duke created.

(3) *Marquis, Marquess* (both spellings are still current). The title, originally an adjectival form, is derived from OF *marchis*, Lat. *marca* 'frontier territory'; the feminine form *marchioness* (from med. Latin *marchio*) did not appear until the sixteenth century. Towards the end of the fourteenth century, Richard II created the marquisate, when he made his favourite, Robert de Vere, Earl of Oxford, Marquis of Dublin.

(4) *Earl*. The earliest known use of the title is in the *Laws of Æthelbert*, early in the seventh century. The title simply distinguished a nobleman from a freeman (OE *ceorl*), and came to be regarded as the equivalent of *Count* (Lat. *comes*) in Romano-Celtic Europe. Norman kings confined the title *Earl* to noblemen who governed counties. If such a person was already a Duke, the courtesy title of *Earl* was conferred on his eldest son. The Earl's original function was to wait on the King for advice.

(5) *Viscount* (deputy for a Count), fourth in rank of the English peerage, was not used in England until the late fourteenth century, when it appeared in Trevisa and Malory's *Morte Darthur*. The title was created by patent for John, Baron Beaumont, in 1440. It lapsed in 1461, was restored in 1485, and abolished in 1509.

(6) *Baron* (OF *barun*, thought to be related to OE *beorn*) was a feudal award for meritorious service to the king. *Great Barons* were those who attended the Great Council, forerunner of the English Parliament. When Henry III was compelled, through absenteeism, to summon members by writ, a distinction arose between barons by tenure and barons by constraint (see *OED*, vol. I, p 677). This fell away when Richard II established baronage by patent, as the lowest order of English nobility, descendable to male heirs. Debrett's *Correct Peerage of England*, 1814, says that the original title was *Vavasour*, the equivalent of a Saxon *thegn*, and that the Normans substituted the title of *Baron*. *Vavasour* occurs in the General Prologue to Chaucer's *Canterbury Tales*, line 360, and is glossed in Robinson's edition as 'substantial landowner'; the *OED* describes the person as a 'feudal tenant'. The Baron's right to wear a coronet was bestowed by Charles II.

The order and duties of manorial officers are set out in a

thirteenth-century French work, *Seneschausie*, translated by E. Lamond (Longmans Green, 1890):

(1) *Seneschal* (lit. 'old servant') an OF derivative of Germanic *seni*+ *scalc*. Kings and noblemen employed such an official as major-domo or chief steward of the household; but his functions were later judicial, especially in the Channel Islands, where seneschals often acted as town-governors. Legal knowlege was necessary, because the seneschal had to give instructions to bailiffs regarding manorial courts, woods, pastures, water-mills and the like. The title first occurs in English in the late fourteenth century.

(2) *Bailiff* (OF *baillif*, med. Latin *bajulivus*). The first usage recorded by the *OED* is in 1297, by Robert of Gloucester. Originally a king's sheriff, with magisterial powers, usually in charge of a *baillie* or hundred, sometimes also the mayor of a town. As an estate official he had to be an experienced husbandman, and was supposed to make daily inspections of operations in his district, particularly at times of ploughing, mowing and reaping.

(3) *Provost*. An Anglo-French word, found in Æthelwold's *Rule of St Benet* (c 961), adapted from med. Latin *propositus* or *praepositus* 'prefect', 'head' or 'overseer'. The title had a large number of applications, even in Middle English; for instance, the ecclesiastical dean of a chapter; the head of a cathedral college; an abbot or prior. Secular uses were, however, the earlier. The word obtained the general significance of 'ruler' in LOE, and in EME was applied to the chief magistrate of a town. In manorial practice the provost combined farming expertise with skill in accounting and property evaluation.

(4) *Reeve* (OE *girǣfa*, *gerēfa*). In Anglo-Saxon times, this man was a regional official of the king, with judicial powers; the title is mentioned as early as the eighth century; *shire-reeve*, the source of *sheriff*, appeared only in the eleventh century. A reeve's duties under the medieval manorial system were seldom those of the Old English official, but rather like the Provost's. Chaucer's Reeve, Osward, apparently had the status of a bailiff:

> Wel wiste he by the droghte and by the reyn
> The yeldynge of his seed and of his greyn.
> His lordes sheep, his neet, his dayerye

243

His swyn, his hors, his stoor, and his pultrye
Was hoolly in this Reves governyng,
And by his covenant yaf the rekenyng
(*Canterbury Tales*, General Prologue, 595–600)

This Norfolk man must have been the manager of a large estate, answerable directly to the Lord of the Manor.

(5) *Hayward* (OE *hege* 'dried grass' + *weard*), an officer in charge of woods, meadows and enclosures, whose special tasks were to protect fences against damage, to attend to the sowing of seed, and to supervise ploughmen and harrowers.

The Ploughman, Waggoner and Cowherd explain their own function, but Shepherds were required, not only to sleep in the fold, but to 'find good pledges' to answer for their doings. The Dairymaid had supplementary duties, such as helping to winnow the corn, and caring for geese and hens. This menial group was, for the most part, illiterate.

Somewhat less than a century before the conquest, the Normans had abandoned Norse for French, a thorough understanding of their neighbours being necessary for survival. This was particularly true of relations with the Franks. After the accession of Edward the Confessor, England was unlikely to avoid Norman and French influence, even had the conquest not taken place. There was also little chance of the English language being submerged, since it possessed a vernacular literature of four hundred years' standing, which was the most developed in Europe.

William the Conqueror preferred Latin as the official language of Norman England, and this was no innovation, since royal charters intended for public display had always been issued in that language. But writs containing instructions to officials and others were in English, and this continued until the northern rebellion, when the king became obdurate. He then replaced all responsible officials with Normans, who were unable to speak the language of the people. Except in court pleadings, English was abandoned as an official medium. French remained for centuries the language of the courts' lawyers. To understand royal indifference in this matter, it should be appreciated that kings after Alfred the Great, if not quite illiterate, were poorly trained in penmanship, so that William the

Conqueror had to use autograph marks to attest his signature. Hence the Chancellor's care of the Great Seal.

Literature in the Middle Ages was produced by the dominant and leisured classes. The Normans had no literary tradition, and such works as appeared in the eleventh and Norman half of the twelfth century came from the clergy, who wrote principally in Latin. Both William of Jumièges and William of Poitiers produced chronicles of the Conqueror's exploits and the rise of his dukedom; the *Gesta Guillelmi Ducis* of the latter is the main, though prejudiced, source concerning Hastings and its aftermath. Nothing of much literary importance appeared before the reign of Henry I, who was nicknamed 'Beauclerk', because, according to Arthur Bryant, he could read Latin (*Makers of the Realm*, p 180). The notable annalists of the early twelfth century were churchmen writing in Latin: Vitalis, Eadmer (who produced a life of Anselm), Simeon of Durham, and William of Malmesbury, whose *Gesta Regum* has considerable historical and critical merit.

About this time the *Anglo-Saxon Chronicle* was continued in the vernacular at the monastery of Peterborough, after the great fire of 1116. Various monks took part, and penned annals in the West-Saxon dialect until 1131. During Stephen's anarchical years, there were no additions; but upon the accession of the Angevin king, Henry II, writing was renewed from the year 1132, and intermittently recorded events up to 1154; the centre-piece of the later entries is the struggle between Stephen and Empress Matilda. The dialect of these additions is a local form of East Anglian in an unexpected orthography, generally regarded as the earliest specimen of Middle English. The manuscript of the *Peterborough Chronicle* is in the Bodleian Library, Oxford, Laud Misc. 636.

The use of the term 'Anglo-Norman' in reference to this period is comparatively late (*OED*, Scott, 1811). An Anglo-Norman, for instance King Henry I, was a person of Norman descent, born in England; but the language introduced first by Edward the Confessor, and then by William the Conqueror's settlers, was Norman-French. This language, which incorporated many Norse words, such as *houle* 'hole', *tourbe* 'peat' and *vraic* 'seaweed', is descended from Vulgar Latin, via the sixth-century Lingua Romana Rustica of western Europe. By then there were two forms of spoken Latin, that of the clerics (descended from the literary tongue), and the vernacular, which had borrowed a number of Gothic, Celtic and

Frankish forms. Romance languages are regional developments of the latter, that of northern France being the *Langue d'Oil*, in which Germanic elements are important. This parent tongue, by the ninth century, had five recognized off-shoots: Norman, Walloon, Picard, Burgundian and French of the *Ile de France*, the area around Paris, from which modern French is descended. One of these French dialects had, by an edict of the Council of Tours (AD 853), to be used by priests in delivering sermons. In the south of France the parent tongue was the *Langue d'Oc*, with the following dialects: Gascon, Provençal, Catalonian and Piedmontese, all spoken south of the Bordeaux-Val d'Isere line.

The use of 'Anglo-Norman' for the sub-dialect of French, which evolved on English soil in the twelfth century, is apt to confuse, though J. Vising in *Anglo-Norman Language and Literature* (1923) did his best to clarify the historical situation for linguists. French speakers of many origins, including Walloons from Flanders, continued to mingle with the English and Norman population for two hundred years, and came in numbers during the reign of King John, being dissatisfied with the French administration of the lost provinces. The clergy (chiefly Cluniac and Augustinian monks) were recruited from even remoter regions, as were mercenary troops hired by the Norman kings. The church under Lanfranc was more influential than the Court in disseminating French, since its country-wide activities and sermons were conducted in French or Latin.

Vising lists the distinctive characteristics of eleventh-century Norman French on pages 27–33 of his handbook, under phonology, morphology, orthography and vocabulary. The divergence of what is called Anglo-Norman from French is marked by an exceptional decay of declensions, accompanied by variations of sound, form and syntax, which Vising illustrates mainly from writings between 1200 and 1400. Under syntax, he notes, *inter alia*, the use of *de* for *pour*, and the imperfect tense where Continental French has the perfect. The Angevin dialect used by the court of Henry II, and the advent of central French from the University of Paris in the reign of Edward III, made a lasting impact by outmoding Anglo-Norman, beginning in the thirteenth century. Though there were still Norman usages in the poet Gower, the dialect survived chiefly through employment in legal documents.

Visitors to the Channel Islands of Alderney, Jersey, Guernsey,

Sark and Herm, soon discover that Insular Norman (with its Frankish elements) is alive, though now a regional dialect greatly modified in vocabulary by modern English. The *patois* of Sark is more closely related to the speech of Jersey than to that of Guernsey. Poems in the Norman-French dialect of Guernsey were published in 1949 by A. T. Henley, entitled *Ichin Nou Pale L'Patouais* ('Patois spoken here'). So far as is known, this dialect was not committed to writing until 1831. Georges Metiviér's *Dictionaire Franco Normand* (1870) and Marie de Garis's *English-Guernsey Dictionary* (1967) remain the principal authorities.

The de Garis family is descended from Pierre, a Gascon, who acquired a Guernsey farm in the thirteenth century. The important families of the States (or legislative council) still bear Norman names, such as Carré, de Sausmarez, de Guérin, de la Mare, Dobrée, Le Cocq, Le Febvre, Marquand, Mourant, Ozanne, Robilliard and Tourtel. The Islands formed part of the Duchy of Normandy in William the Conqueror's time, and were regained for England from Robert II by Henry I. When Normandy was lost to King John in 1205, the islanders remained loyal to the English crown, and were granted a constitution by royal charter, which is still operative.

The poet Wace was a native of Jersey, as he says in line 5322 of *Roman de Rou*, his name being derived from Germanic *Wazo*. He was born sometime between 1090 and 1112, his mother being a daughter of Duke Robert I's chamberlain. Educated in theology in Caen and Paris, he attended the court of Henry I, when it sat at Caen, where he continued to live during the reigns of Henry II and III. As a cleric, he did not achieve high office, but he translated Latin annals and compiled religious biographies in verse. *La Geste des Bretons* (also called *Le Roman de Brut*), was written in 1155. He later became a prebendary at Bayeux cathedral, dying in Rouen about 1174.

Wace paraphrased and augmented Geoffrey of Monmouth's *History of the Kings of Britain* in composing the *Brut*, a narrative poem of sixteen thousand lines in rhyming octosyllables; Geoffrey in turn had based his work on Gildas. About 1200, Layamon, a priest of Worcester, freely translated Wace's *Brut* into English. The common theme is based on the legend of Brutus, grandson of Aeneas of Troy, who is supposed to have visited Brittany before conquering England. Wace's real hero is, however, King Arthur, a rival to Charlemagne, who upholds the order of chivalry; a possible explanation of this anachronism is that Wace pictured the court of the honoured Theodoric, king of the Italian Ostrogoths.

The central figure of Wace's later work, *Roman de Rou* (original title *Geste des Normanz*), was Rollo, first Duke of Normandy; the poet's account depicts the coming of the Norsemen to France, and takes the history to the year 1107 (reign of Henry I). The poet's honesty makes him a dependable historian, and special interest attaches to the British Library copy of the *Geste*, since it came from Battle Abbey.

An extant feudal fief of considerable interest is the Island of Sark, governed since 1563 by its hereditary Seigneur, answerable only to the ruling monarch of Britain, by whom he holds the land for 'the twentieth part of a knight's fee'. The Seigneurie entitles the overlord to tithes on all the island's products, and to a thirtieth part of the price of all property sold. Forty of the islanders are, however, tenants, represented in the Chief Pleas (or feudal Court) by twelve deputies, who are not tenants. The Court Judge is called the Senechal, and some procedures date back to the days of Duke Rollo. Local customs and place-names throw an invaluable light on the history of all the islands, and the French to this day know them as 'les Iles anglo-normandes'.

The transition from Old to Middle English in the latter half of the eleventh century saw some important sound changes. There was no break in language evolution, for most changes ascribed to early Middle English had their origin in the preceding age.

In the ninth or tenth century OE vowels were lengthened or shortened under certain conditions. Short vowels (monophthongs or diphthongs) were lengthened before the liquid or nasal combinations *ld, mb, nd, ng, rd, rl* and *rn*. One explanation is that long vowels are easier to pronounce before liquid and nasal consonants; but the change must have been gradual. OE *feld* > LOE *fēld; word* > *wōrd; camb* > *cāmb; ende* > *ēnde; lang* > *lāng*. It is unlikely that lengthening took place, however, when any such group was immediately followed by a third consonant, for instance in the plural. Thus LOE *cīld* appeared as *cildru*, cf. Modern English *child, children*. Nor did lengthening occur in words which represented weakly stressed syllables, e.g. *and, under* and *wolde*.

At a later state some of these vowels were again shortened before two or more consonants (including double ones); this was regular before *rd*, but sporadic before the other combinations, the *ld* group resisting the tendency strongly. Examples:

	LOE	EME	ModE
	ēnde	ende	end
	hēard	hard	hard
	sīngan	singen	sing
but	clīmban	clīmben	climb
	fīndan	fīnden	find
	fēld	fēld	field
	cīld	chīld	child
	gōld	gōld	gold

Shortening invariably took place when a third consonant was added; but it was inhibited in recognized compounds such as *hāmstede* 'homestead'. Compare, however, ModE *Hampstead*, in which shortening did occur.

OE *ă* before liquid and nasal groups revealed points of special interest. As noted in chapter VII, this vowel was lengthened in OE, and rounded in dialects south of the Humber to [ɔ:], the sound in *laundry*. When shortened in LOE, the sound returned to *ă*; but if shortened in EME, the resultant vowel was [ɒ], the sound in *pot*. Since the shortening took place in different parts at different times, doublets arose, and the form that turns up in EME texts is not necessarily the ancestor of the modern one. Examples of doublets in ModE from OE *ă* are *long*, on the one hand, and *lamb* and *hand* on the other. ModE *old* is not derived from West Saxon *eald*, but from Anglian *āld*, the vowel having being lengthened in LOE.

Some other shortenings of the transition period are worthy of note. In EME long vowels were regularly reduced in length before double consonants or groups of two or three consonants, e.g. OE *cēpte* > ME *cĕpte*; *sōfte* > *sŏfte*; *wīfman* > *wĭmman*; *Ēadward* > *Edward*. Compare ModE *five* and *fifth*; *wise* and *wisdom*; *deep* and *depth*. Exceptions to this phenomenon occur often (though not always) when the two consonants constituting the group *st* can be pronounced as the beginning of the next syllable, as in the inflected forms of *gōst*, *prēost* and *Ēaste*. ModE forms *ghost, priest* and *East* are therefore derived from inflected forms, probably the genitive singular or the nominative plural. In *breast* and *dust* the shortened forms have survived.

Either in LOE or EME (probably the latter) long vowels in initial syllables were shortened in words of three or more syllables; e.g. OE *frēondlice* > ME *frendli; sǣlignesse* > *seliness; hālig* has the radical vowel shorted in ME *haligdom;* and ModE *southern* [ʌ]<OE *sūperne*. Three-syllable words occur mainly in compounds, such as place-names, or in the inflected forms of disyllabic words, such as *hēofod*, plural *hēofodu*, yielding the ME form *hĕvede*.

Lexical additions from Viking sources were late in appearing in English texts, and Eilert Ekwall, the Swedish scholar, endeavoured to supply the reason. In 'How long did the Scandinavian language survive in England' (*A Grammatical Miscellany offered to Otto Jespersen*, Copenhagen, 1930) he says that the Danes who invaded England, and inhabited the Danelaw, were expatriates who had joined the Grand Army to occupy the river estuaries of the east coast of England, as well as the Rhine, Somme and Seine; Norwegians tended to settle in the Celtic areas of Britain, such as Cumberland, Ireland, the Isle of Man and the Hebrides.

As there was no problem of communication in England, Ekwall thinks that the Norse language continued to be spoken mainly in those areas of the Danelaw where Scandinavians predominated through force of numbers, or where the new settlers were extremely isolated. The political independence of the Danelaw was actually of short duration; south of the Humber it ended as early as 920, while the kingdom of Yorkshire terminated in 954. The settlers were more concerned with the possession of land than their personal allegiance; and it is noteworthy that the two peoples were united in resisting the Norman invasion of 1066. What took place was a language amalgamation, rather than a supersession; this is shown by the fact that several inscriptions, authorized by Scandinavians, were written in Old English. The *Anglo-Saxon Chronicle* remained silent on the language problem, because it was compiled in that part of England where the Danes were few. Ekwall believes that in York the Scandinavian language disappeared early; while in the Isle of Man it was still spoken in the twelfth century; the year 1200 must be the limit of its survival in England. In any event the language of the Danes lasted long enough to take part in the sound changes of early

Middle English. Some of these will shortly be considered.

What is found in the vocabulary of Middle English represents only a fraction of the words borrowed by English speakers from Scandinavian sources in the tenth and eleventh centuries. Most loan words found their way into English through Northumbria and the North-East or North-West Midlands. Sometimes borrowed words existed side by side with Old English words from the same Germanic root, e.g. *garþ* and *ʒard* 'yard'; *grā* and *græg* 'grey'. Ekwall has an illuminating account of the evolution of the place-name *York*, from OE *Eoforwic* 'the place of the boar'. The spelling *Íorvík* (under Scandinavian influence) is found as early as 952; this was later shortened to *Íork*. But there is no written evidence of the form *York* until about 1200. An intermediate form *Ĵorvík* is postulated to account for the English pronunciation; the loss of *w* is explained later. The elimination of the semi-vowel in pronunciation, but not in spelling, is exemplified in *Berwick* and *Harwich*.

The phonological treatment of sounds is of some importance, and the Middle English texts that provide the best material for a study of Scandinavian loan words are those of the thirteenth and fourteenth centuries: *Ormulum* (*c* 1200), *Genesis and Exodus* (*c* 1250), *Cursor Mundi* (*c* 1300), *Havelock the Dane* (*c* 1300), Brunne's *Handlyng Synne* (1300–30), Hampole's *Ayenbit of Inwyt* (*c* 1349), *Early English Alliterative Poems* (*c* 1350) and Barbour's *Bruce* (1375).

All the vowels of Old Norse loan words, long and short, which were the same as those in Old English, underwent the treatment of native words; but unusual Scandinavian diphthongs *ai/ei*, *au* and *ei/ey*, not found in OE, appear respectively as *ā*, *ēa* and *ie* (or *y*) in later English speech. It is instructive to follow the phonological development of parallel words:

ai/ei: OE *gāt* 'goat'; ON *bleikr*, OE *blāc* 'pale'. EME borrowings in texts show different spellings, and presumably pronunciations e.g. *geit/gait*, alongside of *gōt* from OE; *bleik/blaik/blayke*, alongside of *blāc*. Cf. Modern English *hale* 'healthy' and *whole* in *wholesome*.

au: in parallel words of OE this diphthong appears as *ēa*, e.g. ON *hlaupa*, OE *hlēapan* 'leap'. In EME borrowings *au* > *ou* or *ow*, but OE *ēa* > ME *ē* [ɛ:]. Thus in ME *loupen* is found beside *lēpen*; *coupen* (ON *kaupa*) beside *chēpen* 'buy'; and *gowk* (ON *gaukr*) beside *gēk* 'fool'.

ei/ey: in parallel words, this appears in West Saxon as *īe* or *ȳ*, but in non-West-Saxon as *ē*; e.g. ON *leysa* 'loosen', Anglian *lēsan.* The commonest ME forms are *leisen, laisen* and *lesen.*

Some Germanic consonants had a different history in Old Norse and Old English:

(1) Germanic *ð* remained in ON, but became *d* in primitive OE. Borrowings from Old Norse often accounted for double forms; e.g. ME *tīþende* 'tidings' from ON *tiðinde,* beside *tidende* from OE *tīd.*

(2) Initial *w* of Germanic was lost in early ON before long and short *o, u* and *l,* but retained in OE. In the place name *Ormsby, orm* < ON *ormr* 'snake'; but OE has *wurm* or *wyrm.* Cf. OE *wlatian* 'gaze', ME *leiten* or *laiten* < ON *leita.*

(3) Germanic *k* (OE *c*) underwent no palatal modification in Old Norse before front vowels, as it did in Old English, e.g.

> ON *kirkja* > ME *kirke;* OE *cirice* > ME *chirche*
> ON *kista* > ME *kist;* OE *cest* > ME *cheste* 'chest'
> ON *dīki* > ME *dike;* OE *dic* > ME *dich* 'ditch'

A considerable number of double forms survived from the combination *sk* (OE *sc*) e.g. *skirt* and *shirt.*

It is worth observing that the historical process by which English asserted itself as the spoken language of the people, even when of foreign descent, did not begin with the accession of Henry II (1154), but in the reign of King John. Nor did the initiative come from that unhappy king, for French remained the language of the Court until the last quarter of the thirteenth century (the reign of Edward I).

About the time of Magna Carta, French became the second language of the universities, Latin remaining the principal medium of instruction.

In 1258 English was restored as an *official* language, alongside of French, by the document already referred to as the Provisions of Oxford. French ceased to be used as the language medium of the schools after the great plague of 1349. In 1362 Edward III opened

Parliament with an English speech. During Richard II's reign, petitions to Parliament began to be presented in English, and statutes of the gilds were framed in the vernacular. Ceremonial use was given an impetus by Henry IV's acceptance of the crown in English in 1399.

Caxton, the first printer, adopted the predominantly South-East Midland dialect of London as the medium of his selective publications, and this undoubtedly widened its influence (see p 429). Even if Chaucer and Caxton had not lived, London English, with the official recognition of the Court, would have become the literary language of the country.

CHAPTER X

Feudalism and
Life in Society

𝕴𝕴𝕴𝕴𝕴𝕴

THOUGH ANGLO-NORMAN FEUDALISM is more often criticized than approved, it was inevitable, as F. W. Maitland has shown in *Domesday Book and Beyond* (pp 267–8):

> At various times and places there emerge phenomena which may with great propriety be called feudal and which come of evil and make for evil. But if we use the term, and often we do, in a very wide sense, if we describe several centuries as feudal, then feudalism will appear to us as a natural and even a necessary state in our history: that is to say, if we would have the England of the sixteenth century arise out of the England of the eighth without passing through a period of feudalism, we must suppose many immense and fundamental changes in the nature of man and his surroundings. If we use the term in this wide sense, then (the barbarian conquests being given us as an unalterable fact) feudalism means civilization, the separation of employments, the division of labour, the possibility of national defence, the possibility of art, science, literature and learned leisure; the cathedral, the scriptorium, the library, are as truly the work of feudalism as is the baronial castle. . . . The process of civilization is often a cruel process.

Chivalry probably reached its height in the twelfth and thirteenth centuries, and not in the age of Froissart's *Chronicles,* which glorify, yet expose, its demise in the time of the Plantagenet kings, Edward III and Richard II (1327–99). The ideal, proper to the class of knights, was one of social service, without regard for reward other than honour; its merit was a code of manners succinctly described as 'courtesy'. Several aspects of this code bore small relation to the actual conduct of life; for the tradition of chivalry was inherited from literature. Medieval knights were happy to be entertained by the marvellous adventures and ballads of their minstrels. The romantic notions of anonymous poets, or prose-writers such as Malory in the *Morte Darthur,* were revived in the nineteenth century by the historical novelist Sir Walter Scott, in *Ivanhoe* and *The Talisman*.

The knights of Norman times were hard-headed, practical men, who used their military experience as a means of livelihood. The early knights were soldiers first, landowners second, and patrons of jousting and warfare only by necessity, in which the concept of ordeal by battle played a significant role. As a social class, knights would be predominantly professional soldiers or country gentlemen, such as were constantly exercised in the skill of arms. Barons, bishops and abbots, the foundations of the ruling class, were required by William the Conqueror to respond to a call for arms by sending him a stipulated number of knights, who became liable to service for a period of forty days. It was often more convenient, however, to substitute hired knights, with little or no land, for the king's muster. Should the exigencies of a campaign exceed forty days, it was the practice of William to hire knights for the extra period, at personal expense, and usually to promise them a share of the spoils, including the ransoms demanded for prisoners. Henry I, who found this system unworkable, required cash payment, known as *scutage* 'shield-money', instead of knights of short-period service; and this meant that the bulk of his army was hired. Richard I, on the other hand, preferred dependable knights to money; yet he also raised scutage.

A son destined to be a knight usually entered the service of a baron, bishop or abbot, as a page, at about the age of seven. In this service he was taught good manners, enjoyed Christian training and some elementary education, and had practice in hunting and the use of weapons. At not less than fifteen years, the boy was advanced to the status of squire or knight's attendant, and accompanied his master to the tournaments or campaigns, as shield-bearer, supervisor of arms, or nurse, should the champion be wounded. At twenty, the squire became eligible for knighthood. In time of hostilities this was usually conferred on the battlefield; otherwise the aspirant had to undertake a church vigil, with arms upon the altar, as well as the ritual of purification, still recalled in the honour of the Order of the Bath.

Knights were thus members of a freemasonry, as well as a military gild; they were indeed regarded as volunteers of an international brotherhood. The origins of the concept are older than is generally supposed, and social historians, such as G. G. Coulton, have traced it to the pagan Germany of Tacitus. The housecarls who rallied round Harold's banner at Hastings were of a comparable order. But knighthood and chivalry did not flourish as a major force in society, until given religious approval. Christendom pledged itself to rid Spain and southern France of the Muslim Moors from north Africa; but it was soon recognized that the latter were a civilized people, advanced in learning as well as human dignity. For centuries their culture influenced French thinking and art, through the Catalonian kingdom which spanned the Pyrenees, embracing Provence.

In the latter half of the eleventh century the monastery of Cluny in Burgundy became the spiritual centre of the Holy Roman Empire, at a time when the papacy was degraded by its preoccupation with temporal and political affairs. The Cluniac monks revived the Benedictine way of life and trained the influential papal administrator, Hildebrand, who in 1073 was proclaimed Pope Gregory VII. With autocratic ability, this cleric set about reforming the Church in Rome, and conceived the idea of a holy war against the Saracens on all Mediterranean fronts. The Normans were already in possession of Apulia in southern Italy, and had established a kingdom in Sicily. The two-century struggle between the Cross and the Crescent (originally a symbol of the Byzantine Empire) was under way when Gregory VII died at Salerno in 1185.

This Pope had caused a large hostel to be built for Christian pilgrims in Jerusalem, which was then governed by suppressive Islamic Turks from central Asia. An appeal to Pope Urban II to liberate the Christian shrines came from the Patriarch of Jerusalem and from an eloquent preacher, Peter the Hermit. The Council of Clermont responded by approving the First Crusade, which in 1096 had the cordial support of the Church; Robert, Duke of Normandy, was one of the leaders. This was a baron's war, under the banners of French, Flemish and Burgundian counts, the most conspicuous figures being Godfrey of Boulogne and Bohemund of Apulia, son of the Norman conqueror of southern Italy, Robert Guiscard. The forces left by different routes and agreed to assemble at Constantinople. After successful engagements in Asia Minor, Jerusalem was taken in July, 1099, and Godfrey became its governor until his death the following year. Under Baldwin I the new state became a Christian kingdom, attaining its zenith when Fulk, Count of Anjou (1130–43), was its ruler.

English participation in the first two Crusades (1095–1146) was private and minimal; the first was the most memorable of the seven Crusader movements, which ended in 1274. The exploits of the 1096–9 campaign furnished material for many medieval tales, and for Tasso's epic, *Jerusalem Delivered*. Geoffrey of Anjou, son of the third king of Jerusalem, married Matilda, daughter of Henry I (see p 234), and their son Henry II of England, became founder of the Plantagenet house, whose heroes, Richard Coeur-de-Lion (1190) and Edward I (1248) participated, respectively, in the third and fourth Crusades. The comparative lack of success of the latter ventures was due to absence of unified leadership, and disagreements among rival commanders.

On the Pope's instructions, crusaders were enrolled as pilgrims, presented with a symbolic cross, and promised absolution from their sins. For this reason, murderers, thieves and criminals joined the volunteers, as Giraldus Cambrensis shows, in his *Itinerary through Wales* (1188), which describes his recruiting campaign with Baldwin, Archbishop of Canterbury.

The pilgrims suffered hardships from famine, fever, plague and dysentry, the nearly insoluble problem of the army being its commissariat. Had not the Crusaders lived by piracy, and been followed by profiteering merchants from Genoa, Pisa and Venice, the campaigns would have been impracticable. The disorganized ventures were foolhardy, in permitting the participation of women and immature children, many of whom were captured and sold as slaves. The richest captives were able to find ransoms for their liberation; others were absorbed into the Levantine population, and swelled the ranks of half-breeds called *poulaines* or *colts*.

The wars against the Saracens exemplified both extremes of the chivalric order. Those motivated by religion were exalted to a piety and self-denial that found an outlet in two dedicated orders, the Templars and the Hospitallers, or Knights of St John, whose members were celibate monks, as well as knights. By 1150 there was a preceptory of Templars on the site of Lincoln's Inn, and five others in England were to follow. There were no less than fifty-three English commanderies of the Hospitallers, the largest of which was at Clerkenwell, just north of the London wall.

Crusaders of less integrity often fell victim to degrading luxuries, while fanatics perpetrated ruthless atrocities. Crusades had the salutary effect of drawing to the East bellicose elements from

European society, who were a menace to orderly government; but they left in their wake hundreds of usurers who lent ready money on the security of the barons' estates, many of which changed hands. The Church, as instigator of the campaigns, consolidated its dominance over western European kingdoms, by demanding allegiance to the Pope.

The spokesman and organizer of the Second Crusade, St Bernard of Clairvaux, used his influence to found the order of Cistercians, whose orthodoxy was designed to counteract the speculations of rising groups of French scholars. The crusading spirit encouraged clerks to become wanderers, on the pretext of widening their horizons, and throughout Europe they began to form themselves into mendicant orders, relying almost entirely on charity. The Franciscan and Dominican friars were first instructed in the thirteenth century by St Francis of Assisi and St Dominic of Castile, later canonized as leaders of movements that were hesitatingly approved by the Pope, because the founders criticized a lack of simplicity, humanism and charity in the Church's established order. 'The hungry sheep look up, and are not fed.'

The brotherhoods of friars were dedicated to contact with, and improvement of, the lot of the common man; they became the physicians and nurses of the very poor. Their ideals were humility, simple sermons and austere living, and they were not allowed to carry arms, except in defence of the Church. The response in southern France and central Italy was remarkable, especially in the districts of Toulouse and Assisi. The Friars Minor, or grey-habited followers of St Francis, wore a single, tattered garment, and went bare-footed, even in the English winters. Both the Black Friars (Dominicans) and the Grey Friars were established in England by 1221, and were followed in the same century by Carmelites (White Friars) and Augustinians (Austin Friars). All such orders were responsible to the Pope, and not to the bishops, except for those friars licensed to act as priests and confessors, who had the power to grant absolution. Friaries arose in the destitute areas of London, Winchester, Bristol, Oxford, Cambridge, Norwich, Northampton, Lynn, Boston, Lincoln, York and Newcastle-on-Tyne. Friars who were given defined areas in which to operate their fund-raising were known as *limitours*. In the thirteenth century they were helped by the monasteries, and championed by Bishop Robert Grosseteste of Lincoln, who regarded them as educators and social workers. They so flourished that a learned Dominican and a Franciscan became Archbishop of Canterbury; Roger Bacon and Duns Scotus were both members of the Franciscan Order.

In time, these foundations received gifts of money and endowments of land, and the austerity of their life gradually ceased. The mendicant orders were open to abuses named by Chaucer, Langland and Wyclif (fraud, deception, luxury and illegal trading), and long before 1400 were roundly condemned by orthodox monks and priests. The Dominican order was closed down in 1559.

The Renaissance of learning began in Italy in the tenth century, and reached Paris, Orleans and Chartres by the twelfth, the age when Peter Abelard, Bernard of Clairvaux and John of Salisbury established their reputations for scholarship. The English scholar, John, was born in Salisbury and studied in Paris, Reims and Chartres, spending much of his life in France and Italy. He was the first renowned English Latinist, procured the Pope's approval for the English conquest of Ireland, and became secretary to Thomas Becket, whose life he wrote; he was, in fact, present at Becket's murder in Canterbury Cathedral and recommended his canonization. John of Salisbury was typical of the international character of learning during the Middle Ages; he paid for his education by taking private pupils, and ended his career as Bishop of Chartres.

One of the proverbs adapted by Chaucer, 'A monk out of his cell is a fish out of water', was not held in regard by secular clerks, and the Church now thought it in the cause of Christianity and progress that scholars and clerics should travel, with the bishop's permission. Besides learning, there were three motives for clerics going abroad: avoidance of military service, exemption from taxation, and freedom from prosecution by the secular courts. The last was a considerable advantage, for it protected Thomas Becket in his dispute with Henry II. The Church itself never imposed the death penalty.

To what kind of university did the wandering scholar or *goliard* go, and how did he travel there? Though there were communities of teachers at Oxford and Cambridge, no such institutions as universities existed in England until the thirteenth century. In *De Gesta Suis*, Giraldus Cambrensis (1146–1220) describes the nature of his *studium generale*. He studied the liberal arts of rhetoric, grammar and logic for six years in Paris, and returned to the university as a lecturer for the period 1176–80. He then became tutor to Prince John, and chaplain, as well as envoy, to Henry II, visiting the Pope in Italy on two occasions. At Oxford, on three successive days he lectured on the theme of his treatise, *The Topography of Ireland*, and was one of the best representatives of academic life in his time.

Universities in Italy and France attracted foreign students through the reputation of particular scholars, whose medium of instruction was universally Latin. They were clerics, who *read with* students with the object of qualifying them as teachers, the master's degree providing the acknowledged licence. At the conclusion of the half-degree course, the *baccalaureus* had to offer an *exemplum* or 'masterpiece' of his training. The badge of every student was his tonsure, although he was seldom in orders; he was usually admitted at the age of thirteen or fourteen, and agreed to a celibate life while attending the university. By 1300 there were fourteen known universities in western Europe. Bologna was eminent for law, Paris for theology and philosophy. They were, in effect, student gilds, to whose regulations the masters were subject, having to provide 'caution money' as a guarantee that they would meet their obligations. The 'halls' of residence hired by students were run on the lines of friars' convents, and later became colleges, whose nerve-centres were the hall, the chapel and the library.

The earliest colleges of Oxford, Merton (1264), Balliol (1266) and University (1280), were in existence a little before those of Cambridge, though the dates assigned are disputable. William of Wykeham proved to be a more ambitious founder than his predecessors, and adopted the quadrangle plan for scholastic buildings, as in New College (1379). Cambridge had no college foundation earlier than Peterhouse (1284), though several, such as Clare, Gonville, Trinity Hall and Pembroke, were established during the first half of the fourteenth century. During the thirteenth century the enrolment at Oxford seldom exceeded fifteen hundred, and at Cambridge a thousand. The annual bachelor-degree passes were about ninety at Oxford and fifty at Cambridge, while the successful masters numbered less than half a dozen. There is not much evidence that these results were regarded as unsatisfactory.

English colleges provided a 'carrier', who accompanied groups of students, for their own safety, at the beginning and end of the academic year; by the fifteenth century this consisted of four terms of twelve weeks each. Most inland journeys were made by river or on horseback, a fair day's journey covering about twenty-five miles. Bridges were constructed so as not to impede river traffic, and ferries were available across estuaries. Other means of transport, such as the horse-litter, borne by two animals, were in use for well-to-do ladies; but most women could ride, and did so astride until the fourteenth century, when Chaucer's genteel prioress is shown seated on a side-saddle. Carriages, costing as much as a thousand pounds, were within the reach of royalty and aristocrats only; there is an illustration of one of these elaborately furnished vehicles in the *Louterell Psalter* (c 1320). To France and to Flanders there was a steady flow of sea-traffic, and armies to the later crusades were transported by ship through the Mediterranean, instead of overland.

Hospitality on the road, especially for the poor, was the subject of several royal proclamations. At first the monasteries provided it in guest-houses, free of charge to the destitute. One of these guest-houses, with central hall and adjoining sleeping compartments, remained opposite the entrance to Battle Abbey. From the thirteenth century priories offered similar facilities, but mainly in the larger towns. Alternative accommodation for the upper classes was the baronial castle or the gentleman's country house, where hospitality was regarded as an obligation of courtesy. But the middle class, consisting principally of merchants, small farmers and transport-riders, were provided for in hostelries of the type illustrated in the *Louterell Psalter*; they offered bed and board, with sleeping room, usually of the dormitory type. Expensive items of fare were always meat and fodder for horses; and lodgings in London cost more than elsewhere. The forerunner of the English public-house was the tavern or ale-house, placed at the junction of important highways. Amenities for travellers in France, described in fourteenth-century manuscripts, were undoubtedly similar to those in England.

Pilgrims were inveterate travellers, not only in Chaucer's England, but in western Europe throughout the Middle Ages; but not all were able to make the journey to the Holy Land. The principal shrines in England were at Glastonbury, Durham, Winchester, Canterbury and Walsingham; in Europe the frequented sanctuaries were those of Rome and Santiago (St James) of Compostella in north-western Spain. Persons from all walks of life embarked on

261

pilgrimages for diverse reasons; some as a cure for sickness, others for the conviviality of casual encounters; while not a few were advised by confessors to visit the shrine of a saint as penance. The veracity of the miracles witnessed by the superstitious at martyrs' shrines was widely accepted, rebuked by Erasmus and Latimer, and honoured by Sir Thomas More. In *Piers Plowman* Langland comments ironically on the pseudo-hermits and their 'wenches', whom he met on 'Palmers' Way, while visiting Walsingham.

Chaucer does not disguise the suspicion with which pilgrimages were regarded by the king's officers. For every devout traveller there was a devious charlatan, such as the Pardoner of Roncevalles, who sold bogus relics and granted indulgences (money exchanged for repentance). This abuse was denounced by Wyclif, but approved by the church in the fourteenth century. Roncevalles was the village on the French side of the Pyrenean pass where Roland died in defending the Christian faith; but Chaucer's Pardoner may have belonged to an Order of hospitallers, known as St Mary Roncevall at Charing Cross, dissolved for its evil reputation towards the end of the fourteenth century.

Santiago (St James) was visited annually by thousands of pilgrims, including kings and bishops. The *Book of St James* (1130) enshrines the legend of how the body of the martyred James came to be buried in Compostella; how the bones were discovered by a hermit in the ninth century; how the apostle, mounted on a white horse, became the supernatural champion of Christendom, nicknamed the 'Moor-slayer'; and how Charlemagne and Archbishop Turpin made the first pilgrimage through Burgos, along a road still important as the meeting-place of Moorish and Christian culture. The place of pilgrimage in Santiago was taken over by clerics from the monastery of Cluny, and visited by St Francis of Assisi and many historical figures until the sixteenth century, when the Moors were evicted.

Besides passports, a party going on a pilgrimage abroad required a licence, and the pilgrims could take no more money out of the kingdom than was necessary for the journey. By the fourteenth century Englishmen had proved themselves to be enthusiastic travellers, and the monk Ranulf Higden, author of *Polychronicon* (1387 – see p 419) wrote: 'they cultivate other regions, and succeed still better in other countries than their own. . . . wherefore it is that they are spread so wide through the earth. . . . They are a race able for every industry.' Many pilgrims were trilingual, and found that French was widely spoken and understood as far East as Palestine, where Norman conquerors had taken it. The most cosmopolitan travel author (though he seldom left his library) was Sir John Mandeville; his *Travels* were full of fictitious wonders, and the book had a wide circulation in several European languages (see p 353). Shiploads of pilgrims annually visited Jerusalem, travelling by sea from Venice, via Famagusta in Cyprus and Jaffa on the Palestinian coast. Others reached the Holy Land via Egypt, in order to experience the wonders of the Nile, where the pyramids were named by Mandeville as 'Pharaoh's granaries'.

The prosperity of England in the thirteenth century was largely due to its self-sufficiency; many goods were imported, but in value they were less than the country's exports of raw materials and handcrafts. Traffic of merchants on the Thames, Humber and Severn did not compare with that on the Rhine, the Seine, the Danube or the Po, nor was the English Channel as busy as the Baltic or the Mediterranean. English imports were largely of fine cloth, weapons, luxuries and wine, though the range of articles was extended after the crusades, when spices, nutmegs and ginger created a demand among those that could afford them, including the monasteries. Trade reached its zenith in the later Middle Ages when the main English export changed from wool to cloth. In the wine trade the initiative was taken by French merchants, principally from Rouen, Burgundy and Bordeaux. Chaucer's father was a London vintner of French extraction.

The Merchant in the Prologue to the *Canterbury Tales* carried on his trade (possibly in wool) between Holland and the English east coast; the main share of Continental trade, however, passed through Bristol, then the second largest town in the country. Merchants were also bankers, influential persons in London and the leading towns, because they lent money at usury rates (French *chevyssaunce*) and employed brokers to bring this business to them. Some dealt illicitly in foreign exchange. Chaucer's Shipman, on the other hand, was a freebooter from Dartmouth, whose licensed seamen were encouraged by the king to rove the seas and commit acts of piracy. He was engaged in the dubious wine trade with Bordeaux, and guilty of petty larceny, sometimes of murder by drowning. Chaucer's uncomplimentary social portraits are backed by historical evidence; for the poet had inside knowledge of the shadier aspects of trade, through the experience of his father.

Foreign trade with England was controlled by borough regulations, which forbad a merchant to stay more than forty days, or to sell goods to anyone who was not a resident of the town; whatever an importer sold was wholesale, that the retail trade might be kept in the hands of English shopkeepers. To overcome such difficulties, certain towns in the cloth trade of Picardy and Belgium made agreements with merchant groups in London, whereby, for an annual fee, they were allowed to store their goods in the city, and sell them later elsewhere to the best advantage. The first *hanse* of Continental trade-gilds was established in London by Bruges in the twelfth century, and joined by fourteen other towns of Flanders and northern France, including Caen in Normandy. This association of merchant gilds did not include craftsmen. Another *hanse* was set up in London by Cologne and the Rhineland in the reign of Henry II, while Lübeck, Hamburg and other Baltic towns formed a third association in the thirteenth century, favouring the English ports of Boston and Lynn.

By Chaucer's time there were more than fifty Continental towns enjoying trading privileges with England, and using other ports, such as Scarborough and Newcastle-on-Tyne. Trade had also developed in goods from the Levant and the Far East. Arab traders, using primitive dhows without nails, sailed round Arabia to India or Sumatra and places where they rivalled the Chinese junks, bringing back exotic products to the Persian Gulf. From there merchandise was transported overland to Constantinople and Trebizond, and thence by road or river to Baltic towns. Italian merchants entered the eastern trade after the first crusade, and the trade-routes were changed. Venetian merchants crossed the Alps to the Rhine, and brought their goods to Flanders; the Genoese preferred Marseilles and the River Rhône and exchanged their goods at the popular fairs of Champagne. These were sold chiefly to French-speaking merchants, and by them placed on the English market.

The outcome of all this international activity by crusaders, pilgrims, mendicant orders, scholars and merchants, was an influx of foreign words, first through Anglo-Norman, then through central French, which found their way into late Middle English. After one hundred years of Norman occupation, miscegenation had produced a blend of culture in which Englishmen were indistinguishable from the French in government or trade circles. The characters of Chaucer's *Canterbury Tales* represent the progeny of a cosmopolitan urban population speaking a form of English in which dialects of French, with other Continental influences, including Italian and Flemish, were assimilated. From Palestine, northern Africa and southern Italy the indirect impact was that of Arabic.

Arab colonization of southern Europe lasted longest in Sicily and Spain, and the enduring evidence of eight centuries of occupation is found in place names, some of which have survived in their products, e.g. *Marsala* (Arabic, 'Port of God'). *Cordoba* in Spain gave its name to *cordwain* of the leather-workers. *Gibraltar* means 'the mountain of Tarik', one of the eighth-century Moorish leaders, who happened to be of Persian blood. The prefix *al*, found in names such as *Alhambra*, represents the Arabic definite article. Saracen invaders used light cavalry, and Tarik's progress was such that he reached the Pyrenees in seven weeks. *Fontarabia*, not far from Biarritz, is evidence of Arab penetration.

In time the Moors occupied southern France as far as the Loire; when defeated by Charles Martel they moved for a generation into Provence. Early in the tenth century they gained possession of the principal Alpine passes into Italy, so that they were able to attack pilgrims proceeding to Rome. *Saas Fe* suggests Arabic origin, and *Pontresina* is said to mean the 'Bridge of the Saracens'. The word *Saracen* occurs in King Alfred's translation of Orosius's *Universal History* (about 893 – see p 116), in reference to the peoples of Judaea and Palestine; the etymology is uncertain, but Jerome associated it with Abraham's wife Sarah, and the children of Hagar, which is Arabic for 'stone'. *Sarcenet* was a silk obtained from the Saracens, and so were the materials *damask* from Damascus, *muslin* from Moussul, *taffeta* from Atab, *gauze* from Gaza, *fustian* from Fostat, near Cairo, and *mohair* from the Arabs in Spain.

Alan S. C. Ross in his study *Ginger* (1952) has shown how complex the etymology of international consumer goods can be; but the midwife at the European birth of *ginger* was probably Arabic; and a similar conjecture is justifiable in the case of *apricot*, a fruit that apparently originated in Persia. *Tamarind*, from Arabic *tamr-hindi* 'date of India' was introduced by Marco Polo in the thirteenth century, and passed from Italian into French, though the word did not reach English until the sixteenth century, when it was employed by Sir Thomas Elyot in the *Castle of Health* (1533).

Western European influences were strong in the progress of English society in the Middle Ages. The French were cultural leaders, and the Holy Roman Empire ensured for the western world a community of religious tradition, ideas and aspirations. International ties were strengthened by the Crusades, and Walter Scott was not alone in noting the influence of Saladin and other rulers on the tradition of chivalry. Understanding of the oriental world, and of Arabic lore, led to discovery of the works of Aristotle, and to the thirteenth-century intellectual revival, based on the force of reason, of which Peter Abelard was the foremost leader. He was not the exponent of free-thinking; but he and Aquinas tried to justify theological doctrine on intellectual grounds.

In England, intellectualism had some bearing on the emancipation of the commons from feudal tyranny, through the granting of royal charters of rights; these were among the instruments of promoting an unacknowledged economic revolution. Some of these documents are considered later; it will suffice here to mention Edward I's Writ of Confirmation of Charters of Liberties (those of 1100 and 1215) which he issued in 1297. There he undertook not to levy any new taxes, without 'the common consent of all the realm'. Many London companies were granted their first charters by Edward III. Industries coincided with the rise of the artisan and merchant classes, growth of the towns and the organization of trade gilds.

The founding of the universities of Paris, Bologna, Oxford and Cambridge gave an impetus, not only to scholasticism, but to humanism. By the fourteenth century there was widespread enthusiasm among scholars for classical Latin literature, and especially for the poetry of Ovid, Vergil and Catullus. Medieval romance seems to have sprung largely from this source, and it flowered in a considerable output of secular verse, Chaucer's *Troilus and Criseyde* being one of the finest English examples.

In late Middle English, secular poetry tended to be bookish in vocabulary, and C. S. Lewis in *The Discarded Image* (ch. I) remarked on its essentially 'clerkly' character:

For one reference to Wade or Weland we meet fifty to Aeneas, Alexander or Caesar. For one probable relic of Celtic religion dug out of a medieval book we meet, clear and emphatic, a score of references to Mars, Venus and Diana. The debt which the love-poets may owe to the barbarians is shadowy and conjectural; their debt to the classics, or even, as now appears, to the Arabians, is much more certain (pp 5 and 8).

The *fabliaux*, favourite reading of Chaucer, are full of realistic and satirical reflections on bourgeois life; they reveal a new attitude, combining the desire for self-knowledge with a critical appreciation of shrewdness in human dealings. This attitude was manifest in the amusing debate of the Guildford poet, who wrote *The Owl and the Nightingale*, and in the spirited poetry and *diablerie* of Villon and Chaucer.

Some art historians consider that the noblest expressions of the age are to be found in other forms than literature, for instance, in Romanesque churches and Gothic cathedrals, of which Chartres and Reims are memorable examples. The mystical fervour and symbolism behind Latin Christianity are manifest in medieval paintings, which are richly endowed with colour and light.

The conditions of fourteenth-century society were such that vernacular literature tended to become a people's art, subject to an author's conventions. One of these was to please the taste of patrons, another to honour the narrative appeal of chivalry, even in the consciousness of its decline. Culture was more widely diffused among listeners than in the age of Henry II, when the tradition rested in the hands of the trouvère and the troubadour, accompanying knights of France to the Crusades. They introduced rhymed, syllabic measures to lyric poetry, which emanated from Provence. Their themes of courtly love motivated the tragedies of Guinevere and Iseult. The cult of women, implicit in devotion to the Virgin Mary, was to enhance the dignity of the sex, and encourage deeds of selfless renown.

In Chaucer's time the number of educated persons who possessed and read books must have been small. Richard II and his first Queen were patrons as well as readers. Froissart presented a sumptuously bound volume of his English Chronicle to the king, shortly after the first Irish campaign. Here are extracts of his account from Berners's English translation (Pynson, 1523):

> Than the kynge desyred to se my booke that I had brought for hym: so he sawe it in his chambre, for I had layde it there redy on his bedde. Whanne the kynge opened it, it pleased hym well, for it was fayre enlumyned and written, and covered with crymson velvet, with ten botons of sylver and gylte, and roses of golde in the myddes, wyth two great clapses gylte, rychely wrought. Than the kyng demaunded me

wherof it treated, and I shewed hym how it treated maters of love; wherof the kynge was gladde and loked in it, and reed it in many places, for he coulde speke and rede French very well; . . .

This kyng Richarde reigned kynge of Englande xxii yere in great prosperite, holdyng great estate and signorie: there was never before any kyng of Englande that spente so moche in his house as he dyd, by a C.M. [100,000] florens every yere: for I sir John Froissart, chanon and treasourer of Chimay, knewe it well, for I was in his court more than a quarter of a yere togider, and he made me good chere, bycause that in my youthe I was clerke and servaunt to the noble kynge Edwarde the thirde his grauntfather, and with my lady Philyp of Heynault, quene of Englande, his grandame; and whan I departed fro hym it was at Wynsore, and at my departynge the kyng sent me by a knight of his, called sir John Golofer, a goblet of sylver and gylte, weyeng two marke of silver, and within it a C. nobles, by the which I am as yet the better, and shal be as long as I lyve; wherfore I am bounde to praye to God for his soule, and with moche sorowe I write of his dethe.

That most Latin chronicles were compiled in monasteries is not surprising. Literacy was largely confined to the clergy and nobility, who enjoyed leisure and access to the best minds. A lay writer was usually a retainer in a nobleman's household, as was Chaucer in John of Gaunt's, one of the many in the reign of Richard II, who belonged to the citizen class. H. T. Riley in *Memorials of London and London Life* from the Guildhall Library (1868) reproduced a number of city records translated from medieval French and Latin, among which was Chaucer's lease with London's Mayor and Aldermen dated May 10, 1375 (see Coulton, *Social Life in England*, Preface, p vi and bibliography). He acquired a life tenancy, at no charge, of the dwelling over the Gate of Aldgate, and was living there when the riotous peasants of 1381 were illegally permitted to enter the city. Although he had been a member of parliament for Kent and held several civil service posts, Chaucer was not in affluent circumstances towards the end of his life. This is surmised from the legal action taken against him for debt in 1398, and the *Complaint to his Purse*, a poem addressed to King Henry IV, which resulted in an increase to his pension.

A remarkable sign of change, by the close of the fourteenth century, was the burial of Chaucer in Westminster Abbey, close to the graves of Edward III and Richard II (see p 426). As noble families were busy extinguishing each other in the pursuit of power, the comfortable middle class, to which Chaucer and John Gower belonged, were coming to the fore. Yet Gower in 1375 could not understand why a villein should want to eat wheaten bread, when his meal had once consisted of beans or coarser corn. 'The world,' he wrote in *Mirour de l'Omme* 'goeth fast from bad to worse.' Gower was, in fact, the last poet of note to write in what was still the language of most of the Court, Anglo-French. G. C. Macaulay describes his verse as a 'combination of the French syllabic principle with the English accent principle . . . alien to English traditions' *(Cambridge History of the English Literature*, vol. II, 1908, p 143).

French loan words in English suffered in stress-emphasis, tone and quantity, from changes for acoustic convenience; a speaker in the context of an English sentence does not usually adjust the mechanism of articulation for a single borrowing. It often happened that French or Latin borrowings duplicated English words already in existence, e.g. *frigid* for *cold*; this is not to be deplored, since synonyms offer alternative rhythmical opportunities, and add subtleties of meaning that enrich the language's resources. No purist can reasonably object to hybrids such as *enfold, cleavage* and *forbearance,* in which borrowed prefixes and suffixes are attached to native words.

In the Middle English period eleven hundred French words are supposed to have entered the English language, 934 of which appeared between 1200 and 1400 (see O. Jespersen, *Growth and Structure of the English Language,* 1940, ch. V); the figures are based on entries in the *OED*. The writer combed the dictionary for examples of words of French etymology, such as *virtue,* and noted all citations from Middle English. In the case of *virtue,* of which there are numerous examples, he found that the earliest was from the *Ancrene Riwle* in 1225, i.e. within the period of greatest borrowing (200 years). As would be expected, the romances and the works of Chaucer account for a high share during the period of maximum importation. It is probable that this tendency reflects the increasing number of texts that were appearing in several dialects. The dialect often indicates the social and cultural climate of a work's origin.

There were two principal waves of importation of French words into English: (1) from Anglo-Norman in the early Middle English period (1150–1300); and (2) from Central French in late Middle English (1300–1450). The largest percentages of loan words from Anglo-Norman are to be found in *Ancrene Riwle, Kyng Alisaunder* and Robert of Gloucester's *Chronicle* (*c* 1295); many subsequently disappeared from the language. Borrowing in the later period continued throughout the fifteenth century, and beyond. Sometimes a borrowed word was repeated in a more refined form in the later period, e.g. *guardian* for *warden*, possibly because the Norman form had been vulgarized by the lower classes. By the end of the fourteenth century the Anglo-Saxon word-count had probably been reduced to half of its original strength; but it is noteworthy that French innovations replacing Anglo-Saxon words have been those most liable to shifts of meaning.

One of the worthwhile reforms that Richard III introduced in 1483 was to cause the proceedings in parliament to be kept in English, instead of French, because the latter was virtually unknown to the English public. In fact, the legal and official form of French had by then degenerated into a mongrel language.

The influence of French upon English after the thirteenth century was stronger in spelling and pronunciation than in syntax. We know, for instance, that a word containing a syllable with the spelling *oi* or *oy* should be of French derivation, because that diphthong did not occur in the Germanic languages. In morphology the lasting effect of French was to increase the number of weak verbs, shown in preterite and past-participle endings, and so indirectly to induce native strong verbs to follow the same pattern. The new orthography that the French scribes introduced, not being familiar with the old conventions, had one merit, that of reflecting sound changes begun in the late Old English period, which were not as yet indicated in spelling. Hence spellings such as *chance*, with initial [tʃ], began to appear in English texts for the first time; though other changes were not equally happy.

At no time was the north of England as greatly affected by the influx of French words as the south; this the literary texts of the dialects confirm. As the major number of the French importations came into the language after 1200, and participated in the sound changes of the thirteenth century and later, it is necessary to deal with one of these first, viz. the lengthening of English vowels in open syllables.

An open syllable is one which ends in a vowel, according to the customary manner of syllable division e.g. *da/gas*; lengthening of such syllables took place in the thirteenth century. When the short vowels *a, e, o* occurred in the open syllables of disyllabic words, (e.g. ME *fader* < OE *fæder, tale* < *talu*) they were lengthened to the corresponding long vowels [ɑ:], [ɛ:] and [ɔ:]. Towards the end of that century, or early in the fourteenth, *i* and *u* were lengthened, too, in open syllables, but the change was accompanied by lowering and tensing of the vowel, the evidence of which appears first in northern texts. Thus *i* > ē, e.g. OE *wicu* > ME *wēke* [wekə]; OE *yfel* > ME *evel* [evəl] in C14 texts of the North and East Midlands. Similarly u > o, e.g. OE *wudu* > ME *wōde* [wodə].

In the North, by 1300, final -*e* had become silent, so that many disyllabic words became monosyllables. Consequently, the lengthening took place only in inflected forms, from which new nominative singulars were formed, with a long vowel, in the fourteenth century; thus *wēkes* and *wōdes* produced new singulars *wēk* and *wōd* at this time. In fact, lengthening took place even in many monosyllabic words that ended in a consonant, e.g. *hol* 'hole', which produced ME singular *hōle*; the analogy caused the appearance of many doublets.

Lengthening in open syllables did *not*, however, take place in the inflected case of disyllabic words, if the inflexion brought about a trisyllabic form. This, too, was productive of double forms. For example, OE *bodig* > C13 [bɒdɪ]; but the plural *bodies* was trisyllabic, and the *o* therefore remained short, as it is in modern English. Cf. the short quality of the vowel in ME *sadeles* 'saddles', *hevenes* and *wederes* 'weathers', as in modern English. On the other hand, note the lengthened quality of the first vowel in *crādeles* 'cradles' and *bēveres* 'beavers'. The spelling *ea* in modern *heaven* and *weather*, indeed, indicates derivation from a lengthened vowel form; this is one of the inconsistencies of historical English spelling.

Lengthening in the open syllables of inflected forms of some OE monosyllabic words (*hol* has already been cited) gave rise to interesting double forms; for instance in the case of OE words *dæl* and *blæc*. The development of these words was as follows:

OE *dæl* > EME *dăl* > plural *dāles*, yielding the new singular *dāl*. OE *blæc* > EME *blăc* > plural *blāke*, yielding the new singular *blāk*, which was written *blake*, the source of the modern proper name; cf. the noun/adjective *black*, also used as a proper name.

In the case of ModE *staff*, archaic plural *staves* (Oe *stæf*, pl. *stafas*) the short form in the singular, and long in the plural, have been correctly preserved.

An important fact in spelling-lore is the origin of final -e to denote length of the preceding vowel. This was indubitably connected with the phenomenon of vowels in open syllables. Scriveners came to regard *final -e* as the sign of length of the preceding vowel, and therefore retained the usage after the ending ceased to be pronounced, as in modern English.

Norman French, on its transplantation to England, underwent little change of sound, when words were incorporated into the English language. Borrowings were mainly legal, ecclesiastic, heraldic or military terms, as the Normans had become the ruling class. Wright in his *Middle English Grammar* (§ 180) reckons that about half a million French-speaking persons must have settled in England in William the Conqueror's reign, and that they killed or otherwise got rid of about an equal number of the English and Danes. The population of England was then about two million.

Central or Parisian French, which became the standard dialect of France, supplanted Anglo-Norman, as the language of the Court, in the thirteenth century, and the Norman dialect then quickly became extinct in England. A knowledge of the sound changes effected on the incorporation of French words into English, from whatever source, is indispensable to the student of the early language. H. C. Wyld's *Short History of English* (§§ 182–200) contains a brief outline. Wright (*M.E.G.* § 185) shows which Old French sounds underwent change in Norman French. The aim here is to consider the pattern of change in the twelfth century, initiated by the speakers of Norman French. Old French sounds that preceded Norman French are indicated in brackets. Some philologists choose rather to trace the history of the sounds from the Old French system; unfortunately, little is known about the quantity of OF vowels and diphthongs. The principal difference between Anglo-Norman and the parent Old French tongue lay in the pronunciation of diphthongs. Only two new diphthongs actually entered English from French sources during the ME period, viz. *oi* and *ui*.

NF *ă* remained unchanged in ME, except in the following circumstances: lengthening took place in open syllables in the same way as occurred with OE *ă*; but it also took place before *st*, as in *paste*, and before a single consonant, as in *debāt*. Nasalization in the combinations *ām, ān*, though at first retained in English, soon gave rise to the diphthong *au*, as in *chaumbre* and *daunce*. The original spelling (and presumably pronunciation) frequently remained, however, e.g. *chambre* and *dance*. Jespersen (*Modern English Grammar*, pp 110-11) ascribes the undiphthongized forms to Continental French; Wyld (op. cit. § 184) to social causes. Wyld contends that the lower classes would have been unacquainted with such a pronunciation as *dāncen* (with nasalization) and would naturally simplify. The phenomena, at any rate, produced the double forms that passed into ModE. In the undiphthongized form *an* before *-ge*, the vowel was lengthened; hence such spellings as *straange*, found in Trevisa's translation of *Polychronicon*.

NF *ě* [ɛ] was retained in close syllables, for example in *clerk, lettre, taverne, werre* 'war'; but it was lengthened before the combination *-st*, as in *bēst* 'beast', and often before *-r* + consonant, as in *sērchen*. It was lengthened, too, in open syllables, e.g. *grēten*, and before a single final consonant, e.g. *squiēr*.

NF *ē* [e] passed unchanged into ME, as in *beautē, daungēr, pēr* 'peer'. It should be noted that OF *ie* > NF *ē* about 1150, the latter retained in ME, as in *manēre*.

NF *ī* passed unchanged into ME in words such as *brībe, mercīe*, and *strīven*.

NF *ŏ* was preserved in close syllables, such as *cofre, fors* 'force', *loggen* 'to lodge'. It was, however, lengthened in open syllables to [ɔ:], as in *cōte, suppōsen, tresōr*, and before *-st*, as in *hōst*.

NF *ŭ and ū* (derived from OF *o* [o]) were retained in ME before two or more consonants, e.g. in *purse*. In open syllables, and before a single final consonant, *ŭ* was lengthened in NF itself, and remained long in ME, the spelling usually being *ou*, as in *flour, labour, spouse*. The *ū* passed unchanged into EME, but was then shortened, if it occurred before two or more consonants, e.g. *touchen*. The sound is also spelt *ou*.

NF *ŭ and ū* = [y]. According to Wyld (§ 193), the French [y] was probably tenser and higher than the OE sound, because it did not undergo the changes in time and place of the native vowel. As this sound remained unchanged in ME, words containing it are readily traced to their French origin. The *u*-spelling was retained throughout ME. Instances of the short vowel are *humble, just* and *sepulchre*. Short sounds were, however, eventually lengthened in stressed open syllables, e.g. in *natūre, rūde* [rydə], *vertū*. In some words, such as *bugle* and *duke*, ū[y]>[iu] or [ju], either in LME or EModE.

NF *ŭ* (before the nasal *n*)>ME [u], generally spelt *ou*, e.g. *abounden, ounce, renoun.*

Norman-French diphthongs were all derived from Old French combinations, but with slight variation. Some combinations, such as the first two following, were merely orthographic, the sounds discussed being really monophthongs:

NF *eo, ue* [ø] (from OF *ue*). The sound resembled that in German *Goethe* and French *peu*, a half-close rounded vowel. It passed unchanged into EME, and then followed the monophthongization tendency of ēo in LOE, usually spelt *e* or *u*, according to dialect. By 14C the sound had become unrounded to [e], reflected in a variety of spellings, e.g. *people, poeple, peple; boef* and *beef*. An unusual representation is *ioparde* 'jeopardy' in line 242 of *Pearl*.

NF *ui* [yɪ] (from OF *ui*). Monophthongization is indicated in the sporadic spelling *u*. This sound >[y] in ME, variously spelt, e.g. *fruit, frut; pu, puw, pew.*

NF *ai* and *ei* (unchanged from OF). These fell together as [ɛɪ] in NF, the sound becoming [aɪ] in ME, e.g. *lai, maire* 'mayor', *obeien*. Later, this sound tended to become [ɛ:] before liquid and dental consonants, as well as before *s* and *v*, giving rise to double forms, as in *frēle/fraile; plēden/plaiden; ēse/aise* 'ease'; *pēs/pais* 'peace'.

NF *au* (unchanged from OF). The original combination was *a + l*. This diphthong passed unaltered into EME, but was later monophthongized to [ɑ:] before labial consonants. Examples, *faute, heraud, paume* 'palm of the hand' later *pāme, sauven* 'to save' later *sāven*. In the C-text of *Piers Plowman*, passus VI, line 51, Langland has the compound verb *vochen sāf* 'vouchsafe'.

NF *eau* (from earlier *eal* + consonant)>EME [eu]>C13 [iu]. Various spellings occur, e.g. *beautē, beutē, bewtē.*

NF *eu* (from OF *ieu*)>EME [eu]>C13 [iu]. The resulting diphthong was spelt many ways, e.g. *Jew/Jiw* and *rewle/reule/ruile.*

NF *oi* [ɔɪ] (unchanged from OF < Latin *au + i*) passed unchanged into ME, e.g. *chois* [tʃɔɪs], *cloistre, joie, poisen* 'to poise'.

NF *ui* [uɪ] (from OF *oi* < Latin *ō* or *u +i*). This sound was preserved in ME, and lasted until the first quarter of the seventeenth century, written either *oi* or *oy*, e.g. *boilen* 'to boil', *point, poisen* 'to poison'. Some words, such as *moist*, entered the language later in ME from Parisian French.

A useful summary of general principles relating to the Norman French vowel system, as it affected Middle English, appears in Wright's *M.E.G.*, § 185. He points out that denasalization of sounds using the nasal cavity, converted nasal vowels into oral ones, which then followed the development of the corresponding English vowels.

Final accented vowels, Wright reminds us, were either long in NF or became so in ME, for instance *imāge* and *grāce*. But although the *ā* in these words was the final vowel in NF, it was not so in ME, since the final *e* was pronounced [ɪmadʒə], [grasə]. In brief, *g* and *c* had now acquired an alternative phonetic quality to what they possessed in OE. Probably medial *c* in words like *grace* was first pronounced [ts] in EME; but the combination was rapidly simplified.

Norman French vowels were short in consonant combinations, other than a plosive + liquid, e.g. in *cacchen, simple, ordre, turnen.* But before plosive + liquid groups, as well as *-st*, they were lengthened, as in *fāble, mirācle, chāste* and *Chrīst.* Short vowels were also lengthened before another vowel in what were correctly regarded as disyllabic words, e.g. in *chaos, lion, quiet, poet*; these words are, of course, borrowings from Latin or Greek. In addition, short vowels were lengthened before a single final consonant in monosyllabic words, such as *pēr*, the reason being that the vowel appeared as long in the inflected forms. This change was analogous to the lengthening of vowels in the open syllables of native words.

The rules that Wyld and Wright enunciate are mainly concerned with the pronunciation of vowels in accented syllables. The treatment of French vowels in unaccented syllables is also important. The latter are distinguished as *pretonic* and *post-tonic*, according to their occurrence *before* or *after* the main stress. The treatment of pretonic vowels is difficult to determine, especially if they remained unaccented in ME. The sounds cannot be subjected to the test of rhyme, which, as Ten Brink reminds us in § 86 of *The Language and Metre of Chaucer*, is the most valuable of all tests. Unaccented vowels or diphthongs of French borrowings often became tonic by shifting of the accent, however, in which case they were lengthened, provided the borrowing occurred early; if late, the vowel tended to remain short. As already shown, the short vowels of early borrowings were invariably lengthened before a following vowel, or in open syllables.

It happens that the vowel in post-tonic positions is always *e*, and this disappeared earlier in French borrowings than it did with native words. The first *e*'s to become mute were probably those which followed *st* (e.g. in *haste*), medial *c* [s] (e.g. in *place*), or were preceded by a vowel (e.g. *folie*). Chaucer's preservation of the final *e*, when it had already passed out of current speech, was an archaism justified by poetic licence. He did not permit words ending in *-ce* to rhyme with words ending in *-s*; or words ending in *-ye* or *-ie* to rhyme with those ending in *-y*. This is regarded as proof that, in his verse, he intended the final *-e* in these circumstances to be pronounced.

The Old French and Norman French accented vowels in words borrowed early, which became post-tonic through the shifting of accent, passed unchanged into ME, but acquired a secondary accent, which was soon weakened. The result was the neutralization of the vowel sound to [ə].

Sometimes weakened medial *e* disappeared between consonants. Thus *chimneie* is found beside *chimeneie*, *kerchef* beside *keverchef*, *pantrie* beside *panetrie*.

Initial unaccented syllables, whether vowels or prefixes, often disappeared. Initial *e* tended to disappear before *s*+any voiceless plosive (*p*, *t*, *k*); hence the forms *scapen* and *escapen*, *spyen* and *espyen*, *staat* and *estaat*. An initial vowel (usually *a-* or *e-*) tended to disappear before consonants, causing the doublets *menden* and *amenden*, *prentys* and *aprentys*. Sometimes prefixes were unaccountably lost, yielding *fenden* and *defenden*, *saumple* and *ensaumple*, *sport* and *disport*.

The time spent on Middle English phonology stands the student in good stead, when he comes to study the development of verse. Unless he has a sensitive understanding of the pronunciation of medieval English words, his appreciation of metrical nuances will be hampered. Of this, Chaucer's poetry is the supreme test.

The weakening of OE vowels in unaccented syllables was a phonological change of the greatest importance to the future of the language. As early as the seventh century OE final *-i* > *e*; and in LOE *a*, *o*, and *u* were similarly levelled to *e*. What the quality of this vowel was in LOE, it is impossible to say; it may have been [ə] in final syllables, but in other positions it probably varied according to the neighbouring sounds.

In ME similar variations seem to be indicated by spellings *i* and *u*, as well as *e*, after 1300. But the *i*- spellings were found mainly in the North, and the *u*- spellings in the W. Midlands. Generally, in other texts, OE *bealu*>ME *bale; brōðor*>*broþer; dǣlan*>*delen; heofones*> *hevenes; macodon*>*makeden; stānas*>*stones*. The vowel was not, however, weakened in certain final syllables, which were suffixes bearing a secondary accent, such as *-dōm, -fast, -fōld, -ful, -hōde, -i* (OE *-ig*), *-ing, -isch, -les* (OE *-lēas*), *-līche, -ling, -lok* (OE *-lāc*), *-schipe, -sum, -ung, -ward*, and *-ēr* (when it denoted an agent). The long vowels were, however, shortened during the ME period.

Sometimes [ə] developed before vocalic consonants *l, m, n* and *r*, where no vowel had existed in OE. These neutral sounds are termed *svarabhakti* vowels, because they replace old hypothetical Indo-European vowels of the vanishing grade of the ablaut (gradation) system (see chapter VIII). The development of this neutral vowel took place in the transition period (LOE – EME). Thus OE *fæþm* >ME *faþem; hæsl*>*hasel; setl*>*setel; swefn*>*sweven*.

Also in the transition period, a neutral sound (usually spelt *u*) developed between *r* and a following back fricative. Thus OE *burh* >*buruʒ*, the inflected form of which was *burowe*; from the latter a new nominative *burough* was developed in ME. Spellings in *-ow* are also found, e.g. *sorowe*.

Svarabhakti vowels developed in medial as well as final syllables, giving rise to trisyllabic forms, beside the old disyllabic ones. The spelling was generally *e* before liquid and nasal consonants, e.g. *evere* (OE *æfre*), and *o* before the semivowel *w* (from earlier *ʒ*) e.g. *morowe* (OE *morʒen*). Double forms found in ME are: *borowen* [ɔ] beside *borgen; breþeren* beside *breþren; dēveles* [e] beside *dēvles*.

Loss of neutral vowel [ə] took place in the following circumstances: It happened much earlier in the North than in the South. Barbour's *Bruce* shows that the loss was complete in Scotland by 1375. In ME many words had a final *-e* which did not exist in OE; it was generally, but not always, a scribal device to indicate length of the preceding vowel, and this, as already shown, resulted from the lengthening of vowels in the open syllables of the inflected forms of monosyllabic words e.g. ME *tide* (OE *tīd*); ME *nedle* [ɛ] (OE *nǣdl*); ME *seke* [e] (OE *sēoc*). Such spellings were retained long after the final *-e* was not pronounced; in fact, are generally preserved to the present day.

In originally disyllabic words with short stem syllables final -e ceased to be pronounced, and consequently written, earlier than in similar words with long stem syllables, e.g. *son* (OE *sunu*). The position by LME was that final -e after short stem syllables had generally ceased to exist. And where it survived after long stem syllables, it came to be taken as an indication of length of the preceding vowel, irrespective of whether it was original or not – a habit which hardened, and became chaotic after the advent of printing. By the latter half of the fifteenth century -e was frequently added to the spelling of any noun ending in a consonant, without regard to the quantity of the preceding vowel.

Regarding the chronological order of loss of final -e in pronunciation, the North preceded (complete by 1250), the Midlands followed (1350), and the Southern dialects brought up the rear (lost somewhere between 1350 and 1400). Kentish was the last to adopt the innovation. Wright (*M.E.G.* § 141) says that in 'all the dialects it disappeared in pronunciation earlier in nouns and verbs than in adjectives, and earlier in the strong than in the weak declensions of adjectives.'

Chaucer's use of the final -e has been described as a poetic archaism; he found it useful for metrical purposes. In fact, the evidence has been adduced largely from a study of his metre. It is probable that in his own speech he did not pronounce the letter, which he meant to be sounded in the reading of his poems.

From the orthographical point of view, final -e has two origins:

(1) It may represent an older final syllable or inflexion (OE -*a*, -*e*, -*u*, -*an*, -*en*, -*um*; or OF -*e*).

(2) It may be a mere scribal device (a) to indicate length of the preceding vowel; or (b) it may be used by the scribe quite capriciously, e.g. in Chaucer's forms *Aprille* and *pytte* 'pit'. This last use represents no real syllable; the final -e was probably never pronounced.

When inflexional, -e could be the relic of grammatical functions:

(1) The nom. sing. of some nouns and adjectives, e.g. nouns: *sone*, *chirche*, *dame;* adjectives: *grene*, *trewe.*

(2) Acc., gen. or dat. sing. of other nouns and adjectives: e.g.

nouns: *sorwe*, *speche*; adjectives: *halfe*. (A final -*e* was often appended to adjectives which occur after *the*.)

CHAPTER XI

Dialect, Literature and Language

ͽͽͽͽͽͽ

PERHAPS the most acceptable account of the class dialect that became 'the received standard of English' is to be found in H.C. Wyld's *History of Modern Colloquial English*. Synonyms for this in Wyld's introductory chapter are 'well-bred English' and 'upper-class English', the boundaries being social rather than regional. Wyld postulated a number of *modified* standards, spoken in the towns of the Home Counties and Midlands, some of which became prominent in post-Chaucerian literature; but the bulk of the modifications occurred in pronunciation, rather than grammar and vocabulary.

Of some significance for the received standard was the progress of Mercian and East Anglian dialects in which much of the literature after 1250 was written. By then the decay of English inflexions was practically complete, and grammatical gender in decline. The diffusion of Midland literature in the fourteenth century was due partly to that area's commercial importance, and partly to the presence of the university towns of Oxford and Cambridge; but the influence of such writers as Chaucer and Wyclif may have been paramount.

The phonology of Middle English is the most complicated part of its evolution, because the recognizable dialects reflect whims of authors who wrote as they spoke, and spelt as they fancied. The literary supremacy of Wessex had disappeared by the beginning of the twelfth century. The broad classification of dialects into Northern, Midland and Southern was first observed by Ranulph Higden, who died in 1364; his Latin history, *Polychronicon*, was then translated into English at Exeter College, Oxford, by John of Trevisa, whose task was completed about 1385.

The distribution of English dialects after the Norman Conquest is manifest in official documents and surviving literary texts. The evidence reveals that OE spelling conventions had been undermined by the impact of Norman French scribes, whose legacy can be seen in the place and personal names of the *Domesday Book*. The scribes attempted a compromise with French, when representing un-familiar English letters or sounds, by using ready-to-hand approxi-mations. Modifications of native speakers during the preceding century, which late Old English scribes had failed to recognize, were reflected in these new spellings. Norman scribes invariably used the Carolingian script of France to replace the Celtic-Latin script that had persisted in Britain. The Caroline minuscule intro-duced into England in the ninth century developed a less pointed art than that of the Anselm tradition, and showed a tendency to flatten letters in the interests of linear appearance.

It is customary to subdivide Higden's tripartite classification of the English dialects, which were simply Northern, Midland and Southern; but in practice it is preferable to discuss texts, rather than their supposed counties of origin. The dream of a normative grammar, which some eighteenth-century grammarians enter-tained, would have foundered on an attempt to apply it to medieval manuscripts. Kenneth Sisam in *Fourteenth-Century Verse and Prose* (p 265) says that the ideal would be to provide a special grammar for each individual text.

Lowland Scots and northern English were differentiated by 1350, and Barbour's *Bruce* gave the Middle Scots dialect a literary status in 1375. The London dialect perpetuated by Caxton proved to be of mixed origin; it preserved South-East Midland as its base, while containing a strong admixture of Kentish and Central Southern forms.

As the lot of Englishmen rose in the social hierarchy, through intermarriage or economic necessity, language barriers disappeared; most people of the gentleman class must have been thoroughly bilingual. When English was reborn as a literary medium, it little resembled the language of late West Saxon clerical authors; as a medium befitting a people emerging from underprivileged condi-tions, it was homely, colloquial and spontaneous, though much of it still emanated from the monasteries. In time the syntax became more complicated, especially in prose, as translations such as Chaucer's *Boece* reveal.

When inflexions were lost, the order of words became syntactically important in every aspect of communication. It is a normal development of synthetic (inflexional) languages, such as Old English, to become analytical; but in Norman England the process was aided by the adoption of relation words for functional ends. It became possible to extend the subtleties of thought through phrasal syntax and idiomatic groupings that convey symbolic relationships. The chief factors in this development were increased employment of the verbs *be, have, come, make, do;* interchange of parts of speech, and the extensive use of auxiliary verbs and prepositional phrases; for instance, the substitute genitive, with *of,* to replace the inflected form. Appositional phrases, expanded tenses and participial constructions became resources of syntax that added to the flexibility of English usage. English syntax owes absolute-participial and accusative-infinitive constructions to Latin; the latter were occasionally found in Old English.

Qualities of mind that contribute to a culture are perhaps more important than linguistic origins. In the Middle Ages the received standard of English in London belonged to the privileged governing class; as a class dialect, it embodied mannerisms, taboos, fads and political prejudices of the social group. At the other extreme there developed, in Tudor times, the class dialect known as Cockney, which began as a regional dialect of a localized underprivileged çommunity.

Frequent causes of linguistic isolation are occupation and social status. People of different strata in society are, to a large extent, out of touch with each other, living, as they do, in separated environments. There were for generations, too, disparate standards of education; and it follows that the speech of different social groups was likely to develop on divergent lines.

Medieval literature in English is so abundant, and of diverse quality, that a critical conspectus is not possible in a chapter or two. The products of different regions have, of necessity, to be taken into account, and the different genres in prose and verse discussed, which leaves little room for the language and style of individual authors, many of whom are unknown. On the whole, creative writers of the fourteenth century were more sophisticated than those of the thirteenth, because they possessed a more resourceful command of their medium. With Chaucer, for the first time, the secular and humane can be said to counterpoise the didactic and religious. Narrative volubility, in things of minor human concern, was the undoubted defect of the thirteenth century; even its lyrical mood was conventionally tied to symbols of religious veneration.

A stimulating introduction to the literature of the period has been written in C. S. Lewis's *The Discarded Image*. He begins by assessing the romances and ballads as 'truancies, refreshments, things that live only on the margin of the mind' (p 9); 'at his most characteristic, the medieval man was not a dreamer nor a wanderer. He was an organiser, a codifier, a builder of systems' (p 10). He sought to synthesize 'theology, science and history into a harmonious mental Model of the Universe' (p 11). His 'spiritual books are entirely practical – like medical books' (p 18).

This is a new outlook; for the old dwelt on the inherent melancholy of medieval literature, in which man is a creature conceived in sin, wholly at the mercy of the divine will. It is mistaken to look upon such beliefs as a gospel solely of punishment. Though the world was beset with powers of evil, the thoughtful writer managed to dramatize them in the imagination. His sense of insecurity was relieved by benign grace, or the practice of religious virtues. Indeed, the stuff of men's hopes and fears became the fructifying material of art, such as Dürer used in his etchings. The same imagination took the great names of antiquity (e.g. Vergil's) and invested them with magical powers. Grammarye (knowledge of the art of language) was a key to such power, granted to gifted persons like Roger Bacon.

The pressure of orthodoxy in the Middle Ages did not inhibit the spirit of revolt. There was a good deal of homely invective and burlesque for folk who needed recompense for their political disabilities. Jean de Meun unrepentantly replaced chivalry, in the latter part of *Le Roman de la Rose*, with realism and satire. Chaucer's Wife of Bath is as perfectly human as amoral; the humanism of this poet's writing is nowhere more evident than in his Boccaccio-like sense of humour. Literature had at last become, not merely recreation, but a stern necessity pressed out of the tedium of life, by those who could joyfully participate in the life of people.

Middle English literature has also songs of pure feeling, in which the senses are refined by appreciation of the beauty of nature. The sombreness of life is balanced by an optimistic sprightliness. Man has to be a brave creature, resilient and elastic in spirit, if the penchant for allegory is to be enriched with graceful fantasies. The purposive writings of the thirteenth century were remodelled in the fourteenth to show that, underneath the travail, there is a living need for men to find the kind of satisfaction that literature alone affords. Its real appeal is that it grows out of the joys, fears, sorrows and perplexities of everyday life.

Piers Plowman, in its preoccuaption with oppressive issues, is not merely an allegory of the spiritually perturbed. The main task of the distressful peasant, who assumes the office of reader's guide, is to introduce us to a perplexed society that has lost its leaders, and is looking for new ones, who are spiritually or more humanely endowed. The typical English allegory is here in contrast to the lighter Latin spirit of reform. The danger of the allegorical mode is always a tendency to lose touch with humanity. The early part of *Piers Plowman* powerfully moves us; the scenes have the same graphic vividness as those of *Pilgrim's Progress*. But in the latter part the humanity seems to have evaporated; abstract signification, with a quasi-philosophical appeal, is all that is left.

The medieval imagination saw all events as contemporaneous; one soon realizes that there is no awareness of perspective. The Morality plays, for this reason, are not historical, but ethical, with the same proneness to allegory, where 'Everyman' is seen to be forever summoned by Death. The organizers of drama, as part of the Easter celebrations in the Church, however, realized, with Shakespeare, that continuity of the past with the present is the life-blood of drama. No one is seriously perturbed by anachronism.

English literature in the Middle Ages is, therefore, far from a collection of bookish curiosities, especially in the writings of Langland, Chaucer and the Gawain-poet. The thirteenth century was an age waiting to be born, whose genesis was not complete by 1400. Lord Buckhurst's contribution to the *Mirror for Magistrates* in the Age of Elizabeth was a gathering up of the threads of Medievalism; if man was still dogged by sinister foes, the allegory of the Fall of Princes was attuned to express, through intuition, his romantic respect for life's indefinable purpose.

'Romance' and 'romantic' are words of ill-defined significance in literature. In English, the noun, meaning 'a verse tale embodying medieval legend', appeared first in *Cursor Mundi*, at the beginning of the fourteenth century; the adjective was not actually invented until the Restoration. But the kind of emotional appeal that narrative poetry inevitably conveys is as old as literature; in varying forms the phenomenon appears in the *Odyssey*, the *Arabian Nights*, *Troilus and Criseyde* and the Arthurian Legend, works written in prose as well as verse.

The distinguishing feature of medieval romance was its Christian, chivalric character; there was no inconsistency in making a pagan environment, for instance that of Troilus and Hector, fit into this incongruously vernacular pattern; nor was there a qualm in grafting Christian dogma on Latin inspired literature. In France, most Roman of the imperial provinces, the *Chansons de Geste,* which were minor epics, glorified traditional heroes, from Alexander the Great to Roland of Roncesvalles; the true romance adopts a lower key, using any and every exotic theme, from the Destruction of Troy to the Marian apotheosis of women.

> Loveless hearts shall love to-morrow, hearts that have loved
> shall love again,
> Spring is young and Spring is singing, Spring is life where
> death had lain.

These are the opening lines of *Pervigilium Veneris*, the Latin poem that coloured the spirit and action of all medieval romance. The French perfectors of the art had no rivals in English, until *Criseyde* and *Gawain*; their skill is to be appreciated in models such as *Aucassin and Nicolette,* a thirteenth-century Provençal legend prompted by the most romantic of religious movements, the Crusades. In analysis of the emotions and sentiments, the indigenous romances of *King Horn* and *Havelok the Dane* are striplings, when compared with the polished Arthurian poems *Ywain* and *Sir Launfal* of Chrétien de Troyes. The earliest of English romances were composed nearly a century after the French prototypes; *King Horn,* which dates from the late thirteenth century, was an adaptation of a French poem, and *Sir Orfeo* was of Breton origin.

There is sound reason why Sir Gawain is the most impressive of the Knights of the Round Table in realizing the romantic ideal. The medieval romancer was not much moved by the merit of originality. Even the new twist given to the supernatural may be regarded as less important than the combination of adventure with the sporting spirit, or the fine sense of landscape, which reveals a deeper awareness of nature than is to be found in the conventional clichés of minor poets. It is clear that the superiority of *Sir Gawain and the*

Green Knight, like that of the General Prologue to the *Canterbury Tales* and the *Nun's Priest's Tale,* is due less to the content than the treatment, a broad term comprehending the language, style and spirit of the piece. On the first of these C. S. Lewis writes feelingly in *The Discarded Image* (p 6):

> Nothing about a literature can be more essential than the language it uses. A language has its own personality; implies an outlook, reveals a mental activity, and has a resonance, not quite the same as those of any other. Not only the vocabulary – *heaven* can never mean quite the same as *ciel* – but the very shape of the syntax is *sui generis.*

An attempt will be made in the remaining pages to trace the intricate development of style in Middle English literature, so far as evidence in the language permits. To say, as some critics contend, that poetry is impassioned language and prose reasoned language, is a false distinction; because there is reasoned poetry, like most of *The Owl and the Nightingale,* and impassioned prose, like Wulfstan's or Hereford's version of the English Psalter. The dichotomy, classical and romantic, is almost valueless in the medieval period; for 'romance', in origin, meant anything that emanated from medieval Rome (or Florence), which had abandoned many of the acknowledged classical disciplines.

In the records of most literary languages there have been revolts against convention and artificiality of diction. At no period in the long history of English poetry was there a greater divergence between the language of poetry and prose than in Old English; this is borne out by the figurative compounding, the use of synonymous epithets and the word order. The Anglo-Saxon poet was not much interested in exercising the inventive faculty; he was too busy with execution. This primacy of ornament was modified in the Middle English period, though the earliest verse products were unattractive. Most of the work of the twelfth century was in Latin prose, historical and theological. Much more verse must have been written in the traditional Old English line than the surviving *Site of Durham, The Grave* and *The Worcester Fragments.*

The first lyric quoted by D. J. Stewart in *Liber Eliensis* (1840), was attributed to King Cnut; only four lines were remembered by the Chronicler, Thomas of Ely, in the twelfth century. The rhyme is so rudimentary as to be merely assonantal:

Mérrie súngen ðe Múnekes binnen Ély
ða Cnút chíng réu ðér by.
Róweð cnítes nóer the lánd,
and hére wé þes Múneches sæng.

This is imperfect verse, but has the semblance of a four-beat line, with minimal alliteration. The interesting morphological forms of an undependable text are: *sungen* (preterite plural), *ching* (fronting), *reu* (preterite sing.), *cnites* (nom. plural), *noer* (prep.), *here* ('hear' pres. plur.) and *sæng* (presumably present tense). There are three instances of the syntactic inversion of subject and verb.

R. M. Wilson says that, whatever its origin, the song appears to have been sung as part of a *carole (Early Middle English Literature*, p 253). This was a dance of the chain variety, accompanied by singing, and directed by a leader – something like one of the figures in Square Dancing. The leader sang the verse, and the rest of the dancers responded in the refrain. A fair description of this pastime, much frowned upon by the Church, is given in 'The Dancers of Colbeck' in Robert Mannyng of Brunne's *Handlyng Synne*, written in the first decade of the thirteenth century. *Brunne* is the ME form of Bourne, the town in Lincolnshire.

Handlyng Synne is a candid account in the North-East Midland dialect of life in medieval England. 'The Dancers of Colbeck' (216–19) contains the following compound-complex sentence, with two relative *that*-clauses in the first line:

Þys yche arme þat was of Ave,
Þat none myȝt leye yn grave,
Þe Emperour dyd a vessel werche
To do hyt yn, and hange in þe cherche

The discontinuity of the syntactic structure is due to anacoluthon. The subject *þys yche arme* has no predicate, and although it is picked up again as *hyt* in the last line, to serve as the object of *do*, the logical requirements of grammar are not met. Certain functions of relative clauses were not yet understood, and could not have been employed without changing the word order, e.g. 'The Emperor caused a vessel to be made and *hung* in the church, *in which* to place this very arm of Ave that no one could lay in the grave.' The major problem was, however, to make such a bald statement poetically acceptable. This was a difficulty that the average narrative poet of the Middle Ages had no inkling how to confront.

Nothing better reveals the international nature of literature and learning in the Middle Ages than the appearance and reappearance of popular metres and verse forms, first in one country, then in another. Ker points out in *English Literature: Mediaeval* (pp 76–7) that the verse-line of that quaint, though long, religious poem, the *Ormulum (c* 1200), comes from Greek, through Latin. It is a seven-foot line with a fixed caesura, which divides it into three and four – the metre of the *Poema Morale* (1170). Accompanied by rhyme, the line turns up in different parts of the Continent, (e.g. Germany and Provence), and soon became a favourite one with ballad-minstrels. The *Ormulum* is, however, unrhymed throughout. Several features show that the poet was a purist and a spelling reformer. He indicates every short vowel by doubling the consonant which succeeds it:

> Nū, brōþerr Walterr, brōþerr mīn
> affter þe flæschess kīnde;
> and brōþerr mīn in Crisstenndōm
> þurrh fulluhht and purrh trowwþe.

From internal evidence the MS is holograph, of remarkable consistency, with virtual abolition of grammatical gender. The East Midland dialect suggests strong Norse influence. Fifteen syllables to the line are rigidly observed, and the ending always has a redundant feminine syllable; as a consequence the poem reads rather monotonously. The poet's evident desire to preserve quantity, when it no longer served his metre, is proof of pedantry.

It has to be admitted, however, that discipline in verse was sorely needed in this early period; for the hesitancy of versifiers tended to make their lines irregular; one perceives the stresses, but there is no rhythmical progression that resembles foot division. For example, the three-beat line of *King Horn* was a thoroughly English measure; but short rhyming couplets were too staccato in effect for a long narrative, as this example shows:

> Hé was whít so the flúr
> Róse réd was his colúr.
> In nóne kínge-ríche
> Nás nóne his ilíche (15–18)

Redundant negatives in lines 17/18 persisted until the seventeenth century, and are common in the plays of Shakespeare. The iterative function, for emphasis, appeared early in Germanic languages, and was not peculiar to them, as Jespersen showed in his monograph (Copenhagen, 1917).

Comely use of accentual measures is first found in the thirteenth-century lyrics of the Harley Manuscript (B.M. 2253), written between 1314 and 1325, and edited by G. L. Brook (1948). This miscellaneous collection of 141 poems contains the work of Midland poets, mostly from the West. There are several poems in which the overworked alliterative convention is combined with regular accent, rhyme and stanza form. Only in *The Meeting in the Wood*, a dialogue resembling the French *pastourelle*, did this measure succeed. Intimations of Wordsworthian feeling are rare in the lyrics; the perception of felicities is formal, and the imagery, when it occurs, somewhat lifeless. In the opening stanza of the following *reverdie* ('welcome to Spring') the italicized words hint at personification or metaphor, by virtue of the figurative value the reader ascribes to them (see, for instance, Brian Stone's free translation in *Medieval English Verse*, Penguin, 1964, p 200):

> Lenten is come *wiþ love to toune,*
> Wiþ blosmen and wiþ briddes roune,°   [song]
> Þat al þis blisse bryngeþ,
> *Dayes-eȝes* in þis dales
> Notes suete of nyhtegales
> Uch foul song singeþ.
> Þe threstlecoc him *þreteþ°* oo°;   [chides] [always]
> Away is huere winter *wo*
> When woderove° springeþ.   [woodruff]
> Þis foules singeþ ferly° fele,   [wondrous]
> Ant wlyteþ on huere wynne wele,
> Þat al þe wode *ryngeþ.*

The Harley lyrics abound in the courtly love of the troubadours, *Alysoun* being a fair example. The last stanza has a single impressive simile to stretch the imagination, *wery so water in wore*. There are three or four stresses in the line of dominantly iambic feet, with trochaic variation to sustain the rhythmical interest.

> Icham for wowyng° al forwake   [wooing]
> Wery so water in wore°,   [turmoil]

Lest eny reue° me my make,   [rob]
Ychabbe yȝyrned ȝore°.   [desired long]
Bettere is þolien° whyle sore   [suffer]
Þen mournen euermore.
Geynest vnder gore°   [Most gracious in attire]
  Herkne to my roun.
    An hendi hap° ichabbe yhent;   [fair fortune]
    Ichot from heuene it is me sent;
    From alle wymmen mi loue is lent°,   [turned]
    And lyht on Alysoun.

Coalescence of the first personal pronoun and verb in *Icham*,
Ychabbe and *Ichot* (ich wot) anticipates the genuine later contractions *I'm* and *I've*. The first four of the twelve lines are in alternate
fours and threes of the ballad.

Ballads have the most complicated genealogy of any poetry in the
Middle Ages, partly because they assimilate the lyrical element to
narrative. The keynote of the usual measures is simplicity, which is
due to oral tradition. Many of the ballads are tragic, and W. P. Ker
says in 'The Ballad is *Form*' (see *Form and Style in Poetry*, p 36 et
seqq) that when ballads first appeared in Denmark, they were the
pastime of the gentry. So they seem to have been in medieval
France, Spain and England; but soon they were taken over by the
people, and became the most impersonal of all forms of poetry.
Older narrative or epical poetry perhaps influenced subject-matter,
but the ballad, for Ker, is a pure formal idea, with a plot that is
never complicated or expanded. The provenance of most ballads
would place them in the fifteenth century; but the consensus of
opinion is that their origin in England belongs to the thirteenth.

The spontaneity of ballad language, and the bareness that followed from whittling away inessential details, is illustrated in *The
Battle of Otterburn* (1388), a poem preserved in Cotton MS
Cleopatra CIV. The ballad was probably not contemporary, but its
economy of phrase may be appreciated by comparing it with the
eye-witness account Froissart provided in the *Chronicles* (IX
237–85). Three of the final stanzas are appended; their date is here
unimportant:

          Then on the morne they mayde them beerys
            of byrch and haysell graye;
          many a wydowe wyth wepyng teyres
            ther makes they fette awaye.

thys fraye by-gan at otterborne,
   bytwene the nyght and the day;
ther the dowglas lost hys lyffe,
   and the perssy was lede awaye.

now let us all for the perssy pray,
   to Iesu most of myght,
to bryng hys sowlle to the blysse of heven,
   for he was a gentyll knyght.

Early in the fourteenth century, Franciscan friars made steadfast pleas for Latin hymns to be sung in the vernacular during English church services. William Herebert of the Convent at Hereford was one of the first to interest himself in translation, and is the earliest known author of religious lyrics. Seventeen poems appear in Phillipps MS 8336, with the translator's name in the margin; they show creditable fidelity to the originals, and were written in the first half of the fourteenth century, for Herebert died in 1333. The language, like that of the ballads, is pure and dignified; but the poems are today chiefly esteemed for their moral and devotional values. The various attempts in religious verse to explain the mystery of the virgin birth of Christ demonstrate a naive simplicity that culminated in the symbolism of that most discussed poem of the fifteenth century 'I sing of a maiden that is makeless'. The third stanza of Herebert's translation of *Conditor alme siderum* is reverently explicit:

> Toward þe worldes ende
> Þy wylle was t'alende°   [take up abode]
> In on maydenes bour;
> Ase spouse of chaumbre al-one
> Out of þat clene wone
> Þou come t'oure honour.

Contraction of preposition *to* before words with initial vowels is of much orthographic and metrical interest.

Analysing fourteenth-century poems compels the critic to establish some norms of style, to which authors seem to have accommodated their writings. Geoffrey de Vinsauf's *Poetria Nova* (c 1200) was too simplistic to influence the practising English writer. If poets wrote predominantly for practical ends, there must still have been aesthetic principles underlying particular acts of creation, either to satisfy the ear, or to stimulate taste for the chosen kind. Why were digressions so admired, not merely tolerated? Why does Chaucer, at the end of *Troilus and Criseyde,* invite 'moral Gower' to improve his work? These are valid questions.

Authors seem to have respected more the integrity of established themes, than fictional novelty; they were inheritors of a tradition the writer was expected to hand on, a little embellished, but not fundamentally altered. Digressions were afterthoughts, comments or historical addenda, which the original author, or chain of authors, was presumed to have overlooked. Chaucer's admiration for the editorial ability of Gower was partly humility, and partly acknowledgement of his colleague's skill in languages, for polyglot Gower composed with facility long poems in Latin, French and English.

The classical division of styles in the *Ad Herennium* into high, middle and low was not really adequate for the genres of Middle English writing; for nearly all were cast in the naturalistic mode that suited the emerging middle stratum of society. The only categories of poems to which a modified high style was appropriate were the elegiac and religious. A low style was adaptable to satire, popular drama and dialogue of the humbler social orders, many employed by the gilds. The speech of the new bourgeoisie in the fourteenth century, not in the clerical orders, was between these extremes. The leading poets were probably Minot and Barbour in the North, Langland and the Gawain-poet (usually identified with the Pearl-poet) in the Midlands; Gower and Chaucer in the South. Each has a distinct literary personality, marked by the themes he favours. Only Chaucer is individualized in Gallic refinement, observation and execution, a mind probing diligently to extend vocabulary with knowledge. It is to Chaucer that one returns constantly for that critical temper, breadth of intellect and technical competence, which are associated with the humanistic Renaissance.

The undervalued martial poet, Laurence Minot, who championed the cause of Edward III, was the first patriotic singer of England to mention his own name in the surviving text. Of northern origin, probably from Yorkshire, he followed the armies of the king to the Scottish border and to France, either as a soldier or a professional minstrel. Eleven poems of some length are preserved in MS B.M. Cotton Galba E. IX; they celebrate the exploits and victories of Edward between 1333 and 1352. Soon after the latter date the poet is presumed to have died. These stark, but spirited, accounts of war in the Middle Ages resemble Froissart's *Chronicles;* but they are extremely partial. Indeed, one reason for Minot's unpopularity with the critics is his fierce, sardonic nationalism, noticeable in his unwavering prejudice against the Scottish-French alliance.

There is considerable diversity in the metrical treatment of these so-called 'war-songs'. Abundant alliteration was a snare to any transitional poet with Minot's journalistic cast of mind, which reveals itself in trite phrases and a want of feeling for heroic simile and metaphor. But he redeemed a general want of imagination by a fine allegorical elegy on the king's death, reflecting the unhappy situation of the country at this time (see chapter XIII). Minot's vocabulary owes much to the romances, and his narrative simplicity to the ballads. The style is notable for fluency, and the syntax for its lack of complexity, as the following stanzas from the *Battle of Halidon Hill* show. The English victory, claimed as a recompense for Bannockburn, took place about thirty miles from Newcastle-on-Tyne in 1333:

> In þis dale I droupe and dare°   [hide]
> For dern° dedes, þat done me dere°.   [dark] [sad]
> Of Ingland had my hert grete care,
> When Edward founded° first to were.   [sought]
> Þe Franchemen war frek° to fare   [daring]
> Ogaines him, with scheld and spere;
> Þai turned ogayn with sides sare,
> And al þaire pomp noght worth a pere.
>
> A pere of prise es more sumtyde
> Þan al þe boste of Normondye.
> Þai sent þaire schippes on ilka side,
> With flesch and wine and whete and rye.
> With hert and hand, es noght at hide,
> Forto help Scotland gan þai hye.
> Þai fled and durst no dede habide
> And all þaire fare noght wurth a flye.

The northern origin of the text is indicated by the form *es* 'is', 3rd pers. sing. pres. indic. of *be*, and by the Old Norse borrowing *frek* 'daring,' 'insolent'. The periphrastic use of *gan hye*, for the preterite form *hyed*, is a metrical licence, and so is the compound preposition *Forto* at the beginning of line 14. The intrusive silent *h* in *habide* is due to French influence, and was probably a device to separate contiguous vowels, one of which should otherwise have been elided.

Three important modes of literary expression attained their most mature form in the fourteenth century, namely, romance, vision and satire. There is space to comment on the first two only. The great poems are long enough to permit the author to dilate upon his chosen themes and reflections e.g. *Sir Gawain and the Green Knight, Pearl, Piers Plowman* and the principal works of Chaucer, *Troilus and Criseyde,* the General Prologue to *The Canterbury Tales,* with such exemplars as the *Nun's Priest's Tale* and *Pardoner's Tale.*

These poems were all written in Midland dialects, including that of London, which was predominantly East Midland. The commercial city had established itself as the centre of cultural and political life. Whether in the alliterative or accentual mould, the liveliest poetry was written for oral delivery; therefore dramatic speech, to match the varied resources of narrative, was a *sine qua non.* No enduring composition is without structural merits of some kind; not a few possess unity of plot. *Sir Gawain and the Green Knight* has a taut atmosphere, because there is no item of its abundant detail that a reader would wish excised.

This untitled romance was formerly part of the B.M. Cotton MS Nero IX, which also contained *Pearl, Cleanness* (often called *Purity*) and *Patience.* It has 2530 lines, and is in four cantos, or *fits* (OE *fitt*), a word derived from Old Saxon, meaning 'division'. After a brief historical introduction, *Gawain* starts dramatically with the 'marvellous' beheading of the Green Knight, Sir Bercilak de Haut-desert. The name itself is of Celtic origin; but *haut-disert* (rather than *desert*) is French for 'high hermitage'. Green is the colour for 'truth' in the contemporary morality play *The Castle of Perseverance,* written in alliterative rhyming stanzas, and of North Midland provenance. Bercilak is able to survive decapitation because he has powers of magic, learnt from Morgan le Fay (Irish Morrigu) the enchantress who resides at his castle. Morgan, who is jealous of Guenevere, is actually of King Arthur's family, and the devoted pupil of Merlin. These explanations are cunningly withheld until the final fit, which is the most dramatic.

In a way, *Gawain* is an atypical romance, because its central event is an ordeal or 'jeopardy' to test the loyalty and courage of the knight. Gawain, son of the King of Orkney, is bound in a twelvemonth's time (the season is the Christmas festivities) to keep tryst at the Green Chapel, in order to 'bide' a similar blow upon his neck by his challenger. The latter's horse is clad in green, so that the colour has obvious mythological significance. In *Gawain*, the Faëry of pagan folklore is subtly transformed into a domestic drama, and finally into a chivalric one, in which the Christian motive is obvious. There is no perceived inconsistency between the religious and magic elements. After each temptation, during the Green Knight's spell of hospitality at the castle, he goes to mass, implying a Christian background at Hautdesert. But the discomfited man, by the sheerest chance, is preserved from harm through another charm, the green girdle which he received as a memento from his host's wife. He returns to court wearing this like a baldric, over the right shoulder and under the left arm, as a reminder of self-confessed weakness.

The two male characters in the romance are admirably contrasted; the one a humble, gracious, dependable member of the order of the Round Table; the other a robust lover of nature, with brusque exterior, but a latent capacity for compassion. It is almost as though the Latin and Celtic virtues are being compared. Bercilak, who describes himself as 'the merriest man alive', had been critical of the luxury at King Arthur's Court; he had called the knights 'beardless boys', and chided them for want of pride and valour. What he ultimately seems to have challenged is not the code of courtesy, which he severely tested, but the tendency to place it before personal honour.

Sensitivity to character and atmosphere makes the *Gawain* story a unique and undidactic romance, enhanced by a grim sense of humour. The poem has the essential elements of the genre, pageantry, expectancy, hunting scenes and temptations; incident and image are so patterned as to produce a series of significant contrasts, between the civilized court at Camelot, and the naturalistic world outside it, where the strangest things happen. To show how graciously language is accommodated to mood, the poet's description of the changing seasons of the year follows (fit II, lines 516–35):

> After, þe sesoun of somer wyth þe soft wynde3,
> Quen 3eferus syfle3° hymself on sede3 & erbe3;   [blows]
> Welawynne° is þe wort° þat waxes þeroute,
>   [very joyful] [plant]
> When þe donkande° dewe drope3 of þe leue3,   [dripping]
> To bide a blysful blusch° of þe bry3t sunne.   [gleam]

Bot þen hyʒes° heruest, & hardenes
        hym° sone,   [hastens] [and becomes severe]
Warneʒ hym for þe wynter to wax ful rype;
He dryues wyth droʒt þe dust for to ryse,
Fro þe face of þe folde to flyʒe ful hyʒe;
Wroþe° wynde of þe welkyn wrasteleʒ with þe sunne,
                                        [fierce]

Þe leueʒ lancen° fro þe lynde° &
        lyʒten on þe grounde,   [fall] [linden]
& al grayes þe gres þat grene watʒ ere;
Þenne al rypeʒ & rotez° þat ros vpon fyrst,   [ripens and rots]
& þus ʒirneʒ° þe ʒere in ʒisterdayeʒ mony,   [passes]
& wynter wyndeʒ° aʒayn, as þe worlde askeʒ,   [returns]
           no fage°,   [in truth]
      Til Meʒelmas mone°   [Michaelmas moon]
Watʒ cumen wyth wynter wage;°   [challenge]
Þen þenkkeʒ Gawan ful sone
Of his anious uyage: [wearisome journey]

There is a fair percentage of Old French and Old Norse loan words in the passage just quoted:

OF origin (8): *sesoun, syfleʒ, erbeʒ, face, lancen, wage, anious* and *uyage.*
ON origin (3): *donkande, roteʒ* and *aʒayn.*

This may be regarded as a representative proportion of words from two language sources in the text. Except where rhyme requires otherwise, the principal accent on French (sometimes Anglo-Norman) borrowings is moved to the stem syllable.

The principal peculiarities of the spelling are as follows:

(1) ʒ is used to represent initial g [j] e.g. in ʒere. When it occurs medially between vowels it serves as a glide sound, e.g. *hyʒes.*
(2) ʒ also finds employment as a voiced sibilant [z], e.g. *ʒeferus;* the latter sound also appears as an inflexional ending, e.g. in *sedeʒ.*
(3) ʒ may stand for a voiceless fricative [χ] before t, as in *bryʒt* and *droʒt.*
(4) ʒ represents [w] in words such as *saʒe* [sɔwə].
(5) In *watʒ* the [ts] combination had been simplified under French influence to [s].
(6) OE initial *hw* usually appears as *wh*, but sometimes the northern spelling is preferred, e.g. *Quen* 'when'.

(7) ME *ch* is often written *sch*, e.g. *blusch*.
(8) In *uyage*, the initial letter represents [v].
(9) *y* is preferred to *i* wherever it represents the sound [ɪ].
Almost invariably, the present participle ending is -*ande*, as in *donkande*.

In the second volume of Wells-Severs' *Manual of the Writings in Middle English* (p 339) *Pearl* is characterized as a 'mystical, elegiac dream-vision', and attributed to an unknown author, probably from South Lancashire, writing sometime in the last four decades of the fourteenth century. One evidence of the North-West Midland dialect is the use of the feminine pronoun *ho* for 'she'. The cryptic nature of the poet's intention, and the obliquity of his style, call for an explanation of the allegorical genre.

Dream-visions were a literary phenomenon in Italy and France, before they became popular in England; their roots lie deeper than Dante's *Divina Commedia*. A principal source of inspiration seems to have been Macrobius's commentary on Cicero's *Somnium Scipionis*. The type of allegory to which *Pearl* belongs is one where the entire poem recounts a mystical experience in the first person. The blend of colloquialism and domestic tenderness the elegy exhibits was the principal reason for the choice of the dialogue form. Four of Chaucer's early poems belong to the same class of visitation, the motive of dream being to remove the events from the world of objective reality. A. C. Spearing in *Medieval Dream-Poetry* discusses the dream-convention thoroughly, and suggests that the prototype for English writers was Guillaume de Lorris's part of *Roman de la Rose*, begun in 1277. This poet was the Ovid of the Middle Ages, and *Pearl*, written a century later, refers to the *Roman* in lines 749-53. The scene of both is a garden, which allegorically represents paradise.

Pearl is regarded as elegiac because it recalls the death of the poet's two-year-old daughter, who in the dream-vision becomes the spiritual guide and comforter of her father. The complexity of the design was made feasible by the writer's extensive vocabulary; section VIII, for instance, is devoted entirely to the religious significance of the word *courtesy*. There are paraphrases of passages from the Gospels of St Matthew and St John, the Psalms and Isaiah, but the great indebtedness is to the Vulgate book of Revelation. Religious people fervently believed in the potentiality of dreams to convey allegorical messages from God.

The joyous solemnity of *Pearl* reflects the autobiographical content, which some interpreters find in the visionary experience. The language is expressive of a genuine sense of loss, calmed by spiritual resignation. The religious aura of *Pearl* (a symbol of purity) suggests an author in some way connected with the Church. The poem remains one of the finest examples of the elevated style in Middle English, one in which pathos makes a healthy entry to English poetry. The high regard of the Queen of Courtesy in the New Jerusalem, is explained by the influence of Mariolatory in medieval art, as well as in the religious lyrics. There was nothing incongruous in a child of two becoming the devout amourist of her father's vision. The poem is a searching test of the critic's ability to attune his judgement to the attitudes and feelings habitual to the medieval mind.

Langland's *Piers Plowman*, in a South-West Midland mixed dialect, is an allegory of different outlook – the poet prefers to deal in personified abstractions of a paradoxical liveliness, and holds to the rhetorician's figurative view of allegory as extended metaphor. He resorts to a dreamer only incidentally, as Dante does. This does not inhibit graphic descriptions of observed individuals, as in the portrait of 'coveytise' (B-Text, Passus V, lines 190-94):

> He was bitelbrowed and   baberlipped° also,   [thick-lipped]
> With two blered eyghen   as a blynde hagge;
> And as a letheren purs   lolled his chekes
> Well sydder° þan his chyn   þei chiveled° for elde
>   [even lower] [trembled]

Many such characters are clearly allegorical fictions. The important difference between the two poets is that the imagery of *Piers Plowman* is cumulative and realistic, that of the Pearl-poet selective and conventional e.g. in lines 73–6 of the latter poem:

> Dubbed° wern alle þo downeȝ° sydeȝ   [arrayed] [hills]
> Wyth crystal klyffeȝ so cler of kynde.
> Holtewodeȝ° bryȝt aboute hem bydeȝ   [woods]
> Of bolleȝ° as blwe as ble° of Ynde°   [tree-trunks] [colour] [indigo]

Langland is no longer regarded as the 'malcontent' of Puttenham's description two centuries later; nor is his occasionally lumbering diatribe a Dickensian satire, to be studied primarily as a sociological document. The poet-critic was thoroughly disillusioned by what he saw; but his pilgrimage to Truth, recorded in a series of visions and debates, shows that he had the larger purpose of a Christian humanist. He dressed as a beggar, and lived in straitened circumstances, probably a member of the unbeneficed clergy class. As a Christian poet, he quickly perceived that the arid routine of the working-man's life led to tendencies that were certainly anti-Christian (see pp 339, 361).

The exercise of moral judgement in *Piers Plowman* involves the stripping from nature of conventional dress, to reveal the underlying human qualities. This was a method often employed by contemporary preachers; for the most searching critiques of fourteenth-century manners and customs were sometimes contained in sermons, and not many poets or writers of Morality plays could escape the stylistic influence of the pulpit's hortatory argument.

There are two main difficulties in reading *Piers Plowman*: its apparent lack of organizational plan; and its tendency to switch, without notice, from narrative to moralizing. The lack of a specific diction is less felt, because Langland is too engrossed with his theme. Being a man of humble origins, he despises literariness; and he never hesitates to digress, if the argument requires illumination. The digressions are not sought for the sake of stylistic variation.

Though Langland confesses to some natural indolence, he is not wanting in imagination or passion. He has an astounding memory for details; as W. P. Ker says 'his mind is never satisfied; least of all with such conclusions as would make him forget the distresses of human life . . . His remedy for the evils of the world would be to bring the different estates – knights, clergy, labourers and all – to understand their proper duty' (*English Literature: Mediaeval*, pp 199–200). Unfortunately, a simplistic remedy of this kind is not the *raison d'être* of the poet's conception; nor does the modern fashion of studying the symbolism do more than distract attention from the plain language of the text. It is obvious that the name *Piers* stands for St Peter (Pillar of Holy Church), and sometimes even for Christ.

The forty-five surviving texts fall into three chronological groups A, B and C, representing the author's first version and subsequent revisions, over a period of some twenty years: A (before 1370) has only 13 books; but B (1379) and C (1390) have 21 and 24 respectively. The entire poem has two thematic divisions: 'The

Vision of Piers Plowman' (the natural world) and the 'Life of Do-Well, Do-Better and Do-Best' (the spiritual world). In the latter, Man is reborn through the acceptance of Christ; the whole work analogically anticipates Bunyan's *Pilgrim's Progress*. The revised texts of over seven thousand lines involve much amplification, and several changes to the original plan, consequent upon deeper understanding of the Scriptures with advancing age. The original poem had only 2567 lines, and Skeat suggests in the introduction to his 1856 edition that the decision to recast what must have been a completed poem may have followed from the death of the Black Prince in 1377. In the words of Arthur Bryant, 'Official Christianity had grown into a gigantic vested interest' (*The Age of Chivalry*, p 458). On the subject of textual development and authorship, the sanity of R. W. Chambers is preferable to the anarchy of disintegrators. The recommended reading is a chapter in *Man's Unconquerable Mind* (1939), and 'Poets and their Critics: Langland and Milton' (British Academy Warton Lecture, 1941).

The syntax of *Piers Plowman* is more natural than that of other Middle English alliterative poems; Langland was writing for a different audience, less acquainted with complex metrical consider-ations. At the same time the three designated texts have been subject to much scribal corruption. There are occasions when the C-text clarifies what was obscure; but at other times freedom from conventions spells diffuseness. An editor who has to decide upon options soon realizes that his author's methods are extremely personal.

For this reason there have been several attempts to discover what kind of a man 'Long Will', the author of *Piers Plowman*, was. He was itinerant, austere and often intolerant of human weakness; a man who mingled with the under-privileged, possessing no ancho-rite's temperament, but a strong sense of the visible injustices of the feudal system. Langland pronounces with Pauline authority the norms of both Holy Church and Lady Meed, two figures that make 'The Vision' the most effective part of his message of salvation. He is a Christian liberal, whose compassion leavens his sternness; no orthodoxy can conceal the evident spirituality of his desired con-duct. Outspokenness in condemning the uncharitableness of those, like physicians, who make a livelihood out of men's infirmities, ranks him as the first moral ironist in English to sense the power of the well-directed word. The dullest passages are those which are overburdened with theological explanation.

R. W. Chambers in his Warton Lecture of 1941 (p 12) believed that the renaissance of English poetry owed more to indigenous Langland than to French Chaucer. One advantage of the Court poet is, however, that he can be read by a modern student with the aid of a glossary, and the knowledge that final -e must, in certain circumstances, be pronounced. What Chaucer helped to bring about was the syllabic future of poetry in English. Alliterative measures were already compromised by the admission of rhyme (see chapter XII). In the improvement of stanza forms and use of the pentameter couplet Chaucer's influence was supreme.

As his name implies, Chaucer was of French extraction, born in London about 1340, the son of a prosperous vintner. His knowledge of astronomy and mathematics suggests a reasonable education, partly acquired as a page in the household of Lionel, Duke of Clarence. In his writings Chaucer probably naturalized more French words than the present language retains. He had married and was a member of the King's household by 1366, and six years later went on a diplomatic mission to Italy, where he met Petrarch and Boccaccio. By this time he was honoured as a poet both in France and England. Passing from one official appointment to another, he built up the extensive experience of men, women and affairs that is everywhere reflected in his poetry. Though the last ten years of his life were probably the most productive, he made a public retraction of his worldly writings at the end of the incomplete *Canterbury Tales*, and died on 25 October, 1400.

Among Chaucer's earliest French enthusiasms was reading the *Roman de la Rose*, part of whose five thousand lines in English, he translated. The importance of this thirteenth-century romance to his art can hardly be exaggerated. The allegory of courtly love was a genre that France brought to perfection, taking the place of classical Ovidian myth. As *Piers Plowman* had demonstrated, realism and allegory are not inconsistent, provided a psychological affinity between natural love and sentiment exists in the mind of the author. Such a relationship Chaucer found at a young age in Guillaume de Lorris; but he was too much the man of affairs to stay overlong with this fashion. Chaucer's talent was for narrative and description, and allegory was eventually to prove sterile to his bent for practical scholarship.

In working on the *Romaunt of the Rose*, Chaucer discovered a fruitful source of medieval fiction, the *Heroides* of Ovid; he also learnt that philosophical sentiments expressed by de Lorris were largely drawn from Boethius's *Consolations of Philosophy*. So he made a thorough study, and a not very good prose translation, of that author. Chaucer learnt from the *Roman de la Rose* the art of graceful narration, and a conventional beauty of nature that appealed to Gallic tastes. *The Knight's Tale,* an early work later revised for *The Canterbury Tales,* has several good examples:

> This passeth yeer by yeer and day by day,
> Til it fil ones, in a morwe of May,
> That Emelye, that fairer was to sene
> Than is the lilie upon his stalke grene,
> And fressher than the May with floures newe –
> For with the rose colour stroof hire hewe,
> I noot° which was the finer of hem two –   [do not know]
> Er it were day, as was hir wone to do,
> She was arisen and al redy dight;
> For May wole have no slogardie a-night.
> The sesoun priketh every gentil herte,
> And maketh him out of his slep to sterte,
> And seith 'Arys and do thyn observaunce.'
> This maked Emelye have remembraunce
> To doon honour to May, and for to rise.
> Yclothed was she fressh, for to devyse°:   [describe]
> Hir yelow heer was broided in a tresse
> Bihinde hir bak, a yerde long, I gesse.
> And in the gardyn, at the sonne upriste°,   [uprising]
> She walketh up and doun, and as hire liste
> She gadereth floures, party white and rede,
> To make a subtil gerland for hire hede;
> And as an aungel hevenisshly she soong.   (lines 175–97)

This is picture-making, with a delicate touch, in the set manner of the Middle Ages. From the Prologue to *The Legend of Good Women* it is clear that this fable existed in an earlier version, as a shortened story from Boccaccio's *Teseida*. The Italian poet had, in fact, borrowed it from the *Thebais* of the first-century Latin author Statius, a Christian poet who figures in Dante's *Purgatorio*. Since the theme originated with the Greek legend of Theseus, it was antique; but Chaucer treats it, in dress and chivalric custom, as a thoroughly medieval event.

As his powers of observation matured, Chaucer's imaginative

insight into character was blessed with a gift of humour. He was fortunate in expressing himself in the London dialect, which was fitfully becoming Court English. The classical refinement of his simple diction, the flair for social satire, owed almost everything to French and Italian sources; yet these had become cosmopolitan virtues by the late fourteenth century. Instinctively, Chaucer chose the best things life could offer within the Lancastrian tradition, which was familiar to him through friendship with John of Gaunt.

Troilus and Criseyde, his longest romance, is in stanza form, a tragedy of character remarkably sustained in psychological insight for its time. Written about 1382–6, it derives from Boccaccio's *Filostrato*, in turn adapted from Benoît de Saint-Maure's *Roman de Troie*. This French author invented the story of Criseyde's faithlessness in love; Boccaccio is said to have added the figure of Pandarus. Successions like these mean as little as the source-material of Shakespeare's plays. The novelty of Chaucer's treatment was threefold: an amusing detachment in portraiture, philosophical irony and a mastery of dramatic dialogue. Such a blend of romance and realism, sentiment and humour, had not previously appeared. Fifty-seven proverbial expressions are quoted by Pandarus, whose colloquial speech revels in parry and thrust, creating the impression of a heretic towards the code of courtly love.

In a secular poem of mixed religious affiliations, Chaucer was careful to close with a complete rejection of the pagan deities, and a warning to youthful readers to avoid the dangers of lust. Stanza 263 of Book V is an example of his narrative ease:

> O yonge, fresshe folkes, he or she,
> In which that love up groweth with youre age,
> Repeyreth hom° fro wordly vanyte,   [return home]
> And of youre herte up casteth the visage
> To thilke God that after his ymage
> Yow made, and thynketh al nys° but a faire   [is nothing]
> This world, that passeth soone as floures faire.

There is very little aestheticism in Chaucer; his manner is modern, even when the forms he employs are archaic. The diction is determined by the verse modes he adopts; he eschews harsh phrasing and turgid rhythms, and seems to have disliked effects in which artifice is the main merit. More than Dryden and Wordsworth, Chaucer chose the language of men and women.

In parodying the pseudo-romanticism of *Sir Thopas*, Chaucer's criticism was destructive; but it was not his purpose to show what romance ought to have been. He could appreciate the reality of chivalry in a person like John of Gaunt; but he did not care much for monotonous picture-weaving. The fun he made of this vulgar degradation in the late fourteenth century, was achieved through metrical skill. The prosodic effects are uncanny in imitation, especially the parody of 'tail-rhyme'.

The Canterbury Tales were begun about 1387, about the time Chaucer was leaving his Aldgate home. Their subject-matter was quite English, but the refinement of tone and dignity of phrase were still French in spirit. At the age of nearly fifty, Chaucer set himself the task of doing something new; for adaptation or translation had been his *métier* to date. A number of the tales had been composed well before Chaucer thought of amalgamating them. The inspirational plan took shape as the General Prologue, and was carried through in a series of linking dialogues and subsidiary prologues. The effect was to convert realism into dramatic entertainment, complete with Chorus, in the person of the genial Host of the Tabard. Chaucer himself assumed the role of Froissart to the social history of his countrymen, at a time when saints, charlatans and knaves were as picturesque and numerous as a writer of comic satire could wish. The inherent selfishness of their lives is brilliantly etched, and justifies the disquieting social commentary found in *Piers Plowman*.

There are twenty-four tales in Chaucer's incomplete *comédie humaine*, which he conceived on a scale that only a medieval author could have contemplated. Three stories were broken off *in medias res*, because the teller had been abruptly silenced. The continual attractiveness of the *Canterbury Tales* has been due primarily to their diversity, and to the studied individuality of the characters who narrated them. Chaucer seems to have sought greater freedom of inventiveness, both in the choice of subject and in the style of narration. A number are still typed, however, in the observance of formal or rhetorical conventions; indeed, many critics prefer the organic wholeness of *Troilus and Criseyde*, arguing that the spell of Boccaccio was more constructive than that of de Lorris or Chrétien de Troyes. There is no evidence, however, that Chaucer was at all acquainted with the *Decameron*.

Throughout his career Chaucer quotes the Bible freely, and

W. M. Thompson has shown that he was as little acquainted with the Wyclifite version of 1382 as he may have been with the Latin Vulgate. Forty-eight citations from the Book of Proverbs reveal that Chaucer himself translated scripture to suit the requirements of his verse (see 'Chaucer's Translation of the Bible' in *English and Medieval Studies*, pp 183–99). He was partial to the Wisdom Books, and many a fable from the Bestiaries he garnished with moral exhortation; for instance at the end of the Maunciple's 'Tale of the Crow':

> My sone, keep wel thy tonge, and keep thy freend.
> A wikked tonge is worse than a feend;
> My sone, from a feend men may hem blesse.
> My sone, God of his endelees goodnesse
> Walled a tonge with teeth and lippes eke,
> For man sholde hym avyse° what he speeke.   [consider]
>
> . . .
>
> A jangler° is to God abhomynable.   [babbler]
> Reed Salomon, so wys and honurable;
> Reed David in his psalmes, reed Senekke.
> My sone, spek nat, but with thyn heed° thou bekke°.   [head] [nod]
> Dissimule as thou were deef, if that thou heere
> A janglere speke of perilous mateere.
>
> (lines 319–24, 343–48)

It is one of the subtleties of the General Prologue, that Chaucer himself is one of the pilgrims, and poses as a gauche observer, of self-effacing humility, who merely reports what he sees. His thirty-two characters, drawn from every stratum of society, are delineated with deference for their degree and professional standing. At a time when that society was far from homogeneous, he was capable of sketching a significant quality in a single line, as when he speaks of the Franklin's hospitality:

> It snewed in his hous of mete and drynke   (345)

No writing of the Middle Ages is as perspicuous as the General Prologue; and no one rendered it with a more enjoyable vivacity than Nevill Coghill. But the first eight lines of the Prologue have been the despair of all translators into the modern idiom. The fluency, vowel variation, and phonetic richness of the derived sounds from French, are lost, until the couplets are recalled to life in their original pronunciation. There is a genuine need to understand the intricacies of Chaucer's language.

When Dryden called Chaucer 'a well of English undefiled', he was speaking as a poetical appreciator of the poet, not as a student of language. For the class dialect that Chaucer naturally elected to use was a hybrid of three provincial ones, East Midland, Southern and Kentish, derived directly from Anglo-Saxon; there was also a sprinkling of Norse words introduced by the Danish invaders. London was the seat of the King's government, but the speech of its citizens was not that of the Court, where French remained the medium of polite conversation; the King was, after all, still ruler of a large portion of France. The incongrous situation was that official documents were drawn up in Latin or French, but the real business of the country was conducted in English; any lacunae in the English vocabulary were automatically supplied by borrowing from French.

The text of Chaucer's works has been considerably improved by a succession of editors; for the scribes of his day who copied from original manuscripts were indifferent spellers. In fact, there were scribal habits, but no rules of spelling; and what editors strove to do was, not to modernize, but to systematize what they found in the Ellesmere and other manuscripts. When written, *u* looked so much like *m* or *n* that the scribal practice was to change *u* to *o* before these consonants; but the pronunciation [u] was retained, e.g. in *sonnè* and *yronnè* in the opening lines of the Prologue.

The inflexional function of final -*e*, explained at the end of the previous chapter, has considerable metrical utility, and its restoration therefore presents problems to the inexperienced. For this reason some editors have placed a dot (as above) over the termination whenever it has to be pronounced, thereby ensuring that the line has the required number of syllables. Skeat's advice in the first volume of his monumental edition of Chaucer was to sound this -*e*, as in the final syllable of *China, except* in the following circumstances:

(a) It is invariably mute after a short stem-vowel, e.g. *ycom(e)*. Many auxiliary verbs fall into this category, e.g. *hadd(e), wer(e), shold(e), wold(e)*; but in *coudè* the vowel combination, pronounced [u:], is long.

(b) Elision takes place before a word beginning with a vowel or *h*.

In the following lines the acceptable reading is illustrated:

> Wel coud(e) he sitt(e) on hors, and faire ryde,
> He coude songes mak(e) and wel endyte.

At the end of lines the final -e is always pronounced in Chaucer's poetry.

Scribal practice sometimes may fail to reflect phonological history, and consequently difficulty arises with the pronunciation of *au* and *ou*. In the word *cause* the first of the combinations is pronounced as in *cows* [kauz]; but in words of French origin, such as *observáunce*, the sound represented is [ɔ:] in *haw*. The combination *ou* in *soul* is sounded in precisely the same way [ɔ:], alternatively written *sawl;* but not in flour, where the monophthong [u:], as in *hoot,* is the correct sound.

The Old English word-list retained in the London dialect had shrunk to about half of its original utility, and Chaucer was the most prolific replacer of lost words from Central French. Anglo-Norman had, by his lifetime, degenerated into the genteel patois of the Prioress, Madame Eglentyne, who spoke 'after the scole of Stratford atte Bowe', a convent dedicated to St Leonard in the eastern part of London. Learned terms were almost always borrowed from French or Latin; and it seems that Chaucer, in translating Boethius, experienced not a few lexical difficulties. This explains why his technical prose style tends to be laborious. The proportion of French and Latin words is, in fact, large in Chaucer's version of the *Consolations of Philosophy,* and many classical borrowings appear to be coinages. Yet his translation is a comparatively modern one, when compared with the Teutonic-looking rendering of King Alfred.

H. C. Wyld in *A History of Modern Colloquial English* (p 52) remarks that Chaucer's prose practice differs somewhat from that of the verse in the use of forms from adjoining dialects. The language of his poetry, besides containing many more southern and south-eastern forms, is somewhat archaic; the prose, though heavy-footed, is more modern, and nearer to the dialect that Caxton was to perpetuate. Southern words had become a little old-fashioned, but they helped Chaucer to many rhymes, and other subtleties of versification, one being the use of the prefix *y-* in past participles.

According to Wyld, there is a sprinkling in Chaucer's poetry of

Kentish (south-eastern) forms, generally explained by his long residence at Greenwich. Examples are *merie, kesse, fest* 'fist', *berie* 'bury' and *fulfelle*. A few of these, e.g. *merie*, remained in modern English; but in the case of *bury*, the southern spelling was retained, with the Kentish pronunciation. On the whole the London dialect of Chaucer is richer in East Midland forms than those of any other dialect. He gave it literary form and charm, and Hoccleve accurately described him as 'the first finder of oure faire langage'.

It took centuries for scholars to establish the Chaucer canon, and the tests that were, and still are, applied, should be known. The poems are judged as authentic from several sources of evidence. There is Chaucer's own testimony in the Prologue to *The Legend of Good Women*, and in the Introduction to the Prologue of *The Man of Law's Tale*. In several manuscripts, including the Ellesmere, which is probably the best, there is a retraction at the end of *The Parson's Tale*, in which Chaucer specifically mentions the 'Book of Troilus', and several other of his works, permitting only the translation of Boethius to stand.

Next comes the evidence of Chaucer's successors, for instance the poet John Lydgate, who died about 1450. In the Prologue to his *Fall of Princes* (see p 403), he provides a list of Chaucer's writings. The professional scribe John Shirley (1366–1456), an ardent admirer of the poet, copied a large number of Chaucer's poems in manuscripts that survive, and these help to authenticate authorship. Finally, testimony comes from early printers, such as Caxton, and editors, such as William Thynne (d. 1546), who assembled the first collection of Chaucer's works in 1532. No dependable edition was, however, available until Thomas Tyrwhitt's (1775–78); whatever its deficiencies, it was of considerable help in establishing the canon.

Methods of examining the authenticity of particular poems are illustrated by tests applied to Chaucer's translation, *The Romaunt of the Rose*. In the *Legend of Good Women*, the poet himself asserted that he translated the *Romaunt* from the French, and the version attributed to him was therefore included in the folio edition of Thynne. Lines 1–1705 are now generally accepted as Chaucer's; they may be tested by his customary use of accidentals. But the next section (1706–5810) contains northern forms unusual to Chaucer, such as the use of the present participle ending -*and*; and there is frequent falseness of rhyme (see Skeat, *The Chaucer Canon*, ch. VII). Furthermore, there is much diffuseness in the style of the latter part, with its stilted rhythm, that is not typically Chaucerian. The vocabulary test, though not conclusive, reveals that there are in the *Romaunt* 840 words which do not occur elsewhere in Chaucer's works. Assuming that poets are apt to use their vocabulary repeatedly, this fact is unusual; but it has to be remembered that a translation may necessitate a special word-list. One hundred of the words referred to here are taken bodily from the original French poem.

In the *Romaunt of the Rose,* the metrical test is not now seen as important as before. Except in *Sir Thopas,* Chaucer's authentic compositions did not rhyme *y* with *yë* [ɪə]; but this rhyme occurs 43 times in the latter part of the MS e.g. 2521/2 *by/folye,* a defect usually corrected by modern editors (for instance F. N. Robinson) as scribal aberrations.

Grammatical tests raise similar issues. In the authentic writings, Chaucer would, if it suited him, omit an inflexional final -*e*. In the *Romaunt,* however, this disregard is proportionally more flagrant, especially dropping the inflexional vowel of the infinitive and gerund – another northern characteristic. The use of *ado* (= at do), in the sense of 'to do', some editors regard as a sign of textual corruption; they do not allow that it reflects a young translator's inexperience.

Saintsbury in *A History of English Prosody* (pp 167–8) reacts with some vigour to philological tests of this kind, as the following observations show:

> There was up to Chaucer's time absolutely no school-instruction even with English as a vehicle, let alone any school-instruction in English itself. . . . There is not the very faintest spark of evidence that Chaucer ever received the smallest instruction from anybody how to spell an English word, to decline an English noun or verb, to construct an English sentence, or to modulate an English line. . . . The earliest grammatical and rhetorical dealings with English that we have date from the sixteenth century; the earliest prosodic observations from its latter end. . . .
>
> The Middle English 'scholar's' problem is to discover the positive and doctrinal principles of a body of documents –
>
> I. Which were written when there is no evidence that any such positive or doctrinal principles existed, and all but a certainty that they did not;
>
> II. Which were transcribed by persons under the same deprivation or limitation;
>
> III. Which include no pedagogic treatise dealing with the matter.

Whether consciously or not, English must have had a systematized grammar in Anglo-Saxon; the gropings and glosses of Ælfric reflect it. The inflexional system that bolstered constructions broke down in Middle English, with the result that language instruction, except in Latin, was pathetically inadequate even by the time of Shakespeare and Ben Jonson. To compensate for this transitional relaxation, however, there came into being a progressively visible orthodoxy of usage, which came to be recognized by grammarians of the eighteenth and nineteenth centuries. The period 1100–1450 shows English plainly in the state of 'becoming' an efficient medium of communication. Language research has concentrated on finding reasonable criteria for assessing medieval practice, and there is now abundant material for pronouncements on morphology and pronunciation, though less on the functions of sentence-structure. All that can be said is that surprising agreement on the major issues exists.

CHAPTER XII

Experiments in Verse

᠁᠁᠁᠁᠁᠁

I THE RISE OF ACCENTUAL VERSE

The difficulty of describing the evolution of accentual verse, first on the Continent, then in England, is largely one of technical information about rhythm, metre, accent and quantity during the Middle English period.

Rhythm may justly be said to have a physiological origin, resembling the beat of the heart or the act of breathing. As an emotional impulse, it reflects the state of feeling of the poet. The artistic use of spoken words carries an emotional overtone. When a poet is at a high pitch of excitement his rhythm is accelerated; when his mood is calmed his rhythm is retarded.

Metre is the external form of poetry, and may be defined as a frame against which the rhythm of verse exerts a degree of resistance. From the contrast of metre and rhythm one derives the experience of beauty in the movement of verse. The purpose of metre is well stated by Gilbert Murray in his chapter on 'Metre' in *The Classical Tradition in Poetry*, p 71:

> The metre is an ideal pattern which is, as a rule, uniform throughout the whole poem, though no single verse or stanza, as spoken, is exactly identical in rhythm with any other. In every verse the words conform to the metre with more or less variation. This variation is not a regrettable 'licence'. It is from the outset an essential element in the total rhythmical effect, and if it were not there, much or all of the beauty of rhythm would be lost.

In many studies of prosody *stress* and *accent* are regarded as synonymous terms; but originally stress was one manifestation of accent, pitch being another. Accent is the habitual emphasis given to a syllable of a word in normal pronunciation; stress may well be thought of as a force specially acquired in the verse, for logical, rhetorical or metrical reasons. Rhythm depends on variation in the incidence of stress, melody on the variation of *pitch* (i.e. the degree to which the voice is raised).

Quantity may be defined as the measure of difference in the time taken to pronounce syllable combinations. Quantitative verse exploits the duration of syllables, disposed in a special order, most significant being the ratio of long to short syllables. In short, metre in the classical system implies regular recurrences of certain mathematical combinations. Accent in Latin and Greek poetry was independent of, and sometimes in opposition to, quantity.

In *accentual verse* the aim is to preserve the natural stress of the language as usually spoken; complete regularity in the incidence of stress is designedly avoided. The monotony found in the earliest examples of blank verse (e.g. in *Gorboduc*) was due to the rigid observance of the syllabic system. Identical rhythms destroy the gentle opposition that makes the reading of verse artistically satisfying.

The terminology of prosodists who treat quantitative, as well as accentual verse, is apt to confuse. At one time 'accented' and 'long', 'unaccented' and 'short', were used interchangeably to denote the function of stressed and unstressed elements respectively. There was some justification for this, because the length of vowel sounds may be determined by the emotional emphasis one puts on them at a given moment. Stress invariably has the effect of lengthening the vowel on which it falls. Because classical quantitative measures lost touch with the emotional rhythm of words, they became artificial and fell into disuse.

Latin and Greek verse were, in the classical period, quantitative. Anglo-Saxon and early Teutonic and Scandinavian verse were both quantitative and accentual. One has to account for the loss of quantity, first on the Continent, then in England, and so to explain the gradual rise and ultimate triumph, of syllabic verse. It is not enough to suggest that English got its syllabic measures from French and Provençal poets. A satisfactory explanation needs to go further back in time.

The transition from quantitative to syllabic measures was gradual, and aided by the fitting of words to music. As W. P. Ker has shown in *The Dark Ages* (1904, pp 199–208) and *English Literature: Medieval* (1928, p 78), the change began with post-classical Latin verse written to be sung in church services. St

Ambrose, in the latter half of the fourth century, is credited with writing the first hymns in accentual verse; for he respected the rights of both accent and quantity in his measures. His four great hymns, written about Easter 387, were the Evening Hymn, *Déus creátor ómnium,* the Morning Hymn *Aetérne rérum cónditor,* the Tierce (or hymn sung at the third canonical hour – 9 a.m.) *Iam súrgit hóra tértia,* and the Christmas Hymn *Véni redémptor géntium.* It will be seen at once that the regular incidence of accent in these opening lines is very important; yet the laws of quantity were not neglected.

The new developments that St Ambrose's hymns foreshadowed were not really innovations. Ker pointed out that the essential elements occur in pre-classical Saturnian verse, and in the post-classical poem *Pervigilium Veneris,* which begins: 'Cras ámet qui númquam amávit, quíque amávit cras ámet.' Strong accent is even more evident in the poem of Tiberianus, commencing: 'Ómnis íbat ínter árva válle fúsus frígidá.' Anyone who reads these lines with a sensitive ear must realize that the rhythmical swing of the verse depends on the regular recurrence of an accented syllable. So marked is this, that one is apt to miss the quantitative factors which are still strictly observed.

Saturnian verse, exemplifying the most ancient kind of Latin metre, is preserved in primitive folk-songs with a lively dancing measure. This measure consisted usually of three iambs, with an extra syllable before the caesura, and three trochees after it. It is the metre of many English nursery rhymes e.g. The quéen|was ín|the pár|lŏur‖éating|bréad and|hóney. Saturnian verse was undoubtedly accentual, and fitted the natural genius of the language. It was driven underground by the introduction to Rome of classical Greek prosody. But the common people probably never lost it; on the authority of scholars, popular poets, when they adopted classical measures, used them accentually throughout the Roman Republic and Empire. As Ker puts it (*The Dark Ages,* p 202) 'in Latin the tunes of common speech interfered with the strict usage of prosody' (i.e. of Greek prosody, of which Ennius was the first to become the master).

One important aspect of the Ambrosian hymns for the history of accentual verse, was that in most lines the metrical stress (or ictus) coincided with the natural stress of the language. But the hymns also have many lines in which the normal word-accent falls on syllables which, metrically, are in unstressed parts of the line; this often happened in quantitative verse. Hymns must be sung to music, and St Ambrose realized that, in church music, which Rome imported from the East, accent and quantity were matters of indifference; the tune could make the syllables do what it liked. Ker points out that the rhythmlessness of the hymn *Adeste Fideles*, when read as verse, is due to this fact.

In this kind of hymn-making St Ambrose was followed by St Augustine; and later by Prudentius and Fortunatus. By the Middle Ages there were a number of Latin poets working in measures which, to the orthodox classical prosodists, must have been regarded as free verse – free in the sense that the poetry belonged neither to the quantitative class nor to the strictly accentual. From Latin free verse came all the modern accentual rhythms of the Romance languages and of the Teutonic languages. The sources of syllabic verse are therefore mainly two (a) popular speech, especially folk poems, and (b) musical accompaniment. The desire of the hymn-makers was that the man in the street should have something to sing in church which was not too learned or too complex.

There is no doubt that the appeal of rhyme facilitated the adoption, in south-western Europe, of syllabic measures. Rhyme was not known in Greek, and extremely uncommon in classical Latin prosody, though accidental rhymes did occur. It was introduced, no one knows how or why, in the fourth century. The Benedictine poet, Leo, in the twelfth century employed it in elegiac pentameters and hexameters, known as 'Leonine verse'; here the word just before the caesura rhymes with the last word of the line e.g.

Post coenam stabis : seu passus mille meabis.

The great Latin rhymed hymns belong to the thirteenth century; they are *Dies Irae* and *Stabat Mater Dolorosa*. They belong to the circle of St Francis of Assisi, authorship of the first being attributed to Thomas of Celano; that of the second to Jacoponi da Todi. Another Latin poem, *Jerusalem the Golden*, by Bernard of Morlaix, dates from the same period.

By this time rhyme had appeared as an adjunct of metre in the vernacular poetry of the Provençal troubadours, whose advent dates from the eleventh century. M. de Sismondi, in his *Literature of the South of Europe* (Bohn, Classical Library, 1846, pp 84–6) thinks that the Provençal lyrical composers acquired rhyme from the Arabian poets and men of learning, who were present in large numbers at the courts and universities of Moorish Spain. The union of the thrones of Catalonia and Provence under Raymond Ber-renger, Count of Barcelona, early in the twelfth century, facilitated contacts between Provençal and Arabian poets. The latter wrote lyrics and didactic verse in stanza form, with a strictly regulated rhyme order.

This theory of the oriental origin of rhyme has been discredited by several scholars. It is just as likely, they argue, that rhyme was learnt by vernacular poets from contact with the universal Church and its services. But the Provençal lyrical poetry shows little trace of the influence of Christianity. In Provence syllable-counting, not quantity, was the practice of the day, whether poetry was written in the vernacular, or in Latin. By the eleventh century the transition was complete, probably aided and accelerated by changes in Latin pronunciation.

Provençal poetry produced no genius; but there were many accomplished craftsmen, the most celebrated being William, Count of Poitou, Bertrand de Born, Bernard de Ventadour, Pierre Vidal of Toulouse, Arnaud Daniel and Arnaud de Marveil. Some 460 poets are named and represented in the twelfth and thirteenth centuries alone, so that the output of verse must have been considerable. The poems fall into two main groups, the *canzo* and *sirvente*. The canzo treats of love, chivalry, gallantry; the sirvente of war, politics or satire. However different the compositions were in spirit, their structure was the same.

As the Provençal lyric is the basis of all European lyrical poetry, the formal structure is worth considering. Provençal was the first of the vernacular languages in literature, an emphatically accented language, in which the predominant metre was disyllabic (i.e. iambic or trochaic, but most frequently the former). This is significant, because Latin metres had been mainly trisyllabic and dactylic. The commonest line in Provençal poetry was one of ten syllables, and it admitted both masculine and feminine rhymes (´×). Rhyme schemes were varied, and so were stanza forms. Compared with that of Latin and Greek, the metrical structure of the lines was simple. The main principles of syllabic verse were firmly estab-lished, even as employed subsequently in non-lyrical forms.

Greater poetry was to follow in France, north of the Loire, in Italy, Germany and finally in England. In the dialect of Northern France the *trouvères* (poets and reciters of tales) brought to a high state of perfection romances of chivalry, lays and allegories. In Italy the poetic art flowered in the work of Dante, Petrarch and Boccaccio, and in forms such as the canzone (cf. Spenser's *Epithalamion*) and the sonnet.

The slow transition from alliterative to syllabic verse took different steps in England, where the Middle Ages came later than in Europe. Chaucer, the first notable English poet in syllabic verse, appeared almost at the end of the medieval period, and some of his experiments had been anticipated in France and Italy. Sometimes described as a French poet writing in English, he was an important figure in the history of English prosody. Because English has a continuous literature in antiquity, it is possible to trace the evolution of literary and linguistic forms without the awkward gaps that obscure their development in other languages, for instance, the growth of Romance poetry from Latin.

With the exception of *Judith* and the *Battle of Maldon*, not much poetry of merit was composed in Old English during the period 900–1100. These two centuries saw a gradual, though at first slow, weakening of the inflexional system of the language, which was accelerated by the Norman invasion of 1066, and by subsequent contact with a moderate-sized population speaking Norman French.

On the authority of Giraldus Cambrensis, alliterative verse continued to be practised, not only in Wales but in England; and since there was a revival of the measures in the West Midlands in the fourteenth century, it may be assumed that the tradition was unbroken; but such poems as were composed are lost. What does survive is cast in a new linguistic mould, that of popular speech; whereas OE verse was in a literary, even artificial, language. Cultured Old English, preserved by a clerical monastic tradition, soon disappeared after the Conquest. There must have existed in OE times a popular tradition of alliterative poetry as well, in which quantity was neglected and accent predominated. This type, it has been suggested, although not represented in OE, outlasted the sophisticated forms, because it belonged to an oral tradition.

In early Middle English, accentual quantity gradually gave way to pure accent; but the transition period was marked by a number of tentative experiments. The most interesting of these is the long pseudo-historical poem, written in the reign of King John – Layamon's *Brut* – in which the alliterative measure clearly breaks down; numbers of the lines scan according to accentual principles; and there is the added adornment of rhyme from Wace's *Brut*, which Layamon was adapting. Ker describes the result as 'a most disagreeable and discordant measure' (*English Literature: Medieval*, p 207).

The commonest practice of the experimenters was to make the two hemistichs of the line rhyme in the form of a short couplet, much like the Leonine verse of medieval Latin. The change from accent *cum* quantity to pure accent was speeded by the example of French and Latin syllabic verse, familiar to English courtiers, clerics and scholars.

The first perfect lyric is a song with accompanying music, in the advanced canon form. It is given pride of place in the *Oxford Book of English Verse*, viz.

> Súmer ís icúmen ín
> Lhúde síng cuccú.
> Gróweþ séd and blóweþ méd
> and spríngþ þe wde nú.
> Síng cuccú.

The date of this poem is *c* 1230–40 and it was set down by a monk in the abbey at Reading.

The religious lyrics of the thirteenth and fourteenth centuries are among the best achievements of English sacred verse. When the Normans began to build churches in England, they brought over a Breton monk, Adam de Saint Victor, described as the greatest liturgical poet of the Middle Ages. He wrote rhymed Latin hymns with a beautiful singing quality, his Marian ones being the source of many 'Hail Marys' and 'Orisons to our Lady' in English.

Two long poems of the thirteenth century deserve mention before passing to Chaucer. These are *Genesis and Exodus* and *The Owl and the Nightingale*. *Genesis and Exodus* (dated about 1250) is a poem of more than four thousand lines in the East Midland dialect, apparently by a single unknown author, who still clings to alliteration. Historical interest lies in the full-scale treatment of iambic dimeter (now styled 'tetrameter'), the *dimeter* being a *half line* consisting of two feet of similar type. The commonest name for the measure of the poem is the octosyllable.

Genesis and Exodus foreshadows the metre of *Christabel*, for which Coleridge claimed originality in his preface. He wrote:

> the metre of Christabel is not, properly speaking, irregular, though it may seem so from its being founded on a new principle: namely, that of counting in each line the accents, not the syllables. Though the latter may vary from seven to twelve, yet in each line the accents will be found to be only four. Nevertheless this occasional variation in the number of syllables is not introduced wantonly, or for the mere ends of convenience, but in correspondence with some transition in the nature of the imagery or passion.

The distinction between syllable- and accent-counting is important, because it serves, in a strict nomenclature, to distinguish syllabic from accentual verse; but the terms have unfortunately been used as though they are interchangeable. This does not do for French verse, which is more rigid, both in the placing of the caesura and in the number of syllables admitted to the line. The gain in freedom of movement displayed in English has been due to the skill in modulation of poets, such as Chaucer and Spenser.

That Coleridge's metre was not an invention appears in the following limited example from *Genesis and Exodus* – limited in the sense that it has not the liberal use of trisyllabic substitution that Coleridge practised:

> Sóne|it wás|king phá|raon kíd|
> Hu ðis né|we tí|ding wúrð|bi-tíd;
> And hé|was blíðe,|in hér|te fágen,
> ðat Ió|seþ wúl|de him ðí|der drágen,
> for lúve|of Ió|seþ míg|te he tímen°   [be prodigal]
> He bád|cártes|and wái|nes nímen

Resembling more the French practice, especially in its adoption of the *debat* convention, was *The Owl and the Nightingale,* also in four-beat lines, with rhyming couplets. This form had already been used in Latin hymns of the fourth century, and was popular in French verse tales. The fable seems to have been written by an unknown author in or near Guildford, Surrey, some time between the death of Henry II (1189) and 1216. The iambic measure indulges discreet licences of modulation, such as trochaic inversion at the beginning of lines, and the use of feminine endings, in order to avoid monotony. The octosyllabic four-stress line was to become one of the staple measures of medieval English romance.

Chaucer, a discriminating student of French and Italian verse, was as delicate an artist in handling syllabic measures as any in English. His early translation of *The Romaunt of the Rose* was in octosyllabic measure of great subtlety and beauty. Dryden, though he called Chaucer 'a well of English undefiled', believed that many of Chaucer's lines were metrically defective (Preface to the *Fables*). Linguistic scholarship has shown this to be untrue. The instability of accent, and the uncertain dissolution of inflexions, afforded the poet considerable latitude. Unfortunately, this led to formlessness in his successors, which the Renaissance poets Spenser, Sidney and Sackville were the first to remedy, by writing scanable accentual verse.

II MIDDLE ENGLISH ALLITERATIVE VERSE

Old English alliterative poetry was kept alive in the West Midlands and Wales, either by oral tradition, or in the form of written poems that have been lost. This area of the country was conservatively English. When the Normans conquered England they drove the heroic traditions and Teutonic memories into the outlying parts, where legends were seemingly preserved. But a taste for alliterative verse with rugged rhythms was probably handed from father to son.

The revival of alliterative poetry took place in the second half of the fourteenth century, the best poems being written in the last quarter. The earliest were *Joseph of Arimathie* (a poem of 709 lines written about 1350) and *William of Palerne* (1355). The poems of the Cotton MS Nero A.X comprise all that survived of the alliterative poetry of the North-West Midlands, viz. *Pearl, Cleanness, Patience* and *Sir Gawain and the Green Knight*, though no titles appear in the MS. The poems were written between 1360 and 1395, but the name of the author is unknown.

These works and *Piers Plowman* show that the sophisticated structural principles, which underlay OE alliterative poetry, had become confused; for instance, the relation between stress and alliteration was neglected. When rhyme was introduced, alliteration lost the last vestige of metrical importance. Only the caesura remained to divide the line into two halves.

The notable differences between the Old English and the four-teenth-century practices are as follows:

(1) In ME the rhythm is accentual only. Owing principally to the lengthening of vowels in open syllables, the OE distinction between long and short syllables fell away, and it was no longer necessary for the primary stress to fall on a long syllable. The metre is sometimes spoilt by the scribe's omission of a final -e.

(2) The foot-combination in ME preserves the first three OE types only, I falling, 2 rising, 3 rising and falling. Whereas falling rhythms predominated in OE (types I and 4), this cannot be said of ME verse.

(3) The number of unstressed syllables is increased in ME, with the result that the minimum half-line of four syllables is uncommon.

(4) Structurally, the second half-line is more limited in ME; it is not expanded, whereas the first frequently has three accented elements, all of which take alliteration.

(5) There is much more alliteration in ME verse than in OE, and mainly because of this, greater freedom is possible in the use of unstressed syllables. Frequently a four-stress line takes alliteration on all the stresses e.g.

þay b̲óȝen bi b̲ónkkeȝ ‖ þer b̲óȝeȝ ar b̲áre

(6) A first half-line with only one alliterating letter, common in OE, is rare in ME.

(7) The second half-line usually takes the alliteration on the first lift, as in OE, but occasionally it is found on the second, e.g.

And álle his v̲ésture v̲érayly ‖ watȝ cléne v̲érdure

Very occasionally there is no alliteration at all in the second half-line, which is then considered to be corrupt. Corrupt lines are not uncommon in *Piers Plowman*, which is the least strict of the alliterative poems. The poem which adheres most rigidly to the old principles is *The Destruction of Troy*.

(8) Double and transverse alliteration in a single line is sometimes found in ME, never in OE poetry e.g.

And wyth a c̲óuntenance d̲rýȝe ‖ he d̲róȝ doun his c̲óte

(9) In ME alliteration is sometimes found on unaccented syllables, such as prefixes, prepositions, auxiliary verbs and pronouns. In recitation, these syllables probably had an artificial stress e.g.

He géte þe b̲ónk at his b̲ák, ‖ b̲ígyneȝ to scrápe

(10) Occasionally in ME alliteration falls on the second element of a compound word e.g.

Þat þou schal s̲ééke me þis̲élf, ‖ wheres̲ó þou hópes

Regarding the letters that alliterate, the following licences are observed:

(a) Though *h* was not silent, words beginning with the aspirate could alliterate with words beginning with a vowel e.g.

Hit watȝ É̲nnias þe á̲thel ‖ and his h̲íghe kýnde

(b) A voiceless consonant could alliterate with the corresponding voiced one, f̲ with v̲, s̲ with z̲ etc. e.g.

V̲érayly his v̲énysoun‖to f̲éch hym bif̲órne

(c) Whenever possible, consonant combinations were made to alliterate, though custom required only the first letter to chime, unless the group was *sp, st, sch* or *sk.*
(d) *W* was permitted to alliterate with *wh* (*qu*), *qu* being the Northern representation of the sound; in the North-West Midland dialect of *Gawain*, *qu* had actually fallen together with *w.*

The following are some examples of scansion; the type of each half-line, 1 (falling), 2 (rising) and 3 (rising and falling) is indicated:

A. *Piers Plowman* (Prologue 1–4)

1 Ĭn ă|sómĕr|sĕsŏn ‖ whăn|sóft wăs thĕ |sónnĕ 1
1 Ĭ|shópĕ mĕ ĭn|shróudĕs ‖ ăs Ĭ ă shépe|wérĕ 3
1 Ĭn|hábĭte ăs ăn|hérĕmĭte ‖ ŭn h̲óly̆ ŏf|wórkĕs 1
2 W̲ĕnt w̲ýde|ĭn þĭs w̲órld ‖ w̲óndrĕs tŏ|hérĕ 1

Note: Scansion according to types admits of much diversity of opinion. In line 2 the final *e* in *shope* and *shepe* merely indicates length of the preceding vowel; it is not strictly syllabic.

B. *Gawain and the Green Knight* (lines 37–40)

> 1 Pis|kýng lày ăt|Cámўlŏt ‖ ŭpŏn Krýst|mássĕ   3
> 1 Wĭth mŏnў|lúflўch|lórdĕ, ‖ lédĕʒ ŏf þĕ|bést,   1
> 1 Rékĕnly¯of þĕ|Róundĕ|Táblĕ ‖ állĕ þŏ rích|bréþĕr,   3
> 3 Wĭth rých|révĕl ŏ|rýʒt ‖ ănd|réchlĕs|mérþĕs   1

Line 39 has three beats in the first half-line. The first half of the last line has a rising-falling rhythm.

C. *The Destruction of Troy* (Prologue 1–4)

> 1 Máistŭr ŏf|mágĕstĕ, ‖ Mákĕr of|állĕ 1
> 1 Éndlĕs ănd|ón, ‖ évĕr tŏ|lást!   1
> 2 Nŏw, Gód,|ŏf þi gráce, ‖ gráunt mĕ þi|hélpĕ   1
> 2 And wýs|hĕ mĕ wĭth wýt ‖ þĭs|wérkĕ fŏr tŏ|éndĕ   1

The first half of line 2 is a relic of OE hemistich, type 5.

Rhyme and stanza. Many poets, for instance the author of *Pearl* and Laurence Minot, used rhymed lines, grouped in stanza forms, in addition to alliteration. *Pearl* is written in stanzas of 12 lines, each with four accents, the rhyme-scheme being a b a b a b a b b c b c. The scansion is by no means regular. The poem has 101 stanzas and 20 sections, each (with one exception) having 5 stanzas, bearing the same refrain. The last word of the refrain is caught up in the first line of the next stanza, and the last line of the whole poem is practically identical with the beginning. This self-imposed linking, plus the ingenuity of the rhyming scheme, makes *Pearl* a metrical *tour de force*. The caesura is well defined, but the alliteration is not slavishly studied.

In *Gawain and the Green Knight* the fittes or stanzas are of irregular length (12–38 lines) and consist of unrhymed alliterative lines, concluding with a lyrical refrain of five short lines, rhyming a b a b a. The refrain or burden calls for special comment. The first and shortest line of the group is called the *bob*, and the next four the *wheel*. The bob, which is syntactically bound to the last alliterative line, has only one stressed, and two or three unstressed, syllables. The wheel has in each line three stressed elements (two or three of which may alliterate) and the structure is metrically the same as an expanded half-line in alliterative poetry. The falling rhythm predominates, but a rising rhythm is not excluded, e.g. lines 1744–49:

And|rádlў þŭs|rĕháytĕd hўm ‖ with hir|rĭchĕ|wórdeʒ
    with chérĕ:
'Á! món,|hŏw máy|þŏu slépĕ, ‖   (rising rhythm)
Þis mór|ning ís|sŏ clérĕ?' ‖   (rising rhythm)
Hĕ wátʒ|in drów|ping dépĕ, ‖   (rising rhythm)
Bŏt þénne|hĕ cón|hir hérĕ ‖   (rising rhythm)

The strict principles of prosody that prevailed in OE verse are thus relaxed in ME. Quantity has disappeared, so that the alliterative metre, while echoing the old combinations of feet, is strictly accentual in scansion. Rhyme and stanza contribute to neutralize the poetry as a distinct form of verse. The habits of alliteration are seen to be irregular, and crossed alliteration makes its debut. Unstressed syllables are admitted so freely that additional alliteration is invoked to stabilize the line. This sets the poet hunting for words beginning with the same letter, one result being that his vocabulary is often far-fetched and unnatural.

The fourteenth-century revival was an attempt to resuscitate a recondite, and difficult fashion. Not only did stock phrases and epithets make for stereotyped verse, but the limits of vocabulary drove poets to foreign sources, such as the Scandinavian and French languages, both of which contributed to the vocabulary of *Gawain and the Green Knight* (see p 296). Alliterative poetry was doomed to failure, but failed magnificently.

III CHAUCER'S TECHNICAL ACCOMPLISHMENT

Artistry of an exceptional kind was reflected in Chaucer's earliest *forms* and *rhythms;* these aspects cannot, indeed, be separated in a study of his versification. Apart from the four-footer, or octosyllabic line, which one meets in the *Romaunt of the Rose,* the *Book of the Duchess* and the *House of Fame,* there was no thoroughly naturalized line, or carefully moulded stanza, to show how rapidly the triumph of accentual verse was being achieved in England. Chaucer read French poetry avidly; and even before he was able to read Italian, he began by aesthetic intuition, to experiment with types of narrative stanza, which Boccaccio had already employed successfully. This discovery was a confirmation of his own taste and skill in that style of composition.

There is no doubt that Chaucer understood the technique of alliterative verse, because he parodied alliterative romances in *Sir Thopas*, his own tale in the *Canterbury* series. Two lines in the sixth stanza read:

> Ful mány a máydė, bríght in bóur,
> They móornė for hym pàramóur

In the prologue to his tale, the Parson, defending the use of prose, says (42–4):

> I am a Sóuthren mán,
> I cannot géestė° 'rúm, rám, rúf' by léttrė, [tell a tale of adventure]
> Ne Gód woot, rým hold(e) I but lítel béttrė

Rym here signifies 'rhyming accentual verse'; but until the seventeenth century the word was used as often in the sense of 'rhythm'.

That Chaucer was mindful of 'numbers' i.e. syllable count, seems to be borne out by lines 1096–8 of *The House of Fame*:

> But for the rým ys lýght and léwėd,
> Yit máke hit súmwhat agreáblė,
> Thogh sòm vérs fáyl(e) in à silláblė

In the touching address to his 'litel bok' at the end of *Troilus and Criseyde* the appeal is as follows:

> And fòr ther(e) is so gréat divèrsité
> In Énglissh(e) and in wrítyng of our(e) tóngė,
> So préy I Gód that nón myswrítė thé,
> Ne thé mysmétre° for defáute of tóngė   [scan badly]
>   (V. 1793–6)

These citations are surely evidence that Chaucer favoured such accentual verse as was practicable to English in his time. His plea was for greater freedom of colloquial expression.

A study of Chaucer's versification shows that his notable successes were achieved in four measures:

(1) the octosyllabic line in which others had preceded him.

(2) *rime-royal*, the seven-lined (nominally decasyllabic) stanza from France, also called the 'Chaucerian' stanza, used in *The Parlement of Foules*, *Troilus and Criseyde* and *The Clerk's Tale* (rhyme-pattern a b a b b c c).

(3) the eight-lined (nominally decasyllabic) stanza employed in *The Monk's Tale*, the rhyme scheme being a b a b b c b c.

(4) the (nominally decasyllabic) couplet, which anticipated the heroic form of later poets, and is used with consummate skill in the General Prologue of the *Canterbury Tales*, as well *The Knight's Tale* and others.

In all these his modulation is most resourceful; but he seems to have had no conscious need for metrical feet (see p 398). Nor, for his purpose, was such awareness actually necessary.

Aware as he was of the alliterative revival mainly in the north-west, Chaucer pressed on with the accentual medium, not because he foresaw the future of a more disciplined aesthetic principle, but because it was practised delightfully on the Continent. The crux of the problem for a user of English was, not the archaic restoration of inflexional -*e*, but the function and placing of the caesura, including the effect the latter would have on the balanced relationship of the parts it separated. Was phrasal or clausal separation necessary at all? Naturalness, as well as grace of movement, might well flow from a fully integrated line or pair of lines. Would there not even be some advantage in expanding the ideal of unity in variety to a sequence of lines, suitably varied, to form the stanza? Or, if the theme demanded, a paragraph of indefinite but limited length, consisting of rhymed couplets?

In Chaucer's longer linear groupings, two matters of importance to readers should be noted:

(a) the frequent occurrence at the beginning of a line of a mono-syllabic foot, which was much deplored by Saintsbury, because he thought it gives an ugly 'jolt' to the rhythm. This did not become a feature of later pentameters, except in the hands of Milton.

(b) The rule enunciated by modern editors that caesural pause inhibits elision, thereby giving rise to a redundant syllable.

Chaucer's caesural pauses, unlike those of his French models, are movable; to this innovation is attributable much of the flexibility and ease. The redundant syllable is usually a light one, such as an unstressed -*e*, for instance in the first line of the quotation from *Sir Thopas* (see p 324). It should be borne in mind, however, that most Chaucer manuscripts belong to the fifteenth century, when Middle English spelling had changed; the forms in them need not represent the poet's spelling, which was probably phonetic, according to the principles of the time.

There is obvious danger in applying to Chaucer's versification the metrical norms of eighteenth- or nineteenth-century poetry; and equally of likening his verse to the natural speech rhythms of the Pound-Eliot era. The rhythmic quality of Chaucer's language within the line, and the organic linking of the pattern by means of syntax, were both individual. The fluency of Chaucer is not only the result of syllabic discipline. In the light of orthodox practice, and even in comparison with Gower, his modulations are libertarian.

What we shall never know is how Chaucer read his own poetry. There are schools of thought that resolve themselves into two main camps: those of Tyrwhitt and Ten Brink, on the one hand, and of J. G. Southworth and Ian Robinson on the other. This is no place to discuss the rhythmical approach contained in *Verses of Cadence* and *Chaucer's Prosody*, respectively. The well-attested claims have already been investigated in pp 28–35 of my *Language of Renaissance Poetry* and the first three chapters of my *Language of Modern Poetry* (Deutsch, 1971 and 1976).

Editors such as W. W. Skeat, F. N. Robinson and E. T. Donaldson, whose linguistic knowledge and experience in handling the entire text of Chaucer give them authority, are sometimes accused of failing to see the wood for the trees. Their explanations of the structure of the verse are said to rely unduly on resolutions and contractions, including such things as elision, apocope and slurring, in order to secure the desired number of syllables in the line. Such contractions have occurred in English, as documents confirm, from Old English to the present day; there are even shortened spellings in Chaucerian manuscripts. If one could have access to Middle English *speech*, it would be surprising to find that elision and contraction were not known to Chaucer.

The minor poems of Chaucer, which cover the major period of his development, tend to be neglected in metrical discussions. He practised lyrical forms (some in a useful nine-line stanza) such as the ballade, roundel, envoy and complaint, mostly of French origin. Their stricter design and concision of expression are of value in placing Chaucer in the accentual school. The roundel at the end of *The Parlement of Foules* is one of the most charming examples of the author's 'maistrye' in the 'art poetical':

> Now wélcom(e), sómer, with thy sónnė sóftė,
> That hast this wíntres wédres overshákė,
> And dríven away the lóngė nýghtes blákė!
>
> Saynt Válentyn, that art fùl hý on-lóftė,
> Thus sýngen smálė fóules for thy sákė:
> Now welcome, somer, with thy sonne softe,
> That has this wintres wedres overshakė.
>
> Wèl han they cáusė for to gláden óftė,
> Sith èch of hem recóvered hath hys mákė,
> Fùl blíssful mów(e) they sýngė when they wákė:
> Now welcome, somer, with thy sonne softė,
> That hast this wintres wedres overshakė,
> And driven away the longe nyghtes blakė!
>
> (lines 680–92)

Ten years later *Merciles Beaute* was written in the same triolet pattern of thirteen lines with a recurring refrain; for both Chaucer was indebted to the octosyllabic examples of Machaut, and other French lyrists.

The Parlement of Foules is generally thought to have been composed in 1382, when Richard II was only fifteen years of age, to celebrate his betrothal to Princess Anne of Bohemia. The date of the allegory is noteworthy, because it marks the beginning of Italian influence, and of Chaucer's *penchant* for humour in debate, which begins in this poem at line 416. One outcome was the adoption of an amusing colloquial tone, the poet's 'elvyssh' way of tempering the mood of a courtly audience to such rhetorical conventions as *contentio*, congeries, *sententiae* and digression. No early poem is so eloquent of the *esprit* to which Chaucer had matured as an entertainer. Assuredly, there is a hint that *amour courtoise* is no substitute for natural love.

The caesura, or internal pause, is only one source of redundant syllables in the Chaucerian line. Phonetic difficulty poses another in line 411 of *The Parlement of Foules*, the first half of which Skeat scans as follows (Works, vol. I, p 522):

This is óur(e) uságe alwéy, ‖ fro yer to yeere

According to the glossary of this editor, *uságe*, being of French origin, was accented on the second syllable, a circumstance that is crucial for the intended rhythm, or what Skeat calls 'speech-waves'. The awkward contiguity of nearly identical sounds in *This is*, which Skeat instructs us to regard as a metrical monosyllable, is said to resemble the contraction *'tis* in poetry, or *it's* in conversation. But it is not possible to utter the combination *this's* [ðɪsəz], except as a dissyllable. My scanning of the line would be:

$$\text{Thís ìs óur(e) uságe álwey, ‖ fro yér tò yéerè}$$

implying two stress inversions, and one redundant syllable.

By modern standards every line of Chaucer's triolet contains some inversion of word order, either for rhyme or rhythm. But it is often beyond factual knowledge to assign a date for the normal order of words. The Germanic ancestry of the language permitted a qualifier to appear after a noun, and in perfect tenses the past participle was invariably disposed to conclude a clause, as in line 2. *Recovered hath* (line 9) is, however, a poetic licence. Whether of metrical stress or word order, inversion has always been a device available to poets.

Narrative circumlocution was for some reason common to all writers of *gestes* or romances; for instance in Chaucer's General Prologue (*C.T.* 43–5):

> A Knyght there was, and *that* a worthy man,
> *That* fro the tymè *that* he first began
> To riden out, he lovéd chivalrye

This is structurally otiose – in word order, in the demonstrative use of *that* (43) and in the sequential employment of the same word for two relative clauses, the second being subsidiary to the first. The subject, *Knyght*, is so distanced from the predicate *loved chivalrye*, that a resumptive *he* has to be supplied. This is what Chaucer probably intended to say: 'There was a worthy knight, who loved chivalry, from the time he first rode abroad' – (15 words instead of 23).

In *The Merchant's Tale* (ll. 2016–18) the following lines puzzle a reader on first acquaintance:

He is so plesant unto every man
(For craft is al, ‖ whoso that do it can)
That every wight is fayn to speke hym good

After the pause in the second line, the words *whoso that do it can*
are obscure syntactically, because the idiomatic collocation *whoso*
that (indef. pronoun + relative) is unfamiliar. The meaning of the
line is surely 'For guile is everything, to anyone capable of it'. *Can*
is transposed to end-position for the sake of rhyme. The complex
evolution of qualifying relative clauses, between late Old English
and the sixteenth century, is one of the most progressive for clarity
in the history of syntax.

Chaucer was critical of his earlier tendency to prolixity, as is
shown by a feigned reluctance to expand in *The Squire's Tale*: (a) 'I
dare not undertake so heigh a thyng./ Myn Englissh eek is
insufficient./ It moste been a rethor excellent,/That koude his
colours longynge for that art' (36–9). And (b): 'Of which if I shal
tellen al th'array,/ Thanne wolde it occupie a someres day;/ And
eek it nedeth nat for to devyne/ At every cours the ordre of hire
servyse' (63–6). Ironically, the Squire is the victim of his own lack
of economy; his long-windedness ends in summary curtailment of
his story.

CHAPTER XIII

The Reigns of Edward III and Richard II

𒀀𒀀𒀀𒀀𒀀𒀀

IN THE LONG REIGN of Edward III (1327–77) and the tragic one of Richard II (1377–99), feudalism and chivalry experienced many changes. Major events of their rule are reflected in Jean Froissart's *Chronicles,* written between 1369 and 1400. Edward was only fifteen when he came to the throne, marrying Philippa of Hainault within a year of his accession. A regency council of noblemen and prelates was nominally in control, under the presidency of Henry of Lancaster, cousin of the deposed Edward II; but it had little political power, which was effectively in the hands of the new king's mother, Isabella, and her ambitious lover, Roger Mortimer. The king, a father at seventeen, courageously threw off this yoke, and even laid claim to the throne of France.

Edward was an attractive young monarch, the flower of chivalry, but also an astute diplomat. Good relations with the Netherlands were fostered by his promotion of the cloth trade, and Edward earned a dubious reputation as 'the father of English commerce'. An ardent believer in pageantry, he was extravagant in taste, but generous in bestowing favours, treating his conspiratorial mother with unmerited magnanimity. His chief mason, William de Ramsey, improved cathedral architecture, and in 1344 seven hundred villeins from surrounding counties were employed to build the Round Tower at Windsor Castle. The outcome of this Arthurian enterprise was the institution in St George's Chapel of the Order of the Garter, in 1348. Shortly after, St George became the patron saint of England.

The Order of the Garter was a fellowship of chivalry limited to twenty-six knights of known prowess, who swore fealty and close friendship to the king; there was also created a similar body of canons and poor knights. A garter is said to have been accidentally dropped at a ball in Calais by Princess Joan of Kent, wife of the Earl of Salisbury; the king appropriated it, with the words *Honi soit qui mal y pense*, 'evil to him who evil thinks', setting the tone of gallantry for which the Order became famous in Europe.

Froissart, a contemporary of Petrarch and Chaucer, himself came from Hainault, and enjoyed the patronage of the queen. He reported the dramatic siege of Calais, and the other victories of Sluys, Crécy, Winchelsea and Poitiers (1340–56). As chronicler and poet, he lived at the English Court for eight years, travelled in Scotland, and revisited England for three months in the latter part of Richard II's reign. Of Flemish origin, he was a humanist, with a middle-class conscience, wavering in sympathy between England and France. He once expressed the view that the proud English were 'affable to no other nation than their own'; but he endeavoured to be impartial in his interpretation of mostly oral testimony. The *Chronicles* are by no means confined to military exploits, and were translated into English by John Bourchier, Lord Berners, in the years 1523–5.

Being a traditionalist, Froissart captured the medieval mind at its maturest, most credulous and tribalistic periods. He does not disguise the brutality of war, while defending chivalry as a moral force. He is a dependable journalist, who recorded that the papacy was the sole authority to protect the Jews, and discredit their persecutors.

In Edward's reign plague, persecution, war and civil disturbance took their toll of the southern European population. Mob rule was to Froissart one of the direst evils that could afflict mankind, and he demanded that it should be stamped out with vigour, for the same reasons as Shakespeare held; namely, that popular risings, like that of the Jacquerie (French peasants) in 1358, were a negation of law, order and political harmony. (*Jacques* was the nickname of the French peasant, who was usually dressed in a short jacket of this name.)

Edward III was a monarch who pursued dynastic ambitions in spite of social change, though not unaware of the decline of the feudal system. The chivalric dedication of the crusaders was virtually over. Edward was himself the instrument of change in strengthening royal ties with the merchant class, and enlarging the peerage, by letters patent, whenever the recipients of honours had done the state some service. Wealthy merchants were befriended because they were a fruitful source of credit, and Edward ensured that their relations with the Crown carried special privileges. Through international trade he was able to borrow money from Florentine bankers to finance his French campaigns.

The costly armies were raised, not by the old feudal levy, but by enlistment. Though cannon were used for the first time at Crécy (1346), they were ineffective. The army's mainstay was not the mounted feudal knight of the preceding wars, but the long-bowmen of England. Their weapons originated in Wales, and were made of wild elm, instead of yew; the yard-long arrows were plumed with feathers of the grey goose that throve on the English commons.

History records that Edward, Prince of Wales (known as the Black Prince) won his spurs and his badge of ostrich feathers at the Battle of Crécy. This crest belonged to the blind King of Bohemia, who was killed in the engagement; and a similar badge seems to have been adopted by the king's other sons, and Anne of Bohemia. The Black Prince's shield-for-peace was decorated with silver feathers on a black field (perhaps the origin of his name), with the surmounting motto *Ich Diene* 'I serve'. The German origin of this is disputed by those who hold the motto to be a corruption of Welsh *Eich Dyn* 'Your Man', an appropriate slogan for the Prince of Wales.

At the time of the Hundred Years War France was a more populous, prosperous and prestigious country than England; the French population was considerably over twelve million as compared with England's four and a half million. Industrial Flanders was a French dependency, but its Count was disposed, by Philippa's marriage and by trade compacts, to sympathize with England's cause. The English economy flourished agriculturally, and quantities of wool, grain and dairy products were exported, in addition to lesser commodities such as dried fish, hides, tin, coal and lead. The fine quality of the wools produced in England made textiles by far the richest commodity, especially with the Low Countries and Italy. There was a substantial settlement of Flemish weavers in East Anglia and the Bristol areas, where a weaver by the name of Thomas Blanket gave his name to this domestic article.

Edward's hunger for deeds of valour was handicapped by a constant shortage of funds, and he devised a plan to make the wealthy wool merchants help him. Taxation, with or without the help of parliament, had always been the king's prerogative. Edward used his power to negotiate directly with the merchants and impose a levy on their exports, known as the *staple*. The merchants responded by reducing the prices paid to the producers, and inducing the latter to buy goods on credit; there was the inevitable outcry through the producers' representatives in parliament. Taxation of all kinds was not collected in rural England without some resistance to local sheriffs; particularly in the midlands there were fraternities like Robin Hood's, which claimed to protect the poor and the victims of injustice.

The Black Death of 1348–51, which reduced the English population by an estimated one third, accelerated changes that were about to take place in the economy. The plague was a bubonic type, with complications of pneumonia; it is said to have spread westwards through the Mediterranean world from the highlands of Persia. King Edward lost his daughter, Joan, in France; and in the recrudescence of 1369 his wife, Philippa. The victims usually died on the third day, and in cities it was difficult to cope with the burials. The problem in the rural areas was to gather the harvest, and attend to the cattle and sheep. Shortage of labour proved the knell of the manorial system, by causing wage prices to rise. The Statute of Labourers was passed in 1351 to reduce wages to the earlier levels, and to uphold monopolies; but inadequate organization made it difficult to enforce. It became obvious to employers that the wage-earners could not be regarded as slaves. Farm-hands moved to improving markets, landowners' rentals fell, and many villeins found themselves possessed of an unexpected freedom that made possible the yeoman class. Lords of manors were compelled to accept a modest rental instead of the obligatory feudal services.

After the Treaty of Brétigny in 1360 Edward took no further part in the French wars, leaving the campaigning in the hands of the Black Prince, whose victory at Poitiers in 1356 had resulted in the capture of King John, the pattern of French courtesy, but an impetuous soldier. The monarch was lodged in the Tower and treated as a guest of honour; but the ransom demanded was so high, and the distress in France so acrimonious, that another army had to be sent to France in 1359, among which was Geoffrey Chaucer. The figure of three million gold crowns was finally agreed upon in the treaty of 1360; Edward was hard pressed financially and had to renounce his title to the French throne. The Prince of Wales then took office in the south of France, as governor of Aquitaine, while four French princes remained in London, as hostages, pending the payment of the ransom. When one of King John's sons escaped, the chivalrous ruler returned to England in 1364, but died in the London residence of John of Gaunt in the same year.

The reign of King Edward now declined into a period of undignified disagreement and dishonour. All his sons had been married to English heiresses, which engendered rivalries within the country, rather than abroad. After the death of the queen in 1369, the king sacrificed his domestic peace, by passing into the exploiting hands of his mistress, Lady Windsor (the notorious Alice Perrers), and his fourth son, John of Gaunt, Duke of Lancaster. (The spelling *Gaunt* represented the English pronunciation of Ghent, where John was born.) There were quarrels with parliament over money, resulting in charges of corruption. Edward had to concede the control of taxation to parliament, but continued to enjoy the support of baronial magnates, many of whom he had created. The Black Prince, broken in health, had been a merciless ruler in Aquitaine, and returned to England in 1370, to spend the last six years of his life at Berkhamsted. His influence was now exerted in support of parliament, against his unworthy father. Internal unrest had enabled the king's old enemies, France and Spain, to attack the seaports of England virtually unmolested. The moral and economic decline was not arrested until the calling of the Good Parliament of April, 1377; but when this was dissolved, Gaunt regained power and packed another parliament with supporters, who nullified the impeachment of corrupt officials.

In this atmosphere of bitter reprisal the Oxford scholar, John Wyclif, was brought to trial at St Paul's in February, 1377. He had the temerity to suggest that the Church was misusing its spiritual powers by meddling in temporal affairs, and was busy accumulating wealth through bequeathed property. Politically, Wyclif was encouraged by John of Gaunt, who intervened in the trial, and turned it into a riot. As early as 1369 Gaunt had joined the anti-clerical movement, which rebuked the Chancellor, Bishop William of Wykeham, for squandering the country's revenues on the wars in France. Anti-clerical feeling was so strong in the late fourteenth century that many high offices went to laymen. William of Wykeham is said to have founded New College, Oxford, in 1379 to offset the heretical influence of the Wyclif supporters.

Wyclif was fifty-seven at the time of his abortive trial, and had been Master of Balliol College, Oxford, as well as university lecturer; he was also rector of Lutterworth in Leicestershire. A staunch opponent of Rome's sole authority on matters of Christian dogma, he was held in great esteem as a preacher and public figure. Jusserand described him, in *A Literary History of the English People* (Unwin, 1895, p 428), as the father of English prose, and a 'partisan of the system of free investigation'. Oxford University saw fit to defend him, when he was charged with heresy by the Pope. Summoned to appear before the bishops in London in 1378, he was the centre of another demonstration that broke up the proceedings at Lambeth Palace. The anti-clerical movement, known as Lollardry, was already strong among the middle class. During the lifetime of Wyclif, and until 1400, there was no move to stamp out heresy by imposing the death penalty.

The nominal kingship had now passed to Edward III's second grandson, Richard II, the eldest son of the Black Prince having died in 1371. Wyclif's radical views against the Church party were addressed in English to the king, not to the Pope. *Of Civil Lordship*, an early plea for Christian socialism, expressed his doubt whether the ordinances enforcing hereditary servitude were 'conformable to the law of Christ' (*English Works*, p 227). Wyclif did not, however, support the insurgents in the Peasants' Revolt (1381), though his 'dominion' theory was the power behind Lollardry. There was a mounting conviction that the feudal system, and the Church of Rome within it, were too hierarchical to countenance essential reforms (see p 435). Wyclif was not to be silenced, even when the diatribe on transubstantiation was disowned by his Oxford colleagues. In spite of harassment, he continued to live in retirement at Lutterworth, until his death in 1384.

Wyclif anticipated Tyndale in holding that the Bible should be within the reach of Englishmen in their own tongue, and collaborated with a group of Oxford scholars in translating the Latin Vulgate. 'Christ came of poor folk,' he argued, meaning to appeal to the lay classes of William Langland in *Piers Plowman*. The first form of the Wyclifite Bible was complete by 1382; Wyclif himself appears to have contributed the Gospels, and Nicholas of Hereford most of the Old Testament. His collaborator was revising the entire translation when Wyclif died. Unfortunately Nicholas was compelled to flee the country and the final version of 1395 was the work largely of Wyclif's secretary and friend, John Purvey. The most vigorous prose of Wyclif comes from the treatises and sermons, however, not from the New Testament, which lacks the rhythm and elegance of Tyndale's version.

Richard II was born at Bordeaux in 1367 and did not come to England until his fourth year. Being only ten at his accession, his widowed mother, Joan, Princess of Wales, acted as guardian, while a Council of twelve was appointed to govern the country. The times were difficult, and the Council, which excluded the trouble-makers, Gaunt (with a large private army), and Lord Percy of Northumberland, was twice changed before Richard began to reign personally, at the age of nearly twenty-two. He was tall, fair-haired, sensitive and solitary; not physically strong, but endowed with a youthful courage, which showed to advantage when he faced the leaders of the Peasant Revolt. The situation was so perilous that the Archbishop of Canterbury was beheaded by the malcontents. The rebellion is graphically described in Book II of Froissart's *Chronicles*.

In 1382 Richard married Anne of Bohemia, whose father, Charles IV, was the Holy Roman Emperor. His principal tutor, Simon Burley, inculcated an exaggerated sense of majesty, which the king never moderated. His coronation was of a magnificence unequalled in medieval history. Two different aspects of Richard's character are portrayed in Gordon Daviot's play, *Richard of Bordeaux*, which romanticizes the earlier part of the king's reign, and Shakespeare's tragedy, which deals only with the last years, but gives an incontestable picture of vacillation, egotism and self-pity. *Richard the Redeless* 'ill-advised' was the people's catch phrase to his memory. Within a decade of his majority, Richard became the victim of baronial bullying, and his own obstinate vanity. Chaucer's poem (of uncertain date), which F. J. Furnivall entitled *Lak of Steadfastnesse*, is said to have been sent to King Richard while in residence at Windsor Castle. The last stanza, in rime-royal, is headed 'Lenvoy to King Richard' and reads:

> O prince, desyre to be honourable,
> Cherish thy folk and hate extorcioun!
> Suffre nothing that may be reprevable
> To thyn estat don in thy regioun.
> Shew forth they swerd of castigacioun,

Dred God, do law, love trouthe and worthinesse,
And wed thy folk agein to stedfastnesse.

Yet the dazzling, extravagant court of Richard II was the centre of music, art and poetry. He encouraged the painting of royal portraits, favoured the perpendicular architecture of Westminster Hall, and adorned his person with embroidered and bejewelled clothes, whose bright colours alternated with a taste for the elegance of white satin. The Court was a curious mixture of French ceremonial and English informality, which came from a new stratum of the aristocracy, the lesser barons, those who supplanted the declining Norman families. Metrical romances, such as *Sir Degrevant* and *Sir Gawain and the Green Knight*, are full of chivalric traditions, which Richard sustained by festival jousting, and recitals of the knight's love of adventure. But the mounted gentleman, as a military force, was already an anachronism. A new element in literature was undoubtedly compassion, which in *Piers Plowman* meant justice for all classes. The Court at which poets were invited to read their narratives, was remarkable for good manners, generosity and hospitality.

The reign of Richard falls into two parts – the minority, when Richard was an uneasy spectator of opposing political forces; and the majority, which culminated in his deposition. The important event of the first period was the Peasants' Revolt, two causes of which were the maldistribution of property, and the accompanying evil of money-power. The Church was implicated in both matters, as Wyclif had maintained.

The medieval economy, in the eyes of the Church, was important from the aspect of human conduct only. Nature (or God) was the universal provider, and labour (either of hand or brain) was essential to make natural resources viable. The Church was equivocal about usury, but condemned it officially as a principal cause of price increases. After the Norman conquest, all inhabitants of England, and what they possessed, were enrolled in a social register, shrewdly designed to keep the feudal rulers in power (see chapter IX). Lords of the manor owned the land, and received from their villeins either services or rent. The labourer was attached to the land; and though the landlord could not get rid of him, his way of life was regulated and enforced by the bailiff and the manorial court. Unpaid services were usually ploughing, harvesting and transportation.

The latter half of the fourteenth century saw villeins or peasants turned into wage-earners, possessing a plot, but not owning it. They were unable to make a reasonable living, because the land-owner usually compelled them to surrender the bulk of their marketable surplus as rent. The day of the fixed rental and cheap commodity prices was passing with the increasing size of estates and the complex labour problems. The peasants' sense of exploitation was justified, and the major offenders were business-like organizations such as the monasteries, some in the south-east of England owning as many as fifty manors. Large Church estates were able to keep under control the heavy managerial costs of the manorial hierarchies.

The Black Death profoundly changed an economy based on the sales of agricultural produce. More and more of the owners' land had to be made available to tenants. The Statute of Labourers was designed to counter migrant labour, and this crippled the smaller estates, because conditions of employment favoured the larger ones. Maximum, but not minimum rates of pay were determined for every farming occupation; any man who did not have enough land to keep him occupied was compelled to accept work at the rates offered, the local landlord having the first refusal. Agreements were not in writing, and were for a minimum period of six months. So large was the number of cases before the courts, and so unfavour-able the judgements to the workers, that resentment against the Statute mounted during the next three decades. The villein remained a victim of the manorial system in his liability for all sorts of taxes, fines and licence fees, payable to the landlord. He could not send his son to school or allow his daughter to marry without permis-sion, as well as penalty, and on his death the family was mulcted in a death duty. Rarely did the courts uphold a peasant's plea that he had legally freed himself of servitude; a third party had always to buy the charter of manumission before a serf was legally free. Such were the major grievances of the peasants before the Revolt of 1381.

The match that sparked off the conflagration was, however, the heavy poll-tax passed by parliament in 1380; there were many defaulters and physical action had to be taken against them. The resistance offered to tax-collectors, officials of the overlords, was an offence to the natural law that separated noble from non-noble classes, among the former being abbots and bishops. Anti-clerical-ism was most rampant among the lower strata of society, for churchmen were apt to hold the highest offices in the state; hence the murder of the Archbishop of Canterbury in the London disturbances. Anti-clerical criticism was as vocal in Chaucer, a member of John of Gaunt's household, as it was in William Langland, who owed his education to a Malvern monastery. This poet seems to have been born in bondage, the illegitimate son of a peasant's daughter, who was freed by the Church. An anonymous poem, *Richard the Redeless* (c 1399), rebuking the king for his want of compassion, was not written by Langland, as W. W. Skeat thought (see EETS edition, 1936).

Langland became a London chantry priest, one of many poor clerks and moderate conservatives whose poverty took a mystical turn, finding in the cloister a haven, where 'no man cometh to chide or to fight'. He was no inflammatory orator, but his allegory was influential some time before the revolt, the first version of *Piers Plowman* having been written shortly after 1362. The rebels' watchword 'When Adam delved and Eve span,/Who was then the gentleman?' might have been a slogan from Langland's vision. It did not originate with John Ball, one of the two excommunicated ringleaders in 1381; it was heard in pulpit tirades against pride several decades before the Kentish dissidents marched on London.

The inequalities of work and wealth in medieval times, condemned by Carlyle in *Past and Present*, created intense dissatisfaction with callous rulers, who would not take steps to ward off social disaster. The grievances of the returned soldier, and the out-of-work artisan were added to those of the peasants, who had few rights. The root of complaints was the deep division between classes, and the Church's connivance at usury, a universally disapproved source of wealth. Neither rulers nor priests seemed to have much understanding of the working of the economy in a feudalist society.

Disturbances over the poll-tax began in Essex in May, 1381, and spread to Kent in June, when a runaway serf belonging to Simon Burley was imprisoned in Rochester Castle. Rioting started immediately, in three Kentish towns, the agitators in the south being Wat Tyler and John Ball, who encouraged looting and arson, as the disorderly peasant workers approached London. The northern contingent, led by Jack Strawe, took over the villages of Mile End and Highbury. In the city prisoners were set free, two palaces sacked, and an attempt was made on the Treasury at Westminster.

The young king, lodged in the Tower with a strong garrison, counselled negotiation, and rode with his mother and retainers to meet the mob at Mile End. According to Froissart he promised to remedy every just complaint, even the emancipation of serfs, and to pardon all rebels who would return to their homes. All except a hard core of the rabble, he says, accepted this offer. But the situation remained tense, and the king had to take refuge in Blackfriars, finding on his return that the rebels had broken into the Tower, and executed leading noblemen.

The next day Richard and sixty retainers met Wat Tyler and the other leaders at Smithfield; the prospect of loot had induced Tyler and a body of thirty-thousand disorderly persons to remain in London. Tyler, confronting the king aggressively, was struck down and killed by the Mayor of London, according to Froissart's account. This effectively silenced the revolt; and the king thereupon issued a proclamation instructing non-citizens to depart from London. John Ball and Jack Strawe were discovered in hiding (the former at Coventry) and executed. Richard's Council revenged itself on the malcontents at leisure. None of the king's undertakings were fulfilled, because he had no power to override the feudal lords, who belittled his efforts at a settlement. The Peasants' Revolt was terminated by stratagem, as well as by presence of mind; some historians are sceptical of Richard's acclaimed prowess as a diplomat.

The state of the realm after the Peasants' Revolt was complex; but that England was on the brink of a new nationhood appears in the sociological literature. William Langland's imaginative self-consciousness has been compared to that of Dante in Tuscany. A poet still using French, like Gower, was an isolated phenomenon. Chaucer, whose name was of Gallic origin, read poems before King Richard in English, and transformed, not only the principles of versification, but relationships of the educated classes. He had pungent criticisms to make on the Church and some of its adherents. These were consonant with the resentment of the Commons at the benefices bestowed by the Pope, and the consequent loss of revenue to the English people. Several statutes were passed by parliament, now seated at Westminster, to counter this intrusion; the struggle was one of the issues that led to the Reformation.

Latymer, at the end of Edward III's reign, was the first minister of the crown to be impeached for corruption. Richard II, declaring himself a ruler and maker of laws by divine right, was the earliest English monarch to be deposed by statutory process. He was not in a position to do as he chose for two reasons: (1) Edward III had already deferred to parliament on the privilege of raising money by taxation; (2) the king had no standing army or police force to ensure his ultimate power. The situation that confronted both Edward and Richard is well described by G. M. Trevelyan in *English Social History* (Longmans, 1946, pp 16–17):

> The Hundred Years' War enriched individuals with plunder and ransoms from France, and swelled the luxury of court and castle, but was a curse to the country as a whole. It increased disorder and violence, by raising the fighting nobility and their retainers above the control of the Crown.
>
> The King was powerless to act against the great nobles, because his military resources were the resources commanded by the nobles themselves. His army consisted, not of his own Life Guards and regiments of the Line, but of numerous small bodies of archers and men-at-arms enlisted and paid by earls and barons, knights and professional soldiers of fortune, who hired out their services to the government . . . They could scarcely be used to suppress themselves, or to arrest the employers whose badges they wore on their coats . . . These evils were partly the result of the bankruptcy of the government.

Richard's first serious brush with parliament occurred in the years 1386–8. Subservience to a Council, not of his own choosing, had become irksome, and a royal party had been formed that consisted mainly of the king's personal friends; among these were Michael de la Pole, Earl of Suffolk, an experienced Lancastrian past middle-age, and Robert Vere, Earl of Oxford, a nobleman of twenty-five, who became the first Marquis created in England. The king's plan was to exclude from the sphere of influence three of the greatest magnates in England: Richard's uncle, Thomas of Woodstock, Duke of Gloucester; Richard, Earl of Arundel, whom the king greatly disliked, and Thomas Beauchamp, Earl of Warwick. They had all served on the regency council, and so had wielded considerable power. Tressilian was to be the king's Chief Justice, John Fordham his treasurer, and Nicholas Brembre, an ex-mayor of London, his link with the victuallers in the city. This curialist group came into office in July 1386; it was ill-matched in age and administrative talent. De la Pole was appointed chancellor, and de Vere nominally chamberlain, the office being actually carried by the deputy, Simon Burley.

The lords in opposition were essentially a war-party, equally at odds with the egotistical John of Gaunt, who was campaigning in Castile when the so-called 'Wonderful' parliament met in October 1386. Pole and Fordham were immediately arraigned for mismanagement of the State's affairs. The king brashly insisted on his prerogative to appoint whomever he liked, and retired in dudgeon to his manor at Eltham. He soon relented, however, and agreed to dismiss his chancellor and treasurer. Pole was thereupon impeached and found guilty of usury, though the charge was undoubtedly trumped up against him. In refusing to participate with the Commons, the king had behaved tactlessly, and permitted a precedent for constitutional action against him. This took the form of a one-year commission of twenty-four noblemen and churchmen, resident at Westminster, to enquire into the king's administration and domestic expenditure. In reality its function was to control the state's finance and to restrain undue use of the king's seal in bestowing offices; Richard, who was still a minor, had to take an oath to abide by the commission's decisions.

A purge of the Crown's lesser officials followed, Chaucer being a victim, when deprived of his controllership of Customs, though with the recompense of a pension. The king, now regarding his presence at Westminster as humiliating, proceeded to York, Chester and other towns of the North Midlands to test the feeling of the countryside regarding his cause. He furthermore took legal advice on the commission's rights, as well as the proper definition of treason, and began the enlistment of a royal bodyguard in Cheshire and North Wales.

There was no real constitution in a state ruled by historical precedents; thus there was, for example, no statutory ground for the deposition of Edward II. Richard was trying to elicit rulings concerning the encroachment on his powers, which were hypothetical, for none had been given. The prerogatives he claimed were delayed until he had attained his majority. Thus the procedure on this tour was incautious, if not provocative. The intent was well known, and the result was that both sides adopted the expedient of raising private armies.

In November 1387, the patriot lords, Arundel, Gloucester and Warwick, took the initiative and lodged an appeal against alleged treasonable actions of the king's five leading officers. Some of these had already been replaced, and four had actually absconded. The king, with reason, referred this to parliament, while de Vere with an army raised in the Chester area, moved down the Severn valley, and was thwarted in a one-sided engagement at Radcot Bridge. This was the first time that Henry Bolingbroke, Earl of Derby, actively opposed the king. The commission's year of office had by now expired; yet before the king attained his majority the threat of deposition was undoubtedly made. Richard, now resident in the Tower of London, was compelled to assent to the arrest of his ministers. The crisis was drastically resolved by the 'Merciless' parliament of February 1388, which met at Whitehall, to consider thirty-nine articles of the noblemen's appeal. Historians are of the opinion that this 'attainder', the declaring of a person guilty by act of parliament, without going through the preliminary legal channels, was *ultra vires*; and Henry IV was later to abolish such procedures. Parliament had no competence to arraign officers of the Crown for treason, on the grounds of administrative inefficiency or the giving of misguided advice.

All the accused, except the Archbishop of York, were condemned to death by the House of Lords, which had assumed the powers of a superior court. The assent of the Commons and the king was wanting; the victims had been undefended, and had not even been given the opportunity of reading the indictment. Burley, being a knight of the chamber, was tried by the Commons; but in spite of the queen's pleading on her knees to Gloucester, he was executed. The appellants were unashamedly awarded the sum of £20,000 for services to the security of the state, and remained in political control until May, 1389, when Richard assumed the right to rule personally. Though he made changes in the personnel of his ministry, in a mood of appeasement he maintained the policy of the 1388 and 1389 parliaments.

Queen Anne, who had been a moderating influence on Richard since the crisis, died in 1394; two years later he was induced, in the interests of peace with France, to marry the French king's daughter, Isabella, who was nine years old. This seems to have been overlooked by Shakespeare, who attributes to Richard's second queen the sentiments of a mature woman. The second crisis arose in 1397, and with this period of neurosis Shakespeare's tragic portrayal of Richard is concerned. The new situation had led to a cautious restructuring of the Court. A number of bishops enjoyed high office, and anticipating further trouble, the king created a liveried force known as 'yeomen of the household'. Among his retainers were the knights, John Bushy, William Bagot and Henry Green, all members of parliament, who had held legal offices on the side of the opposition Lords of 1386. Bushy had on several occasions been Speaker of the House.

The parliament of 1397 was saddled with the unwelcome duty of curtailing the king's household expenditure, which had risen enormously with the celebration of his second marriage. The unpleasantness arose partly from a petition by Thomas Haxey, keeper of the records of the Common Bench, who was not a member of the Commons. In a changed climate of opinion, this man was sentenced to death for treason by the Lords; but the sentence was not carried out, Haxey being reprieved three months later. In Richard's critical reign, treason had become a sensitive constitutional area. Westminster Hall was being rebuilt, and the royal dilemma was, as usual, a shortage of money, which Richard remedied by the device of loan levies; the project had worked well eighteen years earlier. The war party, Gloucester, Richard Arundel and Warwick, mistrusting the king's new conciliatory policy with France, plotted a new confrontation; but Richard, not to be forestalled again, had all of them arrested. When the king's appeal to parliament was heard, Warwick broke down and confessed, thereby saving his life; Arundel was sentenced and executed; Gloucester had opportunely died in a Calais prison, supposedly murdered.

Richard was jubilant at the triumph over his earlier persecutors, using their very methods. Parliament partly relieved financial difficulties by granting him the excise duties of the wool and leather trade. Five new dukedoms, a marquisate and four earldoms were created, the recipients being endowed with the forfeited estates of Gloucester and Arundel. Henry Bolingbroke was now named Duke of Hereford, and Thomas Mowbray, Duke of Norfolk; the quarrel between them, with which Shakespeare's tragedy begins, had a curious origin. In 1398 Richard, possibly aspiring to absolute rule, nominated a parliamentary committee of eighteen, which included Bushy and Green. Jealousies and intrigues were aroused among the king's intimate followers. Norfolk had failed to attend the last parliament, and Hereford accused him of suspecting that the king plotted his (Norfolk's) destruction, as well as his friends', in order to compel them to flee the country. The quarrel was exacerbated by

Hereford's further assertion that Norfolk was implicated in the murder of the Duke of Gloucester. The parliamentary committee's initial task was to resolve this delicate situation; in the absence of proof, a duel was thought to be the honourable way to settle the argument. Richard himself had failed to reconcile the opponents.

The proposed trial by combat was to have taken place at Coventry in September 1398; it was stopped by the king, in favour of the banishment of both parties, with the approval of his committee, one reason being that Richard would gain by the absence of *both* parties.

When John of Gaunt died in February 1399, Richard went back on his word to preserve the eldest son's inheritance; he felt that the house of Lancaster was powerful enough in estates, without the addition of Hereford's. It is now known that the king justified his action by forging an addition to the authority granted by parliament. This perfidy led to his downfall, by making Bolingbroke the champion of the nobility's property rights. Norfolk, banished for life, died within a month at Venice; Hereford's exile of ten years (Shakespeare has 'six') was extended to a life sentence, as soon as his estates were sequestrated.

The king continued his practice of mortgaging land and extorting forced loans in order to pay his increasing number of pensioners and retainers. In June 1399, loaded with the crown jewels, he undertook the second expedition to Ireland, leaving his uncle, the Duke of York, in charge of the government. The warlike barons were poorly represented in his army, but sons of important noblemen accompanied Richard as hostages for their parents' good conduct. One of the sons who went with Richard to Ireland was Henry of Monmouth, afterwards Henry V. The unsuccessful campaign against Art MacMurrough of Leinster was interrupted by Bolingbroke's landing at Ravenspur in Yorkshire, where his greatest support lay. Sending Salisbury ahead, Richard delayed his return to South Wales until the end of July, by which time his treasurer, Wiltshire, as well as Bushy and Green, had been captured at Bristol and summarily killed. The plan to reunite the king's forces at Conway Castle failed, when Worcester and Albemarle (Shakespeare's Aumerle) deserted to Bolingbroke at Chester, and made known Richard's movements.

At Conway, Richard met a deputation under Northumberland from the Lancastrian leader, offering terms of conciliation, provided the king would restore Bolingbroke's inheritance and agree to the parliamentary trial of certain ministers; there was no suggestion of surrender or deposition, and the king accepted what he believed to be a truce. On the road to Chester, he was, however, ambushed, and taken prisoner to Flint Castle – an act of unequivocal treachery. From this time he acted under duress, and was constrained to summon parliament for the end of September. Sending him to the Tower, the usurpers took every step in the king's name, and made as few administrative changes as possible.

Bolingbroke, with an eye to the Upper House, could only claim the crown by descent or conquest, neither of which rights he possessed. Throughout September his consultations with a constitutional commission were frequent. The following were his conclusions: (1) that Richard should not be formally tried; and (2) that he himself could govern only by parliamentary consent, based on the rule of law, with the rights of the subjects properly secured. The negotiations resulted in the king's 'voluntary' abdication on 29 September, 1399, in the presence of a committee of both houses of parliament. Richard at first demanded to appear personally before parliament, but the melancholy state of his health prevented him from pursuing the point. For the first time in English annals a signature was appended to the document, instead of the royal seal. Next day the abdication was accepted by the assembly, which included numerous unauthorized citizens of London; the gathering could scarcely be called a parliament, since the throne was vacant, and no speaker was elected. At this assembly thirty-three charges were preferred against Richard, covering the last twelve years of his reign; they included perjury and the breach of his coronation oath. An objection was raised by Thomas Merke, Bishop of Carlisle, but this was subsequently expunged from the record.

Henry Bolingbroke was enthroned by the archbishops the next day, and summoned his first parliament for 6 October; it consisted of the same persons who had attended on 30 September. There were no punitive acts of expropriation, but Richard was imprisoned in Pontefract Castle by the end of the month. The most plausible account of his end is that he was starved to death the following February by the prison officer, Sir Thomas Swinford. The reason for this seems to have been a rising in Richard's favour, which the new king had to suppress in January 1400. The fictitious account of Richard's killing by Sir Piers Exton was derived by Shakespeare from Holinshed's *Chronicles* (II.517), the ultimate source being the unknown French author of *Chronique de la traïson et mort de Richard Deux* (c 1412). There is no evidence that a blow on the head with a pole-axe killed the king; when the tomb in Westminster Abbey was opened in 1873, it was found that there were no signs of violence, though possibly the end was hastened by smothering.

Historians since Caxton have had to thread their way through a maze of fourteenth- and fifteenth-century chronicles, only a fraction of which were impartial. Most supported either the Lancastrian, or the French and Yorkist points of view. The *Historia Anglicana* of Thomas Walsingham, of the Abbey in St Albans, recorded Richard's and the following two reigns, the last version being written in the third decade of the fifteenth century. A fuller account from the same Abbey, *Annales Ricardi Secundi et Henrici Quarti*, is dated about 1408 (authorship uncertain); this includes important documents relating to Richard's deposition. The St Albans group explicitly favoured the Lancastrian cause, and so did Knighton's continuation of *Eulogium Historiarum* (c 1429), compiled at Malmesbury Abbey. An eye-witness account, entitled *Chronicon Adae de Usk*, was compiled by a legal expert who took part in the negotiations leading up to the deposition. One partisan Lancastrian suggested that Richard died of 'voluntary starvation'.

Another side of the picture is presented in the Ricardian part of the *Dieulacres Chronicle* (c 1403) and the *Kirkstall Chronicle*, from an abbey in Yorkshire. Holinshed relied for some important events on Jean Creton's verse *Histoire du roy d'Angleterre Richart* (c 1401–5). This French squire joined the Earl of Salisbury in Ireland, on Richard's second expedition, and shared the earlier part of the king's captivity. His pen-portrait, while acknowledging Richard's mistakes, regards him as a Christian martyr, and denounces the Lancastrian succession as traitorous and opportunist. Froissart, who knew Richard personally, provides indispensable material for the latter part of his reign (1394–5).

Most Yorkist annalists wrote as late as the reign of Edward IV. The *Chronicles* of Jehan de Wavrin, compiled in the middle of the fifteenth century, lean heavily on Froissart. John Capgrave's *Chronicle of England* (1462–4) contains the information that the starvation of Richard in 1400 was deliberate. The *Chronicles* of Caxton and Fabyan were both derived from the Latin and French sources just mentioned. During the reigns of the three Henrys who

succeeded Richard, the monastery annalists, who wrote in support
of the deposed monarch, had the offending evidence destroyed by
the diligence of authorities.

Feudalism and chivalry, in the medieval acceptance of the word,
probably began to decline with the death of the Black Prince, who
wrote his own epitaph in French verse. It is still to be read on his
tomb in Canterbury Cathedral, and is as appropriate to the memory
of his son, Richard II: 'On earth I enjoyed ample wealth, and I used
it with great splendour. . . Now I am poor and bereft, I lie under
the earth, my great beauty is all gone. . . Were you to see me now, I
do not think you would believe that ever I was a man.'

At the close of the fourteenth century, the *monastic* documents
describing King Richard's end, be it noted, were still written mainly
in Latin, though the ruling classes invariably expressed themselves
in French or English. English prose, as a rule, took the form of
chronicles, theology or didactic literature; but the chronicles differed from history in being anecdotal. Research into sources to
explain cultural and political movements was no part of the feudal
recorder's equipment. He preferred colourful legend, and had
perforce to rely on the books of predecessors, whose credentials
were indifferently tested.

Surveying the literary situation after the Conquest, R. W. Chambers observed that the 'strangling of English prose was a national
disaster, and has much to do with that strange misunderstanding of
their own Middle Ages which obsesses so many good Englishmen'
(Introduction *The Continuity of English Prose*, p lxxxi). The best
one can do to illustrate the prose of this transition is to examine its
essential functions and idiomatic sentence structure. In the ensuing
notes on the period 1150–1350, I have two main principles in mind,
the functions of parts of speech, and the use of indigenous phrases
to ensure the intelligibility of sentences.

The first passage comes from the *Peterborough Chronicle* at the
beginning of the reign of Henry II (c 1154). As the local manuscript
was destroyed by fire, a copy was obtained from St Augustine's,
Canterbury, about the third decade of the twelfth century. It was
thereupon continued in the East Midland dialect, preserving a
number of West Saxon forms. The inconsistent spelling shows that
many modifications of Old English orthography had in the mean-

time taken place, e.g. the occasional use of *th* for þ in *other þe*:

> Wes næure gæt mare wreccehed on land, ne næure hethen men werse ne diden þan hi *diden*, for *ouer sithon* ne forbaren hi nouther circe ne cyrceiærd, oc namen al þe *god* ðat þarinne was, and brenden sythen þe cyrce and *altegædere*. Ne hi ne forbaren biscopes land ne abbotes ne preostes, ac ræueden munekes and clerekes, and æuric man *other þe* ouermyhte. Gif twa men oþer iii *coman ridend* to *an tun*, al þe *tunscipe* flugæn for heom – wenden ðat hi wæron ræueres. Þe biscopes and leredmen heom cursede æure, *oc was heom naht þarof*, for hi uueron al forcursæd and forsuoren and forloren. War-sæ mē tilede, þe erthe ne bar nan corn, for þe land was al fordon mid suilce dædes, and hi sæden openlice ðat Christ *slep*, and his halechen. Suilc and mare þanne we cunnen sæin, we þolden xix wintre for ure sinnes.
>
> (Dickins and Wilson, *E. M. English Texts*, p 5)

OE use of the double negative was pervasive until the seventeenth century. The relative pronoun was invariably ðat. Note the orthographic abbreviation *me* for *men*.

diden The pret. pl. inflexion is *-en*; but cf. *coman* and *flugæn*.

ouer sithon (OE *ofer sīþum*) 'against custom', probably idiomatic.

god (sing.) 'property' (of some value). Modern English would have used the plural. In ME the adjective is often employed substantivally.

altegædere 'everything in it'. Idiomatic.

other þe Idiomatic inversion.

coman ridend 'came riding'. The pres. part. used in continuous tense.

an tun Indef. article is the same as the numeral.

tunscipe Collective noun, singular in form, plural in meaning; hence *flugæn*.

oc was heom naht þarof Idiomatic word order, and partitive sense in *þarof* = 'of that'.

slep Relic of strong preterite of OE class 7 verb *slæpan*.

The next passage, which comes from the *Ancrene Riwle* (not later than 1210), is in direct address. The dialect, probably of Herefordshire, was a descendant of West Saxon. MS Cotton Nero A. 14 was later revised as the *Ancrene Wisse,* to make it available for both sexes.

> Nu, mine leoue sustren, urom al vuel speche, þet is þus þreouold, idel, and ful, and *attri*, holdeð feor our earen. *Me seið* upon ancren ðet euerich mest haueð on olde cwene to ueden hire earen, ane maðelild þet

maðeleð hire alle ðe talen of ðe londe, ane *rikelot* þet cakeleð hire al
þet heo *isihð oþer ihereð*. So þet me seið ine bisauwe, 'Vrom mulne and
from cheping, from smiððe· and from ancre-huse, me tiðinge
bringeð.' Þet wot Crist, þis is a sori tale: þet ancre-hus, þet schulde beon
onlukust stude of alle, schal beon *i-ueied* to þeo ilke þreo studen þet
mest is inne of cheafle. *Auh* ase *quite* ase ȝe beoð of swuche, leoue
sustren, *weren* alle ðe oðre, *ure Louerd hit vðe*.

(Dickins and Wilson, *Early Middle English Texts*, p 92)

In this text there are yet traces of grammatical gender, not replaced
by the natural order in the south-west until about 1350. The
preterite-plural of verbs ends in *-eð*. Some nouns have plural in *-en*,
a relic of the OE weak inflexion. The orthography of OE *f* is
invariably *u* sounded [v]; this was a characteristic of the south-west,
e.g. *urom, ueden*.

attri from OE *ātor* 'poison' + *-ig*.

Me seið 'people say', or 'it is said', the usual impersonal construction, which preceded the passive voice.

rikelot 'chatterbox', a word of unknown origin.

isihð oþer ihereð (OE *gesēon, gehēran*). Prefix *ge-* > ME *i-*, and is
indicative of completed action, as in the perfect tense.

onlukust 'most secluded', a superlative derived from OE *ǣnlic*,
'alone'.

i-ueied 'connected' from OE *fēgan*.

Auh 'but' from OE *ac*.

quite 'free', from OF *quiter* 'quit'.

weren 'would you were' subjunctive in the preterite, for expressed
wish.

ure Leouerd hit uðe 'may our Lord grant it' subjunctive, present,
for the same reason.

The final passage is from Richard Rolle of Hampole's homily,
The Nature of the Bee, from the Thornton MS. Rolle was writing in
the first half of the fourteenth century, and died in 1349. The
reference to Aristotle comes from the *History of Animals* Book IX,
21. In the northern dialect of Yorkshire inflexions were already
much modified. OE *ā* was retained in the North, but became *ǭ* in
the South and Midlands. The 3rd pers. sing. pres. indic. of verbs has
inflexion *-es*, and the pres. participle ends in *-and*. Norse influence
is shown in spellings *k* for initial *c*.

Arestotill sais þat þe bees *are feghtande agaynes* hym þat will drawe þaire hony fra thayme. Swa sulde we do agaynes deuells, þat *afforces thame* to reue fra vs þe hony of poure lyfe and of grace. For many *are*, þat neuer kane halde þe ordyre of lufe *ynence* þaire frendys, sybbe or fremmede. Bot outhire þay lufe þaym ouer mekill, settand thaire thoghte vnryghtwysely on thaym, or þay luf thayme ouer lyttill, yf þay doo noghte all as þey wolde *till* þame. Swylke kane noghte fyghte for thaire hony, forthy þe deuelle turnes it to wormes, and makes þeire saules oftesythes full bitter in angwys, and tene, and besynes of vayne thoghtes, and oþer wrechidnes. For thay ar so heuy in erthely frenchype þat þay may noghte flee intill þe lufe of Iesu Criste, in þe *wylke* þay moghte wele forgaa þe lufe of all creaturs lyfande in erthe.

(Sisam, *Fourteenth Century Verse and Prose* p 41)

are feghtande 'always fight'. Use of the present continuous for habitual action.

agaynes Northern form derived from ON *gagn* (cf OE *onȝean*). The ending -*es* represents the genitive inflexion, which signalled an adverb from about the middle of the twelfth century.

afforces thame 'endeavour' from OF *s'afforcer*. The present plural is used reflexively.

are 'there are'. The verb *to be* is here used in one of its original senses, viz. 'to exist'.

ynence 'towards', a word of probably Saxon origin, cf OE *onefn*.

till prep. 'to', commonly used in northern texts.

þe wylke adapted from French *lequel*.

The progressive loss of noun inflexions, owing to the confusion of their similarities, affected all cases but the genitive, and induced a semblance of fixity in word order. Greater sensitivity to the patterns of speech meant that only the idiomatic formulae of the old language were likely to survive. The substitute genitive, using the prepositon *of* with an uninflected form of the noun, came into being under the influence of French *de* in the twelfth century. On the other hand the OE tense system, consisting of present and past, remained undeveloped in Middle English until the fourteenth century, when the historical present began to make its appearance. The need for a consistent sequence of tenses was not, however, felt; consequently, as a syntactical principle, it was sadly neglected. Compound tenses, with the verb *have*, were present in Old English, but the alternative use of *is* in combination with verbs of motion (e.g. *is come*) was delayed until Middle English.

There was, at the same time, a notable disregard of concord, where the subject happened to be compounded. The principles of subordination in all passages above are elementary, consisting of adjectival, noun and adverbial clauses, all of which were present in Old English prose.

It is doubtful whether English prose would have bridged the gap between the Old and Middle periods but for the devotional requirements of the people. The Church needed to provide homilies and manuals of a religious character in the simple, direct language reflected in the chosen passages; the homely language is not, indeed, without power to move. Though the nuns were not generally as knowledgeable in Latin as in English, the three ladies of Kilburn for whom the *Ancrene Riwle* is thought to have been written, came from gentle stock, and had been maids-in-waiting to the Queen. Their retirement was due to the disturbed conditions of the age. Jocelyn de Brakelond says that the Abbot Sampson was preaching in English at Bury at the turn of the twelfth century. Richard Rolle was actually educated in Oxford, but elected to lead the life of a hermit. Because of his spiritual vocation, he became a respected Christian writer in his lifetime.

CHAPTER XIV

Prose from Mandeville to Malory and Medieval Drama

🆎🆎🆎🆎🆎🆎

AFTER THE APPEARANCE of Marco Polo's book in 1290, a taste for travel literature was in the air. Sir John Mandeville was not himself a traveller of comparable experience; he was more probably an enthusiastic translator of another man's work; but that did not diminish his popularity as a writer of entertaining prose. The distinctive merit of these *Travels* was their personal style, skilfully adapted to the choice of subject. Mandeville claimed that he was an Englishman, and because he inherited his countrymen's liking for a world view, he was a fitting person to undertake the translation.

The original version upon which Mandeville worked was written in Norman French, and is preserved in MS Harley 4383. The definitive English translation (a conflated text of date *c* 1400) is contained in MS B.M. Cotton Titus CXVI, which remained unedited until 1725, when it replaced a much shorter version published by Pynson in 1496. The unnamed author of the *Travels* was an imaginative writer, not content merely to compile from the resources of his own or other men's libraries. The material he used was selective, and undoubtedly improved by passage through the writer's mind. In a decidedly English turn of phrase, he trans- formed crude legend, as well as real travellers' notes, into readable fiction; he was extremely tolerant of alien customs and manners. Indeed, Mandeville had much in common with Chaucer – a love of the marvellous, and a gift for narrative, unspoiled by humorous scepticism.

Over two hundred manuscripts of the *Travels* are recorded in European Libraries; the majority are in French, but several are in Latin; no less than thirty-five editions were in print by the end of the fifteenth century. This proclaims the durability of the Man- deville tradition. Evidence suggests forcibly that the renascence of

English prose in the last century before Caxton resulted largely from the discipline of translating, either from French or Latin, or from languages in which the Bible was preserved. Wyclif's prose talent was vigorous and polemic; but his share in biblical translation proved the more influential.

From dates provided in the French manuscripts, the journey described by Mandeville took place in 1322, and the *Travels* was completed in 1356, the year of Poitiers, in the reign of Edward III. This makes unlikely the once fancied authorship of Jean d'Outre-meuse of Liège, a notorious fabricator, who was then only eighteen years old. Another improbable candidate, supposed to have adopted the pseudonym 'Mandeville', was Jean de Bourgogne, a bearded physician who practised in Liège; in 1365 he wrote a Latin work on *The Plague*, and he is known to have died in 1372. The earliest French MS extant is dated only a year earlier. Recent research has suggested that the Harley MS could well have been prepared in England, rather than Liège, possibly by a clerk in the employ of a French hostage, who accompanied the ex-King John the Good. Its Norman-French style resembles the language and syntax of the poet Gower. In the Prologue it is stated that Sir John Mandeville was born and educated at St Albans, and in the Epilogue that the *Travels* were written thirty-four years after setting out from his native land, because he had begun to suffer from gout and rheumatism. The name Mandeville was common in Hertfordshire, Essex and other parts of England.

Josephine W. Bennet says that by 1400 Mandeville's *Travels* 'was available in all the major languages of Europe' (*The Rediscovery of Sir John Mandeville*, p 220); there are citations from the book in the Gawain-poet, in the alliterative *Morte Arthure*, and in *The Squire's Tale* of Chaucer. There is an interpolation in the Epilogue of the English translation that does not appear in the French original, or any known Continental MS. Its purpose was to forestall sceptics, by signifying that the manuscript was submitted to the Pope in person, and approved by his Council. The consequence has been to raise problems of dating and the relationship of substantive English versions, namely the Cotton, Egerton and Pynson texts, for which there is no space here.

The passage below, from chapter XXXII of the *Travels*, reflects its lively and graceful style, though this is more characteristic of the fanciful second part (the Far East) than the factual first, which describes routes to the Holy Land.

Another yle there is that men clepen Oxidrate and another yle that
men clepen Gynosophe, where there is also gode folk and fulle of
gode feyth. And thei holden for the moste partye the gode condi-
couns and customs and gode maneres as men of the contree
aboueseyd. But thei gon alle naked.   5
Into that yle entred kyng Alisandre to see the manere. And whan
he saugh hire gret feyth and hire trouthe that was amonges hem, he
seyde that he wold not greuen hem, and bad hem aske of hym what
that thei wolde haue of him, ricchess or ony thing elles, and thei
scholde haue it with gode wille.   10
And thei answerden that he was ricche ynow that hadde mete and
drynke to susteyne the body with, for the ricchess of this world that
is transitorie is not worth. But yif it were in his powere to make hem
immortalle, therof wolde thei preyen him and thanken him. And
Alisandre answerde hem that it was not in his powere to don it   15
because he was mortelle as thei were.
And thanne thei asked him whi he was so proud and so fierce and
so besy for to putten alle the world vnder his subieccoun, 'right as
thou were a god and hast no terme of thi lif, neither day ne hour;
and wylnest to haue alle the world at thi commandement, that schalle 20
leve the withouten fayle or thou leve it. And right as it hath ben to
other men before the, right so it schalle ben to othere after the. And
from hens schaltow bere nothyng. But as thou were born naked, right
so alle naked schalle thi body ben turned into erthe that thou were
made of. Wherfor thou scholdest thenke and impresse it in thi   25
mynde that nothing is immortalle but only God that made alle thing.'
Be the whiche answere Alisandre was gretly astoneyed and abayst
and alle confuse[d] departed from hem.
                    (*Mandeville's Travels*, ed. M.C. Seymour, Clarendon, 1967,
                     pp 213–14)

The main sources of this account are the forged *Letter of Prester
John,* which was current in Europe in the second half of the twelfth
century; and Vincent of Beauvais's *Speculum Majus* (Part 3,
Historiale), which relied upon apocryphal letters supposed to have
passed between Alexander the Great and King Dindimus of the
Brahmans. The kingdom of the legendary Christian priest and
monarch, Prester John, was vast, but geographically vague; in the
twelfth and thirteenth centuries it was reported to be powerful in
the Far East, either in northern India or Cathay (China); but from
the fourteenth century Ethiopia was the almost universal location.
   In the accounts of early travellers any exotic Eastern country was

described as an 'island', possibly because the larger rivers determined boundaries. *Oxidrate* and *Gynosophe* need not be one and the same island, as some editors assume; nor need they be associated with *Bragman*, earlier mentioned in the same chapter. Alexander's campaign in the Indus valley brought him into opposition with the *Oxydracae* (see R. D. Milns *Alexander the Great*, Hale, 1968, p 225); while *Gynosophe* is a mis-spelling of *gymnosophe* (Greek 'naked sophist'). The gymnosophists were an ascetic sect of the religion called Jainism, whose adherents wore no clothing, until the Mohammedan conquest compelled them to do so.

The simplicity and naturalness of Mandeville's sentence structure are partly due to the absence of rhetorical effects. The tone is that of a letter writer, who desires to be clear and intriguing, rather than literary. Seven sentences begin with *And*, and three with *But*, after a full pause; but it would be mistaken to view the narrative development as paratactic. Abundant evidence of complexity is to be found in twenty-four subordinate clauses, ten adjectival, seven noun and seven adverbial. The change from indirect to direct speech in the penultimate paragraph was not unusual in Middle English prose (and verse) reporting.

Among the idiomatic functions that date the passage are the following:

(1) line 1, the impersonal construction *men clepen.*

(2) line 2, the collective noun *folk* which, being singular in form, preserves concord by being singular in function.

(3) lines 5, 14 and 25, the growing preference for adverbial compounds, such as *aboueseyd*, *therof* and *wherfore.*

(4) line 7, the use of *hire* before *trouthe*, redundant because of *hem* following.

(5) lines 8–9, *what that* = 'whatever', a transitional relative, with indefinite function.

(6) line 13, the adjectival use of *worth*, without complement.

(7) line 18, the infinitive *to putten*, preceded by *for*, from OF *pur*, meaning 'in order to' (dates from C13).

(8) lines 18, 22 and 23, the idiomatic use of *right* meaning 'just'.

(9) lines 19 and 20, the subjunctive *were*, succeeded by indicative *hast* and *wylnest*, in parallel subordinate clauses.

(10) line 19, the correlative conjunctions *neither . . . ne.*

(11) lines 22 and 26, the forms *othere* and *thing*, with plural meaning.

(12) line 25, superfluous *it*, before *in thi mynde*.

(13) line 27, definite article *the* before *whiche*, influenced by Fr. *lequel*.

Many of these medievalisms were eliminated in the progress of syntax during the next two centuries.

Chaucer wrote in the ..ame dialect as Mandeville (South-East Midland), but his prose is much more rewarding because of its diversity. *Boece* (c 1377–81), the tales of *Melibee* and of the *Parson* (1389–91), and *A Treatise on the Astrolabe* (c 1391), are placed chronologically only by conjecture. There is hardly a style in the individualistic sense, since most of the work varied between close translation and fairly free adaptation. If read for content, much of the prose seems dull to the modern reader. Pattern being the soul of argument, rhetoric was all-important to Chaucer; the rhythmical quality of the prose alone insists that it should not be under-estimated.

Boethius's *Consolations of Philosophy*, the original for Chaucer's *Boece*, was written in Latin (see pp 85, 117); but Chaucer's classical scholarship was not comparable with his skill in French. His latinized vocabulary shows how freely he borrowed from the original, though he relied in the more difficult passages on the French commentary of Nicholas Trivet. Many borrowings have endured in English, e.g. *absolut, coeterne, conjoineth, contagious, convenient, corollarie, demonstracioun, efficient, fatal, futures, imaginabile, impressed, inestimable, infirm, intelligence, manifest, mortal, mutabilitee, obiecte, positioun, propinquitee, sensibilitees, sensible.* Some of these loan words have an obvious Gallic colouring; indeed, borrowings directly from the French translation by Jean de Meun are nearly as numerous as those from the Latin text.

If *Boece* is a laboured translation, this is not because Chaucer made it much longer than the original. As B. L. Jefferson has pointed out in *Chaucer and the Consolation of Philosophy of Boethius* (pp 25–46) there was some difficulty in handling the author's sentence constructions; for instance, the frequent occurrence of the ablative absolute, for which Chaucer sometimes substituted a subordinate clause. As in most prose of the time, excessive use was made of the conjunction *and* and the pronoun *that*. Chaucer took infinite trouble in trying to reproduce the plentiful alliteration, though he retained prose for Boethius's metrical pieces. A persistent use of rhetorical balance in the phrasing sometimes approaches the artificiality of John Lyly; here is an instance:

> The yeer hath eek leve to apparaylen the visage of the erthe, now with floures, and now with fruyt, and to confownden hem somtyme with reynes and with coldes. The see hath eek his ryght to ben somtyme calm and blaundysschyng with smothe watir, and somtyme to ben horrible with wawes and with tempestes. But the covetise of men, that mai nat be stawnched, – schal it bynde me to ben stedfast, syn that stidfastnesse is uncouth to my maneris? Swich is my strengthe, and this pley I pleye continuely. I torne the whirlynge wheel with the turnynge sercle; I am glad to chaungen the loweste to the heyeste, and the heyeste to the loweste.

> (Robinson, p 331, ll 39–54)

The Tale of Melibee was another translation, this time of a French author, Renaud de Louens, who himself paraphrased the Latin version of Albertanus of Brescia. In the Prologue Chaucer speaks of a 'moral tale', 'a litel thing in prose', which is an obvious understatement, since the narrative develops into a 'tretys' larded with proverbial wisdom, put into the mouth of Prudence:

> Salomon seith that right as motthes in the shepes flees anoyeth to the clothes, and the smale wormes to the tree, right so anoyeth sorwe to the herte.

> (Robinson, p 168)

Like *The Parson's Tale*, both probably written in Chaucer's third period, *Melibee* is sententious prose ethically motivated, and makes frequent use of the Vulgate Bible. Chaucer actually mentions the four evangelical Gospels, which his prose obviously imitates. French syntax is much in evidence e.g. 'right so anoyeth sorwe to the herte' and a few lines later 'othere goodes temporels'. R.W.V. Elliott in *Chaucer's English* (p 173), with some reason, sees *Melibee* (the story) as a mild burlesque of the grand style, but not as explicit as its predecessor, which uses the stock-in-trade of the romances.

In the chosen manuscripts of the texts of *The Tale of Melibee* and

The Parson's Tale (though not of *Boece*), the scribal virgules are a feature which few editors deign to notice. They may not, of course, be Chaucer's, since he never saw any MS from which the modern printed text is derived. But their purpose is undoubted, when one studies the following passage carefully. They mark terminal pauses of some length, which correspond with planned cadences, and are therefore intended as a guide to anyone who reads aloud. They do not coincide with *all* the full stops supplied in the modern editions, because punctuation since the seventeenth century has been a compromise between logico-grammatical and elocutionary needs:

Áfter the sýnne of Énvye and of Íre,|nów wol I spéken of the sýnne of Accídie. ‖ For Énvye blýndeth the hérte of a mán,|and Íre tróubleth a mán,|and Accídie máketh hym hévy,|thóghtful, and wráw./‖|Énvye and Íre maken bítternesse in hérte,|which bítternesse is móoder of Accídie,|and bynýmeth hym the lóve of álle góodnesse.‖Thánne is Accídie the ángwissh of tróubled hérte;|and Seint Aúgustyn séith,|"It is anóy of góodnesse and Ióye of hárm."/‖|Cértes, thís is a dámpnable sýnne;|for it dooth wróng to Jhésu Críst,|in as múche as it bynýmeth the sérvice|that men óghte doon to Críst with álle diligénce,|as séith Sálomon./‖|But Accídie dooth nó swich diligénce. ‖ He dooth álle thyng with anóy,|and with wráwnesse, sláknesse, and excusácíoun,|and with ýdelnesse, and unlúst;|for which the bóok seith, |"Acúrsed be hé that dooth the sérvice of Gód necligéntly."/

(Robinson, p 249)

The virgules apportion the prose into versicles, or rhythmical units of delivery, which may be further subdivided into *stichoi*, capable of considerable variation. The stressed syllables are marked, to draw attention to the balanced distribution of emphasis. Chaucer's text resembles that of Hebrew poetry, written as prose, and seen at its best in the *Psalms, Job* and the *Wisdom Books;* he anticipates the liturgical language of the English *Psalter* (1530) and Tyndale's New Testament (1534), the underlying principle of whose syntax was rhythmical balance.

In *The House of Fame* is found Chaucer's single use of the word cadence:

> To make bookys, songes, dytees,
> In ryme, or elles in *cadence*,
> As thou best canst

He is here distinguishing rhymed accentual verse, like his own,

359

from alliterative poetry (free verse), using two different rhythmical principles. But the original meaning of cadence was 'the fall of the voice at the caesura or final pause, accompanying a gradual retardation of the phrasal movement'. In English prose, cadence could operate at any significant juncture, before breathing pauses, *per cola et commata*, to borrow the 'limb' metaphor of Jerome in his preface to the Vulgate version of *Isaiah*. Three significant features characterize the English practice: (a) retardation of the rhythm sometimes begins earlier than the 'classical' sixth syllable; (b) the turning-point is invariably a heavily stressed syllable; and (c) falling rhythm is not indispensable, for English cadences frequently closed with a stressed syllable. The half-dozen cadences in the Chaucer passage above are: (1) *sýnne* ŏf Accídie (2) *hévў̆*, thóghtfŭl ănd *wráw* (3) *lóve* ŏf ălle *góodnĕsse* (4) ănóy ŏf *góodnĕsse* ănd Ióye ŏf *hárm* (5) dilĭgénce, ăs sĕith Sálŏmŏn (6) *Gód* nĕclĭgéntlў̆.

Medieval pointing remains a closed book to most editors, and this is a pity, because,.as Peter Clemoes says 'the indication of cadences to a liturgical reader demanded a special kind of punctuation', which was more influential in prose than in poetry (*Liturgical Influence on Punctuation in Late Old English and Early Middle English Manuscripts*, Cambridge: Occasional Papers, 1952, pp 8 and 20). Writing of the practice of monastic schools, Clemoes adds that by the twelfth century 'a system of punctuation had been made generally available to literature, indicating to the reader inflections of the voice appropriate to the phraseological divisions recognized by the Latin grammarians' (p 13). Prose sentences favoured certain rhetorical patterns of development, one of which was parallel phrases; as in the above passage, for example: Envye blyndeth/Ire troubleth; anoy of goodnesse/ Ioye of harm. The penitential theme of *The Parson's Tale* rendered it imperative that Chaucer should hold the reader's attention by tight oratorical control of the phrasing. In this he succeeded eminently; for, like Gower, he was a pioneer of 'literary' English. What informality Chaucer infused into his writing owed much to his reading of Martianus Capella and the *Ars Dictaminis*, in which punctuation played an important role.

The Parson's is the longest of the *Canterbury Tales*, though it is no 'tale' at all. What Chaucer left is a disquisition on Contrition, the need for Confession, and the Seven Deadly Sins, making free use in the first two parts of *Summa Casuum Poenitentiae* of Raymund of Pennaforte, a cleric close to the Pope, who became head of the

Dominican Order in 1238. This manual was written soon after confession was made compulsory for Catholics by the Lateran Council of 1216. The account of the seven sins is borrowed from the *Summa de Vitiis* of another Dominican, Guilielmus Peraldus; it was also written in the thirteenth century. *The Parson's Tale*, designedly included at the *end* of the collection, leads up to Chaucer's retraction of his 'translaciouns and endytinges of worldy vanitees'. From an honest Catholic, repentance towards the end of his life would have been natural and sincere. Chaucer could not have been a Wyclifite, since Lollards were totally opposed to pilgrimages. Moreover, there is no hint of heresy in the writings, although, since the Schism, the Church had been under constant fire to reform itself.

Piers Plowman was evidence enough of religious disquietude in Chaucer's lifetime. G. R. Owst, accounting for its likeness to manuals and treatises, writes:

> Through modern contempt for a pulpit now shorn of its ancient glory, the one complete clue to the poem is still persistently ignored. In reality, it represents nothing more nor less than the quintessence of English mediaeval preaching, gathered up into a single metrical piece of unusual charm and vivacity. Hardly a concept of the poet's mind, an authority quoted, a trick of symbolism, or a satirical portrait but is to be found characteristic of the literature of our present study.
>
> (*Preaching in Medieval England*, CUP, 1926, p 295)

There were complaints about Church Courts, ecclesiastical materialism, mendicant friars, luxury in high places, and political ambition. Canon Law and the power of retribution exercised by Rome through excommunication, made the task of social reform by Plantagenet rulers extremely difficult. Only a small part of Church revenue seems to have been devoted to education, of which it was the sole agent.

To this state of materialism there was constant reaction from preachers like Wyclif, and activists in minor orders, like William Langland, who was something of a mystic. In the fourteenth century there arose a number of English exponents of mysticism, whose personal or transmitted thoughts were important as literature. The principal figures were Richard Rolle of Hampole (*The*

Form of Perfect Living), Julian of Norwich (*Revelations of Divine Love*), Walter Hilton (*The Ladder of Perfection*) and the unknown author of *The Cloud of Unknowing*, whose hand is traced in the style of several other prose pieces, such as *The Book of Privy Counselling*. Women, who were often the mainstay of the local church, were poorly educated, especially in Latin; but their spiritual development, reflected in an increasing number of nunneries, was remarkable. Rolle, a hermit who kept in touch with the life about him (see pp 350, 364, 420), addressed two books to the anchoress, Margaret Kirkby. Julian of Norwich was herself a dedicated recluse, whose revelation of 8 May 1373 took twenty years to put into manuscript form. She is justly honoured as the first authoress in England, though there is no MS dated earlier than the sixteenth century.

A mystic is one who seeks and usually finds a direct, harmonious relationship with the infinite power of God. Among Dominicans and Franciscans on the Continent (especially in Convents of the Rhineland) an aspiration towards mysticism was common by the twelfth century. In Norfolk, a secular eccentric was the married mystic Margery Kempe, who answered the call to holy living without any attempt at seclusion. Though she could not herself record her visions and temptations, she testified to priests, who believed in her veracity, but significantly referred to her as 'the creature'. Accompanied by her husband or relations, she made pilgrimages to Canterbury, Jerusalem, Rome, Santiago de Compostella, and even visited Norway and East Germany. Many sceptics rejected her because they could not endure her emotionalism.

Walter Hilton, who died four years before Chaucer, was an Augustinian Canon at the Priory of St Peter at Thurgarton in the Midlands; his *Ladder of Perfection*, first published by Wynkyn de Worde in 1594, was essentially a manual for the enlightenment of an anchoress, owing much to *The Imitation of Christ* of Thomas à Kempis. Christians, he said, do not have to choose between the active and contemplative life; both are serviceable to Christ, because they are complementary. The mystic's way is through prayer that involves three stages – purification, enlightenment and oneness with God. These cannot be attained without self-discipline; the will, and not humanitarian sentiment, prompts deeds of charity.

Though Hilton quotes from *The Cloud of Unknowing*, he did not in fact write it, as was formerly supposed. The author, using the

362

East Midland dialect, was a priest of profound understanding and clear observation, lightened by glimpses of humour. *The Cloud of Unknowing* has no equal as neo-Platonic English prose, set out with remarkable tenacity to point. The writer was a disciple of the Greek philosopher, Dionysius the Areopagite, called the father of mystical theology, who, at the turn of the fifth century, propounded the heavenly hierarchies, and greatly influenced both Aquinas and Dante. In *Dionyse Hid Divinite,* the author of *The Cloud* actually made the first English translation of *Mystica Theologica.*

Not often does a mystic reveal himself as a realist, psychologist and writer of pellucid English. This man was trained, with scholastic precision, not to place much reliance on visions and other psychic manifestations. He believes that the aspiring mystic should not be satisfied with ascetic practices; he must learn to concentrate, avoid eccentricity and cultivate grace by putting the spirit to its most courteous active use. Humility is a great mender of life's deficiencies, provided it is combined with acts of love. Man's 'unknowingness' of God, makes it all the more imperative to *feel* His presence through exercise of the affections.

No less than six fifteenth-century manuscripts of *The Cloud of Unknowing* are preserved in the British Library, but no edition came into print until 1871. The book is in seventy-five short chapters, each with three or four closely-knit paragraphs, linked by logic and syntax, so that it is difficult to abstract a brief excerpt. The passages below exemplify two important aspects of the author's style, described by Evelyn Underhill as 'robust common sense' and 'humorous exasperation' (*The Cloud of Unknowing*, 1934, pp 7 and 9).

(A)

Þinkyn may not goodly be getyn wiþ-outyn reding or heryng comyng before. Alle is one in maner, redyng & heryng; clerkes redyn on bookes, & lewid men redyn on clerkes, whan þei here hem preche þe worde of God. Ne preier may not goodly be getyn in bigynners & profiters wiþ-outyn þinkyng comyng bifore. See by þe preof in þis same cours.

Goddes worde, ouþer wretyn or spokyn, is licnid to a mirour. Goostly, þe iӡe of þi soule is þi reson; þi concience is þi visage goostly. & riӡt as þou seest þat ӡif a foule spot be in þi bodily visage, þe iӡe of þe same visage may not see þat spotte, ne wite wher it is wiþ-outyn a myrour or a teching of anoþer þan it-self: riӡt so it is goostly. Wiþ-outen redyng or heryng of Godes worde, it is impossible to mans vnderstondyng þat a soule þat is bleendid in custom of synne schuld see þe foule spot in his concyence. (Hodgson, EETS, pp 71–2)

(B)

For som men aren so kumbred in nice corious contenaunces in bodily beryng, þat whan þei schal ouȝt here, þei wriþen here hedes onside queyntely, & up wiþ þe chin; þei gape wiþ þeire mouþes as þei schuld here wiþ hem, & not wiþ here eres. Som, when þei schulen speke, poynten wiþ here fyngres, or on þeire fyngres, or on þeire owne brestes, or on þeires þat þei speke to. Som kan nouþer sit stille, stonde stylle, ne ligge stille, bot ȝif þei be ouþer waggyng wiþ þeire fete, or elles sumwhat doyng wiþ þeire handes. Som rowyn wiþ þeire armes in tyme of here spekyng, as hem nedid for to swymme ouer a grete water. Som ben euer-more smyling & leiȝing at iche oþer worde þat þei speke, as þei weren gigelotes & nice japyng jogelers lackyng kontenaunce. Semeli cher were wiþ sobre demure beryng of body & mirþe in maner . . . I sey þat þei ben tokenes of pride & coryouste of witte, & of vnordeynde schewyng & couetise of knowyng. & specyaly þei ben verrei tokenes of vnstabelnes of herte & vnrestfulnes of mynde, & namely of þe lackyng of þe werk of þis book. (Hodgson, EETS, pp 99–100)

These citations need very little glossing. In (A) *getyn* has the sense of 'gotten'; *Goostly* means 'spiritually', and *bleendid* represents 'blinded'. In (B) *leiȝing* is 'laughing', *gigelotes* are 'wanton women', and *jogelers* 'buffoons'. One grammatical inconsistency is the occurrence of infinitives with and without final -*n*. The lexical range is not as various as Chaucer's (Hodgson says about 1700 words), but a third of them are borrowed from French.

The second excerpt is illuminating in showing the technique of modulation used in the sentence structure. Alliteration combines with a deft management of lateral, nasal, sibilant and trilled consonants to secure the ease that is characteristic of this writer's rhythm. Antithetical balance of phrases and clauses is not as conspicuous as the sporadic repetition of words (*ploce*). But it is clear that the effects of rhetoric have been well studied, and that Richard Rolle was the originator of this English style, rather than the Latin Church Fathers. It is possible that the stichic pattern of alliterative poetry prompted the measured movement each paragraph contains. The paragraphs are rationally bridged by connectives, such as *and, but* and *for,* and care is taken to make the opening sentence arresting and largely monosyllabic.

So much has been learnt concerning *Morte Darthur* in the last eighty years that its author, Sir Thomas Malory, has become a less shadow figure than Sir John Mandeville. G. L. Kittredge's paper 'Who was Sir Thomas Malory?' published in Boston in 1897, was followed by E. Hicks's brief biography *Sir Thomas Malory, his Turbulent Career* (1928), which added a wealth of facts, and some useful interpretations. The authoritative work of Eugene Vinaver on Malory appeared a year later, and the views there expressed on the romance's compilation were partly confirmed when W. F. Oakeshott in 1934 discovered a fifteenth-century manuscript in the Fellows Library at Winchester College. The effect of this more reliable text, which began in the middle of page 18 of Caxton's version, was to call for Vinaver's new three-volume edition (Clarendon, 1967) to replace Oskar Summer's reprint of 1889; this had included an extensive, but unreliable, commentary on Caxton's earliest printing of 1485. We are now in a better position to appreciate the worth of Malory's achievement.

He was born about 1410, apparently at Newbold Revell in Warwickshire, near the Leicestershire border. He served in France under Richard Beauchamp, Earl of Warwick, and became a member of Parliament in 1445. The Wars of the Roses began a decade later, and Malory at first espoused the Yorkist cause, as the armed supporter of Warwick, his feudal lord. These were lawless times, but Sir Thomas's belligerent seizure of priory property and other dues was apparently unconnected with the civil war. He was arraigned for breach of the peace in 1451, and for the next twenty years spent most of his time in and out of custody. After the law-breaker and his liege, the king-maker, had thrown in their lot with the Lancastrians, Malory's inability to secure a pardon must have been on political grounds. He was actually charged with sedition in 1468, and probably died in prison in 1471, a month before Warwick lost his life at the Battle of Barnet.

Morte Darthur was written during Malory's final imprisonment at Newgate, opposite which was situated the first known London library, founded and endowed by the Lord Mayor, Richard Whittington, in 1421. Being a knight of standing, Malory was virtually on parole, and was able to afford the privileges granted to respectable prisoners. He would never have undertaken his book, but to alleviate hours of boredom. Caxton printed the book in July 1485; the envoy, however, states that the writing was completed in the ninth year of Edward IV's reign. As the year on the old calendar

began on 4 March, the manuscript must have been completed
between 1469 and 1470.

It would be unfair to judge the character of Sir Thomas by the
record of criminal accusations against him. The aristocratic, moral
tone of the writing implies a chivalrous soldier, conscious of his
responsibility to society, who admired an anachronistic code, some
centuries after it had ceased to exist (see p 52). The impression is
confirmed by the physical trappings, courtly manners and Christian
sentiments, subsumed in Malory's advocacy of love, truth and
faithfulness. If the biographical facts were better known, we should
perhaps find that Malory's choice and manipulation of themes
reflects his own moral struggle and penance. He tried to find a
solution to man's lack of stability, in ethical, and not simply the
Church's religious, terms.

The retrospective glamour of Malory's imaginary society contains many analogies to the unhappy state of England in Malory's
time, one of the most moving coming in Book XXI, chapter 1,
when he reflects upon the rebellion of Mordred and the death of
Gawain:

> Lo ye all Englysshemen, se ye nat what a myschyff here was? For he
> that was the moste kynge and nobelyst knyght of the worlde, and moste
> loved the felyshyp of noble knyghtes, and by hym they all were
> upholdyn, and yet myght nat these Englysshemen holde them contente
> with hym. Lo thus was the olde custom and usayges of thys londe, and
> men say that we of thys londe have nat yet loste that custom. Alas! thys
> ys a greate defaughte of us Englysshemen, for there may no thynge us
> please no terme.
>
> (Vinaver, *Works*, p 708, lines 34–41)

Those who espoused the cause of Mordred against Arthur are said a
little earlier to have tired of the constant state of war and strife.
Malory mentions the people of Kent, Sussex, Surrey, Essex, Suffolk
and Norfolk, and Vinaver believes that he had in mind a similar
situation in the Wars of the Roses, 'when the strength of the
Yorkists lay to a large extent in the south-eastern counties' (*Works*,
p 777, last footnote). The intervention of the Pope in the siege of
Joyous Garde, near Carlyle (Book XX) has all the ring of recent
English civil disturbance.

It is unlikely that the manuscript obtained by Caxton bore any
title – few MSS did. The colophon's reference to *The Death of*

Arthur would, therefore, presumably have been Caxton's after-thought. In the excellent Preface he explains that the collection of Arthurian legends was demanded by influential English patrons, though the publisher himself was justifiably sceptical of their historicity. Time has shown that Geoffrey of Monmouth's account of the document he is supposed to have received from Archdeacon Walter of Oxford was without foundation. By convention, how-ever, Arthur was one of the nine worthies of history (pagan, Jewish and Christian), the others being Hector, Alexander the Great, Julius Caesar, Joshua, David, Judas Maccabeus, Charlemagne and Godfrey of Boulogne. The admirers of Arthur pointed to tombs and relics in sundry places to overcome Caxton's misgivings. Five of the sources Malory used were French; but Caxton knew that others existed in Welsh and English; for instance, the fourteenth-century English alliterative poem of 4300 lines, called *Morte Arthure*, written in the northern counties; and a worthier stanzaic poem *Le Morte Arthur* (3800 lines), devoted to the theme of Guinevere and the last battles.

Caxton's Preface praised Malory's didactic intention in choosing materials that contain diverse acts of 'chyvalrye, curtosye, huma-nyté, frendlynesse, hardynesse, love, frendshyp, cowardyse, murdre, hate, vertue and synne'. He realized that all was 'wryton for our doctryne'; but he qualified this by describing the product as a 'noble and joyous (i.e. entertaining) hystorye'. The Winchester MS makes it clear that Caxton did some editing; and he was also responsible for the division of *Morte Darthur* into twenty-one books, and 507 chapters.

Chrétien de Troyes was responsible for gallicizing the Celtic legends about Arthur (e.g. in the Tristan story), and for the popularization of courtly love among speakers of Central French; for the idealism of this code was as exotic in northern France as the British names of Arthurian heroes and heroines. He was either a herald or cleric at the court of Marie de Champagne, daughter of Eleanor of Aquitaine, and a poet of intellectual refinement, active between 1160 and 1190. He was the author of at least four books on Arthurian themes, and the creator of the Lancelot legends, used by Malory, which were written in rhymed octosyllabic couplets of great ease and elegance. Picaresque adventures, for Chrétien, as for Malory, were rendered more attractive by the imaginary dialogues and interpolated comments of the author.

367

Another French author on whom Malory drew was Robert de Boron, probably a knight attending the court of Henry II; he wrote in verse on the Merlin theme and the Grail legend, which he claims to have invented. The so-called Arthurian Vulgate Cycle consists of a number of thirteenth-century prose versions in French, perhaps wrongly attributed to Walter Map, Welsh Archdeacon of Oxford (c 1200–10), whose principal work, *De Nugis Curialium*, was written in Latin, also for the court of Henry II.

By rewriting his source-material, Malory gave a new moral slant to pseudo-history and to supernatural legend, thereby gratifying an English, rather than a French audience. The reasons for Malory's omissions are just as important for criticism as those for his additions. He suppressed many marvels, such as Lancelot's magic shields, and protective ring, because personal prowess can only be reduced by such adventitious aids. He added or adapted events or reflections that would forward his patriotic design; this was to produce a prose epic enshrining the noble ideal of service, for which the Round Table was created, under the influence of Merlin.

Malory's first experiments were often dislocated; but structural coherence was improved in the Quest of the Grail and the Lancelot-Guinevere tragedy. Vinaver observes that his characters 'lack individual complexity and variety' (*Malory*, p 21); and adds that the narrative conception of the author often failed, because 'his mind was reflective, rather than creative' (ibid. p 42). Malory's original treatment of the Quest of the Grail has considerable relevance to the final tragedy, though he does not seem to make this clear. More than a third of the work is occupied by *The Book of Sir Tristram de Lyones,* a section which negates any traces of organic unity that the collection might have possessed.

Malory was a man of strong feelings and convictions; but particularly in 'The Fair Maid of Astolat' it is clear that feelings are not subservient to episodic development. There is a passage in Book XVIII, chapter 13, which again reflects Malory's sensitivity to historical change:

'What knyght ar ye?' seyde the ermyte, ' and where were ye borne?'
'My fayre lorde, ' seyde sir Launcelot, 'I am a straungere and a knyght aventures that laboureth thorowoute many realmys for to wynne worship.'
Than the ermyte avysed hym bettir, and saw by a wounde on hys chyeke that he was sir Launcelot.

'Alas,' seyde the ermyte, 'myne owne lorde! Why layne you youre name from me? Perdeus, I ought to know you of ryght, for ye ar the moste nobelyst knyght of the worlde. For well I know you for sir Launcelot.'

'Sir,' seyde he, 'syth ye know me, helpe me, and ye may, for Goddys sake! For I wolde be oute of thys payne at onys, othir to deth othir to lyff.'

'Have ye no doute,' seyde the ermyte, 'for ye shall lyve and fare ryght well.'

And so the ermyte called to hym two of hys servauntes, and so they bare hym into the ermytayge, and lyghtly unarmed hym and leyde hym in hys bedde. And than anone the ermyte staunched hys bloode and made hym to drynke good wyne, that he was well refygowred and knew hymselff. For in thos dayes hit was not the gyse as ys nowadayes; for there were none ermytis in tho dayes but that they had bene men of worship and of prouesse, and tho ermytes hylde grete house-holdis and refreysshed people that were in distresse.

(Vinaver, *Works*, pp 628–9, lines 37 et seqq)

Books XIII to XXI are undoubtedly the most impressive, because here the action is centralized on the main characters and the passions that motivate them; Lancelot is Malory's hero, an essentially humane man, forced into an ambiguous situation; the tragic flaw is his attitude to love, less urgent to him than dedication to prowess in jousting and adventure. Arthur, the model of truth and fair-dealing, does not exceed Lancelot in courtesy, but in *worship* (honour); in his worldy ambitions Arthur seems to resemble Henry V. Guinevere is the *femme fatale*, against whom Arthur is warned by Merlin, as 'not holsom' (Vinaver, *Works*, p 59, lines 36–9). Gawain of Orkney, Arthur's nephew and counsellor, is obdurate in personal vengeance. The Table Round, a fellowship of one hundred and forty knights, is destroyed by internal dissension, two of the causes being the Queen's jealousy, and the younger knights' envy of the supremacy of Lancelot.

In a splendid essay 'The English Prose *Morte*' (*Essays on Malory*, Clarendon, 1963) C. S. Lewis asks and answers the following important question:

Did any Middle English author conceive clearly that he was writing fiction? . . . They are all, even Chaucer, handing on, embellishing, expanding, or abridging a matter received from some source. . . . They all proceed as if they were more or less historians; unscholarly, decorating, and emotional historians to be sure, like Livy or Plutarch. . . (p 22)

The age of chivalry Malory framed in his imagination flourished vaguely from the reign of Henry II to that of Henry V, but not earlier. It was the product of such sources as Geoffrey of Monmouth, Layamon, Wace, Marie de France, Chrétien de Troyes and de Boron, but not Nennius. Archaeologists, bent on locating King Arthur's seats and activities in the sixth century, write for a fact-loving public, with whom it is difficult for literary historians, like R. S. Loomis, to identify; diverse investigators live in different worlds. But Malory's *Morte Darthur* is an important link between the medieval and the modern world. In the last book, the resourceful Guinevere, simulating a pre-wedding shopping-spree, takes refuge in the Tower of London, and is there beleaguered by Mordred, who 'made many assautis, and threw *engines* unto them, *and shotte grete gunnes*' (Vinaver, ibid. p 707, lines 32–3). This is an instance of what C. S. Lewis calls 'Malorian realism'; but it strongly recalls the siege tactics of Henry V in France after Agincourt.

Whether Malory translates or paraphrases or condenses (as he does in the bulk of his work), the sources are so numerous that one might expect several styles to appear in the *Morte Darthur*. French prose and poetry, English alliterative verse and English rhyming stanzas have, indeed, left their mark on parts of his writing. There is a tendency, however, to overlook Malory's impersonal skill as a manipulator of the thoughts of others; this has two significant aspects, the handling of dialogue and dramatic presentation. He was adept at curtailing long speeches that arrest the lively interplay of thoughts and feelings, and at varying the tempo of narrative to sustain interest in the action. The concision of most dramatic scenes in *Morte Darthur* contrasts admirably with the rambling discussions of some of the sources. Few episodes are more graphic and stirring than Book XX, chapter 4, where Lancelot is discovered by his accusers in the Queen's chamber. One detects a strain of Gallic culture in this 'fair-languaged' knight; always it matches his courteous indignation, and is probably what made him more attractive than his fellows to women.

Malory was, perhaps unconsciously, the first writer of English prose fiction, as well as the earliest to buttonhole the reader by using a colloquial and direct style. The 'chronicle' manner he adopted is not identifiable with any historical period. While deliberately archaic, it is neither latinized nor aureate, as was most prose of the late fifteenth century. The OF word *orgulous* 'proud', of which

Malory was over-fond, was already old-fashioned when Shakespeare used it rhetorically in *Troilus and Cressida*. At its best, the Malorian style relies on nostalgic memories and elegiac tones for its emotive power; it became so popular that four editions of *Morte Darthur* appeared, before the book cast its spell upon Sidney and Spenser. No earlier romance combined so happily graphic fluency and the homiletic note of pathos. The epithets that enliven the narrative abound in motor-activity and monosyllabic strength, while the *longueurs* of Celtic sentiment are tastefully restrained.

Paradoxically, the artist, Malory, was also a man who enjoyed the buffets and brawls he depicts in chivalric terms. Knights, who unseat and wound each other in sport, are apt to weep and swoon as naturally as women. Characters are undistinguished by their apparel and personal appearance, but more by their stoical traits. Only when Malory follows closely the alliterative poem *Morte Arthure* is there a congenial response to weather and natural surroundings. The kingdom of Logres was not the only faery realm associated with no geographical reality. This was surely not merely the result of writing in prison.

The chief merit of Malory's style is its readability; but almost universally praise has been given to its musical cadence. The two paragraphs that follow are characteristic of his technical execution, in the dual role of translator and original thinker:

(A) Book V, chapter 5, 'The Noble Tale of King Arthur and the Emperor Lucius':

Anóne sir Árthure|wénte to his wárdrop|and cáste on his ármoure,‖ bòthe his gesseráunte|and his básnet|with his bróde shýlde. ‖|And sò|he búskys hym tyll his stéde|that on the bénte hóved.‖|Than he stértes uppon lóffte|and héntys the brýdyll,|and stírres hym stóutly,‖and sòne he fýndis his knýghtes twó|full clénly aráyed.‖|And than they tròtted on|stýlly togèdir|over a blýthe contráy|full of mány mýrry býrdis,‖and whan they còm to the fórlonde|Árthure and they alýght on hir fóote.‖And the kýnge commáunded them to tárye thère.‖|
(Vinaver, *Works*, p 120, lines 13–20)

Gesseraunte 'light coat of armour', *basnet* 'light helmet', *buskys* 'hastens', *bente* 'grass', *hoved* 'waiting', *hentys* 'seizes', *clenly* 'completely'.

371

Typical of the original poem (*Morte Arthure*) is the shift from the past to the graphic present tense, and the plentiful alliteration. Vinaver's edition, in fact, indicates by appropriate marks the verse lines that have been taken over bodily. Malory was reducing the length, and simultaneously attending with care to his prose diction, so that stressed syllables would not be as emphatic as they were in alliterative poetry. He wished the prose to have a flexible rhythm of its own, but realized that it would not command continuous attention, unless sufficiently varied for the desired romantic effect.

Punctuation presumably did not help Malory's prose much, since the scribe of the Winchester MS (which is not holograph) used only two stops, the virgule and the period, plus capital letters. In Malory's writing the relative duration of the pauses is important. Resumptive conjunctions, *and* and *then*, are characteristic of his paratactic practice, which preserves the natural order of events, and gives them verisimilitude.

A carefully composed passage is usually balanced in the symmetry of its segments, a method that implies limitations in the number of stressed and unstressed syllables. By and large, shorter pauses denote thought progression; the longer ones are rests for the voice. In its inception, good Middle English prose was a survival of alliterative verse, whose measured phrasing was greatly varied in stress. The loss of unstressed inflexions in early Middle English did not fundamentally alter the rhythm of either prose or verse, because missing syllables were replaced by similarly unstressed Germanic relation words (particles and prepositions). The real continuity of prose, even more than of verse, was made possible by preserving the natural stress of the language, as spoken. The responsive reader recognizes segments as the stressed word-groups the writer composes in acceptable order. In the 'flow of speech' the latter conjures up, through syntactical units, their speed and duration are determined by a heard pattern of intonation and stress, adapted to the matter in hand. Malory's good ear was undoubtedly for prose, Chaucer's for verse.

(B) Book XVIII, chapter 25, 'The Knight of the Cart' (a curtailed story of Chétien de Troyes):

Whérefore|I lýkken lóve nowadàyes|unto sómmer and wýnter:‖fòr,| lýke as the tóne ys cólde|and the óthir ys hóte,|so fáryth lóve

nowadàyes.|||And thérefore|áll ye that be lóvers,|cálle unto youre
remémbràunce|the mónethe of Máy,|lyke as dèd quéne Gwenyvér,|for
whom I make hère a lýtyll méncion,||that whýle she lýved|she was a
tréw lóver, || and thérefor she had a góod énde.|||

(ibid. p 649, lines 30–35)

In this paragraph the syntactic units are a little shorter, but the
pauses are more frequent, the clausal balance being stimulated by
repetition. *Ploce* is only one of a number of schematizations of
word and thought, which accompany Malory's elegiac writing. This
paragraph ends with a superb cadence. A basic paratactic structure
is evident, but there are more subordinate clauses than are usual
with Malory; they are adverbial, noun and adjectival.

The simplicity of the writing in both passages is aided by minimal
employment of descriptive adjectives, those chosen being monosyllabic or common. Malory must have been a judicious reader of such
Latin and French prose as was available to educated persons in the
late fifteenth century; from this source would have come many of
the conventional images. The stock phrases, such as 'wyte you
well', 'ride a walop' (gallop), and 'take no force' must have been
culled from the common pool of popular speech. Malory's unob-
trusive style is unique for its time, because (alliteration and repetition excepted) it is so remote from the clerical tradition of classical
rhetoric. Most of the emotive effects are managed through the
dialogue, of which he has more than the average modern novelist;
yet behaviour, rather than speech, differentiates almost all his
characters.

DRAMA

Medieval drama arose out of the liturgy of the Church, first as
antiphonal dialogue, and then as the impersonation of biblical
figures. The ceremony preceding Mass on Easter Monday tended to
take a primitive dramatic form, though the representations were
necessarily static. One of the seven canonical hours, *Matins* (from
eleventh-century French *matines*) originally came just after mid-
night; but the Church found it convenient to 'anticipate' the
ceremony on the previous evening; hence the nineteenth-century
borrowing *matinée*, for a performance that took place in the
afternoon.

Short plays stemmed from the Corpus Christi procession in June, and from the Christmas festivities that culminated in Twelfth Night; these were at the outset written by monks in Latin. A wandering scholar called Hilarius, composed three amusing biblical sketches, which were performed on the Continent in the eleventh century. Liturgical drama did not, however, incorporate New Testament themes until the twelfth century, when brief scenes were created in Benedictine monasteries, using schoolboys or young clerks as the actors.

One of the earliest Latin depictions was entitled *Descensus Christi ad Inferos* ('The Harrowing of Hell'), which was soon to find expression in vernacular representations. It is really a poem in dialogue form derived from the *Acta Pilati* (later styled the *Gospel of Nicodemus*), an Apocryphal book of the fourth century, in which Christ descends into Hell, after the Crucifixion, to despoil Satan. Into this theme the clerics worked an antiphonal rendering of the last four verses of the twenty-fourth psalm, intoned as question and answer, just when the Palm Sunday procession reached the Church door. A well-known East Midland version of 'The Harrowing' was probably written in the reign of Edward II.

In the thirteenth century dramatic pieces in Anglo-Norman were replaced by short plays in vernacular verse, performed in a public area, such as a churchyard or market-place. The transfer of control from the Church to local authorities was an important step for such centres of play activity as Chester, York, Coventry, Lincoln, Norwich and London. Chaucer's Wife of Bath, we are told, frequented Miracle plays during her husband's absence. Such was their popularity that longer runs were called for by the end of the fourteenth century; and this meant that professional performers took over the secular activities from the clerics. The actual writing of Nativity, Passion and other plays, however, continued under the guidance of better educated churchmen.

The texts of surviving plays differ greatly for two reasons; first, the traditional material had been mainly oral; and secondly, busy Midland and Northern towns frequently borrowed and adapted the versions of plays used by their neighbours. There is a visible association between the Chester and Wakefield-York Cycles, while one Coventry Cycle was of mixed East Anglian origin. The realistic language, and occasional social disaffection, suggest that a master hand was behind some of the compositions.

When the organization of plays passed into the hands of lay authorities, the trade gilds became prominent sponsors. In the *Ordo Paginarum* of 1415, reproduced by L. Toulmin Smith, no less than forty-eight gilds are represented as participants in a Corpus Christi Pageant. At this Feast, held on the Thursday after Trinity Sunday in June, Christ's presence at the Sacrament of Communion was commemorated, from the year 1311, by a solemn procession, in which each of the gilds bore the banner of its patron saint. Every craft was expected to enact a biblical scene in a connected sequence, and to provide actors, as well as stage facilities, suitably decorated. Scenes from the pageant were presented simultaneously in different streets of the town; and this arrangement soon called for portable wooden stages, mounted on wheels. An annual levy, up to four pence per member, called *pageant-silver*, defrayed the gild's expenses, which included items such as 'to the devyll and to Judas, XVIII pence' and 'halfe a yard of Rede Sea, 6 pence'. There are records of a pageant festival presented at Chester in 1328. The word *pageant* was derived from Anglo-Latin *pagina*, a stage platform for tableaux or the performance of dumb-shows, like the one Shakespeare presents in *Hamlet*.

Play festivals could last as long as a week; in MS B.M. Cotton Vespasian, D.VIII, a proclamation by three heralds of the *Ludus Coventriae*, announced in verse a list of forty-one pageants. A complete cycle aimed to cover biblical events beginning with the Creation, and ending with the Last Judgement.

The secularization of drama was considerably helped by the introduction of folk elements, some, like the Mummers' Plays, being of pagan origin. Examples of bucolic graftings in the *Townley Mysteries* are seen in the Shepherds' Plays. The popularity of the folk tradition is reflected also in its dances, which reminded the community of the cyclical significance of the seasons. The Church itself had retained festival ceremonies for spring, summer, autumn and winter. Christmas happened to be the season of the Court Revels, which soon became the pattern of light-hearted entertainment throughout the country. By the thirteenth century farcical incidents were fairly common in plays, and the Church naturally raised theological objection. To Bishop Robert Grosseteste of Lincoln and Robert of Brunne in *Handlyng Synne,* the representation of God on the stage, in white cloak and with gilded face, was not only in bad taste, but likely to undermine the faith of many illiterate spectators. The following protest is from a treatise on Miracle Plays contained in MS B.M. Addit. 24202:

Whanne we taken in bourde [jest] and pley þe most ernestful werkis of god, as ben hyse myraclis, god takiþ awey fro us his grace of mekenesse, drede, reuerence, and of oure bileue; þanne whanne we pleyin his myraclis as men don nowe on dayes, god takiþ more venjaunce on us þan a lord þat sodaynly sleeþ his servaunt for he pleyide to homely wiþ hym.
(R. Kaiser, *Medieval English*, p 258)

Some explanation of terms used in connection with medieval drama seems appropriate. The word *mystery* applied to plays, was not current until the eighteenth century, when Robert Dodsley introduced it (*Select Collection of Old Plays*, 1744). There must have been confusion, at some stage, with the word *maistry* 'mastery of a craft'. The word *miracle* was not, at first, employed for religious plays in general, but only for dramatizations of saints' legends; most surviving miracle plays have been assigned to the reigns of Henry VI and Edward IV. Extant *moralities*, such as *The Castell of Perseverance*, were dramatized allegories, the best of which, e.g. *Everyman* and *The Satire of the Three Estates*, belonged to the Tudor age. *Interludes* were plays performed in the banqueting halls of the nobility, and tended to limit the number of actors in their casts.

The twenty-five plays in the Chester Cycle, probably the earliest of the existing four, belong to the time of Chaucer's youth, and were acted at Whitsun. The fifteenth-century text we have was not, however, transcribed until 1591, by Edward Gregorie. It is therefore useless to suppose that the language and spelling are relevant to the date of composition. The best-known play of this group is *Noah's Flood*, concerning 'the building of the Arke', which has sometimes been wrongly attributed to Ranulf Higden, author of *Polychronicon*. The verse is in the popular romance measure, called by the French *rime couée*, the stanza scheme being a a a_4 b_3 c c c_4 b_3. The iambic rhythm has little alliteration, and not infrequently stanzas are allocated to two or more speakers. For example:

NOYE. Wyffe, in this vessel we shall be kepte:
My children and thou I woulde in ye lepte.

NOYES WIFFE. In fayth, Noye, I hade as leffe thou slepte!

> For all thy frynishe fare°,   [polite talk]
> I will not doe after thy reade°.   [counsel]

NOYE. Good wyffe, doe nowe as I thee bydde.

NOYES WIFFE. Be Christe! not or I see more neede,
> Though thou stande all the daye and stare.

(Pollard, *English Miracle Plays, Moralities and Interludes*, p 11,
lines 97–104)

The comic relief provided by Noah's recalcitrant wife is not in the least unbecoming.

The York Cycle consists of forty-eight plays, all short, because performed on a single day. They seem to have been in vogue a little before 1360, but the manuscript is dated nearly a century later. Signs both linguistic and metrical indicate that these plays were rewritten to their detriment. It is known that Richard II saw them at the height of their esteem in 1397; he would probably have approved of the rhetoric to which the final versions leaned. In style, the plays belong to the alliterative revival, which combined narrative techniques with a complicated system of rhyme. To a modern ear the mixed anapaestic rhythm is often disturbing, though capable of dramatic effect, as in the second scene (in Hell) of *The Creation and the Fall of Lucifer*. The speaker is Secundus Diabolus:

> Owte! owte! I go wode for wo, my wytte es all wente nowe
> All oure fode es but filth, we fynde us beforn,
> We that ware beelded in blys in bale are we brent nowe,
> Owte! on the Lucifer, lurdan°! oure lyghte has thu lorne.   [clown]
> Thi dedes to this dole nowe has dyghte° us,   [prepared]
> To spille us thu was oure spedar,
> For thou was oure lyghte and oure ledar,
> The hegheste of heven hade thu hyght us.

(Pollard, ibid., p 5, stanza 14, lines 105–12)

With the York Cycle is associated the Townley Collection of thirty-two plays, so-called because the manuscript (*c* 1485) was once owned by the Townley family, who lived near Burnley in Lancashire. At one time the MS seems to have been at Woodkirk Abbey, near Wakefield, where most of the plays were almost certainly written and performed (not earlier than *c* 1425). Five plays were borrowed, with some textual changes, from the York Cycle; but the literary merit of the collection is undoubted, centring on the contribution of the supposed 'Wakefield Master'. His strain of realistic humour has been widely acclaimed. The verse is stanzaic, with a discreet use of alliteration; the social outlook favours the peasant underdog, whose underprivileged state is reflected in the satirized hardships of the times. The hand of the 'master' is at its most skilful in the First and Second Shepherds' plays; it is equally at home with the grim comedy of Mak, the sheep-stealer, and the lyrical mood of shepherds who celebrate the birth of Christ:

> Haylle, comly and clene: haylle, yong child!
> Haylle, maker, as I meyne°, of a madyn so mylde.   [think]
> Thou has waryd°, I weyne, the warlo so wylde,   [cursed]
> The fals gyler of teyn°, now goys he begylde.   [sorrow]
>   Lo, he merys°;   [grows merry]
> Lo, he laghys, my swetyng,
> A welfare metyng,
> I have holden my hetyng°,   [promise]
>   Have a bob° of cherys.   [bunch]
>
> (Pollard, ibid., p 41, lines 721-9)

The Coventry plays fall into two groups, confused until 1825, because both were assigned to Corpus Christi festivities:

(1) Two untitled gild pageants, staged not later than 1416, by the Shearmen and Taylors' Company, and by the Weavers' Company, comprise the remains of an earlier group, which originally consisted of ten plays. The manuscripts of the surviving two were destroyed by fire in Birmingham in 1879, but had been published by Thomas Sharp in 1825 and 1836 respectively.

(2) The other group is a cycle of forty-eight short plays, known as *Ludus Coventriae*, preserved in MS B.M. Cotton Vespasian DVIII, which was largely the work of a co-ordinating scribe. The Latin tag was born of misapprehended statements by Robert Cotton's librarian, and the antiquarian William Dugdale, that this cycle was sponsored by the Grey Friars of Coventry. The much-revised MS suggests that the dialect came from East Anglia, but the document cryptically assigns the pageantry to 'N-town'. One of the plays in the collection bears the date 1468. The collection was much too long to be performed at a single festival.

Under the manorial system, delimited areas were empowered by charter to hold leet-courts and keep records of their jurisdictions. *The Coventry Leet Book* (ed. M. D. Harris, EETS, 1907-13) and

T. Sharp's *Dissertation on the Pageants or Dramatic Mysteries, Anciently performed at Coventry* (1825) show that this city was close enough to London to attract large audiences to its Corpus Christi pageants. All ruling monarchs from Richard III to Elizabeth I visited Coventry for this purpose. What these notables came to see was the trade-gild Cycle, not the so-called *Ludus Coventriae*; and it has been suggested that the latter was the repertory of a touring group, in which most of the *Passion* series was adapted from a Northern Cycle. The compiler of the *Ludus* displayed great ingenuity in giving order to the miscellaneous material; but his work sometimes lacks the dignity, and always the humour, of the other cycles. *The Salutation and Conception* is strictly a poem in dialogue form, that leans heavily to the Morality technique.

The dual theme of the Shearmen and Taylors' Pageant in the gild Cycle is 'The Adoration of the Kings and the Slaughter of the Innocents'. Appended is the speech of the first king, based on Matthew II. 1–12:

> I REX. Now blessid be God of his swet sonde,
>   For yondur a feyre bryght star I do see!
> Now ys he comon, vs a-monge,
>   Asse the profet seyd thatt yt schuld be.
>
> A seyd there schuld a babe be borne,
>   Comyng of the rote of Jesse,
> To sawe mankynd that wasse for-lorne;
>   And truly comen now ys he.
>
> Reyuerence and worschip to hym woll I do
>   Asse God and man, thatt all made of noght.
> All the profettis acordid and seyd evyn soo,
>   That with hys presseos blod mankynd schuld be boght.
>   (*Two Coventry Corpus Christi Plays*, ed. H. Craig EETS,
>   1957, p 19, lines 540–51)

This simple, narrative style, has only the humblest literary merit. Yet the not unworthy aim of the Coventry gild plays was imaginative enlargement of the New Testament. Both plays reveal how important a role the Bible played in the life of the people. According to Sharp's *Dissertation* one of the lost pageants, presented by the Smiths, Cappers and Drapers had the naive title of 'Taking down of God from the Cross' (Craig, Intro. p xvi). The value of the *Coventry Leet Book* is the light it throws on the staging, financing and elaborate presentation of plays; some were still being performed when Shakespeare began to write his great tragedies. In Coventry religious folk were zealously devoted to veneration of the Virgin Mary.

The earliest extant Morality is *The Castell of Perseverence*, provisionally dated *c* 1405, but the manuscript belongs to a generation later. Apart from the instructive stage directions, external evidence leads one to conclude that this was a touring venture, of Lincolnshire origin. Several different stanza forms are used, but the bulk of the play is in thirteen-lined groups, of which eleven are four-stressed, and the other two three-stressed. The rhyme scheme (a b a b a b a b a c c c a) having only three rhymes, vocabulary sometimes becomes a problem. All characters are personifications that do not have the status of 'humours'; didactic monologue usurps the function of true dialogue. This makes *The Castell of Perseverance* a highly abstract form of entertainment; a dramatist can hardly sustain much interest in a character styled *Humanum Genus*. His customary mode of speech is verbose soliloquy, for he only *contemplates* action:

> A, Schryfte°, blessyd mote thou be! [absolution]
> This castel is here but at honde;
> Thedyr rathely wyll I tee°, [go]
> Sekyr over this sad sonde.
> Good perseveraunce God sende me.
> Whyle I leve here in this londe!
> Ffro fowle fylthe now I fle,
> Fforthe to faryn now I fonde° [try]
> To yone precyous port,
> Lord, what man is in mery lyve
> Whanne he is of hes synnys schreve!
> Al my dol° adoun is dreve, [trouble]
> Christe is my counfort.
> (Pollard, ibid., p 76, lines 396–408)

Miracle and Morality plays continued to flourish until the end of the sixteenth century, which accords them a life, in England, of some five centuries. Though inspired by the Church, they would not have borne fruit without civic involvement. The major part of play-conception was the task of clerics, whose theological training did not help them to become genuine poets. The stanzaic verse they favoured (a compromise with reformed alliterative rhythms) was not congenial to natural dialogue. Nor did they often realize that there can be no drama without human action and inter-action. When the folk-play intervenes, native humour frequently asserts itself. Wherever didacticism is paramount, however, puppet characters give vent to moralizing, which lacks the dynamic power of the *Book of Job*, a supreme example of the static drama.

CHAPTER XV

The Close of the Middle Ages

🅖🅖🅖🅖🅖🅖

IT IS A TRUISM that there are no breaks in history; all periods tend to be arbitrary divisions, even when the intention is merely to demarcate trends in development. The Middle Age in England did not end with the death of Chaucer, or the dethronement of Richard II, though these events preceded important political changes. The deposition, following so soon after that of Edward II in 1327, imposed severe limitations on the line of Lancastrian kings, who were invariably in financial difficulties, because their household expenses were monitored by parliament. The tragic consequences of Bolingbroke's usurpation were perceived by the chroniclers and by Shakespeare. One result was that the magnates responsible for the removal of Richard grew in strength, until, like most rivals, they fell out, and destroyed their own feudal power. Universal distrust was the inevitable outcome of civil disobedience.

Seven kings ruled in England in the disturbed fifteenth century; but they themselves produced only such change as was forced upon them by social conditions. The break with tradition came from the dissolution of the monasteries and the collapse of the papal connection. The invention of printing foreshadowed educational advance, but the enlightenment of the masses was by no means immediate. The loss of the Church's secular power through home-appointment of ecclesiastical officers was accompanied by a growing scepticism on the part of some English people. English thinkers began to appreciate and employ the resources of their language; becoming more articulate, they enlarged a capacity to reason about the causes of their condition. Merchants grasped the social significance of political economy and used their bargaining power with ruling monarchs to match the feudal lords in government influence. Some saw in the failure of the chivalric ideal a political analogue with the

382

tragedy of King Arthur.

Shakespeare reviewed the signs of decline in reverse order, starting with the Yorkist-Lancastrian struggle for power, which ended in the defeat of both parties. Like Malory and Caxton, he was conservative; by unique insights he identified the fortunes of kings with the destiny of nations; but as a genuine humanist, he forebore to take only a moral view of history. In *Henry V,* by comparing the lot of kings with that of their humblest people, Shakespeare exploited the irony of contrast, and was not troubled whether he wrote chronicles or histories. In the Chronicles, anecdote and events provide the dominant interest; in the Histories the emphasis is on political or private morality, through character.

Langland and Chaucer were aware of the corruptions of their time; but the needed improvement they implied was opposed by Church and rulers, partly through self-interest, and partly because sterile minds fear the consequences, even of peaceful change. It was not realized that forces of disruption lay in the hierarchical structure of feudal society. In whatever sphere, rulers ignored the growing strength of the middle, mercantile and yeoman classes, through *osmosis,* the unconscious assimilation of ideas. The unacknowledged new gentry, largely anti-clerical, demanded and acquired for itself, secular education, better conditions of living and improved techniques of production. Reason was invoked to undermine popular superstitions, and worshippers tended to make the parish church the centre of their religious activities. The lay population was inevitably up-graded by the demise of the self-destructive warrior class; but all were disadvantaged by civil riot, siege and the curtailment of trade with the rest of Europe. In the fifteenth century Burgundy actually placed an embargo on English wool.

The House of Lancaster was dogged by misfortune throughout its sixty-year tenure of the government; and this was regarded by Henry IV himself as due retribution. Henry IV received threatening anonymous letters, and was not allowed to forget that he was a usurper. Every move he made was cautious, until he had suppressed the rebellions of Hotspur and Owen Glendower. In his campaigns he was loyally supported by a recreant son, but declined to agree to his desire for aggression against France, a policy which he considered to reflect the reckless ardour of youth.

The King wanted to be exemplary in tact, patience and mercy, but failed in the last, because his position was largely due to Church support, and this was over-zealous in suppressing heresy. In maintaining good relations with Archbishop Arundel, he was persauded in 1401 to sign a statute aganst Lollardism, *De heretico comburendo*; this law was to have fatal results for Catholicism in England. In 1409 John Bradby, a dissenting tailor of Evesham, was condemned to be burnt at the stake in Smithfield; his offence was outspoken disbelief in the doctrine of transubstantiation (consecration of the eucharist). Young Prince Henry, who was present, was greatly moved by the man's courage, and tried to persuade him to relent. But unlike the aged John Purvey, Wyclif's successor in biblical translation, he refused to recant, and suffered the penalty.

Though driven underground by persecution, Lollardry maintained its hold over a considerable section of the population in London and the Midland towns; it became a major force in preparing the way for the Reformation. The most celebrated, but also defamed, of the aristocratic Lollards was Sir John Oldcastle, Lord Cobham, who had fought for the King on the Welsh Border, and was a personal friend of the Prince. Though a conscientious churchman, he was regarded as evasive when interrogated for heresy, became angered, and fomented a rebellion in 1413 (reign of Henry V). The revolt of his followers was put down with great ferocity, and resulted in more than thirty public hangings at St Giles' Fields. Sir John himself escaped from custody, but was recaptured in 1417, and met the same fate with remarkable stoicism. In medieval tradition, death by hanging was to be publicly disgraced.

Henry V, Shakespeare's hero-king, who removed the crown for safe-keeping before his father's death, was too busy a statesman to brood over dissension at home; he was determined to press his claims to the kingdom of France, which he did with a self-assurance that amazed his contemporaries. He at once rejected the frivolities of his youth, and ruled with a humourless justice that soon gained the approval of the under-privileged classes. One of his first acts to placate the ghost of Richard II was to have the body reinterred beside that of his wife in Westminster Abbey. He was a lover of music, and a patron of poets, such as Lydgate and Hoccleve. Henry had been a soldier since the age of fifteen, and in the storming of Aberystwyth and Harlech had shown some expertise in siege tactics. He was wounded in the cheek at Shrewsbury, but refused to leave the field; he then formed the resolve to avoid pitched battles, as costly expedients. The loss of nearly half his army at the siege of Harfleur, where he used artillery with much effect, was due to disease and desertion, rather than enemy action. He more than compensated for any loss of morale in his men by his personal courage and powers of exhortation, qualities that Shakespeare's portrayal splendidly observed.

The King's success at Agincourt in October, 1415, was credited to divine intervention, being achieved against an army five times the strength of his own; the French were over-confident and divided in leadership. As at Crecy, the victory was chiefly ascribed to the archers; among many aristocratic prisoners, the Duke of Orleans returned with Henry to England a few weeks later. Two years elapsed before the King was prepared for a second invasion; but the risk of Agincourt was not again to be repeated. Siege warfare gave Henry time to use his diplomatic skill in protracted negotiations, which included a solution to the Papal Schism. With the capture of Caen (1417) and Rouen (1419) he was in a sound bargaining position; for the progress made was due partly to strife between Armagnacs (the Orleans party) and the Duke of Burgundy. In 1420 it was agreed that Henry should marry the French King's daughter, Katherine, and succeed to the throne of France upon Charles VI's death. After three years' absence, Henry returned to England to present his Queen. The marriage was not merely politically motivated, but it was genetically unwise, since Charles was periodically insane.

Now a feared and respected ruler, the King was soon recalled to France, because of the death in battle of his brother, the Duke of Clarence. The campaign in support of Burgundy's cause sapped his vitality, and he died of dysentry in his thirty-sixth year. His life, written at the suggestion of his younger brother, the 'good' Duke Humfrey of Gloucester, by Tito Livio of Forli, was translated into English in 1513, and became one of the sources of Shakespeare's play. Henry V appealed to Shakespeare because he was the last of the royal medievalists. When he captured a city, he meticulously observed certain priorities. First he went to church to return thanks for victory; then he examined the treasures of the library. Thereafter, he did what he could to restore trade and to improve the local laws. He had immense confidence in himself as the instrument of God's Will. His was simply the function of a feudal lord to protect the limited rights of humans to enjoy life.

Henry VI was only nine months old when he ascended the throne in 1422, as the nominal head of two kingdoms. The Regency Council was headed by Henry Beaufort, Bishop of Winchester. The Beauforts were descendants of John of Gaunt by Katherine Swynford, legitimized by Richard II, but excluded from the succession by the parliament of Henry IV. John, Duke of Bedford, another brother of the late king, who was his deputy in England during the French campaigns, became Regent in France. During the latter's attempts to suppress rebellion, Joan of Arc was captured by the Burgundians in 1430, and handed over to the English for trial. Shakespeare shows her ignominious treatment as a witch; but there are irreconcilable circumstances and inaccuracies in the play *1 Henry VI*. Joan of Arc had actually been dead for twenty-two years when Talbot was defeated. Whatever view one takes of Bernard Shaw's presentation of Joan of Arc, he does state clearly the circumstances of her arraignment:

> She was tried, not as a traitress, but as a heretic, blasphemer, sorceress and idolater. . . . She was in a state of invincible ignorance as to the Church's view . . . There was a great wrong done to Joan and to the conscience of the world by her burning. . . . The Church should have confined itself to excommunicating her. There it was within its rights: she had refused to accept its authority or comply with its conditions.
>
> (*St Joan*, Preface, pp 28–33)

The collapse of the English cause in France was largely due to lack of funds and reinforcements, and was accelerated by the desertion of Burgundian allies, who rejected Henry VI's title to the French throne. The unhappy Regent, Bedford, died in 1435. Ten years later Henry VI was induced to marry the sixteen-year-old princess, Margaret of Anjou, in order to restore Anglo-French relations; but the price was the final surrender of Normandy and Maine. Public disapproval and the new Queen's forceful personality led to a renewal of the war with France in 1449, and to a further drain on England's financial resources. The French triumphed because of the superior might of their artillery against English archers. The Hundred Years War ended with the defeat of Talbot at Castillon in 1453; this is one of the finest episodes in Shakespeare's *1 Henry VI*. Talbot's was the type of patriotism that redeemed the treachery of quarrelling allies. He is portrayed in the spirit of a medieval crusading Christian, as Henry V aspired to be. Of the kingdom of France, Calais alone remained in English hands, a mere thirty-eight years after Agincourt.

Meanwhile the King's affairs had been sadly mismanaged at home. After the death of Duke Humfrey in 1447, the heir-apparent, Richard, Duke of York, led the opposition to the Beaufort faction, which was now headed by Edmund, Duke of Somerset. The kingdom's rising debt, inability to pay armed forces, and loss of Normandy were principal causes of the animosity towards the government. The chief Minister, William de la Pole, Duke of Suffolk, was impeached, and attempting to reach France, was murdered at sea. Pious Henry VI, who gave away a legacy of £2000 to found Eton College and King's College, Cambridge, had no longer the kind of personality to survive.

The Jack Cade scenes in Shakespeare's *2 Henry VI* show the futility of popular rebellion. This man was apparently an Irish adventurer (some say a doctor), who had served in the French wars, and had considerable qualities of leadership. In 1450 he defeated a detachment of the king's troops, sent to confront him at Sevenoaks, then occupied London for three days, and presented a petition, which voiced a long list of grievances. The government was charged with mismanagement, corruption, burdensome and unequal taxation, wrongful confiscation of property, the maintenance of low wage-rates, and the ruinous conduct of the war about to be concluded with France. National pride was at its lowest ebb. As in the Peasants' Revolt, the supporters of insurrection were placated by promises of pardon that were not fulfilled; and no action was taken on the solid grounds of the petition. The English rebellions of 1381, 1413 and 1450 were significant pointers to the state of public feeling. It was no wonder that public esteem turned to the House of York; for this group had cultivated good relations with the merchants and tradesmen.

Henry VI's hereditary malady began to reveal itself under stress, just before the birth of his son Edward in October 1453. Although he had apparently recovered by Christmas, 1454, York had successfully pressed his claim to take over the Regency, to the great indignation of Queen Margaret. Shakespeare's portrait of her, as a proud and vindictive royalist, is reasonably accurate, except for her impossible role as a chorus in *Richard III*, the purpose there being to comment on the baleful effects of court intrigue. She had, however, been sent to the Tower after the Battle of Tewkesbury

(1471), and remained there for four years, until ransomed by the King of France, on condition that she remained an exile from England.

By 1453 the Crown was in debt to the extent of four thousand pounds. In his introduction to *The Household of Edward IV*, A. R. Myers gives an illuminating account of the conduct of Henry VI's household (pp 2–10). Vast expenses were incurred, owing to the traditional need for ostentation and bounty in a competitive society. The formality of domestic arrangements in royal and noble establishments was at that time modelled on the Court of Burgundy, whose Duke dictated fashions, manners and entertainments. No Lancastrian monarch had the means to compete with him; Henry VI's annual income, for instance, was only £5000.

Through her personal animosities, Queen Margaret incited the Houses of York and Lancaster to test their relative strengths. Trouble on the English-Welsh border was exploited by the opportunist, Richard, Duke of York, who raised his army on Yorkist estates in the Marches of Wales, chiefly Herefordshire and Shropshire, then Welsh areas.

The Wars of the Roses began with Richard's victory over Henry VI at St Albans in 1455. Notable Welsh supporters of the Lancastrian cause were the Tudors of Anglesey, cousins of Owen Glendower; Edmund Tudor and his brother, Jasper, Earl of Pembroke, were half-brothers of Henry VI. This came about because the Queen Mother, Katherine, widow of Henry V, had had a lasting liaison with Owen Tudor, Clerk of the Wardrobe, and bore him four children. When the secret relationship was discovered, the unfortunate Owen was sent to Newgate prison, but subsequently released.

Much of the fighting took place in Herefordshire; and when Henry was captured by the Earl of Warwick (the Kingmaker) in 1460, the Queen and her son took refuge in Harlech. The Welsh enabled her to defeat York and Warwick at Wakefield and St Albans, respectively, in 1461. But the Welsh armies of the Tudors were defeated at Mortimer's Cross by the Duke of York's son, Edward of March, a descendant of Llywelyn the Great, who became the next English king (Edward IV) at the age of nineteen. Owen Tudor was captured in that battle, and afterwards executed; his grandson was to become Henry VII.

Pleasure-loving Edward IV (1461–83) was an able soldier, a

student of alchemy, and the patron of William Caxton, the first English printer. There are several valuable references to events of his reign in the *Paston Letters*. In spite of a large family and nepotism on behalf of his Woodville relations, he was the first English king, since Henry II, to acquire wealth, after paying the debts of his predecessor. When he returned from temporary exile in Holland in 1471, he conducted a brilliant campaign for the recovery of his kingdom, achieved in three months. War now ceased, at home and abroad. In a few years Louis XI of France was to pay him a handsome pension (or bribe); he also made money astutely out of investments in trade. He shocked aristocratic conservatism by fraternizing with the merchant class, for instance in his relationship with Jane Shore; but he undoubtedly stimulated business and increased customs revenue, in the face of the monopolies of the Hanseatic League.

The Yorkist supporters in Wales included notable lords, such as William ap Thomas of Raglan, and the Nevilles of Abergavenny; their losses in men at the battle of Banbury in 1469 were considerable. The final defeat of the Lancastrian cause came at Barnet and Tewkesbury in 1471, where Henry VI lost his son, and soon after his own life. Henry Tudor of Penmynydd in Anglesey, whose father had been created Earl of Richmond in 1452, became the surviving heir of the house. The fact that Owen Tudor had supposedly married Henry V's widow, did not make Richmond's claim a strong one, as the marriage had been declared illegal; what carried more weight was Henry's marriage in 1486 to Edward IV's daughter Elizabeth, and his ability to speak Welsh. He did not want his title to be dependent on this marriage.

For a decade Henry Tudor bided his time in France, and his landing at Milford Haven in 1485 was supported by the French king Charles VII, friend of the Lancastrian refugees. Richmond's advance from Newport to Welshpool was permitted by Rhys-ap Thomas, the king's chamberlain in west Wales. Herds of cattle were driven from the north to feed his forces. The overthrow of Richard III at Bosworth Field was made possible by Welsh support of Henry Tudor, and the defection of eight thousand men under Sir William Stanley, Justice of North Wales. Thirty-five bards are said to have foretold the King's deliverance of his country from its oppressors. The standard he bore to battle was of the design of the mythical seventh-century chief Cadwaladr, consisting of a red dragon on a field of white and green. Henry's loyal supporters from Wales were rewarded in due time with English citizenship, minor offices and sometimes estates; and the 'Yeomen of the Guard', charged with the protection of his safety, consisted largely of Welshmen.

The Wars of the Roses brought important changes in the administration of Wales. The Crown took the opportunity of alienating feudal lordships that had supported the rival cause. But when higher church offices fell vacant, they were generally given to Welshmen. Jasper Tudor, Earl of Pembroke, became Chief Justiciar of Wales; bondsmen tenants were granted their liberty; Henry VII took an active interest in the development of printing.

One of the most dependable recorders of Henry VII's reign, and indeed of English history until the mid-sixteenth century, was Polydore Vergil, an Italian from Urbino, who settled in England about 1502. He was naturalized in 1510, and held many church offices until his death in 1555. Henry Tudor befriended him and encouraged the writing of his *English History*, published in Latin in 1534. Its twenty-six books took the historical record up to 1509; but twenty-nine years were added in the second edition of 1555. Polydore was the first historian of England to grasp the necessity of research among records, and to disabuse the public mind concerning the veracity of popular tradition and folklore, having in mind the so-called 'history' of Arthur found in Geoffrey of Monmouth. He actually edited the work of Gildas.

John Gower (c 1330–1408), the friend and, some say, the mentor of Chaucer, foresaw the decline of the Middle Ages. There is good reason why Caxton, after printing *The Canterbury Tales*, followed it with Gower's *Confessio Amantis*. Both poets were 'courtly makers', as well as humanists ahead of their time. Gower is perhaps the most neglected English poet of the fourteenth century; so argues J. H. Fisher in his scholarly biography. His reputation continued to be high until the English Renaissance and he figures in several works including Shakespeare's *Pericles*, and Jonson's masque, *The Golden Age Restored*.

Gower was of Yorkshire extraction, but settled in Kent and lived nearly all his life in London, where from 1376–86 he was in close contact with Chaucer. They exchanged literary confidences, when both were at the height of their achievement. Gower's poetry contains many of the characteristics of medieval thinking; but he lacked creative talent, and had not the acute observation and humour of Chaucer. He wrote for the aristocratic class, and his outlook was essentially moral. There was no difficulty in getting his message across in Latin and Anglo-Norman, because his style in all three languages he used was simple and often attractive. Gnomic wisdom compensates for fulsome complaint and prosaic length, which were responsible for most of his tedium. Gower's importance to the understanding of the late Middle Ages cannot be overestimated. He offers the most satisfactory critique of courtly love in early English; for he demolishes both its pretensions and artificiality, and argues for the greater stability of the married state.

John Leland, in his mid-sixteenth-century *Itinerary*, described Gower as a lawyer, who practised in London; he may have been one of the earliest poets to grace the Inns of Court, which had become a 'Lawyers' University' by the late fourteenth century. He was well-to-do, purchased property in nearby counties, and devoted himself fully to poetry after 1377, when he retired to St Mary Overy's Priory at Bridge Gate in Southwark, not far from Chaucer's Tabard Inn.

The three major works of Gower's life are interdependent, completing a philosophical picture of his moral attitudes to medieval society. The first work was *Mirour de L'Omme* (Gower himself styled it *Speculum Hominis*), a poem of some thirty thousand lines, written in Anglo-Norman (1376–8); in line 18825 he refers pointedly to the disastrous Schism of the Roman Church, which began in 1378. The MS of the *Mirour* (Cambridge University Library, Additional 3035), was not discovered until 1895, when G. C. Macaulay, the editor of Gower's works, had his attention drawn to it by the University Librarian. Then came *Vox Clamantis*, in Latin elegiac couplets, of which there are early (*c* 1382) and later versions. In its 10,265 lines Gower's careful revision of texts first becomes apparent. Eleven manuscripts are extant, four of which contain *Cronica Tripertita* (an account, written in 1400, of the last years of Richard II), together with three 'laureate' poems presented to Henry IV at his coronation (October 1399). The third major work, this time in English, was *Confessio Amantis*, of which there are many MSS, representing different stages of development, the earliest about 1390, and the latest (the Fairfax MS) dated about

1393. This contains over 33,000 lines, and 141 tales in regular octosyllabic couplets. It was originally written at the behest of Richard II, to extol courtly love; the theme is not unlike that of the French authors of *The Romaunt of the Rose*.

There were lesser works, such as the *Cinkante Balades* of the Trentham Hall MS, written in Anglo-Norman before 1374; they advocate married love, and were probably intended for the merchants' *Pui*, a London club resembling the Rotary, to encourage composition. The *Traitié*, another sequence of ballades on the same theme, must have been penned at various times after 1385; a translation into Northern Middle English was made by Quixley, about the year 1400. The Provençal ballade was a poem of limited rhymes, usually written in three stanzas, concluding with an envoy; the last line of the opening stanza is repeated as a refrain. Gower's last work in English (also in the Trentham MS) was addressed to the new King, Henry IV, and now bears the title *In Praise of Peace*. It was composed in rime-royal, (a named derived from the occasion of this poem), and contains fifty-five stanzas. By this time (c 1400) Gower had become afflicted with blindness. *The Major Latin Works* were translated by E. W. Stockton in 1962.

It is clear that Gower had transferred his loyalties from King Richard to Henry Bolingbroke by 1393, so that until the present century he was often regarded as a medieval Vicar of Brae. This charge is unjust, since he was disillusioned, after the murder of Thomas of Woodstock, by the misrule and avarice of the Court group, and made the duties of kingship, and the right of the people to justice, dominant themes of his poetry. The political philosophy of the Three Estates (the Lords spiritual, the Lords temporal, and the Commons) looms large in his poetry, and especially in *Vox Clamantis*, which opens with a graphic description of the Peasants' Revolt in 1381. Gower was a believer in the classical slogan *Vox populi, vox Dei*, and said 'Nothing I write is my own opinion. Rather I shall speak what the voice of the people has reported to me' (*Vox Clamantis* IV. 19). Like Chaucer in *Troilus and Criseyde*, he regarded London as the 'New Troy'; but he detested Lollardry. Throughout his life he expressed dislike of continuous warfare, which the country had experienced since the reign of Edward III, and he urged the advantages of peace:

The werre bringth in poverte at hise hieles,

Whereof the comon people is sore grieved;
The werre hath set his cart on thilke whieles
Wher that fortune mai noght be believed.
For whan men wene best to have achieved,
Ful ofte it is al newe to beginne:
The werre hath no thing siker, though he winne.

Forthi, my worthi prince, in Cristes halve,
As for a part whos feith thou hast to guide,
Ley to this olde sor a newe salve,
And do the werre awei, what so betide:
Pourchace pes, and set it be thi side,
And suffre noght thi poeple be devoured,
So schal thi name evere after stonde honoured.

(Verses addressed to Henry IV)

The effigy on Gower's tomb, now in Southwark Cathedral, bears a double 'S' collar, clasped by a swan, which was once the emblem of Thomas of Woodstock, Duke of Gloucester. After his death (or even before), the symbol in the form of a silver collar was adopted by Henry Bolingbroke, Earl of Derby, who presented it to Gower, in recognition of the dedication to himself of *Confessio Amantis*. It is worth noting that the Lancastrian troops in the Wars of the Roses wore an 'S' on their tunics, and not the symbol of the red rose. The scene in Shakespeare's *1 Henry VI* of the symbolic plucking of the white and red roses is a pretty sixteenth-century fiction.

Amans in *Confessio Amantis*, who stands for reason and perception, is a persona for Gower himself, as well as a symbol for natural love. The poet writes candidly of his own experience; but though an admirer of Ovid's *Ars Amatoria*, he was incapable of that writer's cynical circumspections. In making his Confessor, named Genius, a priest of Venus, he was not entirely original, since the idea had occurred in de Meun's contribution to the *Romance of the Rose*. Venus is not the goddess of the Greek pantheon, which Gower as a churchman was at pains to reject in favour of Christian ethics. It is part of the wisdom of maturity, he concludes, that the *eros* of youth should give way to the *caritas* of age.

Several of the tales that Gower selects from the past to illustrate his elaborate classification of the Seven Deadly Sins appear also in Chaucer's *Legend of Good Women* and other writings; they were retold, with a moral twist, perhaps to gratify the taste of King Richard's queen. As stories, they give the impression that Gower was dealing with Augustinian abstractions, rather than persons.

393

C. S. Lewis in *The Allegory of Love* (p 210) thought that 'Gower is "romantic" in the nineteenth-century meaning of the word'; but John Lawlor in an essay 'On Romanticism in the *Confessio Amantis*', takes a different view (see *Patterns of Love and Courtesy*, pp 122–40). Lawlor seems to think of *romance* in the Coleridgean context, an extension of consciousness through the sensuous application of words; whereas Lewis speaks of it as a bridge between the conscious and unconscious mind. Gower principally deplores love as sexual cupidity. What is irrational is a lover's self-delusion about the uniqueness of feminine beauty, usually expressed in emotive terms.

The penitential tradition evident in Gower's work may be the result of his reading in the library of the Priory at St Mary Overys. On pages 36–7 of Russell A. Peck's critical exposition, *Kingship and Common Profit in Confessio Amantis*, the writer presents a list of the progeny of the Seven Deadly Sins, and their Remedies, which Gower's tales were intended to illustrate. Such terms as *Orguil* 'pride', *Surquiderie* 'presumption', *Fals Semblant* 'deception', *Contek* 'strife', *Accidie* 'sloth', *Covoitise* 'dispossession', *Ravyne* 'seizure', and *Simony* 'trading in benefices', occur frequently as personifications; all are of Latin-French origin.

The homiletic strain is strong in Book VII of *Confessio Amantis*, and Gower does not shrink from discussing openly desirable principles for the education of a king. One is instruction in rhetoric, regarded as the study of words and their meanings. Lines 1507–1640 suggest that one of the functions of rhetoric is to urge citizens to lead better lives. Thus Ulysses and Catiline are condemned as perverters of words for political ends. The argument demonstrates the practicality of medieval ethics, and shows the extent to which Gower's thinking was influenced by Boethius's *Consolations of Philosophy*. Gower's understanding of human nature is distinctly bookish, and he follows the conventional line in blaming Pope Boniface VIII for the worldliness of the medieval Church.

Chaucer inhabits the same intellectual world, but his criticism is more economical, less doctrinaire. The relationship between these two writers is complex, and resembles that of T. S. Eliot and Ezra Pound. Fisher thinks that Chaucer owed more to indigenous sources of inspiration than he did to Italy, and that Gower's social critiques were influential (op. cit., p 205). Chaucer is easily distinguishable from Gower by the merits of his style, chiefly urbanity, raillery and greater variety. In Fisher's view, *Confessio Amantis* and the incomplete *Legend of Good Women* (c 1386) 'appear to stem from the same royal command' – that of Richard II and his Queen (op. cit., pp 235–6). *Troilus and Criseyde*, and especially the fabliaux element in the *Canterbury Tales*, set Chaucer apart from Gower; the author of *Confessio Amantis* could never have created a character like the Wife of Bath.

Gower's poetic language is less figurative than Chaucer's, but more correct metrically. The rhythms of verse in the contemporary languages, Anglo-Norman and English, that Gower employed, might be expected to differ considerably; but this is not the case. Gower was a syllabist in both media, which suggests that his French dialect tends to follow the principles of English accentuation, in which strong stress alternates with weak. One does not find in Gower the evenness of Central French poetry. This, as G. C. Macaulay pointed out, had a considerable effect on the future of English metre, as practised by Chaucer and Hoccleve. The inter-action, this editor says, 'was so alien to English traditions that it could not survive the changes caused in the literary language by the loss of weak inflectional syllables; and, therefore, in the fifteenth century, English metre, for a time, practically collapsed' (*Cambridge History of English Literature*, vol. II, p 143).

Outside Chaucer, the most cultivated development of Middle English is to be found in Gower. His spelling is fairly consistent, and his use of the final -e reflects either length of the preceding vowel, or a rudimentary inflexion, sometimes both. Gower never permits the initial monosyllabic feet of Chaucer, and tries to avoid imperfect rhyme. The regularity of his lines accounts in some degree for the sameness of his rhythms, though he is careful to vary the position of internal pauses, and to cultivate syntactical enjambement.

Towards the end of *Confessio Amantis,* Venus addresses her suppliant, Amans, in the following lines, the supple movement of which amply displays the Gower technique:

> A peire of bedes blak as sable
> Sche tok and heng my neck(e) aboute;
> Upon the gaudes al withoute
> Was writ(e) of gold,| *Por reposér.*
> 'Lo,' thus sche seide,|'John Gowér,
> Now thou art ate laste cast,

> This hav(e) I for thin ese cast,
> That thou nomor(e) of love sieche.
> Bot my will is that thou besieche
> And prei(e) hierafter for the pes,
> And that thou mak(e) a plein reles
> To lov(e),│which takth litel hiede
> Of olde men upon the nede,
> Whan that the lustes ben aweie:
>   . . .
> And gret wel Chaucer whan ye mete,
> As mi discipl(e) and mi poete:
> For in the floures of his youthe
> In sondri wis(e), as he wel couthe,
> Of ditees and of songes glade,
> The which(e) he for mi sake made,
> The lond fulfild is overal:
> Whereof to him in special
> Above all(e) othr(e) I am most holde.
>   (Book VIII, lines 2904–17, 2941–9)

There is a natural charm in Gower's simplicity, which is preferable
to rhetorical striving for effect, as in *Vox Clamantis* (V.53).
Stockton translates the sophisticated oxymorons as follows:

> Love is sickly health, troubled rest, pious error, warlike peace, a
> pleasant wound, a delightful calamity, an anxious joy, a devious path, a
> dark light.

No doubt, Shakespeare, Lyly and Spenser knew Gower; they all
seemed to approve the medieval cast of his mind.

One of the enduring tributes to Chaucer's genius was the influence
he exerted on poets in the fifteenth century and beyond. His impact
on English has been excelled only by Shakespeare; while in the
technicalities of verse, the contribution Chaucer made was unique,
though often misunderstood. The dispute concerning his followers,
Thomas Hoccleve and John Lydgate, dubbed the English Chaucerians, proves this to the hilt.

Hoccleve (c 1368–1430) was an entertaining Londoner, whose
autobiographical verses described him as a scrivener, serving in the
office of the Privy Seal. In *La Male Règle* (1406) the eight-line
stanzas (rhyming a b a b b c b c) tell of a misspent youth, its effects
on his health, and final breakdown, where the symptoms are of

considerable psychological interest. The longest and most lively work of Hoccleve is the *Regement of Princes* (1411–12), which was written in rime-royal for Prince Hal, a year before his coronation as Henry V. The first two thousand lines consist mainly of a dialogue with an old beggar in colloquial style, whose simplicity and variety reveal Hoccleve at his best. Stanzas 16, 130 and 143 are quoted from F. J. Furnivall's edition for the EETS, 1897:

> Þe smért of þóght, | Í by experiénce
>   knówe as wéll as ány man do lýuỳnge;
> His frósty swóot|& fýry hote feruénce,
>   And tróubly drémes, | drémpt al in wákỳnge,
>   My máyzed héed sléeplees han of kónnỳnge,
>   And wýt dispóylyd, |& só me be-iápỳd,
>   Þát after déþ|ful óften haue I gápìd.
>
> "Þóu þat yclómben art in hý honoúrès,
>   And hást þis wórldes wélth at thy deuýs,
> And báthist now in yóuthes lústy flóurès,
>   Be wár, | réde I! | þou stándist on þe ýs:
>   It háth ben séen, | as wéleful and as wýs
>   As þóu, | han slíde: | and þóu þat no pítèe
>   On óthir fólk hast, | whó schal réwe on þé?"
>
> "A wríter mòt thré thýnges to hym knýtte,
>   And in thó may be nó disseùeránce;
> Mýnde, ée, and hánd, | nón may fro óthir flítte,
>   But in hem mót be ióynt contìnuánce.
>   The mýnde al hóole|with-outen vàriánce
>   On þe ée and hánd awáyte moot alwáy,
>   And þéi two eek on hým; | it is nó náy."
>
> (pp 5, 33, and 37)

One difficulty here is to determine the relative weight of stress on polysyllabic rhyme-words.

Hoccleve's output amounts to only some thirteen thousand lines; but, despite its didacticism, there is much of social and historical value. Nearly all the poems are in stanza form, consisting of seven or eight lines; these are of no less than nine, and no more than eleven syllables, the bulk being decasyllabic.

Hoccleve is pleasing to read, as his diction is even plainer than Gower's; he is as free from aureate terms as Chaucer, though a much less gifted poet. Clearly, his verses were not what metrists call iambic pentameters. To think of the fifteenth-century heroic line in terms of feet is futile, as the locus classicus of C. S. Lewis in *Essays and Studies of the English Association* (vol. XXIV, 1938, pp 28–41) shows conclusively. Language change, Lewis maintains, has little to do with the metrical shortcomings of Hoccleve and Lydgate; they were not aiming to do what nineteenth-century critics and editors have claimed to be their purpose. They merely wanted, like Chaucer, an English approximation to the French hexameter or the Italian *endecasillabo* of Dante and Boccaccio, both of which had strict syllable-count, but no metrical pattern of accentual syllables.

Anyone who reads Hoccleve carefully will find lines of approximately ten syllables, with four strong beats, so disposed as to secure the rhyme-scheme of the stanza he favoured. His decasyllabic lines do not reveal the sophistication of a medial caesura; for Chaucer had taught fellow artists that no such break was essential, English syntax being better accommodated to a flexible distribution of internal pauses. Chaucer is invariably praised by his successors as a 'rhetor', not as a metrist. Indeed, it was two centuries before metrical feet were mooted by Gascoigne, as a means of detecting the rhythmical movement of groups of verses. Lewis observes (p 32): 'If Chaucer meant his lines to be read as the modern scholar reads them, it is extremely likely that he was disappointed.' A twentieth-century reader speaks the verses as modern editors determine, largely because he is trained for metrical analysis, and finds it much more satisfying to do so. It was John Urry who first proclaimed the normalizing of Chaucer's text in his edition of 1721.

We cannot yet be certain how late Middle English was pronounced, or whether the final *-e* of verbs, nouns and adjectives was an editorial spelling device, or a rudimentary inflexion (see the end of chapter X). Therefore it is difficult to determine precisely the number of syllables in a line, or where the stress fell in words of more than one syllable (see my *Language of Renaissance Poetry*, pp 31–4). But if foot division, which was unknown to poets of the fourteenth and fifteenth centuries, is eschewed, their lines are rhythmically intelligible. Several factors have, however, to be borne in mind. Lines of poetry should not be taken in isolation. The virgules of MSS are rhetorical signals, not caesural pauses, which means that the delivery of the lines was considered more important than theories about structure. The *count* of stresses and syllables is as important as their accentual disposition. Elision is not indicated by symbols, and seldom by spelling.

Seymour Chatman in *A Theory of Metre* (Mouton, 1965, p 113) regards syllables as *events*, and holds that metre is a 'complex secondary rhythm, since it contains not only grouped events, but also groups of grouped events (lines) and even groups of groups of grouped events (stanzas)'. On the same page, Chatman groups Chaucer with Spenser, Shakespeare, Milton, Pope and others, as a 'member of the syllable-counting tradition of English verse'.

Hoccleve was apparently a man of timid nature, full of humility, even self-disparagement, concerning his verses. Here is his ballade to the Duke of Bedford, Regent of France, in the reign of Henry VI. The virgules are preserved in MS Huntington 111, from which the text is taken (see E.P. Hammond, *English Verse between Chaucer and Surrey*, p 76):

Vn to the ríal égles èxcellénce
Í|húmble Clérc|with al hértes húmblèsse
This bóok presénte/& of your réuerènce
Byséeche I párdon and foryéuenèsse
Þt of myn ígnorànce & léwdenèsse   5
Nát haue I wríte it in so góodly wýse
As þt me óght vn to your wórthynèsse
Myn yén|hath cústumed býsynèsse
So dáswed°|þt I máy no bét souffýse   [dazed]

2

I dréede lést þt my máister Mássỳ   10
Þt ís of frúctuous intélligènce
Whan hé behóldith hów vncónnynglỳ
My bóok is métrid/how ráw my sénténce
How féeble éek been my colóurs his prùdénce
Shal sóre encómbrid béen of my folíe   15
But yit trúste Í/þt his benéuolénce
Compléyne wóle myn insípiènce
Secréetly/& what is mís réctifiè

3

Thow bóok/by lícence of my lórdes gráce
To thée speke Í/and thís I to thee séye   20
I chárge thee/to shéwe thów thy fáce
Befórn my séid Máister/& to him préye
On my behálue/þt he péise and wéye
What mýn enténte is/þt I spéke in thée
For réthorik hath híd fro mé the kéye   25
Of hís tresón/nat déyneth hir nòbléye
Déle with nóon so ígnorant as mé

Hoccleve makes generous use of alliteration, but not as a

determining factor in the rhythm. The movement is not that of free verse; it is wholly controlled by the interlocking rhymes of the stanza form. Although the juxtaposition of accentual elements is occasionally harsh, as at the end of lines 14 and 18, the total effect of the stanzas is not unpleasant.

There is no mistaking Hoccleve's discursive individuality; his candour in dialogue, disarming femininity and courtly manners were an unusual combination for the harsh times in which he lived. He is conservative in politics, as the *Address to Sir John Oldcastle* shows (see p 384), and the abundant religious verse of the age is well represented in his *Ars Moriendi*. Where Hoccleve disappoints is in metaphor and other imagery; one may observe conventionality in all its decorative or formulaic pedestrianism, in *frosty swoot, fyry hote, mayzed heed, lusty floures* and *fructuous intelligence*. But Hoccleve is not as guilty of 'thwarted stress' or 'broken-backed doggerel' as Furnivall and Saintsbury suggest; their concept of the scansion of isolated lines, as demonstrated in examples, is sometimes naive. Southworth claims that 'Hoccleve had caught the surface rhythms of Chaucer's verse, but did not have within himself the ability to feel them deeply, and incidentally, to modify them to fit his own inner needs' (*Verses of Cadence*, p 78).

The English Court, from Richard II to Henry VI, was notable for its patronage of letters. Lancastrian kings encouraged and used poets in an attempt to emulate the culture of French and Burgundian Courts, on lines instigated by Queen Katherine of Valois and Margaret of Anjou. Humfrey, Duke of Gloucester, was another patron, to whom poets, such as Lydgate, were deeply indebted. In London, the scrivener, John Shirley, initiated the novel enterprise of copying, selling and lending manuscripts, which anticipated the printed book trade. Production could harldy keep pace with demand, and this may account for the quantity, if not the quality, of poetry in circulation. Some of the best came from two royal prisoners, James I of Scotland, and Charles, Duke of Orleans; after Agincourt they mixed freely in Court circles, and were influential in creating a wider taste for a cultivated courtly style.

Nevertheless, it was the monk of Bury St Edmunds, John Lydgate (1370–1450), who became the consulting poet of royalty for festive occasions. Josef Schick, who edited his *Temple of Glas* for the EETS, described him as 'a vast storehouse of medieval lore' (p xii); for he was a voluminous writer, whose verse quadrupled the output of Chaucer. By his contemporaries this Oxford scholar was regarded as the successful poet of the age; yet his stature has been progressively diminished by academic critics since the nineteenth century.

A close association between the Crown and the monastery at Bury, where Lydgate resided, meant that kings sometimes visited and rested there. The poet's choice of themes was invariably determined by the taste of his patrons, who included the leading political figures of his time. But the scope of several romantic-epic ventures was too ambitious for Lydgate's humble talent. Though he was intrigued by pseudo- and genuine history, in the art of narrative he was insufficiently selective. The stylistic sins were prolixity and wordiness. Lydgate's aimless repetitions, ornate vocabulary and ponderous syntax were the result of personal mannerisms, one of which was a fondness for participial clauses. Yet he was the author of a fine and influential dream-vision in the *Temple of Glas* (*c* 1403), a poem much indebted to Chaucer's *House of Fame*.

The minor poems have been allowed to contain some spontaneous writing; but the *Testament of Dan John Lydgate* is a different kind of autobiography from Hoccleve's. Stanzas 43 and 44 offer an instructive contrast with the style of Chaucer; the first is indebted to the opening lines of the Prologue to the *Canterbury Tales*, the second is Lydgate's own:

> First Zepherus with his blastes sote
>   Enspireth ver with newe buddes grene,
> The bawme ascendeth out of euery rote,
>   Causyng with flowres ageyn the sunne shene
>   May among mon[e]thes sitt like a quene,
> Hir suster Apryll watryng hir gardeynes
> With holsom shoures shad in the tender vynes.
>
> This tyme of Ver Flora doth hir cure,
>   With soleyne motlees passyng fressh and gay,
> Purpel colours wrought be dame nature,
>   Mounteyns, vales, and medewes for tarraye,
>   Hir warderobe open list not to delaye
> Large mesure to shewe out, and to shede
> Tresoures of fayre, whiche she doth possede°.

[possess, OF *posseder*]
(*Minor Poems*, Part II, EETS pp 341–2)

Notice Lydgate's conventional personification in *Ver Flora* and *dame nature;* prosaic expressions, such as *doth hir cure, for tarraye,* and *shewe out;* the jejune intensifier *passing;* and the banal metaphors *warderobe* and *Tresoures of fayre.* Only a decline in popular taste could explain the approval of such verses.

The development of syntax in English poetry was not helped by Lydgate's unexplained addiction to inversions. The *Ballade at the Reverence of Our Lady, Qwene of Mercy* contains many stanzas such as No. 3:

> Allas! unworthi I am both and unable,
> To loffe suche on, all women surmountyng,
> But she moost benygne be to me mercyable,
> That is of pite the welle and eke the spryng:
> Wherfore of hir, in laude and in preysyng,
> So as I can, supported by hir grace,
> Right thus I say, knelyng to-forn hir face
>
> (ibid., p 255)

There is no reason for the word order of 'unworthi *I am both* and unable'; for the awkwardness of line 3; for the unpoetic transposition of phrases in 4 and 5. Nor can the stilted language be ascribed entirely to a love of archaism. The aureate language seemed to demand decorative epithets and latinized words in order to appear unusual.

In the *Court of Sapience,* rhetoric is hailed as the mother of eloquence, whose sustenance begets the perfect pleasure of *beauperlaunce* (fine language). Lydgate speaks of the 'colours *purpureate* of rhetoric', which may be the origin of the phrase 'purple patch'. The high style of eloquence had a similar function to pigmentation in painting, falsely regarded as a reflection of colour in nature. But Lydgate, in some of his earliest verse, is polysyllabic for the sheer joy of flexing his rhetorical muscles. Here is the opening of *The Churl and the Bird:*

> Problemys, liknessis & ffigures
> Which previd been fructuous of sentence,
> And han auctoritees groundid on scriptures
> Bi resemblaunces of notable apparence,
> With moralites concludyng in prudence, –
> Lik as the Bible reherseth bi writyng,
> How trees somtyme ches him-silf a kyng
>
> (*Minor Poems,* part II, p 468)

But for line-segmentation and multiple rhyme, any reader might be excused for taking this verse as prose. Only the first, second and last lines have ten syllables; the third and fourth have twelve apiece, and the fifth and sixth, eleven.

The mature *Fall of Princes* (1430–38) has the distinction of being the longest of Lydgate's compositions; it was written at the behest of Duke Humfrey of Gloucester. The following stanza, in rime-royal, has ten syllables to the line in all but 1 and 5, where there are eleven:

> Whér is Túllius, chéeff lánterne off thi tóun,
> In réthorik all óther surmóuntỳng?
> Móral Sének, or prúdent sád Catóun,
> Thi cómoun próffit álwei preférrỳng,
> Or ríhtful Trájan, móst júst in his démỳng,
> Whích on no párti líst nat to declýne?
> But lóng procésse hath bróuht ál to rúỳne
>
> (Book II, lines 4488–94)

Lydgate's technique is the time-honoured one of cataloguing rhetorical questions; but the rhyming of polysyllables is palpably rough. The rhythm of the line-grouping is, however, more satisfying.

This *magnum opus* was the forerunner of the much more skilful *Mirrour for Magistrates*; its monotony is in part due to lack of planning in the narrative procedures. In his zeal for historical information, Lydgate becomes insensitive to the overall quality of his verse. Opinions still differ on the way many of his lines were spoken. Margaret Schlauch (*The English Language in Modern Times*, pp 41–2) has this to say on the Chaucer-Lydgate dilemma of metrical intention:

> If an occasional -*e* is demanded here and there by scansion, we may assume that it was preserved as a literary archaism.
> In medial unstressed syllables, the -[ə]- between consonants persisted longer. In the 15th century it is in general practice dropped only in the neighbourhood of liquids and nasals, as in the word *appalled* in the following lines from Lydgate's *Fall of Princes*, iv, 1646:
>
> > Law haddę perisshęd naddę be writyng;
> > Our feith appallęd, ner vertu of scripturę;
> > For al religioun and ordrę of lyuyng
> > Taketh ther examplę by doctryn of lettrurę.

[the dots under the *e*'s indicate that they are not pronounced]

The accentual status of other syllables is less clear, but such lines as these illustrate the reduction of stress on the suffixes in French words, and on -*ing* of English verbal nouns. An awkward amount of elision, syncope and slurring is sometimes necessary to make such lines by Lydgate and his contemporaries conform to the pattern of octosyllabic couplets. An exhaustive study of metrical practice at the time would probably reveal that they often permitted two or more unaccented syllables to intervene between those accented. Hence it is difficult to determine the precise status of those not receiving main stress.

Here again one has the fallacy that an acceptable rendering of the lines may be found by trimming the syllables to the theoretical pattern of scansion. If this writer's interpretation is correct, the syllable count is 8, 10, 11, 11, which implies greater latitude than usual with Lydgate. The lines are, indeed, claimed as octosyllabic, whereas the poet's probable intention was to make them decasyllabic.

Lydgate was not an original poet; he followed in the footsteps of Chaucer, even adopting his measures in three principal forms: (a) seven-line stanzas of rime-royal, (b) rhymed couplets of nominally five beats, for poems conceived on the epical scale, and (c) octosyllabic couplets, as used in the translation of *The Romaunt of the Rose*. In the minor poems only does he deviate from this practice, for instance in the use occasionally of an eight-line stanza. Lydgate's confession in the *Troy Book* clarifies his technique of translation – a happy chance, since most of his longer works are of this nature. The descent of the work, commissioned by Henry V and commenced in 1412, is complicated; but the greater part was translated from the Latin prose *Historia* of Guido delle Colonne (c 1287), who had himself condensed Benoît de Sainte-Maure's *Roman de Troie* (c 1160). Lydgate's procedure is volunteered in Book II, lines 180–85:

> I leue þe wordis and folwe þe sentence.
> And trouþ of metre I sette also a-syde,
> For of þat arte I hadde as þo no guyde
> Me to reducyn, whan I went a-wrong;
> I toke non hede nouþer of schort nor long,
> But to þe trouþe
> (*Troy Book*, ed. H. Bergen, EETS, part I, p 149)

There is little doubt that 'short nor long' refers, in English verse, not to quantity, but to unstressed and stressed syllables. Editor

Bergen's comment (Intro. p xvii) is:

> ... His somewhat arbitrary inclusion or omission of unaccented syllables shows plainly enough that the tendency he followed (quite aside from his merits or demerits as a metrist) was to return from Chaucer's and Gower's syllabic purism to the rougher and readier traditional usage of his countrymen.

There is a consolatory note in Schick's observation (*Temple of Glas*, p lvi) that 'hardly a good critical text of Lydgate's writings' exists.

That Lydgate lacked Chaucer's 'good ear' is an understatement, and the problem is aggravated by the unfortunate system of rhyme he practised, to the permanent disablement of his stanza form. Sometimes he is content simply with assonance; but mostly, he ventures to rhyme on the unstressed or weakly stressed elements of words having more than one syllable. This may throw the harmony of rhythm completely out of gear; which is a pity, because in the *Siege of Thebes* Lydgate indulged an ambition to supplement Chaucer's *Canterbury Tales*. Against the quoted conclusion of Margaret Schlauch, Schick expressed the conviction that 'the final -*e* is sounded by Lydgate nearly in all cases which Chaucer sounds it' (op. cit., p lxiii).

Much more attention might have been given to Lydgate's language than his metre, for his vocabulary is extensive. He wrote a dozen poems of more than a thousand lines each, and his complete extant writings exceed 140,000 lines. He borrowed freely from Latin and French, rarely from Scandinavian languages, and several of his anglicized words are still in existence. Here are some of his probable innovations, with dates of first citation in the *OED*; in many instances Lydgate's use of the word antedates the examples there offered:

Nouns (mainly abstract): *adolescence* (1430), *agregat* (1430–8, *OED* 1656), *collik* (1420–2, *OED* 1483), *confidence* (1430), *conspyratour* (1413), *credulite* (1430–8), *decepcioune* (1430), *dilusioun* (1420), *dyal* (1430), *duplicite* (1430), *gallery* (1430–8, *OED* 1500), *granmoder* (1412–20, *OED* 1424), *incydent* (1412–20), *magnate* (1430–40), *paganysme* (1433), *pretens* (1412–20, *OED* 1425), *pyrat* (1426), *solicitude* (1412), *tolerance* (1412-20), *transgressioun* (1426)

Verbs: abuse and *admit* (1413), *atempte* (1430–8, *OED* 1513), *countermaund* and *debar* (1430), *delude* (1430–8, *OED* 1493), *depend* (1413), *disapere* (1412–20, *OED* 1530), *dyverte* (1430), *interrupte* (1412–20), *provoke* (1412–20, *OED* 1432–50).

Adjectives: adiacent (1430), *arable* (1430–8, *OED* 1577), *auburn* (1430), *avaricious* (1430–8, *OED* 1474), *circumspect* (1430), *condygne* (1413), *cremynall* (1430–8, *OED* 1474), *equivalent* (1430–8, *OED* 1460), *fallible* (1430), *fraternal* (1430–8, *OED* 1494), *fraudulent* (1430), *immutable* (1412–20), *impre(g)nable* (1430–40), *incredible* and *ineschuable* (1412–20, the latter obsolescent), *infallible* (1412–20, *OED* 1491), *invyncyble* (1412–20), *massive* (1410), *musical* (1420), *passionat* (1412–20, *OED* 1450), *powerless* (1412–20, *OED* 1552), *rural* and *tedious* (1412–20), *terrible* (1430), *unperturbed* (1420–2)

Adverb: gentylmanly (1412–20)

This incomplete list is impressive, and tells the tale of Lydgate's latinity, even if the poet was not the coiner of all these borrowings. Many other words may be added from glossaries of the major poems, such as the *Troy Book* and the *Fall of Princes*.

If Lydgate founded a school of rhetoric at the monastery of Bury St Edmunds, it is difficult to account for his sprawling sentences and grammatical untidiness. Perhaps his learning was wide, rather than deep. For a poet of standing, he wrote too much, to please too many patrons. The poetry is disquietingly burdened with stock-phrases and makeshift expressions. All that may be said in his defence is that the English inflexional system had become uncertain, and that a new analytical era in the order of words was taking shape. He was the successor of Chaucer by hardly a generation; but there can be little doubt that the London English he used admitted much flexibility, including several pronunciations of polysyllabic loan words.

It is hard to credit that the same poet could have written lines such as these:

> Floures open vpon euery grene,
> Whan the larke, messager of day,
> Salueth þ'uprist of the sonne shene
> Moost amerously in Apryl and in May
>
> ('As a Mydsomer Rose', lines 17–20)

Lydgate realized that he could not match the artistry of Chaucer, and chose 'to refourme the rudenesse of my stile with aureate colours' (*Fall of Princes* VIII, 80–81). His procedure was not merely lexical, but liturgical; he borrowed extensively from the vocabulary of Vulgate Latin, which he may have acquired during two periods of residence at Oxford. Many critics think that Lydgate reached the summit of his achievement in his early period (1398–1412), during which the *Complaint of the Black Knight* and the *Temple of Glas* were written. By the reign of Henry V he was widely acknowledged as the laureate successor of Chaucer. An anonymous poet, before 1450, said as much in his 'Reproof' of Lydgate's attitude to women in the *Fall of Princes*:

> O noble chaucer passyd ben thy dayse
> Off poetrye ynamyd worthyest
> And of makyng in alle othir days the best
>
> Now thou art go/thyn helpe I may not haue
> Wherfor to God I pray ryght specially
> Syth thou art dede and buryde in they graue
> That on thy sowle hym lyste to haue mercy
> And to the monke of bury now speke I
> ffor thy connyng ys syche and eke thy grace
> After chaucer to occupye his place
>
> Besechyne the my penne enlumyne
> This flour to prayse as I before haue ment
> And of these lettyrs let thy colours shyne
> This byll to forthir after myn entent
>
> (Hammond, ibid., p 200, lines 19–32)

Lydgate's influence with the aristocracy, especially Katherine, the Queen Mother, Duke Humfrey and Guy of Warwick, is shown by his secondment to Paris in 1426, as senior liaison-clerk to Thomas Montague, the Deputy to the Regent of France. This bibliophile persuaded him to translate Guillaume de Guileville's *Le Pelerinage de la Vie Humaine* (written about 1331). Lydgate's *Pilgrimage of the Life of Man*, which expanded the original's eighteen thousand lines by at least a third, became the forerunner of a number of didactic allegories, such as Bunyan's *Pilgrim's Progress*. Both the *Temple of Glas* and the *Pilgrimage* made a considerable impact on the first of the Scottish Chaucerians, King James I, whose *Kingis Quair* was highly regarded in the latter half of the fifteenth century.

For security reasons, King Robert III of Scotland planned, before he died, to send his heir, James, to France. The prince, aged eleven, was captured by Yarmouth merchant-pirates and brought before Henry IV. From 1406 he lived, under restraint, in the Tower of London, along with other Scots prisoners, but was removed to Nottingham, Pevensey, Kenilworth and Windsor during recurrences of the plague. After the death of Henry IV in 1413, he was befriended by Henry V, and accompanied the King on his French campaigns, after the English reverses of 1421. There was a large contingent of Scottish soldiery in the French army, and the presence of the rightful king of Scotland on the English side was designed as a gesture to discredit their integrity. The truth is, however, that the Scots under Buchan were not deflected from their purpose, and had played a notable role in the English defeat at Baugé.

James I of Scotland attended Henry's marriage to Katherine of Valois, and was a chief mourner at his funeral in 1422; the following year he married Joan Beaufort, daughter of the late Earl of Somerset. Negotiations were then opened for his return to the Scots kingdom, and this was effected in 1424, for a ransom of forty thousand pounds, which was claimed as the cost of maintenance and education during the king's eighteen years in captivity. One sixth of the sum was remitted by the Beauforts, who were Henry VI's regents, as a dowry to Joan. During his time in England, James I became enamoured of the works of Chaucer, Gower and Lydgate, and the beginning of his real-life *amour* is described in *The Kingis Quair* ('Book'), an autobiographical allegory in 197 seven-line stanzas, probably written between 1430 and 1435. The manuscript, dated *c* 1505, is preserved in the Bodleian Library, Oxford, along with three major poems of Chaucer (MS Seld. Arch. B24), among them *Troilus and Criseyde*.

At the age of thirty James I returned to Scotland, which had been governed by the Duke of Albany until 1420, and then by the latter's son, Murdoch. The king is said to have been an athlete who excelled at field events, such as throwing the hammer and wrestling, sports still practised at the Highland games. Besides a taste for English poetry, he was a capable musician, and proved himself to be a strong ruler in restoring order among the warring earls and Highland clans.

The *Kingis Quair* is a sensitive, inward-looking poem, whose love-theme is different from that of other medieval allegories, in

breaking with the *amour courtois* tradition. A delicate res-
ponsiveness to nature enlivens its neo-Platonism. Though the
philosophico-narrative style owes much to Chaucer's *Knight's Tale*
and Lydgate's *Pilgrimage*, particularly in the latter's conflict between body and spirit, personal involvement is a new departure; for
it gives immediacy to the quest for happiness through spiritual
freedom. Order in the universe is likened to the motion of the
planets. This is a Boethian notion, but James's philosophy is given a
Christian slant. Divine grace renders obsolete the belief in human
destiny's being at the mercy of Fortune's wheel, one of the
tenacious medieval symbolisms. Two of the more significant aspects
of the King's marriage were the absence of political motivation, and
the sought-for counsel of Minerva, Goddess of Reason, which
proved more fruitful for conjugal fulfilment than the sexual entice-
ments of Venus.

James's style is seldom rhetorical; it tends rather to the colloquial, and this is one of its principal charms. The rime-royal stanza
is consequently handled with a feeling for rhythm, of which
Lydgate was rarely capable:

> Go litill tretise *nakit* of eloquence,
> Causing simplese and pouertee to wit:
> And prey the reder to haue pacience
> Of thy defaute and to supporten it.
> Of his gudnese thy *brukilnese*° to knytt,   [frailty]
> And his tong for to reule and to stere,
> That thy defautis *helit* may ben here.

> Allace, and gif thou cummyst in the presence
> *Quhare* as of blame faynest thou wald be quite,
> To here thy rude and *crukit* eloquens,
> *Quho* sal be *tháre* to pray for thy remyt?
> No wicht, bot geve hir merci will admytt
> Thee for gud will, that is thy gyd and stere,
> To *quham* for me thou pitousely requere.
> . . . .

> Vnto [th'] impnis° of my maisteris dere,   [religious songs]
> Gowere and Chaucere, that on the steppis satt
> Of rethorike *quhill thai* were *lyvand* here,
> Superlatiue as poetis laureate
> In moralitee and eloquence ornate,
> I recommend my buk in lynis sevin –
> And eke thair saulis vnto the blisse of hevin.
>   (Envoy, stanzas 194, 195, 197, Norton-Smith, pp 49–50)

[Scots and northern forms and spellings are indicated in italics.]

The language of this poem is a curious blend of Middle English and Scots forms and spellings; this is not surprising, in view of the mixed influences upon the king's education. The dialect is not artificial, as Skeat claimed, but predominantly northern. Words of a literary character are usually reminiscent of the spelling of Chaucer or Hoccleve. The two scribes who worked on the unique manuscript have been held accountable for some inconsistencies in the orthography; the name of one is known, James Gray, who undertook the major share of transcription. He worked for Henry Sinclair, third Earl of Orkney, who originally owned the manuscript.

W. A. Craigie, himself a Scot, and one of the editors of the *OED*, drew attention to some of the Scottish spelling, accidental and rhyming peculiarities:

> As mere matters of spelling which are mainly or exclusively Scottish may be noted the use of *i* for *e* in such forms as *othir, seruantis, thinkith, biddith* (but *preyeth* is retained); also *sum* for *som, quhich* for *which*.
>
> Displacing of English forms by Scottish occurs in *haue* for *han, thame* and *thaire* for *hem* and *her, or* for *er(e)* 'before', and *dirknesse* for *derknesse*. . . .
>
> In the whole poem there appear to be only two forms attested by rhyme for which a Scottish origin can reasonably be claimed. The one is the past tense *begouth* for *began*, which in stanza 16 rhymes with *youth* and *couth*; the form appears to be purely Scottish. The other is *regne* in stanza 39 in rhyme with *benigne* and *digne* . . .
>
> (*Essays and Studies of the English Association*, XXXV, 1939, pp 27, 30–31)

The Scots dialect was an off-shoot of northern English (Northumbrian), and its evolution is usually divided into three periods: Early (before 1424), Middle (1425–1603), and Modern (after 1603). The court poets of the Middle period, such as Henryson and Dunbar, cannot be described as adherents to this dialect; they preferred to model their literary language on the style of English predecessors, such as Chaucer, or of contemporaries, such as Lydgate. A distinctive dialect did, however, develop north of the River Forth, but was only recognized when the scholar-poet, Gavin Douglas, Bishop of Dunkeld, made his famous translation of the *Aeneid* in 1525.

The influence of Norman French on the northern dialect of

'ynglis', in the areas between Newcastle and Edinburgh, was small, but the impact of French literature, through diplomatic and educational channels, was considerable. A Scots College had been founded at the University of Paris as early as 1326. The poets who followed James I were as familiar with the works of Machaut, Deschamps, Chartier and Villon, as they were with Chaucer. In Henryson and Dunbar, Scotland found poets of different, but higher, calibre than Hoccleve and Lydgate; for their artistry was the outcome of French inspiration, in poems of much shorter length.

The term 'Scottish Chaucerians' is an unreliable literary tag, if it implies that the principal Middle Scots poets were derivative. Robert Henryson (c 1425–1505), though there is little biographical background, is typically Scots in the pathos, humour and practicality of his observations. He was apparently a teacher. At the Benedictine Abbey school of Dunfermline, a small town north of Edinburgh, he was sufficiently close to the country to explain his intimate acquaintance with the life of the peasantry. The 'canny' but amusing, *Moral Fables of Aesop the Phrygian* (Harleian MS, dated 1571) are not all from the perennial source of French *fabliaux;* Henryson gave them a personal, yet popular, character quite extraordinary for the Middle Ages. These moral fables were probably written to familiarize abbey colleagues with the society in which they lived; they serve equally as a cloak for shrewd comment on the intrigues and abuses of James III's government. The narrative is so fluent, the dialogue so crisp and original, that the tales present one of the liveliest portraits of social conditions in Scotland in the fifteenth century. In the lines that follow the fondness of northern poets for alliteration may be seen in lines 1, 2 and 6.

> Than *l*ychtlie in the bukket *l*ap the *l*oun°; [fellow]
> His *w*echt but *w*eir° the uther end gart ryis; [without doubt]
> The Tod come hailland° up, the Wolf yeid doun; [quickly]
> Than angerlie the Wolff upon him cryis:
> 'I cummand thus dounwart, quhy thow upwart hyis?'
> 'Schir' (quod the Foxe), 'thus *f*airis it off *F*ortoun:
> As ane cummis up, scho quheillis° ane uther doun!' [wheels]
> (H. H. Wood, *Poems*, p 82, lines 2413–19)

Henryson the humanitarian, as well as the humanist (one who acknowledges 'the dignity of the common man'), reveals himself as an uncompromising critic of the disintegration of the feudal system. This is how he pictures the poverty-stricken small farmer in the *Tale of the Wolf and the Lamb*:

> His Hors, his Meir, he man *l*en to the *L*aird,
> To *d*rug° and *d*raw in Court or in Cariage;   [pull]
> His *s*ervand or his *s*elf may not be *s*paird
> To *s*wing° and *s*weit, withoutin Meit or wage   [labour]
> Thus how he standis in labour and bondage,
> That scantlie may be purches by his maill,°   [rent]
> To leve upon dry breid and watter caill°.   [broth]
> *(Moral Fables*, lines 2749–55)

The moral concern of his poems, and their religious feeling, lead us to assume that Henryson might have been a cleric in lower orders.

The other aspect of Henryson is his craftsmanship, his outstanding performance being *The Testament of Cresseid*. This is an imaginative sequel to Chaucer's tale, preserving all the main characters, except Pandarus. Henryson by-passes the statement in Book V of Chaucer's narrative that Troilus had been killed in battle. 'Who knows,' he asks in line 64, 'if all that Chaucer wrote is true?' His is a well-structured, but pessimistic narrative poem, remarkable for its smooth versification in rime-royal. The writer depicts physical suffering with a stark realism. Cresseid, not for the sin of wantonness, but because she cursed the 'craibit Goddis', is afflicted with leprosy, the symptoms of which are minutely described. This is unusual in medieval literature, since the term was applied to any disfiguring disease of the skin.

The especial merit of Henryson's art is its concision and concentration of expression. He was not a Court poet, and modestly claimed in the Prologue to the *Fables* (stanza 6) that he was compelled to use 'homely language' and 'rude terms', because he did not understand eloquence or rhetoric – a characteristic example of Scots understatement. The truth is that Henryson was an urbane Renaissance poet ahead of his time. He was certainly read by Shakespeare for *Troilus and Cressida*, and is nearly as able as Spenser in the modulation of vowel sounds, for instance in the following lines:

> Throw out the glas hir bemis brast sa fair
> That I micht se on everie syde me by
> The Northern wind that purifyit the air

And sched the mistie cloudis fra the sky
(Testament of Cresseid, lines 15–18)

The extent to which Henryson modelled his technique on
Chaucer is evident from his constant adherence to that poet's
metrical forms. He has a finer sense of the dependence of rhythm
upon stress than either of the English Chaucerians already considered. He achieves national distinctiveness, not through his
settings, but his language, and remains the finest introduction to
Alan Ramsay and Burns. He has, like the latter, a visual gift much
stronger than his sense of locality. The theme of *Robene and
Makyne*, fashioned on the model of the French pastourelle, is
original, and anticipates in a brief compass the splendid insights of
poetic reasoning that were to distinguish the Renaissance tradition.

Marshall W. Stearns in his study *Robert Henryson* (Columbia
University Press, 1949, p 129) echoes the invariable critical dictum
that 'the dialect of Middle Scots was never spoken'. This is surely a
denial of the fundamental meaning of 'dialect'. Henryson's poetic
language is a northern class-dialect, a counterpart to the London
English of Chaucer; it was close to the speech of the educated
gentry living in the south-eastern region of Scotland, and assuredly
alive. It would be erroneous to imagine that the social level of the
poet's audience could have been merely that of his classroom. The
scotticizing of Henryson's English was a remarkable achievement,
that was recently recognized by John MacQueen in 'The Case for
Early Scottish Literature' (*Edinburgh Studies in English and Scots*,
pp 234–47). As MacQueen reminds us, the crux of the difficulty is
that 'English in the form of Lowland Scots has never been the only
Scottish vernacular . . . Gaelic, as has been well established, is no
more native to Scotland than is Lowland Scots; the linguistic
ancestors of both languages were imported at much the same time'
(pp 236–37).

William Dunbar (*c* 1460–1520) became the most versatile of the
Scottish courtly 'makars'; thanks to James IV's interest in printing,
a few of Dunbar's poems were printed during his lifetime. He was
probably educated at St Andrews University, and M. P. McDiarmid has suggested that he served as a chaplain to Queen Margaret,
daughter of Henry VII, and consort to the King, who died at
Flodden Field in 1513 (see *Historical Review* XXXIII (1954) pp
46–52). The poet was a city-dweller, who loved Edinburgh, but
complained of its polluted atmosphere. He had been sent on a

mission to London in 1501, and wrote in praise of that city on his return. Though his metrical experiments were more diverse than Henryson's, he was essentially a poet of French or English conventions, whose immense energy made him a force in the succeeding age. The French allegorical convention he mingled freely with Lydgate's aureate style, to produce that curious impressionistic poem *The Goldyn Targe*. Dunbar is, however, an indifferent narrator; he lacks the insight into character that enlivens Henryson's *Fables*. Nor is he a genuine allegorist; the situations he contrives are much too objective to come from a dreamer.

In the variety of his moods and themes Dunbar was unique. He could be obsequious, comic, complaining or religious, with a craftsman's solicitude for diction in the handling of his subject. He was an extravert who relied on sense impressions for his emotive effects. Liturgical language was responsible for his discreet Lydgatian latinism. His masque-like poem, *The Goldyn Targe*, begins as follows:

> Ryght as the stern of day begouth to schyne,
> Quhen gone to bed war Vesper and Lucyne,
>   I raise and by a rosere° did me rest;   [rose-garden]
> Up sprang the *goldyn candill matutyne*,
> With clere *depurit° bemes cristallyne*,   [purified]
>   Glading the mery foulis in thair nest;
> Or Phebus was in purpur cape revest
> Up raise the lark, the hevyns menstrale fyne
> In May, in till a morow myrthfullest.
>
> Full angellike thir birdis sang thair houris
> Within thair courtyns grene, into thair bouris
>   Apparalit quhite and red wyth blomes suete;
> *Anamalit* was the felde wyth all colouris,
> The perly droppis schake in silvir schouris,
>   Quhill all *in balme did branch and levis flete°;*   [float]
> To part fra Phebus did Aurora grete,
> Hir *cristall teris* I saw hyng on the flouris,
>   Quhilk he for lufe all drank up wyth his hete.
>   (*Poems*, ed. W. M. Mackenzie, lines 1–18)

The florid conceits of these nine-line stanzas (indicated in italics) are not without a certain fanciful charm; they herald a new age, too sophisticated and pretentious to be medieval.

Dunbar's numerous petitions (complaints to his purse) were remonstrances to a parsimonious king; but they are typical of his egotism and frustration. The much-desired church benefice never came his way, possibly because of his caustic comments. His life at Court reflects some solace in a fatherly relationship with the young Queen, who was only thirteen when she married. But Dunbar had little of Henryson's sympathy with the poor and oppressed. The satires on the insanitary and gloomy aspects of city life, especially in Edinburgh, reflect the least of his spleen. The bitterness of his attitude to Walter Kennedy, a rival at Court, is tempered with flashes of humour, but it is invariably of the insulting kind, familiar to the spirit of the age.

It has been suggested by K. Wittig (*The Scottish Tradition in Literature*, p 61) that Dunbar 'had Celtic blood in his veins', because he recalls the strophic technique of the Gaelic bards. But Edwin Morgan thinks differently (see his acute study 'Dunbar and the Language of Poetry', *Essays in Criticism*, II, pp 138–58); he explains the poet's brilliant use of the alliterative technique as follows:

> Alliteration on the 'popular' side of poetry recommended itself to the Scots because it was an apt medium for racy narrative, because it established an immediate link between verse and the fund of alliteration in common proverbs, tags of speech and phrases from ballads and songs, and because it encouraged the peculiar Scots leaning towards the wild and the outspoken, the vituperative and the incongruous. Alliteration on the 'art' side of poetry is one aspect of a larger movement which affected all the poets of the time: the wakening consciousness of language as a ground open to deliberate enrichment and of literature as a growth springing from that prepared soil. . . .
>
> Much of the makars' poetry is a lyrical run or lilt of a peculiar kind which comes from a nice fusion of native alliteration and French-based verse-form. The fact that the alliteration does not always coincide with the syllabic accent, but leads the reader on with a sinuous stress of its own, gives the writing a chatoyant and dance-like quality which is very attractive. . . . The alliterative form of writing was no strain on the range and resource of Dunbar, nor on the other hand was it an excuse for mere wordy excess, with epithets empty of everything except the requisite sound.

(pp 143, 145–6, 154)

The astonishing vocabulary and the evident extravagant enjoyment of *The Tua Mariit Wemen and the Wedo* are helped by the unrhymed long lines of the alliterative measure, which contain many gnomic utterances, such as 'Faith has a fair name, but falsheid fares better' (line 457). It would be hard to find in any other Scots poet a polarization of art so striking as this coarse-grained extravaganza, set beside a ceremonial poem like *The Thrissil and the Rois*, with its striking heraldic figures.

The conventional lyrics of Dunbar, for instance *Meditatioun in Wyntir* have an artistic unity of their own, reflected in singleness of mood and lexical simplicity:

> I walk, I turne, sleip may I nocht,
> I vexit am with havie thocht;
> > This warld all ouir I cast about,
> > And ay the mair I am in dout,
> The mair that I remeid have socht.
>
> I am assayit on everie syde:
> Dispair sayis ay, 'In tyme provyde
> > And get sum thing quhairon to leif,
> > Or with grit trouble and mischeif
> Thow sall in to this court abyd.'

(ibid., lines 11–20)

Austerity of phrase also dignifies the seven religious poems of Dunbar's maturity, which are moving, partly because they are so impersonal. *On the Resurrection of Christ* illustrates his remarkable capacity to weave a liturgical Latin refrain into his stanzas.

> The grit victour agane is rissin on hicht,
> That for our querrell° to the deth wes woundit;   [cause]
> The sone tha wox all paill° now schynis bricht   [waxed
> And dirknes clerit, our fayth is now refoundit;   all pale]
> The knell of mercy fra the hevin is soundit,
> The Cristin ar deliverit of thair wo,
> The Jowis° and thair errour ar confoundit: [Jews]
> *Surrexit Dominus de sepulchro.*

(ibid., lines 25–32)

The language of Dunbar is not valued alone for its interest to the lexicographer or the student of prosody. If one concentrates on the sounds, and not on the scribal spelling, the artistry of the verse soon emerges. In long poems like *The Tua Mariit Wemen and the Wedo* (530 lines) Dunbar's verbal vivacity is the source of his gusto and raciness, whether in description or dialogue. Most of the words of impact are not of Celtic, but of Anglo-Saxon, French or Latin origin. The flyting epithets add a savour that betokens a way of thinking, feeling and reacting. The satiric impulse could not have been realized in any other form of speech.

The movement to claim respectability for the Lowland Scots dialect in translating the classics, was largely the work of Gavin Douglas, as shown in Prologues to his Books of the *Aeneid*, which are masterpieces of their kind, and of great philological interest. But Douglas's writings lie outside the scope of the present study; they were produced in the early sixteenth century.

CHAPTER XVI

The Significance of the
Fifteenth Century

🙚🙚🙚🙚🙚🙚

IN THE FIFTEENTH CENTURY English prose was used for three principal ends: (1) dissemination of knowledge; (2) religious controversy; and (3) introducing the reader to newly published authors, especially through translation. In these activities the authors who mattered most were Trevisa, Pecock and Caxton. The development of prose in the 'century of the commons' is one of the neglected areas of English language history. The continuity of prose which R. W. Chambers extolled was confined to one aspect, the homiletic tradition of Anglo-Saxon, beginning with the tenth century. Significant changes in the reigns of Henry VI and Edward IV were introduced by secular writers of distinct types; those sponsored by humanists of the aristocratic class, who were collectors of manuscripts and books; clerics involved in the Lollard heresy; and aspiring *literati* among the merchant class, whose presence was widely felt in the promotion of medieval drama.

The eminence of Chaucer and Langland, as poets, made the impact of poetry upon prose inevitable. There were two influential currents of prose at work: French treatises and romances, and the imitation of indigenous alliteration as a means of cohesion and quaint decoration. The habit of thinking in doublets, (e.g. *time and tide, bag and baggage*) came from the native source also, because there were plentiful parallel terms of Germanic and French origin.

Two prominent humanist noblemen, Thomas, Lord Berkeley in Gloucestershire, and Duke Humfrey, became literary patrons. Berkeley sponsored John of Trevisa (*c* 1342–1402), a Cornishman by birth, who was educated at Exeter, but became a Fellow of Queen's College, Oxford (1369–74). Trevisa was expelled in 1379, probably for his part in heretical biblical translation, and he then became Lord Berkeley's chaplain. One of his duties was to translate such Latin works as his lordship favoured, the best being the English version of Ranulf Higden's *Polychronicon*, in seven books. Higden, who died in 1364, was a Benedictine monk of St Werburg's, Chester; his world history, in Trevisa's English, was completed in 1387 and printed by Caxton in 1482. Trevisa's own contribution was not considerable, but important; the chronicle ends with the year 1360, not 1357 as stated by Caxton, who himself continued the history up to 1461. Trevisa wrote in the Gloucestershire dialect, which preserved many south-western forms.

Quite as instructive for studying the Middle Ages are Trevisa's translation of Bartholomew's *De Proprietatibus Rerum* (*Of the Properties of Things*, 1398) and his *Epistle to Lord Berkeley on Translation*, prefixed to *Polychronicon*. In the latter his lordship argues that, for the purpose of translation, prose is preferable to rhyme, since it is clearer and consequently easier to understand. Such generalizations were common in the thinking of the time. Higden's description of Wales in the *Polychronicon*, Book I, is actually in rhymed Latin octosyllables, and Trevisa followed suit in verse of supple simplicity. Here is an example of his skill in translation:

Higden

Si foret qui penitima,
Terrae venas et viscera,
Transpenetrare sedula
Novisset arte praevia.
Occulta latent plurima
Naturae beneficia;
Quae, hactenus incognita
Humana pro incuria,
Per posterorum studia
Patebunt sub notitia

Trevisa

ȝif me kouþe by craft vndo
Þe veynes of þe erþe, and come þerto.
Many benefices of kynde
Beeþ now i-hidde fro manis mynde,
And beeþ vnknowe ȝit,
For defaute of manis wit.
Grete tresour is hid in grounde,
And after þis it schal be founde
By greet studie and besynesse
Of hem þat comeþ after vs.

                    (Babington, Rolls Series, vol. I, pp 414–15)

Beeth and *i-hidde* in line 4 are characteristic forms of the south-western dialect; it should be noted that Trevisa's French and Latin borrowings are surprisingly few. The singular virtue of Trevisa's writing is his naturalness and adherence to the forms of common speech. The style tends to become laborious only because the matter-of-factness of medieval pseudo-historians was slavishly perpetuated. Trevisa was accounted a good scholar, but his capacity for originality was limited.

Alice D. Greenwood speaks of the 'fairy-tale science of Bartholomaeus' (*Cambridge History of English Literature*, ch. III, p 72); yet the thirteenth-century encyclopaedia, *De Proprietatibus Rerum*, became one of the popular handbooks of the Middle Ages. The main interest in Trevisa's English version centres on its specialized terms; the translator was sometimes verbose in rendering these into English. A count of the latinized words he introduced into the language runs to several hundreds; and he coined others, such as *stretchable*, from native sources. Successive publishers of Bartholomew's book in English modernized the text, and much might be learnt from a language study of the various renderings.

The alliterative tradition in English prose, which Trevisa often invoked, began with Richard Rolle of Hampole, and was a thoroughly Germanic trait. It has never quite been extinguished, as R. L. Stevenson observed; generations of English writers have used it with greater subtlety than John Lyly. Word-play of initial letters did not arise simply from the desire for an elevated style. The practice was deeply rooted in the dialectal habits of the north and west of England, and clearly related to the secularization of prose in the fifteenth century. The *fin de siècle* saw a rapid increase in public readership, and consequently in the number of professional scribes to replace the declining monastic scriptoria. A new class of copyists was actively disseminating its own productions.

The popularity of Trevisa's *Polychronicon* is proved by the number of manuscripts extant, and of editions printed before the end of the sixteenth century. The Trevisa MSS differ much in orthography, and even in the choice of words. Four were collated by Churchill Babington for his edition of *Polychronicon* in the Rolls Series (1865). He offered not only Higden's Latin text, and Trevisa's translation, but another English rendering of the mid-fifteenth century (Harleian MS n. 2261) written by an unknown translator, who used a bombastic and florid style, belonging to no recognizable class of society.

A. J. Perry, in an edition of Trevisa's (?) *Dialogues* for the EETS (1925) gives sound reasons for attributing to him the translation of a *Sermon against Mendicant Friars,* delivered by Archbishop Fitz Ralph of Armagh on 8 November 1357. The following passage throws unexpected light on the educational discontent of the times:

> Paul þe apostle hoteþ, þat no man schuld ouer passe noþer begile his broþer, for oure Lord is wrecheful in alle siche dedes (I Thess. 4:6). Here of comeþ grete damage boþe to þe peple & to þe clergie; . . . for now in þe Vniuersitees of þe rewme of Englonde, for children beþ so y-stole from her fadres & modres, lewed men in euereche place wiþholdeþ her children & sendeþ hem nouȝt to þe Vniuersite, for hem is leuer make hem eerþe tilyers & haue hem þan sende hem to þe Vniuersite & lese hem. So þat ȝet in my tyme in þe Vniuersite of Oxenford were þritty þousand scolers at ones, & now ben vnneþe sixe þousand. And me trowiþ þat þe grettest occasioun & cause why scolers beþ so wiþdrawe, hit is for children beþ so bigiled & y-stole; & y se noon gretter damage to al þe clergie, þan is þis damage.
>
> (p 58, lines 16–31)

A certain Celtic tolerance in Trevisa was echoed in another Oxford student Reginald Pecock (*c* 1390–1460), who was a Welsh-man, and a much more controversial figure. By using the vernacular for large-scale philosophical reasoning, he hoped to reach a wider audience, especially among the heretical Lollards, who inveighed against the abuse of Church privileges, and the unwillingness of bishops to preach, because of their preoccupation with administra-tive affairs.

Profiting intellectually from his long residence at Oxford, Pecock was awarded the degree of Doctor of Divinity and elected to a fellowship at Oriel College, until ordained as a priest in 1421. Duke Humfrey liked his alertness of mind, and induced him to come to London as Rector of St Michael Royal, which was attached to Whittington College, a foundation of the one-time Lord Mayor of London. Duke Humfrey then fell out of political favour with the Queen (see p 387), and it was left to his successor, the new Duke of Suffolk, to fulfill Pecock's ambitions by making him Bishop of St Asaph in 1424. The cleric had to share much of the Chief Minister's unpopularity, and probably for this reason was translated to Chichester in 1430. He was a prolific writer, and has been credited with more than forty works, though only seven have survived.

Personal vanity and excess of zeal in combating lost causes were ultimately responsible for Pecock's ignominious downfall. In about 1449 he published a book that had been written several years previously, entitled *The Repressor of over much blaming of the clergy*; in 1860 a two-volume edition was prepared by Churchill Babington for the Rolls Series. History has shown that Pecock's unfortuante attempt to undermine the Lollard's belief in the literal wording of Scripture foundered on an untimely resort to reason, which neither contemporary clerics nor his detractors were capable of understanding. He neither persuaded the puritan followers of Wyclif, nor allayed the suspicions of orthodox churchmen, whose views on clerical privilege and the raising of money had long been under attack. Catholics everywhere (none more conservative than Pecock himself) felt it unwise to exacerbate existing tensions by requiring that faith should be reconciled with reason. Duns Scotus and William of Ockham had undoubtedly started a flood that orthodoxy was struggling to contain, and the Church had done no more than weaken its case by insisting on papal infallibility.

An inflammatory sermon at Paul's Cross led to an enquiry by the Archbishop of Canterbury. Not only the *Repressor*, but other writings of Pecock, were examined and condemned in his presence, and he was faced with the alternatives of recanting publicly or burning at the stake; shamefacedly he accepted the first. He was deprived of his office, and spent the last two or three years of his life in seclusion at Thorney Abbey, Cambridgeshire, without access to the means of writing and to books other than those used in church services. At his examination, he at first declined to accept responsibility for any of his writings that were more than three years old, on the ground that unauthorized copies (possibly erroneous) were in circulation. He was so confused about what he had actually said, that he recanted many things that were true. One of the charges levelled against him was simply that he had chosen to write in English instead of Latin; but the principal objection was casuistry, Pecock's syllogistic treatment of the arguments for ecclesiastical authority. This was held to be a greater peril than Lollardry; for it meant that any Christian might claim the right to interpret Scripture for himself.

Pecock's other important works were: (a) *The Reule of Crysten Religioun* (1443), and (b) two English dialogues, *The Donet* (1440) and its sequel *The Folewer to the Donet* (1454); both the latter were edited by E. V. Hitchcock for the EETS (1918 and 1924 respectively). OF *Donet* (also spelt *Donat*), a fourteenth-century borrowing, was adapted from the Latin grammarian's name, Donatus, signifying an 'elementary grammatical treatise'; the dialogue in the *Donet* books takes the form of a treatise on the Christian religion. All three books were theological in conception, designed to inculcate the moral and intellectual virtues. In content, they present a more favourable picture of Pecock than the *Repressor*, and are easier to read. The *Folewer*, in chapters V to VII, gives an extensive account of the psychology of the *bodily wits* (senses), and distinguishes between the 'inward' and 'outward' kinds. Pecock here employs two unusual technical terms, *meenal* meaning 'instrumental', and *eendal*, meaning 'final' or 'ultimate'. He explains in an introductory chapter that the dialogue is between a father (representing himself) and his son (whose status is that of a pupil, seeking enlightenment). In part I, chapter 27, the son's comments include some autobiographical sidelights:

> I wote wel, fadir, þat now late in londoun a book of ȝowre writyng which þe kunnyngist and wijsist clerkis in ynglond maken ful mych of and preisen it mych, and in which þei fynden noon yuel, was scornyd and reprouyd of mercers servauntis, whanne þe book came into her handis and was of hem rad. But what þerfore, schulde ȝe haue left vnwrite þilk book, if ȝe hadde bifore knowe suche vnpristis detraccion? goddis forbode! . . . What eny notable good werk or word euer ȝit lackid his enemy, his hyndrer, his letter or his detracter? Noon or fewe! . . . Þerfore suche men more schewen whiche þei ben in hem silf, þat is to seie, yuel disposid, þan þei hurten ȝow.
>
> (*Folewer*, pp 176–7)

Not often does Pecock write with such clarity and ease. The weightier, syllogistic style has two drawbacks, tautology and a lack of feeling for sentence rhythm. The following is a characteristically latinized excerpt from the *Repressor*:

> Of whiche first principal conclusioun thus proued folewith ferther this corelarie, that whanne euere and where euere in Holi Scripture or out of Holi Scripture be writen eny point or eny gouernaunce of the seide lawe of kinde it is more verrili writen in the book of mannis soule than in the outward book of parchemyn or of velym; and if eny semyng discorde be bitwixe the wordis writen in the outward book of Holi Scripture and the doom of resoun, write in mannis soule and herte, the wordis so writen withoutforth ouȝten be expowned and be interpretid

and brouȝt forto accorde with the doom of resoun in thilk mater; and the doom of resoun ouȝte not forto be expowned, glosid, interpretid, and brouȝte for to accorde with the seid outward writing in Holi Scripture of the Bible or ouȝwhere ellis out of the Bible.

(Babington, part I, ch. 5, pp 25–6)

To the modern ear, this language sounds archaic, even legalistic, and the syntax is deliberately complex. Hitchcock, in her introduction to the *Folewer*, counters such criticism in these words:

Where there is a more complex relationship of main and dependent facts, Pecock is accurate enough, and mature enough, and modern enough to express these facts in their right shades of importance, that is to say, by the complex sentence, and by the complex sentence justly balanced and subordinated, for Pecock's syntax is very rarely defective or slovenly. . .

Where Pecock can best claim to be a stylist, even a great stylist, is in order and arrangement, and in the power of marshalling his ideas. . . . Then there is the steady essay-like building up of evidence – the careful ordering, not merely stringing, of statements, the proofs of these statements, the deductions from them. And his long laborious treatises are natural wholes and therefore works of art.

(*Folewer*, pp lxiv, lxx, lxxi)

This sounds like overpraise, but the arguments must be respected. When Pecock wrote, there was not a vocabulary extensive enough to meet his intellectual needs. He therefore invented a number of abstract compounds, such as *un-to-be-thought-upon*, which are quaint, but clumsy. Richard Hooker, with whom he is sometimes compared, was fortunate in writing a century and a half later, when many dignified words were available to express his weighty thoughts.

Hitchcock was just in praising Pecock's freedom from provincialism, and closeness to the standard language of London, which was predominantly East Midland. Like Wyclif, he favoured for inflexional suffixes the *i-* type of spelling common to the south-western dialect of Oxford. Surprisingly, he seldom used the western preterites of strong verbs, which cultivate radical vowels of the past participles; he seems to have preferred the northern preterite system. Except for *þei*, third-personal pronouns are invariably found in the *h-* forms (*hem, her*), rather than *them, their*. His word order is much addicted to adjectival inversions.

In argument, Pecock was no match for Aquinas, by whom he was influenced. The scholastic philosopher realized clearly that truth was of two kinds, one reached by faith, through revelation, the other by reason, through evidence. The two, Aquinas thought, might live in harmony, provided reason, which was an instrument of orderly living, did not presume to be supreme.

William Caxton, the last of the medievalists, belonged to the rising middle class of the fifteenth century. He was born about 1421 in the weald of Kent, given a sound education and apprenticed to a London mercer, Robert Large, in 1438. The middle period of his life was spent as an agent for the cloth trade in the Low Countries, then part of the Dukedom of Burgundy. By 1463 Caxton was Governor of the English Merchant Adventurers at Bruges, and he was in contact with the Burgundian Court, at its apogee, when in 1468 Charles the Bold married Margaret, Duchess of Somerset, sister of Edward IV.

By this time Caxton was a man of considerable means, and he seems to have dabbled in the export of Dutch and German illuminated manuscripts. In 1464 he began his English translation of *Le recueil des histoires de Troyes*, by Raoul Lefèvre, who had been chaplain to Philip, Duke of Burgundy. Trained as he was in the wool trade, Caxton did not think of himself as a literary figure, but was encouraged by the duchess to finish his translation; the Court of Burgundy apparently employed him in some capacity from 1470. Several Englishmen at Margaret's court wanted copies of this *History of Troy*, and Caxton hit upon the labour-saving notion of printing them.

The invention of European printing began in Mainz (*c* 1450), and twenty years later had spread to Brabant, Flanders, Paris and Italy; by 1472 Caxton had spent two years in Cologne studying the art. He then acquired a printing press, with two type-founts, engaged Colard Mansion as calligrapher and illuminator, and in 1474 began what was initially a small venture in Bruges. The following year appeared the first book printed in English, the translation entitled *Recuyell of the Histories of Troy*. The initial title-word illustrates Caxton's invariable method of borrowing; *recuyell* means 'collection' or 'miscellany'. The printer showed himself to be an ardent admirer of French prose, who had early acquired the Burgundian taste for potted history and traditional romance. Two further books were printed at Bruges, before Caxton finally changed his vocation, and set up his printing business at Westminster in 1477.

The first book printed in England was *Dictes and Sayings of the Philosophers;* and like all of Caxton's volumes, it contained no title-page. Eventually Caxton acquired six founts, all in Black Letter, or modified Gothic. The types were based on the current practice of manuscript books, Caxton's resembling the style of writing used in the Mercers' trade. The new publisher had no special design in choosing texts, except the law of supply and demand, and a desire to concentrate on the English market. The popular favourites in Court circles were the works of Chaucer, Gower and Lydgate, and French romances, including *Morte d'Arthur.* He did not have to translate the last, but freely altered Malory's version, shortening Book V, because of its alliterative bias. The printed translation of Ovid's *Metamorphoses* (1480) has unfortunately not survived; but there is a partial MS in the Pepys Library, Magdalene College, Cambridge. The largest volume Caxton produced was *The Golden Legend*; commissioned by the Earl of Arundel, it ran to 499 folio leaves. Two of his principal patrons in Edward IV's reign were the Queen, Elizabeth Woodville, and Earl Anthony Rivers.

The fullest and most dependable account of Caxton's fifteen years as a printer is to be found in N. F. Blake's *Caxton and his World.* This writer states that the total number of known publications from the Westminster press was 106, and that twenty-eight were Caxton's own translations from the French. When Caxton died in 1491, the press passed to his foreman, Wynkyn de Worde, who was not English born. Though Caxton sought to combine entertainment with instruction, he was no scholar, and did not publish for the academically-minded reader. Most of his original writing is contained in the prologues and epilogues, expressing his own restrained point of view (see N. F. Blake, *Caxton's Own Prose*). There are constant confessions of want of skill in rhetoric, the quality he most admired in Chaucer. In his edition of Chaucer's translation of Boethius, Caxton described the poet as the 'first foundeur and enbellisher of ornate eloquence in our English'.

Chaucer was buried in Westminster Abbey, probably because he spent his last years in its precincts, the house being demolished for the building of Henry VII's chapel. The present monument was not erected in the Poet's Corner until 150 years after Chaucer's death. Before that a leaden plaque was hung on a nearby pillar, with an

THE SIGNIFICANCE OF THE FIFTEENTH CENTURY

epitaph by Surigone of Milan, to which Caxton added, in Latin, the following four lines:

> After your death, renowned poet Chaucer, the care of William Caxton was that you should live, for not only did he print your works in type but he also ordered these your praises to be placed here.
>
> (Blake, *Caxton's Own Prose*, p 150)

Caxton's important contributions to the study of English literature were undoubtedly the seven volumes of Chaucer (most of the complete works), five works of Lydgate, Gower's *Confessio Amantis*, Trevisa's *Polychronicon* and his adaptation of *Le Morte Darthur*. It is very likely that the later Scottish Chaucerian poets (see pp 411-13) read these publications in Caxton's texts. Caxton's second edition of Chaucer's *Canterbury Tales* greatly improved on the first, which was based on an inferior manuscript. But it has to be admitted that Caxton's editorial work was indifferent; one improvement to Trevisa's *Polychronicon* was, however, the supplying of a table of contents.

Characteristic examples of Caxton's ornate style are to be found in his *Prohemye* (Prologue) to the *Polychronicon*; here are two passages from consecutive paragraphs:

> Historyes also have moeved ryght noble knyghtes to deserve eternal laude, whiche foloweth them for their vyctoryous merytes, and cause them more valyantly to entre in jeopardyes of batayles for the defence and tuicion of their countrey and publyke wele. Hystorye also affrayeth cruel tyrauntys for drede of infamye and shame infynyte bycause of the detestable actes of such cruel personnes ben oftymes plantyd and regystred in cronykes unto theyr perpetuel *obprobrye* and *dyvulgacion* of theyr infamye, as th'actes of Nero and suche other. . . . Historye is a perpetuel conservatryce of thoos thynges that have be doone before this presente tyme and also a *cotydyan* wytnesse of bienfayttes, of *malefaytes*, grete actes, and tryumphal vyctoryes of all maner peple. And also yf the terryble, feyned fables of poetes have moche styred and moeved men to pyte and conservynge of justyce, how moche more is to be supposed that historye, *assertryce* of veryte and as moder of alle philosophye moevynge our maners to vertue, reformeth and reconcyleth ner hande alle thoos men whiche thurgh the infyrmyte of oure mortal nature hath ledde the mooste part of theyr lyf in *ocyosyte* and myspended theyr tyme, passed ryght soone oute of remembraunce; of which lyf and deth is egal oblyvyon.
>
> (Blake, *Caxton's Own Prose*, pp 129–30, lines 49–58 and 68–81)

[*obprobrye* 'shame', *dyvulgacion* 'propagation', *cotydyan* 'daily', *malefaytes* 'evil deeds', *assertryce* 'advocate', *ocyosyte* 'idleness']

The style employed indicates that Caxton was not writing in his natural voice; in fact, his personal vocabulary was limited. According to Blake (op. cit., p 32) he was here thinking in terms of a French version of prologues by Poggio (the Italian humanist) and Diodorus Siculus. This chameleon-like trait affected most translations from the French, in which Caxton simply anglicized, as best he could, difficult words for which he knew no English equivalents. This is a reason, too, why Caxton's spelling is so inconsistent. It does not seem that his press developed what is known as a house style. Nor did he learn from his reading the art of sentence construction, the ability to control subordinate clauses in complex syntactical paragraphs.

When translating, Caxton worked at incredible speed, in order to keep his press-men fully occupied. But he found time to modernize Trevisa's vocabulary: for instance *travaille* becomes 'laboure', *lese* 'pasture', *nostrilles* 'nose thirles', *battes* 'staves', and so on.

The tale of the two priests, with which Caxton winds up his translation of *Æsop's Fables* from a French version, is regarded as his own, and reveals that he could write unaffectedly, if he chose. Here is some part of it, produced only two years later than the *Polychronicon* Prologue:

> This worshipful man, this dene, came rydynge into a good paryssh with a x or xii horses lyke a prelate, and came into the chirche of the sayd parysshe and fond there this good symple man, somtyme his felawe, whiche cam and welcomed hym lowely. And that other badde hym 'Good morowe, Mayster Johan', and toke hym sleyghtly by the hand and axyd hym where he dwellyd.
>
> And the good man sayd: 'In this paryssh'.
>
> 'How?' sayd he. 'Are ye here a sowle preest or a paryssh preste?'
>
> 'Nay, sir,' said he. 'For lack of a better, though I be not able ne worthy I am parson and curate of this parysshe.'
>
> And thenne that other avaled his bonet and said: 'Mayster Parson, I praye yow to be not displeasyd, I had supposed ye had not be benefyced. But, mayster,' sayd he, 'I pray yow, what is this benefyce worth to yow a yere?'
>
> 'Forsothe,' sayd the good, symple man, 'I wote never, for I make never accomptes thereof, how wel I have had hit four or fyve yere.'
>
> 'And knowe ye not,' said he, 'what it is worth? It shold seme a good benefyce.'
>
> 'No, forsothe,' sayd he, 'but I wote wel what it shalle be worth to me.'

'Forsothe,' sayd he, 'yf I doo my trewe dylygence in the cure of my parysshens in prechyng and techynge and doo my parte longynge to my cure, I shalle have heven therfore. And yf theyre sowles ben lost or ony of them by my defawte, I shall be punysshed therfore. And herof am i sure.'

(Blake, ibid., p 56, lines 29–57)

When Caxton began to print, he was faced with a major difficulty in the choice of language. He was conscious of a want of uniformity in the regional dialects of English, but anxious to produce reading material in such homely speech as his own class would be able to appreciate. Children of the trade gilds were educated in the new merchant schools, such as that founded a little later by the Merchants Taylors in London. Fortunately, he was a business expert of eclectic tastes, and knew the meaning of compromise. His clientele was largely drawn from noblemen, such as Earl Rivers, Since he had chosen vernacular literature as his exclusive field, he wisely decided to emulate the language of the preceding generation of successful writers, Trevisa, Chaucer, Gower and Lydgate. But their style was never acquired, since Caxton's ear had become attuned to the rhythms of French prose. Spelling and punctuation, when he thought of them, were derived from the practice of reputable scriveners. Caxton had not the acoustic knowledge to attempt spelling reforms that might lead to orthographic consistency.

After the death of Chaucer, the dialect of London, as used by the courtly class, became the accepted literary language, although by no means recognized as standard. For Court English was itself in a fluid state, especially as concerned pronunciation. In the crucial fifteenth century important sound changes occurred over a lengthy period, now described as the Great Vowel Shift. Often there were two or more pronunciations of the same word. The Court language was, as yet, comparatively localized; for it reached the outlying counties chiefly through the medium of noble representatives at the King's councils.

When Chaucer was active, vowels probably still had their Continental value (as used in Italian); but when Caxton printed, many changes had already taken place. It is not just to suppose that the problem of unphonetic English spelling is to be blamed upon Caxton and his style of printing. He accepted the main principles of Middle English spelling, as they appeared in London English. One

429

test of Caxton's unphonetic ear is his unresponsive spelling of
neutralized vowels in unstressed syllables. The inflexional system
he retained clings to that of Chaucer, but it was mostly outmoded
by the close of the fifteenth century. The spelling question was little
better in contemporary presses operating in London, as well as in
Oxford and St Albans; none was conscious of the benefits of
uniform spelling.

In *English Pronunciation from the Fifteenth to the Eighteenth
Century* (Intro. p x) Constance Davies writes: 'No matter how
unphonetic a system of spelling may be, it possesses phonetic
significance in the minds of its users.' She illustrates by reference to
occasional improvisations of letter-writers, such as merchants and
housewives, who were largely uninfluenced by the literary language; their spellings are of considerable interest to the language
historian. One such correspondent was Margaret Paston, who
wrote to her husband in a serviceable, homespun style, devoid of
figures, but ample enough for the narration of momentous events in
the life of a Norfolk family:

(1) Ryth worchipful hosbon, I recomande me to yow, desyryng hertely
to her of yowr wilfar . . . be my trowth I had never so hevy a sesyn as I
had from the tyme that I woste of yowr sekenesse tyl I woste of yowr a
mendyng, and *ȝyth* myn hert is in no grete esse, ne nowthe *xal* be, tyl I
wott that ȝe ben very hal. . . .
  I pray yow hertely that [ye] wol wochesaf to sende me a letter as
hastely as ȝe may, yf wry[t]yn be non dysesse to yow, and that ye
wollen wochesaf to sende me worde *quowe* your sor *dott*. Yf I mythe
have had my wylle, I *xulde* a seyne yow er dystyme; I wolde ye wern at
hom. . . lever *dan* a goune, ȝow it wer of scarlette.
Sept. 1443   (Davies, op. cit., pp 24–25)

(2). . . Than I prayd her *aȝyn* that sche wuld *teryn* tyl ȝe kom hom, and
I seyd I trostyd veryly that ȝe wuld don *qhan* ȝe kom hom, as itt longeth
to ȝw to don; and if ȝe *myth* have very knowleche that sche awyth of
ryth for to have itt, I seyd i wyst wel that ȝe wuld pay it with ryth gode
wyl, and told her that ȝe had *sergyd* to a fownd wrytyng thereof, and ȝe
kwd non fynd in non wyse. . .
  The Holy Trynyte have ȝw in hys kepyng, and send ȝw helth and
gode spede in all ȝour maters twchyng ȝour ryth.
  Wretyn at Norwyche, on the Wedenys day nexst after thatt ȝe partyd
hens.
April 1448   (ibid., pp 31–2)

Margaret Paston wrote from the countryside, where she supervised farming operations; her East Anglian dialect leaned strongly to the north. Significant spellings are:

(1) *ȝyth* 'yet', *xal* and *xulde*, *quowe* 'how', *dott* 'doth', *dan* 'then'
(2) *aȝyn*, *teryn* 'tarry', *qhan* 'when', *ȝw* 'you', *myth* 'might', *ryth* 'right', *sergyd* 'searched', *kwd* 'could'.

The form *aȝyn* was probably spoken as [agɪn]. The ENE pronunciation [agɛn], found in rhymed verse until the nineteenth century, seems to have been a mixture of northern *again* and southern *ayen*. In several places Chaucer employed the form *ayein*, alongside the northern type.

At the end of Book II of R. L. Stevenson's *The Black Arrow* (about the Wars of the Roses) Ric Shelton writes a letter to Sir Daniel Brackley, which shows that the Scots novelist was less skilful than Thomas Chatterton in archaizing language through orthography. The syntax, not to mention the atypical tone of the dialogue, should convince any reader that the language is an artefact; for he is not to be deceived by such spelling oddities as *fynde*, *wasshe*, *gentyl* and *therinne*, by the catch phrase *let you to wytte*, or by the singular use of *ye* for *you*, irrespective of grammatical function. The Rowley poems were a feasible imposture in the mid-eighteenth century; they would not have been attempted in an age better supplied with linguistic information.

The simplicity of Margaret Paston's syntax is not unlike that of early biblical translation, dating from the West-Saxon gospels. In the fifteenth century compound tenses, using auxiliaries *have* and *be* to form the perfect and pluperfect, became increasingly common; and so did the employment of *shall* or *will* to form the future perfect tense. The latter auxiliaries were, however, interchangeable for all grammatical persons; *shall* tended to suggest obligation, and *will* volition. The periphrastic auxiliary *do*, which had been extremely rare in the fourteenth century, suddenly became acceptable in the fifteenth, even when emphasis was not intended.

On the other hand, the subjunctive, in subordinate objective clauses, fell into disuse, and was often replaced by periphrastic compounds with *may/might* or *shuld* (and sometimes *wold*). The sequence of tenses continued to be poorly observed, and concord remained faulty, especially when a compound subject was preceded by the verb. The gerund, with suffix *-ing*, preceded by a preposition, was much used by the Pastons, Pecock and Caxton.

The transitional period before the English Renascence was marked by a number of still more useful syntactical modifications. Connectives or prepositions became indicators of types of phrase or clause, and this made possible greater complexity in the range of sentence structures. In dialectic, this also added to the use of abstraction. The paragraph, as a means of grouping related ideas, became a feature of all kinds of prose writing. But the more sensitive concept of a well-wrought paragraph, the pattern of a rhythm in completion, was not generally understood.

By establishing colloquial, rather than literary, habits of expression, the Paston and Stonor letters did for prose what popular drama had achieved in verse. Non-formal notions of style were developing a more virile command of prose in the south of England. The acknowledged writers still clung tenaciously to rhetoric, because there were no valid principles of grammar in a vernacular which tended to discard inflexions.

Sound, as well as extraordinary, observations were sometimes made concerning the 'art' of grammar. In *Didascalicon* (ed. C. H. Buttimer, 1939) Hugh of St Victor wrote in the twelfth century, more in the guise of a rhetorician:

> He practises the art of grammar, who treats of the rules concerning the use of words . . . It befits everyone to speak or write grammatically . . . Not everything should be said which we are able to say, lest those things that we should say are said less profitably . . . Do not multiply the byways until you have learnt the highways. You will travel safely when you are not afraid of making mistakes.

Hugh was, of course, referring to Latin, as the universal scholar's medium. The genuine grammarians of the Middle Ages were Donatus and his successor Priscian, but their 'art' was considered by many vernacular writers to be irrelevant to their own practical difficulties. The other side of the picture was, indeed, presented by Sir Thomas Elyot in *The Booke of the Governour* (1531):

> Lorde God! howe many good and clene wittes of children be nowe a days perisshed by ignorant scholemaisters! . . . I call nat them gramariens, whiche onely can teache or make rules, wherby a childe shall onely lerne to speake congrue latine, or to make sixe versis standyng in one fote, wherein perchance shal be neither sentence nor eloquence . . . Nowe a dayes, if to a bachelar or maister of arte studie of philosophie

waxeth tediouse, if he have a spone full of latine, he wyll shewe forth a hoggesheed without any lernyng, and offre to teache grammer and expoune noble writers . . . he wyll, for a small salarie, sette a false colour of lernyng on propre wittes, which wyll be wasshed away with one shoure of raine.

(Ed. H. H. S. Croft, Book I, ch. 15)

There seems to have been no worthwhile reform, even in the teaching of Latin grammar, until John Stanbridge, master of Magdalen College School, Oxford, published his *Accidence*, just before the close of the fifteenth century.

A periodic structure of sentences was one useful function of cohesive writing that rhetoric managed to inculcate. A growing consciousness was already in being that prose should be the proper medium for scientific and technical writing, in fact, for all utilitarian purposes. Dante's *De Vulgari Eloquentia*, though written in Latin to reach a broad spectrum of readers, securely advocated the use of the mother tongue; for any sincere utterance, it was the *natural* form of speech. The loose structure of sentence, beside the periodic one, provided an extremely useful form of modulation. Many thinkers on style rejected the theory that formal rules had to be memorized before a speaker could express himself adequately. Educated Londoners, in particular, were humorously voluble on the dangers of pedantry. There is not the slightest doubt that a literate society has always been a prerequisite for the rise of an important literature: and evidence in plenty suggests that such a society existed in the southern counties of England in the fifteenth century.

One inhibiting aspect of rhetoric in the Middle Ages was its formulaic character; writers tended to think of rhetorical skill as 'science' (knowledge), while grammar was commonly referred to as 'art'. There was, in the medieval mind, no clear distinction between art and science. Anyone aspiring to 'endite' (compose) had to master the rules of his profession; but a genuine critical faculty was, as yet, undeveloped. This may have been because theology was regarded as the pinnacle of academic attainment; it involved much training in the skills of disputation. The University of Paris, which specialized in scholastic logic, as taught by Thomas Aquinas, Albertus Magnus and Peter Abelard, was at the centre of this activity, the basis of which was the *Organon* of Aristotle. Oxford, by Wyclif's time, was motivated by similar principles; but as Bishop

433

Pecock subsequently showed, these were not productive of literary resilience. 'Augmenting' the vernacular vocabulary from Latin and Greek sources, usually through French, proved to be useful for polysyllabic variation of a paragraph's movement, but it was seldom used with discrimination.

By the fifteenth century latinism in England had temporarily lost some ground; even monks were not always qualified to teach Latin adequately. Cultured Englishmen had usually gone abroad to complete their education, which meant that they came back thoroughly trilingual. Language, in medieval Europe, was a cultural inheritance, with no indication of national or political affiliations. In Italy and Germany, citizens of quite independent principalities spoke the same language, as did those of France and Burgundy. No European language could then be said to enshrine the 'soul' of a nation; but Latin was still the international language, which made it possible for medieval students to pass from one famous university to another. What was recognized in England was undoubtedly that Latin, the highroad to the Catholic faith, need not be the sole medium for acquiring knowledge. Printing might become the means by which the new vernacular language would be given stability, and a wider local currency; it was first used as a medium of education at the elementary stage. There was one unfortunate result, however; printing tended to separate the written and spoken media of communication; it may even have been responsible for accelerating the Great Vowel Shift in England.

Despite the disastrous civil war of the latter half of the fifteenth century, the state of English education seems to have improved; there were few people in the southern counties, above the villein class, who could not read or write. Printing made it possible to distribute reading matter at a more reasonable cost than hand-copied script. Within a generation of Caxton's innovation, prose communication outstripped writing in verse, which had been the vehicle of creative writing, as well as history, for centuries. But the classics remained the criterion of excellence. The principles of Christian doctrine were all bent to support the ideals of feudal society. Italy supplied much of the talent for new writing, northern France the good taste, dominated by the Germanic spirit. According to G. G. Coulton, feudalism was a compromise between Germanic individualism and Roman collectivism (*Medieval Panorama*, pp 45–6). Feudal nobles had become the patrons of literature long before the introduction of European printing; but in England, after 1350, the aristocratic class probably did not provide the main body of readers; they came, as students, from the leading universities, Paris in France, Oxford and Cambridge in England.

In 1432 William Sevenoaks, a grocer, provided in his will for a secular school to teach grammar; he saw that no proper provision was made for the education of middle and labouring classes, only for the élite. It was left to monastic and cathedral choir schools to educate commoners. Until the invention of printing, books were so scarce that the teaching consisted largely of question and answer.

Printing transformed educational attitudes to literature, and consequently some of the author's creative aims, which are reflected in the attitude to style. H. J. Chaytor observed in *From Script to Print* that there was a 'gradual substitution of visual for auditory methods of communicating and receiving ideas' (p 4). The Church that had been mainly responsible for perpetuating the dominance of the Latin language, and its stability as a universal medium, was unhesitatingly used in restraining current innovations. Chief of these was the daring suggestion that everybody should be able to read and think for himself. Chaytor adds the further observation that 'when speech and orthography fail to agree, script or print usually gains the upper hand' (p 35).

As the circulation of books spread, literature came to be looked upon as a reliable expression of the state of society. A printed page gave the reader more time than an oral communication to reflect upon ideas presented to him. No effective criticism of writing was possible until a large and intelligent *reading* public had been created. When such a stage has been reached, the reader tends to repose more confidence in the realism of prose than the imaginative liberties of poetry. Reliable knowledge was indispensable to the medieval student of literature; his interest, as Chaytor explains, was seldom in the literary personality of the author.

By the thirteenth century the University of Paris had become the fountain of western ideas; it was also the alma mater of William of Ockham. Oxford University, which came into being about 1167 and produced Duns Scotus, did not make such an intellectual impact, until William of Wykeham, Bishop of Winchester, and Chancellor to Edward III, in 1379 injected new blood. By the time of the Peasants' Revolt (1381) Wyclif, ever in the forefront of schoolmen at Oxford, had been named a Lollard and heretic, because he advocated political and religious changes that were inevitable. The Great Schism of the papacy indisputably brought this Christian socialist into the arena of secular controversy as well; his *Of Civil Lordship* presents a revealing picture of medieval social anomalies. The vast possessions and the immunity of the Church were Wyclif's principal targets; but he also assailed, with abrasive vigour, compulsory confession, indulgences and the doctrine of transubstantiation, and argued sensibly for the vernacular in biblical reading and elucidation.

The real issue of Lollardry, in Coulton's inimitable phrasing, was 'the soul's direct responsibility to God; the comparative irrelevance of human mediators and of traditional forms' (*Medieval Panorama*, p 490). Persecution was unable to suppress the truth of Wyclif's pleas. Yet successive Lancastrian kings, for security reasons, supported the established Church, their own title to the throne being shaky. Scepticism, as Erasmus showed, was not incompatible with genuine faith, and the need for it was a moral conviction by the fifteenth century. The growth of secular knowledge undoubtedly helped to expose the Scribes and the Pharisees of institutional religion. Desiderius Erasmus (1466–1536) arose out of the general fermentation of ideas; but the New Learning, beginning as Christian humanism, was late in coming to England. The Church, which was wealthy, condemned usury, and continued to do so; but the powerful gilds saw that trade and industry could not expand, unless given a periodic injection of loan capital.

In a lecture delivered at Oxford in 1948, Arnold Toynbee said that 'the study of history is enquiry into events of people trying to civilize themselves'. Something like this was Erasmus's mission; like Toynbee, he achieved through the study of Greek, a critical attitude of mind and a healthy scepticism regarding the claims of material progress. The Dutch individualist cultivated detachment, when it was precarious to do so, and was not deflected from his path by the influential connections he had made with Italy, England and France. At the invitation of Lord Mountjoy, he came to England (mainly London and Oxford) for five years in 1499. He induced Oxford Englishmen, like William Gray, who went to Italy to study under Guarino of Verona, to purchase manuscripts, such as the Ferrara collection which Gray donated to Balliol College. From 1470–75 Greek had been taught at New College, Oxford, by an Italian scholar, named Vitelli. Erasmus himself lectured on the subject at Cambridge from 1511 to 1514, and his edition of the Greek New Testament was then prepared. His culture, not merely latinity, was international, with the result that European vernaculars had no special appeal for him. It was through Erasmus and Renascence humanists in Italy that the study of Greek and Roman literature was placed on a proper classical foundation.

The impact of the classics upon the Middle Ages had unfortunately never been direct; such knowledge as there was came through French versions, which were adaptations, rather than translations. The acceptance of these versions in England was uncritical. There was consequently little sensitivity to form and style in writing; moreover, what the ancients designed as fiction, was mostly mistaken for historical truth. The more marvels a tale contained, the greater was its appeal to medieval audiences, because most were steeped in the chivalric misconceptions of the time. For instance, attitudes to love were at variance with the expressed experience of the Greek masters of classical literature.

In the fifteenth century, the concept of a united Christendom was sadly fragmented; so was the effectiveness of the mounted knight as a military force. *Amour courtois*, a gracious fiction of feudal life in self-contained castles, was disappearing in favour of married love. Ovid's *Ars Amatoria* was seen, in perspective, as the art of trifling. The harsh realities of the Hundred Years War were responsible for the simultaneous introduction of nationalism to many European countries.

Coulton, writing on 'Chaucer and Malory' in *Medieval Panorama* (pp 248–57) says: 'Not brevity, but verbosity, was a note of highest culture' in medieval English society. He instances Chaucer's long discussions on predestination in *Troilus and Criseyde,* and the Wertherism of the love scenes, which he attributes to the lack of privacy in Court and castle life. The moralist in Chaucer, he concludes, grew weary of the sordid elements in the illicit love situation.

Coulton recalls, too, Roger Ascham's reaction to *Morte Darthur*: that the major interest lies in the Knights' bold bawdry, and willingness to slaughter each other without a quarrel. Malory, retorts our critic, has all the 'violent antitheses' so characteristic of medieval life, which was by no means as simple as some imagine. These antitheses are captured through colour contrasts. For harmony was achieved, 'not by blending, but by the balance of opposite factors' (p 255). What is remarkable about Malory's book, in spite of the constant letting of blood, is the sense of religion that pervades it. To the fifteenth century, the romance was as much an archaic idealization, as it is to our own time.

Many aspects of the Middle Ages appear to the modern reader irrational or strained. Except in Chaucer and Malory, one misses personal touches in the handling of a story; the dialogue seldom induces belief that real persons are conversing. When realism *does* depict an abject society, the result is probably meant to represent satire. There is so little fidelity in medieval history. But with all the oddities there exists a certain charm and freshness to offset the naiveté, natural innocence in the midst of acquisitive sin and bourgeois lust mingled with aristocratic lavishness. No age later than the Elizabethans managed to portray crude life with so much relish.

Bibliography

Chapter I

Anthony, I. *The Roman City of Verulamium*, St Albans, English Life Publications, 1970.
Birley, A. *Life in Roman Britain*, Batsford, 1964.
Birley, E. *Roman Britain and the Roman Army*, Kendal, T. Wilson, 1961.
Blair, P. H. *Roman Britain and Early England*, Nelson, 1963.
Burckhardt, J. *The Age of Constantine the Great*, New York, Pantheon Books, 1949.
Burn, A. R. *Agricola and Roman Britain*, English University Press, 1953.
Cary, M. *A History of Rome*, Macmillan, 1960.
Charlesworth, M. P. *The Lost Province*, Cardiff, University of Wales Press, 1949.
Collingwood, R. G. *A Guide to the Roman Wall*, Newcastle-upon-Tyne, Reid, 1933.
Collingwood, R. G. & Myers, J. N. L. *Roman Britain and the English Settlements*, Oxford, Clarendon Press, 1936. 2nd edn, 1937.
Cottrell, L. *The Great Invasion*, Evans, 1958.
Cunliffe, B. *Fishbourne*, Sussex Archaelogical Trust, 1971.
  The Regni, Duckworth, 1973.
Fox, G. E. & Morris, J. A. *A Guide to the Roman City of Uriconium at Wroxeter*, Shrewsbury, Shropshire Archaeological Society, 1931.
Frere, S. *Britannia: A History of Roman Britain*, Routledge & Kegan Paul, 1967.
Gibbon, E. *The Decline and Fall of the Roman Empire*, ed. J. B. Bury, OUP, World's Classics, 7 vols, 1914.
Grant, M. *Tacitus: The Annals of Imperial Rome*, Penguin, 1959.
Haarhoff, T. J. *Schools of Gaul*, Johannesburg, Witwatersrand University Press, 1958,
Haverfield, F. *The Romanization of Britain*, Oxford, Clarendon Press, 1915.
Jackson, K. *Language and History in Early Britain*, Edinburgh University Press, 1953.
Kenyon, K. K. & Frere, S. S. *The Roman Theatre of Verulamium*, St Albans, English Life Publications, ND.
Mattingly, H. *Tacitus on Britain and Germany*, Penguin, 1948.
Merrifield, R. *The Roman City of London*, Benn, 1965.
Moore, D. *Caerleon, Fortress of the Legion*, Cardiff, National Museum of Wales, 1970.
Moore, R. W. *The Romans in Britain*, Methuen, 1954.
Mothersole, J. *The Saxon Shore*, John Lane, The Bodley Head, 1924.

Palmer, L. R. *The Latin Language,* Faber & Faber, 1954.

Richmond, I. A. *Roman Britain,* Penguin, 1955.

Roman and Native in North Britain, Nelson, 1958.

Rivet, A. L. F. *Town and Country in Roman Britain,* Hutchinson, 1958.

Salway, P. *The Frontier People of Roman Britain,* CUP, 1965.

Simpson, G. *Britons and the Roman Army,* Boston, Gregg Press, 1964.

Thompson, E. M. *An Introduction to Greek and Latin Palaeography,* Oxford, Clarendon Press, 1912.

Todd, M. *The Coritani,* Duckworth, 1973.

Wacher, J. S. (ed.) *The Civitas Capitals of Roman Britain,* Leicester University Press, 1966.

Webster, G. & Dudley, D. R. *The Roman Conquest of Britain,* Batsford, 1965.

Wilson, D. R. *Roman Frontiers of Britain,* Heinemann, 1967.

Chapter II

Alcock, L. *Arthur's Britain,* Allen Lane, 1971.

Anderson, G. K. *The Literature of the Anglo-Saxons,* Princeton University Press, 1949.

Anglo-Saxon Chronicle (trans. G. N. Garmonsway), Dent, 1953.

Ashe, G. (ed.) *The Quest for Arthur's Britain,* Paladin, 1971.

Bede, *The Ecclesiastical History of the English Nation* (trans. Stevens & Jane), Dent, 1939.

Blair, P. H. *An Introduction to Anglo-Saxon England,* CUP, 1956.

Chadwick, H. M. *The Origin of the English Nation,* CUP, 1924.

Chambers, R. W. *Man's Unconquerable Mind,* Cape, 1939.

Clemoes, P. (ed.) *Anglo-Saxon England,* vols I–III and VI, CUP, 1973.

Giles, J. A. *Six Old English Chronicles,* Bell, 1891.

Hodgkin, R. H. *A History of the Anglo-Saxons,* 2 vols, OUP, 1939.

Kirby, D. P. *The Making of Early England,* Batsford, 1967.

Loomis, R. S. (ed.) *Arthurian Literature in the Middle Ages,* Oxford, Clarendon Press, 1959.

Malone, K. (ed.) *Deor,* Methuen, 1933.

Morris, J. *The Age of Arthur,* Weidenfeld & Nicolson, 1973.

Norman, F. (ed.) *Waldere,* Methuen, 1933.

Oman, C. *England Before the Norman Conquest,* Methuen, 1910.

Stenton, F. M. *Anglo-Saxon England,* Oxford, Clarendon Press, 1943.

Thomas, C. *Britain and Ireland in Early Christian Times,* Thames & Hudson, 1971.

Tolkien, J. R. R. *Beowulf, the Monsters and the Critics,* British Academy, OUP, 1936.

The Lord of the Rings, 3 vols, Allen & Unwin, 1954–5.

Wallace-Hadrill, J. M. *Early Germanic Kinship in England and on the Continent,* Oxford, Clarendon Press, 1971.

Ward, A. W. & Waller, A. R. (eds.) *The Cambridge History of English Literature,* CUP, 1907.

Whitelock, D. *The Beginnings of English Society,* Pelican, 1952.
Williams, H. (ed.) *De Excidio et Conquestu Britanniae,* Cymrodorian Society, 1899.
Wrenn, C. L. *A Study of Old English Literature,* Harrap, 1967.

Chapter III

Baugh, A. C. *A History of the English Language,* New York, Appleton Century, 1935.
Campbell, A. *Old English Grammar,* Oxford, Clarendon Press, 1959.
Contard, F. *The Popes* (trans. A. J. & E. F. Peeler) Barrie & Rockliff, 1964; original edition 1959.
Deansley, M. *Sidelights on the Anglo-Saxon Church,* A. & C. Black, 1962.
The Pre-Conquest Church in England, A. & C. Black, 1961. 2nd edn, 1963.
Irwin, R. *The Origins of the English Library,* Allen & Unwin, 1958.
Ker, W. P. *The Dark Ages,* Edinburgh and London, Blackwood, 1904.
MacGillivray, H. S. *The Influence of Christianity on the Vocabulary of Old English,* Halle, Max Niemeyer, 1902.
Meillet, A. *General Characteristics of the Germanic Languages,* Florida, Miami University Press, 1970.
Migne, J. P. *Patrologiae Cursus Completus,* Paris, In Via Dicta: D'Amboise, Près la Barrière D'Enfer, où Petit Montrouge, 1844–55.
Sandys, J. E. *History of Classical Scholarship,* 3 vols, 3rd edn, New York, Hafner, 1958.
Taylor, H. O. *The Classical Heritage of the Middle Ages,* New York, Ungar, 1957.
Trench, R. C. *On the Study of Words,* rev. A. L. Mayhew, Kegan Paul, Trench & Trübner, 1910.
Winston, R. *Charlemagne,* New York, Random House, 1960.

Chapter IV

Clemoes, P. & Hughes, K. *England Before the Conquest,* CUP, 1971.
Duckett, E. *Alfred the Great and his England,* Collins, 1957.
John, E. *Land Tenure in Early England,* Leicester University Press, 1964.
Ker, N. R. *Catalogue of Manuscripts Containing Anglo-Saxon,* Oxford, Clarendon Press, 1957.
Mawer, A. *The Vikings,* CUP, 1913.
Mitchell, B. *A Guide to Old English,* Oxford, Blackwell, 1965.
Potter, S. 'King Alfred's Last Preface' in *Philologica,* ed. Kirby, T. A. & Woolf, H. B., pp 25–30, Baltimore, Johns Hopkins University Press, 1949.
Sawyer, P. *The Age of the Vikings,* Edward Arnold, 1971.
Schram, O. K. (ed.) *The Old English Orosius,* Methuen, 1939.

Sedgefield, W. J. (ed.) *King Alfred's Old English Version of Boethius' De Consolatione Philosophiae*, Oxford, Clarendon Press, 1899.

Sisam, K. *Studies in the History of Old English Literature*, Oxford, Clarendon Press, 1953.

Stenton, D. M. (ed.) *Preparatory to Anglo-Saxon England*, Oxford, Clarendon Press, 1970.

Stevenson, W. H. (ed.) *Asser's Life of King Alfred*, Oxford, Clarendon Press, 1904; OUP, 1959.

Sweet, H. (ed.) *King Alfred's Orosius*, EETS (O.S.79), 1883. (ed.) *Oldest English Texts*, EETS, 1885.

Thompson, A. H. (ed.) *Bede, his Life, Times and Writing*, Oxford, Clarendon Press, 1935.

Wilson, D. *The Vikings and their Origins*, Thames & Hudson, 1970.

Wright, T. *The State of Literature and Learning under the Anglo-Saxons*, Royal Society of Literature, Charles Knight, 1839.

Wyatt, A. J. *Anglo-Saxon Reader*, CUP, 1919.

Zandvoort, R. W. 'Three Notes On King Alfred's Boethius', *Collected Papers*, Groningen, J. B. Wolters, 1954.

Chapter V

Almgren, B. A. & Cagner, E. (eds.) *The Viking*, Watts, 1966.

Arbman, H. *The Vikings*, Thames & Hudson, 1961.

Craik, H. (ed.) *English Prose Selections*, vol. 1, Macmillan, 1893.

Chambers, R. W. *On the Continuity of English Prose*, EETS, 1932.

Crawford, S. J. (ed.) *The Old English Version of the Heptateuch*, EETS (O.S), 1922.

Garmonsway, G. N. (ed.) *Ælfric's Colloquy*, Methuen, 1939.

Goolden, P. (ed.) *Apollonius of Tyre*, OUP, 1958.

Jespersen, O. *Growth and Structure of the English Language*, Oxford, Blackwell, 1940.

Kinard, J. P. *A Study of Wulfstan's Homilies: their style and sources*, Baltimore, J. Murphy, 1897.

Logeman, H. (ed.) *The Rule of St. Benet*, EETS (O.S), 1888.

Morris, R. (ed.) *The Blickling Homilies of the Tenth Century*, 3 vols, EETS (O.S), 1874–80.

Shearin, H. G. *The Expression of Purpose in Old English Prose*, New Haven, Yale Studies in English, XVIII, 1903.

Skeat, W. W. (ed.) *The Holy Gospels in Anglo-Saxon*, 3 vols, EETS, Cambridge, 1871–87.

Lives of the Saints, 4 vols, EETS (O.S), 1881–1900.

Sweet, H. (ed.) *Selected Homilies of Ælfric*, Oxford, Clarendon Press, 1901.

Thorpe, B. (ed.) *Homilies of the Anglo-Saxon Church*, 2 vols, Ælfric Society, 1844–6.

BIBLIOGRAPHY

White, C. L. *Ælfric: A new study of his life and writings,* New Haven, Yale University Press, 1898.
Whitelock, D. (ed.) *Sermo Lupi ad Anglos,* Methuen, 1939.

Chapter VI

Baker, T. *The Normans,* Cassell, 1966.
Chadwick, H. M. *The Study of Anglo-Saxon,* Cambridge, Heffer, 1941.
The Nationalities of Europe, CUP, 1945.
Chambers, W. W. & Wilkie, J. R. *A Short History of the German Language,* Methuen, 1970.
Chevalier, C. T. (ed.) *The Norman Conquest,* Eyre & Spottiswoode, 1966.
Douglas, D. C. *The Norman Achievement,* Eyre & Spottiswoode, 1969.
Lockwood, W. B. *An Informal History of the German Language,* Cambridge, Heffer, 1964. Rev. edn, Deutsch, 1976.
Kaiser, R. *Medieval English,* 3rd edn, Berlin, 1958.
Loyn, H. R. *The Norman Conquest,* Hutchinson, 1965. 2nd edn, 1967.
Trench, R. C. *English Past and Present,* Parker, 1855.
Wrenn, C. L. *The English Language,* Methuen, 1949.
Wright, C. E. *The Cultivation of Saga in Anglo-Saxon England,* Edinburgh, Oliver & Boyd, 1939.

Chapter VII

Andrew, S. O. *Syntax and Style in Old English,* CUP, 1940.
Barrett, C. R. *Studies in the Word-Order of Ælfric's Catholic Homilies on Lives of Saints,* Cambridge, Dept of Anglo-Saxon, Occasional Papers III, 1953.
Brook, G. L. *An Introduction to Old English,* Manchester University Press, 1955.
Crystal, D. *Linguistics,* Pelican, 1971.
de Saussure, F. *Course in General Linguistics,* trans. W. Baskin, Owen, 1960.
Ekwall, E. *Selected Papers,* Lund, Studies in English, 33, 1963.
Gray, L. H. *Foundations of Language,* New York, Macmillan, 1939.
Jespersen, O. *Progress in Language,* Sonnenschein, 1909.
Language, its Nature, Development and Origin, Allen & Unwin, 1922.
Kirby, T. A. & Woolf, R. B. (eds.) *Philologica,* Baltimore, Johns Hopkins Press, 1949.
Kispert, R. J. *Old English, an Introduction,* New York, Holt, Rinehart & Winston, 1971.
Onions, C. T. *Advanced English Syntax,* Swan Sonnenschein, 1904.
Quirk, R. *The Concessive Relation in Old English Poetry,* New Haven, Yale University Press, 1954.
Quirk, R. & Wrenn, C. L. *An Old English Grammar,* Methuen, 1955.
Sandman, M. *Subject and Predicate,* Edinburgh University Press, 1954.
Sapir, E. *Language,* New York, Harcourt Brace, 1921.

Sievers, E. *Old English Grammar,* trans. A. S. Cook, Boston, Ginn, 1899.
Strang, B. M. H. *A History of English,* Methuen, 1970.
Wright, J. & E. M. *Old English Grammar,* OUP, 1925. Reprint 1934.
Wyld, H. C. *Historical Study of the Mother Tongue,* Murray, 1906. Reprint 1926.
  A Short History of English, Murray, 1914. Reprint 1924.

Chapter VIII

Andrew, S. O. *Postscript on Beowulf,* CUP, 1948.
Bessinger, J. B. & Kahrl, S. J. (eds.) *Essential Articles for the Study of Old English Poetry,* Connecticut, Hamden, 1968.
Bliss, A. J. *The Metre of Beowulf,* Oxford, Blackwell, 1958.
Bloomfield, M. W. *Essays and Explorations,* Cambridge, Mass., Harvard University Press, 1970.
Brodeur, A. G. *The Art of Beowulf,* California University Press, 1960.
Chambers, R. W. *Beowulf, An Introduction* (supplement, C. L. Wrenn), 3rd edn, CUP, 1959.
Crossley-Holland, K. & Mitchell, B. (trans.) *The Battle of Maldon and other Old English Poems,* Macmillan, 1966.
Dickins, B. & Ross, A. S. C. (eds.) *The Dream of the Rood,* Methuen, 1934.
Fox, C. & Dickins, B. *Chadwick Memorial Studies: Early Cultures of North-West Europe,* CUP, 1950.
Gordon, E. V. (ed.) *The Battle of Maldon,* Methuen, 1937.
Gordon, R. K. (ed.) *Anglo-Saxon Poetry,* Dent, Everyman, 1926.
Gradon, P. O. E. (ed.) *Cynewulf's Elene,* Methuen, 1958.
Klaeber, Fr. (ed.) *Beowulf and the Fight at Finnsburg,* 3rd edn, Boston, D. C. Heath & Co., 1941.
Krapp, G. P. & Dobbie, E. V. K. (eds.) *Anglo-Saxon Poetic Records,* 6 vols, New York, Columbia University Press, 1931–53.
Pearsall, D. *Old English and Middle English Poetry,* Routledge & Kegan Paul, 1977.
Pope, J. C. *The Rhythm of Beowulf,* New Haven, Yale University Press, 1942.
Sisam, K. *The Structure of Beowulf,* Oxford, Clarendon Press, 1965.
Timmer, B. J. (ed.) *Judith,* Methuen, 1952.
  The Later Genesis, Oxford, Scrivener Press, 1948.
Wardale, E. E. *Chapters on Old English Literature,* Kegan Paul, Trench & Trübner, 1935.
Whitelock, D. *The Audience of Beowulf,* Oxford, Clarendon Press, 1951.
Wilson, J. H. *Christian Theology and Old English Poetry,* The Hague, Mouton, 1974.
Woolf, R. (ed.) *Juliana,* Methuen, 1955.
Wrenn, C. L. (ed.) *Beowulf with the Finnsburg Fragment,* Harrap, 1953.

Wyatt, A. J. (rev. ed. R. W. Chambers) *Beowulf with the Finnsburg Fragment*, CUP, 1933.

Chapter IX

Adams, G. H. & Stephens, H. M. (ed.) *Select Documents of English Constitutional History*, Macmillan, 1918.

Brooke, C. *The Saxon and Norman Kings*, Fontana, 1967.

Bryant, A. *Makers of the Realm*, Collins, 1953.

Clark, J. W. *Early English*, Deutsch, 1957.

de Garis, M. (ed.) *English-Guernsey Dictionary*, La Société Guernesiaise, 1967.

Ekwall, E. 'How Long did the Scandinavian Language Survive in England', *Jespersen Miscellany*, Allen & Unwin, 1930.

English Historical Review, vols VI and VII, 1891–2.

Finn, R. Weldon. *An Introduction to Domesday Book*, Longmans, 1963.

Hall, J. (ed.). *Layamon's Brut* (Selections), OUP, 1924.

Herlihy, D. *The History of Feudalism*, Macmillan, 1970.

Honigmann, E. A. J. (ed.) Shakespeare's *King John*, Methuen, 1954.

Langenveldt, G. *Select Studies in Colloquial English of the Late Middle Ages*, Lund, Gleerupska 1933.

Maitland, F. W. *Domesday Book and Beyond*, CUP, 1897.

Morris, R. (ed.) *Cursor Mundi*, EETS, 1874–93.

Onions, C. T. (ed.) *Oxford Dictionary of Etymology*, OUP, 1966.

Plummer, C. & Earle, J. (eds.) *Two Saxon Chronicles Parallel*, OUP, 1892.

Pollard, A. F. *The History of England*, OUP, 1947. Reprint of 1912 edition.

Powicke, M. *Medieval England*, OUP, 1950. Reprint of 1931 edition.

Round, J. H. *Feudal England*, Sonnenschein, 1895.

Stephenson, C. (ed. B. D. Lyon) *Mediaeval Institutions*, New York, Cornell University Press, 1954.

Vising, J. *Anglo-Norman Language and Literature*, OUP, 1923.

Wardale, E. E. *An Introduction to Middle English*, Kegan Paul, Trench & Trübner, 1937.

Wyld, H. C. *A History of Modern Colloquial English*, Oxford, Blackwell, 1920. 2nd edn, 1921. 3rd edn, 1936.

Chapter X

Arthurian Chronicles, Wace and Layamon, (trans.) Intro. L. A. Paton, Dent, ND.

Chaucer, G. *Works*, ed. F. N. Robinson, OUP, 2nd edn, 1957.

Coulton, G. G. *Social Life in Britain from the Conquest to the Reformation*, CUP, 1919.

Fisher, J. H. (ed.) *The Medieval Literature of Western Europe*, New York University Press, 1966.

Froissart, J. *Chronicles* (trans. G. Brereton), Penguin, 1968.

Giraldus Cambrensis. *Itinerary through Wales* (1188), ed. T. Wright, Bell, 1892.

Gower, J. *Works*, 4 vols, ed. C. G. Macaulay, Oxford, Clarendon Press, 1899–1902.

Jusserand, J. J. *A Literary History of the English People*, Unwin, 1895.
English Wayfaring Life in the Middle Ages, Unwin, 1909.

Ker, W. P. (ed.) *Froissart's Chronicles*, trans. Lord Berners (1525), 6 vols, OUP, 1927–8.

Lewis, C. S. *The Discarded Image*, CUP, 1967.

Mitchell, R. J. & Leys, M. D. R. *A History of the English People*, Longmans, 1950.

Riley, H. T. (ed.) *Muninenta Gildhallae Londoniensis*, 3 vols, Longman, Green, Longman and Roberts, 1859–62.

Ross, A. S. C. *Ginger*, Oxford, Blackwell, 1952.

Ten Brink, B. *The Language and Metre of Chaucer*, 1884 (2nd edn, revised F. Kluge, Macmillan, 1901).

Trevelyan, G. M. *English Social History*, Longmans, 1946.

Wright, J. & E. M. *An Elementary Middle English Grammar*, OUP, 1928.

Chapters XI and XII

Bolton, W. F. (ed.) *The Middle Ages*, Barrie & Jenkins, 1970.

Bowden, M. A. *A Commentary on the General Prologue to the Canterbury Tales*, Macmillan, 1954.

Brewer, D. S. *Chaucer*, Longmans, 1953.

Brook, G. L. *The Harley Lyrics*, Manchester University Press, 1948.

Brown, Carleton F. *English Lyrics of the Thirteenth Century*, Oxford, Clarendon Press, 1932.
English Lyrics of the Fourteenth Century, Oxford, Clarendon Press, 1924. Reprint 1952.

Bryant, A. *The Age of Chivalry*, Collins, 1963.

Chambers, R. W. *Poets and their Critics: Langland and Milton*, OUP (British Academy), 1941.

Clemen, W. *Chaucer's Early Poetry*, Methuen, 1963.

Coghill, N. *The Poet Chaucer*, OUP, 1949. Revised 1960.
(trans.) *The Canterbury Tales*, Penguin, 1951. Revised 1977.
(trans.) *Troilus and Criseyde*, Penguin, 1971. Reprint 1977.

Cowling, G. H. *Chaucer*, Methuen, 1927.

Davenport, W. A. *The Art of the Gawain-Poet*, Athlone Press, 1978.

Davies, R. T. *Medieval English Lyrics*, Faber & Faber, 1963.

Davis, N. & Wrenn, C. L. (eds.) *English and Medieval Studies, presented to J. R. R. Tolkien*, Allen & Unwin, 1962.

Dickins, B. & Wilson, R. M. *Early Middle English Texts*, Cambridge, Bowes & Bowes, 1951.

BIBLIOGRAPHY

Elliott, R. W. V. *Chaucer's English*, Deutsch, 1974.

Emerson, O. F. *Middle English Reader*, Macmillan, 1905. Revised 1932.

Everett, D. *Essays on Middle English Literature*, Oxford, Clarendon Press, 1955.

French, R. D. *A Chaucer Handbook*, New York, Crofts, 1927. Reprint 1947.

Gardner, J. (trans.) *The Complete Works of the Gawain-Poet*, Chicago University Press, 1965.

Gibbs, A. C. (ed.) *Middle English Romances*, Edward Arnold, 1966.

Goodridge, J. F. (trans.) *Langland, Piers the Plowman*, Penguin, 1959.

Gordon, E. V. (ed.) *Pearl*, Oxford, Clarendon Press, 1953.

Gradon, P. *Form and Style in Early English Literature*, Methuen, 1971.

Hadow, G. *Chaucer and his Times*, Butterworth, 1914.

Hussey, M., Spearing A. C. & Winny, J. *An Introduction to Chaucer*, CUP, 1965.

Kane, G. *Middle English Literature*, Methuen, 1951.

  (ed.) *Piers Plowman, the A-Version: Will's Vision of Piers Plowman and Do-Well*, Athlone Press, 1960.

Kane, G. & Donaldson, E. T. *Piers Plowman II: The B-Version*, Athlone Press, 1975.

Ker, W. P. *English Literature: Mediaeval*, Butterworth, 1912.

Form and Style in Poetry (ed. R. W. Chambers), Macmillan, 1928.

Kittredge, G. L. *Chaucer and his Poetry*, Cambridge, Mass., Harvard University Press, 1915. Reprint 1946.

Lawrence, W. W. *Chaucer and the Canterbury Tales*, New York, Columbia University Press, 1950.

Legouis, E. *Geoffrey Chaucer*, Dent, 1928.

Lewis, C. S. *The Allegory of Love*, OUP, 1936. Corrected reprint, 1946.

Lowes, J. L. *Geoffrey Chaucer*, OUP, 1934.

Luria, M. S. & Hoffman, R. L. *Middle English Lyrics*, New York, Norton, 1974.

Moorman, C. *The Works of the Gawain-Poet*, Mississippi University Press, 1977.

Morris, R. & Skeat, W. W. *Specimens of Early English*, 2 vols, Oxford, Clarendon Press, 1886. Impression 1935.

Mossé, F. *A Handbook of Middle English* (trans. J. A. Walker), Baltimore, Johns Hopkins University Press, 1952.

Rhys, E. *Lyric Poetry*, Dent, 1913.

Robbins, R. H. *Historical Poems of the Fourteenth and Fifteenth Centuries*, New York, Columbia University Press, 1959.

Robinson, I. *Chaucer's Prosody*, CUP, 1971.

Root, R. K. (ed.) *The Book of Troilus and Criseyde*, Princeton University Press, 1926. Reprint 1952.

Rowland, B. (ed.) *Companion to Chaucer Studies*, Toronto, OUP, 1968.

Saintsbury, G. *History of English Prosody*, vol. 1, 1908. Reprint, New York, Russell & Russell, 1961.

Schipper, J. *A History of English Versification*, Oxford, Clarendon Press, 1910.

Sisam, K. *Fourteenth Century Verse and Prose*, Oxford, Clarendon Press, 1921.

Skeat, W. W. *The Vision of William concerning Piers Plowman*, 2 vols, Oxford, Clarendon Press, 1886.

The Works of Chaucer, 6 vols and supplement, OUP, 1894–97.

The Chaucer Canon, New York, Haskell House, 1965.

(rev. K. Sisam) *The Lay of Havelok the Dane*, Oxford, Clarendon Press, 1915.

Southworth, J. G. *Verses of Cadence*, Oxford, Blackwell, 1954.

Spearing, A. C. *Criticism and Medieval Poetry*, Edward Arnold, 1964.

Medieval Dream-Poetry, CUP, 1976.

Speirs, J. *Medieval English Poetry*, Faber & Faber, 1957.

Stanley, E. G. (ed.) *The Owl and the Nightingale*, Nelson, 1960.

Stone, B. (trans.) *Medieval English Verse*, Penguin, 1964. Reprint 1971.

(trans.) *Sir Gawain and the Green Knight*, Penguin, 1959. Reprint 1977.

Tolkien, J. R. R., & Gordon, E. G. (eds.) *Sir Gawain and the Green Knight*, Oxford, Clarendon Press, 1925. Impression, 1930.

Turville-Petre, T. *The Alliterative Revival*, Cambridge, D. S. Brewer, Rowman & Littlefield, 1977.

Wells, H. W. *Langland's The Vision of Piers Plowman*, Sheed & Ward, 1935.

Wells, J. E. *Manual of the Writings in Middle English* (ed. J. B. Severs) 2 vols, Connecticut Academy of Arts and Science, 1970.

Whittock, T. *A Reading of the Canterbury Tales*, CUP, 1968.

Wilson, R. M. *Early Middle English Literature*, Methuen, 1939.

Wright, T. *Political Poems and Songs relating to English History*, vol. 1, London, 1959.

Chapter XIII

Carlyle, T. *Past and Present*, Dent, 1912.

Duls, L. D. *Richard II in the Early Chronicles*, The Hague, Mouton, 1975.

Hilton, R. H. & Fagan, H. *The English Rising of 1381*, Lawrence & Wishart, 1950.

Jones, B. *The Royal Policy of Richard II*, Oxford, Blackwell, 1968.

Loomis, R. S. & Willard, R. *Medieval Verse and Prose*, New York, Appleton-Century, 1948.

Mathew, G. *The Court of Richard II*, Murray, 1968.

Schlauch, M. *The English Language in Modern Times*, Warsaw, Państwowe Wydawnictwo Naukowe, 1959.

Skeat, W. W. *Richard the Redeless*, 1873. Also EETS, 1936.

Steel, A. *Richard II*, CUP, 1962.

Sweet, H. *First Middle English Primer*, Oxford, Clarendon Press, 1884. 2nd edn, 1890. Reprint 1931.

Trevelyan, G. M. *England in the Age of Wycliffe*, Longmans, 1909.

Tuck, A. *Richard II and the English Nobility,* Edward Arnold, 1973.
Wyclif, J. *English Works,* ed. F. D. Matthew, EETS, 1880.

Chapter XIV

Bennett, H. S. *Chaucer and the Fifteeenth Century,* Oxford, Clarendon Press, 1947.
Bennett, J. A. W. *The Rediscovery of Sir John Mandeville,* New York, MLA of America, 1954.
Benson, L. D. *Malory's Morte Darthur,* Cambridge, Mass., Harvard University Press, 1976.
Block, K. S. (ed.) *Ludus Coventriae,* OUP for EETS, 1922.
Bramont, J. *The Travels of Sir John Mandeville,* Dent, 1928.
Chambers, E. K. *The Mediaeval Stage,* 2 vols, Oxford, Clarendon Press, 1903. Reprint 1925.
  English Literature at the Close of the Middle Ages, Oxford, Clarendon Press, 1945.
Chaucer, G. *The Works* (eds. A. W. Pollard, H. F. Heath, M. H. Liddell & W. S. McCormick) Macmillan, 1898. Reprint 1932.
Craig, H. (ed.) *Two Coventry Corpus Christi Plays,* OUP for EETS, 1902. 2nd edn, 1957.
England, G. & Pollard, A. W. (eds.) *The Townley Plays,* OUP for EETS, 1897.
Field, P. J. C. *Romance and Chronicle,* Indiana University Press, 1971.
Gordon, I. A. *The Movement of English Prose,* Longmans, 1966.
Hamelius, P. (ed.) *Mandeville's Travels,* 2 vols, OUP for EETS, 1919 and 1923.
Hicks, E. *Sir Thomas Malory, His Turbulent Career,* Cambridge, Mass., Harvard University Press, 1928.
Hilton, W. *The Ladder of Perfection,* Penguin, 1957.
Hodgson, P. (ed.) *The Cloud of Unknowing and the Book of Privy Counselling,* OUP for EETS, 1944.
Jefferson, B. L. *Chaucer and the Consolation of Philosophy of Boethius,* New York, Haskell House, 1965.
Krapp, G. P. *The Rise of English Literary Prose,* New York, OUP, 1915.
Letts, M. *Sir John Mandeville,* Batchworth Press, 1949.
Loomis, R. S. *The Development of Arthurian Romance,* Hutchinson, 1963.
Loomis, R. S. (ed.) *Arthurian Literature in the Middle Ages,* Oxford, Clarendon Press, 1959.
Lumiansky, R. M. *Malory's Originality,* Baltimore, Johns Hopkins University Press, 1964.
Meech, S. B. & Allen, H. E. (eds.) *The Book of Margery Kempe,* OUP for EETS, 1940. Reprint 1961.
Moorman, C. *The Book of King Arthur,* Kentucky University Press, 1965.
Owst, G. R. *Preaching in Medieval England,* CUP, 1926.
  Literature and Pulpit in Medieval England, CUP, 1933. Oxford, Blackwell, 1961.

Partridge, A. C. *Tudor to Augustan English*, Deutsch, 1969.
English Biblical Translation, Deutsch, 1973.
Pollard, A. W. (ed.) *English Miracle Plays, Moralities and Interludes*, Oxford, Clarendon Press, 1890. 8th edn, 1927.
Reid, M. J. C. *The Arthurian Legend*, Oliver & Boyd, 1938. Reprint 1960.
Saintsbury, G. *A History of English Prose Rhythm*, Macmillan, 1912. Reprint 1922.
Scudder, V. D. *Le Morte Darthur of Sir Thomas Malory*, New York, Haskell House, 1965.
Seymour, M. C. (ed.) *Mandeville's Travels*, Oxford, Clarendon Press, 1967.
Stone, R. K. *Middle English Prose Style*, The Hague, Mouton, 1970.
Thomas, R. G. *Ten Miracle Plays*, Edward Arnold, 1966.
Underhill, E. *The Cloud of Unknowing*, Watkins, 1912. 3rd edn, 1934.
Vinaver, E. *Malory*, Oxford, Clarendon Press, 1929.
Malory, Works, 3 vols, Oxford, Clarendon Press, 1967. OUP (1 vol) 1954.
Young, K. *The Drama of the Medieval Church*, 2 vols, Oxford, Clarendon Press, 1933.

Chapter XV

Aitken, A. J., McIntosh, A. & Pálsson, H. (eds.) *Edinburgh Studies in English and Scots*, Longman, 1971.
Bennett, J. A. W. (ed.) *Selections from John Gower*, Oxford, Clarendon Press, 1968.
Dunbar, W. *Poems* (ed. W. M. Mackenzie), Edinburgh, Porpoise Press, 1932.
Poems (ed. J. Kinsley), Oxford, Clarendon Press, 1958.
Essays in Criticism, II.2., Blackwell, 1952.
Essays and Studies of the English Association, XXIV and XXV, Oxford, Clarendon Press, 1938, 1939.
Fisher, J. *John Gower, Moral Philosopher and Friend of Chaucer*, New York University Press, 1964; Methuen, 1965.
Gray, M. M. *Scottish Poetry*, Dent, 1935.
Hammond, E. P. *English Verse between Chaucer and Surrey*, New York, Octagon Books, 1965.
Henryson, R. *Poems* (ed. C. Elliott), Oxford, Clarendon Press, 1963. 2nd edn, 1974.
Poems and Fables (ed. H. Harvey Wood), Edinburgh and London, Oliver & Boyd, 1968.
Hoccleve, T. *Works*, 3 vols, (ed. F. J. Furnivall & I. Gollancz), Kegan Paul, Trench & Trübner for EETS, 1892, 1897, 1925.
James I of Scotland. *The Kingis Quair* (ed. J. Norton-Smith), Oxford, Clarendon Press, 1971.
The Kingis Quair of James Stewart (ed. M. P. McDiarmid), Heinemann, 1973.

Lawlor, J. (ed.) *Patterns of Love and Courtesy,* Edward Arnold, 1966.

Lydgate, J. *Minor Poems* (ed. N. H. MacCracken), Two Parts, EETS, 1911, 1924.

   Siege of Thebes (ed. A. Erdmann & E. Ekwall), Two Parts, EETS, 1911, 1930.

   Temple of Glas (ed. J. Schick), EETS, 1891. Reprint 1924.

   Troy Book (ed. H. Bergen), Three Parts, EETS, 1906, 1908, 1910.

   Fall of Princes (ed. H. Bergen), Four Parts, EETS, 1924, 1927.

   Poems (ed. J. Norton-Smith), Oxford, Clarendon Press, 1966.

Macaulay, G. C. (ed.) *The Works of John Gower,* 4 vols, Oxford, Clarendon Press, 1899–1901.

Mitchell, J. *Thomas Hoccleve,* Urbana, Illinois University Press, 1958.

Myers, A. R. *England in the Late Middle Ages,* Penguin, 1952.

   The Household of Edward IV, Manchester University Press, 1959.

Patch, H. R. *The Goddess Fortuna in Medieval Literature,* Frank Cass, 1967.

Peck, R. A. *Kingship and Common Profit in Gower's Confessio Amantis,* Southern Illinois University Press, 1978.

Peter, J. *Complaint and Satire in Early English Literature,* Oxford, Clarendon Press, 1956.

Rowse, A. L. *Bosworth Field and the Wars of the Roses,* Macmillan, 1966.

Schirmer, W. F. (trans.) *John Lydgate,* Methuen, 1961.

Scott, T. (ed.) *Late Medieval Scots Poetry,* Heinemann, 1967.

Stearns, M. W. *Robert Henryson,* New York, Columbia University Press, 1949.

Tillyard, E. M. W. *Shakespeare's History Plays,* Chatto & Windus, 1944.

   Five Poems, Chatto & Windus, 1948.

Wittig, K. *The Scottish Tradition in Literature,* Edinburgh and London, Oliver & Boyd, 1958.

Chapter XVI

Blake, N. F. *Caxton and his World,* Deutsch, 1969.

   Caxton's Own Prose, Deutsch, 1973.

   Selections from William Caxton, Oxford, Clarendon Press, 1973.

Chaytor, H. J. *From Script to Print,* Cambridge, Heffer, 1945.

Coulton, G. G. *Medieval Panorama,* CUP, 1938. Reprint 1949.

Davies, C. *English Pronunciation from the Fifteenth to the Eighteenth Century,* Dent, 1934.

Davis, N. *Paston Letters,* Oxford, Clarendon Press, 1958.

Debrett's *Correct Peerage of England, Scotland and Ireland* vol. I, London, 1814.

Higden, R. *Polychronicon,* with Trevisa's translation, 9 vols (ed. C. Babington & J. R. Lumby), Longman, Green & Roberts, 1865.

Mumby, F. A. *Publishing and Bookselling,* Cape, 1930. Revised 1949.

Pecock, R. *Repressor of Over Much Blaming of the Clergy*, 2 vols (ed. C. Babington), Longman, Green & Roberts, 1860.
  Reule of Crysten Relegioun (ed. W. C. Greet), OUP for EETS, 1927.
  The Donet, (ed. E. V. Hitchcock), OUP for EETS, 1918.
  The Folewer to the Donet (ed. E. V. Hitchcock), OUP for EETS, 1924.
Ross, J. B. & McLaughlin, M. M. (eds.) *The Portable Medieval Reader*, New York, Viking Press, 1949.
Thomson, J. A. K. *The Classical Background of English Literature*, Allen & Unwin, 1948.
Trevisa, J. *Dialogus* and *Sermon by FitzRalph* (ed. A. J. Perry), OUP for EETS, 1925.
Troutbeck, G. E. *Westminster Abbey*, Methuen, 1900.

Index

⌘⌘⌘⌘⌘⌘

453

Ulfilas, 62; Gothic Gospel of St Mark, 59, 90
*Umlaut,*170, 178
Usher, Archbishop of Armagh, 196

Vere, Robert de, Earl of Oxford, 341, 343
Vergil, 21, 30, 86, 200, 266, 283
Verner, Karl, 'An exception to the First Sound Shift' of Grimm, 182; Verner's Law, 174–5, 182–4
Vespasian, Emperor, 2, 3, 18–20
Vespasian Psalter, 114, 209
Victor, Adam de Saint, 317
Vincent of Beauvais, *Speculum Historiale,* 166, 355
Vinsauf, Geoffrey de, *Poetria Nova,* 291
Vitalis, (*see* Ordericus)
Volund (*see* Weland), 63
Vortigern, 10, 11, 28, 35–6, 38, 43, 51, 55
Vulgate Bible, 89, 111, 335, 360

Wace, *Le Roman de Brut,* 247–8, 370; *Roman de Rou,* 155, 247–8
Wakefield-York Cycle, 374, 377
Waldhere, 55, 58
Walter, Hubert, Justiciar and Archbishop of Canterbury, 236
Waltheof, Earl of Northumbria, 161
Wanderer, The, 59, 196, 201, 211–12
Wanley, H., *Catalogue of Anglo-Saxon Manuscripts,* 196
Warenne, William de, Abbot of Lewes Priory, 233

Wars of the Roses, 240, 388, 390, 393
Warwick, Guy of, the Kingmaker, 388, 407
Weland, the Smith, 58
Widsith, 43, 55, 57–8
Wife's Complaint, The, 196, 212
Wilfrid, St, x, 67, 75–6, 79–81, 83
William FitzOsbern, Earl of Hereford, 159–62
William of Malmesbury, *Gesta Regum Anglorum,* 166, 233, 245; *Gesta Pontificium,* 195
William of Ockham, 422, 435
William of Palerne, 319
William of Poitiers, *Gesta Willelmi Ducis,* 154, 157, 245
William of Wykeham, 260, 334, 435
William II, Rufus, 163, 233
William the Conqueror, Duke of Normandy, 48, 146, 149–66, 227, 229–30, 232–35, 244, 247, 255, 272
Wisdom Books (Old Testament), 201, 305, 359
Worcester Fragments, The, 286
Wulfhere, King of Mercia, 49
Wulfstan, Archbishop of York (Lupus), 54, 108, 113, 126, 135–6, 142; *Sermo Lupi ad Anglos,* 142
Wulfstan, Bishop of Worcester, 229, 232
Wyclif, John, 259, 262, 280, 334, 337, 354, 361, 422, 424, 435; *Of Civil Lordship,* 335, 436
Wynifrith of Exeter (St Boniface), Archbishop of Mainz, 87